From
To: Cl
3/9/2019

The Keeper of the Land

The Spirit of the Ancestors

Bun Phuong

First published by Dog Ear Publishing
4011 Vincennes Rd
Indianapolis, IN 46268
www.dogearpublishing.net

ISBN: 978-1-4575-5669-2

This book is printed on acid-free paper.

Printed in the United States of America

CHAPTER 1

Bun Chhoeun was walking behind two full-grown Italian breed oxen along the wagon road. Skinny and dark, he stood slightly taller than their knees. Another ox was trotting from behind. In Kampuchea, also known as Cambodia, the Italian breed oxen were known to be big and tall.

"Huy! Huy!" He commanded the oxen, tapping the hind leg slightly with a bamboo stick, steering them away from the rice paddies along both sides of the road.

It was a hot day. Bun Chhoeun was wearing shorts and no shirt. His shorts were filthy from the daily routine. He got splashed with small puddles and then coated with dust as he walked along the wagon road. He usually rinsed off the dirt at the end of the day by jumping into the ponds or bathing at the nearby well. His shorts were once dark green all around when Mother first sewed them from the scraps of fabric that the wealthy Chinese used to make curtains. The green color had faded, leaving only the dark brown from the mud and dirt stains. It was too hot to wear a shirt. There was no reason to get the shirt dirty anyway. Besides, he only owned two shirts. Most of the children in the village don't even have one.

His exact date of birth had never been certain. Many of his friends used April 13, the Khmer New Year, as their birthday. That would mean he was turning eleven, as rumor had it that the New Year was coming up. The current date was wasn't relevant; at least not in the city of Tram Knah, the Province of Takeo, located deep to the south of Kampuchea. Everone's daily task was simply farming and fishing and there never a need to know what day it is

The current year was 1970. Everyone knew the New Year because that's when the school was closed and when the elders made good food for the spirits for the angels and for the spirits of our ancestors.

Food was scarce here in Tram Knah. A poor family like ours would only have one meal a day. Our family never had a whole chicken for a meal before. Mother would chop up one chicken thigh and stir-fry the chicken with cabbages. The New Year was the only time food was abundant. Unfortunately, the food could not be eaten. The children were told not to go near the food because it belonged to the spirits and the angels. Nearly every front door in the neighborhood had a tray with a whole chicken decorated with fruits. The burning incense sticks were poked right in the middle of the chicken and fruits. Touching the food was sinful and could taint your body for a long time. After several days, the food was relocated somewhere behind the house to let the spirits and angels finish it.

The city of Tram Knah was far from Phnom Penh, the capital city of Kampuchea. The roads were mostly made for the ox wagons. Once in a while, cars and motorcycles were seen passing by. Most children in Tram Knah had not seen the vehicles up close before. When they saw one coming, they flocked around the vehicles. The kids (and some adults) were very impressed with the cars and motorcycles. Their lack of knowledge made them think cars and motorcycles were made from magic. There was no other explanation for an object that roared so loudly and moved with such high speed without the help of humans or oxen. Sometimes they even saw one with wings flying in the sky.

"Here, I caught three lizards. Clean them up and cook them. I'm very hungry," Bun Chhoeun said to Kim Chhorn.

He tossed the lizards near the fire. Kim Chhorn, my eight-year-old sister, picked them up, gutted them with a cooking knife and skillfully roasted them in the fire. Mother had not taught her how to make stir-fry yet. As a younger sibling and a girl, Kim Chhorn obeyed every word from Bun Chhoeun because he was the oldest child in the family. My other younger sisters were Kim Chhoy and Kim Chhom. They were seven and five respectively. Kim Chhoy had light skin and long dark hair. She inherited the light skin from father. Unlike Kim Chhorn, she didn't like to follow orders and instead did things on her own will. She was sitting on a log next to the fire, not paying attention to Bun Chhoeun at all.

"What's wrong with Kim Chhoy?" Bun Chhoeun asked.

"Today was her first day of school. She got whipped by the teacher because she couldn't write the alphabet, and the whipping made her fingers bleed," Kim Chhorn explained.

"Stupid teacher! How could she write if she hasn't learned anything yet?" Bun Chhoeun said.

"That's what I said to the teacher when I went to her class and asked the teacher. Well, I didn't say the word 'stupid.' He said he whipped her very lightly. He insisted that Kim Chhoy scratched her own finger and bled," Kim Chhorn said.

"That was why I have just quit school. I'm very bad in math. Every time I was called to add some numbers, I always made mistakes and got whipped," Kim Chhorn said.

"If Mother finds out that you quit school, she's going to whip you even harder," Bun Chhoeun warned.

"Mother whipped me before, and it didn't hurt as much. Plus, she has no time to whip me every day," Kim Chhorn replied.

A about a month later, Mother found out that both Kim Chhorn and Kim Chhoy had stopped going to school when she accidently walked into their teacher, Ouwk. He was known as Kroo (teacher) Ouwk. She was very angry when she heard the news. She marched straight home and whipped and chastised Kim Chhorn. "Without school, you're going to be poor the rest of your life. Because of you, your younger sister quit school too."

Kim Chhorn stood still as she received the whip, hoping it would be over soon. She figured not having to wake up early in the morning and walk about two kilometers just to get whipped by the teachers was worth the one-time pain of this whipping. The teachers whipped the students every day for nearly any reason. She got whipped mostly for forgetting to bring the chalk from home and for making a mistake adding numbers or spelling on the board. As the younger sister, Kim Chhoy did not even get yelled at by mother.

The Khmer (people of Kampuchea) culture believed punishing students would help them do better in school. "All I want back from my kids were their eyes, their bones, and their skins," the parent normally said to the teachers when they met, assuring them they could punish the students as needed.

The teachers became creative with making new whips. They discovered the rare and high-quality tree branch that would last for years.

"Well, since you were no longer going to school, you can help me catch fish and collect clams. This was the perfect time," Bun Chhoeun said as Kim Chhorn stood weeping from the pain.

The Khmers only considered two types of seasons, the raining season and the dry season. The raining season allowed them to plow and plant rice. The dry season was when the rice was ready for harvest. In Kampuchea, whenever there was rain, there were always fish in the ponds, puddles, or in the rice paddies. In fact, somehow the fish existed wherever the water was. Most people believed the fish fell from the sky.

The raining season gave the families the opportunity to eat well and even make some money by selling the abundant fish. When the water dried up, it gave another opportunity for the villagers to catch the stranded fish. Catfish were the most abundant of all.

Bun Chhoeun loved the raining season for many reasons. He didn't have to carry water from the well about one kilometer away to fill the water vases. The rain filled the vases. During the dry season, he had to carry two buckets of water from the well and fill many huge vases around the house. Each bucket could hold up to five gallons of water. It took him one whole day to carry the water from the well and fill up all the vases. Sometimes he tripped and spilled all the water when he was just a few steps away from the vases. It had been his responsibility since the day he knew how to carry a bucket. From time to time, our neighbors and travelers would come and drink the water, but they understood the tradition not to use the water for any other purposes.

The rain also helped the grass flourish, making it abundant for the oxen. That made it easier for Bun Chhoeun because he didn't have to walk the oxen far to find the healthy grasses. He could tether the oxen around the house and use the time to play with his friends. If Father was there, Bun Chhoeun would work by his side catching fish. Unfortunately, he was out there somewhere driving trucks. He was away from home most of the time. His job required him to drive all over Kampuchea.

Bun Chhoeun was fond of being around Father. Unlike himself, Father was a giant compared to many Khmer men. His height and size dwarfed most of the Khmer adults who stood near him. He looked very daunting to those who'd never met him, especially when they looked into his murky left eye that had been blind since childhood. He came home from time to time loading and unloading rice bags from the truck. As his co-worker was struggling with one bag of rice, Father would carry two bags without an effort. Bun Chhoeun would stand and watch Father works with awe.

Mother left shortly after she'd finished chastising Kim Chhorn. She was a merchant. She didn't have a stationary business. She went around different cities and bought anything ranging from chicken to Italian oxen for a low price and sold them for profit. Like many other Khmer women, Mother had never been to school in her life. She'd grown up helping the family to make a living. Besides the trading skills, Mother had learned a few things about the ancient remedies to heal simple illnesses. It was important to know a few remedies because there was no hospital nearby.

Her main focus was to save as much money as possible. Over the years, she had bought about ten acres of land. When she had extra money and extra time she would buy material to bake desserts and various foods for my sisters to sell in the open market. She had saved enough money and transformed our once tiny house into a mansion, built with large and strong wood and with a tiled roof. Our house was about a hundred feet long, fifty feet wide, and was two stories high. It was a castle compared to the surrounding houses that were mostly made from palm leaves. Many of Father's and Mother's siblings and their families were living under different sections of this house.

Our family was heading toward a promising future. Mother was doing well in trading, Father's income continued to flow in steadily, Bun Chhoeun was working tirelessly caring for the oxen, and Kim Chhorn was home looking after the family, which gave Mother more time to trade. If things continued to go this way, Mother thought our family would be wealthy one day.

CHAPTER 2

It was around late 1971. The Communist organization was gaining popularity, as the majority of people believed the organization could provide equality and opportunity to every family in the country and eliminate the current government system that most people believed was corrupt. The new organization was known as the Red Khmer and was building up its forces inside and nearby the Takeo province. The current government, led by Lon Nol, was well aware of the situation. They were fighting hard to maintain the control. Backed by the United States of America, Lon Nol had nearly unlimited amounts of money to maneuver his armies. Our big and strong house was the perfect place for the solders to gather and monitor the suspicious activities. Mother and Father didn't mind the soldiers in our house, as they helped protect our families.

The Red Khmer continued their small skirmish attacks here and there, showing off their might around our town. Sometimes they killed the soldiers, decapitated them, and placed their heads on pikes. The soldiers did the same to the Red Khmer, but only to learn that the heads of the Red Khmer were the sons and daughters of the local villagers.

The battle between the Red Khmer and Lon Nol's army continued and grew worse every day. It was becoming very dangerous to live in Tram Knah. Father and Mother decided to move to the city of Bakaeng, located north of Phnom Penh, far away from Tram Knah. Grandma on Mother's side and Mother's older sister promised to take care of the house, the land, and the oxen.

Bakaeng was one of the cities located along the Tonle River. It was Father's birthplace and his hometown. Most of his side of the family was living there. Our grandfather on Father's side owned land on a large island.

Most people who lived here were fishermen. The Tonle River connected to two other main rivers. The north was Tonle Sap. The south connected to the Tonle Mekong that flowed from Thailand and Laos. Tonle flowed south during the dry season into smaller rivers that led to the ocean. In the rainy season, Tonle Mekong overflowed, forcing Tonle to flow back north toward the Tonle Sap. Either way, the current swept the fish along and made it abundant for fishermen.

Unlike Takeo, each of the houses here in Tonle were oversized and elegant, surrounded by trees of all sorts and sizes. There weren't very many rice paddies around here, but the trees grew everywhere. The people here wore nice clothes and talked with slightly different accents. This was where Father had gotten his accent from.

Grandpa also had another piece of land that he used to plant vegetables. The land was located between two mansions that belonged to other families. Each mansion was nearly the size of our house in Takeo. Grandpa allowed Father to use the land to build a temporary house using bamboo trees as the frame and the pre-woven palm leaf planks as the walls and roofs. With the help of Chhoeun and Grandpa, he finished the temporary house in less than two days.

Bun Chhoeun was thrilled to see the river. From the look of the surroundings, he'd rather go fishing here than feed the oxen. Just days after we arrived, Mother bought him three fishing nets and a roll of fish lines and a few dozens of hooks.

Mother realized that she had not had the chance to speak to the two neighbors on both sides of our house for one reason or another. As busy as she was, it had just dawned on her that the neighbors on both sides had been behaving very differently in an eerie way. They avoided talking to our families, and they seemed to hang out and chat among one another every evening. They seem to talk a lot, but their tone of voice was low and secretive. Even the children seem to behave the same way as if they had been trained to do that. Mother informed Father what she thought of the two neighbors, but he thought maybe they didn't like the fact that he'd built the funny-looking house between their mansions.

It was awkward at first, but Mother managed to speak to the families and tried to understand them better. She learned that the two families living in the two mansions were one big family. She explained to the family the reasons we had moved here and the situation at Takeo, where the Red Khmers were getting more and more powerful. Mother expected concern from the families, but she noticed their contentment instead.

When Mother came back home, she shared her thoughts with Father. "During my conversation with them, they never mentioned anything about our house. Anyhow, this was our property. We can do whatever we want with it, and we have told them that it was a temporary house. We will save the money and build a bigger house soon. I could care less of what they think of us. But there was something about this family that gives me a chill. I cannot explain why."

"Just ignore them. We will show them that we were not poor and will not live in a shack forever," Father replied.

Despite growing up here and catching fish with Grandpa all his childhood, Father had no intention of doing that again. He showed Bun Chhoeun the area where Grandpa kept all his canoes. He spent a few days showing Bun Chhoeun how to set the fishing net and how to retrieve the fish later at night, and then he returned to his truck driving job. Once again, Bun Chhoeun was responsible for all the important tasks at home. With his new skills, he was looking forward the catching fish and making money to help Mother.

Bun Chhoeun woke up in the middle of the night. It was colder than usual but not cold enough to wear a shirt. He walked over to Kim Chhorn and Kim Chhoy who were still sleeping soundly.

"Kim Chhorn! Kim Chhoy! Get up, and let's go catch some fish!"

Kim Chhorn woke up startled and immediately knew what she had to do. She had no choice but to go. There were several ways that Bun Chhoeun would make her go. One of them was knuckling her head. Kim Chhoy, on the other hand, always had more options. It wasn't that Bun Chhoeun treated her any nicer, she just would not obey him easily. She would rather take the punishment and cry than follow orders. She came along because it was part of her responsibilities to help out Kim Chhorn.

"Here, hold this." He handed one basket to Kim Chhorn and one to Kim Chhoy with a brand-new fishing net neatly rolled inside.

Bun Chhoeun held three fishing rods on his shoulders and a coconut shell where he placed all the fishing hooks and led them down to the river bank where all the boats were anchored.

"Put the basket in that boat over there and help me find the worms for bait," Bun Chhoeun ordered.

Kim Chhorn and Kim Chhoy squirmed in disgust when they heard the word "worms."

"I'm not touching any worms. You know I'm afraid of worms," Kim Chhoy replied.

"Me too. I'm scared. I can't even look at one, let alone touch it. I will get nightmares," Kim Chhorn added.

"I don't care if you're scared or not. I need your help finding worms. If you were don't help me, I will shove them in your mouth if I found any," Bun Chhoeun threatened. "Here, follow me and do what I do to find them."

From past experience, they knew Bun Chhoeun would do what he said. Afraid of Bun Chhoeun shoving the worms in their mouth, they walked after him obediently. They each grabbed a short stick and grudgingly walked toward the muddy area along the shore. They jumped when they saw movements in the mud. Bun Chhoeun knelt down and dug the dirt with a stick. Kim Chhorn and Kim Chhoy pretended to follow his technique, hoping not to find any worms.

Bun Chhoeun found a worm in less than a minute. He held the worm on its end with his finger and lifted it up proudly as the worm curled and wiggled in the air.

"You see, they were harmless. They don't do anything to you," Bun Chhoeun said sarcastically.

Kim Chhorn and Kim Chhoy jumped and screamed and nearly fell in the mud. They stood up and shivered, turning their faces away from the worm.

"Both of you were useless," Bun Chhoeun said as he continued to dig for more worms. He placed all the worms he found in the coconut shell.

After he collected enough worms, he led them to the canoe. He placed the two baskets in the canoe and hopped in.

"Kim Chhorn, come with me. Kim Chhoy, stay here and make sure to keep the birds away from the worms," He ordered.

Kim Chhoy was glad he didn't ask her to go along. She hated riding in the canoe. It looked very unstable. Kim Chhorn didn't like it any better, but she had no choice. Bun Chhoeun rowed the canoe down the river and found a spot where he could lay the net overnight. Then he took the net out from the basket and tossed one end in the water and held the other end.

"Get out and lay the net. Tie the other end over there," Bun Chhoeun said.

"I'm not going in the water. It's cold, and there were leeches. I'm afraid of leeches," Kim Chhorn replied defiantly.

"Get out of the canoe, or I will kick you out myself," he yelled.

Nearly in tears, Kim Chhorn got off the canoe. Fortunately, the water was warmer than the air. She laid the two nets along the water as Bun Chhoeun unrolled them.

When she finished laying the net, she climbed back in the canoe and checked every spot on her body to make sure there were no leeches. Kim Chhorn feared the leeches more than the worms. Not only did they look so much like worms but they clinched to your skin and sucked your blood. Terrified by the thought, she moved to the high end of the canoe, far away from the spot with water.

Bun Chhoeun rowed the boat back to shore where Kim Chhoy was waiting. Then he started working on setting up the fishing hooks. He tied five to six hooks per string. He severed the worm into smaller pieces and then hooked part of the worms onto each hook. Then he tied and anchored the strings to the tree branches along the shore. When finished, they returned home to continue their sleep.

Just before sunrise, Bun Chhoeun led the two back to the river. Kim Chhorn held the oil lamp, and Kim Chhoy held the baskets. Both were still half asleep as they walked grudgingly.

When they reached the river, Kim Chhorn and Bun Chhoeun got in the canoe and rowed toward the fishing net they had set up last night. Once again, Kim Chhoy refused to get in the canoe and waited at the shore instead.

Bun Chhoeun lifted the net off the water. Kim Chhorn raised the oil lamp to help him see better. Hundreds of fish were wagging and flipping as they tangled in the net. Bun Chhoeun nearly fell out of the canoe from the thrill.

"Wow! Look, Kim Chhorn. We caught so many fish," Bun Chhoeun exclaimed as he pulled the net into the canoe.

"We caught all types of fish," he added.

"I can't wait to sell them. I'm going to sell them, and we were going make a lot of money," Kim Chhorn said.

After the entire net was inside the canoe, they rowed the boat back to shore.

"Kim Chhoy, help untangle the fish. I will go retrieve the hooks," Bun Chhoeun said.

Kim Chhorn and Kim Chhoy untangled the fish and filled all three baskets. Kim Chhoy did not complain. She was very excited herself. Never before had she seen so many fish.

Bun Chhoeun brought over a dozen more fish that were caught on the hooks. They returned home a little after sunrise with three baskets full of fish. Bun Chhoeun did not expect to carry any basket of fish. That had been Kim Chhorn's and Kim Chhoy's task since Takeo. This time, however, he had no choice. Kim Chhorn helped him place the basket on his head, and then he walked clumsily behind the two with the basket on his head.

Mother was thrilled when she saw the fish. She picked a few large fish and placed them aside. "I will dry these snakehead fish and sell them for much more money." she said and then collected a few smaller fish and placed them in a pile. "We will eat these, and we can sell the rest."

Kim Chhorn wasted no time. She coiled the scarf in a circle to make a cushion and then placed it right on top of her head. Then she placed the basket on top of the coiled scarf. The scarf was large and thin and was used by most Khmers for multiple purposes such as blocking the head and face from the sun or wiping the sweat off the face. Some Khmer even wear it like sarong by wrapping it around their body.

Kim Chhorn and Kim Chhoy walked around with the fish baskets on their heads. They had done this many times in Takeo and became very skilled at walking with the baskets on their heads without using their hands to assist.

"Fresh fish! Fresh fish! Who wants to buy fresh fish?" Kim Chhorn hollered to attract attention.

It was common in Khmer to see the vendors walking around calling their product out loud. Some were more descriptive and catchy than others.

They walked for two hours; only three people were interested and bought some fish. All of them were elders. Kim Chhorn was disappointed and confused at first why no one wanted to buy their fish. Then it dawned on her that her that most people who lived here were fishermen. Despite the disappointment, Kim Chhorn and Kim Chhoy didn't return home right away. They were new to the area and curious to see more. They were very fascinated by the atmosphere and continued to walk toward new parts of town. Unlike Takeo, Tonle had so much to see. She came across two concrete bridges busy with cars and motorcycles. One of the bridges was just about five minutes of walk away from our house. There weren't any children on the street at this time. All the children were in school.

They returned home just before sunset. Kim Chhorn explained to Mother where they went and what she thought about why no one wanted to buy the fish. Mother didn't seem too concerned.

"That's all right. I knew that from the beginning. I will take the fish and sell them in Takeo myself. I have other things for you to sell here. It looks like this town needs beef and pork. I went to the nearby market today, and all I saw were fish and vegetables but very few meats. Meats were very expensive here, but the fish and the vegetables were cheap. I will buy the meat from Takeo and sell it here. Continue to help Bun Chhoeun catching fish. The fish and vegetables were rare in Takeo because they don't have much water. I will buy the vegetables to sell them with the fish for cheap. This will be my new way of trading from now on. I will find the taxi that will take me every other day," Mother explained her plan.

Kim Chhoy and Kim Chhorn continued to help Bun Chhoeun setting up the net and catching fish every night. My other sister, Kim Chhom, beginning to learn how to sort the fish and carry baskets and fishing net. She couldn't do much but any was better than nothing for the three. She also helped them many other ways, such as carrying light loads of fish in the buckets and collecting firewood.

Kim Chhorn and Kim Chhoy continued to sell the fish around the town for now until Mother got the meat for them to sell. Besides, they had nothing else to do, and this was their excuse for not starting school again. This was probably the same reason why Kim Chhoy worked without complaining. Fortunately, they found many people who did not like to catch their own fish and preferred to buy them instead at a low price.

Mother took the taxi to Takeo to sell the rest of the fish. Sometimes she traded the fish for the meat directly. She returned a few days later with beef and pork. Since Mother knew the meat was rare and in such a high demand in Tonle, she carried all the meat in a basket and visited each house and introduced herself to establish her clientele. On her first few trips, she sold all the meat in two days after she returned to Tonle. She tripled the profit from the money that she made from selling the fish each time. Since the trip from Tonle to Takeo was expensive, she would wait several days to transport lager amounts of fish and vegetables all at once. Then she would stay in Takeo for a week before returning.

Within a few months, her business became stable. Most of the clients came directly to our house and bought the meat wholesale and then went to sell in another location. Kim Chhorn and Kim Chhoy would sell any leftover meat in the open market or from house to house.

Mother became pregnant in mid-1971. She continued to work on her business tirelessly. In early April 1972, Mother gave birth to me. I was named Bun Chhun and was the second boy in the family. The family was excited to have me, especially Bun Chhoeun. He was happy to see a baby brother. They said my face looked a lot like Father. They said I had a big belly and small arms and legs.

"He's going to be someone important," Mother said. "All the high officials have big bellies and small arms and legs,"

Mother rested for two months as recommended by Grandma, and then she continued to make trips to Takeo to trade, taking me along with her. She continued to prosper, multiplying her profit each week. The fish that she got from Bun Chhoeun, Kim Chhorn, and Kim Chhoy was not enough to meet the demand. She bought extra fish from the local fishermen. She also purchased enough vegetables to fill two taxies. She had four taxies that were dedicated to work just for her.

Even though Mother had a lot of money now, our family still did not eat any better than before. Mother is trying to save money as much a possible. They continued to eat a simple meal of rice and fish. Once in a while, Mother would make stir-fried pork for everyone to eat.

It was now late 1973. The United States was still in the middle of the Vietnam War fighting to suppress the Communist North Vietnam. At the same time, the United States was aware of the quickly growing numbers of Communists in Kampuchea. It was a threat that the United States would have to deal with soon. Without consulting Lon Nol, the United States conducted a series of air raids in the southeast of Kampuchea and dropped a million tons of bombs. The bombs did very little damage to the Red Khmer, but they killed thousands of civilians and destroyed thousands of homes. Our house in Takeo was hit by the bomb. The family of Mother's older sister was living there. One of their daughters died, and some were badly injured. Everyone, including the Lon Nol's soldiers, helped put the fire out using the water that was reserved in the big vase. Fortunately, only a small section of the house was destroyed. The rest of the house still stood strong and undamaged.

Father urged his brothers and sisters to move to Tonle with us. Most of them decided to come along. It was safe and peaceful there. Since our house in Takeo was made from expensive wood and Father had a truck, he decided to salvage the wood from the house and transport it to Tonle and to rebuild our existing temporary tiny house. With the help of his brothers and brothers-in-law, Father removed the wood from the house and transported it to Tonle within days. Father even bought extra wood because he decided to build the house bigger than the one in Takeo.

When the house was completed, it was nearly twice the size of the house in Takeo. The floor of the house rose more than ten feet off the ground, high enough for the oxen to stay under at night.

Since our house could fit up to eight families, most of Father's and Mother's siblings and their families came to live with us. Father returned to his truck driving job a day after the house was completed. His job was busier than ever, as the turmoil of the country had gotten worse and the government needed more transportation of ammunition and food supplies all around the country. Unfortunately, the jobs became a lot riskier. Some truck drivers were afraid to drive far and resigned, leaving Father in high demand. He received bigger pay raises accordingly.

About three weeks after the bombing, Mother went back to Takeo and bought several Italian bred oxen and several full-grown pigs. The price of the livestock had dropped drastically after the bombing incident. Everyone wanted to sell their cattle and move.

Early one morning in Takeo, Mother decided that she wanted to transport an ox to Tonle. Father was not around. Mother paid the tux-tux taxi that had a big open-top cargo large enough to fit one ox. She left the rest of the oxen and pigs with her older sister who still wanted to live there. With the help of the villagers, she had the ox on the taxi laid on its side with its feet tied together so that it couldn't move. Mother took a final look at the ox and took a deep breath. Then she walked over and sat in the front seat holding me. The taxi began to move along the wagon road.

After about ten minutes, the taxi merged into the national road that was large and paved and busy with all sorts of transportation vehicles ranging from the makeshift powered bicycles to the expensive Mercedes. But nothing drew more attention than an ox tied up on the tux-tux taxi. The adults and children from every vehicle couldn't help but stare and point their fingers at the ox.

About thirty minutes later, a police officer on a motorcycle pulled us over.

"Ming (auntie), it's against the law to transport oxen in that small taxi," the police officer said.

Mother was nervous. She had never been pulled over by the police officer before. She was afraid they would take her to jail. She knew absolutely nothing about the law. She was hoping she didn't have to read anything because she couldn't read. It was a well-known fact that people who couldn't read usually got the worst punishment. The officers could accuse them of nearly anything and often would threaten to take them to jail. The best and most common way to avoid the threat was bribery.

"I'm sorry, Loak Kmuy (respectful young man). I didn't know that's against the law. My cousin Phon never told me that. He's working in the police department in Phnom Penh. He told me once that he was an important man. He told me if I came across another police officer with any trouble, just let him know. Now this was the time. Could you find out where he is? I want to talk to him. I want to swear at him for not telling me," Mother said. All the things she said were true, including the intention to swear.

"Ming, what is your name?" the officer asked.

"My name is Yorn," Mother answered nervously, but she managed to maintain her smile.

"What is your last name?" the officer asked.

"I don't have a last name," Mother said, hoping he would not ask her to write her name.

"Ming, I need your last name to inform your cousin," the officer said.

"He would know the name Yorn right away. You don't have to tell him that I'm his cousin or anything. If you want, you can tell him my husband's name is Chhay, but I don't think you need to," Mother said confidently.

The officer returned to his motorcycle and used his walkie-talkie to communicate. Mother waited in the taxi. She turned to the taxi driver who had been speechless all along. "I'm sorry, Loak (sir). I will take all responsibility," Mother said, hoping there will no trouble.

The taxi driver's face was white as a ghost. He had been trying to avoid speaking directly with the officer and happy that Mother was dealing with the situation.

After several minutes, the police officer returned. "Ming, I'm sorry for pulling you over. Please give this note to any officer that would pull you over. It has my name and my identification number along with Loak Phon." The officer handed her the note.

Mother sighed and smiled. She slipped the note in her pocket, hoping she wouldn't have to deal with this again.

"Let's go. We should be all right from now on," Mother said to the taxi driver.

"I thought you made up the name, and I thought we were going to jail for sure. Who is Loak Phon? He must be very important that they let us go that easily and guaranteed our privilege with a note," the taxi driver said.

"Phon is my cousin. Unlike me, he is well educated. He works at the police department. He told me to mention his name if I get in trouble with the law. I'm uneducated; therefore, it is embarrassing to ask him for a favor. I hope this is the last time I have to deal with police officers," Mother explained.

The taxi driver looked relieved and resumed driving. They got pulled over one more time about halfway home. Mother handed him the note, hoping it would help. The office took the note and reviewed it.

"Ming, I'm sorry for your inconvenience. I will escort you to avoid further interruption," the police officer said apologetically.

When Mother arrived home, she and the taxi driver untied the ox and tethered it underneath our house. With the size of the space beneath the house, she could fit a dozen more oxen.

A week later, Mother paid a transportation company to transport the rest of oxen from Takeo. Grandma and Grandpa assigned my aunts and uncles to tend the oxen when they saw Bun Chhoeun was overworked. Some of our uncles were even helping Bun Chhoeun with fishing. For the first time in a while, Bun Chhoeun had some extra time on his hands. He used the opportunity to enjoy time with friends and relatives. He spent more time with Pu Ream, who was our uncle and only about a year older than Bun Chhoeun, than anyone else. Pu Ream was about the same height as Bun Chhoeun. He had been putting in as much effort as Bun Chhoeun, from fishing to tending the oxen.

When Mother was away to trade, Grandma looked after Bun Chhoeun and my three sisters. Bun Chhoeun and Grandma became so attached they were like mother and son.

The hot season arrived again. With the help of our aunts and uncles doing the house chores, Kim Chhorn, Kim Chhoy, and Kim Chhom also had a lot of free time. Like Bun Chhoeun, they spent their free time wandering around the city. Kim Chhorn normally led the way. Kim Chhoy and Kim Chhom would go wherever Kim Chhorn went. Today, Kim Chhorn was leading them toward the nearby bridge to watch the cars and other motor vehicles passing by. They stood at a distance staring at the busy traffic. They could never get tired of the sight. After our family moved from Takeo, Kim Chhorn had not had a chance to look around the area or talk to any children. When she walked around selling the fish and meat, she longed for the opportunity just to sit and watch the cars passing by or play with other children her age. She wanted to enjoy her time like other children instead of selling all the time. Now was the perfect time.

After a long moment of staring at the vehicles, the sisters switched their attention to the soldiers holding all sorts of weapons and patrolling the bridge. About a half-dozen military tents were put up on both sides of the road. Women and children swarmed the area like they were planning to live there permanently.

"Who were those people?" Kim Chhoy asked.

"I don't know, but let's go take a look. I didn't see them here before. They must have just arrived. There are a lot of kids there too," Kim Chhorn said and continued to lead the way.

The three approached the new settlers. Except for the armed men, the families appeared ordinary. They also seemed not to be bothered by their presence.

When they got closer, Kim Chhorn heard the muffled conversation from inside the tents. "... Khmer Luh (Upper Khmer). My husband joined the military because we got paid. Where we use to live, there was nothing for us to do except for hunting. The government assigned my husband to guard this bridge. My children and I came along. He cannot afford to move back and forth," the woman said. She spoke with the accent was so strange that Kim Chhorn could hardly understand.

They looked around and saw boys and girls scattering the area doing what any normal children would do with their free time. Some were playing jump square. Others were standing close to the river and throwing rocks, and some were just standing around chatting. Closer to the base of the bridge, women were hand-washing their clothes in a bucket of water while others were bathing their babies.

Kim Chhorn was curious and tried to focus her attention on the conversation coming from inside the tent.

"We need the money... We go wherever they tell us to go...We are here to prevent the Red Khmer from blowing up this bridge." Chhorn was trying to understand everything the woman said. She was amazed how people could speak with such accent and how she could even comprehend the conversation. The Khmer Luh woman kept going with her life stories.

Kim Chhorn had heard Father tell stories about the Khmer Luh when they used to live in Takeo. They lived way up north of Kampuchea and spoke with an accent known as "un-dun." Some of them could even speak Thai. These people normally walked around naked with their face painted with mud and celebrated around the fire. In Khmer, generally people believed deeply in communicating with the spirits. They believed the spirit would protect them from danger if summoned properly. The Khmer Luh, however, practiced their ritual every day as part of their lives.

Kim Chhorn wanted to speak to the children, but something told her that she shouldn't. She continued to walk around the camp, possibly looking for potential customers to sell the meat to.

The three returned home just before nightfall. They didn't do much besides walk around and see new people and places. It was a big break by not having to carry a basket full of fish or vegetables on their heads. Strangely, it was a nice day for families to sit outside and chat, but our two neighbors were nowhere to be seen. They must have decided to stay inside the house for the entire day. Our families were outside chatting after everyone was done with their tasks. Bun Chhoeun and Pu Ream had just arrived from the lake. They were both soaking wet. As usual, they were standing outside chatting with the families until their clothes were dry.

The hot evening eventually surrendered to the cooler night. The families were finishing sharing their daily stories and preparing for the night. Everyone fell asleep soon after the nightfall. Our entire house was in complete silence.

It was about midnight when the gun battle erupted. *Tat tat tat....tat tat tat...tat tat tat...BOOOOOOOOOM!*

"Charge! Comrade!...Charge!.......,"

"Charge!..."

Tat tat tat...tat tat tat...tat tat tat...BOOOOOOM!..BOOOOOOM!.. BOOOOOOOM! The sound of the guns rattled followed by loud explosions.

"Ahhhhhhhhhhhhhh!," An adult male screamed in pain and then was silent.

"Ahhhhhhhhhhhhhh!" Haunting screams with mixture of the fear, confusion, and pain of the children and adults erupted.

All of us woke up in confusion. Mother picked me up and secured me in her arm.

"Get to the ground! Get to the ground! Everybody, get to the ground. The Red Khmer are attacking," Mother said frantically.

Bun Chhoeun and all my sisters woke up and bolted down the stairs. Mother was behind them ensuring that all of them were all right. We were the first to reach the ground since we lived closest to the stairs. The rest of the families were making their way down.

"Lie flat on the ground and keep your head down," Mother said as she laid me down on the ground.

Our grandma, grandpa, aunts, uncles, and their families all made it safely to the ground around us. Several oxen were lying down and chewing on the hay, heedless of the sounds. Everyone was lying behind the oxen silently, listening to the sound of the guns and the explosions. The sound of human screams of pain pierced through the dark night.

Someone was curious and lifted his or her head up, looking around for any sign of movements.

"Keep your head down!" said one of my uncles.

Then there the sounds of a long whistle approaching from the distance. The whistle got louder and louder, and then the sound changed to *rak rak rak...* like a giant malfunctioning gear mesh, then *BOOOOM!*

Another whistle was approaching. Once it was somewhere above our house, the sound changed again to the *rak rak rak...* and then ended with the loud explosion.

"That's the rocket propelled grenade," one of our uncles whispered.

Another one came so close and was so loud that everyone cringed and moaned in fear, bracing for a hit. When the explosion was somewhere else, everyone sighed loudly.

The sound of the battle and the painful screams went on for nearly two hours. Everyone was still lying flat on the ground feeling very vulnerable because there was no wall around. The oxen were the only objects that were blocking us from the possible explosions. They were still lying down and chewing on the hay like nothing happened.

"They must be the Red Khmers," Mother whispered.

When the battle subsided, we all slept on the ground under our house until the glimmers of the dawn shined in our eyes. Kim Chhorn peeked at one of the neighbors beside our house and expected to see them on the ground in confusion like our families. Instead, they were nowhere to be seen. The lower, opened part of the house was empty.

Bun Chhoeun was the first person to get up and walk out of the base of our house. Then many other residents emerged from their houses as curious as he, walking toward the direction where the battle had taken place last night. They were looking at one another not knowing what to expect. Bun Chhoeun started to follow the crowd. Kim Chhorn sneaked after him. Mother was still asleep. She'd stayed up all night to feed me so that I wouldn't cry. She was afraid I might attract attention from the attackers.

Not too far from our house, they came to a crowd standing around a big crater. Kim Chhorn was looking for our neighbors to see if they knew anything about the attackers. Two men who were living beside us finally walked out of their house and then stood wordlessly not looking curious or worried, as if they had been expecting this. Bun Chhoeun and Kim Chhorn follow the crowd toward the bridge. They could hear the humming sound of the vehicles similar to sound of Father's truck. Hundreds of people were flocking to the scene. From a distance, Bun Chhoeun and Kim Chhorn saw solders carrying charred and disfigured human bodies and then tossing them onto a truck.

Overwhelmed by curiosity, Bun Chhoeun ran closer toward to the scene. Kim Chhorn trailed behind him swiftly and cautiously. Along with the crowd, they stood and stared at the entire camp that had been very lively just yesterday but was now burned to the ground. The bodies of the bridge guards were scattered lifelessly around the bridge entrance. More bodies of the adults and children were scattered around the tents. Most were charred and mutilated. Some were sprawling on the ground, soaked with blood.

More soldiers were carrying the charred and curled-up bodies and tossing them onto the truck. One soldier was holding a body of a mutilated infant, looking away to hold his grief. Bun Chhoeun and Kim Chhorn continued to scrutinize the camp area. They saw more bodies still lying at the burning spot.

"I feel very bad for them, especially the children. They are innocent. Why would they kill children?" one of the adults said.

"These killers are gruesome. They killed without sympathy. I wonder if they would do that to the family of the civilians like us?" a woman asked. But no one was answering, as they were all busy looking.

"What made that whistle and the *rak-rak-rak* sound?" another added.

"No one but the families of the soldiers seem to be the victims. They use mostly the AK rifles, the grenades, and the rocket propelled grenade. When you hear the whistle, the propelled grenade is flying. The *rak-rak* sound is when the propelled grenade is about to land," another explained.

"Bun Chhoeun, let's go back home. If Mother finds out we were here, she will whip us," Kim Chhorn said.

"Let's go. Don't tell her we saw dead bodies. If you want to tell her anything, just say we heard it from other people," Bun Chhoeun said.

They walked back home and found Mother was talking to a woman who appeared traumatized.

"I had moved all the way from Takeo to avoid these kinds of problems," Mother said to the woman. "There will be no more peace from now on. They will come and attack every night like they did in Takeo. Where could we go this time? They are everywhere. If we want to be safe, we should dig a ditch below the house," Mother said.

Bun Chhoeun and Kim Chhorn sneaked past Mother and went straight home, as she was busy talking. When Mother returned home that evening, she instructed Bun Chhoeun and all my uncles to dig several ditches below our house, one for each family.

It took two days to dig all the ditches. Knowing the attacks would continue and get worse, Mother made sure the ditch was deep enough for us to sit and sleep. The excess dirt was stacked around the perimeter of the ditches to make extra protections.

About a week later, another group of soldiers and their families settled at the same location at the end of the bridge. Except this time, there were more of them. They even had military vehicles and some type artillery mounted on the back of the vehicles.

It was only a little past noon. Kim Chhorn and Kim Chhoy had sold all the pork in the open market. They returned home and gave all the money to Mother. They found Father chatting at home with the families, and he said he was staying for several days. He parked his transportation truck in front of our house. Mother had explained to Father about the Red Khmer's attack incident. He's very nervous about the family living here, but he had no choice. There was no other place he could think of that we could move to. Besides, Mother was making good money, and he had just finished building the house.

Kim Chhorn and Kim Chhoy left the house and walked toward the bridge looking for something to do for the rest of the evening. Many children and adults were already congregating at the water front socializing. Every adult was talking about the previous week's attack. Kim Chhorn noticed that the new people had the same accent as the previous families. They must be the Khmer Luh as well.

"I am not afraid of the Red Khmer," said one of the soldiers. He was heavily armed and wore all kinds of necklaces with pendants ranging from a carved Buddha to plain hogs' tusks.

"No one can touch me and my family. We have protections that no one else has," he said to the local town person with confidence while caressing his pendants.

Father was right about the Khmer Luh. They believed they were protected by some type of spirits and truly depended on the spirits. Kim Chhorn felt a surge of relief to see they were more heavily armed than the previous guards. More importantly, they were aware of what the Red Khmer was capable of. The number of soldiers patrolling the bridge had tripled. There was no way the Red Khmer could defeat them this time.

Several nights later, the similar sound of the gun battle erupted. Fortunately, Father was still here at home, which gave the family some comfort.

"Wake up! Wake up! Get downstairs!" Father shouted. Then he picked me up and rushed down the stairs.

Everyone in the house rushed down the stairs and slid into the ditches. This time everyone was safer than before. Not only was the ditch was deep, but the rim was stacked with thick and compacted dirt to give extra protection. Everyone made it to into the ditches safely.

Unlike before, this time there were more explosions. The sound of multiple whistles flew directly toward our house and then exploded elsewhere. More whistles flew one after another trailed by the loud explosions. Some of them landed so close that our house shook, and the debris crashed nearby. Our house could be hit at any time.

After a long moment, the whistles and explosions subsided. Then the familiar sound of the attackers shouted, "Charge! Comrades! Charge!"

The haunting screams of torment and pain erupted in the night once more. They were from the father, mother, and the boys and girls that Kim Chhorn and Kim Chhoy had seen that evening. They could imagine them being shot, stabbed, or burned to death.

The sound of the explosions and gunfire exchanged between the two sides seemed to go forever as our families braced for any explosion that could hit our house.

After a long moment, the sound of the gun battle subsided. The families were relieved and felt safe for the moment.

"We should sleep here until morning," Father said.

Everyone except for Father slept sitting up with their backs leaning against the side of the ditch. Father couldn't fall asleep because he was very curious to see any sign of the attackers. He crawled slowly to the front side of the house and hid behind the oxen. He peeked out and looked around. He was shocked to see two of our neighbors assisting two men who were wearing all black. One of them was limping, with one hand holding his right leg, and the other hand holding a rifle. They must be the attackers, Father thought.

"Help our comrade. Our comrade is injured. Take them to the boat," one of the attackers said to the neighbors.

The two neighbors rapidly assisted the injured attacker, hobbling to the other side of the river. The night was so quiet after the battle. Father could hear his own breathing. He tried to be calm and stay hidden. "Bravo, comrades! You killed all the enemies. I will help you get back on the boat safely. Soon, my family will go live with the comrades."

Father waited several minutes after they'd disappeared and then crawled back into the ditch. He remained shocked from what he had just seen. Mother was still awake and heard all the conversation but she hadn't seen who they were.

"Both of our neighbors are the Red Khmers. They are assisting the attackers," Father said.

Mother turned to Father in shock. "What are we going to do?" she asked.

"I saw them very clearly. They helped the injured Red Khmer. We have to be careful what we say from now on. They are living on both sides of our house. Now I understood why they don't like to talk to us," Father said

"That explains why they seem so strange. The ways they communicated are strange too. The children spoke to their parents like they are friends. We must tell our kids not to talk to them," Mother said.

After sunrise, Father told everyone to go sleep upstairs. Shortly after, he came along upstairs and slept for a couple hours. He woke up when he heard a voice calling his name. "P'own (Litle Brother) Chhay! P'own Chhay! Are you there?"

"Who's that? Sounds like Loak Bong (Respectful Big Brother)?" Father replied as he recognized the voice hollering from the outside. He walked out to the door and saw his boss standing by the stairway.

"Is your family all right?" his boss asked.

"I thought we were going to get hit so many times, but luckily the bombs landed somewhere else," Father replied.

"I got the message from the office. They informed us to transport the bodies away since we are the closest to the area. It is an order from the government. They will triple our paycheck. I have never done this before. I'm a little nervous, but they will pay us triple," the man said.

"I'm a little nervous too. I have never seen dead bodies before. I hope their spirits will not stick to us. What if we walk and turn around and then all we see are the dead standing behind us, staring at us?" Father said.

"Here, I brought one bottle—half for me and half for you. From my experience, this works all the time. I bought this on the way here. The office will pay me back," the man said lifting the bottle up to show Father.

"Then come up and have a drink first," Father said.

Father and his boss sat in the kitchen and filled two large glasses with the liquor. They each chugged down their whole glass in one shot. They refilled their glasses and drank until the bottle was empty.

Father and his boss then hopped on the truck that they'd parked in front of the house and drove toward the bridge.

Bun Chhoeun and Kim Chhorn were awake when Father and his boss were talking. They looked at each other and then got up and sneaked out quietly down the stairs. Bun Chhoeun was leading the way.

When they arrived at the bridge, the area was already crowded with hundreds of people who were confused, frightened, and curious. The bridge that was once beautiful and busy with bicyclists and motor vehicles was now collapsed and half submerged into the river.

The crowd was surrounding the broken base of the bridge and exchanging questions. Father and his boss were among the workers who were collecting the corpses and tossing them into the trucks. The bodies of the men, women, and children who were lively just yesterday were now scattered everywhere in a pool of their own blood. Many of them were charred beyond recognition.

"The Red Khmers are ruthless. They killed even the women and children. I wish I had guns. I want to shoot every single one of them," Bun Chhoeun said to himself loudly enough that Kim Chhorn could hear very clearly.

Father, his boss, and other crew members filled the truck with corpses and then transported them away using the bridge on the other side of the island. He came back home that day and explained to Mother all about his trip.

"Even though I was a little drunk, I could still feel the creep. Every time I looked at the rearview mirror, I saw the corpses' hands sticking out as if they were telling me where to go. When the truck hit a bump, their bodies moved as if they'd all come back to life all at the same time. The hair on my neck stands up on the way there and back. I think the spirits were still on my truck. I think they were upset that they were set up to die and were not getting a proper funeral.

"I need more drinks tonight. If they come to squeeze my throat, at least I will be less frightened before I die. I don't want to die like that. They said if you die like that, you will be a mad ghost and come to kill all your own family," Father said.

"Is this your excuse to get more drinks? The ghosts will not come after you. You didn't kill them. You helped them to find a place to rest their bodies," Mother scorned.

"I think some of them were asleep when they got killed. They wouldn't know who killed them. I'm the last person they saw holding their arms and legs and tossing them into the truck," Father continued.

"If they wanted to break your neck, they would have done that already. Maybe they just want to say thank you. I will get you one container of palm ale. Maybe you can see them better when you are buzzed," Mother said with a laugh.

Days later, there were many similar incidents reported throughout the country. Father had been called to collect the bodies. The government simply ordered them to dig the mass graves and bury them without any ritual. Things had changed dramatically around Tonle. The Red Khmers had been attacking, trying to destroy all the bridges to disable the government military supply movements. The reason behind the killing of women and children was still questionable. The government recruited more soldiers to guard all the bridges and streets. The soldiers made camp in the guarded area with their families. The government seemed to have unlimited resources. The Red Khmers attacked and wiped out the entire camp each time.

Besides the attacks, all sorts of chaos began to spread throughout every town in Tonle. Some family members around the town had gone missing. Some believed they went and joined the Red Khmer. Some believed they were kidnapped and then brainwashed to become the Red Khmer. Rumor had it that the Red Khmers had kidnapped, tortured, and killed anyone related to the high-ranking officials. Among those who went missing were our cousins who were living nearby.

Our family noticed that our two neighbors' houses were empty except for the two men Father had seen the other night helping the attackers. The two men spent most of their time sitting on the front porch observing the passersby. They rarely talked to anybody but themselves. They didn't seem to worry or care what was happening around the town.

Not long after, there was an attack that destroyed another bridge nearby. That was the last bridge that connected the island to other cities. Now there was no other way to cross the river but to use the ferries. The sound of gun battles and explosions continued nearly every night. By now, our families could identify all types of rifles and could even tell if it was the Red Khmers or the military doing the shooting or bombing. Unfortunately, most of the gunshots were from the Red Khmers.

Just before noon on a very hot day, Kim Chhorn and Kim Chhoy were sitting in the canoe helping Bun Chhoeun gather the fish from the net that they had set up the night before. They noticed a couple of airplanes swirling above the forest in the far distance on the other side of the river.

Suddenly, loud explosions rocked the sky. They turned and stared at the airplane. Black smoke could be seen rising from the thick forest into the clear sky. The airplane then released more bombs onto the forest below causing a deep, loud blast. The ground shook from the explosion. Mushrooms of smoke with flames rose up from the distance. The sound was so loud and the shock was so strong that the canoe flip-flopped on the surface of the water. The smokes and flames expanded quickly, engulfing everything around the area.

The three tossed the net back in the water and frantically rowed the canoe back to shore. They left the fish and the baskets on the canoe and darted straight up the hill toward home. They dashed through alleys of the city without looking back, afraid the airplane might come their way.

When they got closer to our house, they saw the two men standing side by side sobbing in grief as they stared at the bombed site.

"You corrupt bastard! I will get revenge for my family and kill every single one of you!" One of the men yelled.

"You watch and wait! I will kill every single one of you," the other added.

Bun Chhoeun knew by now that the men had moved all their families to live with the Red Khmers in the jungle on the opposite side of the Tonle River. It was just the two of them living here taking care of their houses.

Bun Chhoeun was happy to see the Red Khmer was being attacked by the military forces for the first time. He stood in front of our house and enjoyed every moment of the bombing operation. He wished he was that pilot of that airplane. He would destroy all the Red Khmers. He enjoyed seeing the two neighbors mourning as well. This would teach them how it felt to have their families be attacked.

CHAPTER 3

The Red Khmers continued to attack and gained control over many cities and towns, destroying nearly every bridge and blocking many of the main highways. Father was no longer transporting rice and logs. He was working directly for the government, transporting the soldiers and weapons all over the country. He could no longer drive his truck home because all the bridges around our town were had been destroyed. We had not seen Father for months, and we had no way to communicate with him either. Every city in Tonle had been attacked nearly every night. So far, our house had not been hit by the bombs. We might run out of luck if we stayed here any longer. Mother discussed with the families that she wanted to move away from Tonle to Phnom Penh, maybe somewhere near the base of the government military. It should be safer there. She had a younger sister who had moved to Phnom Penh about a year ago. She was married to a high-ranking official living near the military base. Unfortunately, Mother didn't know exactly where she lived and had no way to find them. No one had any solution. They could not think of a place to go.

One night, a grenade landed just a few yards away from our house, sending the debris crashing into the wall. Mother was determined to move to Phnom Penh regardless of the uncertainty of her destination. She discussed her decision with the families about taking the chance to move. Um Yeun, Mother's older sister, Ming Sain, Mother's younger sister, and their families were coming along. Grandma on Mother's side and our uncle, Pu Ream, were also coming. Grandma was a widow. She had been living with Mother since Mother and Father were married. Mother had been taking care of her well. She was confident that Mother could make a living wherever she went.

Pu Ream was not only our uncle but also Bun Chhoeun's best buddy. They were together and doing everything together every single day.

Grandpa and Grandma on Father's side did not like the idea. They believed the Red Khmer were not hurting the civilians but only attacking the military. Therefore, they decided to stay in Tonle. Besides, they liked the house that Father had built.

We took the ferry across the river. Mother brought three oxen and two pigs along. She knew she could trade them for nearly anything. Our families couldn't bring much on the ferries other than our clothes, pots and pans, and the mosquito nets. The ferry was crowded with families just like ours fleeing the city to go to Phnom Penh.

After we crossed the river, we all got on the taxi, except for Bun Chhoeun and Pu Ream. They had to wait and find a taxi with big cargo to transport the oxen and the pigs. Our aunts and uncles got their own taxi. Shortly, we rode toward Phnom Penh together.

When we approached Phnom Penh, we saw long lines of refugees from all over the country flocking to seek safe shelter. Their hometowns were probably being attacked just like ours. Some families were walking on foot—mothers and fathers holding their infants and toddlers in one arm and carrying their personal belongings in the other. Children ranging from the age of four and up were walking and holding the handmade backpacks or sacks. Some families were riding on bicycles with makeshift cargo for their children to sit. Items ranging from animal cages to mosquito nets were dangling around the bicycles.

The oxen wagons were moving slowly along the middle of the road, taking most of the space. The families sitting on the wagon were looking around at other refugees content that they didn't have to walk. Some of the oxen left their dropping along the road as they walked. Fortunately, Mother had the money to pay for the taxi. We were moving smoothly along the road, passing everyone like they were not moving.

When we got further into Phnom Penh, temporary houses made of palm leaves and plastic sheets were had been or were being built along the national road. Women and children were cooking and bathing with buckets of water along the edge of the road. Men were continuously fixing their equipment, preparing for where they might have to go next.

Instead of looking for any open space nearby, Mother decided to go deeper to the center of Phnom Penh. The further we rode, the more crowded the area became. Our aunts and uncles were right behind us on their taxis.

We came to a crowded place near Pochengtung Airport. It was once an open field where there was nothing but grass and small trees. Mother pointed to an open spot up ahead. The taxis stopped in the open spot that was large enough for our family and all my aunts' and uncles' families to build shelters. The entire field was already packed with temporary shelters, but Mother decided to stay here because there was a well-known large pond nearby called Tuk Tla (Clear Water). From her experience, living near the water was the best thing.

Mother knew the area well. She came to Phnom Penh a lot to trade. The airport could be seen in the distance. Large airplanes were taking off or landing continuously. Sometimes, a plane flew over our heads so low and so loud that everyone thought it was going to land on us.

When we got off the taxis, the adults positioned their items around the area to claim the vacant spot. Mother looked around and saw everyone was using the palm leaf lattice to make walls and roofs.

"Kim Chhorn and Kim Chhoy, go find out where they bought the palm leaf lattice. I'm going to wait here with your grandma so that no one can take our spots," Mother said.

Mother also asked our uncles in-law to look for Bun Chhoeun and Pu Ream, as they were transporting the oxen and pigs. Somehow, our uncles were able to locate them among the sea of refugees. They arrived with the pigs and oxen just before noon.

Kim Chhorn and Kim Chhoy came back with the information about where the palm leaf lattice was being sold. It was easy to find. Palm leaf lattices had the highest demand in the market right then. Everyone needed them to build the shelters. Mother asked Bun Chhoeun and Pu Ream to buy enough bamboo trees and palm leaf lattices to build the shelter for everyone. They returned at sunset, too dark to begin building the shelter. Bun Chhoeun and Pu Ream secured several of the bamboo sticks on the ground and used them to tie the mosquito nets. We slept in the mosquito net for the night in the middle of the crowd. The night was uncomfortable and different for everyone.

The next morning, Pu Ream and Bun Chhoeun started to build our shack. Neither had ever started building a shack themselves before. Last time it was Father who had started building our small house at Tonle and did most of the work. The two spent half the morning figuring out where to start. A nearby elder man saw them struggling to begin building the frame and offered a hand and advice. The man helped plant three main columns and explained what they needed to do next. It took them all day to complete the frame. We ended up sleeping out in the open in the mosquito net for another night.

The next morning, they completed the frame and began stacking the palm leaf lattices. With the help of Kim Chhorn and Kim Chhoy, the shack was complete early in the afternoon. As usual, Kim Chhorn and Kim Chhoy got knuckled on the head by Bun Chhoeun a few times each as they misunderstood his instructions and made a few mistakes.

After the shack was completed, two windows were made by piercing rectangular holes through the walls. The shack was large enough to fit up to ten people. There were eight of us including Grandma and Pu Ream. Our aunts and uncles managed to build their own shack nearby.

Bun Chhoeun and Pu Ream also built a small temporary corral behind the shack for the pigs and a strong pole to tether the oxen.

In the evening, Bun Chhoeun and Pu Ream took the oxen to the small pond to feed them water and wash them up. When they finished, they took the oxen to the meadow nearby and allowed them to graze the grass. Once again, Bun Chhoeun ended up tending the oxen like he'd done in did in Takeo.

Mother spent her time chatting with the current settlers, trying to get more information about the situation of the country and to find our other relatives. Most of the settlers had been here over a year. Many had spent weeks migrating on foot from their hometowns. Some had lost their love ones from illness and from the cross fire between the Red Khmer's and the Lon Nol's soldiers.

Many settlers considered themselves fortunate enough to afford to move. Many families were too poor to take the risk and had no option but to stay where they were. Many did not move because they thought the Red Khmer would not harm them. So far, it had been proven that the Red Khmer were only attacking the Lon Nol's military camps and compounds and not the ordinary citizens.

After several days, Mother got the information about her younger brother, Neang, who was responsible for distributing Father's check. He had moved to Phnom Penh several weeks before us. Mother had lost contact with Pu [uncle] Neang after his hometown was attacked and after the main road was blocked. Like us, his family abandoned their house and moved to Phnom Penh for safety. He was residing in a shack a few kilometers away from us.

Pu Neang was still working for the same company as Father and continued to distribute Father's pay checks to Mother.

Mother also found her younger sister, Ming Sarai. She had moved to Phnom Penh about a year ago after her husband got promoted to a three-star general. They were living in an apartment complex with their three children. Her husband was not making a lot of money, but it was enough to pay rent and provide a good meal for the family.

It took nearly two weeks for our family to get back to normal. Mother had spent a lot of money paying the taxis, building the shacks, and buying food for our family as well as our aunts' and uncles' families. She was running low on the money that she had earned in Tonle. It had been over three months since the last time Mother had made any money. If she didn't start making more money soon, she would run out. She missed her trading in Tonle. She would never find such opportunity again as long as the country was in this situation.

After she found her brother and sisters, she started to look for ways to make money again. Mother had spoken to the local residents to seek opportunities to trade but could not come up with anything that would make money. Then, on the way home, she came across merchants selling fresh mustard greens. Mother decided to purchase the mustard greens and pickle them. Pickled mustard greens were very well liked among every Khmer social class. They could be eaten raw or cooked. She bought one basket full of mustard greens and pickled them in a bucket. She fermented the mustard greens for several days. When they were ready, Mother arranged them in two small buckets. Kim Chhorn and Kim Chhoy carried a bucket each on their head and walked around the new shelters calling out the pickle mustard green and the price in a sing-song fashion. It was a lot of work to walk around shelter to shelter with the heavy bucket on their heads, but it was a convenience for the customers.

They sold all the pickled mustard greens in one day, but they had to walk from morning to late evening. Mother was excited that she was starting to make money again. She bought several more baskets of mustard greens and pickled them. Kim Chhorn and Kim Chhoy continued to sell them. Unfortunately, they didn't have as much luck as the first day. They only sold half as much, and they had to walk farther, but overall it was still was worth the work.

After several days, they got tired of walking and decided to sell the pickled mustard greens in the open market instead. They found a spot to sit and sat with other merchants, waiting for the customers. The market was always busy. Most merchants were a lot older than Kim Chhorn and Kim Chhoy. They would wait for the customer to approach them to bargain. Kim Chhorn was not embarrassed, and she had been asking anyone passing by. Many people were interest in buying pickle mustard greens, but most of them didn't have enough money. Kim Chhorn learned that many customers preferred to wait until dark to buy the product because the sellers would want to get rid of their produce by selling it at a reduced price so that they could go home.

Kim Chhorn and Kim Chhoy saw more new settlers continue to pour in the area each day and claim any open spots. The land could belong to a private owner or the government, but so far, no one had witnessed any complaints by the landowners. Because the country was in turmoil, getting kicked out of the land was not a big deal at all. The settlers could always move to another spot. The area around our shack became more and more crowded each day. It was a good thing for Kim Chhorn and Kim Chhoy. New settlers were their new customers. They began walking from house to house again, carrying the bucket of pickled mustard greens on their heads to sell to the new settlers. This time they didn't have to walk far to sell the pickles. Most of the time, they sold all the pickles before noon. Right now, Mother could not keep up making the pickles.

With Kim Chhorn and Kim Chhoy making the money, Mother had a steady flow of income once again. She was taking advantage of the situation in Phnom Penh. The city was crowded but peaceful and safe. There was no sign of the Red Khmer attacking. Mother was urging Bun Chhoeun to start school again. He was now around fourteen years of age. The school system here was much better than in Takeo. Besides, there was not much for Chhoeun to do. Our aunts and uncles were helping with the oxen and pigs. Bun Chhoeun and Pu Ream found a nearby school in Phnom Penh and attended full-time. Bun Chhoeun had always loved school, as he believed one day he could become someone important and make Mother happy. He still helped tend the oxen and feed the pigs after school, but it was optional for him.

Kim Chhorn and Kim Chhoy, on the other hand, were still afraid of the teachers and tried to stay away from school.

With so much time on his hands after school, Bun Chhoeun spent a lot of time hanging out with new friends and cousins chatting and playing soccer. He became very close friends with our cousin named Vann who was about two years older than him. Vann was the son of Father's cousin and known to be a bad influence to all his friends. He was known to be very manipulative and untruthful. In Tonle, he'd stolen and sold things ranging from the radios to firearms and had been caught many times. His Father spent thousands of Khmer dollars in bribery to keep him out of jail. One day in Tonle, he'd managed to persuade Bun Chhoeun to help him steal coconuts from the neighbors and got caught. The neighbor did not report the incident to the police but came to tell Mother to discipline him instead. Mother scolded him for days and warned him not to hang out with Vann again.

Vann and his families were now living a few shacks away from us. No one but Pu Ream knew that Bun Chhoeun was hanging out with him again. Vann was obsessed with firearms and even owned several different ones. He talked about firearms and war every day and even took Bun Chhoeun to test shots many times. Bun Chhoeun had loved firearms himself since he was six years of age but had never had the opportunity to fire one.

The friendship between Pu Ream and Bun Chhoeun was fading, as Pu Ream was putting more effort into school and Bun Chhoeun was spending all his after-school time hanging out with Vann and talked mostly about firearms and militaries. Bun Chhoeun had always wanted to join the military since the day he saw one in Takeo when was just five years old.

Earlier that morning, Mother had left home early to purchase more mustard greens from a remote farm. Kim Chhorn woke up and saw Bun Chhoeun quietly fold his clothes and wrap them in a scarf. He tried not to wake anyone up, but Kim Chhorn was already awake.

"Where were you going? Aren't you supposed to be in school?" Kim Chhorn asked.

"I'm going to shoot all the Red Khmers," Bun Chhoeun replied.

"Where?"

"You don't need to know."

Kim Chhorn stood still, not knowing what to do or what to say. She knew that Vann had a bad influence on him. He should have not mingled with him at all. Now it was too late.

Kim Chhorn was too worried to go sell the pickles that day. Even though Bun Chhoeun had been mean to her and knuckled her head many times when she made mistakes, he was still her older brother and that's just how older brothers were. He had been the one who looked after the entire family while Father was away. Father was still out there working for the government and had not returned home since the second bridge in Tonle was destroyed. It had been months since the last time she'd seen Father. And now Bun Chhoeun was gone too.

Mother returned home just before noon with a taxi full of mustard greens. Finally, she could afford to hire the taxi again. She was smiling as she got off the taxi and unloaded four baskets full of mustard greens.

Kim Chhorn ran up to Mother and said, "Mother, Bun Chhoeun was gone. He said he's going to shoot the Red Khmer. He won't tell me where he went."

"Are you sure? He must be joking. Where could he go to shoot the Red Khmer?" Mother asked.

"He was serious. He packed all his clothes. He wouldn't tell me where he was going," Kim Chhorn added.

"Why didn't you try to ask where he was going?" Mother scolded.

"I was afraid he might knuckle my head if I asked too much questions."

"You deserve a harder knuckle for not asking. Do you know that he will die? God has mercy. What was he thinking? How could he do anything? He was so small. That's what happens from hanging out with Ah Vann too much. He's a bad kid. Bun Chhoeun was never like this before. Now he's become stupid. What I'm I suppose to do now? I raised him all these years just to let him go die like that," Mother said and wept.

Kim Chhorn did not want to stay around Mother. She was afraid she might get knuckled on the head for not asking where Bun Chhoeun went. She usually got knuckled on the head from Bun Chhoeun and Mother when things went wrong. She seemed to be responsible for nearly everything.

Feeling hurt and guilty, Kim Chhorn walked aimlessly out of the house. She worked very hard to make Mother happy, but somehow things always went wrong. She had decided not to go sell any pickle at all, regardless of the possibility that she would get knuckled on her head when she returned home.

After a long walk in the hot sun, she reached the outer boundary of the Puchentung Airport. She walked slowly along the fence watching the airplanes taking off and landing. The sight of the enormous and loud airplane lifting into the air like a bird was always astounding to her and made her forget about the situation at home. She couldn't get over the fact that such an enormous piece of metal could fly.

She went further into the actual street of Phnom Penh city, away from the temporary shacks and canopies, not knowing where else to go. Then she thought of Ming Sarai, who lived not too far from here. She had been to Ming Sarai's house once after Mother discovered where she lived.

Ming Sarai was a nice person. She was much younger than Mother. She was very talkative and friendly. She had three children between the age of three and seven. Her husband had an important job working for the government. Kim Chhorn never understood what he did for work, but Mother said he was a three-star general. He must've known how to read and do math well to do those kinds of jobs, Kim Chhorn thought. It was something she would never be able to do. She could never go back to school. She got hit by the teacher the most out of all the students in the class because she always made mistakes.

As she took a turn into a busy street with mostly cars and motorcycles, she saw a woman standing by a large window selling some type of silver and gold metal rings to a Chinese man. The rings were too big to be bracelets. Kim Chhorn stood watching the woman and the Chinese man, as she has nothing else better to do—anything to take her mind off her guilt and the absence of Bun Chhoeun.

The Chinese man counted two sacks full of rings, and then he took a large bundle of money from some type of drawer on the side of the desk and held them in one hand. Then he used his other hand to count and stack the Khmer dollar bills on the flat surface inside the glass window.

If Kim Chhorn saw the money correctly, they were all twenty reals (Khmer dollars) bills. Kim Chhorn stood frozen with her jaw dropped. She had never seen so much money in just one trade.

Kim Chhorn walked up to the woman and asked, "Ming, what were those?"

"Oh, these were called 'L'boh Ate Jai'. It's the metal scraps that flew off the artilleries after the fires. It's very hard to find. You have to pick them up after the battle or buy them from the local town near the battle sites. It's very dangerous. I have seen people get killed by stepping on the mines trying to collect these rings." The woman explained all this to Kim Chhorn without worrying about creating a possible competitor because Kim Chhorn was way too young to attempt such risks.

"I will pay you two reals for each ring," the Chinese man added with a broken Khmer accent.

Kim Chhorn pretended she was not interested after the lady had spilled out the secret of making the money. She walked quickly back home, very eager to get some money from Mother to buy some artillery rings. She wondered why the rings were so valuable and what they are used for. Maybe the military would buy them and reused it.

She walked quickly toward home with all kinds of trade plans in her mind. She could buy the artillery rings and guarantee to sell them to the Chinese man. From her experience, seeking the customers was the most difficult part of the trade. This was the opposite. The customer was waiting for the products. All she has to do was get the products.

Kim Chhorn came home and explained what she saw and what the lady and the Chinese man told her. Mother listened but looked at her with doubt.

"You can't make money that easily. It must be a lie or a trick. The Chinese will trick you if you don't use your head," Mother said. It was a well-known belief throughout many generations of Khmer.

"The Chinese shop located near the airport guaranteed the purchase, Mother. It can't go wrong. Just give me one hundred real, and I can triple the money in one day. I have some money for the taxi already. I can buy them for a cheap price, Mother. You know I can bargain. I will not get tricked by the Chinese man," Kim Chhorn pleaded.

Mother paused for a moment and then said, "You can try. Besides, you and Kim Chhoy made all the money." She took the money from her pocket and gave Kim Chhorn one hundred reals.

Kim Chhorn had no idea what the mines were, but she was not going to search for artillery rings. She was going to buy them from the residents of the town as one of the lady's suggestions. Since the battles were going on in all the cities around Phnom Penh, she would have no problem finding the source.

She took a small taxi heading south of Phnom Penh where she though the battles occurred the most. After just over an hour, she arrived in a small and isolated village that seemed fit for the battleground. She got off the taxi and looked around the village. She saw a woman walking and carrying a basket over her head.

"Ming, do you know where I could buy the L'boh Ate Jai?" Kim Chhorn asked.

"I don't know what that is, but I have seen people go in and out of that big house over there." She pointed to a house on the far end of the village.

"Then I will take a look to see if they sell them," Kim Chhorn said.

Kim Chhorn walked to the house and went right in. She saw a woman rocking a baby in the scarf hammock tied to two opposite ends of the walls.

"You're coming to buy the L'boh Ate Jai?" the women asked.

Kim Chhorn was happy that she had come to the right house. "Yeah, do you have any left?"

"I have a lot left. How many do you want?"

"I have one hundred reals. How many can I get?"

"I sell two for one real. So, you would get two hundred."

"Ming, give me ten extra because I came a long way. I spent a lot of money on the taxi. I have been searching all day for your house. When I get home, I will bring more money and come again tomorrow," Bon Kim Chhorn bargained.

"Well, all right. It's your first time here. I will give you ten extra."

The women took out two stacks of rings that were tied together with long grass stems and the extra ten that Kim Chhorn had bargained.

"Here are two hundred and ten. I have only about three hundred more left until my husband brings some more. He fights the Red Khmer very far this week. He might not return home for several more days, but I have other people that will bring me more tonight. If you come early tomorrow, they might be available for you, but I'm not guarantee."

"Then, if you do get more, don't sell them to anybody. All right, Ming? I will come tomorrow. I promise. Maybe I will return today if all goes well," She spoke in a soft and friendly voice that the adults seem to like and trust.

Kim Chhorn was around eleven years old now. She was slightly taller than the average girl her age. She had grown so fast for the past two years. It must have been rare to see a talkative young girl who went around different cities to trade. Kim Chhorn saw the sympathy in the woman's eyes, and she would take the full advantage of it. Besides, this was business. She was bargaining and not stealing anything.

Kim Chhorn took a taxi straight to the building where the Chinese man awaited. She carried the artillery rings wrapped in the scarf and walked toward the Chinese man who was sitting and watching the traffic through the window.

"Here were the rings that you wanted to buy. I got two hundred and ten," Kim Chhorn said handing the Chinese man the rings.

The Chinese man jerked his head back in astonishment and said "You were serious. I like that."

The Chinese man unwrapped and counted the rings. He took out a bundle of money and counted. "This was four hundred and twenty reals," the Chinese man said and handed her the money. Kim Chhorn's hand was trembling from excitement. She didn't have to recount the money; she was counting with the man when he was counting the money. She had made so much money in just one trip.

"What time do you close? I will try to get more today," Kim Chhorn asked.

"I normally close just before dark. If I don't have any customers, I usually close early. Since you were planning to come back, I will wait until dark. If you return tonight and the window was close, you can knock on the door but not too late at night. I'm old, and I need to sleep early," the Chinese man said.

"Don't close too early. I will come back," Kim Chhorn said. She wanted to call him Pu, but there was a class title for the Chinese man. Kim Chhorn was not certain what that was and decided it was best not to use the class title at all.

She took the taxi home and gave Mother one hundred and fifty reals. She told Mother she was keeping the rest of the money to buy more of those rings. Mother was content that she had pocketed fifty real in profit in less than half a day plus the two hundred and seventy real that Kim Chhorn was keeping to make more money. Selling the pickle mustard greens would only profit about fifty real a day by both Kim Chhorn and Kim Chhoy.

There was a lot of daylight left. Kim Chhorn took the taxi back to the village right after she handed Mother the money. The woman who sold the artillery rings was surprised to see her back so soon.

"Ey ya! You came for real! You were serious and bold," the woman said. She took out the rest of the artillery rings that were already tied in a bundle plus some loose ones. Each bundle was one hundred.

The women had three hundred fifty left. Kim Chhorn did the math quickly in her head using her fingers and toes to help. Since two rings cost one real, she would slash the number by half, and it came to one hundred seventy-five reals.

"Then the total was one hundred seventy-five reals?" Kim Chhorn asked. If the teachers were to ask her to solve this type of problem in class, she would never be able to and would get so many whips. For some reason, though, it was very simple for her to solve it here.

"That's right, but just give me one hundred and fifty real because you rode here twice on the same day. The twenty-five reals were for the taxi expense and your effort," the woman said kindly.

"Ming, I'm coming back in three days. If your husband brings any more, please save six hundred for me. All right, Ming? Don't sell the six hundred to anybody, all right, Ming?" Kim Chhorn reassured her with an outgoing and friendly tone of voice.

"Don't worry, Kmuy (niece). Ming will save more than six hundred for you."

Kim Chhorn rode the taxi back to Phnom Penh. She arrived just when the man was closing up the window. The Chinese man paid her seven hundred reals for the three hundred fifty rings. Now she had more than eight hundred reals in her pocket in just one day of easy work. She had never felt so happy in her life.

She decided not to spend money on a taxi and walk home instead. She was in no rush. Even thought it was getting dark; the street was still busy with merchants and buyers bargaining the wholesale price and children playing all sorts of games on the street. She bought herself some desserts and coconut juice on the way back. She would normally not spend any money on miscellaneous food except for rice, vegetables, and meat for Mother to cook. This was her first time spending money on herself.

When she got home, Grandma was sitting outside chatting with our aunts and our neighbors. Mother was sitting alone on the bamboo plank floor breastfeeding me and staring at the open door as if waiting for Bun Chhoeun to come back. She didn't seem to take notice when Kim Chhorn entered the door. It was too dark to see her face, but Kim Chhorn sensed that she was weeping.

"Here, Mother. Take one hundred reals. I'm keeping the rest of the money to buy more rings," Kim Chhorn said handing Mother the money. She could have kept it and use it to buy more artillery rings, but she wanted to prove to Mother that her business was for real.

Just before bed, Kim Chhorn explained to Kim Chhoy her new method of making money. Kim Chhoy was excited that Kim Chhorn was making a lot more money now, but she thought it was too dangerous having to travel to remote villages and buy those rings. She didn't want to be part of it. She liked selling the pickled mustard greens. It was safe and kept Mother happy. Besides, she didn't have to walk far anymore. There were so many people living nearby with a lot of money who wanted to buy the pickles.

Kim Chhorn woke up early the next morning. She took the taxi further down south toward Takeo looking for any village that might have the metal rings. She observed the area from a distance as she was riding in the taxi. She made a stop at a town that seemed to be very busy with people.

She began walking looking for the suitable person to ask, and then she saw a girl around her age walking and carrying two buckets of water on her shoulder using the popular bamboo shaft called *dong raek,* where both ends of the shaft hooked onto the handles of the metal buckets. "Me Own (little sister), do you know where they sell the 'Lboh Ate Jai'?"

The girl stopped and lowered the bucket onto the ground. The weight of the water, the bucket, and the Don Raek were probably twice her weight.

The girl straightened her body and stretched her arms and legs and then replied, "I think it's any one of those big houses over there. Their husbands were in the military, and they had people come to buy those things all the time." She pointed to the houses further down the block.

It was always the people living in a big house that had the artillery rings. Probably only the high-ranking soldiers got to keep them. Most soldiers were paid well by the government and able to afford to build better houses than the common citizens. It was well-known that soldiers would use multiple fictitious names to claim more than one paycheck. The Lon Nol's government was not doing anything to prevent the fraud. The money could be used to help the common citizens, but it went to the hand of the Lon Nol's officials instead. This was one reason why the poor stayed poor, and the wealthy kept getting wealthier. This was one of the reasons hatred was building up within the poor toward the current society—and one of the reasons the Red Khmer was formed and why they were getting stronger every day.

Kim Chhorn walked down the alley questioning the adults and children and discovered several residents who sold the artillery rings. She had over seven hundred reals after she'd given Mother one hundred reals last night. Kim Chhorn entered the large houses and purchased all she could afford and told them she will come back later on that day.

She returned to the Chinese man and sold all the rings. She made over 2,800 reals. The Chinese man paid her in hundred-real bills. She had been thrilled the night before for making over 800 reals. No words could describe how good she felt now. Her throat and lungs seemed sore from the continuous exhilaration. She could have had the same taxi wait for her and had him transport her back to the same town, but she didn't want anybody to know that she had a lot of money. More importantly, she didn't want anybody to know what she was doing. She wanted to keep this business a secret.

She hadn't realized until now that she quadrupled her money each trip. She calculated and recalculated using all her fingers and toes and verified that she really was quadrupling her money on each trip.

It was not even noon yet. She had all day to make more money. She stuffed all the money in her pockets and called the taxi. She rode the tax back to the village and bought all the artillery rings that she could afford. She now had over 3,600 artillery rings. Unfortunately, the village had no more artillery rings to sell to her. They told her to come back in a week or so.

"Don't sell them to anybody, Ming. I will come back in five days," She said politely to her suppliers.

"Don't worry, Kmuy. I promise to save them for you," many would say.

Kim Chhorn rode the taxi back and sold the rings to the Chinese man. This time, the Chinese man gave her mostly five hundred-real bills. This was the first time she had ever touched such bills. She took one of them and examined the detail. She was intrigued by the picture and the design. She now had over 14,000 reals. She really wished she could find more people who would sell the artillery rings. It was past noon now, and she wasn't sure she could find anyone else before dark. She decided to head home and think of another place to go.

Mother was pickling the mustard greens in front of the shack when Kim Chhorn arrived. Kim Chhoy was holding me while Mother was working. Kim Chhom was probably out playing with other children.

"Mother, here's some money," Kim Chhorn took out some money from her pocket. She was careful not to take out too much because Mother might have wanted more than she'd planned to give her.

She counted 4,000 reals and handed the money to Mother. "This was four thousand reals," Kim Chhorn said with a big smile that she couldn't suppress.

Mother opened her eyes wide in shock. She dries her hands with the scarf and took the money. "Jum! This was a lot of money. How could you make so much money in half a day?" Mother asked. She appeared excited when she saw the money but then frowned slightly afterward with concern.

"It's easy. I bought the rings and sold them," Kim Chhorn said.

"How far did you go today?" Mother asked.

"About ten kilometers toward Takeo."

"You went that far? Kim Chhorn, that's very dangerous. You were too young. People might want to hurt you. There's a lot of fighting going on over there," she spoke with shock.

"It seems to be fine to me. The city was very calm. People were walking normally."

"Your Aunty Sarai came here earlier. She asked where you were and what you were up to. I told her that you were buying and selling the L'boh Ate Jai. She said she's been doing exactly the same thing, but I think she doesn't go as far. I told her to go with you from now on. I think it was safer if you were with her."

"Going with Ming Sarai was good in a way. I need someone to talk to anyway. I'm scared of riding the taxi with people that I don't know," Kim Chhorn agreed. Even if she didn't agree, she had to do what Mother said. Mother normally didn't give her the option.

Kim Chhorn went to bed with so much eagerness for the morning to arrive. She was trying to think of a place where she could buy more rings. She was not familiar with any road except to the south of Phnom Penh toward Takeo. She couldn't help but to think of the stacks of money the Chinese man handed her and the people who sold her the metal rings. It took her a long time to fall asleep.

Kim Chhorn was still asleep when Ming Sarai walked in, "Chhorn! Wake up! Why do you sleep so long? What type of merchant was that?" She said out loud and laughed.

Kim Chhorn woke up and squinted her eyes. She paused for a moment, hoping the money-making frenzy from yesterday was not just a dream. She remembered Mother had mentioned that Ming Sarai was going with her to buy the artillery rings. After she was satisfied that it was real and she was resuming her business, she sat up and smiled at Ming Sarai.

Ming Sarai dressed heavily to protect herself from the sun. She was holding several empty garment bags on each hand. She must have sewn them herself. She had a light skin tone similar to the Chinese. She was much bigger and taller than Kim Chhorn. Her lips were thick and her cheek bones were wide like Mother's. Her voice was similar to Mother's except she talked a lot louder.

"Here, eat some dessert and drink some coconut juice. I bought them last night. It will be a long ride," Ming Sarai said handing her a package of round rice cake called Num Ah Kouh and a fresh coconut with the top cut open. "Also, I figured you'd need bags, so I brought some for you."

Kim Chhorn ate the dessert. She felt a sudden surge of energy after eating the Num Ah Kouh. She drank the coconut juice carefully so as not to spill it on herself. It had been a while since the last time she had eaten in the morning. She would only eat in the morning when there was left-over rice from dinner. The Khmer called the leftover rice "Bai Kok" (Frozen Rice). Bai Kok was rare. Our family would normally eat until the pot was empty.

Ming Sarai and Kim Chhorn took the taxi to the nearby city. They walked around the city and asked the local residents for sellers. They found a few. Unfortunately, they didn't carry many artillery rings. They were harder to find being were far from the battle sites, but it was a lot safer. The sellers were hesitant to sell at first, as Kim Chhorn and Ming Sarai were new to them. For some reason, they would only sell the rings to the familiar customers. After Kim Chhorn spoke a few polite words with her charismatic tone, they were more than willing to sell and promised to save the amount Kim Chhorn requested the next time they got more.

Ming Sarai was glad that Kim Chhorn was with her; she could have come home empty-handed. They continue to search for the other sellers in the same town. They found only two more and bought everything they had. It was less than a thousand rings total.

At the end of the day, Ming Sarai and Kim Chhorn made about two thousand reals each. It was a lot of money but was less than what she'd made yesterday. But there not much she could do. Ming Sarai would never go farther than a twenty-minute ride.

Kim Chhorn continued to work with Ming Sarai for about eight weeks, buying from the local sellers around Phnom Penh. Ming Sarai had introduced her to several more Chinese buyers. She referred to them as "Chen Ate Jai."

Kim Chhorn sneaked out a few times after dark to her first customers near Takeo that had made the promise to save some artillery rings for her.

It was getting harder and harder to find the sellers nearby. More people had learned about this business and started buying and selling the artillery rings as well, making it more and more difficult for Kim Chhorn and Ming Sarai to find them. Sometimes they made just five hundred reals each. Even though it was a lot more than selling the pickled mustard greens, Kim Chhorn wanted to make more.

Frustrated with the problem of finding new sellers, Kim Chhorn suggested going farther from Phnom Penh. According to the rumors, all the cities and towns farther away from Phnom Penh were being attacked by the Red Khmers. It was a great opportunity for Kim Chhorn to buy more artillery rings. She constantly urged Ming Sarai to take her there. Ming Sarai was nervous and refused to go any farther. She determined not to take the risk and instead stay local.

Kim Chhorn finally decided not to go with Ming Sarai anymore and resumed her lone-wolf trades. She thought of Mother's words to work with Ming Sarai, but Mother had not been asking anything about the trades.

Kim Chhorn had given about seven thousand reals to Mother within the last eight weeks. She still had over thirteen thousand reals with her right now. She bought herself a big jacket with a lot of pockets to store the money.

Kim Chhorn looked around for a vehicle that could travel fast. The common tuk-tuk taxis seemed to move too slowly, and they would pick up more people along the road. Kim Chhorn didn't want to sit with other strangers, afraid they might see her pockets full of money. She also wanted to make at least three round trips a day.

With her desperate need to travel fast, the idea dawned on her that she could hire a car driver to drive just her alone. She believed she could afford to pay them. She looked around, and there were plenty of cars. She gazed across the street and found a car with a man standing next to it. He was holding some type of communication device speaking to someone.

She walked over to the man and asked, "Pu, could you drive me?"

"Of course! That's my job. Where do you want to go?" The man asked.

"Down south, toward Takeo."

"Takeo? It's kind of dangerous there. I normally charge a little bit more to travel that far," the man said.

"How much would it cost me just to drop me off there?"

"Normally, I would charge around fifty reals, but now I have to charge around one hundred reals depending on how far I have to drive."

"I'll pay you three hundred reals to take me there, but you cannot pick up someone else along the way. Is that all right?" Kim Chhorn asked to make sure.

"Of course it's all right, but I have to see the money first. Kids your age are sneaky. What if I get there and you have no money to pay me?"

"I'll give you the money in the car," Kim Chhorn said.

"Then get in."

The man led Kim Chhorn into the car. She took the money out of the pocket, careful not to reveal that she had more money. She handed the money to the man and looked away trying not to get any more of his attention.

Kim Chhorn was once again taking the taxi alone further down south. She wanted to go north, east, and west of Phnom Penh as well, but she didn't know the way or how to read the signs.

She liked cars more than the tuk-tuk taxis. Even with the window was rolled down, she felt a lot safer. She was being protected all around.

She was glad that the man didn't seem to be interested in talking to her. He was busy communicating with another person using the electronic device that was attached to the car. She didn't like talking to men when she was alone. More importantly, she didn't want to reveal that she didn't know how to read. She was afraid he would threaten her and cause problems. He could do anything to her if he knew how to read. He could make things up and report her to the police and put her in jail. The thought frightened her.

In just about twenty minutes, she had passed her previous towns where she bought the artillery rings. The car was traveling nearly twice the speed of the tux-tux taxis but felt like it was not even moving. Despite the fighting going on, Kim Chhorn saw taxis traveling both directions. She was relieved to see other taxis on the road. She would need a ride back. She gazed through the window of the car, observing the region, looking for a suitable town to buy the artillery rings.

"Pu, stop!" she said when she reached a town that was large enough to hold more than one potential seller.

She got off the car, holding several garment bags, and looked around trying to memorize the location using the trees and houses as the references. It was important to know where she was for the next time she would come here.

Boooom! Boooom! Boooom! She heard a thunder-like sound in the distance. She knew it was not thunder though. The sky was bright and clear. She had heard this sound before in Tonle and in Takeo. It was the sound of shelling. She was not afraid though. It was still far away.

The local residents didn't seem to worry about the distant explosions either. They were going about daily life. People were riding bicycles, some were walking and talking, some were cooking in their backyards, and some were bathing with the bucket of water.

She approached and asked a passerby where she could buy the L'boh Ate Jai. Sometimes, they didn't know. Then she asked where she could find the house of the military leaders instead. After asking several people, they led her to a house three times larger than the rest, made of large strong wood similar to our house in Tonle but only half the size. The seller was an elderly woman who was wearing all kinds of gold necklace and a pair of glasses. Her hair was neatly tied and coiled on the back. She was chubby and well-dressed.

"What brings you here, Me Tooch (tiny one)?" the woman asked nicely.

"I'm looking to buy the L'boh Ate Jai. Do you sell them?"

"You were brave for a little girl. People don't come here anymore. They are scared. I'm used to it. How many do you want?"

"I have ten thousand real. How many can I get?"

"That's enough for twenty thousand rings. I have much more than that if you need to come again. My husband and his army were shooting the bastard Red Khmers. All his subordinates brought the rings to me."

Kim Chhorn took out the money out trying to conceal her excitement. She saved $3,000 in her pocket for the taxi and just in case she needed it on the way back. The woman counted the money. Then she counted the rings that were already separated into thousand-ring bundles. Good thing Kim Chhorn had sturdy garment bags with tough handles. The bags also had covers so that no one could see inside. The woman placed the rings into four of Kim Chhorn's bags. She still had two more empty bags just in case she needed them.

Kim Chhorn told the woman she'd be coming back to purchase another twenty thousand. She wanted to buy forty thousand more, but after she lifted the bags, she nearly broke her back. She wished she was stronger, although she was already able to carry as much as any adult woman could.

She carried the bags back to the road and waited for a taxi. She remembered when she was moving from Takeo to Tonle that the road was jammed with all types of vehicles. Now the road was light with traffics. There were still families walking or riding on the ox wagon traveling toward Phnom Penh.

After a short wait, Kim Chhorn found a taxi that had no other passengers. She offered to pay the man four hundred reals for the ride as long as he did not pick up anyone else along the way. She told the man that she was carrying desserts that might get squashed by other passengers. The man didn't seem to care what she's carrying. He got paid much more than he would have from all other passengers combined.

When she arrived in Phnom Penh, she sold the rings to the closest Chen Ate Jai and made forty thousand reals. She stuffed the money into the large pockets in her jacket. She didn't pay much attention to the Chen Ate Jai, who was staring at her in disbelief after he'd handed her the money.

She walked into the open market nearby, wearing the large jacket full of money, and bought herself a couple of packages of Num Ah Kouh and other desserts that she had been dreaming of eating since Takeo. Somehow, the idea of making even more money was more appealing than food. She would have gone straight back to buy more artillery rings had her stomach not been growling and churning for food. She spent less than twenty reals for all the desserts.

She hung all the empty bags on one arm and held the dessert package at the same time. She used her other hand to shove the dessert in her mouth while her eyes were scanning for a suitable taxi. She waved for a nice taxi and paid the driver two thousand reals and asked him to drive her to the same woman's house and informed him to wait for her.

The man agreed and didn't seem to raise any suspicious. Kim Chhorn bought the rest of the artillery rings from the woman. She forgot to bring more bags, but fortunately, the woman had extra bags of her own and gave them to Kim Chhorn. She even helped her carry the bags back to the taxi.

The driver was standing on the other side of the taxi smoking and paid no attention to Kim Chhorn at all. He drove her back to Phnom Penh without asking a single question.

Kim Chhorn sold the rings to two different Chen Ate Jais. She thought it was safer that way. She didn't want anyone to know she was carrying so much money.

She stuffed the money in every pocket in her jacket and also placed some in the bag. She decided to return home because she had nowhere else to put the money. Besides, it was too late in the evening to search for other sellers. She probably would have to travel over an hour to find new sellers. If Mother found out she went that far, she would forbid her from doing this trade again.

She returned home as Mother was just arriving home herself with two new Italian bred oxen. She was no longer making the pickled mustard plant. She had gone back to buying and selling oxen and pigs with the money that Kim Chhorn had made.

Kim Chhoy was studying her schoolwork. She had returned to school full-time now. She didn't need to walk around and sell the pickled mustard greens anymore. Kim Chhom was holding me as Mother was washing the oxen and speaking to my uncle about tending the new oxen. Pu Ream was there as well. He was responsible for tending the oxen after school since Bun Chhoeun was gone.

Because Kim Chhorn had started the new trade, she had not been home much. She just came to eat dinner and sleep. Then she returned to do her tasks. She had not had a chance to speak to Kim Chhoy or Kim Chhom at all.

"Mother!" Kim Chhorn called softly.

Mother turned around and saw Kim Chhorn wearing a thick jacket on a hot evening. One of the bags was half filled, and the rest were empty.

"You didn't come and eat today. Did you eat anything yet?" Mother asked.

"I ate dessert."

"How could the dessert fill you up? If you continue to skip meals like that you will starve to death. Now get inside and eat. I saved you some rice and some stir-fry pork."

"I want to show you what I got you first. Then I will eat," Kim Chhorn said, looking away to hide her smile.

"What did you bring me?" Mother asked as she followed Kim Chhorn inside the shack.

Kim Chhorn walked to the corner of the shack where no one could see from the outside. She laid down all the empty bags on the ground and handed Mother the bag that was half filled with the money. "Look in here."

Mother took the bag and peeked inside. She saw bundles of money, all in five hundred-real bills. Her hand shook uncontrollably. She reached in the bag and grabbed as much as she could with one hand and lifted the money up closer to her face.

"So much money. How much is in here?"

"I don't know. I just showed you what's in there. You think that's a lot? Take a look at this." She unbuttoned her jacket, and all the inner pockets were filled with bundles of five hundred-real bills. Kim Chhorn pulled out stacks of money. The money hidden in the jacket was about five times more than the money in the bag. "If the Chinese man paid me correctly, it should be a little over one hundred thirty thousand reals," she said proudly and tried to be funny at the same time.

Mother was overwhelmed with so much money. As Kim Chhorn was unloading the money from her jacket, Mother arrange it neatly in larger stacks. Then she started to count the money and stacked the bills in groups of ten thousand. When she finished counting, she set up a scarf by the corner of the shack and neatly piled the money on the scarf. Then she gathered all her clothes nearby to cover the money.

Kim Chhorn asked Mother for forty thousand reals to resume her trades. Mother counted and stacked forty thousand reals for her and placed the money in a bag.

"Don't tell anyone that we have a lot of money. Not even your grandma. I will save all the money. I'm thinking of buying land and building a new house somewhere," Mother said.

Kim Chhorn ate her food that Mother saved for her. Then walked outside the house checking the new oxen and spoke to Pu Ream and Grandma. She pretended that nothing she did was out of the ordinary. However, she could not take her mind off the money she'd made, the people she'd traded with, and how she'd paid the taxi just to ride all by herself. She felt so good and so eager to make more money.

She went to bed early and woke up before the sunrise. She put on the big jacket with a lot of pockets and hid her money in the pockets. She went straight to the taxi and paid extra money so that the driver would not pick up any other passengers. This time she was not in rush and took her time to bargain for the price of the cab. The cab driver wanted only two hundred and fifty reals to drop her off down south, near Takeo.

She got out of the cab and started to seek the artillery rings sellers. Unfortunately, she found only one woman who had only about a thousand rings for her to buy. Other buyers had come a day earlier and bought most of them. She had to get another taxi and rode to another town nearby.

At the end of the day, Kim Chhorn had made just over five thousand reals. It was still a lot of money, but she was extremely disappointed. She had expected a lot more than this.

Kim Chhorn resumed her trading daily using the same path but only ventured slightly farther away from the familiar roads. She found new sellers, but none carried more than two thousand rings. She wished she could read street signs and take different routes to find new sellers. The pace at which she was finding new sellers was slow. She was averaging only about four thousand real per day.

Three months had passed. Kim Chhorn did not seem to break more than ten thousand reals per day, even after she had ventured further south. Each day, she got closer and closer to the battle site, and the sound of the explosions became louder and louder. If she continued to get any closer, she would get caught in the cross fire and be killed. She needed to go further east or west of Phnom Penh.

Kim Chhorn had been very frustrated and angry at herself for not being able to read. She had made an attempt to take a risk but changed her mind every time she thought of being lost in an unfamiliar place.

Today she determined to take a chance. She wanted to come home with one hundred thousand real like she had before. She went to the taxi and bargained with the driver. She paid him one thousand real to driver her. She didn't tell the driver her destination. Instead, she told him to keep driving and she would tell him when to stop. She promised to pay more if necessary.

She instructed the drive to start going south for a long time, and then she instructed him to turn right onto another main road. The taxi moved along the paved road where the traffic was busy in both directions. She was looking through the window trying to remember the road as much as possible, especially any trees or houses that were unusually distinct from the others.

She was too focused on remembering the landmarks and forgot to pay attention to the traffic. She came to a quiet town where there was not a single vehicle on the road beside the taxi she was in—not even a bicycle. It was a fairly large town though. The houses were built closely together as if they were all relatives. After she realized the surroundings, she yelled out to the driver, "Stop! Stop! Stop right here!"

The driver stopped the taxi in shock, "Are you sure you want to stop here, Me Own (little girl)? With the amount of money you paid me, I could drive you back home and more. This place is dangerous. See? No one comes here."

Kim Chhorn paused for few seconds and then said, "I need to come here, but I don't know how I'm going to get back home."

"There's a bus stop about two kilometers back. There's even a bench for you to sit. I know for sure the buses still come this way. In fact, we just passed one on the way here. So, if you know this place, you could take the bus home," the man explained.

"I'm getting off. I will take the bus home when I'm ready," Kim Chhorn said and got off the taxi.

The driver turned his taxi around and sped off. Kim Chhorn was alone on the road. She started to trot toward the quiet town. When she got closer, it surprised her to see many local residents were still going about their business. It was still early morning. The children were probably still in bed. The men and women were carrying water on their shoulders.

A few minutes later, Kim Chhorn heard a deep and powerful sound of explosions from somewhere not too far away. The villagers seem unconcerned. This was the reason why no one wanted to drive this far. However, this was a good opportunity for Kim Chhorn. She approached an old woman who was tossing the rice grain to a horde of hungry chickens and their little chicks.

"Um, do you know where I could buy the L'boh Ate Jai?" Kim Chhorn asked.

"You were coming to buy L'boh Ate Jai? I don't know what they are, but I heard they sold them in those houses over there. Walk straight and turn right, and you will see the houses with the banana trees in the front. If that's not the right house, you can ask them," the old woman said pointing.

Kim Chhorn followed the directions and came to a large house built entirely from large wood with a tiled roof. The house was surrounded with flowers of all sorts. The grasses and small plants were neatly trimmed. Large banana plants grew neatly in columns. Only the wealthy could afford to live in a house like this.

Kim Chhorn knocked on a large hardwood door and peeked through the nearby window. A middle-aged woman dressed like she was going to the king's welcoming, heavily smeared with makeup, opened the door.

"Um, do you know where I can buy L'boh Ate Jai?" Kim Chhorn asked, taking a risk to assume she was older than Mother.

"You came here to buy the L'boh Ate Jai? How much do you want to buy?" The woman asked without showing any sign of being insulted by the title.

"How much do you have?" Kim Chhorn asked.

"I have a lot—over twenty thousand—and I sell them two for one real like everyone else," the women said.

"Then I want to buy all of them," Kim Chhorn said.

Like every adult she did business with, the woman was stunned when Kim Chhorn said she wanted to buy all of them. It would cost her over ten thousand reals.

Kim Chhorn took a bundle of money that had Mother wrapped neatly in a rubber band. Each bundle was ten thousand reals. Kim Chhorn has three more bundled in the other pockets.

The woman counted the rings in bundles where each bundle has one thousand rings. The number of rings was twenty-one thousand. The woman kindly let Kim Chhorn keep the extras. Kim Chhorn paid her ten thousand reals, and she still has over thirty thousand reals left in her pockets. Once again, she was thrilled to be making big money again. She filled four of her bags and then carried the bag toward the main road, hoping a taxi or car would come by. There must be someone who would still travel here.

Unfortunately, after she walked half kilometer along the road, not a single vehicle or person was seen on the road. She has no choice but to walk to the bus stop that was about two kilometers away. She wished she had a dong raek right now where she could carry things on her shoulder instead of holding the bags in her hands. Her knees and back was working hard to maintain the weight and balance. She stopped when she could no longer keep her palm curled up. She looked back to the town each time she stopped to see the progress of the distance she had walked.

Nearly two hours later and after many stops, the road curved around the hills and trees; the town was no long visible. She reached another road that intersected the current road. Then she saw a few cars moving swiftly on the other road. She felt a little relief.

Kim Chhorn saw an old bench that stood solemnly on the corner of the intersection. This must be where the buses stopped. She placed all the bags on the ground with relief and sat on the bench, waiting for the bus. As she relaxed she heard the sound of explosions from somewhere in distance. The battle was somewhere many kilometers away, but it had gotten louder than the ones she'd heard in Takeo.

A moment later she saw a bus coming toward her. She had never ridden a bus before, but everyone said it was easy as long as you knew where the bus was heading. Every bus had the final destination sign on them. The only problem was that she couldn't read the sign on the bus. She was hoping there was another way to find out where the final destination is. She needed to go Pochentong Airport.

The bus stopped in front of her. Kim Chhorn got up looking around for clues. There was a big sign on top of the windshield that said the final destination, but she couldn't read the sign. She continued to look for any type clues that would help indicate the destination.

She found nothing that pertained to the Pochentong Airport.

"Are you getting on, or were you going to stare all day?" the bus driver asked impatiently.

Kim Chhorn hesitated, but she got in the bus and kept searching for clues. She sat in the first open seat on the aisle just in case she needed to get off the next few seconds. She didn't want to ask the driver or the passengers, afraid they would find out that she couldn't read and harass her.

The bus started to move. Kim Chhorn's heart was pounding in fear of being taken further from home and getting lost. She sat down and continued to observe the road carefully. So far, it was heading in the direction that she had come on the cab.

A moment later, the bus made a few turns, and the road no longer looked familiar. Kim Chhorn didn't feel this was the right bus. If she waited any longer, it would be too far to walk back to the bus stop.

"Pu, where is this bus heading?" Chhorn asked the driver.

"This bus is heading to Steung Mean Chey."

"Oh, I want to go to Pochentong Airport. Please stop the bus. I need to get off."

The driver pulled the bus over, and Kim Chhorn walked off the bus. "Why didn't you read?" he asked.

"Sorry, Pu. I was in a hurry," she replied.

"Pay the fees!" the man demanded.

"But I just got on," Kim Chhorn replied.

"Well, you disrupted the business and wasted my time."

"But Pu, I only have enough money to pay for my trip back home. If I pay you, then I don't have the money to get home," Kim Chhorn lied. She didn't want to show she had money being alone in a remote place.

"Then get off!" the man yelled angrily.

Kim Chhorn stepped off the bus and stared at it as it sped off. She started walking back to the bus stop again carrying the heavy bags. She was about one kilometer away from the bus stop. It was now past noon. If she didn't get the right bus soon, she would be stranded here, possibly until dark. The fear made her walk hastily to the bus stop without thinking that she was carrying the heavy bags.

She reached the bus stop, very exhausted and terrified. She sat on the bench waiting impatiently not knowing what to do next. She decided to take the next bus even if it didn't take her to the Pochentong Airport. She needed to leave this remote place.

She waited for two hours and was ready to burst out crying when she saw the bus approaching from the distance. When the bus stopped, she pretended she knew exactly what she was doing and got on the bus. The passengers were all adults. She wished there were children on the bus that she could ask without revealing that she didn't know how to read.

As the bus started to move, she looked around for clues again hoping to find out where the bus would take her. She found nothing. She carefully paid the driver without revealing her bundles of money. Good thing she'd brought some small bills.

She sat down keeping her eyes on the road and hoping the bus would take her to Pochentong Airport.

The bus moved and stopped a dozen places but nowhere Kim Chhorn was familiar with. She continued to wait and wait for a familiar place.

It was nightfall when the bus finally stopped completely. There was not a single person on the bus except for the driver and herself.

"This bus is done for the day. When were you planning to get off the bus?" the driver asked.

"I wasn't paying attention; my house was way back. I thought this bus would go another round," Kim Chhorn lied.

"You have to get off! Can't you read? This was the final stop!" the driver added angrily.

Kim Chhorn got off the bus frantically looking for a way to get home. The bus had stopped in a quiet town somewhere in the border of Phnom Penh. Kim Chhorn carried the heavy bags looking for a taxi.

She walked and hollered around for a taxi. After a dozen tries, a taxi finally stopped for her. She told the taxi to drive her to Pochentong Airport. This time she didn't have to worry about reading any signs. She should have gotten off the bus earlier and taken the taxi, but she was too nervous and couldn't think straight.

When she arrived home, she saw Mother sitting by the door in the dark weeping as she was waiting for her. Kim Chhorn had arrived home late before, but Mother was never like this.

"Why were you home so late?" Mother asked.

"I was lost. I took the wrong bus."

Kim Chhorn placed the bags of artillery rings along the wall. Mother walked over and examined the bags.

"How far did you have to travel?"

"I don't know. I just continued to go further until I reached a remote town where they sold a lot of rings," Kim Chhorn replied. She didn't want to tell her that she went far, but she couldn't lie. She had returned home so late and gotten so many artillery rings in one trip

"Sarai told me that you went further than anyone dared to go, and you were not afraid of anything. I took a taxi to the south looking to buy some oxen; I heard the sounds of shelling so close. All I could think of was you. I was so worried. From now on, you are not going to do this trading anymore. Sarai and I will continue your business. I will do it locally. Although it's less money compared to the amount you made, it is still a lot. I want you to go back to school and help tend the oxen and feed the pigs. I will sell these rings," Mother said. "And how many rings do you have here?"

"A little more than twenty thousand," Kim Chhorn said.

"That's a lot. Sarai said she could only find five thousand at most in a week," Mother said.

Kim Chhorn was upset that Mother was not allowing her to go make more money, but she was happy to be home. She thought she would never see home again. She ate the food that Mother saved her and went to bed.

Mother woke up early in the morning and took all the bags of rings with her. She sold all the rings and made over forty thousand reals. She took five thousand reals and invested with Ming Sarai to resume the trade.

Kim Chhorn didn't want to go back to school, afraid of getting whipped by the teachers. Instead, she spent all her time taking care of me, tending the oxen, and feeding the pigs. Mother was right. It was too dangerous out there. She could have been killed by going too far from Phnom Penh. She had become so greedy about making money and forgotten all about the dangers.

CHAPTER 4

It had been over six months since Bun Chhoeun left home. Father was finally able to come home for a short period of time. Mother had to pick him up at the truck station, as he was unable to find where we lived. He explained to Mother how much worse the war had gotten. The Red Khmers had taken over many of the major cities, destroying bridges and blocking the main roads. Their forces were getting bigger and stronger every day. Mother told him about Bun Chhoeun joining the army, and there was no news about him at all. Father worried about him, but he didn't know what to do either. Plus, he was very busy. The government needed him more than ever. They increased his salary every three months and offered him all sorts of gifts on the side. Father informed the office about us living in a shack and told him we deserve a better place to live since he was risking his life for the government. The office offered us a bunker house right inside the military compound. They gave us a house that sat on a big piece of land with open space all around. The house only accommodated our immediate family, not our aunts and uncles. Mother bought a lot of wood and had my uncles expand the house. With the money that Kim Chhorn made, she still had over two hundred thousand reals left after she'd bought all the wood. The money was enough to feed all the families for many years. She invited all my aunts and uncles who were living in the shack to live with us, including Grandma and Pu Ream.

Mother continued to buy and sell the artillery rings with Ming Sarai. At the same time, she continued to buy and sell oxen and pigs. She traveled around the outer boundary of Phnom Penh a lot and heard the sound of the explosions every time. The sound used to be faint, but it got a little louder and louder each day, indicating the Red Khmer was getting closer and closer. She was hoping Bun Chhoeun was nowhere near the shelling. She wept nearly every day, especially when she heard the radio about the Red Khmer attacking the nearby cities. Despite the fact that the Lon Nol's armies were losing the war everywhere, she believed that Bun Chhoeun was still alive. She really wanted him back home.

Nearly every evening when the dinner was ready, Mother would make a plate of rice and with pork or chicken. Then she would burn the incense sticks and place them on the plate. She would place the plates on a high chair and kneel down in front of the food praying, "I'm begging the keeper of the land and keeper of the water, the spirits of all the ancestors from all cardinals, please look after my son, Bun Chhoeun. Please keep the dangers away from him."

Sometimes, she would add more details to her prayers. After she finished praying, she would bow three times slowly where her palms would touch the ground with her forehead atop the back of her hands.

A week after Father left home to resume his duty for the government, Mother woke up early in the morning dressed in long pants and a long-sleeve shirts with a scarf draped down from her neck. She was also wearing flip-flops. She would normally walk barefoot. She woke Kim Chhorn up and whispered, "Kim Chhorn, take care of Bun Chhun. I'm going get Bun Chhoeun back."

Kim Chhorn woke up looking confused. How was she going to get him back? He was probably somewhere out there either fighting or prepare to fight against the Red Khmers. With the Red Khmers attacking every city and town, he probably was not even alive right now. It was common that the children as young as ten years of age went to join the armies. Some had died from the battle. Some returned home without their arms or legs. There were many cases where they accidently triggered their own grenades and got killed or seriously injured.

Mother looked determined and ready. She also knew that Bun Chhoeun had always been a stubborn boy. Even if she found him, she would still need to convince him to come home. She discarded thought of the difficulties and determined to carry out her mission. That was the least of her concern. For now, she needed to find him.

She walked over to the military base office not too far from where we lived. She entered one of the buildings, unsure if it was the right place for her to ask the question. She saw a young man sitting in his office speaking on the telephone.

"Loak P'own, my son sneaked away and joined the military without asking me. He's only fourteen. I want him back home. How can I get him back?" Mother asked.

"Ming, normally, once he joins the military, he cannot resign without approval. What was your son's name?" the young man asked politely.

"My son's name is Bun Chhoeun. He's very short. He's about this tall," Mother replied and raised her arm to demonstrate his height.

"Let me check for you, Ming. Wait here," the man said and walked to another area.

He returned about thirty minutes later holding a piece of paper with an uncertain look on his face. "I'm sorry, Ming, but he has been taken to the Kompung Speu province. According to the information here, he's in the second line of defense in the area. He will be in combat if the first line of defense breaks down. The first lines are in the middle of combat right now."

"My God! My son! Why would my son wanted to do that? He's so young and so small. He probably can't lift a rifle off the ground. I need to get my son back," Mother said and wailed.

Her hands were shaking in terror. Tears were rolling down her cheeks uncontrollably. Bun Chhoeun was in a grave danger. Mother thought he was still in training. She had been hoping he would give up and return home.

"Loak P'own, I want to get my son back. Tell me where in the Kompung Speu," Mother pleaded. "He's so small. He had been talking about joining the military with his friends many times, but I never thought he would really do it," Mother added.

"Ming, the road to the location is very dangerous. There are reports of Khmer Rouge's ambushing along the way. It's very dangerous for Ming to go," the young man informed her.

"I want my son back. I'm going, even if Loak P'own won't tell me where he is. I will search until I find him or die trying, but if Loak P'own would tell me the location, consider you saved Ming's life."

"He's in the area called Tum Paeng Kalueng." he told Mother with hesitation.

"I wish Loak P'own longevity. For this life and all your next life, peace and happiness will always be with you," Mother blessed the young man and then marched out of the office. Kompung Speu province was located to the southwest of Phnom Penh and adjacent to the northern part of Takeo. Ma went to trade in many parts of Kompung Speu, but she had never been in the Tum Paeng Kalueng area before.

Mother returned home to get some money for the taxi. She didn't expect Bun Chhoeun to be out in the battle field. When she arrived home, she saw Ming Sarai waiting for her to go with her to do their usual business.

"Sarai, please look after my children. I'm going to find Bun Chhoeun. He's at Tum Paeng Kalueng in Kompung Speu. The place was under attack, but he's in the second line. If he stays there, he will die for sure."

"You are planning to go there? The entire province is in the middle the battle. And do you know how to get there?" Ming Sarai asked.

"I don't know the exact place, but I know where to look."

"I'll go with you. You know how Bun Chhoeun is. His head is hard as a rock. He will not listen to you. If you let me go with you, I will drag him by his neck, Yorn. You just watch," Ming Sarai said. "I'm not asking you. I'm telling you that I'm going with you."

"He is a hard-head like you said. It's too dangerous for you to go. If anything happened to you, who will take care of your children?" Mother asked, trying to discourage her from going.

"My husband could take care of them. Don't think too much. Let just go."

"Then you can wait in a safe place while I will do the searching when we get there," Mother replied, reluctantly agreeing.

Mother and Ming Sarai walked out of the military base and tried to get a taxi. Every single one of them refused to go when they heard the destination. They thought it was too dangerous.

Mother returned home with Ming Sarai and brought out a large stack of money all in five hundred-real bills and put some her pocket. It must have been at least twenty thousand reals. She went back to find the taxi. When the first available taxi stopped by, she asked normally to take her to Tum Paeng Kalueng. The taxi driver refused immediately. Mother took out about an inch-thick stack of five hundred-real bills and showed it to the driver.

"Here, Loak P'own. If I give you this much, would you take me? I'll give you more when we return. My son secretly joined the military, and I'm going to bring him back home. You can wait for us two kilometers away from the site, so you'll be safe," Mother bargained.

"All right, let's get going," the man said. It was a big risk, but if he returned home safely, he wouldn't have to work for several years.

The man drove them out of the military base of Phnom Penh and headed down south with the tuk-tuk taxi. The traffic become lighter and lighter the further they rode. A long moment later, they arrived at the foot of the mountain in Kompung Speu. The sounds of the explosions resonated from somewhere in the distance then subsided. Mother was hoping the driver wouldn't change his mind. The man drove his taxi along the main road that led further into the mountain. Another sound of explosions erupted much louder than before.

Kompung Speu was once a beautiful place. Before the war, Mother would ride the taxi along the mountain and visit small villages looking for the right people to trade with. Sometimes she would spend many nights in the village chatting with the families she had just met, mostly about none business related.

The view of the mountain still looked the same, but as she gazed far up the mountain and around the area, she got an eerie feeling. Anywhere in those thick forests could be infested with the Red Khmer waiting to attack. They could be hiding and making plans or ready to ambush anyone that would pass by.

The taxi continued move along the road that ran along the side of the mountain. Sometimes the road would cut through the thick forest and then emerge on the edge of the cliff. There was no sign of a single motor vehicle on the road. The road was quiet except for a few random families migrating on foot toward Phnom Penh.

When they got deeper into the mountains, they heard more explosions trailing one after another. Some were louder than others. It was ironic that they were driving toward those dreadful sounds.

"They are in the middle of combat right now," the driver said with great concern.

"If Loak P'own will help me get me there and get my son back, not only you will get more money but you will be blessed forever. Angels will look after you the rest of your life. Angels have eyes. They are looking upon us all the time. The keeper of the land and the keeper of the water will help you as well," Mother said, encouraging the man to continue this trip.

The road became narrow, and the asphalt suddenly disappeared leaving just the gravel and shrubs. The road was worn by the ox wagon on two sides leaving the shrubs and dirt in the middle untouched. The sounds of the explosions were loud and close. The sound of the battle rifles could be heard clearly.

"Bong Srey, I cannot go any further. The shelling is too close. It could hit us any time. I'll wait here, and please be quick," the man said after he stopped his taxi.

"P'own Sarai, you wait here. If you don't see me in an hour, you should return home. If I'm still alive, I know how to get back home," Mother said as if she was ready for her last day of her life.

"I'll go with you, Bong Yorn," Ming Sarai said.

"You shouldn't go. It's too dangerous. The shelling is too close."

"I said I'm going, so I'm going," Ming Sarai insisted.

"Then let's go," Mother said. She knew she could not change her mind.

The sounds of the rifles erupted from somewhere close by. Mother and Ming Sarai instinctively stopped and crouched and then began to pick up their pace along the side of the wagon road.

They walked along the dirt road searching for any kind of movements. After about one kilometer, they spotted a soldier in a camouflage uniform and a helmet, heavily armed, standing on the left side of the wagon road. Mother was exhausted but relieved to see the soldier with a uniform and not the ones that dressed in black. It was known that the Red Khmer dressed in black and wore red and white checkered scarves around their necks.

Mother led Ming Sarai toward the soldier hoping not to cause any stir. The soldier was in his mid-twenties. He's stood much taller than Mother. His entire body was strapped with grenades, bullet belts, and handguns. The soldier saw Mother and Ming Sarai immediately and jumped with surprise, but he didn't appear suspicious.

"Ming, where are you coming from and where are you going? It's very dangerous here. Please go back," he said politely.

"Loak P'own, I need your help to get my son back home. His name was Bun Chhoeun. He's about this tall, and he's only thirteen years old. I was told he's in this area. Have you seen him?"

"Of course I know him. He's the smallest one that insisted he was sixteen and wanted to shoot the Red Khmers. I like his attitude, but he is so young. You will have to convince him yourself. He is very determined to stay and fight. He would not listen to us," the soldier said. "I'll have one of my men take you to him. Maybe you can convince him to go home."

Suddenly, there was a loud explosion from somewhere nearby. Mother and Ming Sarai instinctively dove to the ground for cover. They could hear debris caused by the explosion crash back to the ground.

The soldier walked quickly toward one of his men crouching nearby and whispered the instruction. The other soldier signaled Mother and Ming Sarai to follow. "Ming, follow me. Stay low and walk fast."

Another loud explosion went off so close that Mother thought she was going to get hit. Everyone dove to the ground. The escorting soldier got up and walked with his head stooped down low with one hand securing his helmet. Mother and Ming Sarai followed him closely, moving in the same manner.

After about twenty yards of crouching and running through the thick brush and trees, Mother and Ming Sarai spotted a little boy with his body curled in a fetal-like position, holding an oversized rifle and looking the other direction. He was wearing faded blue shorts and a dirty green t-shirt. The helmet covered most of his head and face. There was a small bag of rice and a small pot with a long handle lying right beside him.

Mother recognized the shorts and t-shirt. She had sewed them herself. The little boy heard the sound of the movements behind him and he turned around. He lifted the helmet up so that he could see better. He scowled and jerked back in disbelief. "Mother... Ming! What were you doing here?" he asked softly and angrily.

Mother and Ming Sarai kneeled down next to Bun Chhoeun, staying low to the ground.

"Chhoeun, son, come home with us. You are too young and too small. Let the big people fight. Come home with Mother," Mother pleaded.

"I'm not going back. Mother and Ming should go back home! It's dangerous here! We're in the middle of a battle! There's a shell just landed around here," Bun Chhoeun said.

"That's why I want you to go back home. I'm afraid of the shells," Mother said.

"Mother, leave now!" he screamed.

"You are coming back home with us!" Ming Sarai replied trying to keep her voice low.

"Bun Chhoeun, please come back home. I'm begging you," Mother said.

"Mom, I said I'm not going back. We're going to kill the Red Khmer," Bun Chhoeun insisted.

"Bun Chhoeun, you are so young and small. The war is for grown-ups. I know you liked school. We made a lot of money now. You can go to school without having to work hard like before. I have thought about you every day. Haven't you thought of me?" Mother said and wept.

Ming Sarai watched Mother weep with a heartbroken look, and then she turned her face to Bun Chhoeun with an irritated stare. Unexpectedly, she reached out and snatched his rifle and tossed it aside. Then she quickly took off her scarf and thrust herself forward on to Bun Chhoeun. She wrapped her scarf around his skinny body and yanked him up. Bun Chhoeun struggled to get free, but Mother immediately grabbed both of his hands. Ming Sarai hauled him with her scarf as Mother held his hands tightly so that he couldn't free himself.

"Since you were hard-headed, I'm dragging you home. You will be shot in the head if you stay here any longer," Ming Sarai said angrily.

They hauled him along until they reached the wagon road. Bun Chhoeun, embarrassed by the look of his fellow soldiers, decided to walk willingly. He was walking between Ming Sarai and Mother like a prisoner of war.

"The taxi is up ahead waiting for us," Mother said.

Bun Chhoeun kept his head down as he walked, embarrassed and angry. He was trying to avoid the conversation.

"Your sister Kim Chhorn made over two hundred thousand reals in less than six months. We have enough money to survive for many years. I'm not allowing Kim Chhorn to go out and make money anymore, but

I'm still making money from trading pigs and oxen. Also, me and Ming Sarai were buying and selling L'boh Ate Jai locally. You can concentrate on school. I want you to be someone important. You are smart. I don't want your life to end meaninglessly," Mother explained as they walk.

They arrived where the taxi had been waiting. Mother was relieved to see the taxi was still here, and the taxi driver was very glad to see them as well. He knew he would get the rest of the money when they got back home.

A loud explosion went off very close to them when Ming Sarai took the first step onto the taxi. Everyone ducked for a few seconds and then scrambled onto the taxi. They heard several more explosions and gun battles as they were leaving the area.

They rode home without saying a word. Mother gave another twenty thousand real to the taxi driver as she'd promised. She couldn't stop thanking the man for the favor. Bun Chhoeun was surprised to see things had changed a lot. We were no long living in a palm leaves shack. Our new house was made of wood and bricks, surrounded by the military buildings. He could see the newly added sections all around the original house.

When he entered the house, Kim Chhorn was sitting in the kitchen chopping up a large pork belly and keeping an eye on a pot of rice cooking on the hearth. Pork was very expensive. Normally, Mother would only buy a small slice of pork once a month and stir-fry it with a lot of vegetables. Kim Chhoy was lying on the wood plank floor doing her school work. She got up and walked over to Bun Chhoeun. Kim Chhom was rocking me in a hammock that Father had made when he was here. She was trying to make me go to sleep.

Inside the house, Bun Chhoeun noticed that Mother had bought more pots and pans and silverware and hung them on the wall and shelves.

Grandma, Pu Ream, and the rest of our aunts and uncles poured in from the other sections of the house to our kitchen.

"Where have you been, Grandson?" Grandma asked.

"He was seeking death, but Bong Yorn and I hauled his neck back," Ming Sarai announced.

"You make things up, Ming. I was not looking for death. I was looking to shoot the Red Khmers," Bun Chhoeun said trying to redeem himself.

"My nephew was trying to defend his country. Don't yell at him like that," one of our uncles said.

"Defend the country how? The rifle was heavier than him. The Red Khmers don't need to shoot to kill him. They could just throw a rock and kill him," Ming Sarai added sarcastically.

Bun Chhoeun appeared to be very uncomfortable with everyone around and being scorned by Ming Sarai. However, Grandma and some of the aunts and uncle responded in his defense. They believed he had been brainwashed by his cousin Vann. Mother agreed and told Bun Chhoeun not to talk to him again if he ever came back home alive. Vann had joined the army with Bun Chhoeun on the same day, but he was deployed to a different location. There had been no word of him since he left.

Bun Chhoeun went back to school the next day. He did his schoolwork immediately after school. Once finished with his schoolwork, he took over the tasks with the oxen and pigs from Kim Chhorn. Since we were no longer living near the pond, Bun Chhoeun took over the task of carrying water from the well to fill the vase and feed and bathe the oxen.

The grass had become scarce. It was now late in the dry season, and most of the grassland had been claimed by the new settlers. He couldn't even walk the oxen along the paved road like he'd done before. He had to walk over two kilometers just to find the grassland.

Three days after Bun Chhoeun returned home, Mother got the news from the military office that all the defensive lines in Tum Paeng Kalueng had been destroyed. Only less than a dozen out of about a thousand soldiers survived the attacked. Bun Chhoeun could have been easily one of the dead.

Mother wept for the soldiers that she saw preparing for the combat. She was thankful that she had made the decision to retrieve Bun Chhoeun on time. She believed it was the work of the spirits and the angels that urged her to go and helped her find him. She went to the market and bought a whole chicken, fruits, and palm ale and made a decorative tray as a gift and prayed.

Two weeks after she brought Bun Chhoeun back home, her business of buying and selling the artillery rings was going well. She found new sellers every time she ventured further away from the border of

Phnom Penh. Now she understood why Kim Chhorn had to go so far to seek the sellers. It appeared easy and safe.

Today, Ming Sarai was looking more excited than ever when she arrived at our house in the morning getting ready to make a trip to purchase the artillery rings.

"Bong Yorn, my husband is working in Tuel Sleng. I want to visit him before we go anywhere today," she said.

"There has been an attack in Tuel Sleng recently. It might not be safe," Mother replied.

"It's a military fortress there now after the attack. They made sure it won't happen again. If anything, my husband would know because he's the general. He would know anything before anyone else."

"We can go there then. Besides, I would like to visit him anyway," Mother said. She had not seen him for years since the Red Khmers had begun the attack. He had been away from home most of the time.

Tuel Sleng was not too far from our house. Mother and Ming Sarai took the taxi and got there in less than an hour. They got off the taxi when they reached the front gate and began walking on the dirt road toward the new fortress. The road was clear of any vehicles. No one came here besides the soldiers.

"Bong Yorn, what was that? It looks like some type of missile," Ming Sarai said pointing to an object about thirty feet away about twice the size of a coconut.

"It looks like a missile that has not yet exploded," Mother replied.

"That's dangerous for the soldiers. They drive cars and motorcycle this way all the time. If they drive over it, it will explode and kill every single one of them. I'm going to move it off the road," Ming Sarai said, walking toward the object.

"Don't touch it—it might explode!" Mother yelled.

"It's OK. The missiles will not explode unless you drop them a thousand feet from the air. Plus, my husband works here, and he drives this way all the time."

Ming Sarai walked over toward the missile. She grabbed the top part of the missile with both hands and lifted. *Click!* The flurry of flames shot upward like the breath of demons. The flame engulfed her entire body. Ming Sarai screamed in agony. Mother was in a panic not knowing what to do. She ran toward Ming Sarai and used both her hands to vigorously brush the fire off. The flame leaped over and caught on Mother's clothes. Ignoring her own burning pain, Mother continued trying suppresses the fire on Ming Sarai. The flame was spreading on Mother's clothes. She couldn't withstand the pain and began brushing the fire off herself. When she finished putting the fire from her clothes, she saw Ming Sarai collapsed to the ground.

"Help! Help! Please help my little sister!" Mother screamed and begged for someone to help.

Mother sat beside Ming Sarai's unconscious body and wailed. Several minutes later, a car passed by. The driver and the passenger rushed out to help. They drove Ming Sarai to the military base and requested an ambulance. The ambulance arrived twenty minutes later and took her to the hospital.

The hospital was packed with mostly severely wounded soldiers. Ming Sarai was lying on the ground waiting for her turn. Mother was not allowed to get on the ambulance for some reason. Her clothes were completely burned. She was given the cloth to cover herself. Most of the skin on her hands and body was burned, but she did not seek medical treatment. She took the taxi home and explained the nightmarish incident to the families. Our aunts and uncles went to the hospital immediately to see Ming Sarai.

Two days later, Ming Sarai passed away. Mother spent most of her time sitting on a chair staring at the wall and weeping. She spoke only when spoken to. Every single one of our aunts and uncles were not doing any better. They too were hurt from the loss of Ming Sarai.

Many weeks later, Mother's behavior had not changed much. She frequently murmured to herself, blaming herself for allowing Ming Sarai to touch the missile. She also blamed herself for not putting out the fire fast enough.

Mother decided to stop buying and selling the artillery rings, not because she scared but because she missed Ming Sarai. She could not do the business alone after spending so much time with her.

CHAPTER 5

In January 1975, Mother gave birth to a baby boy and named him Makara, which means "January" in Khmer. The fighting around Phnom Penh intensified. The Red Khmers fired the artilleries in to Phnom Penh every single day. They won over most of the eastern parts of the Kampuchea and the surrounding area of Phnom Penh. They destroyed all the main bridges around Phnom Penh. Everyone knew it was in a matter of time until the Red Khmers would take over Phnom Penh.

Bun Chhoeun was turning sixteen. Kim Chhorn was turning thirteen. Kim Chhoy was twelve. Kim Chhom was turning nine. I was turning three.

Father sent us a telegram through the military office and informed us that he was far down south in the city of Kompung Som. All the roads to Phnom Penh had been blocked by the Red Khmer. He instructed Mother to buy a plane ticket and fly to Batambang City in Batambang province, one of the largest cities in Kampuchea, located about 140 kilometers to the west of Phnom Penh. The plane tickets were now sky-high since everyone wanted to flee from Phnom Penh. It was fortunate that Mother had saved a lot of money to purchase the tickets for all of us. However, having enough money to buy the tickets was one thing, but actually purchasing the ticket was impossible. Not everyone could buy the tickets. Most of the planes had been destroyed by the Red Khmers. Fortunately, Mother had a cousin who worked at the airport. Her cousin made it possible for her to buy the tickets.

Bun Chhoeun decided not to come with us yet. He had been studying very hard. He had just graduated from the middle school and was waiting to receive his diploma. He also wanted to take care of oxen and pigs and sell them when he found the right people to buy them. In addition, Grandma wept every time Mother mentioned Bun Chhoeun going with us to Batambang. He had spent majority of his time with Grandma. They were bonded like mother and son. Grandma decided to stay, as the rest of her children were not planning to go anywhere.

On February 1975, we went to the airport ready to depart. Grandma was coming along to help us carry our bags. Mother had just had a baby last month. She didn't feel well and was barely able to walk. The Red Khmer had been shelling Phnom Penh relentlessly. The airport had been their main target for the last several weeks. Most of the planes hand been destroyed, leaving the broken parts scattered everywhere on the open field.

An explosion went off on the other side of the airport spewing up the dirt and flames high in the air. Another explosion went off several dozen yards from the last one and then another...

We were crouching behind the door of the building with other families waiting for the opportunity to run to a small plane about 160 yards away, humming loudly and waiting for us. Kim Chhorn was holding my hand getting ready to run toward the airplane. Kim Chhoy was holding the baby Makara. Kim Chhom and Mother held the bags of clothes and the cooking ware.

"Run!" Mother shouted.

Grandma wailed "Good bye, daughter Yorn and grandchildren. Go with peace and happiness."

"Good bye, Mother," Mother replied in tears.

We ran along with other families toward the airplane. A shell landed a few hundred feet away causing a volcanic-like explosion and sending the dirt and liquid fire about fifty feet up to the air.

"Crouch!" Mother screamed.

We all dove to the ground and covered our heads with our arms.

"Run!" Mother shouted again.

We got up very quickly and darted toward the airplane. We got on the airplane and sat wherever we could find an open seat. We looked out the window and we saw Grandma kneel down, weeping as if she was begging us to stay.

Mother and all my sisters wept. With the country in such chaos, they thought this was the last time they would see her. They had been living with Grandma for most of their lives. This was the first time they had departed away from her.

The flight attendant hastily shut the door. The plane roared louder than before getting ready to take off. It was the first time on a plane for everyone. We had seen planes taking off from the distance but never gotten close to see how it was done or, better yet, from the inside. We were all anticipating the airplane taking off.

The plane started to move. After a short moment, the plane started to lift up causing a strange gut-wrenching feeling. We held on tight to our seats hoping the plane would not drop back down. Mother and my sister had stopped crying and embraced the terrifying experience of getting lift-off from the earth by this mystifying flying object.

The plane ascended higher into the sky. Everyone looked down and saw objects below start to shrink smaller and smaller. In just a few minutes the buildings and the field of the airport diminished out of sight. Below us laid clusters of trees, spots of open land, rivers crisscrossing, and tiny figures of houses and buildings. It was nice and peaceful up there, other than the monotonous sound of the engine. No one spoke much as every adults and children alike were busy gazing down to the earth below, dazed by the view.

About forty minutes later, the plane started to descend. I felt like I had been tickled from inside out. Everyone appeared to experience the same feelings. It was scary and fun at the same time.

Batambang Airport was busy like Phnom Penh, but there was no sign of war here. We walked out of the airport and took a taxi. Mother explained the destination to the taxi driver, and he knew exactly where to take us. The city was spacious and beautiful. Similar to Phnom Penh, there were big buildings and nicely paved roads, busy with vehicles and bicycles. Just outside of the airport, refugees from all over the country had built shelters along the roads and fences and the sides of the buildings. The military tanks and jeeps roamed the roads with soldiers marching all around them. In spite of all the movement, Batambang was a lot more spacious than Phnom Penh. Buildings and house were much newer with nicely maintained gardens. The roads were wider, and the buildings stood farther apart.

There was no sign of any damage by the Red Khmers at all. Maybe the government was rebuilding the military strength here and then would try to fight and get the rest of country back.

A short while later, we arrived at the trucking station located just across the street from the superior court call Sala Dom Boang.

Like in Phnom Penh, settlers were living in the temporary shelters along the road sides. Shacks of all sorts clustered along the fences and buildings. Women were cooking and bathing their children along the side of the street. Men were building and fixing the shelters. Children were playing with sticks, bicycle wheels, pebbles, and rubber bands. This was how exactly how Phnom Penh was.

As we entered the gate, we saw Father standing and chatting with a dozen of other men. Every single one of them was wearing a uniform. Behind them were several dozen freight trucks parked neatly in columns.

Father and his friends walked over to greet us when we got off the taxi.

"Mae Vea [Mother of the family], you are here. Did you remember my friends, P'own E, Pon, P'own Poo, and Kloat? The others are over there."

"Greeting, everyone! Of course, I remember. All of you came to visit us in Takeo, and Pon was your cousin," Mother said happily holding baby Makara. She was excited to see Father again after months of separation and uncertainty.

"I thought we would never see each other gain. We nearly got killed driving from Kompung Som," Father said, happily reaching down to rub the baby's face.

"Let's get the kids to the trailer over there. Then we can talk," Father said pointing to columns of trailer behind all the trucks and led the way.

We followed Father and came to our trailer. The other trailers were occupied by the families of the other truck drivers. Mother and Father sat down and exchanged the news between the Phnom Penh and Batambang. Mother explained the situation in Phnom Penh and how lucky we were to be able to make it here. Father informed us that the government was paying for the trailer because he had accepted the risky job of transporting the soldiers and weapons around the country. They even provided him multiple bags of rice.

While Mother and Father and chatting, Kim Chhorn immediately started wondering around the area for trading opportunities. Kim Chhoy came along because she has nothing else to do. There were nearly as many soldiers as civilians in Batambang. They marched in groups up and down the street along with tanks and jeeps. Some stood guarding the buildings. Others stood guarding the crowded areas.

On the second day, Kim Chhorn and Kim Chhoy decided to buy two baskets of oranges from the local farmers and sell them. They carried the baskets on their heads and walked around the area. They sold about half the basket each at the end of the day. Most of the customers were soldiers.

Batambang was safe. We hadn't heard a single explosion or gun battle. Soldiers patrolled every corner of the street, each carrying all types of weapons ranging from rocket propelled grenades to machine guns. Children as young as five years of age knew these weapons very well and frequently boasted their knowledge to others.

Bun Chhoeun arrived several weeks later. He'd sold most of the cows and used the money to buy the plane ticket. Without the help of Mother's cousin, it would have been impossible for him to purchase the ticket. He described how Grandma did not want him to come because it was too dangerous. He was only sixteen and travelling alone in the time of war. She really wanted to know that he had arrived there safely. He'd promised to send a message back once he reached Batambang. When Bun Chhoeun arrived, he scrambled to send a message to Grandma, but all the communication in Phnom Penh had been destroyed. Bun Chhoeun knew how Grandma was, and she would not settle until she knew that he was safe. He was feeling unsettled and bearing the pain for not being able to tell Grandma that he'd arrived safely. She would spend the rest of her life waiting for the answer.

A few weeks later, we began to hear the faint sound of explosions from the distance. It was still too far to hear the sound of the rifles. Rumor had it that the Red Khmers were trying to take over the city of Anlong Vil.

The sound of the explosions became louder and louder every day. About five weeks later, we began to hear the gun battles along with the explosions from the distance. The sound of the gun battles indicated the Red Khmers were making progress. Batambang was no longer the safe place it had seemed at first. Once again, we were living in fear. It was inevitable that the Red Khmer would make their way here and attack the city. Father and Bun Chhoeun dug a ditch near the trailer similar to ones they'd made in Tonle. The ditch was large enough to fit all of us and deep enough where we could sleep sitting upright. The excess dirt was used to make a thick border for extra protection.

The same day after the ditch was completed, a loud explosion and gun battle erupted in the middle of the night. All of us woke up and scrambled to the ditch. We slept in the ditch until the battle subsided. During the day, the adults and children flocked to see the damage done by the shells.

Day by day, the gun battles intensified and were getting closer and closer to our trailer. It was a matter of time until it reached us.

"If the rumor is correct, tonight is the night the Red Khmer will make its' final move. Tomorrow morning is the April 17 that everyone is talking about," Father said while we were eating our dinner.

Mother and Father were staying awake after dinner. They knew what was about to happen. The rest of us couldn't help but to fall asleep. Just when I was about to close my eyes, a loud explosion went off somewhere near our house. We could hear the shattering sound from the falling debris on to the trucks and trailers. Then the monotonous whistle-like sound whizzed somewhere in the air, followed by the rak-rak-rak then ended in an explosion. We ran out the door and into the ditch like we normally did. Explosions went off all around us hitting trucks and other trailers. There was one that landed so close that the small debris flew into our ditch. We all crouched tighter in the ditch covering our heads with our hands.

Then the sound of the battle rifles trailed after the explosions, then the machine guns, then more explosions. The battle went on until morning. Fortunately, with hundreds of explosions all around us, we were lucky that we didn't get hit. Besides baby Makara, all of us had been awake all night. None of us said a single word to one another throughout the entire night.

The battle subsided when the sun rose. There were a few gun shots here and there but no more explosions. I felt very drowsy from the lack of sleep. This was a good time for me to go to sleep.

Then I heard an announcement from the loudspeaker somewhere near the front gate, "The King Norodom Sihanou is back and has ordered all the soldiers to drop their weapons. He's welcoming those who wanted to see him."

The man repeated his phrase over and over again. Befoe this, the King Norodom Sihanou had vanished without a trace. No one knew where he'd gone. Some believed he'd fled the country. Many believed he had been captured by the Red Khmer. He was still loved by many citizens. Many elders still believed in his divinities.

We all came out of the ditch and observed the area. There was no sign of resistance from Lon Nol's force. Thousands of soldiers were walking in lines with their hands over their heads, without their weapons, surrendering. Some soldiers were ordered to get on the trucks.

Some local citizens cheered, "Bravo the savior! Destroy the corruption!"

Many people appeared terrified and kept quiet. The corpses of civilians and soldiers were sprawled everywhere on the streets and beside the buildings. The majority of the dead civilians were the ones who'd been living in the shelters along the streets. They were out in the open and had no place to take cover. Families mourned besides the corpses of their love ones. Houses and building were wrecked and burned. Black smokes spiraled up from all directions. The Red Khmer walked around each block using the loudspeakers and ordered the evacuation. "All civilians! You must evacuate! Leave all your belongings here! Come back in three days!"

It was April 17, 1975. Besides the New Year, dates were never important to our family, not even our birthdays, but today was different. Every adult was very conscious of the today's date. Several weeks earlier, everyone had been talking about today's date in every single conversation. The Red Khmer had made their final move. This was why April 17 had been the subject of discussion every day. They marched into the city using loudspeakers to order the Lon Nol soldiers to drop their weapons.

There were a dozen heavily armed Red Khmers standing by the gate. They wore all black including their sandals, save for the red and white checkered scarves that hung loosely around their necks. The entire city was ordered to evacuate, except for us and all the families of the truck drivers. They ordered us to stay where we were. They seemed to know everything about us. They ordered all the men to come forward. Father and the rest of the men walked nervously forward and crowded around a man in charge. The man in black talked for about thirty minutes in front of Father and his friends. Each man nodded as he spoke. Once the man finished speaking, all the men returned to their families standing near the trailers and waiting anxiously. Father and all the men appeared relaxed.

"They gave us an option. If we stay, they will not harm us, but I have to work for them to transport people around the country. They let us pick a place to live. We can choose to live anywhere in the Batambang province. If we choose to leave Batambang, they will not promise us anything," Father explained.

"I chose to stay because I don't know where to go. And if we chose to leave, we would have to walk like everyone else; we could not take the truck. Since they want me to work for them, I don't think they will harm our family. Besides, they sound very friendly."

"It seems like we have no choice but to stay. I can't walk with the baby, and Bun Chhun is too small to walk. We'll stay then," Mother said.

Father walked over to his friends and discussed. All his friends decided to stay as well. Like us, they didn't want to walk. Besides, they didn't know where to go. They thought the Red Khmer were harmless. They just need adapt to the new system.

Father knew that the Red Khmers hated the military and the wealthy. Something told him to dispose of all belongings that related to the military, such as his uniforms and backpacks. It was well understood by nearly everybody that the Red Khmer hated the current system. Although we were not wealthy and Father had never registered as the military, all of our names were long and would make them think otherwise. Father quickly assigned us all new names.

"Bun Chhoeun, you were now Chhoeun."

"Kim Chhorn, you were now Chhorn."

"Kim Chhoy, you were now Chhoy."

"Kim Chhom, you were now Chhom."

He pointed at me. "This one, just call him Bun."

He pointed at baby Makara. "Ah, Makara, call him Pech because he's little."

"You and I should keep the same name because our names are short. If they ask us what we do for a living, you are all farmers and I'm a truck driver working for a Chinese business man—because we all know the Red Khmer are backed by the Chinese. Therefore, they must like the Chinese. If you can't remember this simple thing, we will all be dead," Father finished.

The next morning, the adults gathered and decided to pick a place to live. Among them was a man Father called Kloat. He was one of Father's close friends. Um Kloat use to live in a village called Stung Chah (Old River) in the Batambang province. He said Stung Chah had plenty of fish, and the lands were nice and flat. He was planning to live there and suggested everyone go live with him. Since all the truck drivers wanted to live close together, they all agreed to live in Stung Chah.

Immediately after the elders confirmed our destination with Red Khmer, they ordered us to load our stuff into the trucks and start moving. Each man could drive his own truck with his family.

Chhoeun loaded three bags of rice that he'd found in the storage room. Father filled the fuel tank and examined the truck. He was ordered to remove the cover to prevent suspicion along the road. We all hopped onto the truck.

In minutes, we were all ready. Um Kloat led the way because he knew where he was going. Father and the rest of the drivers followed. It was an exciting day for me as I got to ride in a vehicle again.

We rode along the paved road. Many houses and buildings had been destroyed. Black smoke was rising to the sky from the burning buildings and vehicles. Continuous lines of families were walking along the side of the road with children of all ages. The majority were walking empty-handed because they had been told not to bring anything except for their clothes.

The trucks stopped several times to pick up families that begged for a ride. Some had newborn babies. Father had allowed several families to get on the truck. Most had children about my age. They were happy to learn that we were all ordinary civilians just like them. We crowded together in the truck not knowing much of what to come.

After approximately one hour of a slow ride and frequent stops, we turned onto a narrow gravel road with trees branches hanging over from both sides. It would be impossible for another vehicle travelling from the opposite direction to pass by. It appeared the road had been made for the ox wagon and not for the motor vehicles. Thick shrubs and trees of all sorts grew along both sides of the road.

The road became very bumpy from the wagon marks. About ten minutes later we saw a river running parallel to the road. There were small houses sitting on the hill along the other side. There had been no sign of people in the area since we'd gotten off the main road. The town was completely quiet. All the residents must have been forced to evacuate just like us.

We rode along the river for several more minutes and then saw a large white bridge arched over the river. The truck stopped just after a bridge where the road intersected with a large open alleyway where the previous residents must have used it to access the river.

"We were here. The adults said. This is where we decided to come and live," Mother said.

Everyone jumped off the truck. My attention was immediately on the river that was just ten feet off the road, with the span of about sixty yards from bank to bank. The water level was high up to the bank of the river, flowing slightly. Trees of all sorts and sizes stooped over the river, except for the large bare spot where it appeared to be worn out from frequent access.

On the other side of the river, large buildings stood behind thick trees exposing only the roof and the high wall sides.

Families of all the truck drivers and those who were picked up along the road got off the truck and stood on the large alleyway with their families waiting for the instruction. About a dozen of the Red Khmer that we saw earlier walked over and stood on the upper side of the alleyway. Half of them were women. Each one was holding a rifle with grenades strapped around their waist and shoulders.

"Everyone! Listen to me," a woman who appeared to be in charge spoke. "Today is the beginning of the new country. You have chosen to live here. This area is called Stung Chah (Old River). All the houses here are empty. This place was your new home. Each family can choose any house in this place. Choose carefully because the house will be your permanent home."

Everyone suddenly turned their heads, eyeballing the houses in the area. The first house sat on the right side of the path near the wagon road, made mostly from bamboo trees and palm leaves, raised about four feet off the ground. A similar house was located up the hill to the left of the alleyway.

"There are more houses up there. You can start choosing now. Everything in the house belongs to you. We will be back another day and meet here to discuss other plans."

All the Red Khmers walked up the hill and vanished.

The adults started to walk up the slope to see other houses. Not many people were interested in the nearby houses. Most of them were very small.

Father and Mother looked around. There were much larger houses that could be seen up ahead. Some even had tiled roofs and mortar walls. Mother and Father walked and spoke softly together. Then they walked into the third house to the left. It's was about ten yards in length and five yards in width. The house was raised about four feet off the ground supported by rows of bamboo trees. The walls and roofs were made of interlaced palm leaves planks. It's one of the smaller houses that no one seemed to be interested in.

We followed Father and Mother up the stairs into the house. Inside, the floor was made of bamboo trees, tied together with vines and stripes from palm branches. The house was empty. There wasn't even a room. There were a few pots and pans hanging on the wall and a bag of rice that the previous owner left behind. The previous owner must have been very poor.

Chhoeun carried all the rice bags from the truck and stacked them on one side of the wall. Chhorn, Chhoy and Chhom placed all the clothes in the center of the house and went outside. I followed them to the alleyway that ran further up the hill. We saw more houses scattered throughout the village like a hidden city. I noticed a large building about 100 feet away to the right where the front door was facing the river. Tall trees grew over the building, spreading their branches and providing shade to the building. It was the only building of its kind around here.

Further passed the building; there were more houses sitting in random positions. Most of them were the same size as the one that Father and Mother had chosen. Each house was surrounded by tall trees and thick bushes.

To the left of the alleyway, we found more houses, but they were more organized. The houses sat next to one another in columns along the alley.

I continued to follow my three sisters along the main alleyway. We came to an open plain, blanketed by interconnected rice paddies of all shapes and sizes. The plain stretched far to the horizon and then ended by the tiny contour of the gray mountains. The coconut trees randomly scattered the plain, standing tall and dwarfing everything around them.

Bong Chhorn led us into the field, walking on the rim of the rice paddies. Since this was only April, the rice irrigation cycle had just begun. Farmers had just plowed and spread the rice seeds; leaving rice paddies bare and muddy.

After we crossed several rice paddies and observed the area, we returned to our new house. Father and Mother were chatting with other families that had chosen the houses nearby. Among them was a man proudly describing his new house.

In early evening, the heat of the sun was easing. Kim Chhorn carried me to the river to bathe. There were already a dozen women and children there swimming in the river. Eventually, nearly everyone came to the river to bathe, wash their clothes, or to take the water home to cook. Mother carried the water home using the abandoned bucket and filled the large urns around the house.

While we were enjoying bathing in the warm water, a dozen large trucks stopped along the river. Each truck carried as many as fifty passengers. Within seconds, the passengers began to climb off the truck and stood in groups of families waiting for instructions.

A dozen armed Red Khmer walked over from another truck and stood on a higher ground, calling everyone to come closer. Once all the families crowded together around them, the Red Khmer began to give instructions.

Minutes later, the families began searching for available homes to stay in permanently just like us. Most of the houses around us were still vacant.

The next day, more trucks had been seen dropping off more civilians and more Red Khmers all over the town. Within days, the town of Stung Chah was no longer a quiet place but busy with people of all ages socializing in every corner.

A few days later, the Red Khmer ordered Father and all the truck drivers to go to other cities to pick up all the foreigners such as French, American, Thai, and Japanese and drop them off at Thailand's borders.

He returned home three days later and described his trip to Mother. The foreigners thanked him for getting them safely to Thailand and gave him all sorts of gifts such as shirts, belts, silk garments, and fancy lighters.

"Mae Vea, they want me to go back and pick up all the people who want to meet the Prince Sihanouk," Father said.

"I thought the prince fled the country," Mother said.

"I don't know, but they said he came back. They said he wanted to meet people in a remote place. I was told there were many people here in this village who wanted to meet him as well. They were told to wait in a certain spot and I'm to go around and pick them up and then drop them off in a certain place. They have not told me a specific drop-off location yet."

Just before noon, Father left to pick up groups that wanted to meet the Prince Sihanouk. They were waiting on the wagon road along the river. One of them was his boss from the trucking company. They made him drop off these people in a remote site that didn't appear to be any sort of meeting place. Hundreds of armed Red Khmer were there waiting for Father and other truckers to drop off the pro-Prince Sinhanouk people. Then he was ordered to leave and wait for more instructions.

When he returned home, he was instructed once again to pick up more people in other cities who wanted to see the Prince. But the drop-off places were always different. Most of them were empty grass fields surrounded by trees. Some of them were in large abandoned buildings, quiet and distant from the city. Father knew something was wrong, but he was not quite sure what. From his understanding, the Prince Sihanouk and the Red Khmer were allies since they both despised the Lon Nol's Party.

Father became nervous about the Prince Sihanouk ordeal. He explained and described his task to Mother, who also praised Prince Sihanouk highly. Mother has the same thought—the fall of Lon Nol should bring joy to both the Red Khmer and Prince Sihanouk. There was no reason to fear being a supporter of the Prince Sihanouk.

Father's transportation tasks eased after about three weeks. He spent the rest of his time with us and socializing with the truck drivers. He also observed the river and saw fish swimming within reach, but it was impossible to catch them by hand. Unfortunately, he didn't have any sort of fishing net to catch the fish.

While we spent our time wondering around the area, Mother spent some of her time chatting with the families of the truck drivers and most of her time preparing the family for what might be coming. So far, the Red Khmer didn't seem to bother anyone. In fact, they had not returned since the first day they'd arrived here. But Mother was still feeling uneasy about the whole thing. The Red Khmer had been fighting the Lon Nol, slaughtering women and children without mercy for years. It was too good to be true that they would just leave us alone like this. She wanted to be ready for whatever the Red Khmers were planning. We only had about four bags of rice, which would last us a few months. If we didn't find a way to bring rice home, we would starve. There were open lands everywhere, but no one was allowed to do anything with it.

Mother went around rummaging the vacant houses and found an abandoned fabric weaver and all the materials to make the fabrics. With the help of Father's friend, she brought the weaver home and started learning how to weave.

It was about noontime. I was sitting beside Mother watching her weave. She tossed the yarn back and forth through the weaver and used her feet to pedal. A woman dressed in black came and stood by the doorway.

"Mit [Comrade], there is a meeting this evening before sunset at the warehouse. I'm inviting everyone to go to the meeting. You, your husband, and children are required to come," the woman said and marched away.

This woman was different from the ordinary women. Besides the black outfit, her hair was tied up in a bun, the red and white scarf hung loosely from her neck, her slippers were made of carved-out car tire laced with trimmed tire tube. She had a determined face and intense stare. She did not greet when she came nor said good bye when she left.

"Yes, we will go, Me Own (little sister)," Mother replied, trying to be polite.

The woman paused and replied, "From now on, you will call me and everyone Mit. We will explain in the meeting."

"Really... then...Mit," Mother said to assure her she was cooperating.

Mother informed Father, Chhoeun, and all my sisters to ensure we made it to the meeting before sunset. Mother told Father and Chhoeun about the woman who came to notify us. She warned Father and Chhoeun not to talk about any politics with other families. She was feeling very nervous about what was to come.

When the evening arrived, about fifty families congregated in front of the warehouse waiting for the meeting. We sat close to all the families of the truck drivers. About five women marched in and stood in front of the warehouse. All of them were wearing black. Some of them had the red and white checker scarf caped down from their neck. Some tied the scarves loosely around their waist. They walked swiftly and synchronously like soldiers. Besides the youngest one, the rest had short hair trimmed up to their shoulders, probably to avoid having to deal with their hair while in battle.

"All Mit," said a woman who appeared to be the leader of them all. "Today we will start talking about our plans for the future. We got rid of the enemy. We got rid of the corruption and inequality system. Everyone is now equal. You must approach each other as Mit regardless of age and gender. However, you must call us Mit Bong (Elder Comrade) because we joined the new community first and fought for our freedom. You can also refer to us as the Khmer Rumdoh (Khmer Savior).

"We will refer to you as the April Seventeenth because this was the day you were freed. We have the right to be your superior because we risked our lives to fight the enemy. Since we are all equal, we all have to work equally and eat equally. If you don't work, you will not get your share of the day you missed work. We all shall wear black, the color that represents bravery and unity. The scarves shall be red and white, the colors of hard work and commitment, but the scarves are not required. It is only for your convenience.

"We have worked hard in the jungle experimenting with new things and discovered a plant that we can extract to make black dye. We all shall dye all our clothes black starting tomorrow. Anyone wearing colored clothes is considered an enemy.

"The most important people in our lives are our government. They are the higher level of hard workers who have spent the last several years putting plans together for the new society. Under the government, we are all equal. We shall share everything we have. We will work together and eat together. We all will work for government to meet the same goal and for the same purpose. Our government will see to it that we get our share equally. Our government will assign us work and decide what is best for us and our families.

"Today I will give each family the seeds of various fruit plants and vegetables. Each of you should take them and grow them around your house. Once they are ready to be harvested, you need to ask permission from the government. The government will decide if it is all right or not, to make sure no one is taking too much. The crops that you plant are public and belong to government. Anyone found breaking the law will be taken to trial by the higher officials.

Also, you must give up all your belongings, such as watches and bracelets, to Mit Bong. We were too busy training and learning in the jungle and never had a chance to own such things. Now it is a good time to bring us gifts for all our hard work.

Anybody who doesn't agree or doesn't obey the rules is considered enemy. We will get rid of the enemy immediately to prevent the spread of corruption.

"Today we brought you the seeds and tools to grow crops," The woman ended her speech and then pointed to a pile of tools lying in the warehouse.

When the woman finished talking, they handed out a metal bucket containing various seeds in bags and a hoe to each family.

On the way back home, the adults walked and complained about the whole government ordeal. No one was happy. Some even cursed softly. "That demon! What kind of freedom is it when we have to agree on everything the government wants?"

Mother woke up early the next morning and began digging to loosen the dirt around our house. She was given many types of seed such as corn, watermelon, taro, potatoes, bananas, and many other vegetables. She had been doing this all her life in Takeo. She knew exactly what to do. Fortunately, the previous owner of the house had removed all the wheat and grasses from the land around the house. The ground was soft and easy to dig. Chhoeun, Chhorn, and Chhoy helped her dig later in the morning and carried the water from the river to water the newly planted seeds.

At the end of the day, the land around our house was formed in neat columns of raised soil with small aisles in between for space to walk to prune and water the plants.

While Mother was working on the farm around our house, she discovered dozens of yucca trees. She called them the tree potatoes. Not many people knew about this tree; it appeared to be a wild and useless tree that could grow over fifteen feet tall and had long, narrow green leaves. One yucca tree could produce dozens of roots that grew up to two feet long and three times the size of the ordinary potatoes.

When the roots were harvested, the yucca tree continued to produce more roots as long as it was still alive. The roots were bitter when eaten raw and could cause sickness. Once cooked, however, they tasted much better than any ordinary potatoes. The yucca trees were easy to grow; simply cut the branches, stick them into the ground, water them regularly, and they would grow.

Mother got up early again the next morning and continued to loosen the soil around our house to plant more seeds. She also cut the branches from the yucca trees and planted them in all the open spots. She made sure not cut too much off that could kill the trees.

"Mit, we want to talk to you," the voice of a woman materialized behind her.

Mother jumped and turned around. She saw three women dressed all in black standing by our house.

"We came here to collect anything that government might be interested in. As we discussed the other day, it is time for everyone to pay back to government for their hard work in turning this country into a peaceful state. Do you have anything to offer like watches and bracelets?" one of them asked.

"Wait here, Mit Bong, let me check inside." It was difficult enough to use the word Mit when she didn't even like them in the first place, but to add the word Bong to a person that was much younger than her was very awkward and inferior.

Mother went inside the house and brought out a watch and a belt that Father had brought home the day he transported the foreigners to Thailand. She was thinking of giving them the colorful silk garments as well, but on second thought the Red Khmer would dye them black and ruin the garments anyway. Mother decided to keep them instead and hoped one day she could trade them for something useful.

"There's a meeting tonight before dark. We will toll the bell when it's time," the woman said and marched off.

Mother continued working on her farm. She was feeling uneasy about these women walking around demanding things.

I was playing with my new friend named Tien just a few dozen yards away from where Mother was working. Tien was about two years old. He was Pu E's son. Although Tien didn't know how to talk yet, we still had a lot of fun. He laughed very loud, and he liked to run. I would chase after him until we both ran of breath. When there was nothing else to do, we would pick up a rock or a stick and throw it as hard as we could and laugh.

Mother, Chhoeun, and all my sisters came to visit Pu E and Tien's mom every day. Pu E's wife was known as Tien's mom. In Khmer culture, the married women normally got nick-named by the name of the oldest or the most well-known child along with the word "mom".

Tien's mom was thin, light skinned, and stood slightly shorter than the average Khmer women. She was easy to recognize by her unusually loud voice. She never hesitated to swear. In fact, she swore nearly every other phrase, but for some reason no one found it offensive at all. Her husband, Pu E, was almost the opposite in many ways. He was dark and tall. He talked very softly and pleasantly.

Tien and I squatted around a critter about a foot long with thousands of tiny legs moving slowly. Both of us were curious but scared to touch it. Tien stuck his finger out, nearly touching it, but he got creeped out and jerked his finger back. I looked around for an object that I could use to arouse the critter. I found a small stick and used it to poke it softly. The critter curled instantly....then the sound of a loud clank resonated in the air as if it was caused by the critter. Tien and I leaped backward in shock. I nearly cried from the terror.

"It's time! All of us! They want us to meet at the dining hall," someone hollered.

Mother paused and stood still holding the hoe. She was busy working and had forgotten all about the meeting.

"Chhorn, get all your brothers and sisters," Mother said.

Chhoeun and Pu E were chatting and walking along with the crowd. Chhorn carried Pech on her waist and followed Chhoeun and Pu E.

"Bun Chhun…I mean Bun…follow me." Chhorn said.

Tien and I were still recovering from the shock. We thought the critter had made that loud sound, but it was from something else.

We came to a large crowd in front of a warehouse. Some adults were looking nervous. Most were curious.

"What do they have to say after all the war?" one of them said.

"Just wait and see." another replied.

"I need everyone to stop talking!" a woman shouted.

The hum of the crowd subsided. Everyone turned and stared at the same group of women who made speech the other day. Although it was easily noticeable that the spokeswoman had changed her clothes, they were similar to what she wore the other day. She was wearing a black long-sleeve shirt and long black pants. She buttoned her shirt up to her throat, covering most of her neck. Her black pants were loosely fitted and perfectly trimmed just above her ankle. There were as many pockets on her pants as on her shirt.

"All Mit!" She started talking. "When government is ready, we will start gathering all the boys and girls between the age of nine to fourteen and the single men and the single women from age fifteen and up. All the girls will go live and work with all the other girls. All the boys will live and work with other boys. They will be in the next town not too far from here. They are not allowed to come back home without permission. They are allowed to come home once a week. Anybody getting caught breaking the rules will be taken to trial. Each day, the boys and girls will have one hour of school time, then work, then lunch break, then work. This will make them become smarter, stronger, and make our country better.

As for the single men and women from the age of fifteen and up, they will be taken a little further away from home. They are young and strong. They will be taken to work harder and more important tasks. The married men will live and work with other married men. The married women will live and work with other married women, but they remain here in the primary residence."

Tomorrow morning, we will go around each house and take information from each family and report to the government. Then the government will decide what to do with each family.

All the adults will meet here in the morning and to get ready to work. We will begin to eat together in this dining hall when the designated cook is assigned. We will toll the bell around noon. Come and line up for your share when you hear the sound of the bell...That is all I have to say for today," she finished and walked away.

We walked back home after the meeting. The darkness was looming as the sun was about to set. We followed Mother and Father home. Mother was looking very nervous. Maybe she was worried about Chhoeun and my sisters going away. Chhoeun had just turned sixteen and would be taken away to work hard with the adults.

"Chhoeun, what are we going to do? They will take you far away from me, and they will make you work hard."

"I was just thinking about that, and I have an idea. I'm going to tell them that I'm fourteen so that I don't have to go far. I'll be around for one more year before I get taken away."

"That's a great idea! Tell them you are fourteen then," Mother said happily.

Mother seemed a little less worried after Chhoeun brought up the idea. She made steamed rice and steamed potatoes she'd found in her garden for dinner. She would normally stay up until midnight weaving or stitching clothes under a faint glint of the oil lamp, but tonight she went to sleep immediately after the dinner.

I woke up in the morning to the soft, radiant of the sun casting through the open door. Mother had left home to work. Chhoeun had left home as well. Chhorn made us rice for breakfast. Chhom and Chhoy were home looking after Pech and I.

"We only have half of bag of rice left. It's running low, and there's no sign that we are getting more soon. We should be careful not to eat too much," Chhorn said.

Just after we finished our meal, three women in black came marching into our house. One of them was carrying a notebook and a pen. Chhorn recognized her as the daughter of one of the truck drivers.

"Hey, Mit Chhorn. I'm Mit Phon. You probably know me. I'm the daughter of a friend of your Father. I have been promoted to Mekong (horde leader). The two comrades here will ask you questions about your family."

Chhorn stood up and replied, "I remember you from the trucking company near the airport, Bong."

"Call me Mit Bong," she corrected.

"Oh, Mit Bong," Chhorn said.

"Who's living here?" one of them asked.

"Mother, Father, Bun Chhoeun—I mean Chhoeun, me, Chhoy, Chhom, Bun Chhon—I mean Bun, and the little baby here name Mm… Pech," she said, nearly giving away all of our real names.

"What did your mom do for a living?"

"She's a farmer."

"What did your Father do for a living?"

"He drives truck for the Chinese men."

"Did he ever join the military?"

"No."

"How about Mit Chhoeun? Did he ever join the military?"

"Yes"

"Did he ever join the military?" The two took another step forward and stooped lower to confirm the answer, exposing Mit Phon, who was standing right behind them. Her face was white as a ghost, and her eyes were wide open in fear. She winked multiple times to signal Chhorn.

Chhorn suddenly understood the signal and quickly said, "I meant they took him to join the military, but he ran away. That means he never joined the military."

"All right. We are done with you for today," the woman said.

Phon, the new Mekong, sighed and turned to Chhorn. She almost broke a smile, but she turned and left with the two women.

The neighborhood had become very quiet. All the adults had gone to work. Chhorn and Chhoy were taking me and Pech around. We stopped by Um Phon's family. Mother had mentioned that they were our cousins. Um Phon was a truck driver as well. He had a big family. There were over six young children alone. All the adults had gone to work, including Um Phon and his wife.

Um Phon's kids were all busy dyeing their clothes black and did not have time to chat. Chhorn remembered being told in the meeting that eventually, we all would need to dye our clothes black.

"You should start dyeing your clothes, or you will get in trouble," one of our boy cousins hollered.

Chhorn asked where they got the black dye from, and they kindly explained. We left Um Phon's house and came to another house just a dozen yards away from ours. We found a couple that had a three-year-old daughter name Phate. The wife was known as Phate's mom, and the Father was known as Phate's dad. They had both left to work, leaving their Phate home alone. They didn't have a choice.

I had seen Phate's mom many times. She spoke with a funny accent. They said she was from Laos. Everyone made fun of her accent, including myself. I picked up a few words with the funny accent like "walk" and "eat" and repeatedly said them out loud. Mother and Father would laugh.

Chhorn took us to bathe in the river and returned home in late evening. When we returned home, we saw Father chatting with Mother in a soft tone almost like a whisper.

"Mae Vea, the people that they told me to pick up and drop off every day at the remote location are all dead. There were at least thirty people I picked up from this village included Loak Ktean, my former boss in the trucking company. I didn't know until the last day when I accidentally drove back the same road where I had dropped them off. I saw thousands of dead bodies on the same spot. I was curious then and drove to the other spot about ten kilometers further and saw the same thing. They tricked these people. There was no Prince Sihanouk to be met. They killed anybody who wanted to see the Prince Sihanouk. And on the way back, I saw a large pile of dead soldiers I transported one trip a day for thirty days to different locations. Each day I transported nearly forty people. That means I drove at least one thousand, two hundred people to their death.

I have brought great sin to myself. I think I'm going to hell. I hope God would understand. I didn't know their plans. I was just doing what I was told to do. Even if I knew, I couldn't tell them anything because the Red Khmer were riding in the truck with them. While I was driving, I heard the radio stating that Prince Sihanouk returned from China and he'd been captured.

I think they were killing anybody who had anything to do with Lon Nol and Prince Sihanouk. Then I thought of the documents that we brought with us. We have to get rid all of them," Father finished

"I'm going to burn all the documents, but what about our pictures?" Mother verified.

"Let's keep our pictures because there is nothing wrong with pictures," Father said.

"Puk Vea [Father of the family], you wore nice clothes in those pictures. They might suspect us of being part of Lon Nol," Mother said.

"The pictures are the only things we have left. We can't retake the pictures of the past."

"But our lives are more important. We can take more pictures anytime in the future. We need to stay alive."

"How about burn any of the pictures that you think are risky to keep and keep some that aren't risky. Hide the pictures underneath the kitchen area," Father suggested.

"All right, I'm going to do that tonight," Mother finished. "By the way, they really liked the way I worked, especially the woman name K'ouen who lives in the house in that corner near the dining hall. They promoted me to become Mekong. Today they made me *stoong* (pluck and replant the rice buds). It was very easy. I even trained many women in our group how to do it. Starting from tomorrow, my new responsibility is to cook for our horde."

Mother spent the rest of the evening gathering all the documents and burning anything that might raise suspicion. Most of the documents were associated with Father's transportation company in Phnom Penh. Mother found a heavy backpack that belonged to Chhoeun. She checked the backpack and found several dozen brand-new notebooks. Chhoeun must have brought them from school or from the trucking station. Mother thought the blank notebooks would cause no harm to our family and decided to keep them. She planned to hide them just to be safe.

CHAPTER 6

I was standing by the door looking outside as the families reunited after the long, hard work under the sun. Mother and Father must have just returned from work as well. Their conversation caught my attention. Father was chatting softly with the man known as Ta Kloat, one of the truck drivers. Father called him Bong Kloat because he was much older than him. I didn't understand most of the things they said, but I picked up a few words like "American", "militants", "rifles", and "bombs." When United States dropped the bombs on the civilians by accident, the Red Khmer used the opportunity make the Khmer believe the United States was really the bad guy and the Red Khmer were the saviors. Over time everyone learned otherwise. Now everyone was waiting for the Americans to come and rescue us from what was to come. Everyone was feeling uneasy about the Red Khmer. They praised the current government highly and daily. There were rumors that the Red Khmers shot and killed the local workers who were working too slowly or failed to follow instructions.

"The Americans dropped the bomb," I said out loud. I had heard this phrase so many times and finally understood what it meant.

"What do you know about Americans?" Ta Kloat said sarcastically.

"The Americans live across the ocean," I replied extending my arm up, pointing my fingers trying to express how far away the Americans were. I didn't know what the ocean was, but it sounded so big, so far, and so dangerous.

Father, Mother, and Ta Kloat laughed. I was curious why they were laughing. It wasn't even funny. Then I realized that I might have spoken with the Laos accent like Phate's mom. But then I wasn't sure if I had or I hadn't. I could no longer tell if I was speaking normally or with Phate's mom imitation. I felt a sudden surge of fear. I didn't want to get stuck with Laos' accent.

"Mother!" I said out loud testing my accent. But I still couldn't tell if was real or imitation. I didn't want to be laughed at when I spoke. I nearly burst out crying, but then I decided to stay calm and continue listening to Mother, Father, and Ta Kloat speak and focus on how to say each word the correct way. I promised myself not to imitate Phate's mom's accent ever again.

I woke up early the next morning and saw Mother splitting wood. I got to see Mother a lot now since she was working around home. She would cut the wood and carry them to our house then split them with an axe. Mother thought she was fortunate that they assigned her as a designated cook. It was still hard work, as she has to wake up early in the morning like everyone else to attend the meetings, but she gets to work around home and take care of us.

The upper leaders gave Mother a small container of rice every day to cook for the horde. The entire village had been eating together for several weeks now.

Although not required, Mother started her routine early in the morning picking vegetables like water spinaches and amaranths by the river bank and around the rice paddies to make soup.

I was standing beside Mother as she split wood. As usual, I was crying, pleading to be held or maybe just to stand closer to her.

"I can't hold you. I'm busy," she said.

I continue to cry and clung to her pants as she split the woods. I stood so close to the wood that the small splinters flew and hit me in the face. I got scared after I saw what the axe could do to the wood. It could easily sever my arms if I got any closer.

"Move away! Do you want your arm to get cut off?" Mother yelled and shoved me aside.

I stood clear of the axe but continued to cry. I knew it was wrong, but I couldn't help it.

After Mother finish splitting the wood, she carried the wood to the dining hall and began to cook. I clung to her pants every single step.

"My rice and soup are ready," Mother said to the village leader.

"Mine are done also," several other women hollered.

A woman picked up a hammer-like object and struck the bell that was the size of the cooking pot hanging from a post, making a simple rhythm. She repeated the same rhythm a couple of times before she stopped.

Just minutes after the bell was tolled, thousands of workers flocked from the field lining up behind the pots. Mother was standing next to the pot getting ready to distribute the rice and soup.

Chhoeun and all my sisters came and lined up behind the pot that was managed by Mother. Everyone was holding a plate and a spoon. Chhorn was holding Pech on her waist. She was carrying two plates, one for Pech and one for herself.

I walked over to Chhoy as soon as I saw her. She had been helping me with my share. The upper Mekong was standing next to Mother counting heads and making sure no one was cheating.

After we got our share, we sat on a bench and ate our lunch. Father didn't eat lunch with us. He had left to work early in the morning. He and a few of his friends had been assigned to drive the bulldozers that were found in a nearby village. The Red Khmer leaders had been searching for people that knew how to drive and operate the bulldozers. Mother found the job for him. When she first heard the news, she thought it was a good opportunity for Father and requested the job for Father and his friends that knew how to operate the bulldozers.

He no longer needed to transport people around. He had been feeling very sinful after he learned that he had transported over one thousand civilians to their death. He was happy that he got to operate the bulldozer and work in a village very close to home. He didn't have to move far like the government had planned. He got his friend named Chhay and another friend named Long to work with him.

All the excavations were currently being done by the hands of men and women. Father and his friends were the only people who got the easy job, operating the machine along with thousands of manual laborers. The bulldozers were very handy. The Red Khmers were amazed of the efficiency of the machines. Each bulldozer could outperformed more than a hundred men.

A few days later, he and two his friends were forced to train the Red Khmers how to operate the bulldozer.

"Mae Vea, I have a bad feeling about teaching the Mit Chah [Old Comrade] how to drive and operate the bulldozers. When they knew how to drive, what do you think they would do with me?" Father asked.

"When the time comes, you would look for another task. You didn't do anything wrong. You were doing them a favor," Mother said with assurance.

"I have a bad feeling about this. The person that I'm teaching was very strange. He would never look me in the eyes when he spoke to me. He seems to hide something," Father explained.

"Just do what you were being told and you should be fine. They like hard workers. They were our leaders. That's why we called them Mit Chah. We were the April Seventeenth," Mother said.

Father couldn't help but continue to explain his uneasy gut feeling to Mother about the Red Khmers that he and his friends were training. They acted as though it was urgent that they learn. All of them had been acting eerie as if they were hiding something. Father had no choice but to continue the training. Like all the workers, he returned home every evening, just a little after the sunset.

The Red Khmers continued to come door to door in the evening nearly every week to ask questions and take notes about the family's past. They were mostly women. They seem to be harmless. No one had heard of anyone getting into any kind of trouble pertaining to their pasts.

Mother learned that nearly everyone she chatted with told them their true past. Many admitted that they had joined the military before. Some admitted they lived in Phnom Penh and bragged about having a big mansion. Some admitted they had worked in professional fields, such as teachers and health professionals.

Mother determined to stick to her and Father's idea of concealing our family's past no matter how trivial it sounded. Father had been driving trucks for the military for several years transporting soldiers and ammunition from city to city, and Chhoeun had joined the military for several months when he was just thirteen years old.

Early in the morning, shortly after the sunrise, a medium-height woman dressed in black marched into our house. "Where were all the girls? Are they ready? Let's go," she hollered.

"We are ready, Mit Bong," Chhorn replied.

There were about thirty girls between the ages of ten to fourteen crowded outside our house supervised by two Mekong women. The Mekong don't look anything like the woman who made the speech at the warehouse. They dressed all in black but with normal clothes. They seemed to be friendly. They must have been assigned by the Mit Chah to do this job.

Today was the day Chhorn and Chhoy were departing our home to go to live with the other girls. They were no longer eligible to get a share of rice in Stung Chah. If they stayed, they would have nothing to eat. Mother had packed them extra pairs of clothes and a mosquito net.

Fortunately, Mother took the chance and requested Mit Chah to have Chhom stay home and look after us. She convinced K'ouen, one of the leaders, that babysitting was a real job just like any other job on the field. Chhom would still get her share of food.

"There is rice inside your backpack. Eat it when you are hungry," Mother said.

She knew well by now that they would be walking all day without food. No one in the upper- level leaders seemed to care about the well-being of anybody. Chhorn and Chhoy joined the horde of girls. They were excited to meet new kids.

"Everyone line up! The first person stands right here!" the Mekong hollered.

There was a slight confusion at first, but then a line started to form. Chhorn and Chhoy followed the flow and stood in a line.

"Be ready to give me your name, your family name, and your age," the Mekong said.

"What is family name?" one girl asked.

"The family name is the name that you inherited from your ancestor. If you don't have one, you can use your grandfather's name," the Mekong answered.

"What was our family name?" Chhoy asked Chhorn.

"I don't think we have one, but we could use our grandfather's name. Remember Ta Phuong, Father's Father that we lived with in Bakaeng?" Chhorn answered.

The Mekong started to ask for everyone's first name and family name and their age. Many girls stumbled with the family name. Most of them ended up using their father's name. About half of the girls got their age right. Many of them did not know the year they were born, but they knew their zodiac animals. The adults and children alike often bragged about their zodiac animals. The zodiac animals were important in Khmer culture. It was frequently used to describe a person's behavior, intellect, and destiny.

After the Mekongs finished taking names and ages, they started walking in single-file lines along the river. One Mekong was leading the way, and the other was trailing behind.

After a long walk, Chhorn and Chhoy begin having a simple and short conversation with two girls walking in front of them. They appeared to be between twelve and thirteen years of age and seemed to be sisters. They spoke with an accent that neither Chhoy nor Chhorn had heard before. Both had light skin, much lighter than Chhoy. Normally, Chhorn could tell if they were from China, but these two girls were not.

With nothing else to do besides walk, Chhorn, Chhoy, and the two girls continued to chat and exchange some of their stories. Like Chhorn and Chhoy, the two girls paused many times to ensure they didn't reveal certain things about their past. The two girls were from Vietnam. Leng was the older sister, and Chu was the younger sister. They came to Kampuchea with their families when they were little. This was the first time for Chhorn and Chhoy to speak to a Vietnamese descendant.

They marched along the river and then crossed a bridge that led to another path on the other side of the river. The road gradually swayed away from the river and cut through the plain of the rice paddies.

The afternoon sun was hovering straight above the clear sky, baking the air and the ground, making it difficult walk. Everyone, including each of the Mekongs, was walking barefoot. Shoes and sandals were rare. Only Mit Chahs were seen wearing sandals.

They stopped and rested under a large and isolated tree. Chhorn and Chhoy unpacked their lunch and begin to eat. Leng and Chu had brought their own lunch as well. Only a handful of other girls brought their lunch; many did not. The two Mekongs had brought their rice, but they gave it all away to the girls that they thought needed it most.

They rested for about an hour and then continued their march. They arrived in a village just before the sunset. They entered a gate and came to a well-maintained temple surrounded by all types of plants and flowers. The palm trees stood tall by the gate, and many more scattered around the temple. One side of the fence was a pile of broken statues of

Buddha and debris from some sort of structure. Girls were seen lining up behind the large pots sitting on the giant hearths for their supper. Others were congregating in front of three large temple structures in the center of the compound. Each structure was decorated with gold and red color carved woods from the wall corners to the roof top. The buildings were surrounded by a garden full of various types of flowers, mango trees, sugar cane plants, and banana trees. The grasses and hedges were nicely trimmed.

"This was Wat Basaet," the Mekong said. "You will live and work here. Go line up over there for your rice. After you finish eating, go find a spot to sleep in that building right there. We will wake you up tomorrow morning, and we will start working."

Chhorn, Chhoy, and all the girls rushed to the line. They were hungry from walking all day. As they approached the line, many of the girls currently in the lines turned and stared at them.

"Here comes the April Seventeenth! They're going to steal our food," one said out loud.

"People like that don't deserve to live. They must be infected with corruption," the other added. "I'll take it back. I think they were useful for something. Their flesh makes good fertilizer for the banana trees."

A loud mocking laugh erupted.

Chhorn and Chhoy were scared. After walking all day, they had been hoping to get a good rest and a good meal and a good place to stay. Instead they were facing a bunch of girls that wanted them dead. Everyone in the group nervously lined up behind the girls that had just mocked them. They kept their faces down to avoid any eye contact. These girls must have lived here all along. They must be the children of the Red Khmers.

Chhorn and Chhoy took out their plates that Mother had packed for them. They each got a large scoop of steamed rice and then walked over to a quiet area to eat. Leng and Chu were sitting closely with Chhorn and Chhoy. They ate without saying a word. Chhorn gazed around with a distressed face as she ate. She has a bad feeling about this place.

After Chhorn and Chhoy finished eating, they walked over to the building to find a place to sleep. Inside the building lay rows of rugs made from of interlaced leaves call called Daum Kok in Khmer. Most of the rugs had clothing or backpacks rested on top of them indicating it had been taken by someone. Some had a mosquito net suspended on top. All the inside walls of the building had been removed leaving just the columns and the supporting beams.

Chhorn picked an area where the rugs were most available. Leng and Chu chose the ones right beside them. Mother packed one mosquito net for Chhorn and one for Chhoy in case they slept separately. Neither Leng nor Chu had a mosquito net. Chhorn lent them her mosquito net, as she could share with Chhoy.

Chhorn didn't waste time and started to set up the mosquito net.

"Hey, Chhorn," someone called her name.

Chhorn turned to the where the voice came from and saw a girl that she had been walking with from Stung Chah.

"Remember me? I'm Ah Nee. I live two blocks away from your house. My dad was a truck driver just like your dad."

"I remember you, but I didn't know your name. I was afraid to speak to you on the way here," Chhorn said.

A girl sitting a few rugs away rushed in. "You have such a nice name. My name was Araja. I'm an Islam. I want to change my name. I don't know if the government likes Islam or not. Can you guys call me Ah Nee as well? It's such a beautiful name."

"All right, then…we'll call you Ah Nee," Chhorn replied with a smile. She found it funny to just simply name yourself.

"My name was Ah Vee," another girl introduced herself.

"And mine was Peak Lee," a light-skinned girl pronounced her name happily.

"What city were you guys from?" Chhoy asked.

All the girls started to speak at the same time, eager to tell their stories. The word "Ah" was a friendly syllable that appended to a person's name that had only one syllable. In Khmer, sometimes it was awkward to call a person's name with just one syllable.

They all told a brief story of themselves. Most of them came from Phnom Penh. The others came from the cities that Chhorn and Chhoy had never heard of. They chatted for several hours before falling asleep. Some fell asleep while leaning against the wall listening to the others' stories.

"Wake up! Wake up! It's time to go to work," someone hollered and jingled a small bell.

Chhorn and Chhoy woke up looking around in confusion. It took them a moment to recall that they were in the youth compound, away from home. Everyone got up and started walking outside. Chhorn, Chhoy, and all their new friends followed. They found the same two women that led them here from Stung Chah, standing with a paper and pencil.

"Line up right here in front of me. Reply 'yes' when I call your name," the Mekong instructed.

After everyone flocked out of the building, the Mekong called out the names and then instructed the group of about thirty girls to follow them. The women led them to an open area where all the other groups were assembled in multiple straight columns, facing several high-rank women, neatly dressed. Despite the black color, their clothes were made of high-quality garments. They buttoned their shirts from the sleeves to collar. Every single one of the women was wearing the red and white checkered scarves. Some had their scarves draped around their neck, and some wrapped them around their waist. The most noticeable of all was standing in the middle, both hands held behind her back, scanning around the assembly with a light grin. She has dark skin with her long hair tied back. She had a large body frame similar to a man.

After everyone arrived, the woman begins to speak. "All Mit, listen to what I have to say. I'm speaking on behalf of our government. We got rid of the previous government of corruption and inequality. You are here because our new government has a great program for you. We, as the fighters, worked hard and have gone through a tough time to get us to this point. You no longer belong to your parent. You now belong to the government. The government will teach you and guide you to be a better person. Under the new government, we will share everything we have. We shall work together, eat together, and sleep together. For those who don't work, they will not get anything to eat because it will not be fair for those who had worked hard. It is a simple logic that we don't need to explain further. After many years of fighting for equality, we finally succeeded. Let say bravo to our brave comrades that fought for this freedom."

"Bravo! Bravo!" everyone cheered, led by the Mekongs.

"However, beware that we still have enemy among us. The enemies were those who don't believe in our system. The new government was well developed. It was designed to oversee everything in our country. The government has the eyes of the pineapples. They see things all around, including the enemies. If anyone tries to break the rules, the government will see and government will punish accordingly.

"The enemies were the people that wanted to take our equality away. They were contagious and must be gotten rid of. If you discover any enemies among our comrades, report to us immediately or get rid of them yourself.

"Today, I will teach you how to fight the enemies. We can make a weapon as simple a breaking a bottle into pieces and mixing the sharp bottle pieces with mud and rolling it into a ball." The woman continued to talk and demonstrate how to make weapons. Then she demonstrated how fight in hand-to-hand combat.

The woman added many other subjects and extended the time until mid-morning. After she finished the speech and her demonstrations, the Mekong lead the group to a storage room and distributed out hoes and some sort of interlaced baskets.

"Today we will dig a water channel. Line up in front of me after you get the hoes and the baskets," the Mekong said.

After everyone got the hoes and the baskets, they began to walk. One of the Mekongs began to walk, leading the way. The others followed behind. The hoes were heavy for most girls to carry. They were made for the adults who would carry the hoes on their shoulders. The girls simply held the hoes below the blades, dragging the shaft on the ground while holding a dirt basket in the other hand.

The two Mekongs were walking without saying a word. They seemed to be very nice and helped anyone who struggled. After about a quarter of mile, they came to an open field filled with men, women, and children as young as nine, all wearing black, roaming the field like the ant colonies.

Among them were the guards carrying rifles, walking slowly and monitoring the workers. Each guard dauntingly walked along the higher ground with shiny machetes wrapped around their waist with the scarves, reflecting the sunlight as they walked. Fear surged through Chhorn and Chhoy when they arrived.

They walked deep into the crowd and came to a spot nearly a hundred yards in length where the ground was still untouched. Both ends were being excavated by a group of boys. The boys were there first probably because they didn't have the long meeting.

"We are going to dig from this end to that end over there. Spread out so you have room to dig. Be careful not to hurt one another with your hoes. Do as I do. Work hard and don't talk. We will take turns digging and carrying the dirt," the Mekong instructed.

The Mekong splits the group into two. The first group was to dig, and the second group was to carry the dirt away.

"I'm hungry already, and we haven't started working yet," Chhoy murmured to herself.

Chhorn methodically lifted the hoe up and sunk the blade into the ground and move the dirt into the basket with blade of the hoe. A few older girls knew what to do and started digging with ease. Chhoy and the younger girls stood and watched Chhorn and the older girls dig. Then Chhoy and the smaller girls tried. They were awkward at first but got better at it very quickly. After the basket was filled with dirt, the girls in the other group carried the basket to the higher ground and dumped the dirt there. The baskets had one handle on each side and were designed to be carried by two people.

The day was hot and dry as usual. Chhorn and Chhoy were digging and carrying the dirt along with thousands of other workers. Within just a couple of hours, they were soaked with sweat. Their shirts and pants were smeared with dirt. They wished they had scarves with them to wipe off the sweat from their faces. Now they understood why all the Red Khmers wore the scarves.

After a long and hard session of work, someone hollered, "Break time...Come and line up here. We will walk to get our lunch."

Chhorn and Chhoy dropped their basket and hoes and lined up with their group. They walked back to the temple where the rice was ready to be served. Chhorn and Chhoy grabbed their plates and lined up in front of the large pot with a woman standing beside the pot ready to distribute the rice. Everyone was too tired to talk and looking forward to eating. After they got their share of steamed rice, they ate quietly and rested under the trees.

A short while later the Mekong ordered everyone to line up, and they marched back to work. They continue digging the water channel and carrying the dirt until sunset and then returned to the temple for supper.

The darkness swept in shortly after they finished eating the supper. Chhorn and Chhoy went straight inside the building and lay down in the mosquito net. Leng and Chu did the same.

"My arms and my back are sore," Chu said.

"My entire body is sore. I don't know how I'm going to work tomorrow. My arm will fall off tomorrow if I have to work that hard again," Leng said.

"If we continue to work like this, we're all going to die," Chu said

On the second day, the Mekong announced that they would have one hour of school every morning before work starting from today. The classroom had been set up yesterday while they were working. They had cleared one of the storage rooms just for the group. The Mekong did not ask any student if they had attended school before. She simply started teaching the Khmer alphabet. Chhoy already knew the alphabet well from attending school in Phnom Penh. The school was a big break for the girls. They didn't have to work for an hour. The Mekong started teaching the alphabet, assuming this was first time for everyone in school. Fortunately, she didn't yell or scold the students.

They went back to work right after school and then returned to the temple for lunch at noon. They stopped working at sunset and ate supper. They worked in the same place for about four weeks, and then they were reassigned to another location to cut grasses and shrubs along with the women. The work was much easier. Rumor had it that they had brought more men from other villages to take over the difficult tasks.

The two Mekongs continued to teach one hour every morning, but they and all the girls seemed to have absolutely no motivation in education. They were simply taking advantage of the time off from work.

Four weeks later, more of Red Khmer leaders arrived. They liked the Wat Basaet a lot and decided to keep the buildings for themselves. They forced all the girls to move to other locations. Chhorn, Chhoy, and the entire group had been assigned to live in a nearby village called Ta Pon. When they arrived at Ta Pon Village, a group of boys between nine and fifteen years of age were working on demolishing the inside structures of abandoned houses, leaving just the roof, the walls and the supporting frames to get more space. All the girls helped move all the debris out of the house. It took a few days to complete the task. Chhorn and Chhoy had to sleep outside a couple of nights. Just after they completed demolishing and removing all the debris from the inside of the house, several more groups of girls arrived and were assigned to sleep in the same house. The house became very crowded very quickly, forcing everyone to squeeze in every small gap.

In Ta Pon, each horde were responsible to cook for themselves. Every three to four weeks, the Mekong would select three to four girls to cook as the rest would go to work. On the first week, Chhorn, Chhoy and the other two girls in the group were among the four to cook for the group. Chhorn and Chhoy volunteered to collect crabs and vegetables. The other two girls were to collect firewood, make the fire, and cook.

Chhorn and Chhoy had gotten familiar with many edible plants very quickly. There were two abundant vegetables called water spinach and amaranth. The water spinaches grew anywhere from the river bank to the rice paddies. The amaranth was the second most abundant vegetable in the area that grow around the house and along the river.

Chhoy and Chhorn carried a basket each and walked around the village and along the river picking the vegetables. It took them just one hour to fill up the basket and return to the compound early in the morning. Two baskets were enough to make a large pot of soup, but they returned to picked more vegetables for supper.

"We were lucky that we get this job," Chhorn said.

"This is a lot better than digging the water channel," Chhoy said.

On the second day Chhorn was leading Chhoy further along the river picking mostly the water spinach. So far, not a single person had been seen around the area, as they were all working in the rice paddies or deep in the woods somewhere. Chhorn had just realized their house was not too far from here. She had not been home for a couple months now, and they really missed home.

"Chhoy, should we try to give Mother a quick visit?" Chhorn asked.

"I don't know. I'm afraid we might get caught," Chhoy replied.

"They never told us how far we could go to pick the vegetables. They only asked us to pick one basket each. Plus, we have four extra baskets from yesterday. If we return with baskets full of vegetables, we should be all right," Chhorn explained.

Chhoy didn't say a word. She seemed unsure about the idea, but she didn't disagree either. She missed Mother too. She simply followed Chhorn's lead.

"We should walk very quickly so we can get there fast and return before noon," Chhorn said and started to pick up her pace.

Chhorn and Chhoy were excited about seeing Mother again. Chhorn wanted to run and get home sooner, but she was afraid they might raise suspicion. No one over the age of nine was allowed to walk freely.

The two arrived home in midmorning. Mother was splitting wood with the axe in front of the house, and I was standing beside her clinging to her pants.

"Where did you come from? Did you sneak out?" Mother asked in surprise.

"Our job was to pick vegetables and collect crabs. They never told us where to go or where not to go. We decided to come here for a visit," Chhorn explained.

"You spent all morning walking. How are you going to have time to pick vegetables and collect crabs?"

"We missed you so much, we hadn't thought of that yet. Maybe we could work fast," Chhorn said.

"Mother will help you then. I know a spot to pick the water spinach and collect crabs. Get inside the house before they see you here."

When Chhoy and Chhorn walked in the house, Pech was lying alone on the floor. Chhorn picked Pech up and cradled him in her arm.

Mother stared at Chhorn and Chhoy for a long moment.

"Both of you got a lot darker, and you seem to have lost a lot of weight," Mother said. "Don't they give you food to eat?"

"They gave us rice twice a day, but they made us dig the dirt for four weeks," Chhorn said.

"You got skinnier too, Mother," Chhoy said.

"There's never enough to eat here," Mother said.

"Where are Chhom and Chhoeun?" Chhorn asked.

"Chhoeun was taken to live with the boys just a few days after you two left. He has not returned home since then."

"Chhom was here earlier looking after Bun and Pech, but when I got home she told me she was going to look for food. Chhoy, you stay home and keep an eye on Bun and Pech. Make half of can of steam rice, enough for you and Chhorn to eat before heading back. Chhorn, you follow me. We are going to pick the vegetables and catch some crabs."

Mother took Chhorn to pick the vegetables and returned just a short moment later with two baskets full of water spinach and about two dozen crabs. The steam rice was ready. Chhoy and Chhorn took a scoop of steam rice each and begin to eat. The long walk from Ta Pon made them very hungry.

"Chhorn, what happen to your shirt? You lost a couple of buttons," Mother asked.

"They got ripped off when I lifted the heavy dirt basket back in Wat Basaet," Chhorn replied.

"I will stitch them for you. I have a lot of buttons," Mother said.

Mother walked to the corner of the room and rummaged through a pile of clothes behind a large vase. She brought over a fancy-looking shirt with at least a dozen pockets. Each pocket was sealed with a button.

"What are you doing with the shirt, Mother? There are colors on that shirt, and it's a man shirt," Chhorn asked.

"You naïve child, I'm not letting you wear this shirt. That's like asking them to kill you. I'm taking the button from the shirt and stitching it onto your shirt. You are fourteen years old. You shouldn't walk around with missing buttons," Mother scolded. "Move closer to me."

Mother removed two large, black, glossy buttons from the fancy shirt with scissors and quickly sewed the buttons onto Chhorn's shirt. When she finished, she hid the scissors, needle, and thread beneath the pile of clothes. It wasn't clear what the government approved of or prohibited those days, but she decided to be safe and keep most things out of sight when possible.

"The buttons are very large, but they are beautiful. Now you have something new on you," Mother said.

Chhorn and Chhoy returned to the compound just in time for lunch. They were both nervous for leaving the village and, more importantly, for visiting home. No one was allowed to go home. They handed the two baskets full of water spinach and the fresh crabs underneath the vegetables to the Mekong, hoping they would not get in trouble.

"The crabs are under the water spinach," Chhorn said.

The Mekong examined the basket and said, "You guys are good with catching crabs. We will have good crab soup for supper."

"I have to go far to find these crabs," Chhorn said and then looked at Chhoy and grinned.

"I don't care how far you go as long as we get good food. Go get your share of rice before it's gone," the Mekong added. Then she stooped down and examined Chhorn's shirt. "Where did you get those buttons? They are beautiful."

"My Mother stitched them for me," Chhorn replied and realized she had just given herself away for visiting home.

She turned around quickly hoping the Mekong would not catch what she said but only come face-to-face with a tall, dark woman standing with both hands held behind her back. Chhorn jumped from the unexpected encounter. The woman was wearing clean and high-quality black clothes. Her shirt extended past her torso. She buttoned her shirt up to the collar. Her scarf was neatly wrapped around her waist, strapping a long machete. Chhorn shivered when she saw the long machete hanging down from the woman's side. She must be a person with high authority.

The women stooped down and examined the button on Chhorn's shirt and said, "The buttons are beautiful. Where did you get them?"

Chhorn stared at the woman's face in terror. Not only had she given herself away to Mekong but had given herself away to the Mit Chah (Elder Comrade) as well.

Even though everyone was wearing black, it was easy to identify the Mit Chah. Their clothes were usually very clean. They normally didn't have to work. They would walk around investigating the compound for any unusual activities. Very often they reminded everyone to acknowledge them as Mit Chah because they were the first to join the new system.

"My Mother stitched it for me. I lost my button from working, and she replaced them with these large buttons. Do you really like them?" Chhorn asked. Once again, she had just given herself away.

"Could you get me one? You have my permission to go home and get me the button," the woman said with a cold grin.

"You can go home and get her a button," the Mekong said.

Chhorn felt a surge of relief and also felt special for having the privilege to visit home. Every girl she knew wanted to go home. In every meeting, the Mit Chah attempted to brainwash everyone to forget their parents and to regard them as nothing more than their comrades.

"You can have one of mine. I can have my Mother stitch me another one. I will go home another day. Do you have a knife where I can cut the thread?" Chhorn asked and then immediately regretted asking for such a deadly thing.

The woman looked down at the machete hanging off her waist and said, "My knife is too big to cut the thread off the button. It might ruin the button. Just go home tomorrow and get me a button."

"Then tomorrow on the way to work, I will go home and get you a button, Mit Bong." She said it out loud so the Mekong standing right behind her could hear the deal between her and Mit Chah. She could have said more than one button, but her instinct told her to save each one button for a pass to go home one day.

Chhorn was thrilled for the opportunity to visit home. She woke up early in the morning and walked straight home. Unfortunately, she was afraid to bring Chhoy along.

When she arrived home, she found Chhom was home looking after Pech and me. Chhorn picked Pech up and cradled him in her arm and played with him. Mother was away somewhere, probably picking vegetables or cutting firewood.

About an hour later, Mother arrived. "You came again? They did not say anything?" Mother asked with concern.

"They let me come because of the button you gave me," Chhorn said. "They liked the fancy buttons, and they asked me to bring them a button. If you plan to throw any fancy clothes away, make sure to keep the buttons."

"I should have known they'd like the buttons. Every single one of the Mit Chah button their shirt up to the collar. The buttons stand out the most," Mother said.

"I was thinking all night. I will only give them one button at a time so then I get to come home more often," Chhorn said in excitement.

Mother was still worried but couldn't help but to break a smile. "Be careful, daughter. They might accuse us of conspiracy between children and parent. I have a lot fancy clothes. I had burned a lot of them months ago, but your Father had brought more from the trips. They were too beautiful to throw away. I hid them behind the vase and underneath the old clothes. Besides, there was no sign that they would search the house."

Chhorn returned to the compound with the button and handed it to her Mekong. The Mekong delivered the button to the Mit Chah who had requested the button.

"She was very happy with the button," the Mekong said when she returned.

Chhorn and Chhoy saw the woman in the evening walking around the compound with other Mit Chahs, wearing the fancy button on her collar. The fancy button made the rest of the buttons look tiny and dull.

"Ah, our Mit likes the button a lot. It matches her pretty face and her dark heart," Chhorn whispered to Chhoy.

The Mekong came to Chhorn just before night fall and informed her that another Mit Chah would like a button as well. Chhorn was very excited once again. This would give her another opportunity to come visit Mother.

Chhorn took Chhoy along the next day and told Mother the good news. Mother was content with the opportunity, but she warned her not to abuse the privilege and suggested she save it for an emergency.

CHAPTER 7

Chhoeun was at home standing by the door waiting to get picked up. A moment later, two men with about three dozen boys walking in a single-file line stopped in front of our house. One was leading the line, and the other followed from behind.

"Come and line up," the man leading the line hollered.

Chhoeun picked up his backpack from the floor and swung behind his back. He descended the stairs and walked to the line smiling. He was a little nervous, but he was kind of bored staying home doing nearly nothing besides chatting with new friends. The man asked for his first name, family name, and his age. Chhoeun provided all the information he needed, including his fake age and the family name, Phuong. His new age matched well with his short height.

Chhoeun tagged onto the line with a horde of boys. Half of them looked so young that Chhoeun thought they should be at their Mother's side all the time. Chhoeun immediately spotted a few familiar faces. One of them was our second cousin named Noy. He was the son of Um Phon, Father's cousin. It just struck him that he was not the only one who'd faked his age. All the boys he knew were the same age as he or older.

"Hey, Noy," Chhoeun hollered and grinned.

Noy returned a guilty grin. Noy was a few months younger than Chhoeun. His thin frame made him look tall, but he was about Chhoeun's height.

"Let get moving. Follow me in a straight line." said the Mekong who was leading the line.

They marched toward the river, and then crossed the bridge that arched over the Stung Chah River. At the end of the bridge, three buildings stood tall and wide, surrounded by the thick and broad trees called Ampel Tuk. Their branches extended out, and the leaves were drooping sluggishly down. Ampel Tuk trees were famous for their thin, long, edible fruit. Up ahead, the coconut trees rose elegantly displaying their slender and remarkable height. Despite the coconut trees grow randomly, they appeared associated with the three buildings. The elder called this place Wat Samdach (the Temple of the King). There was no trace of the statues of Buddha anywhere. They must have been removed.

The men led the group to a small path that cut through the sugar cane orchard. The orchard once belonged to someone, but now it was covered with thick grasses and ivies. The banana trees flourished among the sugar canes.

A long moment later, they came to an open rice field blanketed with thousands of men, women, and children working. Chhoeun and the horde walked along the rim of the rice paddies, eyeing the workers. Some of the men were riding on the single blade plow, commanding the oxen to haul while the women were stooping over plucking and wrapping the rice sprouts. Small girls were working alongside the women. The guards were armed with long machetes strapped to the sides of their waists and were walking around monitoring the workers.

Chhoeun was overwhelmed with fear. This was what he would spend the rest of his life doing—working in the mud and being monitored by the guards walking around with the machetes. He had been working hard since he turned five. He didn't mind working hard to make money for Mother, but this time he would have to work hard to stay alive. These guards were here not just to idle around. They were here so that everyone would work hard. And the machetes were not just for display either.

No one said a word. Chhoeun could tell that everyone was bearing the same fear, except for the two Mekongs, who seem content with what they were seeing. There was something different about the two Mekongs. Even though they dressed in black, their clothes were clean, smooth, and neatly tucked. Their shirts were buttoned to the collar. They walked with pride and confidence. Chhoeun was unsure whether the two were trying the hide their fear of what was to come or they really were content with the intense labor agenda. If they were hiding their fear, they were doing a very good job.

Chhoeun and the horde came to a village. Small houses were randomly located along the wagon road. All the houses appeared to be empty; not a single person was seen in the area.

The Mekong led them deeper into the village and came to a well-prepped compound with multiple oversized houses crowded by hundreds of boys walking in lines supervised by two to three men. They seemed to be newcomers as well.

They stopped in front of the door of the nearest house. "Find a spot to sleep and come back to meet me outside. Make it quick. We will eat lunch, and then we will discuss our plan," the Mekong said.

There were no rooms inside the house, only the bare columns and beams to support the roof and the side walls. The floor was made of bamboo trees raised a few feet off the ground. Half of the spots in the house were taken. Scarves, clothes, and sacks were being used to mark the spots. Chhoeun walked further into the house searching for a favorable spot.

He found many random open spots in the center of the house, but he wanted a spot near the wall, away from entrance. He had to choose a spot quickly, as another horde had just arrived at the front door.

"Chhoeun, over there! There were two open spots over there," Noy said pointing his finger further into the house by the wall.

Chhoeun and Noy quickly walked over to the open spot and laid down their backpacks. The boys in his horde picked the open spots nearby. There was a window just a few feet away giving plenty of light.

Chhoeun and Noy returned to the Mekong outside the house as instructed. Within minute, everyone stood around the two Mekongs waiting for further instruction.

"Everyone, this is the place where you will sleep and work. The government has arranged this place just for you. Today is the day when we begin to work together, eat together, and sleep together.

"By the way, my name is Narong. I have joined the Khmer Savior and fought very hard for our country to save our country from the corrupted system. I am extremely pleased that the corrupted society has been abolished. It is time to start living where everyone is equal. There will be no more drunken soldiers walking around harassing civilians. There will be no more policemen pulling us over demanding money. We will be free from all kinds of corruption. From now on, all we need to focus on is work. We will work hard to build our country. We will show the foreign countries that we don't need the technology to farm and to build bridges. We will find ways to control the water and use the water to farm.

"I was a three-star general and a pilot, but I was also working secretly for the Khmer Savior. The Lon Nol's force ordered me to drop the bombs on the suspected village to destroy the Khmer Savior, but I drove the aircraft over the military base and dropped the bombs on them instead. Me and my comrade here caused significant damage to the Lon Nol's force. With just us two alone, we destroyed several military bases. The military was a bunch of fools," Norong said and rested his arm on the shoulder of the second Mekong who stood wordlessly beside him.

The second Mekong nodded and grinned in satisfaction.

"It is lunchtime. Today, someone is cooking for us. Tomorrow we will cook for ourselves. I will organize our group after lunch so that we share the responsible evenly. Go line up over there and get your share," Narong said and pointed to a large pot sitting on a giant hearth. Then he walked off.

The steam was rising vigorously from the large pot. The fire was burning slightly beneath the pot. There was a man standing by the pot holding a long scoop, waiting.

"Let's go get our bowls," Chhoeun said to Noy.

Chhoeun and Noy went into the house and grabbed their bowls from their backpacks. They came to line up with the horde to get their share of rice.

"I don't like this equality thing. We have to line up like cows to get our food," Noy said.

"What can we do? We just have to go along with everyone else," Chhoeun replied.

Back in the village, Mother was the Mekong. She would sit down with her horde and eat with them. Narong and his comrade took off to eat somewhere else. Narong had just stressed in the introduction that he was not an ordinary Mekong. He was the Mit Chah, or the Khmer Savior.

A moment after Chhoeun finished his rice, Narong and his comrade returned. He stood outside the dining hall and hollered, "All Mit, come and line up in front of me. It's time for me to divide our horde into groups."

After everyone had lined up, he walked along the line and examined each individual.

"Mit! Come and stand right here." He pulled Chhoeun from the line by his arm and guided him to stand to one side.

"Mit! You come and stand right here," He pulled an older boy and guided him to stand beside Chhoeun.

Then he grabbed another two older boys to step out and said, "I'm assigning the four of you to become the Mekrum (group leader)," Narong said. "Since you look older than the rest, you should be able to handle more responsibilities. Your main job is to organize the daily tasks for your group. I will select your crews shortly. You are also responsible to cook when it is your turn. Each week or so, I will select another group to cook for our horde."

After Narong explained the Mekrum's responsibility, he randomly selected and ordered nine boys to stand behind Chhoeun. Then he selected nine more boys for each of the Mekrum.

After splitting the horde in to four groups, Narong continued with his speech, "Since we are now all equal, everyone is required to refer to another person as Mit, including myself. However, my comrade here and I are known as Mit Bong because we joined the Khmer Savior and fought the war.

"Under the new government, we are now living as one big family. There are no more mothers and daughters. There are no more fathers and sons. We were all comrades. The government will take care all of you from now on. Under the new system, we will rotate our tasks every two to four weeks. Each group will responsible to do a specific task. The tasks include fishing, farming, collecting wood, digging trenches, and tending the cows. We will work from sunrise to sunset. We will eat lunch at noon, and we will eat supper after work.

"Another thing, the government wants to see that everyone is educated. There will be class every morning. School is important for us. Our country will need knowledge to continue to improve and grow.

"Even though we have gotten rid of the corrupted, there are still many who are still opposing our new government. They are considered enemy. Since we are now all brothers, we should look after one another. Report anyone whom you suspect as enemies. We will take the enemies to trial.

"When things get settle down, we will go around asking questions about your past. Answer the questions truthfully. The government will not tolerate lies. Anyone who lies to the government is considered enemy."

Narong continued to explain the ideological aspects of the new government and stressed his commitment to help prove the system was going on the right track. He had so much pride about his accomplishments during the war and continued to mention them over and over again in his speech.

Narong's speech ended about two hours after lunch. His speech seemed to last forever for Chhoeun. He would've fallen asleep several times had it not been for Mit Narong mentioning about getting rid of anyone who was lazy and anyone who didn't follow orders. The remarks made his skin prickle and kept him wide awake.

After Narong ended his speech, he began to assign the tasks to each group. Chhoeun's group has been assigned to dig the dirt on the rice paddies. Normally, the majority of the rice farmers would use the single-bladed plow hauled by a pair of oxen to loosen up the dirt to farm rice but it was obvious that the plow and the oxen were limited. Therefore, the workers would have to dig the dirt manually. It was extremely hard work. Fortunately, it was not permanent.

"Meet me right here first thing in the morning," Narong said before he dismissed everyone.

Noy walked over to Chhoeun after the meeting and said, "I got lucky. My team will cook this week."

Chhoeun spent the rest of his evening chatting with Noy and the older boys. The younger boy within his group stayed by Chhoeun, listening to the conversation, trying to get to know him. They seemed to like Chhoeun.

At nightfall, Chhoeun went to sleep on the crowded space just big enough for him to turn. He shared his mosquito net with Noy. He wished Noy was in his group so that he could talk during work. Most of the boys in his group were around nine and ten. They were too young to have a good conversation.

The entire floor had been taken. Some of boys within the horde that had arrived later in the day had to set up the mosquito net outside and sleep outside the shelter.

Chhoeun sleep almost immediately after he laid down. He was exhausted from the long walk from home. Since no one was wearing a watch beside Mit Narong and his comrade, Chhoeun had no way of telling what time it is. He didn't care either. Time was not important anymore.

Someone brought a lamp and left the lamp on to make it easy for everyone to navigate in the large, dark house.

Chhoeun was woken up multiple times by the crows of the roosters. It was a sign that the sunrise was near. He went back to sleep and was woken up soon by the voice of a man, "Wake up! Wake up! It's time to get up."

Like a corral full of cows, he woke up at the same time as everyone else and trudged outside. He found Narong and his comrade standing outside. Narong was holding a long, thin carved stick. He must be ready to teach the class. Chhoeun blended in the line in front of Narong.

"All Mit! Today is our first day of class. I will be your teacher. My comrade will assist me," Narong said. "Follow me. The classroom has been prepared."

Narong led them to a dining hall. Multiple sections had been set up in the dining hall. Other hordes were using the other sections for their classes.

Narong began to teach the Khmer alphabet right away, as if this was the first time in school for everyone. Chhoeun had attended school for many years in Takeo and Phnom Penh. He and many of the older boys ended up assisting Narong by helping the younger boys with the alphabet.

After class, Narong's comrade ordered Chhoeun to get his group ready. Narong's comrade was a quiet man. He hadn't said a word since yesterday. Narong had not mentioned his name either. So far, he seemed to be a normal man.

"Order your crew to grab a hoe each then line up over there. The hoes are in the storage room over there. You should be the last in line. I will lead the line," the man said pointing to an isolated shack where other groups were retrieving their tools.

"Whoever is in my group, come over here!" Chhoeun hollered. He remembered some faces but not all. He did not get a chance to know their names yet. Eventually, he would need to remember their names.

All nine boys in his group rushed forward and lined up right in front of him. Chhoeun was relieved that he didn't have to look for them. Chhoeun stared at their faces as they formed a line. These boys were too young to be here. Every single boy stared at Chhoeun smiling as they wait for the instruction. Chhoeun felt like he was their older brother already. His mind immediately drifted away and thought of Chhorn and Chhoy. They were in the same situation, away from home with people who didn't really care about them. Chhoeun determined to make the best effort to care for these little boys like they were his little brothers. If the angel had eyes like the adults always said, good things would happen to Chhorn and Chhoy in return.

"Follow me," Chhoeun said and led the line to the storage room.

Chhoeun walked into the storage room and picked out the hoes. He tried to look for the smaller and lighter hoes for his crew. These hoes were newly crafted. The blades were free of dirt, and the handles were freshly carved.

"Be careful with the blades. They are sharp. Make sure you keep your distance from the person in front of you and behind you," Chhoeun advised as he handed out the hoes to his crew.

The boys took the hoes and clumsily carried them in their hands. Some held the hoes by the blades and some held them by the opposite end from the blade. One of the boys dropped the hoe, and the blade landed just a few inches away from his bare feet. The blade of the hoes could cause a severe cut if it landed on someone's foot. He wouldn't know what to do if that ever happened.

"Hold your hoes like this when you walk," Chhoeun said placing the hoe on one side of his shoulder where the blade hung behind his back to demonstrate.

Chhoeun had been using hoes before he even turned ten. He helped Mother loosen many acres of land in Takeo to plant vegetables and rice. Over the years, he had learned how to lift the hoes up and dig the dirt with minimal effort.

He organized his crew in a line as instructed. Everyone held the hoes comfortably on their shoulders.

"These boys are smart! They are standing like the militia," the man said and smiled. "Let's go. Follow me."

Bong Chhoeun was happy to see the man smile. He didn't know much about the man. A smile indicated that he had some heart.

The man led Chhoeun from the compound to an open field. Hundreds of other groups of boys and girls emerged from the village hidden by the forest. Most groups were carrying the hoes just like Chhoeun's group. Only a few groups were carrying shovels and baskets.

They walked along the rim of the rice paddies as thousands of men and women spread throughout the field digging dirt and clearing the wheat. The adults started work early since they don't have class. The guards were walking slowly among the workers monitoring.

Narong's comrade led them deep into the crowd and stopped at empty rice paddies. "This is your job for today. Dig this area," he said and left without giving any further instruction.

Chhoeun took a deep breath. This was the first time he had to lead nine boys to work. He felt very terrible to see how the new government required these young boys to work. They could barely carry the hoes.

"Mit, I know how to dig," a boy about eleven years old said out loud and smiled.

"Very well. You can help me teach the ones who don't have the experience," Chhoeun said and rubbed his head. "What is your name?" Chhoeun asked.

"My name is Ra," the boys responded with pride.

"I know how too!" another boy said raising his hand.

"That's good. You can teach too."

"All right, everyone, spread out," Chhoeun said. "Mit Ra, come over here and stand right here," Chhoeun ordered.

"We will start from here," Chhoeun said and positioned the boy the way he wanted. "The next person will stand right here. Make sure you don't stand too close to one another or you will get hurt," Chhoeun said and grabbed one of the boys standing nearby.

"Mit Ra, show everyone how you dig the dirt," Chhoeun said.

Mit Ra methodically lifted and thumped the hoe to the dirt with ease. He did it repeatedly as if no energy was required. He stopped after a fourth time, waiting for comments from Chhoeun.

"That's the way to dig," Chhoeun said.

Chhoeun arranged the rest of the boys in a horizontal line with plenty of space in between. He saved a spot in the middle for himself so the boys on both side of the line could see him in case they needed help.

Chhoeun and all the boys begin to dig the rice paddies. He noticed Ra still trying to impress him by digging faster than he should.

"Mit Ra, take it easy. Save your energy. We are not in a rush," Chhoeun said.

He liked Ra. It was great to have a boy dedicated to work hard. He made good example for the group. Chhoeun didn't really care how much his group produced as long as everyone worked consistently. Narong's comrade never said how much land they should dig. The guards were walking and monitoring the workers. He would not want to attract their attention.

Chhoeun was impressed how diligently the boys worked. Every single one of them was working without slacking off. He was saddened to see these young boys have to work so hard. He could picture Chhorn and Chhoy doing exactly the same thing.

Chhoeun and his crew inched their way further into the rice paddies. The flat ground became puffy and muddy after being struck by the blades. Sweat was rolling down from Chhoeun's face. His back was soaking wet. The women working in the adjacent field frequently paused and stared at the boys. They must have children too, working somewhere far away, Chhoeun thought.

It was noontime. The sun edged straight above, giving off the warmer heat. Chhoeun noticed most of the groups nearby had been dismissed for lunch break. Then Narong's comrade appeared from the distance and hollered, "All Mit! It's lunchtime. Form a line."

"Let's go. Form a line," Chhorn said softly.

The boys immediately dropped their hoes to the ground and formed a line as instructed. Narong's comrade led them back to the compound where the rice has been cooked by another group in their horde.

After a long and hard morning of work, Chhoeun was very hungry. Unfortunately, each person could only have one large scoop of steamed rice. Narong and his comrade stood by the pot to ensure that everyone had an equal share.

After he got his share, Chhoeun sat with his crew and ate his rice. The rice would be sufficient if Chhoeun hadn't had to dig the dirt all morning. The long and hard work directly under the sun made him crave for more.

"Mit, you want some of my rice? You are bigger than me; you need to eat more," Ra said.

"No, that's all right. You worked very hard. You need to eat too," Chhoeun replied.

Chhoeun felt a surge of sympathy toward Ra. He figured Ra was sucking up to him so that he would treat him well. He probably would do the same if he was Ra's age. He would try to prove that he didn't have to do that.

Chhoeun and his group repeated the same job for several weeks. They worked more efficiently each week and finished more area each day. They worked three times faster than the first day.

Chhoeun found out soon after that there was a river nearby. Someone also returned with a turtle. He didn't wait long and began looking for the river before it got too dark. He found the river not too far from the compound. He began searching for turtles. As he stooped around searching, he found a roll of nylon string with the loose end tangled in the bush. He felt like he'd found a mountain of gold. Chhoeun untangled the string and salvaged every inch of the string. Using a short knife that he'd found in the storage room, Chhoeun immediately crafted a fishing rod with a long and thin bamboo tree that grew by the river. Fish were impossible to catch without a fishing hook, but Chhoeun was not planning to catch the fish. He was looking forward to catching frogs instead. After a short observation, he knew there should be plenty of frogs. He knew exactly what to do to catch the bullfrogs without using the fishing hook. He had done it many times in Takeo during the rainy season.

Chhoeun searched around the shrubs and mud and caught a several tiny frogs and stored them in a sack. He tied a tiny frog to his newly crafted fishing pole as bait and tossed it in to the river. Then he methodically jerked the pole back in a way to make it appear that the tiny frog was hopping across the river. Just seconds later, a bullfrog appeared from under the water and began chasing the bait. Chhoeun skillfully made a final jerk, causing the bait to suspend in the air longer. The bullfrog leaped after the bait and engulfed it in midair. He yanked the fishing pole back, and the bullfrog flew right into him. He used his free hand to catch the bullfrog while it was still in the air and then removed the bait from the frog's mouth. He held the bullfrog by its hind legs and whacked its head against the nearby tree branches. The bullfrog instantly became lifeless. The bait frog was still alive after being swallowed.

Chhoeun smiled with joy. He wasted no time and continued to catch more frogs. He caught the second frog almost as fast as he caught the first. He was aware the night was creeping in fast; he hurried to catch more frogs before dark. He didn't want to stay near the water after dark. There could be poisonous snakes around.

He stopped when he thought it was too dark to continue. He had a pile of frogs beside his feet. If he kept track correctly, he had caught over forty frogs. He hated to stop when he was in the rhythm but it was getting dark. The poisonous snakes could be anywhere. He took off his shirt and used it wrap the frogs and returned to the compound.

Many of the boys were still outside roasting their catches and vegetables in the fire. Noy was among them, sitting with his group chatting and waiting for his catches to cook.

Ra and a few of Chhoeun's crew were sitting around another fire nearby.

"Noy, look what I got," Chhoeun said lifting his makeshift sack.

"What's in there, crabs?" Noy asked.

"Not crabs," Chhoeun replied. He placed the sack on the ground and began to untie the knot.

Bong Chhoeun drew one frog out and lifted it up like a trophy.

"Whaaa…! That's a huge frog!" Ra said.

"These are all frogs," Chhoeun pointed to the sack. "They are all nearly the same size. Some are even bigger than this one."

"I can have one, right?" Noy asked.

"Of course. I caught enough for everyone in our horde," Chhoeun said.

Everyone suddenly surrounded Chhoeun hoping to get one. Ra was standing right next to Chhoeun, proud for being so close to him. Chhoeun handed the one he had in his hand to Ra.

Ra smiled and leaped slightly in joy. Then he darted back toward the fire.

Chhoeun distributed the rest of the frogs to his horde, and he still had two medium-sized frogs left for himself. Instantly, the aroma of the charred frog skin filled the air making Chhoeun's stomach growl violently.

Chhoeun looked around for a spot to roast his frog. He noticed the boys were competing for space in the fire to cook their frogs.

"Come sit here," Noy said.

Chhoeun looked at Noy's group, but there was no space to sit. "No problem. I will sit with my little crew instead," Chhoeun said and came to sit next to Ra. He wanted to be with his young crew. He wanted to comfort them and show them that he was no threat.

The next morning after class, Narong asked everyone to gather outside for a meeting. Narong and his comrade were standing side by side. Chhoeun noticed they both glanced at his face and turned away.

"All Mit, I have heard good news from many of our comrades. They praised Mit Chhoeun for his skill of catching frogs to feed the entire horde in just one evening. Not only he was skilled, but he was also generous. This was what the new system is all about. We share everything we have. I would like to promote him and his group to cook starting today. Chhoeun can go wherever he needs to catch frogs or any other animals or even pick vegetables. The task is not permanent, but I will decide when to switch the task back to the other groups.

Mit Chhoeun, you will have to retrieve the rice from the rice storage department. Tell them my name, and they will give you the rice accordingly. Everyone, let's get back to work," Narong said and walked away.

Chhoeun was shocked. He did not expect the promotion. After digging the dirt for several weeks, he finally got the break. He never had enough to eat. The cooks only made steamed rice and nothing else. On top of that, he was relieved that Ra and the rest of his boys would get a break from digging dirt for a while.

Ra and the rest of the boys gathered around Chhoeun waiting for the instructions. Chhoeun walked over to the dining hall where all the cooking wares were stored for his group.

"No more digging dirt. I didn't think I could go on for another day," Ra said happily.

Every single one of them appeared relieved. Then Chhoeun felt a surge of panic when he thought about cooking for the entire horde. He just realized he didn't know how to cook rice in the giant pot. He had experience cooking rice in a tiny pot when he'd joined the Lon Nol's military years ago, but this pot was about a hundred times bigger. Not only did he have to cook rice, but he had to cook the frogs as well. Chhoeun tried to remain calm. He didn't want to show fear to his boys who were heavily relying on him.

"Let's get started," Chhoeun said.

Chhoeun divided the tasks to each of his group and returned to the river immediately with his fishing. He returned to the compound after catching dozens of bull frogs. He had to cook the rice before the other group returned.

The next morning Chhoeun heard someone complain about his rice. He was not surprised; he need some advice. He went to Narong and asked for permission to go see Mother.

"You may go. You need a lot of advice," Narong said teasingly.

Chhoeun headed straight for home and arrived there shortly. Mother was surprised to see him.

"How did you get permission to come home?" she asked.

"They assigned me to cook for the horde, but I don't know how to cook rice," Chhoeun replied.

"You naïve child. It's easy," Mother said.

Mother quickly explained to Bong Chhoeun how to cook steamed rice properly. She included the steps to drain the water when needed and reduce the fire when the rice was nearly cooked.

Chhoeun returned to the compound with a lot more confidence. When he arrived, his sub groups had already completed their tasks, and they continued to work to get ready for the next day. Chhoeun had plenty of time on his hands. He went back to the river to catch the frogs. He caught over two dozen frogs, as well as several catfish that were stranded in the muddy area of river.

The entire horde enjoyed having Chhoeun's group as the cooks and praised him daily. After four days of cooking, Chhoeun got very comfortable. His subgroup had brought a surplus of water, firewood, and vegetables. They even assisted Chhoeun catching catfish and crabs. Chhoeun attempted to teach some of them how to catch the frogs using his method, but none of them seem to get the grasp. It was too complicated. It was a very difficult skill to train.

Rules were changing slightly every day. Some were better, but most were worse. Everyone was allowed to visit home every other weekend. Each visit was recorded to ensure everyone returned to the compound on time. Each Mekong was required to meet every day and pass the messages from the higher authorities. Worst of all, the country was running low on rice stock. The rice had been reduced from ten cans a meal to five for the horde of forty. Fortunately, Chhoeun and his crew were providing enough frogs, fish, crabs, and vegetables to replace the loss of rice.

Fortunately, Chhoeun's group was the first group allowed to visit home. He arrived when I was standing in the front door watching animals, including snakes, crossing the wagon path from one side to another. Chhoeun emerged from the distance carrying a backpack and a long pole on his back. It seemed forever since the last time I saw him. I ran to Chhoeun and clung to his leg. He stopped and rubbed my head.

"What are you doing out here by yourself?" he asked.

I didn't answer but continued to hold one of his feet with both of my hands. Chhoeun picked me up and carried me inside the house.

Mother was splitting wood on the other side of the house. She was very surprised to see Chhoeun. He explained why he was here, and he sat down and chatted with Mother as she continued to work. He explained his living conditions at the compound and how things were changing very rapidly. Mother explained that things had changed at home too. Rice had been reduced by half as well here at home. Meetings were held daily before work. The government was forcing everyone to work harder. People who were found slacking off had been taken to trial, and sometimes they were punished.

"Bun, I have a task for you. Go catch me some tiny frogs or tadpoles," Chhoeun said.

I was very happy. Not only I get to see my old brother, but I also got to do him a favor. Without asking why, I darted toward the river. I knew exactly what the tadpoles were, and I knew exactly where to catch them.

Chhom had caught them a few times for fun when she took me to the river. They looked similar to frogs except they had a large tail and couldn't hop like frogs. They lived in small puddles and were very easy to catch.

I returned within minutes with half a dozen of tadpoles. Chhoeun looked at me and said, "Well done!" He took the tadpoles and walked inside the house. He picked up an empty glass jar and placed the tadpoles inside the jar. He stepped out of the door toward the river holding the jar, the fishing pole, and a metal bucket.

I followed Chhoeun, curious what he was about to do with the tadpoles. A short moment later my jaw dropped when I saw how Chhoeun caught his first bull frog. He made it look so easy and effortless. I stood and watched him catch more frogs until I got bored.

In the evening, Mother skinned and gutted the frog, and then she made frog soup mixed with rice. It was the best meal I ever remembered having. We had been eating plain rice with water spinach and amaranth for the past several months. Frog soup was delicious.

Bong Chhoeun returned to the compound the next evening. Things continued to change at the compound. Narong decided to stop having the morning class. Instead, he used the time to meet and give lectures. The government had new messages to pass every day. They were mostly bad news.

"We are running low on rice because we don't work hard enough. The government would like us to put more effort into our jobs," Narong said.

Noy couldn't help but make a loud comment, "If we are all equal, why do the Mekongs get to eat unlimited rice when we have to eat less, and why aren't the Mekongs and all the Mit Chahs coming to work with us?"

He was the only person who was not afraid to object to the message from government.

"If you have questions, you should go ask the high authority yourself," Narong said angrily and continued his speech.

"Noy, don't say anything. Let them say what they want. They have more power than us," Chhoeun whispered.

"It's not fair. They eat well, and our rice gets reduced every day, and we have to work harder every time," Noy added out loud.

"I know, but they are different."

"But they said we are equal."

"Noy, you cannot keep on saying that. They just said we are the April Seventeenth. They said we were the ally of the Americans and the Lon Nol. We were their enemies. We are like their prisoners. We have to listen to what they say, or they will kill us all. My suggestion is to do as we are told."

"I will continue to talk back. This is not right," Noy continued.

"I repeat. If you don't agree, go talk to the high official, which I don't recommend," Narong smirked.

Chhoeun gave up trying to convince him not to resist, although he agreed with Noy one hundred percent. He wanted to complain too, but his gut feeling told him not to say a word. A couple more of the older boys were complaining too but not as loudly. Chhoeun was determined to follow his instinct to just work hard and share everything he had.

"Starting today, my comrade and I will go around and collect data from your past. I have told you my past, and now it's time to tell yours. I will start with Mit Chhoeun and his group since they are the cooks," Narong said.

After the meeting, Narong came with his comrade with a pen and a notebook.

"Mit Chhoeun, during Lon Nol's time, what did your Father do for a living?" Narong asked.

"He drove trucks," Chhoeun answered.

"Did he ever join the army?"

"No, he never joined the army."

"What did your Mother do for a living?"

"She was a farmer and a trader."

"What did she trade?"

"She traded cows, chickens, and pigs."

"What did you do during Lon Nol's time?"

"I went to school and herded the cows after school."

"Have you ever joined the army?"

"Yes, when I was thirteen."

Narong took notes and nodded slightly.

"All right, that's all the questions I'm required to ask…next person."

After the brief interview, Chhoeun fetched his fishing pole and a woven basket to catch the frogs and fish. Most of the time Chhoeun did not need to instruct his crew on what to do. Their tasks were the same as usual.

Several weeks later, Chhoeun saw hundreds of boys transported by trucks to live in the same compound. Every single spot in the house had been filled. Many of the boys could not find a spot to sleep; they ended up sleeping outside the house. During the raining days, they flocked inside the house curling between others to sleep. Many became seriously ill.

The Red Khmers continued to transport many more boys to the compound as if they were livestock. Within weeks, the compound had become overcrowded. The higher authorities began to order the existing boys to relocate.

Chhoeun was randomly selected to move out of the compound along with several hundred other boys. He hid the nylon string in his backpack and discarded the pole. He didn't want anyone to know what he carried with him.

He marched out of the compound with his horde of forty, plus two new Mekongs. One Mekong was leading the line, and the other was trailing from behind. Rows of other hordes were marching before and after. None of the boys in his previous horde were in his new horde. He was selected that morning and ordered to get ready by noon. He didn't get a chance to say goodbye to Ra and the rest of his crew. He felt like he had been with his group for years even it had been only several months. It just struck him how much he missed them already. He was leaving the young face that looked up to him like a big brother. Their new Mekrum might not be the same. They might be nice, but as everyone was trying to survive, the new Mekrum might not put in extra effort like he did. Chhoeun was picturing each of their faces, the faces of trust, friendliness, dependence, and submission. Chhoeun's throat tightened, and his eyes became watery as he walked along the line with his new horde, thinking about his young crew.

CHAPTER 8

Chhom was washing Pech and Mao by the river after they had gone to potty. She was cleaning Pech and laying Mao beside her on a rag. Tien and I were throwing rocks at the small fish swimming around the shoreline while we waited for Chhom to finish. When we first arrived in Stung Chah, the water in the river was full and flowed constantly. Now, the water had retreated leaving behind mud and the underwater plants.

We followed wherever Chhom went. For the last several months, Chhom had been taking care of Tien and Mao as well while Pu E and his wife went to work. Like many other men, Pu E had been forced to work far from home. He had only been allowed to visit home about once a month. Tien's mom had left to work since the sunrise. The new government didn't care how she managed it, but she had to work even if she had a baby. Many women would take their babies or toddlers with them.

Mother had asked Chhom once to look after Tien and Mao, and then Chhom took the responsibility to care for them herself afterward. She found it difficult to abandon a baby and a toddler home alone. Chhom was around ten now. She was naturally skinny, dark, and tall. She possessed a bad temper, presumably form Mother. She yelled and spanked us if we didn't do what she said.

It was fortunate that Mother was able to convince the Mit Chah to allow Chhom to stay home to look after Pech and me. All the boys and girls around her age had been forced to live in the youth compound. Chhom bathed us and took us to line up for lunch and supper when the bell was tolled. Not all the children were lucky enough to have a sister like Chhom. All the children were to stay home and responsible to line up for food when the bell was tolled. Parents had to remind their children to pay close attention to the bell. Most women were working nearby their house. Some would have to come home first to pick up their children who were too young to go line up themselves. The last person in line might not get anything to eat.

As a cook, it was difficult for Mother to distribute the rice equally. The amount of rice given to her varied daily. It was important that she make a good estimate. Giving too much to one person would cause a shortage, and the last person or people in line might not get anything to eat. She came across the situation many times when she just began to cook. She had to give up her share to the last person who did not get any rice. Other times, she had to take some rice back from multiple people. She had been avoiding the issue by giving less on the first round so she would always have a surplus. Then anybody who finished their rice first could get seconds.

It had been roughly over eight months since we arrived in Steung Chah. The way of life for adult and youth was to work from dawn to dust, seven days a week, in the scorching sun or in the pouring rain. It became a standard that meetings were held every day before and after work to praise the current government and to pass the messages from the higher authorities. The government informed us that the country was moving on the right track and believed that having full control over the citizens would benefit the country. All the personal belongings had been taken away. Our homes were nearly empty except for a few pairs of black clothes and the cooking utensils. Mother had dug the ground to hide anything that she thought she may need in the future. She had given the watch away to the Mit Chah. The crow of the rooster was the only way to tell time during the night. The position of the sun was the only way to tell the time of the day. The weather and the stars were ways to estimate the season. The day of the week, the month, and the year were no longer relevant. What was really important was to subdue the hunger and to stay out of trouble. The amount of energy expended during work was never replaced by the rice consumed. The neighbors and relatives appeared thinner and frailer every day. We still had half a bag of rice left at home. When we'd first arrived in Steung Chah, we had three bags of rice that Chhoeun scavenged from the truck station. Mother had been cautious not to use it all up. It was difficult, but Mother managed to save some rice in a small bag.

The sound of the bell echoed through the air. After she'd finished cleaning Mao, Chhom knelt down, scooping Pech up while securing

Mao to her waist with her other hand. She normally didn't have to carry them both at once, but today Mao and Pech went to potty at the same time. She walked swiftly uphill toward our house. Tien and I knew it was lunchtime, and we walked closely behind Chhom.

When we reached the slope, we began to see other children emerge from their houses, flocking toward the dining hall like an army of ants to their nest. Some walked alone. Some walked with siblings rushing to the dining hall. The toddlers were standing by the door of their house waiting for their mothers to pick them up. Women were rushing from the field to meet up with their children. It was fortunate that we lived just a short walk away from the dining hall. We had never missed a single meal.

We stopped by our house to get our bowls. Chhom handed me three bowls and Tien two bowls, as she had to carry Pech and Mao.

When we reached the dining hall, we saw Mother standing on one side of the giant pot, stirring the rice porridge. She looked very important. She instructed the children to line up correctly in a single file line. She tries to avoid having the Mit Chah get involved giving orders. Their tone and words were usually intimidating. Each line had a couple of Mit Chah who were monitoring the lines to make sure no one was cheating.

"All right, begin!" Mit Chah ordered.

Mother started scooping the rice porridge with a large scoop and poured it in to the bowl of the children in line. Tien's mom had arrived, and she took over Tien and Mao. Chhom was holding her share and Pech's share. After we got our share we walked over to the available benches in the dining hall. Chhom sat between Pech and me. She started to blow the rice porridge to cool it down. I was waiting for my rice porridge to cool down after being tired of blowing. Today Mother had made rice porridge with taro and amaranth.

"Eat!" Chhom yelled and slapped me on my back.

Afraid that I might get spanked harder, I began to slurp my rice porridge slowly. Mother came and sat beside us. She scooped a spoonful from her bowl and poured it in Pech's bowl, and then she scooped another spoonful and poured into my bowl.

"Eat faster! Look around. Everyone has almost finished theirs," Mother scolded.

I got scolded every day for eating too slowly. I was always the last one to finish my meal.

We came back home after we'd finished eating. Chhom left Pech and Mao inside the house and sat on the stairway taking a break as Tien and I were looking for interesting things to do.

As Chhom was sitting and relaxing on the stairway, she caught a glimpse of a person moving slowly on the wagon path that led to the river. She didn't pay attention at first, but the person was wobbling slightly from side to side. She gazed and squinted and then immediately recognized it was Father. Chhom leaped off the stairs and tripped, nearly falling on her face. She ran to Father.

"Father, what's wrong? Where did you come from?" Chhom asked.

"I'm dizzy and tired. I'm very sick. I need to rest."

Chhom was too small to assist. She held Father's hand and led him up the house. Father walked up the stairs slowly and lay down on the floor using one of the shirts nearby as a pillow.

Without asking further questions, Chhom immediately built a fire in the hearth. She filled a small pot with water and a handful of rice that Mother had hid. The rice porridge was cooked in less than fifteen minutes, but Father had already fallen asleep. Mother had always made rice porridge when any of us got sick. It helped keep our body warm and gave us energy. When finished, Chhom scooped some rice porridge into the bowl to let it cool down.

Chhom decided to stay around the house in case Father woke up and needed her help. Mother was out there somewhere working.

Father woke up just before sunset. He sat up and looked around. He grabbed the bowl of rice porridge and began to eat slowly. The rice porridge was cold, but he didn't mind. After he finished, he poured the rest of the rice from the pot into the bowl and continued eating.

"Mit Chhay, where were you?" a man standing by the door hollered.

"Who's that? I'm in here. Come in," Father replied.

"It's me, Chhay." The man who had the same name as Father replied.

"Oh, Mit Chhay. Aren't you supposed to be working? Come in and sit down."

"I can't come in. I smell. My pants smell. Our friend Mit Long is dead. I returned from lunch, and I saw the Red Khmer that he'd trained kill him. I saw everything. He was hit on the head by the Red Khmer with a rock. He fell to ground and was struggling to get up. The Red Khmer used the bulldozer and buried him alive. When I saw that, I was horrified to death and pooped my pants. I was lucky I came late from lunch. Who knows what would have happened to me if I was there. They would have killed me too. You must not return to work. You must find another place to work. I have to go home and change. I'm done with that place."

"Thank you, pal. You saved my life. I would have gone back if you didn't tell me. Have a bowl of rice porridge before you go."

"No, I'm afraid it's sinful to eat while your other end is filthy. I have to go."

The news of his dead friend made Father shiver. His head was pounding from the illness. He sat up trying to comprehend the situation. Father had known Long for many years. Long and his friend Chhay were the only two friends who knew how to operate the bulldozers. Once again, Father felt guilty for recruiting Long to drive the bulldozer.

"Oh, my good friend. You died and left me. I have known you for more than ten years. I wish your spirit would leave in peace. We'll meet again in our next life," Father said to himself.

Chhom was standing next to the door. She was there the whole time listening. She wasn't sure what to do and decided to stay out.

Mother arrived later in the evening from her trip to another village. She didn't have to cook today. The village leader had requested her to carry a basket of rice from another village. She was surprised to see Father home. Father explained why he was here and what had happened to Long.

"Those cruel demons! I hope they are going to hell. How could they kill an innocent man? Long was a good man. Thank God that you were sick. They would have probably done the same to you if you were there today. I don't think you should operate any more vehicles from now on. First, they made you transport thousands of people to slaughter, and now they slaughter a man after he taught them how to drive. Maybe it's a good idea to work like everyone else," Mother suggested.

"No more driving for me. It's better off to dig ditches. It will be hard work, but I don't have to cause any more death," Father said in despair.

"Puk Veah, you should rest for now. Don't think too much, or you will never recover. I will tell my leaders that you are big and strong. You have experience with logging, fishing, farming, and hunting. Maybe they could find something important for you to do besides digging ditches."

"If you could do that, it would be great. I hope they can find me something," Father replied and went back to sleep.

Mother went to the morning meeting as usual with the hordes and the higher-rank leaders. One of the Mit Chahs gave a short speech and dismissed everyone to work.

"Mit Bong, my husband has completed his task in another village. He is open for another task. He is currently sick. He will be well in a few days and ready to work. My husband is big, tall, and strong. He has experience in logging, fishing, farming, and hunting. I hope you will make good use of him. It will be a waste if we let him work in the rice field all day. If you know any the position available, you should assign him the task," Mother spoke quickly after the meeting, hoping they would not ask for more detail of his last work.

"I know a village that needs a person like him. It's called Tuol Snai. They produce charcoal. They need people who are strong and have experience in logging and making charcoal. They will use him for other tasks if needed. It's less than a day's walk from here," one of the Mit Chahs responded.

"Then, that's perfect. I will let him know and have him prepare," Mother said with excitement.

The job matched Father's experience well. Father used to log for the majority of his life. He knew many things about trees. In his early adulthood, Father used to cut logs and transport them throughout the country. He could identify nearly every tree in Kampuchea. Sometimes he could even identify the name of the tree from smelling the wood.

Mother returned home after the meeting and passed the good news to Father. "Puk Veah, you don't have to dig ditches. There's a place called Tuol Snai less than a day's walk from here. They said they need a logger who knows how to make charcoal. Do you know where it is, and do you know how to make charcoal?"

"I have never been to Tuol Snai before, but I know where it is. Charcoal is easy to make. I have transported logs to the charcoal maker before and helped him make charcoal a few times. It's very easy. The only problem is, we don't have the machine to cut and lift logs, and we don't have any trucks to transport logs. Everything will be done manually. I will have to saw and lift the logs manually and use ox wagon for transportation," Father explained.

"It still sounds like hard work. Do you still want to do it?" Mother asked.

"It's still a lot better than digging ditches. It'll be hard for the government to supervise me because I will be deep in the woods. Plus, if they give me trouble, I would have an ax with me."

Mother was happy that Father liked the thought of working in Tuol Snai. She had been using the reserved rice that she'd hidden to make the rice porridge for him.

Father felt a lot better the next morning after a long sleep and after he'd eaten a lot of rice porridge. He packed his mosquito net, spoons and bowls, and extra clothes in a sack that Mother had sewed and began walking toward Tuol Snai. He still felts a little sick, but he could not stay home too long. He didn't get a share of rice because he wasn't registered in any of the hordes. We were almost running out of rice at home.

Father crossed the Stung Chah River and followed the path along the river. He came across laborers and asked for directions. He arrived at Tuol Snai just before the sunset. Unlike Steung Chah, Tuol Snai was scattered by small hills surrounded mostly by water. He noticed the tree called Snai grew everywhere. Now he understood where the name Tuol Snai came from. Tuol means "hill" in Khmer.

One side of Tuol Snai was thick forest. Ahead, Father saw a cluster of houses and buildings with people going about their duties. He kept walking, looking forward to speaking with the village leaders. When he got closer, he noticed these people were not the ordinary laborers but the Red Khmer militia. They were doing some sort of training. Father panicked. He felt like he was walking into a pack of tigers. He was determined to stay calm and show no fear. If they suspected him of escaping from any type of hordes, he would be executed immediately.

He kept going. Then a moment later he came across a group of elder laborers clearing shrubs and branches. They appeared to be in their fifties.

"Mit, my name is Chhay. I'm from Steung Chah, and I was told to come here to work."

Father wanted to speak more politely, but he remembered the government's rule. He must treat everyone equally no matter how old they are. These laborers could report him to the government if he broke the rule. He wanted no trouble, especially when he was right in the militia's base.

"I don't know if they need any more laborers, but if you walk over that way for about one kilometer, I have seen men transporting logs and have seen smoke rising from some sort of dome?" That might be what you are looking for," one of the men instructed.

"Then I must go," Father replied.

Father headed toward the direction the man suggested. Trekking along the uneven terrain made it difficult to keep his sense of direction. One minute he was below the hill, the next minute he was on top of another hill. Just when he thought he was lost, he saw an isolated house in the distance. There was no sign of smoke as the man had described, but he saw dozens of buffalo grazing nearby. He walked toward the house hoping to meet nice people.

He arrived at the house, and he saw an elder man working in a garden alone. Father spoke politely. "Mit, my name is Chhay. I came from Stung Chah. I was told by my leaders that this village might need people with logging and charcoal experience."

"Oh, you came to the right place. We need as many men as we can get. We could use your size and strength. It's hard work. Our main task is to cut logs, transport the logs from the forest, and burn the logs to make charcoal. Our secondary task is to catch fish to feed the militia. Our third task is to tend these water buffalo. Our fourth task is to grow tobacco plants. You will like it here. We don't have Mit Bong ordering us around. We do what we please, but we must prove that we work hard. If they think we are lazy, they will assign one of them to supervise us."

Father looked around and saw over two dozen buffalo scattered across the field. He'd tended cows before when he was a child but never buffalo. They were a lot bigger than the cows, and their horns were long and pointy. They had a reputation for unexpected aggressiveness. They attacked other buffalo and sometimes the humans.

"You must be hungry from walking all day. I know where Stung Chah is. I have not made anything to eat yet. I was about to cook for the group in a little while. But I will start now since you are here and must be hungry."

Father was relieved to meet such a nice man. He hopes the rest of the crews were as nice.

"And call me Bong since I'm the oldest around here and we don't like the Mit thing. Since I'm the oldest, they assigned me to stay home to cook and tend the buffalo," the man added.

"This place is surrounded by water; Bong must have caught fish every day. If you have fish I could make fish soup," Father offered.

"You can cook? I have fish, but I don't know how to make soup. I usually thrust the stick into them and roast them in the fire. Sometimes I just toss the whole fish directly in the fire. The crew complain I make the same food every day, but that's all I know how to make. I still have problems cooking rice. Sometimes I put in too much water, and it becomes porridge. Sometimes I put in too little water, and the rice becomes dried and hard. I wish my wife and kids were around to teach me, but they were at Phnom Penh before the Peace. I have no way to communicate with them. I don't know where they are right now. I'm not sure if they are even alive." His voice became coarse when he mentioned his family. Many people referred to the postwar as "the Peace."

Father felt bad for the man, but he had not had anything to eat all day and was very hungry. He didn't want to question him further to delay time. Maybe another day, he thought to himself.

"Then I will cook rice and make fish soup. You can watch me. I cooked rice almost every day when I drove the trucks. Besides cooking rice, I only know how to make a few dishes, mostly my favorite soups." Father nearly forgot that he was not supposed to reveal his past.

"How many people are coming, Bong?" Father asked.

"Eight individuals. They all eat like pigs, so make enough for twenty. Come, follow me. I'll show you where the hearth is. The rice is over there."

Father followed the man into the house. There were two kitchens and multiple large rooms. The hallway was neat and spacious. About a dozen great-snakehead fish were hanging on the wall to right of the hearth. This house must have once belonged to a big and successful family.

Father quickly built the fire using a lighter that lay on the wood shelf above the fireplace. Father was a smoker himself. He hadn't smoked for months. Holding the light made him think about the tobacco. He really wanted a roll or two.

"You can show me how to cook some other day. I have to feed the rest of the buffalo before they go wild," the man said and left Father to his work.

Father scooped enough rice to feed twenty people into a large pot as suggested and skillfully rinsed the rice and added just enough water. Then he gutted and cleaned all the fish and tossed them into another pot. He filled the pot with water and added a handful of rice and the rock salt he'd found near the fire pit. He went outside the house to the garden and picked a handful of basil and scallions. Father saw many other herbs growing in the garden. The man was taking good care of them.

The sun was about to set behind the large hill in the distance. The rice and the soup were done. The laborers would be here any moment. Father didn't hesitate to take a sample. His mouth watered in anticipation. He was so hungry that his hand shook as he held the scoop. He took a big scoop of rice into his bowl and scooped up the fish soup and poured in to another bowl. He sat on a stool near the hearth, hoping to finish it before anyone saw him eating. He sipped the soup from his spoon and paused. Satisfied with the taste, he began to eat. His tongue danced around the hot rice and soup. He was too engrossed in the meal and missed the sound of the approaching ox wagon and the men's footsteps.

As he took the last sip of the soup, a cluster of silhouetted figures flooded the doorway.

"Ah… I smell a delicious fish soup! Please grant me a bowl," one exclaimed.

Father stood up, towering over everyone in the room.

The elder man introduced Father. "This is P'own Chhay. He came from Stung Chah volunteering to work with us. He's big and strong and obviously knows how to cook."

"Greetings, Pu[uncle]," the younger men greeted and bowed slightly.

"Greetings, Bong," another man greeted and shook his hand.

Everyone could not help but to stare in Father's murky left eye. He would be very intimidating if he didn't smile. Despite the smile, he still retained the stern and serious glare. Father had gotten used to that long ago.

It had been awhile since the last time Father had encountered traditional greetings. This type of greeting was forbidden elsewhere. Father have never gotten used to treating everyone equally and tired of being spoken to at equal level by children. It was like living in an upside-down world. He was glad to see these men had preserved the Khmer tradition. He felt right at home, the home before the Peace.

"Let's all eat together. We can talk later. Here, I will give you a bowl each. Bong said you eat a lot, so I made enough for your third bowls," Father said and chuckled.

"Pu, don't serve us. It's sinful to let the elders serve the youth. Let us serve ourselves," one of the young men suggested.

"All right. Then help yourself."

Everyone swarmed the pots all at once. Each grabbed two bowls from the shelf; one for the rice and one for the soup. They scooped the rice and soup and sat on the dining table. They stooped their heads over the bowls and begin to eat vigorously. Everyone focused on eating, and no one said a word.

Since Father had already had some samples, he waited until everyone had their share, and then he scooped another bowl of rice and soup for himself.

"This is so good," one of the young men said.

"This soup is unbelievable. We haven't had fish soup for nearly a year. Pu, you should teach Um how to make fish soup and make perfect rice like this." He referred to the oldest man who was designated to cook.

"I will teach him when he wants to learn. There's a lot more you could do with the fish, and I will teach him that too."

After the meal, the younger lads found spots on the raised floor and sprawled, except two elder men.

"Say, Bong Chhay, what city were you from prior to Peace?" one of the older men asked. Although the man might be older than Father, it was respectful to call Father Bong until Father's age was known.

Father told his story starting from his childhood life at Bahkaeng, Tonle Mekong as a hunter, fisherman, and a farmer. Then he told his adult life stories as a logger and a truck driver when living in Takeo and Phnom Penh, but he skipped the parts where he worked for the government.

The older men exchanged their stories with Father. All of them were hard workers, but they had experience only in a few fields. Most of them were loggers and farmers. They were excited to have Father in their group. They needed a good fisherman and a good hunter. They were surrounded by rivers, but they were only using the basic methods to catch the fish. None of them were hunters. They came across so many animals in the forest and didn't know how to catch them. Father explained his experience as a hunter and the types of animals he trapped.

Father and the men caught up with sharing stories and didn't go to sleep until midnight. They were planning to take another trip tomorrow morning to log in a deep forest. The men informed Father that they would stay overnight and return the next day.

"I don't have any equipment to make the traps yet, but there are a few types of animals that I could hunt without using traps, such as snakes, giant lizards, and crocodiles, and I have a few good recipes for each one of them. We will start tomorrow." Father finished his conversation.

The night was warm. There was no need for blankets, but the swarm of mosquitos hummed like bees. Father took out his own mosquito net and suspended it in the corner of the room. He slept among his promising new comrades.

Father was woken up by the crows of the distant roosters. Everyone else was still asleep. He walked outside the house. The morning sky gave enough light for him to see two ox wagons and four oxen tethered nearby. He untied the oxen and yoked them to the ox wagons. He noticed a pile of tools in one of the ox wagons. Father stepped closer and found logging tools, such as the two-man saws, giant axes, machetes, bundles of ropes, and oil lamps. There were also pots, bowls, and a bag of rice. He sighed in relief. This was like back in the days when he used to work in the woods.

When the men woke up, everything was ready. He had even fed the oxen the water. They began the trip as soon as everyone was up. The two elder men were driving the wagon while the rest were sitting in the cargo. The two younger men were lying comfortably resting their heads on the bundled hay resuming their sleep.

Father took one of the machetes and walked ahead of the wagons. He had also made a guiding stick about a meter long from a tree branch.

"Why aren't you riding the wagon? There are a lot of snakes," the driver said.

"That's all right. I'm looking for snakes. Plus, I want to protect the oxen from the snakes," Father replied.

"That's good that you are skilled with snakes," the man said.

"I will walk too then," another man said and jumped off the wagon.

They rolled along the open terrain. Just before noon, Father came across dozens of termite hills. He suggested the men to take a rest as he looked for cobras. He searched for a cobra known as a termite hill cobra that commonly dwelled in a din made below the termite hills. In less than half an hour, he found and killed two large cobras curling in a small den below the termite hills. He chopped the heads off and hung the cobras to the side of the wagons.

They resumed their trip under the morning sun. They arrived at an abandoned house at noontime and decided to rest and cook. Father asked the men to help start the fire and cook the rice while he skinned and gutted the snakes. Father searched inside the house and found a small bag of rock salt. Then he picked a handful of herbs in the abandoned garden. The men had stopped here to rest many times before, but since none of them knew how to cook they had never bothered to search the house.

Father made stir-fry chopped snake with few types of herbs and the rock salt. Despite the lack of spice, the stir-fry came out good. Everyone enjoyed the meal. They scraped every bit of rice and the stir-fry.

They didn't waste any time and resumed their trip right after the meal. They wanted to reach the woodland as early as possible. Father caught another cobra that crawled across the road along the way. The younger men caught a couple of large lizards that were aroused from the sound of the footsteps and the squeaky wagon.

They arrived in the woodland late afternoon and followed the road that cut right in the forest. Within minutes, tropical animals of all sorts sent warning to the others. The monkeys made the most noticeable sounds. The men spotted many more snakes along the way and were able to capture two. Most of them were seen too high up in the trees. Lizards of all sorts and sizes were visible, but trying to catch them in the forest was a waste of effort and time. Father planned to make traps instead. He liked the lizard meat more than snakes. He made mental notes of all the animals he saw and planned to make straps when time allowed.

Father and the men pulled into a spot where the trees had been previously cut down. The plan was to simply cut the logs into smaller pieces and load them into the ox wagons. Father used the two-man saw and cut the tree with another man.

"You are skilled," the man on the opposite end of the saw said.

"I have done this for many years," Father replied.

With superior strength and skill, Father and his partner did the majority of the work. Having Father on the team was like adding three more people. He lifted one cut all by himself and tossed it into the wagon with ease. The two wagons were filled. Their job was completed much earlier than expected. Father took the advantage of the time and cut the bamboo trees to make traps.

While he was making traps, Father instructed the men to dig the bamboo shoots. The bamboo shoots were abundant and a good vegetable that could be used to make nearly any type of dish. Father also found several other edible plants and roots and instructed the men to collect them.

Within a couple of hours, Father had completed over a dozen simple traps using the bamboo trees and ropes. With the help of his friends he set all the traps before nightfall.

Father cooked the snake meat with the bamboo shoots for dinner. The men helped build the fire and cooked the rice. The two younger men were eager to help with whatever Father needed. So far, Father had not learned anyone's name except for the youngest one known as Bao. He'd been teased by the older man for being sneaky and clever. Father wasn't sure if it was his real name or a newly given name. Bao meant "rice bag" in Khmer. The Khmer often teased a fat person by saying they were as big as bao, but Bao was very skinny and short. It might have been his real name after all.

Father and his comrades ate dinner and prepared to sleep in the warm, dry night. Most of the men made space in the wagon, on top of the logs, to sleep. A bonfire was lit around the oxen to keep insects and other animals away. More importantly, they needed to be able to see at night.

A moment after Father and the men dozed off, a squeal of some sort ripped through the night. Father and the men woke up startled.

"What was that?" one of the men asked.

"I think a wild hog got trapped. Light the lamps and let's check it out. Grab the machete. The wild hogs are dangerous. We have to be quick. The traps were not meant for them. They could get free anytime soon," Father informed them.

All the men woke up in the middle of the night. They traced the squealing sound and found a small hog trapped by its hind legs. It was partially hung up with both of its hind legs lifted up off the ground. It was using the front paws to pedal the ground trying to get free. The bamboo post arched down from the heavy weight. The men quickly hacked the hog to death with the machetes.

Father and the men returned to camp and hung the wild hog onto the side of the wagon. They went back to sleep for the rest of the night.

They made the trip back home early in the morning and arrived home at nightfall. The trip home took longer since the wagons were heavy with logs.

Since Father was a major contributor to the group and could handle the majority of the loggings, the men decided to split the group into two subgroups and switch the tasks when the time came. Father was to lead a couple of men to return to the woodland and cut some more logs and check the traps at the same time. The other group would stay and burn the logs to make charcoals. The oldest man suggested they offer the wild hog to the militia. If they found out about not sharing the catch, all the men will be in a lot of trouble.

The next day, Father and his men returned to the forest to cut some more logs and check the traps. Every single trap was triggered and caught all sorts of animals, including a large unidentified bird, a giant lizard, and a monkey. The men told Father that the giant lizards and monkeys were very common here. They had never thought of catching the lizards before, as they appeared to be very dangerous. The men had encountered the giant lizards before. They were at least four feet long walking fearlessly across the open land.

Father and the men added more traps in the area and spent a night in the woodland. They transported the logs and the animals home early in the morning and arrived home long before the sunset. Half the catches were given to the militia to indicate they were doing their jobs.

They repeated the same routine over and over again for several weeks. Father trained all the men to make traps, but many of them didn't like to handle the catches, especially the giant lizards.

It was Father's group's turn to stay home. Besides burning the charcoal, the main duty was to catch fish. The fish were also to be distributed to the villagers and the militia as well. The village leader had provided the men a boat and three sets of fishing nets. Father allowed the men to take the lead as he observed. Father had grown up in Tonle and spent majority of his childhood fishing with grandpa. The men cast the gill nets across the river and waited overnight for the fish to tangle in the net. They returned in the morning to collect the tangled fish. They caught hundreds of fish in one night. This was a great way to catch fish if there was only one person to do the job. Father had better idea. The next day Father suggested making a simple modification to the net in a way to enable two men to haul the net and flank the fish against the river bank. Although a specific net, called a dragnet, was designed just for that method, Father's makeshift nets worked nearly as well. In two hours, they caught more fish than they had in one whole night. The men were thrilled with the new method. They worked from morning until dark to catch the fish and filled up the wagon until there was no more room. Most of the fish were distributed to the village and to the militia.

Father and his group had been acknowledged by many other villages for their skills and contributions. A few Mit Chahs from another village offered a trade of the real dragnet and a cast net for a wagon of fish. The dragnet was used to replace the gill nets that Father had temporarily mended together. The militia and the local villages were happy and never questioned Father and his comrade's activities. Father thought about home a lot and was waiting for the opportunity take some fish and the trapped animals home. The risky part was carrying fish and the animals from here and walk through the militia site on the way home.

CHAPTER 9

I was standing in front of my house, gazing down the main alley observing the laborers working in the rice field. The dark clouds were hovering so low that I thought I could throw a stone and hit them. The thunder rumbled ominously somewhere above the cloud. Then a bolt of lightning flashed straight down and struck a nearby coconut tree, severing some of the branches, which caused them to crash down to the ground. The workers appeared not to be bothered by the deathly sound of the thunder. In the old society, the adults would call this the Pkoh Luahn Daum Chnam (Thunder of the Begining Year). The thunder was the sign of promising rain that would help the crops to flourish. I didn't think the adults saw the thunder the same way anymore. The dark and thick clouds with the ominous sound of the thunder was only reflecting resemblance of this new hellish life and what was to come.

A surge of strong wind swept in, causing all the leaves on the trees to shift to one side. Large raindrops began to drip here and there. Suddenly, the rain began to pours down like buckets. Within minutes, streams of muddy water begin to form, snaking their ways down to the river. Chhom was running uphill from the river securing the vegetables in her arms. She had left us home so she could pick the vegetable along the high-rise river. It has been raining hard and very often for the past few weeks. The Stung Chah River had risen significantly and submerged part of the wagon path along the river. Snakes of all sorts and sizes were hanging on the tree branches along the river as the water submerged most of the tree trunks.

As the rain began to pour, the thunder and lightning eased. Tien and I had been waiting for this. We ran in the rain allowing the pure and warm water to wash the dirt off our bodies. We ran around like the wild horses. It would be a perfect day were it not for the hunger lingering in our minds. The rice harvest season was over months ago. Our village should have had plenty of rice in stock, but instead our share had been reduced by half. The rumor was that the rice had been exported to China in exchange for weapons. Whatever we had left was what we had to survive on until the next harvest season. It also appeared the Mit Chah were becoming more hesitant to give out rice. They were no longer seen eating in the public anymore. They segregated themselves away from us more and more as if we were nothing more than laborers. We had to eat what they decided to give out. Mother had been receiving only ten cans of rice or less to cook for a hundred people. It wasn't enough to make steamed rice. Mother had to make rice porridge, using a lot of water and vegetables to replace the lack of rice.

Water spinach and amaranth were the main vegetables, as they were the most abundant. Mother had learned about new vegetables and roots to mix with rice porridge. Despite the additional vegetables, it was still not enough. We were always hungry, even right after the meals. Along with everyone else in the village, we were searching to find anything that was edible, such as snails, crabs, insects, and any edible plants. Children that were under the working age swamped the river bank picking the lotus and searching for frogs and crabs at the same time. New edible plants and insects had been discovered nearly every day by friends and neighbors. It was a big risk to eat unknown plants, but waiting for someone else to try them first took very long, and they might not be available after the discovery. Some lushly green plants looked edible, but the tastes were intolerable. Some plants offered a friendly taste in the beginning but left a nasty aftertaste that stuck in your throat for hours. Some plants offered edible fruits, but their leaves and stems were known as poisonous.

After the rain subsided, Chhom quickly rushed back to the river. She left Mao and Pech home. They were both sick, lying feebly side by side in our bed. Tien and I followed Chhom in case she found something good to eat. Chhom went into the river bank and picked vegetables within her reach. She kept her eyes on the frogs that usually hopped across one plant to another. Frogs were a great source of food. They offered a lot of tasty meat, and their bones were tender. They were easy to cook; just toss the entire frog into the fire and a wait a few minutes.

Chhom picked the lotus stems and water grass and placed them the basket. Mother had stitched more pockets on her shirt for her to store small collections of food, such as rice, insects, and fruits. She was wearing a ragged sarong strapped by a worn-out elastic band. She was wearing the same clothes that she had been wearing for months. Maybe those were the only clothes she had.

"Snakes! Snakes!" I yelled pointing at a long and thin snake swimming in the river. I wasn't afraid of snakes. I wished Chhom knew how to catch them and cook them.

"That's a frog-killing snake. They are not poisonous," Chhom said and resumed picking the vegetables.

After Chhom filled the basket with vegetables, she returned to shore. She laid the basket on the ground and began searching for frogs and snails. The frogs and snails were normally found roaming the bush and ground right after the rain. She picked the snails that were crawling slowly on the ground and on the wood. Tien and I walked behind her, but we were more interested in other insects, especially the crickets. They were a lot more fun to chase.

Chhom traced after the loud croak of the frogs and provoked them out of the bush and then caught them with her bare hands. After she'd caught several frogs, she hurried back home to check on Pech and Mao. When she got home she crumbled a handful of straw that she'd saved to make the fire. We used to have a lighter once, but the flint had worn out and the lighter had disappeared. She had no quick way to make the fire anymore. She placed the crumbled straw on a piece of rock. Then she tapped the rock with another rock to create sparks. Within minutes, a light string of smoke swirled up from the straw. She blew until the flame came to life. As usual, she only had to build a fire from scratch in the morning. The fire continued to sustain itself throughout day on the wood under the ashes. Later on in the day, Chhom would only need to add straw and more wood to revive the flames again.

She tore the vegetable into small pieces and tossed them into a small pot filled with water. She poured some saltwater from a small vase that Mother had placed in the back door. The government did not allow anybody to have salt at home. Mother put the salt in the vase and filled the vase with water to make it appear like it was a drinking water vase. She placed the vase next to the door to make it appear like it was not something we wanted to hide. Everyone in the village was desperate for salt. It was believed that salt prevented one's body from swelling. Many villagers burned the bamboo and used the salty-tasting ashes to mix with their food.

Chhom tossed the frogs and snails in the fire and waited hungrily for them to cook. Within seconds, the aroma of the charred flesh and skin of the frog filled the room, followed by the sweet smell of the snails' juice and meats. She squatted and monitored her cooking, using a small stick to flip the frogs and the snails in the fire. Tien and I were standing behind her waiting to get some. Our pants were still a little wet. My mouth was watering. I'm sure Tien was as hungry as I was.

Finally, Chhom used the stick to roll one frog out of the fire. She picked up a sizzling frog from the fire and broke a leg off and popped it in her mouth. Her tongue danced around the hot frog leg as she chewed.

"That's mine," I said moving closer to Chhom.

Tien didn't know how to talk yet, but he reached his hand out in anticipation.

Chhom handed the frog to me, as I was bigger and closer to her. Tien shrieked in anger and jumped up and down demanding for some.

"Yours is right here!" Chhom said with aggravation.

Tien didn't understand what she said and continued to wail for his share. Chhom finally got the frog out of the fire and gave one to Tien. After he got his share, he laughed instantly with his eyes still full of tears.

I liked to eat the limbs first. They got cool faster, and I didn't have to worry about the organs. Nearly every part of the frogs were edible, including most of the organs except for the intestines. Most of the time, I didn't bother removing the intestines. Depending on what the frogs had eaten, the taste of the intestines was never the same. Some frogs' intestines came with a tasty bugs or grains, but some intestines were mushy and smelled like rotten animals. The rest of the organs offered an expectedly delicious taste.

After we'd finished eating our frogs, we began eating the snails. The shell of the snail stayed hot for a while after it was taken out from the fire. I liked snail almost as much as the frogs. They offered a dense and juicy meat. Unlike the frogs, the tastes of the snails' organs were much better and consistent. Some even had crunchy baby snails inside.

Chhom was helping Tien pick the meat off the snails using the tip of the crab legs she'd found in the ashes from the previous day. He was too young to do it himself. I liked to pick my own snail meat. I wanted to make sure I got every part of the snail out from the shell.

"Awg...awg..awg..." I'd tried to swallow a whole piece of snail meat, and it was stuck in my throat.

Chhom noticed I was choking and came to rub my back. The snail meat was still stuck in my throat, and I couldn't breathe.

"Why don't you chew before you swallow?" Chhom scolded as she continued to rub my back.

Just when I thought I was about to die, the meat popped out from my throat and onto the ground. I gasped for air and then wailed. Tien continued to eat, as he was too young to understand what was going on with me.

"Here, eat the soup instead. You will die if you continue to eat like that," Chhom continue to scold and handed me a bowl of vegetable soup.

Tien wailed, pointing to the soup because he wanted some as well. Chhom was aggravated, but she poured Tien a bowl of soup.

"Be careful. It's very hot. Don't touch it yet. I will blow it and feed you," Chhom said to Tien.

When Chhom turned around to scoop another bowl of soup for herself, Tien grabbed a vegetable from the bowl with his hand and he shrieked in pain.

"Now you know what I mean?" Chhom said.

Mao and Pech began to cry and cough vigorously. One was waking up the other. They both had been sick for several days now. They haven't eaten since Mother and Tien's mom left for work. They must be very hungry. Mother was not home today. She must have travelled far and would not be home on time to feed Pech milk. They were too young to eat the vegetable soup. Tien's mom would not be home until sunset either. They would continue to cry for who knew how long. Feeling frustrated, Chhom decided to carry them and look for a nursing mother. Chhom had learned that any woman who gave birth to a new baby would get four weeks off from work. They should be home and would have milk. They should understand and help. Chhom had an idea where to seek the nursing Mothers. She remembered seeing them feeding the babies while she explored the village seeking food, but she didn't remember the exact location of their houses.

Chhom set up a scarf and strapped it loosely down from one side of her shoulder. Then she placed Pech in the scarf. Pech was small and light. He had been sick very often, and Mother only got to feed him after work. Chhom picked Mao up and placed her on the side of her waist. Mao was slightly heavier than Pech. She had been sick almost as often as Pech. They continued to cry uncontrollably.

Chhom begin walking down the alley very quickly searching for the nursing Mothers. Mao and Pech stopped crying when Chhom began to walk. Tien and I followed, not sure what Chhom was up to.

After about ten minutes, we came to a house where a thin and dark-skinned woman was nursing her infant by the front door.

"Ming, I have two babies with me here. They are very hungry, and they need milk. Could you feed them?" Chhom asked using the term Ming instead of Mit hoping to get some sympathy.

"I have a little milk. I don't have enough to eat, but I could try...bring them to me," the woman said as she laid her baby aside.

Chhom smiled in relief and began walking up the stairs. She knew the woman was frail from having a baby. She positioned Pech and Mao in a way so they both could drink milk at the same time. Chhom sat in front of the woman helping her hold Pech and Mao as they suckled the woman's breast. They both had not cried since Chhom had taken them out of the house.

The woman stared at Pech and Mao as they fed. She looked very tired. She closed her eyes and dozed off for a minute. Then her body twitched as she regained consciousness.

After a short while, the women detached Mao and Pech from her breasts and said, "That's all I can give them. Maybe there is no more milk for my baby."

"Yes," Chhom replied softly.

Chhom secured Pech back in the scarf and held Mao on her waist and began walking home. Instead of taking the same path through the alley, she decided to take the longer route along wagon road where she could get the opportunity to collect snails and possibly crabs.

The ground was still wet from the rain. The insect were swarming the wet shrubs. The snails were crawling everywhere, leaving their slimy trails. Frogs of all sizes were still croaking. The size of the frogs could be determined by the sound of the croak. The deeper the croaks, the larger the frogs were.

Tien and I trailed after Chhom. I picked up one of the largest snails around and examined it out of curiosity. I liked to eat snails, but I had never thought of collecting them.

"Put that in my pocket and find some more," Chhom yelled angrily. Her hands were busy holding Mao and securing Pech in the scarf; she could not collect the snails. The ground was too wet to lay them down. I did as she told me to, but my attention swayed to something else almost immediately. I collected the snails along road and on the tree barks. Chhom continued to yell when I goofed off.

"Forget it. Let just go home," Chhom was frustrated with me and decided to go straight home.

When we reached home, she placed Mao and Pech on the bamboo plank floor and returned to search for food. She decided to search for crabs and snails near the rice field instead of the river bank, as the snails were easier to collect and the crabs were more abundant.

Chhom continued to search for food every single day to feed us. She took care to Tien and Mao like her brother and sister. The most difficult part was cleaning up after us when we go to potty. She still had not gotten use to that yet. In return, Tien's mom had given us food that she found during and after work. Chhom had gotten a lot skinner than before. Her clothes became loose. Her skin had turned very dark. Her hair became light brown from the excessive sun.

Each week, the share of rice in the village became less and less. Mother had been adding more and more vegetables in the porridge she cooked for the horde. The vegetables were not same as rice. They didn't fill you up or give you that much strength. Every day after the sunset, the villagers of all ages flocked to the river and the rice field searching for food.

Mother returned home long after dark. She was assigned to retrieve rice from another village. A small handwritten note had been given to her. Mother didn't know how to read, but she knew the alphabet. She was told to show the note when requested along the way. She could use the note to travel a short distance. She was aware that Pech needed milk, but she had been looking for people who were willing to trade. Within the last couple of weeks, she discovered several nearby villagers who were interested in trading. Mother still had a good amount of clothes and accessories hidden underground that she could use to trade. She thought trading would help her get more food and the things that she needed like the oil for the lamp and herbs for medicines. Among the many people she met, there was a widow woman who was once married to a wealthy doctor. Her husband had been taken away to execution. Somehow, she had managed to save large quantities of cigar lighter flints. Mother thought they were valuable goods to have and offered to trade for them. The widow woman was interested in Mother's silk garments and other goods. Mother used half of her stocks that she'd hid under the ground to trade for the flints. On the next trip, she used the flints to trade for rice. She was surprised to learn how valuable the flints were. She got half a can of rice for three flints. The rice was enough to make three meals of rice porridge for us to eat. So far, Mother had not been questioned along the way at all. She was given several more different notes. She took the chance and sneaked out at night to trade. She was confident that if she was questioned, she could use any one of her notes. Plus, she was aware that the majority of the Red Khmers, especially the militia, did not know how to read. As long as she had some type of notes and as long as she appeared confident, she knew she would be safe. Mother normally returned home at midnight. Sometimes she had to travel far or got caught up in a long conversation and would arrive home just before the sunrise.

Several weeks ago, Mother learned that she was not the only one who was using the notes to travel at night to trade. At least a dozen men and women were doing the same. Several of them had been bitten and killed by snakes when they travelled during nighttime. Mother had come to close encounters with snakes many times, but luckily, she heard the hisses of the snakes and was able to avoid them.

Mother was still a designated cook, but another woman had been assigned to do the task when Mother was assigned to do other important tasks. Dry wood became scarce over time. Mother had to saw down the live trees, cut them up in smaller pieces, and then carry them to the kitchen. The logs of the live trees were much heavier than the logs of the dead trees. After she brought the logs home, she would split them into smaller pieces and then dry them in the sun. Mother also had to carry about a dozen buckets of water to cook and fill up the giant vases for laborers to drink. Sometimes she wished she could just work on the field instead, focusing on just one task, but the fact that she got to work around the house outweighed the job in the field significantly.

Mother had gained a lot of trust from Mit Chah and the hordes. She had been assigned to raise a pig and several chickens. Her tasks were to the feed the pig and the chicken. The pig ate a lot, but it ate nearly anything. She fed the pig using the water that she used to wash the rice mixed with many newly discovered edible and abundant vegetables that were disliked by most people.

The chickens were easy to raise. They would search for their own food. Mother just needed to make sure they didn't stray too far from the house and ensure they were back by dark. The chickens normally would not go too far from the house and usually returned home by dark. When they didn't return home by dark, Mother would go around to the neighbors looking for them.

Like Chhom, Mother spent her time by the river picking vegetables and catching crabs and snails when she didn't travel. Unfortunately, she was too slow to chase after the frogs. She also continued to take good care of the small farm around our house. The vegetables were flourishing, but she was not allowed to pick them at will since everything belonged to the public. She had to ask for permission every time. She did ask quite often and was denied nearly every time. However, if she continued to follow the rules, we would all starve to death. She took chances and picked the vegetables at night and cleverly used the soil to hide the evidence. Many of the neighbors didn't know how to grow the vegetables and had nothing other than the meal they were given in public. Somehow, the rumor of Mother stealing from the public had emerged unexpectedly. K'Oeun, one of Mit Chah, was the one who informed Mother about the rumor when she bumped into Mother just after the lunch break.

Weeks later, one of Father's old friends named Ta Panh revealed himself as an accuser and requested the Mit Chah to put Mother on trial. He used the term "thickly private" with the farm to describe Mother. In the new system, no one is allowed to harvest their own produce without permission. Everything belongs to the public. Ta Panh is accusing Mother for harvesting her own produce. Ta Panh lived alone in a house that sat on a small hill distant from everyone. He didn't plant anything around his house. Somehow, he managed to stay and work locally.

After the trial, Mother was found guilty of being too thickly private with the farm. We were asked to move out of our house to live in the warehouse that was used to store rice. Ta Panh was allowed to move in to our current house along with the small farm. Our other option was to live in Ta Panh's house, but Mother was too upset with him and did not want to live in his old house. Plus, it was too far from the river, and it sat on a small hill with no space to farm.

Over a year ago, the warehouse had been stacked with rice bags. Now there was nothing but stacks of hays. We didn't have many belongings except for a few pots and pans and a few pairs of clothes. Mother waited until the sunset to start moving so that no one could see what we had. Mother and Chhom carried our belonging to the new house, trying their best to conceal them from the neighbors. They brought the pig and chickens along. Not only did the warehouse have no land to grow crops, but it was also surrounded by Red Khmer officials. Among them were K'Oeun and Ta Watt, the well-known Mit Chah, living just a few dozen yards from us. K'Oeun was one of the Mit Chah who'd agreed on the trial's verdict, but she seemed to have no choice. K'Oeun was also the responsible for Mother getting to be the Mekong and for Chhom getting to stay home. Many had feared K'Oeun, but for some reason she seemed to be pleased with Mother. K'Oeun's hometown was Takeo, the same town where Mother had been living most of her life. Maybe that was the reason.

I was too young to understand why we were moving, but anything new was fun. I was playing outside with other children when Mother and Chhom carried the pots and pans from our house to the warehouse.

"Bun, it's getting dark! Come in and find a place to sleep!" Mother hollered.

I walked into the warehouse and found mostly haystacks scattered throughout the large and spacious room. The floor was not made of bamboo plank like our old house but rather some sort of hard mortar that was layered directly on top of the ground. The surface of the floor was smooth and cold. I walked to the corner of the room. Behind some haystacks I found a cat curled on its side nursing her four tinny kittens. What caught my attention the most was that the cat was patched with the black, white, and yellow colors on her face and body. I had seen cats before, but I'd never gotten this close to them, and for some reason, I loved them. They were such mature and peaceful animals. I stooped over and rubbed its back.

"A three-colored cat!" Mother said. "Don't hurt them. Three-colored cats are smart, and they bring us good luck. We should let it live with us."

Chhom came over and examined the cat, "The kittens are cute. They look like baby rats."

Mother and Chhom resumed cleaning up our new home, and then a familiar voice hollered, "Mae Veah, where are you?"

"This is your new house now, Bong Chhay. That house over there is no longer yours. There are some jealous and lazy people who took that house," Tien's mom said. She was standing proudly right beside Father.

I ran to the door and saw Father and a couple of his friends carrying some dead animals. Some had them hung down both sides of their shoulders. Each man was holding different types of dead animals on both of their hands. One man had an animal that looked similar to a human but had long orange fur. The animal was hanging behind his back as if it was piggy-backing the man.

"Everyone... come in!" Mother exclaimed.

The men stepped in the house and piled the dead animals on an open spot on the floor. I couldn't help but to step closer and examine the animals.

Mother squatted next to the pile and used her hand to move the dead animals around. "These look like the giant lizards. These were monkeys, and this was an orangutan. And what was this?"

"I don't remember what they are called, but their meat was good," Father said.

"I will begin to skin them and gut them," Mother said.

"Skin the lizards, but you should use fire to burn off the fur from the rest of the animals. Their skins are good," Father informed her.

Mother continued to sort through the animals determining what to do with them. The lizard skin didn't look edible like the monkeys. She stared at the monkey's face for a few seconds and then looked away. During Lon Nol's time, Father had brought home a monkey on his trip from the jungle. Mother refused to have anything to do with it. Father had to skin and gut the monkey himself. After Father cooked the monkey, Mother was very disgusted and segregated a set of pots and pans and silverware just for herself for several months. Today she didn't seem to be disgusted by the monkeys at all.

"Don't forget about me, Bong Yorn," Tien's mom said smiling. She was not shy about saying such things.

"Don't worry, I will not forget about you. I will give you the most," Mother said.

"Say, what is the exact reason we are living here now?" Father asked.

"You friend, Ta Phan, took me to trial, accusing me of being too Thickly Private by taking the vegetables in our farm. I worked hard for my vegetables. I asked for permission before I picked them. He had the choice to choose any house he wanted, but he chose the house sitting on the tiny hill with no land to farm. The crops were also given to him, but he didn't do anything with them," she said.

"Bong Yorn seems to be calm about it. If I was her, I would swear at him like a hurricane," Tien's mom said furiously.

"That bastard! He's been a very jealous person since I first knew him. He's single and should be able to care for himself easily, but he's lazy. I will not dip my mouth into any conversation with him from now on," Father said angrily.

"Well, wait a little. I will skin the monkey and will roast it for all of you to eat. Just to let you know, we don't have any rice. You'll have to eat just the plain meat," Mother said.

"The meat should be enough. No need to eat rice," one of Father's friends said as he leaned against a pile of hay, relaxing after the long walk.

Mother started the fire on the new simple hearth that she'd just assembled using just three similarly sized stones. One of Father's friends carried a lighter. It saved her a trip to grab a piece of burned wood from the public hearth.

As Mother started to burn off the fur of the monkey, she noticed Father and all of his friends were rolling a cigarette. She could smell the strong scent of the tobacco, but she was too busy to ask. Besides, it indicated that Father had found the right place to work. Father hadn't smoked since we'd left Phnom Penh when everything was in chaos.

Chhom was helping Mother burn the fur off the monkey. Tien's mom gutted it. The aroma of the charred skin made my stomach growl. It smelled like cooked frogs but much stronger. I was standing next to Father listening to the conversation between him and his friends. I didn't understand most of the things they said, but I felt good just being next to him.

"This one looks like you, Bong Chhay," a man sitting across from me said.

"He's my family generator," Father replied.

"He's a copy of Bong Chhay," Tien's mom added.

The adults liked to tease me. Everyone thought I looked a lot like Father. I hoped it was true. I hoped to grow up big and strong.

"We should be cautious not to let too many people know about this. We should quietly distribute the meat to the families that really need food first. Then, whoever comes and asks for some, we can give them a little," Mother said to Tien's mom.

"It's good that we share. If not, we will see a lot of death soon by the ways things are going. But make sure we have enough for our children too," Tien's mom added.

Mother quickly began roasting the monkey. She had removed the intestines and placed them in a bucket. Everything else was intact, including the head. The aroma of the roasting monkey filled the house. My mouth watered. I watched Mother turning the monkey on the fire, hoping it would be done soon.

After what felt like an eternity, Mother finally informed us the monkey was cooked. She cut a small piece of meat for me and Chhom. The men flocked around the hearth picking the meat off the monkey while it was still hovering over the fire.

"Come, Tien's mom. Don't be shy," Father teased.

"I'm never shy around food," Tien's mom said and joined Father and the men.

"Bong, you are the cook, we should leave the head for you," one of Father's friends said to Mother.

"I accept your offer, but if you want some, I could share," Mother replied.

"During Lon Nol's time, she swore at me for cooking monkeys. You all should watch. She will eat everything, including the brain," Father joked.

"With the gut twisting-hunger, everything is good," Mother replied as she bit meat off the monkey's head.

After we'd finished eating, Father and his friends found a place by the haystacks to sleep. Our house hasn't been organized yet. It was still looking like a warehouse, except there's nothing here but haystacks. I decided to sleep near the cat and her kittens. The monkey meat was good, but I was still hungry. I wished I could have some more.

When I woke up in the morning, our house was empty and quiet again, except for Father, who was still sleeping. All of his friends had left. I could hear Mother chopping the wood outside. Chhom was sweeping and clearing the house. Mao and Pech were lying quietly on the floor. Tien must have been outside playing with other children.

I spent the rest of the day playing around the house. Mother had cooked some more meat but not as much as last night. We ate roast lizard meat and vegetables for lunch in addition to the rice porridge we got at the dining hall.

At sunset, as I was playing with Tien and other children our age, I saw a man carrying a child in his arms with his wife following him from behind walk into my house. I got curious and followed. The man laid a young boy about my age on the floor. The boy's eyes were closed, but he was still breathing. His forehead was sweaty. Mother and Father were sitting on the floor chatting.

"Mit Yorn, my son is very sick. I don't know what to do, but I heard Bong Chhay brought meat home. I'm here to beg you for some meat for my son. Maybe the meat would help make him feel better," the man pleaded.

Mother moved closer to the boy and touched his forehead with her palm.

"His head is very hot. We don't have much meat, but you can have some. Do not tell anyone. If the Mit Bongs hear about this, I might get in trouble," Mother said and picked out a small slab of meat from the basket right beside her. The basket was covered with a cloth so that no one could see how much meat was inside.

"Hold on. Let him drink some medicine that I boiled earlier," Mother said and scooped a small bowl of warm water from the pot and walked up to the boy. She knelt down beside the boy and tilted his head up with her arm.

"Drink this medicine, little boy. It will help you get well," Mother said softly.

The boy opened his eyes and struggled slightly. He appeared confused and frightened. Then he began to weep.

"Drink the medicine, son. Don't be afraid. It will help you," his Mother said.

The boy became a little calmer after learning that his mom was beside him, but he turned his head to the side, refusing to drink. There were more people entering our house. Most of them were carrying a child in their arms. They had all come for the same reason. Mother knew every single one of them. Most were the families of the truck drivers. Some were new acquaintances. Mother had expected this, and she had prepped the meat into small pieces to share.

"Here, try to feed him the medicine. He's afraid of me. I have more guests," Mother said and handed the bowl to the woman.

Mother distributed the meat to each person that represented their family. She gave the bigger pieces to the families that had more children or were less fortunate. She gave smaller slabs to the families who had fewer children or were well off. A slab of meat was about four meals for three people if eaten efficiently with rice. It wasn't really much, but anything was good, especially the red meat. Mother was refraining from giving away meat to the single men or the single women, as they could survive themselves and had no children to feed.

After Mother distributed the meat, the guests wanted to stay and chat to thank her for the meat, but Mother kindly urged them to leave to avoid attracting more attention, especially when our house was now surrounded by the Mit Chahs.

After all the guests had left, I lay down beside Father on the nice, cold floor preparing to sleep. The wind began to pick up, flapping the leaves of the trees that surrounded our house. The haystacks beside me were giving off a light heat that was just enough to offset the cold wind. The aroma of the delicious meat was lingering in the house, making me very hungry. I was still hungry even after Mother has given me a piece of meat earlier. Then I dozed off shortly after.

After a long, deep sleep in the quiet night, I woke up to the sound of a cat meowing next to my ear. "Meow…meow…meow."

I opened my eyes and looked around, but it was too dark to see anything. I could sense the cat's warm body and its breath; my nose picked up some sort of fishy smell. Maybe the cat had just eaten fish. Father stretched closer to the cat. After a short moment, my eyes could see a little better in the dark, and I saw the cat was staring at Father in the eyes, trying to tell him something.

"Meow…meow."

"What's the matter, little one? Where did you come from?" Father reached out his hand to pet the cat.

"What's this in your mouth?" Father said and grabbed the object in his mouth.

"It smells like dried fish," Father said.

"Meow."

Puk lifted the object closer to his eyes with one hand and then lit his lighter beside the object with his other hand.

"Mae Veah, the cat brought us a dried fish from somewhere," Father said softly to Mother.

"I have never seen anyone eat dried fish around here. Only the well-off people could afford to make them, like the leaders," Mother said. She was concerned at first when she thought the cat had stolen from another hungry family, but after she realized that it was not the case, she felt a sudden surge of joy.

"Meow." The cat appeared satisfied and walked away.

Father lit the oil lamp. He was curious about the cat and followed her.

"Mae Veah, I didn't know the cat lives here. She even has kittens. And look, she brought food for her kittens too," Father said in disbelief.

Father reached out his hand to pet her kittens, but the cat crouched defensively and hissed with warning.

"Ey Ya! You have a bad temper there. I'll leave you alone because you are smart. And you are a three-colored cat. That's why you are so smart. I'm going to call you Me-Laek [the dyed one] since you have multiple colors."

"We have to cook the dried fish tonight. If they find out about it, we will be in a big trouble. Right now is a good time because everyone is asleep," Mother said.

Mother revived the fire in the hearth and roasted the dried fish in the middle of the night. The aroma filled the house instantly with a strong, unique smell of charred fermented meat mixed with the sweet smell. I got up and squatted next to Mother in front of the fire.

"The Khmer elders were right. The three-colored cats are smart and bring us good luck," Mother said as she sat and rotated the dried fish over the fire.

Father turned to the cat, "You be careful, all right, Me-Laek? Don't get caught, or they will kill you. I hope the luck will be on your side as well as ours."

After a short while, Mother took a small bite of the dried fish to ensure that it was cooked and then broke it in half.

"Here, eat this meat. I'm saving this for Pech. Chhom could feed him with rice porridge tomorrow," Mother said.

I snatched the dried fish from Mother and took a bite. The meat tasted as unique as smelled. It tasted so good. I didn't want this to end. I took my time eating it; picking the meat with my tiny fingers and eating it slowly.

When I finished eating, I cried for more. "Meat! Meat!" I said lifting my palm up, demanding more meat from Mother.

Mother laughed at how I pronounced the word meat. "No more meat. I'm saving it for Pech."

I didn't care what she's doing with it; I wanted more. "Meat! Meat!"

Mother ignored me and continued her conversation with Father about the cat. I continued asking for more meat until I fell asleep. When I woke up the next morning, I didn't see Father home. He must have returned to work. The meat that Father brought us lasted over five days. Mother managed to use very little meat each day to cook and eat with rice porridge. Chhom continued to search for food as usual when the meat ran out.

I liked our new house a lot. It was spacious. I didn't have to play outside all the time. I began to take notice of the cat and the kittens and observed their activities. After Mother and Chhom rearranged the house, Me-Laek moved her kittens to a new spot located by the other end of the wall. She carried the kittens it her mouth. At first, I thought she was biting the kitten. I darted over and removed the kitten from her mouth, but learned that there was not even slight force on the kitten. She continued to bring us dried fish almost every night. She would normally leave the dried meat near Mother's feet and meow until Mother woke up. Each night, Mother roasted the dried fish and woke me up to eat. I didn't know where she got it from, but I didn't care. I was very happy with the meat.

After a few months, the kittens grew nearly as big as Me-Laek. She spent a lot of time lying outside watching her kittens play.

I was sitting in front of the front door holding a long string I'd found on top of the haystack. It caught my attention when Me-Laek carried a live mouse with her mouth from somewhere and released it in front of her kittens. All of kittens dashed toward the mouse. The first kitten that caught up with the mouse pinned the mouse with its paw and bit the mouse then released it. Just when I thought the mouse was dead, it sprung back to life and began to run again. Another kitten chased after the mouse and did the same thing. It appeared that Me-Laek was training her kittens how to hunt. She sat with watchful eyes on the mouse as the kittens were training. When the mouse had gotten too far, Me-Laek leaped up and chased after the mouse. She pinned the mouse and used her mouth to carry it back to the kittens. The kittens resumed their training.

When the mouse was no longer able to move, Me-Laek came over and devoured the mouse. I learned shortly that the kittens liked any small moving objects. I got creative and tied the string to a small short piece of stick and had the kitten chase after it. I bounced the stick everywhere on the floor and on the hay stack, inside the house. One of the kittens leaped after the stick like it was a mouse.

"Bun!" A man's voice called my name.

I looked around, and I saw Chhoeun and Chhom standing by the door. I hadn't seen him for a long time. In fact, I'd almost forgotten that I even had an older brother. I ran to him and hugged him on his leg. Chhoeun stood still and rubbed my head.

"Why are there so many cats?" Chhoeun ask.

"The cats were living here before we moved in. Father name the mom Me-Laek. She brings home dried fish almost every night. Sometime she brings home fresh fish and fresh chicken meat. Bun was living off her. Anytime Bun would cry at night for meat, that mean Me-Laek didn't bring home anything," Chhom explained.

It was true that I cried when there was no food at night. I was used to having Mother wake me up almost every night to eat. When there was no meat, I would sit up in the middle of the night and wail for roast meat until I fell back to sleep.

"It's a three-colored cat. They are smart and gifted," Choeun said.

Chhoeun had come from the youth compound to visit. I noticed he was holding a long and smooth bamboo stick. Chhom explained why we were living in the warehouse. He was furious at Ta Phan for taking us to trial and making us lose our house and the crops that Mother had worked hard for.

He wasted no time and asked me and Chhom to catch him some tadpoles he could use to catch the bullfrogs. He spent the rest of the day catching the bullfrogs in the river using his fishing rod that he'd brought with him. Mother cooked most of the frogs with the rice porridge for her horde for supper. Everyone was thankful and at the same time wondering how Mother had gotten so many frogs. Mother told them about Chhoeun.

Mother made some more soup at night for our family, and we each had one whole frog to ourselves.

"I'm going to give a bowl to our neighbors. Our children and children of others are the same. We shall help others to survive," she said to us before she left. She probably said that to fight off the urge to keep all of it for our family.

She knew exactly who needed it most. Mother walked over to a house about two blocks away. A woman was sitting in a circle with her children having dinner. Mother saw nothing but a large plate with a pile of water spinaches and amaranths in the middle of the circle. The woman and the children looked up at Mother all at once. Every single one of the children seemed to be ill and tired.

"Here is a bowl of frog soup. Don't tell anyone I gave this to you," Mother said as she entered the door.

"Is that true?" the women asked in disbelief.

"I want some soup," one of the children said.

"Give me some first," another one said.

All of them were demanding some soup all at the same time, fearing that they wouldn't get a share. A girl about three years old wailed, lifting her bowl for her share. Mother had given them exactly five whole frogs in the soup, one for each.

Mother returned home and made more bowls of soup and then walked over to other families that she thought would need it most. She had a few frogs left in the soup and decided to take a risk and offer a bowl to K'Oeun, Ta Watt's wife. Even though K'Oeun was being kind to her, she was still the leader of the Red Khmer and was living next door. Mother was certain that she knew everything we did.

"What's this? It smells so good," K'Oeun said.

"It's frog soup. We caught a few frogs and made soup. I would like to offer half of what we made to Mit Bong. You can have it," Mother said.

"Ah, Mit Yorn. You eat nasty stuff. I don't like frogs, but my husband might like it," K'Oeun said.

K'Oeun was tall, light skinned, and chubby. K'Oeun began to tell her story after she learned our family was from Takeo. She and her husband were also born and raised in Takeo. She explained how she became the Khmer Savior. Mother found it ironic for these people to call themselves the savior. It was difficult for Mother to continue the conversation. She was trying her best not to reveal too much about our family history. For the most part, Father and Mother were nothing more than farmers, but toward the end of Lon Nol's time, Father had worked directly for the military and we'd ended up living inside the military base. If Mother accidently slipped this part of her life story, we were in grave danger. Mother ended the conversation by carefully choosing the part of her life where she had to work hard for a living.

Just before she stepped out, K'Oeun added, "By the way, Mit Yorn, I have seen many visitors to your house lately. It doesn't bother me, but it might be wise for your family to move to another location. There are too many Mit Bong living around your house, and they might not like what they are seeing, and I might not be able to help you. I suggest your family to move to Ta Panh's old house. Many families have been asked to attend private meetings. If you don't want to attend the meeting, you should go live in Ta Phan's house." K'Oeun spoke without looking Mother in the eyes.

Mother's skin prickled from the warning, but she calmly replied, "Ta Phan's house is all right. I will move to that house."

Moving to Ta Phan's house was the last thing she wanted to do. The man had taken her to trial and claimed her house and all her crops. Ta Phan's house sat a on a hill that barely had any land to plant crops. On the bright side, Ta Phan's house was isolated from other houses and away from all the Red Khmer's houses. Mother returned home and told us about moving. She didn't understand exactly what K'Oeun meant by the private meetings, but it didn't sound good. There was always a meeting every morning and sometimes after work. Why did it have to be private? Mother was angry every time she thought of Ta Phan. We didn't have much to carry to our new house, and we brought Me-Laek and her kittens with us.

Chhoeun helped us move and then returned to his compound right after. Mother was sad that he'd left again. She really wanted him to stay so that he could catch more frogs to feed us, but staying here was dangerous as well. She would never know what the local leaders would want him to do. She could talk to them and get him a job somewhere nearby like Father, but something told her that it was not a good idea. The new government had made it clear that your family members were nothing more than your comrades. If we were to stay close together, they might see it as a conspiracy against them.

The next morning, Mother was splitting wood in front of our new house when she heard a voice of a young boy speaking to her frantically. "Ming! Ming! Are you the Mother of Mit Chhoeun?"

Mother turned around and saw a dark and thin little boy about ten years of age standing right behind her. His clothes were ragged and torn. His face was swollen and bruised.

"I was looking all over for Ming's house. I thought Ming still lived in the house back there. Are you the Mother of Mit Chhoeun?" the boy added in distress.

"I'm his Mother. They made us move out of that house. And what is the reason you ask, Mit? And what happened to your face?" Mother asked.

"If you see Mit Chhoeun, tell him not to come home ever again. They are looking for him. They will come to your house very soon," the boy said and sobbed. "They hit me and used a plastic bag to suffocate me and asked me if I knew him or not, but I said no. I like Mit Chhoeun. I would rather die. I would never allow them to kill him. They killed everyone. They executed all of them right in front of me. When they come, tell them you don't know where he is. I have to get back. I have to go, Ming."

Mother's heart stopped a few beats. She stooped down in front of the boy with both of her hands cupping his face and began to weep, "God have mercy, Mit! They tortured you that much?"

"I have to go, Ming. They are on their way here. I don't know when...maybe today or tomorrow or another day. They found everyone they were looking for except for Mit Chhoeun. If they catch me here, they will kill me," the boy said and walked away quickly.

Mother stood and watched the boy walk away. She wanted to ask for his name and offer him something to eat. She wanted to thank him. He was sacrificing his life to save Chhoeun's life. He was so young but so brave and so loyal. He must be tired and afraid after being tortured and had to walk so far to get here. The thought made her feel sympathy and also gave her an unsettled feeling for not able to help him.

Mother stood shaking in terror staring until the boy vanished from her sight. The Red Khmers were seeking to kill Chhoeun. If they found him, it was the end of his life. She wanted to warn him and tell him to hide, but she couldn't leave and didn't know where to find him. Not knowing what to do, Mother wept. She continued to split woods. Her mind filled with bad thoughts as she worked.

The next morning, three men, all dressed in clean black uniforms, approached her while she was splitting wood. One of them was carrying a rifle.

"Mit, where is Mit Chhoeun? The government has an assignment for him," one the men asked politely.

Mother froze for a few seconds trying to figure out what to say without giving Chhoeun away. It was a matter of life and death depending on what she was about to say.

Mother calmed herself and replied, "My son's name is Chhoeun, but you might have mixed it with someone else. There are so many people named Chhoeun. He had returned to work with the youth. I don't know where he stays nowadays. That disobedient son never tells me anything. He had been very sick when he left. He could barely walk. I'm not sure if he's even alive right now," Mother said extending the truth.

The men looked somewhat disappointed and replied, "Then we are heading back."

Mother felt a surge of relief that they did not interrogate her. She wouldn't know what to say and would probably get herself killed as well. After they left, Mother went to the house and prayed, "I plead to the keeper of the land and the keeper of the water. Please protect my son from harm and from illness from now on. When I have the opportunity, I will offer you food."

Mother resumed her work feeling a lot better. She hoped the men would believe her that Chhoeun was very ill and would not make it alive.

CHAPTER 10

Chhoeun walked from home along the river across many villages and arrived at his compound before nightfall. He was away from Mother again. He had been forced to move many times as the compound got overcrowded or another village needed more workers. When he got split up from Ra and Noy, he came across another good friend named Sok. Somehow, he and Sok had been selected to go live in the same places several times. Sok was a couple of years older than Chhoeun. He and Sok shared whatever they had like brothers. They told their life stories when they were out from work. Sok was a lot bigger and taller than Chhoeun. He was raised in a wealthy family while living in Phnom Penh. His Father was a high-rank official. Like many other high-rank officials, his Father had been killed when the Red Khmers took over.

Early in the morning, Chhoeun and Sok had been informed to move again. Chhoeun was packing his clothes and mosquito net. Sok doesn't have much. He was outside ready to leave. The current place was small and isolated. It was set up for the youth only, but Chhoeun and his group had to stay here temporarily to clear out trees to make space for farming. Chhoeun was now considered an adult and could no longer stay with the youth. Unlike the married adults who would have a designated home and spouse or children, the single adults had no designated home or family. They were prone to be moved very frequently and far. On record, Chhoeun had turned sixteen. He was actually seventeen.

Chhoeun was packing his clothes when he heard a boy whisper his name. "Mit Chhoeun! Mit Chhoeun! It's me, Mit Ra."

Chhoeun turned around and saw a familiar but bruised and swollen face. "Mit Ra, what are you doing here? What happen to you?"

Ra broke out crying softly, "They killed all of them."

"They killed who?" Chhoeun asked in confusion.

"Remember Mit Narong? They killed Mit Narung, his wife, and his daughter. They tracked down and captured everyone that was in his group. You are the only one left. They are looking for you."

"Yeah, I remember him clearly. He was the man that bragged about his duties as the former Lon Nol's three-star general pilot who secretly worked for the new government. He was the man who betrayed Lon Nol and dropped bombs on Lon Nol's soldiers," Chhoeun said.

"They searched and captured us one by one and tied all of us up. They use a plastic bag to cover our heads to interrogate us. If you don't say anything, you will be suffocated to death. They questioned and tortured every single one of us for the list of names. Then they killed them all, right in front of me. I was the last one. They captured everyone except you, Mit Chhoeun," Ra paused and began to weep.

"They hit me and said I knew you more than anybody. I told them there were too many people with the name Chhoeun, and I told them I didn't know which Chhoeun they were referring to. They are still looking for you. You have been very nice to me. I didn't want them to hurt you. I'd rather die than let them kill you. For some reason, they let me go. They will go to your house, but I went to your house and told your Mother already," Ra finished and continued to weep.

Chhoeun stood motionless as Ra was standing just two feet from him. He reached out and touched Ra's face and wept. He remembered Ra well. He was only nine when he'd first met him. He was the youngest one in the group. Now he was a lot taller. He'd gotten thinner and darker as well. This little boy had gone through pain and great risks to save his life.

"Thank you for saving my life," Chhoeun said. It was very awkward to say the word "thank." Under the new government, the word was rarely used. In the new government, everyone was expected to work hard without credit or reward.

"How about Noy, my cousin? Did you see him?"

"Yes, Noy was one of them. Mit Chhoeun, you must leave this place when you have a chance. It's too close to our old village," Ra finished, not used to responding to the word "thank."

"They are letting me leave today. I'm gathering my clothes right now."

"I have to go to back to my group before they get mad at me for leaving too long," Ra said and then ran off.

Chhoeun wished he could do more than just say "thank you". He could be his godbrother and look after him. He was such a brave and smart boy. Under this circumstance, there was not much he could do. Chhoeun recalled the memories of Ra's smile when they first met, a small boy who had been taken away from his Mother. He was too young to do anything but to seek friendship and comfort from the older boys.

Chhoeun walked outside, keeping his head down in case someone was looking to capture him. He came to a line and squeezed in behind Sok.

"Why did you take so long?" Sok asked.

"I was busy," Chhoeun said. He couldn't hide his dreadful-looking face.

"What happened?" Sok asked.

"I will tell you later."

"All Mit *yuk veh jun* (the single men). Let's begin our walk. We have an important task to do. It will be hard but you were selected because you were strong," The Mekong said.

It was midmorning. The horde began to march after the Mekong. Chhoeun was walking right behind Sok, still shaken from the terrifying news. At the same time, he was glad to see Ra again and alive. He began to miss him again. He wished he could take Ra with him.

"This is the end for all of us. They are going to make us work to death. We are never going to see our parents again," Sok said.

"I know. We have to get ready for this," Chhoeun said in despair.

No one really said much. Everyone was hungry and tired, but they still had to watch what they were saying. The Schlope might be among them. More and more boys joined the Schlope to spy for the government because they got to eat better and have more chances to live.

They rested every two hours or when the Mekong felt like it. Just before dark, they reached an isolated village hidden behind a thick forest. Two cottages stood side by side along with a couple of small shacks. Many young men around his age were scavenging for food nearby. They paused and stared at the line of the new horde. Bong Chhoeun noticed how incredibly skinny these people were.

"Go find yourself a spot to sleep in one of those shelters. Meet me right here in the morning," the Mekong said and walked away.

After a full day of walking, everyone was tired and there was no sign that they would get anything to eat soon. Suppertime had passed. No one was to cook rice for them. Bong Chhoeun entered the cottage along with his horde. The current occupants were preparing for bed. A few oil lamps were lit, giving a faint visibility throughout the room. Most of the spots had been taken. Chhoeun walked around but couldn't find an open spot. He walked around again and decided to take a small gap between the two other mosquito nets.

"Mit, I beg to squeeze in here. Me and my comrade here couldn't find an open spot," Chhoeun said.

"Come on in, if it's possible for you to set up the mosquito net," a young man replied softly.

Chhoeun and Sok wasted no time and began setting up the mosquito net. Everyone was sleeping in the mosquito net. They either shared or had their own. The mosquitoes had already begun to swamp the night. Without the mosquito net, it would be impossible to sleep. Chhoeun and Sok were sharing the mosquito net.

"I'm hungry. I'm wondering when we are getting anything to eat," Sok grumbled.

"It's dark, and I don't see anyone cooking. I guess we are having nothing to eat today," Chhoeun replied.

"We all just ate just before you all came," one of the men responded.

"I bet they are going to make us work in the morning before giving us anything to eat," Sok said.

"We never have breakfast here, so don't expect anything to eat in the morning. It's best if we go to sleep early and save our energy for work tomorrow," the other added.

The conversation ended, and the room became quiet. Everyone appeared very tired and hopeless. Hungry and in despair, Chhoeun and Sok squeezed themselves into the small space. The men adjacent to Chhoeun and Sok had to move a few inches to make room. Inside the cottage was hot and stuffy. The mosquitoes were buzzing outside the net looking for a way in. Bong Chhoeun drifted away to sleep almost instantly from exhaustion. Sok must have been same. He hadn't moved once since he lay down. The mosquitoes were buzzing every inch of the warm air. The buzzing stopped when they found spots of flesh that were exposed against the wall of the nets.

Chhoeun woke up to the sound of a whistle followed by a loud voice. "Get up! Get up! It's time to get up."

He sat up and gazed out front door. He noticed it was still dark. He heard the first crow of the roosters. He and Sok got out of the mosquito net and followed everyone outside in front of the cottage.

"I didn't have a good sleep last night. I slept for a little, and then my stomach was growling all night," Sok said.

"I slept all right, but all I dreamt about was roasted fish. I woke up once after you kneed me so hard in my stomach," Chhoeun replied.

Outside the house, the men were beginning to form a line in front of the Mekongs. Chhoeun and Sok found their Mekong and formed a line with their horde. Everyone murmured among their comrades, mostly complaining about their hunger and sleeplessness.

"Silence!" a man yelled after everyone lined up. "All Mit. Today we have more new workers that came to join us. The new men will work hard and help us build a good reputation for our village. We can cover more land area and finish the tasks more quickly. The government will be pleased. We will set up the newcomers into groups. They will become efficient like us. Since we learned that many had tried to escape our horde, forming the groups will help ensure the no one tries to escape. The Mekrum (group leader) will responsible to monitor their crew. The Mekong will monitor the Mekrum. And the higher official will monitor the Mekong. This system will help us identify any enemy and any lazy people that try to escape and avoid working. The lazy and corrupted people will be discarded. We have no room for them. There are villages around us that are well-known for their hard work. We need to work harder than them," the man spoke very loud and was very serious. Chhoeun thought he had escaped death, but this place was a death sentence. The man added other subjects that took nearly an hour. Chhoeun had heard them all before.

It was the time of the year to burrow the rice paddies again to soften the ground to spread the rice seeds. After a group had been arranged, Chhoeun was assigned to burrow the rice paddies using an ox and a single-blade plow.

The plow was designed in a way to rest the front end to the cow's shoulder and the rear had a place for the operator to stand and put pressure on the blade. All the wood was tied together using cowhides. Cowhides were one of the items that were being used to hold nearly every object together. It was made from cow skin and didn't require any technology. It was well know now that the government despised technology.

Ox plowing was much more efficient than the manual burrowing, but it was usually done by a man who knew how to command the oxen. The new government expected every man to know how to command the cows. There weren't any lessons available. If the person took too long to learn how to plow, they would be taken to trial.

A plow and a pair of oxen had been assigned to Chhoeun. The oxen were skinny and dirty from negligence and being overworked. The grasses were abundant, but no one had the time and energy to feed them. The oxen were mostly dehydrated, as water was given only when they came across the puddles.

When Chhoeun began to plow, the oxen moved very slowly no matter how hard Chhoeun whipped them. Chhoeun had been around oxen all his life. He felt a lot of sympathy for them, but if they don't move he would die. These people had warned them in the meeting. If he was found guilty of being lazy, they would kill him. Now it made him wonder why he had been recruited here; maybe not because they needed more people but to replace the dead. It was a dreadful thought that he hoped was wrong.

At lunchtime, the rice porridge was distributed. Chhoeun only got about six ounces of rice porridge that contained mostly water and very little rice grain. After having nothing to eat all day yesterday, this didn't do anything. He was very tired and still hungry. After a short lunch break, the Mekong came and ordered everyone to get back to work. Chhoeun barely had the energy to get up.

He kept an eye on the ground searching for snails and crabs as he walked back to work. He didn't expect to find anything along the path, as other people been walking on the same path ahead of him.

He got back on the plow when someone yelled out loud, "Someone stole my cowhide. Did anybody see who stole my cowhide rope?" A young man was running around frantically asking for his cowhide rope.

Everyone was avoiding his look because they feared they might be accused. Cowhides were useful and rare. It was also edible, although they were very chewy. When burned, the cow hide smelled like roast beef. Without the cowhide, the plow could not be mounted on the oxen. The plow and the oxen were useless until the cow hide was replaced.

The man went to inform his Mekong who was chatting with the guards. After a short conversation, the Mekong walked him out of the worksite. Chhoeun thought he was getting a new cowhide and resumed his work until someone said, "That's it for him."

Chhoeun didn't understand what he meant. Maybe he would get lectured. A moment later, the Mekong walked back alone with a hateful smirk.

"Everyone, listen!" the Mekong said.

Chhoeun and Sok paused and stared at the Mekong like everyone else.

"Today we have lost one comrade. He was careless with his cowhide. It is not acceptable to lose the most important object for your job. Now we have one cow and one plow that sit idle and useless until we find another cowhide. This will delay our plan. He was our example if we lose the cowhide. It is your responsibility to keep it safe. Today our leaders would like us to come back to work after supper."

Chhoeun was stunned by how a man's life was gone just like that. He was terrified but also tired and hungry. He had collected some snails and crabs as he plowed. He noticed the water was slowly seeping up the crevice of the burrow. He let the oxen the drink the muddy water when the opportunity allowed. He was looking forward to cooking the snails and crabs after supper, but he was very disappointed to learn that he had to go back to work. He had to wait until he returned from work. He didn't know when that was, maybe long after nightfall.

All the workers had been dismissed to supper after sunset. Unlike the other village, where a person in a group was assigned to cook, here the Mekong was the cook. It appeared all the Mekongs here were the Red Khmers. Like everyone else, Chhoeun could finish the whole rice porridge in one slurp, but he took his time. He ate the rice porridge slowly to enjoy every ounce of it. He sat with Sok and the rest of his group hoping to have a conversation that would help him forget about the hunger and exhaustion, but after the today's incident, everyone was afraid to say anything.

A short while later, the Mekong called up his group. There was another man standing beside him waiting to speak.

"All Mit. The seed spreading time has arrived. We need to plow more. We are far behind schedule. There are thousands of paddies left to plow. The adjacent villages nearly completed their tasks, and we are not even halfway done. We are ordered to work tonight. We need to prove that our village works harder. We must keep the government happy. They have worked hard putting the plan together. We must believe in the government's plan. We need to prove to other countries that we don't need technology to do the job.

"My message is very important. All of you are required to listen carefully. I will continue to pass on this message every day so that all of us will have the same mindset. Anybody who does not heed my message is considered enemy. This is all I have to say for today. It's time to get back to work," the man said and walked away.

It was nightfall. Chhoeun was exhausted and still hungry. He still had several snails and small crabs in his pocket and couldn't wait to cook them. His stomach rumbled when he thought of cooking the snails and crabs. Now he had to go back to work, uncertain when he would be back at the cottage.

He walked back to the rice paddies along with the horde. He stepped on the plow and tapped the oxen on the rear. The oxen budged a little but didn't want to move. He tapped the oxen a little harder, and they started to move slowly. They stopped moving just a moment later. Chhoeun was frustrated and afraid he might get in trouble. Chhoeun decide to lighten up the plow by just pressing the plow with his hands to make it easy for the oxen to haul. The oxen still didn't want to move. Chhoeun whacked the oxen with the stick, and they start moving again. He struggled with the oxen every moment. It was very dark. The oxen normally had a break and grazed by this time.

When Chhoeun was halfway done with one rice paddy, the Mekong hollered from somewhere in the dark, "Everyone may stop now. Go get some rest, and we'll continue the work in the morning as usual."

Chhoeun was relieved that he didn't have to finish the entire rice paddy. It would have taken until midnight. He could hear the murmur of complaints among the workers. He walked sluggishly with the rest of the group toward the cottage. When he got there, he walked directly toward the hearth that the cook used to cook the rice porridge. He picked a piece of small wood that was still hot and used that to start a fire close by. Several of his co-workers, including Sok, swiftly joined him to roast their catches.

"I caught two frogs this morning. The plow ripped the den open, and both jumped out at the same time. I caught both of them. Here take one," Sok said and offered Chhoeun a frog.

As his stomach was twisting and turning inside, Chhoeun was delighted to take the frog.

"Here, take one of my crabs. You take the big one. I hope it has a lot of eggs and fat," Chhoeun said and handed Sok a crab.

"I worked so hard. I'm so tired and hungry," one said.

"I'm so hungry that I feel like my intestines are tearing apart," another added.

"I'm wondering if they will make us work until midnight again tomorrow," Chhoeun said.

"We have to go sleep soon. It's almost midnight, and we have to get up early in the morning," Sok said.

The aroma of the charred frog mixed with the sweet crabs filled the air. Chhoeun turned the frog carefully with a stick avoid breaking its limbs. His mouth watered as he anticipated eating the frog. He had been waiting for this for two days.

After a short moment, Chhoeun removed the frog from the fire with a stick. Without bothering to dust off the ashes, he bit the entire head off the frog and chewed with bliss. His tongue danced around the hot frog head.

"The frog smells so good. Could you give me one of the legs? I didn't catch any frogs today," a man sitting across Chhoeun begged.

Reluctantly, Chhoeun ripped off one leg and handed it to the man, "Here."

"I will pay you back when I get a frog," the man said as he popped the entire leg in his mouth.

"That's all right. You don't have to pay me back."

They ate quietly, enjoying the taste of the food. Chhoeun took the crabs and snails out of the fire and picked off each leg and popped them in his mouth. He chewed and swallowed the entire crab legs. Then he popped the shell open and slurped the hot juice off the shell and munched on the rest of the crab.

After he ate all his catches, he wishes he had a basketful more.

"I'm going to sleep. Tomorrow will be another harsh day," one of them said.

Chhoeun returned to the cottage getting ready to sleep. Most of the people were already asleep. They must have not caught anything to eat, Chhoeun thought. He lay down in the small space with Sok. He was too tired to talk to Sok. His mind was racing race back to the things that had occurred recently and how far he was from Mother. He didn't think he would leave this place alive. The work was hard, and they didn't give them enough rice to eat. Chhoeun dozed off and drifted away.

He slept through the crow of the roosters and woke up by the sound of a whistle followed by a shout. "Wake up! It's time to work."

"I have only gotten one hour of sleep. My whole body aches," someone nearby said in misery.

"Here we go again," another added.

Chhoeun got up and walked along with everyone else toward the front of the cottage. He saw several men standing in outside. He recognized his Mekong was one of them. The line was starting to form in front of them. Chhoeun walked to his line where his Mekong was standing.

"Starting from the first person in the line, I want you to say your name out loud," the Mekong said.

When the Red Khmer first took over, there were plenty of people that could read and write. His first Mekong, Narung, used paper and pencil to write down their names on their first day. Then he took attendance each day by calling his crew's names out loud. No one was seen using paper and pencil anymore.

The Mekong counted the students and then exclaimed, "I have only thirty-eight! Where is another person?"

"I tried to wake him up, but he wouldn't wake up," a man in his mid-twenties in the front of the line replied. "I think he passed away."

"Then it is your job to bury him," the Mekong said as if the dead man was nothing more than an object.

"Mit!" He pointed at Chhoeun. "Help him bury the body! After you finish, come to plow!"

Chhoeun's knees nearly gave out from the unexpected task. "Yes," he replied. Chhoeun followed the man into the cottage and found several other men lying on the floor. They all appeared to be in a deep sleep.

"Where was he?" Chhoeun asked.

"Over there. He's my good friend. He looked after me ever since we met. He's a nice man. He gave me food when I had nothing to eat," the man said in sorrow. He knew well by now that weeping was prohibited, especially for friends.

Chhoeun walked closer to the motionless body and was shocked when he saw who he was. "He sat and ate with us last night. He asked me for a piece of frog leg, and I offered him one. He said he would give me back a frog. I wish he hadn't said that. Now his spirit will follow me trying to pay me back."

The Khmer believed that once you promised to pay somebody something, you were obligated to pay for the debt in this life and the next life if you still owed the debt. The thought gave Chhoeun a chill.

Chhoeun followed the man and found a convenient spot outside the perimeter of the compound. They dug a shallow grave with their hoes. They were aware not to use too much energy to dig the grave and to carry the body or else they would need another grave for themselves if they couldn't work.

"How were we going to carry him?" Chhoeun asked.

"This is your first time?"

"Yes, it's my first time. I have seen many dead people since the beginning of the Peace but never had to carry one," Chhoeun replied.

"A lot of people have died here. Some died in their sleep. Some were taken to execution. I heard they torture people in the worst way. They don't shoot and waste their bullets anymore. They use machetes, axes, or ox-wagon shafts. I'm glad my elder friend here died in his sleep. He's lucky, right?" the man said as if he was happy that his friend had passed away.

"In a way, he was lucky. Why do they take people to execute them so much?" Chhoeun asked.

"The government tried to hide this, but we learned that if they knew anybody had joined the military, they were taken away. To me, you seem to be too young to have joined the military before the Peace, so you are safe."

Chhoeun's heart skipped a few beats when learned the bad news. He stood and froze. He remembered his first few days in the youth group proudly telling Narung that he had joined the military. He never thought it was serious until now. He was terrified. Just two days ago he'd learned from Ra that nearly everyone except Ra and himself had been taken to execution in the most brutal way. Not only were they after him because he was in Narong's class but also because he had a record of joining the military. He was now a fugitive. This man was right. The dead man was lucky to die in his sleep. It was not a bad idea to starve and die after all. Chhoeun thought about killing himself, but he dismissed the idea. According to the elders, if you killed yourself, you would become the most vicious ghost and your spirit would be stranded in this world forever. The way things were going here, maybe he could die from starvation and from hard work without trying. One day maybe he would be lucky to die in his sleep too without having to commit suicide.

"What's the matter, Mit? Are you not feeling well? Bring the hoes with you," the man said.

Chhoeun did not want to say anything. This man seemed to be very nice, but according to the government's rule, they were to report any suspicions. They walked back to the cottage. The man and Chhoeun made a stretcher using the dead man's scarf.

"Let's pick him up," the man said.

"I'll hold his legs," Chhoeun said.

Chhoeun grabbed the dead man by his ankles. His skin was as rough as the tree bark. There were cracks on the bottom of his feet from long hours of standing on the harsh ground. This was the creepiest feeling he'd ever had. If he had a choice, he would rather dig a hundred ditches than pick up a dead person. He was alive just last night talking to him. Now Chhoeun was burying him. The man's eyes were shut as if he was sleeping.

They lifted the makeshift stretcher. Chhoeun was surprised how light the man was on the stretcher. They carried him to the shallow grave, taking their time burying him. They were in no rush to go back to work but also aware not to take too long.

Chhoeun and the man were walking back to work after they finished burying the body. Chhoeun's thought drifted back to the day he told Narung happily about joining the military. He thought of all the faces of all his comrades, especially Noy, who was once alive and happy. All of them were now dead. He thought about how each of them had to suffer before death. Chhoeun remained silent as he walked. If he had an option, he wanted to die in his sleep like this man. It was awkward to think about death. He wondered where those people were who were looking for him right now. Maybe they didn't even know where he was. No one seemed to read or write anything anymore. They relied heavily on interrogations, but everyone was dead now. There was no one to interrogate beside Ra, and he would not tell them anything. Plus, he was far away from that village.

Despite the small odds of being discovered, he still didn't feel settled. He finally snapped back from his deep thoughts and realized that he should be scavenging for food. The man didn't appear to mind.

When they arrived at the worksite, Sok was looking his way and smiling. Chhoeun smiled back hoping no one was paying attention to their friendship. The government didn't like friends to work together, as they were afraid of conspiracies. They wanted everyone to turn on each other and report any suspicious activities. They want everyone to spy for the government.

Chhoeun un-tethered the oxen and yoked them to the plow. He still embraced the thought of working hard and hoped to die in his sleep. He would not want to be taken to execution. He pressed the plow down with both his hands and pushed the plow forward, helping the oxen. Normally, he would only have to stand on the plow to keep the blade below the surface and keep the plow upright. It was the oxen's job to haul the plow.

After a moment, he noticed everyone was looking at him. They must have thought he was insane to use excessive energy to plow when he barely had anything to eat. There was no point for him to use his own energy to plow when the oxen were hundreds of times stronger than he was. He was exhausted but committed to work hard.

As he pushed the plow and took each brutal step forward, he noticed a bullfrog lying flat on its back, half of its body buried in the mud, struggling to free itself. Chhoeun grabbed the frog by the hind legs and whacked its head against the frame of the plow. He slipped the frog in the slack of the scarf that he had wrapped around his waist. He thought of the roasted frog he ate last night. He remembered the taste and the smell very clearly. His saliva squirted in his mouth from the thought. He thought of postponing his attempt to work to death until after he could eat the frog.

He found many more frogs and crabs as he continued to work like a mad man. Maybe God didn't want him to die yet, he thought. The Khmers believed there was a balance between good deeds and the bad deeds. If the good deed surpassed the bad deeds, Gods and angels would like you and always protect you. If the bad deeds surpassed the good deeds, then God and his angels would punish you every chance they got until you worked hard enough to repay with good deeds and surpass the bad deeds. He was trying to determine where he stood on this. The Khmers believed that that killing of any sort of life was sinful. He realized he had killed countless fish and not to mention hundreds of lizards when he was a child. If that was the case, Gods and his angels were punishing him right now. They had offered him food to make sure he was alive so he could be tortured before he died. Chhoeun was confused, and he was feeling worse than before. It was logical but somehow illogical. Life could not be like that. He was alive now because he killed the animal to eat. There must be a teaching near the end of the book somewhere that explained it was all right to kill the animals to survive. He was not settled with his theory.

"Lunchtime! All Mit, it's lunchtime!" The Mekong hollered.

Time flew when he was busy working hard and deciding whether he should die of working hard or stay alive and possibly be taken to execution. He walked along in line with the rest of his group looking for Sok. Then another group joined in the line making it more complicate to spot him. He needed to talk to Sok. He was the only one he could trust. Sok always looked after him and offered him half of his food.

Chhoeun turned his head in every direction, but there was no sign of Sok anywhere. Maybe Sok had been taken away when he was too busy with his silly suicidal attempts. He was worried a little, but on his second thought he would have noticed if anyone had come to escort him. Chhoeun took a big step to the side as he walked and turned his head around. Then he saw Sok smiling at him from the back of the line. Chhoeun was relieved to see him.

When he reached the compound, hundreds of people poured in from all directions, walking among their horde toward their designated dining area. Chhoeun walked to back of the line to stand in front of Sok.

"What were you doing earlier on the rice paddies? You acted like you were an ox. Your butt was up as high has your head. Everyone was watching you. I thought my comrade here was possessed by the dead man's spirit," Suk said and laughed. Another person standing behind Sok laughed as well.

"Don't say that. I still have the creepy feeling. I hope he will leave me alone tonight. He promised to give me a frog back when I offered him the frog leg. Come to think of it, you gave me that frog; therefore, he should thank you instead," Chhoeun said.

"I think the spirits would only remember the last person they contacted, and it wasn't me," Sok replied.

Sok wasn't joking. Chhoeun remembered Grandma used to say the same thing. The spirits of the dead remember mostly the last person they saw.

"I caught two big frogs, bigger than my calves and some little ones. I'm going to give you the big one," Chhoeun said, changing the subject, pointing to the bulging objects covered by his scarf.

"Really? I have not caught a single frog yet. I found one in front of me as I was plowing, but it hopped away so fast and went to another man's working space. I didn't want to get in trouble chasing after it. I caught only one crab today," Suk said.

"Tonight, our mouths will have a good treat," Chhoeun said with a smile.

After Chhoeun got his share of rice, he walked over and sat with his group. He took his time eating the rice porridge, allowing every corner of his mouth to taste the flavor.

"I keep on thinking of the frog that I have right now. I want to roast it and eat it right now if we have enough time. My stomach didn't even budge from the rice porridge," Chhoeun said.

"There are too many people around, and we might not have enough time to cook," Sok said. "And don't forget my share. You promised to give me one."

"I still remember the smell and the taste of the frog you gave me last night. It's so good. This time the frogs are much bigger. You want to see? I'll show you." Chhoeun revealed the frog.

"Ey-ya! Those frogs are big! Make sure you don't lose them."

"Don't worry. It's not going anywhere."

"It's time to get back to work!" the Mekong shouted.

Everyone was tired. The break was too short. The rice porridge could barely provide the energy to walk. They got up reluctantly and walked along the line led by the Mekong. Chhoeun was walking right behind Sok.

They got back to the rice paddies and continued working. The memory of the dead man was still lingering in Chhoeun's mind. He was trying to forget it by working extra hard and keeping an eye on the frogs and crabs. Maybe chatting softly with his co-workers would help, but they were too far away. He felt so lonely and afraid.

He was deep in thought when he saw two men in clean black clothes escorting Sok off the field. No, this couldn't be real, he thought to himself. One of the men was holding a rifle with the machete strapped on his waist where the shiny blade was hanging down. Chhoeun felt like his guts were in his throat. The cowhide rope slipped off his hand. He stood frozen, watching Sok taken away. Sok didn't turn his way, afraid to get Chhoeun in danger. Instead, he turned slightly and tilted his head up diagonally as if he's looking at the sky. Then and waved his right hand slightly behind his back, careful not to let the two men know that he was saying goodbye.

Chhoeun stood frozen with confusion and disbelief. Then his entire body shook violently. Everyone feared to notice what was going one and kept their heads low, but Chhoeun couldn't help looking at Sok as he was walking between the two men. His black clothes were stained with mud. His scarf was wrapped around his waist. It just dawned on him that Sok had been a soldier once. He still walked like a soldier, strong and steady.

Chhoeun stared at the machetes that hung down from the waists of the militia and cringed. He hoped it would be a quick death for Sok.

Chhoeun lost all his hope that he had regained just after lunch. There was nothing else he cared about anymore, not even his own life. He'd rather die of starvation and overwork than to be slaughtered.

He continued to work extra hard from the rage of anger, fear, and sorrow. He wished he would just drop dead right now. He didn't care about eating. He had lost his appetite completely.

Later in the evening, the Mekong came and told everyone to stop working. The Mekong informed everyone that they were responsible for tending their own oxen after hours, before supper. There was no longer a crew to tend them at night.

Chhoeun took his oxen to the nearby grass field to feed them along with everyone else. He let the oxen graze freely. This was the only time when the workers were able to search for food. Tending the oxen was taking away precious time. It was very difficult to find food at nightfall, and it was dangerous. The cobras could be anywhere.

Chhoeun walked the oxen to a nearby shallow pond of water and allowed them to drink. He didn't bother searching for more food. When the oxen were finished drinking water, he tethered them by the tree where they could graze the grass all night. He walked with his group back to the compound.

"They took Mit Sok away. I wonder what he did wrong," one asked softly.

"I didn't see him do anything wrong. He's a hard worker, but I heard a rumor that they were taking away anybody that used to be in the military or had a wealthy family during Lon Nol's time," the other replied.

Chhoeun didn't say anything, and no one else mentioned Sok. It might be the fact that they'd gotten used to this sort of incident. They talked about their hunger and what they'd caught instead. As he lined up for his rice porridge, he was still wondering what they would do to Sok, hoping he didn't have to suffer. He cringed every time he thought of the Red Khmer's machete.

After he got his rice porridge, he sat by himself and ate quietly. A few of his peers attempted to speak to Chhoeun, but he could not make himself respond. He took his time eating the hot rice porridge. He doesn't care how little he had.

After he finished his rice porridge, he walked to sit with his peers around a fire. He unwrapped the scarf, and all his catches fell to the ground.

"Those are big frogs," one said

"You want some?" Chhoeun asked.

"Are you kidding? I'm so hungry right now. I caught three to four crabs, but they are so tiny," the man replied.

"If you're sharing, I want some too. He doesn't deserve to eat it all by himself," another one said.

"We could all share," Chhoeun said, not really caring who got what anymore.

Chhoeun tossed the frogs in the fire where it was easy for him to see. He looks around at the people around the hearth briefly then stared into the burning fire. It was eerie in an unexplainable way that Sok was not here in this world anymore. He felt so empty. He turned the frogs several times in the fire while his mind was somewhere else. He picked one up and bit half of one to the legs without giving much thought to it, and then remembered the man squatting across from him waiting for the share that he'd promised. He tore the frog in half then handed it to the man. He gave the upper part of the frog to the other man and saved the bottom part for himself.

"This is all I'm eating. You guys take the rest." Chhoeun said. Then he got up and walked away.

If Sok was here, he would have given him the bigger frog. Chhoeun went to his sleeping spot in the cottage getting ready to sleep. He gathered Sok's clothes and piled them in one corner of the mosquito net. The entire room was half empty. Most men were still out scavenging for food.

He lay down on his back staring at the ceiling through the mosquito net, feeling frightening and hopeless. He missed having Sok sleeping beside him sharing the mosquito net. He felt like there was a void where Sok used to be. His head began to spin, and then he dozed off slowly and was consumed by the night.

Chhoeun slept through most of the night. He woke up a couple of times wishing that Sok's ordeal was just a dream, but it turned out that it was real.

"Wake up! Wake up! It's time to go to work," the Mekong shouted.

Chhoeun woke up walking like a zombie, listening to what the Mekong had to say before work and plowing after the morning meeting. As much as he wanted to die of starvation and overwork, his body didn't seem to agree. He continued to work and keep his eyes on the ground looking for food.

At the end of the day, he hadn't caught any frogs or snails at all. He fed the oxen and went to search for food. He came across a termite hill with many dens. He dug the den and caught a small snake and a lizard. He didn't care if the snake was poisonous or not. Maybe dying from a snake bite was not a bad idea at all, but catching snakes had become very easy.

Each day, Chhoeun witnessed one to two people escorted away while they were working. Sometimes even after work when they were resting from the hard work. He knew many of them very well.

There was a man about Sok's age lying in his mosquito net when two men came and politely asked him to gather his belongings and follow them. "The government has an assignment for you," one of them said nicely as if it was really true. Several days later, they brought his clothes back and distributed them to whoever wanted the clothes.

Chhoeun didn't have another close friend like Sok, but he made new friends very quickly. He didn't want to be too close to another person and experience the same pain again. It was highly likely that many of these people would die.

Each day after, Chhoeun spent most of his evening time searching for food and making traps. He continued to share his food with anyone that would ask. Friendship was the only thing that helped to occupy his mind and forget about this hellish place. Many of his acquaintances and friends were found dead in their sleep. Some had been escorted out while they were working. Chhoeun was living in fear every waking moment.

Many weeks had passed; the hot season was approaching. There was less and less rain each week. The land became dry. Most of the fields were blanketed by the rice stalks. Women and children were flocking the rice field doing their task. The Red Khmers must have transported them from other villages.

Chhoeun was working very hard as usual to distract his mind from fear and to distract himself from the sorrow of losing of his new friends.

Ironically, hunger and the ongoing fatigue occupied his mind and helped him forget some of those things. One day, while he had his face down pushing the plow and helping the oxen, Chhoeun noticed someone was approaching him. The man was wearing black sandals made of car tire, laced with elastic from car tire tubes.

Just before he got to see his face, the man spoke out politely, "Mit Chhoeun, please come with me. Our leader wants to speak with you."

Chhoeun knew their scheme. They spoke nicely to you so you wouldn't panic and cause a stir. They wanted him to walk normally. He couldn't help but panic. This was it, he thought. He should have died of starvation, but he'd let the opportunity get away. The worst thing that could happen to him was right now. He would be executed by the method that he feared the most. Then he noticed there was only one of them, and he wasn't even carrying any weapons. Normally, there were two, and at least one of them would carry a machete and a rifle. Maybe they saw Chhoeun was too young and too skinny to pose any threat, so only one was needed to escort him to his execution. There was no other reason he could think of for being escorted away.

He walked a few paces in front of the man. His legs were weak. His knees were trembling. He stepped in a small puddle and fell. He had mud all over his pants.

"Mit Chhoeun, could you be a little more careful? You nearly splattered mud on my shirt," the man said.

"Yes," Chhoeun replied.

The man escorted him to a large house, further away from the field. He had never been this way before. He walked up the stairs as instructed. When he took the first step in the door, he saw another man standing, expecting him. Chhoeun looked around the house and saw no one else here except the man himself. More interestingly, there was no sign of previous execution. He was relieved for a second that he was not in the execution chamber yet. He glanced around and saw a machete hanging on the wall. His mind lit up with an idea. There were only two of them. If he moved fast enough, he could grab the machete from the wall and strike them first. He had wanted to kill the Red Khmers since he was thirteen. This was his opportunity. He could cut off their heads, and they would die instantly.

Just when he was ready to dash toward the machete, the man standing in front of him said, "Mit Chhoeun, we called you here because we recognize your hard work. We like the way you work. I have never seen anybody help the oxen push the plow before. You were the first. We want to promote you to become the Mekong."

Chhoeun stared at the man in disbelief.

"You will be leading forty people, including the Mekrums."

Chhoeun stood speechless.

"Your responsibility is to remember all your crew's names, take daily attendance, and report any missing or sick crew members to me. And of course, report anyone that breaks the rules," the man said.

"Yes, Mit Bong," Chhoeun replied.

At the end of the day, the higher Mekong held a brief meeting to inform everyone that Chhoeun was the new Mekong. They were told the previous Mekong has been taken away to work on special assignment. Everyone knew well what that meant. It proved that the Mekongs' lives were no better than the others', and they were simply there to keep track of people and assign jobs.

Chhoeun already knew half the men's names in his horde. The rest were the newly arrived. Most of them were very young. They must have just turned fifteen.

The higher official sat down with Chhoeun and explained his responsibilities and their goals. The amount of work the official planned for the horde was basically a death sentence. He had been a group leader before, but they were the youth. Now he was managing men age fifteen and over. Normally, he would be nervous, but after what he had gone through for the past few months, there couldn't be anything worse. He had just escaped death once again. If he was meant to die, he would have been dead by now. He was still unsure if God intended to punish him or spare his life.

The next morning, forty men were standing before him waiting for instruction. Two of his crew were sick and unable to get up. Chhoeun had to take a mental note and report it to his superior. The sick were not supposed to get anything to eat on that day because they didn't work. He also knew that reporting the same person frequently put their life at risk. He wished he could make a decision and change that rule. The sick would need to eat more than anyone else. He would never forgive himself if death was caused by him. He became panicked at the thought. Then an idea shot in his mind.

He divided the horde into four groups of ten. He assigned the better-off people to begin the usual harsh work and the sick to collect wood and cook. The sick just needed to sit up and do light job or at least pretend to. He could help prevent his group from dying of starvation. Other types of deaths were out of his control. As the Mekong, Chhoeun could be the dedicated cook, but he decided to rotate his job as well.

It took him nearly two weeks to get used to his new tasks. He still felt awkward managing adults, some of whom were twice his age. But so far, no one had been reported sick, and everyone got to eat.

About two months later, plowing season was over, but there were still hundreds of rice paddies that needed plowing. The higher authority had a quota of land they needed done. Chhoeun and his horde were forced to work until midnight to finish up the nightly quota. Sometimes the meeting was held by the higher authority after the midnight work. The Red Khmer were praising the new government and wanted everyone to feel the same. Everyone was required to pay attention during the speech. If they were caught sleeping or not heeding the lecture they would be taken to execution. New rules had been implemented to force people to work harder. Chhoeun and his crew slept for a few hours and were then forced to return to work before sunrise.

The harvest season was several months away, and the stocked rice was getting low—according to the Red Khmer anyway. The share of rice had been further reduced. The cooks had to add more water to make it easier to distribute. A scoop of rice porridge now contained mostly water. The rice grains were like gold nuggets in the bowl. Everyone was getting noticeably skinnier each week. Chhoeun had no more energy to work extra hard like he used to. Frogs and snails were getting scarce. Most days, he didn't catch anything at all due to the long hours of work. He was now hungrier than ever. So far, three people in his horde had been taken away, and two people died of illness since the day he became the Mekong. A lot less than he expected, but that was still a lot. Five more men had been recruited to fill up the spots the next day.

The dry season had begun when all the rice paddies were plowed. It was too late to spread any seeds. The lands were left unused. The hard work was really for nothing. Chhoeun and several members of his horde had been selected to move to another location to do logging. They had chosen three elder men that had recently joined Chhoeun's horde.

Chhoeun and the men were being escorted by the militia to another location early in the morning. They arrived in a thick forest in late afternoon. Chhoeun didn't see any houses or villagers but met a couple dozen current loggers living in their makeshift shelters under the trees. Unlike any other compounds where he had stayed, this place was lead directly by the militia. It indicated that there might be a militia base nearby somewhere. It gave him a chill to think of it. Chhoeun had no logging experience. He'd helped Mother split wood several times in Takeo, but that was it.

The militants that led them here instructed him and the men to begin building their own shelters. The militia had recognized Chhoeun as the Mekong from the previous compound and assigned him to lead the entire horde. The subgroups had already been organized before he arrived. Each person was given a machete or an ax to do their job. Each group was also given three of the giant two-man saws and a wagon but no oxen.

After walking all morning, there was no sign of getting anything to eat at all. Chhoeun and the men didn't bother asking. Instead, they began building their simple shelters, and then they took the opportunity to hunt for animals with the tools they'd been given. This forest was thick and appeared undisturbed. Even the wagon path was covered with thick grasses. Animals were making all sorts of sounds, including the monkeys. Wild birds could be seen roosting on the nearby trees. Chhoeun was overwhelmed by the anticipation of catching these animals.

Just before nightfall, Chhoeun caught four good-size lizards. He came across many snakes, but it was too dark. He didn't want deal with snakes in the dark. If everything went well, he would catch snakes and begin making traps tomorrow.

"Mit, I made a fire. You can use my fire if you give me a piece of your lizard. My eyes are bad after the sunset," a skinny old man said.

It was now very dark. Chhoeun needed a fire. He could make his own, but it would take some time. He was hungry, and he wanted to eat as soon as possible. Besides, this man was so skinny, he could die of starvation anytime if he didn't eat. Chhoeun would rather share his food than bury this man.

"You can have one. I'm keeping the rest because I walked all day without food," Chhoeun said and gave the man one of his lizards.

"One is fine," the man said.

Chhoeun cooked the lizards and ate with the old man. Other men came and joined Chhoeun and the old man.

"Did he ask you for a share to use his fire?" another man about Chhoeun's age asked. "He can't catch his own food. He does that to us too."

"I'm old and cannot see after the sunset. If I could see, I would be better than you at catching lizards. If you knew me when I was young, you would be amazed," the older man said.

Chhoeun and several men were sitting around a fire cooking their catches. One of them caught a snake that was nearly four feet long. After the snake was cooked, the man gave a large piece to the old man and smaller pieces to other men.

Chhoeun was already starting to like this place. He hoped they didn't treat the workers brutally like the previous place had. Somehow, the forest was giving him a lot of comfort and hope.

Early in the morning, everyone gathered in an open spot waiting for the instruction. One of militants arrived and explained the task and the expectations from the horde. The tasks were to simply cut the logs and pile them on the wagon road. Even though the subgroups had already created, he suggested Chhoeun could rearrange them any way he liked. When the meeting was over, Chhoeun divided his group into four, ten in each group. He tried to evenly mix the young men and the elder men. He learned that nearly all elder men had experience with logging. He assigned the most skilled men to become Mekrum to lead the group. He assigned three people to cook rice porridge and to find additional food if possible.

Chhoeun volunteered to join one of the logging groups. He allowed the experienced men to scout for good trees and then begin cutting the trees. Chhoeun was surprised to learn that sawing used much more energy than plowing. With plowing, he would just stand on the plow and let the oxen do all the work. With sawing, he was using his own energy to do the work. Chhoeun and the men became exhausted just after five minutes. The men took turn resting after they couldn't go on. When it was his turn to take break, he walked around the area searching for small animals. Unlike frogs and crabs, which were easy to catch, the forest animals were fast, and the thick trees and shrubs made it very difficult to catch anything. He began making traps using the bamboo trees and small vines. He wished he still had the nylon string. He had to discard it at the previous compound, afraid he might get in trouble for carrying such things.

Later in the afternoon, Chhoeun and his crew loaded the logs onto the wagon and hauled the wagon to the open area. They unloaded the logs on the spot where another group in another compound would come to retrieve them.

Chhoeun rebuilt his shelter by making it higher and sturdier. He made the roof with thick layers of leaves, assuming he would stay here long. The newly built shelter could withstand heavy rain and strong winds.

He returned the next day to the worksite. Most of his traps had been triggered. A few animals had chewed the vines off and escaped. He ended up with a squirrel and a good-size bird. The elder men identified the bird as a wild chicken. Chhoeun added some more traps to the area during rest time.

Like the previous place, the amount of rice was very little. The rice porridge contained mostly water. Fortunately, the cook caught snakes and other small animals to share with the group. They were all experienced men who knew what they were doing.

About three months later, Chhoeun and his horde became obviously healthier and stronger from eating a good amount of meat. The men nearly doubled in size. Chhoeun caught most of the animals since he was the only person that had the time to make the traps. He shared everything he caught with the horde.

In a hot evening after work, after Bong Chhoeun finished eating, he crept into his shelter, getting ready to sleep. He kept appreciating the place for the opportunity to find food. Everyone in his group was becoming healthy very quickly. He took a long, deep breath. He's always thinking of making new traps to catch bigger animals that lived deeper in the forest.

Just when he was getting ready to sleep, he saw two militia members standing in front of another shelter right across from his shelter. The militia members were speaking to the two men who were living in the same shelter. Chhoeun sat up and stared through the open door. Chhoeun had not spoken to the two men directly, but they were both his subgroup. He knew the two men well from the morning meeting. They were known to be generous and skilled loggers. They appeared to be relatives or very close friends.

Minutes later, the two men exited the shelter and followed the militia members. Neither of the militia members appeared aggressive or intimidating. Chhoeun knew well it was the end of their lives. He crawled to the back end of his shelter and sat quietly. He was terrified to see his crew get taken away again just after he'd thought he was safe here. After a moment of thought and reminiscing about the two gentle and hardworking men, he began to weep. His hopes had just vanished into thin air. This time, the men would not die of starvation but from brutal execution.

Chhoeun began to think of the day when he told Narong about joining the military. Soon, they would come to escort him and take him to execution. Then he thought of a plan to strike back. At least he could take two lives before he died. He had a long machete with him all the time. He was determined not to allow them to come and escort him that easily.

Three days later, the militia member that Chhoeun reported to every day arrived early in the morning and asked him to take a walk with him, away from the horde. This was unexpected. Chhoeun would normally carries his machete in the meeting, and then he would go straight to work. Today he tossed his machete on the wagon when he was gathering the tools for work. Besides, he wouldn't know what to do even if he had the machete. He had been reporting to the same man for months, and they had become almost like friends.

"Mit, our record shows that you admitted you joined the military. You are now around sixteen, and the record shows you joined the military more than three years ago. It doesn't make sense that you joined the military at the age of thirteen, but I'm going with the record. The government does not want to see you yet. However, I was asked to demote you to Mekrum. You will be managing just a group of ten. You are no long managing the entire horde. I will inform the group in the meeting," the militant said briefly then walked back to the horde that was waiting for in the instruction for the day.

Despite knowing that he was safe for now, Chhoeun was still very nervous. He felt very dizzy all of a sudden. It was like another nightmare all over again. It happened so fast. The militant's words were short but terrifying. The end of his life was coming soon. It was only a matter of time before they decided to kill him. He began to walk and follow the militant to the meeting. His feet became heavy. He felt ashamed and afraid.

"All Mit, today is Mit Chhoeun's last day of being the Mekong. We got a message from another village indicating that Mit Chhoeun joined the military at the age of thirteen. He used to be our enemy. The Mekrum should lead each group until another Mekong is assigned. I will be your temporary Mekong until we find a qualified person. Resume your work," the militant said and walked away.

Everyone stood frozen and stared at Chhoeun. He could see the sympathy in their eyes. They knew as well as Chhoeun that it was the matter of time before the militant would come and take him to execution.

Chhoeun and his current group began their walk and hauled the wagon to work as usual. No one was asking Chhoeun any questions. He couldn't help but to think of what was going to happen next. The next time they came to see him would be his last day.

When Chhoeun returned from work, he picked up a small slab of stone along the road to sharpen his machete. He sat quietly eating with the horde. His eyes were staring at the fire. The men couldn't help but to stare at him.

When Chhoeun finished eating, he went straight to his shelter and began sharpening his machete. He made sure every inch of the blade was sharp. He had been thinking of several different methods of striking, assuming both the militia members would carry rifles.

From his experience, they appeared to be friendly and pretended to be harmless to avoid complications. Chhoeun was planning to act the same way. Before he went to sleep, he laid his machete beside him and covered it with a scarf. He also had a plan in case they came to wake him up in the middle of the night.

CHAPTER 11

Chhoy woke up to the faint crow of the roosters. She wasn't sure if it was time to get up. Some roosters crowed earlier than others. She was hoping it was the earlier one. She closed her eyes, hoping to gain a few more hours of sleep. The room was very crowded. Everyone had to sleep on their sides to make room for others.

"Get up! Get up! It's time to get up," the Mekong shouted.

Disappointed, Chhoy got up and looked around.

"Chhorn, get up," Chhoy said softly.

"I need more sleep. I'm so tired," Chhorn said as she got up.

Chhorn and Chhoy got up, walking like zombies and following the crowd. Leng and Chu were right behind them. The two girls both named Ah Nees were already up and walking ahead. They had been friends since the day they met.

Dozens of lines were forming outside the building. Chhorn and Chhoy joined their group in a line. The Mekong briefly counted the girls in the line and ordered them to grab their tools and reform the line. When everyone was ready, the Mekong led the way with another Mekong trailing behind the line. They marched along the worn path among other hordes to the field. Several of the Red Khmer were walking along the side of the long lines chatting and monitoring. The Red Khmer women always wore their clothes nicely and buttoned their shirts to the collar to show orderliness and authority.

Once they reached the site, laborers from all directions poured in at the same time like an army of ants. Another day of hard work had begun. Chhorn and Chhoy began digging the soil in the same location where they'd left off yesterday. The girls were aware of the guards walking around in the distance monitoring. They chatted softly as they worked.

Three months ago, all the youth had been working with the adults harvesting the rice. The rice was abundant. It was the best time of the year, as everyone got to eat steamed rice once a week, then they got to eat thick rice porridge for the rest of the week. That time was over very suddenly like a dream. Now, the rice porridge contained mostly water. Everyone was hungry. They had been collecting crabs, snails, and water spinach as they were walking to work or while they were working. It was prohibited to collect food when they walked to work, but everyone still did it here and there. As an older sister, Chhorn needed to collect food for Chhoy as well. Crabs and snails became scarce in the dry season. Chhorn, Chhoy, and the horde had been moved to different compounds multiple times to do various tasks, ranging from plucking shrubs to clearing the forest. Fortunately, the entire horde got to stay together. They were now living in compound called Wat Ta Pon. It had once been a nice temple, but now everything had been stripped out leaving just the structure of the building. Thousands of youth had been transported here, mostly from Phnom Penh. They were taking up every inch of space in all the buildings. Everyone had to squeeze in by sleeping on their sides.

Their current main assignment was to build new rice paddies on the land that had just been cleared of shrubs and trees. The rice paddies were normally formed by a rectangular-shaped damp. Depending on the land, the rice paddies normally linked to the adjacent rice paddies.

Chhorn was turning fifteen. On record, she was fourteen. Chhoy was turning fourteen. She was twelve on the record. The government appeared to be more organized in tracking the girls' identities and their activities to prevent conspiracies and to prevent anyone from attempting to escape. Three new subgroups and ranks had been added to the current horde. The subordinates of the Mekong were Mekrum, Anuvatean, and Samagic. Each position had been handpicked by the Mekong or the higher official. Each position was to report to the upper rank the status of their subordinates, including absenteeism and suspicious activities. The government implemented new rules regularly to ensure no one was slacking off. It made it nearly impossible for Chhorn and Chhoy to visit Mother. Today they were working side by side. Having a sister working together offered some comfort for both of them. Those who did not have a sister would normally have a close friend to work with.

Digging and carrying dirt drained their energy very quickly. They stopped for a short break at noon to eat a scoop of rice porridge for lunch and return to work until the sunset.

Chhoy and Chhorn returned from work without finding any food that day, and they were too tired to search for food. They decide to go straight to sleep. All their friends were doing the same.

"I miss the Lon Nol's time. I got to eat good every day. Sometimes, my Mother had to force me to eat. We had chicken, beef, pork, or fish to eat every day. If I'd known this ahead of time, I would have eaten until my stomach inflated like a balloon," Ah Vee said softly.

"Me too. I still remember the day my dad made sour fish soup. I got a whole fish to myself. I only ate half of the fish because I was angry at my Mother for some stupid reason. I want to go back in time to finish that fish right now," the Islamic Ah Nee said.

"Imagine sipping the fish soup right now. It must taste so good. My mouth is watering just thinking of it," Chhoy said.

"Stop talking! Be quiet and go to sleep!" the Mekong shouted as they walked by.

Everyone stopped talking and went to sleep. The hot night and the small space made it difficult to sleep. Everyone was tossing and turning trying to get comfortable. Many had been sick for the past week. It was common to hear younger girls deliriously beg for their mothers.

Early in the morning, someone blew a whistle loud enough to wake up the dead. It turned out that one of the Mekongs managed to find a whistle from somewhere. The crow of the roosters were rare nowadays and no longer reliable.

"Chhorn, I don't feel good. I have a bad headache," Chhoy said when she tried to get up.

Chhorn reached out and touched Chhoy's forehead with the back of her hand. Mother always did that when they told her they didn't feel well.

"Your skin is very hot. I think you have a fever. You think you will be able to walk to work? If you could, you wouldn't have to work hard. Just pretend. I will be next to you to help you," Chhorn said.

"We'll all be around you to help you," Linh said.

"Yeah, we will help you," Chu added.

"I will help block, so they don't see you standing," Ah Nee, the Islamic girl said.

"I don't know, but I will try. My head hurts, and I feel dizzy," Chhoy replied.

Chhoy had to try. If she didn't go to work, she would not get her share of rice. She was very hungry. She pushed herself to get up and walk along with the group. Everyone was forming a line in front of Mit Ra and Mit Rate. The two Mekongs had been managing the same girls since the beginning. Today they had a special guest. A woman wearing clean black clothes with her shirt buttoned up to the collar was waiting to make a speech. Chhorn noticed the women well, not only from her face but also from the buttons on her shirt that ran from the collar all the way down to the bottom. Those buttons represented the number of days she used to visit Mother. She'd run out of buttons long ago. She regretted spending her buttons lavishly. She could have used that to take Chhoy home right now, if that was even possible anymore.

"All Mit, I came to bring good news. Today, the government is rolling out the ultimate plan. Since we have been relying heavily on the rain to grow our crops, we were only able to grow crops once a year. The new plan will allow us to grow crops all year round. The solution is simple. We create the canal that channels the water from the river to the field. This method will allow us to control the water from the river. To make this possible, every village will work together to dig the canal to channel the water from the river to remote land. Our comrades are working very hard as we speak building dams in the river to control the water. The river will provide unlimited amounts of water. The rain was inconsistent, and it was not reliable. Starting from today forward, we will focus on digging the canal connecting from Ta Pon to Ohmany." the woman announced.

Chhorn noticed Chhoy's head was drooping down, and her eyes were shut. Her posture was very unstable. She would collapse at any time if she continued to stand up.

"Chhoy, try your best to open your eyes for now. You have to pretend to listen," Chhorn whispered.

When the Red Khmer were talking, it was mandatory to listen. If anyone was found not paying attention, they would get scolded and maybe taken to trial. There was one girl in her group several months back that had problems paying attention. She had a habit of turning away and picking up objects off the ground and playing with the objects. After many warnings, the Red Khmer came and tapped her on the back then asked her to gather up all her belongings. The Red Khmer led her away. In the same evening, the same Red Khmer returned the girl's clothes and tossed them in the temple and said the clothes were a gift from the government if anyone was interested. The memories made Chhoy try very hard to hold her head up as the woman continued to speak.

"I would like to remind everyone about the rules and the consequences if the rule is broken. There was one person in this village caught stealing rice from the warehouse. She has been taken away to trial. Stealing is a serious crime. We do not want to form a country full of thieves. Everything belongs to the public. If you steal, you are using it for personal gain. Nothing is personal in our new system." The woman paused and then continued. "One person was caught loving a boy in a nearby village. Both the boy and the girl were taken to be disciplined. The government decides who you should marry with. It is not your decision. Keep that in mind. We do not want to return to the old, corrupt society where boys and girl married whoever they wanted. People made bad decisions. They might see that person was a fit for them, but at the end they might be wrong. The government knows who is a best fit for each and every one of you. The government is the best when it comes to making a decision. Let the government make the decision. We should praise the great government. Let's hear everybody say bravo!" the woman said and paused.

"Bravo!" Everyone pretend to cheer, including Chhorn and Chhoy.

The women continued to report all the new crimes and the consequences. Even though she didn't mention the types of consequences; everyone knew the punishment was normally death, especially when someone returned a pile of clothes.

The woman walked away after she'd finished speaking. Everyone applauded, led by the Mekongs.

"Chhorn, I cannot make it. I'm going to fall if I try to walk. I'm going to stay and rest," Chhoy said feebly.

"All right, then stay here. I will try to get your share of rice, and I will find food for you," Chhorn said.

Chhorn walked over to Mit Ra, the Mekong, and said, "Mit Bong, my sister is sick. She will not be able to go to work. I will work twice as hard, so she can get her full share of rice. Is that fine with you? If not, I can work twice as hard today and tomorrow."

"All right, you can work harder, but not twice as hard or you will die," Mit Ra said.

Based on the meeting, the work would be a lot harder. Chhorn fetched the hoe as instructed and formed a line with her friends preparing to march to work. When everyone was in line, they began to walk. Today the Mekongs were leading them to a different location from yesterday. Chhorn kept her eyes on the ground as she walked hoping to find frogs or crabs. She kept in mind that today she really needed to get food for Chhoy.

They came to a vast, open bare land where thousands of laborers, including men, women, boys, and girls from other villages, were walking in line, pouring in from all directions.

"Wait here. I will be back," the Mit Ra said and walked toward other Mekongs and the project leaders.

After a brief discussion, the Mit Ra walked back to the group and said, "Follow me. Our spot is over there."

They followed Mit Ra toward an open spot. Two other groups were gathering on both sides of the spot.

"Dig along this line here. The depth has to pass your head," the Mit Ra explained.

They were to dig a channel like the woman had described earlier. Chhorn remembered she had to work harder than usual in order to get Chhoy her share of rice. While other girls were taking their time starting their jobs, Chhorn wanted to be the first one to start. Chhorn was bigger and taller than most girls her age. She lifted the hoe up above her head and brought it down with a strong force. The entire blade went all the way in the dirt. She prided the dirt up and a big chunk of soil came loose. She repeated the same process over for several minutes. The sweat was rolling down her face vigorously.

"Mit Chhorn, take it easy. You might collapse. No one will help you if that happens," Mit Ra said.

She was not joking. No one was to help another person when they were in trouble. Both the helper and the sufferer would get in trouble for wasting time. Chhorn wanted to continue working hard so that Chhoy could get her share, but she had no energy to go on. It was still morning and she'd had nothing to eat yet. She slowed down and worked at a normal pace like everyone else, hoping the Mekongs didn't see that. Even though Mit Ra was very nice, she had to follow the rules. Certain things she would not be able to bypass.

Just before noon, her energy was drained. Unlike any other jobs she had done in the past, digging the channel was much harder than anything else. Mit Ra began to assign a subgroup to carry the dirt away. She knew Chhorn was exhausted, so she did not select her.

Chhorn was so tired and barely had the energy to lift up her arm to wipe the sweat off her face. She rubbed her face against her shoulders to get rid of the sweat. Her stomach was empty, and she felt like her belly and her spine were touching. She could no longer lift the hoe past her head.

Just when she was about to collapse, the Red Khmer who were monitoring the workers hollered, "Everyone, it is now lunchtime! Line up and get ready!"

Everyone gathered behind the Mit Ra and Mit Rate forming a line. Mit Ra was leading the line and Mit Rate trailed after marching the group back to the compound for lunch.

When they entered the perimeter of the compound, they approached three armed militia escorting a boy walking directly toward the group on the same path. The boy had a banana hanging from his neck with a string as if he was wearing a necklace with the banana as a pendant.

"All Mit, this person is a thief. We caught him stealing bananas. We don't want thieves in this society. We will use his corpse to make fertilizer for the banana tree. This was what happens when people steal. If we catch you stealing, you will become fertilizer," one of the armed escorts announced.

Chhorn couldn't help but to stare at the face of the young man. He was about fifteen years of age. His hands were tied behind back. There were traces of tears and bruises on his face. He appeared weak and frightened. He sobbed as he walked, knowing that he would be executed after they finished showing him to the entire village.

"Don't look at them. Just walk straight," Mit Rate whispered.

Chhorn tried not to look and continued walking, but it was too late. The face of the boy was now imprinted in her mind. She could only imagine what they would do to him.

When the group arrived in the temple, Chhorn used her last burst of energy and ran inside the temple. She found Chhoy lying on the floor breathing slowly. She didn't have time to check her; instead, she grabbed two bowls and dashed back outside to line up for rice porridge. Many of the girls were staring at the two bowls on Chhorn's hands.

"One is for Mit Chhoy," Ah Vee said to let everyone know.

"Mit Chhorn worked extra hard for Mit Chhoy, so Mit Chhoy could get her share," Leng said.

The girls in the line did not seem to be jealous. They probably wished they had a sister to work for them when they were sick.

Chhorn returned from the line with her share and Chhoy's share of rice porridge. "Here, I got your share of rice porridge." She handed the rice porridge to Chhoy.

Chhoy struggled to sit up right. Her hands shook as she held the bowl and the spoon. If not for hunger, she would not have attempted to sit up. She began to slurp the rice porridge slowly with her eyes half closed. Chhorn sat beside Chhoy looking at her eating her rice porridge.

Chhorn ate a little and stared into her own bowl and saw no more than six spoons of rice porridge left. She was about to eat another spoon, but she stopped herself. "Here, take my rice porridge," Chhorn said and poured the rest of her rice porridge from her bowl to Chhoy's bowl.

Chhoy was half delirious. Without saying a word, she slurped the rest of the rice porridge and went back to sleep.

"I will get you something to eat after I get out of work," Chhorn said with assurance that she would take care of her.

Chhoy was too tired to reply. She fell back asleep instantly. Chhorn sat next to her thinking of the girls that had passed away from illness recently. No one cared about them besides their close friends. The mothers had no clue about the death of their children. They died like animals. She didn't want that to happen to Chhoy, but she didn't know what to do.

One of the Mekong blew the whistle and shouted, "It's time to get back to work."

Chhorn stepped outside and found her group gathering outside the temple, ready to walk back to work. The rice porridge had barely nudged her hunger. She was starving right now. She gained her strength back a little from the rest, enough to walk back to work but unsure how she was going to keep up the work. She just remembered that she had to work harder than everyone else to get a share of rice for Chhoy for supper. She felt even more exhausted just thinking of it.

When she arrived at the field, she knew she could not work twice as hard for the rest of the day. She just need to show that the Mekong was aware that she was working extra hard. She kept her eyes on the Mekong. When the Mekong was not facing her direction, she relaxed and worked at a slow pace. When the Mekong was facing her, she added extra effort. Within an hour, Chhorn was exhausted, hungry, and thirsty. Her clothes and her face were filled with mud and dust.

Just before sunset, the Mekong shouted, "Let's go. We get to leave early today. Because we worked so hard and we are so dirty, Mit Bong is allowing us to stop early so we can go bathe in the river after supper."

Chhorn was relieved to hear that. She's hoping she would have enough time to find snails and crabs. When she returned to the temple, she found Chhoy still lying on the floor, but she was awake. Chhorn was able to get Chhoy's share of rice porridge and poured half of her share into Chhoy's bowl, hoping it would help her feel better.

"They let us out early today because we worked so hard and we all need to bathe. I didn't find any food at work today. I had to work in one spot all day. I'm very tired. We are going to walk to the river and bathe. I will search for vegetables and collects some snails," Chhorn said.

Chhoy nodded. After she finished eating her rice porridge, she lay back down. Chhorn was relieved to see her getting better. Chhorn walked outside and lined up with her group to get ready to march to the river.

Like Chhorn, everyone was scanning the ground as they walked, looking for food, including Mit Ra and Mit Rate. Since this was not a trip to work, everyone was free to collect food as they walked. No one was around to monitor them. Some stopped by the side of the road and picked vegetables. Some dashed after a small frog hopping away. There were no sign of snails or crabs, as the ground was too hot.

When she arrived at the river, Chhorn didn't care too much about bathing. She swam straight toward clusters of vegetation that had been swept over by the current of the river and began searching for the edible plants. There were water spinach and lotus floating in the deep water. She grabbed as much as possible and then swam back to the shallow area. Then she began searching for small edible animals. Many girls began to swarm for food with her when they'd finished bathing.

Chhorn brought back water spinach along with several giant water cockroaches that she recently learned were not only edible but also delicious when cooked over the fire. Since they didn't have any pots, Chhorn roasted the water spinach along with the water cockroaches for Chhoy to eat.

The next morning, Chhoy still felt miserable, but she was able to walk. She was determined to go to work. Chhorn and all her friends assured her that they would work closely by her and help as much as they could.

About a week later, as Chhoy was still recovering from her illness, Chhorn suddenly become very sick. She woke up in the morning and nearly collapsed when she tried to stand up. She went back to the floor and sat up.

"Chhoy, I don't feel well. I think I'm sick. I woke up to go to potty last night, and I nearly collapsed. I don't think I can walk to work today," Chhorn said.

"Then I will tell the Mekong that," Chhoy replied.

Unable to say another word, Chhorn lay back on the floor and went back to sleep. Chhoy went outside to the group and reported to the Mekong that Chhorn was sick. Unlike Chhorn, Chhoy didn't talk much, especially with the adults. She was hoping things would go the way she wished.

As a younger sister, Chhoy felt comfortable with Chhorn working by her side all the time. Without Chhorn, she felt very different. Chhorn had always been around her all her life. Fortunately, Chhoy had a lot of good friends. They would chitchat every chance they got to forget about the hunger and the fear.

Leng and Chu were working on her right side. The two Ah Nees were working on her left. The Islamic Ah Nee still had a heavy accent after two years. Islam wasn't common in Kampuchea, but they were well known to be very different from Buddhism. Not too many Khmers understood their beliefs.

Pehk Lee and Seung were working on the opposite side of Chhoy, talking while they worked. Pehk Lee was around fourteen years old. She had very light skin like Chhoy. Her Father had died on April 17, the day when the Red Khmer took over. He had been a soldier battling the Red Khmer until that day. When all the soldiers surrendered, he'd tried to sneak away to change his uniform. He was a few feet away from the door of his house when the Red Khmer shot him from behind. Her Mother ran out and mourned beside him, but the Red Khmer shot her as well. She collapsed and died right on top of him. Pehk Lee and her sixteen-year-old sister witnessed the entire ordeal through the window. The two sisters moved to live in Stung Chah. After Pehk Lee was taken to work with the youth, she never saw her sister again. She went back to her house in Stung Chah several times, but her sister never showed up. She assumed her sister had been taken to work very far away because she was sixteen and single.

Seung had dark skin like Chhorn but was much shorter. She was around fourteen years old as well. She was closer to Chhorn than Chhoy. Seung was raised in a wealthy family in Phnom Penh. Her Father was a three-star general back in the day. She had many older siblings who'd been taken away to work at different places.

"All Mit! It's lunchtime!" the Mekong called out.

Everyone dropped their hoes and formed a single line. Mit Ra and Mit Rate led them back to the temple. No one said much. Everyone was hungry and looking forward to eating.

When they arrived at the village, the cook was stirring the rice porridge to keep the rice grain floating evenly. Chhoy had never been assigned to cook because she could not lift the pot when it was full of rice and water. The cooks got a lot of advantages. They were closer to food, and they didn't have to work as hard. To be chosen as a cook was like winning the jackpot.

Chhoy wasted no time and ran inside the temple to get Chhorn's bowl and returned to the line, hoping not to be the last person in line. The last person in line might not get anything to eat. Some girls brought the bowl with them to work so they could run straight to the line, but it was difficult to work carrying the bowl around.

It's Chhoy's turn to get the rice porridge. She held one bowl on each hand. Then an angry voice shot out from somewhere, "Hey Mit! Why do you have two bowls?"

Chhoy froze for a few seconds. The voice was not often heard but very familiar. When she turned to the source of the voice, she saw the woman with the fancy buttons. Chhoy was terrified and didn't know what to say. She turned to the Mit Ra and Mit Rate for help.

"Mit Chhorn is sick. One of the bowls is her share," the Mit Ra replied.

"Who said a sick person can eat? Is it fair to the comrade that worked hard while she laid down sleeping? Just get your share for now. Finish your share. If there is any left over, she can have some," the woman said.

Chhoy shivered after being scolded and avoided eye contact with the woman. She didn't want to upset the Red Khmer. They had the power to do anything. She thought they were the living demons.

The cook appeared as nervous as Chhoy. Her hands were trembling as she scooped the rice porridge from the pot and poured it into Chhoy's bowl. Chhoy quickly sat down on a bench and ate her rice porridge. She wanted to slurp the entire bowl so she could go line up to get Chhorn's share, but the rice porridge was extremely hot. She blew the rice porridge as hard as her lungs allowed and forced herself to eat it while it was still burning hot.

It seems forever for her finish her hot rice porridge. She hurried back to the pot to get a share for Chhorn, hoping there was still some left. The cook was eating her share near the pot. She stood up quickly and prepared to give Chhoy the share for Chhorn. The demon-like women came up and snatched the scoop off from the cook's hand. Chhoy and the cook flinched as they thought they were going to get hit by the woman.

"People who don't work do not deserve to eat at all. I'm being kind to give you some," she scolded out loud and scraped the bottom of the pot. She poured some back when she thought it was too much.

Everyone couldn't help but stare at Chhoy, the cook, and the woman. It was a common incident, but it was hard to get used to. Chhoy was nearly in tears, but she fought to keep herself from crying. She walked with her head down toward the temple delivering about three tablespoons of rice porridge to Chhorn.

"Chhorn, here is the rice porridge. This is all they gave me," Chhoy said softly.

Chhorn sat up and took the bowl and stared at the bowl as if she was hallucinating. "Where is the rice porridge? There are only a few drops," Chhorn asked in confused.

"That's all they gave me," Chhoy said, not knowing what else to say.

"What am I going to eat? There is nothing!" Chhorn said angrily. She tossed the bowl to the floor and splattered the rice porridge.

Chhoy stood motionless looking down to the floor. She was not sure if Chhorn was mad at her or at the person who gave the rice porridge. Chhorn lay back down and covered her face with the scarf. Then she began to weep.

Feeling hurt and guilty, Chhoy walked out of the temple and joined her friends under the canopy of a tree. No one had caught anything during work. They had nothing else to eat besides the rice porridge. Everyone was exhausted. Leng and Chu were sleeping with their heads resting on the tree trunk. The two Ah Nees were sitting down staring at the ground without saying a word. Chhoy sat next to Phek Lee who was still scraping her bowl with her spoon to get every last drop of her rice porridge.

A moment later, the Mekong shouted, "It's time to go back to work."

Chhoy and the girls reluctantly got up, forming a line. Mit Ra did a quick roll call and then began to lead them back to the field. As she was walking, Chhoy couldn't help but to think of the whole ordeal. She felt very guilty and sad for not being able to help Chhorn.

They returned for supper after sunset. Chhoy saw two girls cooking the rice porridge. One was stirring, and the other was adjusting the firewood. Chhoy hastily ran to the line so she wouldn't be too far in the line. After she got her share, she darted to the bench and started eating as fast as she could. She kept her eyes on the demon-like woman who was busy talking to the Mekongs in another horde. She tried to finish her rice porridge before the woman returned. She forced herself to slurp each spoonful of the burning hot rice porridge. She nearly spits it out a few times. She fought the burning pain and continued to slurp. She could not waste any time. Chhorn was sick and really needed to eat.

After she finished her rice porridge, Chhoy walked hastily toward the pot. The two cooks were still sitting behind pot eating their share.

"This is for my sister, Mit Chhorn. She is sick," Chhoy said.

Both cooks turned their heads to the demon-like woman who was still busy talking. One of the cook hastily scooped the rice porridge from the pot. Chhoy could hear the scoop scrape against the bottom of the pot indicating the pot was nearly empty. When the cook raised the scoop up, Chhoy was relieved to see rice in the scoop.

Chhoy stared at the cook pleading for more. The cook turned her head toward the woman and shook her head. Chhoy understood and took no chance to lose it all. She glided past her friends and slipped inside the temple.

Once inside, she found Chhorn still lying on the floor sleeping.

"Chhorn, here, eat your rice porridge," Chhoy said softly.

Chhorn got up very quickly when she heard the words "rice porridge." She was very hungry and thought she would never see the rice porridge anytime soon. She got a bad headache as she sat up, but she was overwhelmed by the aroma of the rice porridge and it made her forget about everything else. She began to eat the rice porridge slowly.

Chhoy sat and stared at Chhorn as she ate. She felt very relieved that she could help her back for the first time. They didn't talk much when they were alone. After Chhorn finish eating the rice porridge, Chhoy got up and walked toward the river alone to search for food. She rarely went anywhere without Chhorn. She did what Chhorn did. This time, she was on her own. She longed to have her friends with her for comfort, but she's afraid they might be too fast for her and collect all the food. She needed to get food for Chhorn and fast.

When she arrived at the river, she found nearly all her friends were already there in the shallow water, dipping their hands in the mud fishing for any moving creatures.

Chhoy spend the evening fishing for edible water bugs and small frogs. She also collected what she believed to be edible plants. She even caught one giant water cockroach. It was dark when she arrived at the temple. She roasted the vegetables and her catches and brought the food to Chhorn, who was still lying on the floor.

"Chhorn, get up. I brought you some food," Chhoy said softly.

Chhorn struggle to sit up. She picked the small frogs first, as their aroma was hard to resist, even when she was sick. She popped the whole frog in her mouth

"You can eat the rest yourself. That's all I need. You worked hard all day," Chhorn said.

Chhoy knew Chhorn was still hungry. She also knew Chhorn was determined when it came to abstaining from eating so that she could have more eat. Once her decision was made, she would not change her mind.

Four days had passed. Chhorn was still sick and could not make it to work. She had been lying in one spot all these days. She no longer got her share of rice porridge. Chhoy tried to give Chhorn her share, but she refused to eat. Chhorn would only eat the food that Chhoy collected from the river. Chhoy was getting better at collecting food each day. She even caught some grasshoppers and crickets. She also learned about new types of vegetables from her friends that grew along the river bank that appeared in-edible at first.

The next evening, Chhoy returned from the river, eager to show Chhorn how much food she'd collected and hoping Chhorn was feeling better. Unfortunately, Chhorn was lying on the floor breathing very slowly. She barely noticed that Chhoy was here. Chhoy didn't want to wake her up yet. She went back outside to cook the food. She was very worried about Chhorn, but she didn't know what to do or what to say. She was hoping the food make her feel better.

When Chhoy finished roasting all her food, she brought the food to Chhorn.

"Chhorn, look what I got," Chhoy said and placed the cooked food in front of Chhorn's face.

Chhorn weakly lift her hand and picked up the burned insect and chewed.

"That's a cricket. I know how to catch them. They only come out when it's getting dark," Chhoy explained happily.

"Chhoy, I want to go home. I don't think I'm going to make it. I'm so tired, and my whole body is in pain. If anything happens to me,

Mother will be there. Ask the Mekong for me tomorrow morning," Chhorn whispered softly.

Chhoy did not like what she had just heard. She's overwhelmed with sorrow and fear. "I will ask the Mekong tomorrow morning, then."

When Chhoy woke up in the morning, her whole body was aching from digging and carrying baskets of dirt the last couple days. Thinking of work was like preparing to travel to hell. Chhoy remembered from yesterday that Chhorn was still gravely ill and that she might die from this illness. She was hoping Chhorn's assumption was wrong, but many girls had died of illness recently. Chhoy had to ask the Mekong for permission for Chhorn to go home. It was nearly impossible to get permission to go home nowadays. She didn't like the idea of Chhorn leaving her, but there was nothing she could do to help cure her sickness. Mother could probably help. She used to treat sick children everywhere we lived. Chhoy gazed over to Chhorn again. Her hair was messy and dirty. Her face was covered with sweat. She was lying on her back with her eyes closed as if she was lifeless.

Chhoy walked outside along with her friends and lined up waiting for the opportunity to speak. Mit Rate began the roll call. When Chhorn's name was called, Chhoy nervously said, "Mit Chhorn is sick. She's requesting to go home."

"I will ask for permission for you" said Mit Ra, who was standing beside Mit Rate, and she walked toward a group of Red Khmer chatting nearby.

As Mit Rate continued to take attendance, Chhoy glanced over at the group of high-rank Red Khmer speaking. She got a chill from staring at them. They were like the hell servants that came to kill and take the souls back to hell. Chhoy held her breath as Mit Ra approached the women. She appeared very uncomfortable and inferior. Chhoy became too nervous to see what their reaction might be; she looked away and just waited for Mit Ra to deliver the news.

She changed her focus to her friends to distract herself from thinking of losing Chhorn. She wanted to talk to her friends, but they all looked very tired. Leng and Chu were standing right behind her trying to stay awake.

"How is Mit Chhorn going to get home?" Leng asked.

Chhoy hadn't thought of that. They usually walked home back when they were allowed to. Chhorn couldn't even get up. Walking home was impossible. She was in deep thought when Mit Ra tapped her shoulder.

"Mit Chhorn is allowed to go home. There's an ox wagon coming this way at noon. She could try to ask them for a ride," she said.

"I will go tell her then," Chhoy said happily.

Chhoy ran back inside the temple and delivered the good news. Chhorn assured her she would be able to walk and hoped the ox wagon would arrive as they said. Chhoy ran back outside, not looking forward for another day of grueling work. She would be digging the canal all day again. She wanted to report sick, but she would not get anything to eat.

When she returned to line, Ah Nee whispered, "You missed the good news. We don't have to dig the canal anymore. They said we were too slow, and they have recruited more adults to do our jobs. We will help the adults clear out the grass around the rice field instead."

"That's much better," Chhoy said with relief. "Digging the canal was tiring. I feel like I'm going to die every day."

CHAPTER 12

Chhom poured all her share of rice porridge into Pech's bowl. Pech had just recovered from his illness, and she wanted to make sure he got well fast. Plus, he ate a lot. Chhom was hoping to find something to eat later in the day. It was getting difficult to find food near the end of the dry season. The river had been dried out completely until the last few days of rain had brought back a small stream. According to the adults, the river should have never been dry like this no matter what season. They believed a dam of some sort must have been built to stop the water. The river was no longer a feasible place for Chhom and Mother to find food. The vegetables were very difficult to find. Only certain types of water spinach grew in this condition. Instead, Chhom trekked around the rice paddies side of the village. She carries a small stick poking the crevices of the earth, underneath the rocks and logs, around termite hills and trees for edible animals. She had caught small lizards and salamanders and saved them in her pockets. Unlike crabs and frogs, these animals were small and fast.

She walked further into the open field and encountered a flock of quails feeding on a rice paddy. She charged them with her stick. The quails took off almost immediately. She noticed the quails had large bodies and small wings. They flew very low to the ground and landed almost immediately. She thought it would be possible to catch them. If she could be faster and stealthier, she probably could catch the quails. She wonders what the quail taste like. Then she pictured a small version of roast chicken. It made her even hungrier. She dismissed the thought immediately.

Chhom continued to walk and came across several trees with thick leaves and low-hanging branches. She searched the ground below the trees and found nothing but animal droppings. She began to feel despair for not finding any more food except the tiny lizards and the salamander. Then she caught a slight movement from the corner of her eye. She focused her eyes on the movement and saw a cluster of bats hanging upside down below tree branches. Her hands were trembling form excitement. She sneaked quietly toward the bats and struck the bats with her sticks multiple times as fast as she could, not quite sure if she even hit the bats or just the leaves. She stopped when all the bats flew off. She began to search for the bats on the ground. She was almost certain that she'd struck at least one of them. A dozen feet away, she saw several bats lying lifelessly on the ground. She walked over and picked up the bats and tucked them in her clothes. She didn't want anyone to see them, especially the Schlopes. They might harass her and take the bats from her. Chhom was excited to learn that the bats sleep during daytime. She would come back tomorrow hoping they'd return to sleep on the same tree.

Chhom returned home quickly and cooked the bats for all of us. For some reason, Tien and Mao were not with us today. Only Pech and I were home. Chhom returned the next morning, hoping the bats would return. As she walked, she tried to figure out a way to catch more bats without provoking the entire nest. On the way there, she came across another flock of quails, probably the same quails she saw yesterday. She crouched down and moved stealthily toward the quails, then hurled her stick. Unfortunately, the stick flew and spun in the air and landed just inches away from one of the quails. The entire flock flew off almost immediately. Chhom was disappointed that she didn't hit any quail, but it was very close. She believed it was possible if she was able to get closer and get a better aim. She continued to walk and arrived at the tree where the bats slept. She sneaked closer to the tree and scanned around the tree branches. She was thrilled to see the bats had returned. She had decided not to use her stick. Instead, she crept closer and reached her hand. Quietly, she uses her finger to grab a bat by its neck and squeezed it. The bat died instantly without making any noise. Chhom eagerly repeated the same method and picked about a dozen bats until she stepped on a twig and aroused all the bats from their sleep. All the bats flew off instantly.

Chhom returned every day for nearly four weeks to catch the bats until there was not a single bat left. Each trip she came across the flocks of quails and attempted to hurl the stick. She managed to strike the quails a few times and caught them while they were still struggling to fly. She discovered that quails were over three times larger than the bats, and their meat was much tastier.

After the bats were gone, Chhom had no choice but to go after the quails. She was getting stealthier and better with aiming the stick, but it was still very difficult to get them. She had managed to catch a quail almost every other day. She missed the river. She preferred catching the frogs and crabs instead. Sometimes, she had to walk two to three villages away paying close attention to the sun to make sure she returned home on time to take us to line up for lunch. It was fortunate that Mother was the cook and worked near the house. There were a few times when she went too far and returned home too late for lunch. Mother angrily gathered us to line up for lunch herself.

Each day, after feeding Pech and me, Chhom wasted no time and continued to search for food. The catches were never enough to subdue our hunger, but it was enough for us to live another day. There were many times when she returned home empty-handed. Our meal for the day was a couple of spoons of rice. Sometimes, Mother managed to bring home some water spinaches and amaranths. Pech was getting taller very quickly. He ate more water spinach than Chhom and I combined. His stomach inflated like a balloon. The rest of his body was nothing but skin and bones. Pech began to talk a little using mostly the words to get food. He was sick most of the time. He would either get a high fever or diarrhea. This might explain why he had a grumpy face and cried all the time. He was known to have a bad temper. He was not afraid to talk back to the adults when they teased him. There was a man known as Pu Kuem. Somehow, he was very chubby. He was the only one around that was chubby. He lived alone, not too far from our house. He came by our house very often to chat with Mother and the next-door neighbors. Everyone was happy to see him, hoping he would tell his secret about how he found his food.

"Hey, the Depressing One! What are you crying about today?" Pu Kuem said teasingly.

"Mother, chop Ah Kuem to make spicy and sour soup" Pech said pointing to Pu Kuem and then continued to cry.

Everyone, including Mother, couldn't help but laugh. Pu Kuem unsuccessfully tried to hide his anger by laughing along, but there was no amusement in his face. It was beyond insulting to call an adult with the prefix Ah.

"Ah Pech, don't call him that. It's very rude," Mother said and tried to hold her laugh. "Mit Kuem, he's very mean when he's mad."

"That's all right, Mit Yorn. I don't blame him for wanting to eat me because I have a lot of meat," he said proudly, patting his belly with one hand.

"The Depressing One, stop crying or I will call the monster to come eat you!" Pu Kuem continued to tease Pech.

Pech was scared of the monster; he cried even louder and ran to Mother. Tugging on Mother's sarong, he pointed to Pu Kuem and said, "Mother, cut Pu Kuem and make spicy and sour soup. Mea, cut him."

Everyone was in tears, laughing. Pu Kuem was a little satisfied that he'd scared Pech. But he still looked angry at the fact that Mother did not chastise Pech enough.

"And you there!" Pu Kuem pointed at me.

"You look exactly like your Father. I should call you The Breeder."

I was too curious to see how a man could be so chubby when there was barely anything to eat. I couldn't help looking at his chubby round face and his bulging belly.

"What are you looking at? Are you looking at my belly? Do you want to eat me too? You don't look depressing like your brother. Your new name, The Breeder, fits you."

I was afraid he would pick on me and call the monster on me, so I smiled and walked away. I didn't cry as much as Pech, but I did cry some of the time. I cried when I wanted to stay close to Mother. I felt very comfortable and safe when I was next to her.

Besides the brief socializing after work, the entire village was living under starvation. Over the past two years, hunger had consumed the minds of everyone. The urge to eat to fulfill the hunger kept many people from everything else that was once important to them, such as affection and purpose. It was common to hear our neighbors argue among their family members over food or spot a mother or father eating their children's share. The children were upset with their parents for not splitting the food equally between siblings. To make the matters worse, parents were away at work all day, leaving the toddlers home alone to care for themselves. The family bonding time was nearly nonexistent. Any small conflicts could easily build animosity among family members. Many small children were forgotten. Gradually, nearly everyone was for out only for themselves, even some toddlers.

There was a little girl around the age of three. She stayed home by herself when her mother went to work. The girl was usually wandering around the house alone. The rumor from the neighbors was that her Mother ate most of her share. My Mother brought her to our house for supper when she had extra food. It became more and more difficult to help her when food became very scarce. Offering her food meant less food for us. Mother had invited her less and less frequently, and it was a painful decision to see her starve. She had passed away a few weeks ago of starvation and illness. Mother wept every time she thought of the little girl and blamed herself for her death.

Malnutrition caused sickness across the villages. Mother used to nurse the sick in Takeo by collecting well-known herbs and tree bark for medicine. In this village, it was different. She was not familiar with the native herbs and trees except for the coconut and few types of tree bark. Mother was overwhelmed by the number of sick children and overcome with despair for not having the medicine or food. In some cases, the illnesses were well treatable if the medicine was available, or maybe even a bowl of hot rice porridge. In most cases, she was unable to help; she could only watch as they died. Every death was painful for her. She mourned secretly with the family and helped them with proper burial.

It was late afternoon. Chhom was just finishing washing me, Pech, Tien, and Mao at the dwindled river. Chhom was holding Pech on one side of her waist and holding Mao's hand as she walked slowly toward our house. Mao was slight older than Pech. Tien was about a year younger than me. According to Mother, Chhom was now around ten.

Tien and I were walking right behind Chhom, examining trees and small bush for any sign of edible fruits or insects. I was holding a frog that I'd caught between the crevices of the dried mud. I had been observing Chhom catching frogs when she took us to the river. We thought the frogs had all disappeared until we saw a girl about Chhom's age digging a den with a stick and pulling out a large frog deep within the mud. Chhom began to search for the frogs in the mud immediately after she saw how the girl did it. I found it fun and began to do it too. Chhom warned me a couple times not to stick my hand in the mud, as she feared it might not just be frogs living in the mud. It could be poisonous snakes a well.

Chhom put Mao on the ground and walked stealthily toward the banana trees. She reached over to one of the short banana trees and squeezed the newly-gown leaf that was still coiled in conifer shape. Then I heard a short, loud shriek from the banana leaf. Chhom stuck her hand in the coiled leaf and then pulled out a small bat.

It was like magic to me. I went to the shorter banana leaf and stuck my hand in the coiled leaf. A bat flew out the instant my hand touches the leaf. I leaped backward with fright.

"You wasted a bat. You should have let me do it. Next time, don't do that. The bat will bite you," Chhom scolded.

Chhom shoved the bat in her pocket and continued to walk us home.

"Scorpion!" Tien yelled in excitement.

I saw a black scorpion crawling across our path. I grabbed a stick and pinned down the tail and ripped the stinger off. I picked it up with caution, not to get pinched by its claws. I handed the scorpion to Tien because he was the one who saw it first. I knew Tien would not allow me keep what belonged to him. He would scream until my ears hurt. Besides, I already had two frogs in my hand.

We reached the house, looking forward for Chhom cooking us the food that we'd caught. When we stepped in the house, we saw Mother weeping softly. She had a scarf caped down from her neck and used it to wipes her tears.

It was scary to see her weep. Normally, she wept when someone passed away. This must be serious. Since she was secretly known as the healer, she cried every time her patient passed away. She would come home and sit in the corner of the house and weep. Mother appeared tired, drained, and in despair. Chhom was afraid to ask. She might not like the news.

"Don't tell anyone I cried," Mother said.

Crying was prohibited by the government. Crying indicated excessive care for another person when everyone should be equal.

"Chhorn is very ill. She has been transported by the ox wagon. She's being dropped off at Wat Samdach. Go see your sister. Leave your brothers here. I can't go. I have to finish my tasks," Mother explained.

Chhom nearly dropped Pech off her waist when she heard the news. She hadn't seen Chhorn much, and now she was dying. She tossed all her catches near the hearth.

"Then, Mother, can you roast these for them to eat?" Chhom asked.

"I will feed them for you," Mother replied

Chhom ran outside the house back to the river toward the bridge. She stopped just before the bridge to catch her breath. She felt light-headed and nearly collapsed; she hadn't eaten anything since last night. Too tired to run, Chhom began to walk at a fast pace. The thought of Chhorn dying made her want to run.

After she crossed the bridge, she entered a building that was once a temple currently being used as a hospital. Inside, she saw nearly one hundred sick people lying on the floor. They were mostly children. There seemed to be only one elder woman to care for all of them. She was busy caring for a young boy who was crying very loudly. Most of them were lying still as if they were in the verge of death. Chhom's eyes bounced around from one person to another expecting Chhorn to look back and call her name. She started from the first person on the left and until the last person on the right to make sure she didn't miss anybody. There was no sign of Chhorn. Maybe she'd passed away before she arrived. Chhom's heart was pounding from the thought. She stepped closer, inspecting the girls starting from the opposite end. The first girl was about five years of age, so she didn't bother inspecting. The second girl was too thin and too dark to be Chhorn. As she was about to check the third girl, the second girl moved her head slightly exposing more of her face. She knelt down and lifted the long hair covering the side her face.

"Is this Chhorn?" Chhom asked.

There was a slight nod from the girl. "It's me, Chhorn," She whispered and turned her face slowly to Chhom. Chhom nearly cried when she saw how skinny Chhorn was. Her face was swollen and sweaty.

"There is no hope for me. I might not make it. Don't waste too much time on me. Just make sure you help Mother take care of your brothers," Chhorn said softly with great effort.

"Don't say that. It might come true. I will make you something to eat," Chhom said.

"You don't have too. Don't waste your energy. I'm going to die anyway," Chhorn insisted.

Chhom got up and marched out the door. She walked down the river across the worn path from the Wat Samdach. She picked the water spinaches and the lotus that were once abundant but now found randomly among other inedible plants. After she collected a bundle of each, she started searching for frogs. The frogs were now living deep in the mud. Chhom stuck her hands in the dens hoping she would find frogs and not snakes. She had never encountered snakes in the muddy holes before, but she could never get rid of the thoughts. After fishing through a dozen of holes, she caught one frog slightly larger than her fist.

She got out of the dry river and ran across the bridge. She was very tired, but she didn't care. She wanted to get back home and cook for Chhorn. She could pass away anytime if she didn't hurry.

It's suppertime. Mother was serving the villagers and took me and Pech with her. Chhom thought this was a perfect opportunity when everyone was at the dining hall. She started the fire using the burning wood in the hearth. She made a simple frog soup with water spinach. She also added some saltwater that Mother disguised as the drinking water. She wished she has some rice grain to add to the soup. She still had handful of fresh water spinaches in case Chhorn wanted to eat them raw.

When the soup was done, Chhom strode across the bridge cautiously to avoid attracting attention. If she got harassed by the Schlopes, they might take her soup away. The hope for Chhorn's life would be over, and she would live in regret forever. She believed that all Chhorn needed was food. Besides, if she died, she would at least die with food in her stomach.

Chhom arrived at the Wat Samdach safely. She placed the soup gently to the side of where Chhorn was lying.

"Chhorn. Here, I made you soup. It has vegetables and a frog. I put some salt in as well. You will like it," Chhom said.

Salt was scarce. It was rarely used in public cooking.

"Don't waste it. I'm going to die anyway. Eat it yourself or share with Pech and Bun," Chhorn said weakly.

"Eat it. It will make you feel better," Chhom said. She remembered Mother usually said that to her patients.

"I'm not eating. You are so skinny yourself. You have already wasted so much energy on me. Eat it yourself."

Chhom paused for a moment and said, "Are you going to eat or not? I spent so much time searching for food. I missed supper, so I could make food for you."

"I don't want to put a burden on you," Chhorn insisted.

"Are you going to eat or not?" Chhom said out loud.

Chhorn didn't reply. Chhom looked around and grabbed a handful of fresh vegetables beside the pot and whacked Chhorn on the head.

"You want to die that much? I'm going to kill you myself!" Chhom screamed and continued to whack Chhorn's head with the vegetables.

"I'll eat! I'll eat! You will kill me if you continue to hit me like that," Chhorn said submissively.

Chhom stopped hitting her and wept, feeling angry and guilty for being out of control.

Chhorn struggled to feed herself while lying down. She grabbed the spoon that Chhom laid on one side of the bowl and scooped the soup and took a sip. She was surprised by the delightful taste. She took another sip…then another…then she ate the frog meat and vegetables.

Chhom sat and stared at Chhorn eating her soup, concerned that Chhorn would burn her mouth eating too fast.

In minutes, Chhorn seemed to have so much energy. She sat up and grabbed the whole bundle of roasted water spinaches and devoured them. Then she grabbed the fresh water spinaches and munched.

After she finished eating, she took a big breath and wiped the sweat off her forehead and said, "The soup was delicious. I felt so much better now. I don't think I was sick, I was just starving. I think I can go home now."

Chhom was thrilled and broke out laughing. Then she cried and laughed at the same time.

"Let's go home then," Chhom said as she picked up the bowl and the scarf. "Do you need my help to walk you?"

"Nope, I'm fine. I can walk on my own."

"Follow me then."

The woman who was nursing the children stood frozen staring at Chhorn walk like she had never been sick.

"Mit, you were not sick?" the women asked.

"I was sick, but I'm well now. My baby sister gave me medicine, a good one. I'm leaving!" Chhorn informed her happily.

"All right, then," the woman responded.

Chhom happily lead the way home. Chhorn followed, looking around the surroundings. She was very happy to be well and even happier to be at the home village.

"How come it's so quiet?" Chhorn asked, hoping for a good answer.

"It's suppertime. Everyone is at the dining hall."

"Does that mean you missed your supper?"

"Yeah, but that's all right. I can find something to eat."

Chhorn was impressed by how Chhom had changed. She sounded grown up and confident. She was only around ten years old. She felt like she was missing out seeing her growing.

They walked across the bridge and slipped in the house without being noticed. Mother arrived moments later. "Chhorn, is that you?" Mother asked.

"Yes, it's me."

"Are you all right?"

"After a bowl of soup and a harsh medicine, I'm fine," Chhorn said as she turned to Chhom smiling.

"She didn't want to eat at first. I had to whack her on the head with the water spinach. If you don't like the cold medicine from me, I will give you a harsh medicine," Chhom said using the Khmer cliché.

Mother laughed. "I have such a mean daughter."

"If I wasn't mean, she would be dead."

"You are right. If you didn't force me to eat, I would be dead," Chhorn said in agreement.

"Stay here another day and pretend you are sick. I will give you my share of rice porridge," Mother said.

"What are you going to eat then?" Chhorn reply.

"They assigned me to feed a pig and chickens. I asked to take the water that I use to wash the rice home to feed the pig. I took the water along with a few grains of rice home," Mother explained.

"They didn't say anything when there was some rice in the water?" Chhorn asked.

"The water was very murky. They cannot see the rice at the bottom. Plus, it's not much. Only a few rice grains are all I need. If I get caught with too much rice, I'm as good as dead," Mother added.

"And don't worry about me. Besides, I will find you food to eat. I catch frogs and pick vegetables every day. You can watch your brothers while I go find the food."

"Then I will stay. I want to see Pech and Bun. I have not seen them for months. Speaking of them, where are they?"

"They are outside the house running around. Pech is sick every day. He has no meat but skin and bones. He eats like a pig, but he never gains any meat," Mother said.

Chhorn walked to the front door and found us playing on the other side of the house. The kids from the neighbors were walking toward us, looking for someone to play with. There used to be a lot more children around my age long ago. They disappeared one by one each week. Many had died of sickness.

"My little brothers are so skinny," Chhorn said sadly. "I wish I could bring rice for them to eat. Look at Pech. His stomach is inflated like a balloon."

"I don't know, but I think he got a worm in his stomach. He eats a lot too. He could finish a basket full of water spinach in one sitting."

"Where are the cats?"

"She's still around. She doesn't come out that much during day-time. I feel so bad for her. All her first kittens disappeared. She had more kittens, and they all disappeared too. I'm sure that they were eaten. She's the lucky one. I don't know how she could sneak around without getting caught," Chhom explained.

"Does she still bring food home?" Chhorn asked.

"Nearly every night. She is so smart. Without her, who knows how Bun would be. All he eats is meat. You just watch, if Me-Leak doesn't bring food for one night, he will cry until morning." Chhom said.

"She's a three-colored cat. They are all like that," Chhorn said.

"Hey, Chhorn. Don't stay outside too long. If they see you staying home well and healthy, they might question you. Get back in before they see you," Mother warned.

Chhorn appeared very happy to be home again. She kept inside the house, afraid to be seen. Chhom asked her to watch us, and she left to search for food. Chhorn stay for one whole day and walked back to her compound in the evening.

The sun had dipped behind the trees and houses but was still casting the yellowish radiance. Mother was lying down inside the house after a long of hard work. I was playing with Pech near the warehouse. Just when I was about to run to the river, I saw Chhom from a distance, holding a handful of food. I was hungry and curious to find out what she had. Peach was closer to her and ran after her. Before I could make it in the house, Chhom was already walking out of the house still holding the food. I wanted to be the first person to get what she had to eat. The first person normally got better things. When I got closer, I was surprised to see that Chhom was not cooking the food. Instead, she walked out the door and still had the food in her hands. She normally tossed the food in the fire and shared with us.

I followed her. Then I saw something drop from her hand to the ground and roll under the house. Pech normally would chase after the food and pops it in his mouth. For some reason, he didn't even bother looking at the loose food. I was very sure he saw it too.

I ran to investigate. I crouched and tilted my head, peaking under the stairs and found what looked like a mushroom lying under the house. I crouched and walked under the house and picked the mushroom up. I was happy that no one bothered trying to fight for it. Not even Pech, who ate a lot more than I. But he was right behind me like a spy. He seemed to know something that I didn't.

"Pech, follow me. I'm going to roast this mushroom."

"Don't," Pech said. Pech wanted to explain something to me, but he didn't know the word.

"Follow me if you want half," I said and ran toward the dining hall.

Pech followed me. I knew of a place to get some fire. The dining hall was just a short walk away. I had been watching Mother cook food for the horde nearly every day. She didn't put out the fire. Children usually used the fire to cook their frogs and insects after lunch and supper.

"What are you up to, Bun and Pech?" the lady named K'Oeun asked. She was bathing with a bucket of water beside her house.

"I found a mushroom. I'm going to roast it and eat it," I replied.

"Are you sure it's not poisonous?" she asked out loud.

"No!" I replied loudly.

I continued to walk toward the dining hall. I could see slight smoke rising from a distance. I was happy that the fire was still alive and no one was there to bother me. I picked up a small twig and poked it in the mushroom. I squatted in front of the hearth and dipped the mushroom into the leftover fire, hoping it would cook. Pech was right behind me behaving very bizarrely. He didn't seem to like what I was doing. I waited for a few minutes and then took the mushroom out from the fire. I split the mushroom in half. I handed half to Pech and popped the half in my mouth. It tasted almost like any mushroom that I had eaten before, but this one had a very strong, woody aftertaste. My nostrils were filled with the lingering smell of mud and rotten tree.

"Mother! Bun ate mushroom. Mother!" Instead of eating it, Pech hollered and dashed toward home with the mushroom in his hand. I didn't know that Mother had forbidden us to eat the mushroom. If she found out, I'd get whipped. After pausing for a moment, I started to run after Pech, hoping to catch him before he reached Mother.

Pech got home before I caught up with him. I was about to reach the stairs when Pech was inside the house yelling, "Mother, Bun ate mushroom! Bun ate mushroom! See! He ate this mushroom!" He lifted his hand up showing the mushroom that I offered him.

"He ate the mushroom? I thought I told Chhom to throw them away. How did he get it?"

Mother walked down the stairs looking very angry, "Bun, did you eat the mushroom?"

I was too scared to say anything, but Pech said loudly, "He ate it! He ate it! He gave some to me."

"Chhom, I thought I told you to throw them away. That was 'Pset Sonkung Kreal'! They are poisonous!"

"I threw it away. I don't know how he got it." Chhom was right behind me, looking terrified.

Mother ripped a branch off one of the shrubs nearby. She scraped all the leaves off with her fingers and began to walk toward me. She whipped me several times on my back and arms. I wailed so loud that all the kids in the area came and watched me cry.

All of a sudden, I had this strange feeling in my stomach. I thought because I cried too hard, my stomach was churning or maybe from being too scared of Mother. Then I began to vomit. Even though my eyes were full of tears, I noticed there was blood in the vomit. I also noticed the red lines across my arm. I looked closely and realized they were blood marks as if someone drew a line across my arm with red dye.

I expected a few more whips, but Mother stopped. She stooped down and examined my back and my arms.

"My son was poisoned! My son was poisoned!" She screamed out loud and picked me up off the ground. She held me in her arms, panicked. She started running down the hill toward the river. She was taking me to Wat Samdach. She needed to cross the river, but the bridge was too far to the left. Instead, she rushed downriver and walked across the small stream of water.

She came to a spot where the water was just below her shoulders. She lifts me up above her head and continued to walk. Everyone, mostly children, watched as Mother carried me cross the river.

After Mother carried me up the steep bank, she came across a Schlope about thirteen years of age carrying two buckets of water on his shoulders using the simple crafted rod called a dong raek.

"Mit! Mit! Help my son! He has been poisoned. Please pick me a coconut," Mother said frantically. She kneeled down on the ground from exhaustion still holding me in her arms.

Without asking a single question, the Schlope lowered the buckets to the ground instantly. One of the buckets flipped over and spilled all the water. He dropped his machete on the ground and climbed the nearby coconut tree skillfully using the scarf to help maneuver. When he got to the top of the tree, he yanked down two coconuts. The coconuts fell to the ground with a loud thud. Normally, only the authorized persons were allowed to climb and pick the coconuts; everyone else was prohibited. Most coconut trees were over fifty feet tall. Fortunately, this one was very short.

The Schlope carefully descended the coconut tree. He picked up the coconut from the ground and chopped the top part off with his machete.

"Here Mit, let him drink," the Schlope said, handing Mother the coconut.

I was conscious, but I felt like I was being eaten alive from the inside. Mother lifted my head up and tilted the coconut for me to drink. I drank every single drop of coconut juice. It was cold and delicious. After I finished, the Schlope gave me the second one. I drank the second one as fast as I did the first. I had not had coconut juice since we lived in Stung Chah. I didn't know it would taste this good. Either I forgot all about my pain, or I was well again. I felt so good and refreshed.

The Schlope cut the coconut in half and used his machete to scrape the pulp of the shell.

"Here, eat the pulp. Make sure to finish it all, and do not carry them back with you," the Schlope said, handing me the two halves of the coconut.

Mother understood that it was not a good idea to walk around holding a coconut. The Mit Chah might accuse her of stealing. Without Mother's assistance, I took the coconut and ate the pulp that was already scraped off the shell. I could still feel the pain in my stomach, but I didn't care. I continued to eat the coconut pulp.

"Mit, you should eat too. You are tired. Take this." The Schlope handed the coconut to Mother.

"I'm going take a few bites. I'm very tired. I have no energy to walk," Mother said.

The Schlope stepped aside and poured the water from the one bucket to the empty bucket that was spilled. He secured the machete on his waste with his scarf and hooked the bucket handle to the dong raek. He stooped down and then lifted the dong raek with his shoulder and resumed his trip.

Mother wanted to say "thank you," but it was extremely awkward to say such words to a Schlope. Instead, she said politely, "Then you may continue your trip. I will take my son back home."

"Then I must get going," he replied politely.

Mother took a bite of the coconut to show the Schlope that she was eating. Then she slipped the rest of the pulps in her pocket to bring home.

"Are you almost finished?" Mother asked.

I didn't say anything. I just showed her the coconut that I was eating. I'd eaten all the lose pulp, but I was still picking at the pulp that was stuck to the shell.

"That's good enough. Toss them away. We have to go before people see us eating coconut," Mother said.

Reluctantly, I tossed the coconut shell away. Mother and I walked across the bridge home. I still don't feel right, but I was glad to be alive and get to drink and eat the coconut.

"Next time, do not eat a mushroom on your own again, do you understand? Next time, I might not be able to help you, and you will die," Mother lectured.

I didn't reply but looked down as I walked beside her. The water looked very shallow from the bridge. The sunlight reflected as the water moved slowly down the stream. I could see our old footprints in the mud when Chhom took us to bathe and search for frogs and crabs.

When we arrived home, Mother gave Pech and Chhom the coconut pulp. Pech grabbed the coconut with two hands. He took a bite of the coconut and then jumped up and down with joy. He shoved the rest in his mouth when he saw mom had some more in her pocket, hoping to get some more. Mother gave Chhom a slice. Chhom finished the whole slice in one bite.

"Take another one," Mother handed another slice to Chhom.

"It's all right. Give them to Bun or Pech," Chhom said.

"Don't worry about Bun. He had one whole coconut all by himself. You eat it," Mom explained.

"Give that to Pech," Chhom said.

"I have another slice for him right here."

"How about you, Mother?"

"I had some also," Mother made it sound like she'd had a lot, but she only had a bite just to satisfy the Schlope.

Chhom took the slice and popped it in her mouth. Mother handed the other slice to Pech. He used two hands to hold the coconut pulp, afraid it might drop to the ground. He took small bites, taking his time to enjoy the taste, knowing that Mother didn't have any more, and he was in no rush to finish it.

Mother picked the small scraps of coconut that were in her pocket and ate them herself. She was very good at hiding her hunger. Chhom could never tell when Mother was hungry. Normally, Mother brought the food home, and often she saved it all for us. She didn't eat it herself. How she was able to survive without food was a mystery.

It took several days for me to feel better again. I was feeling hungry as usual. The taste of the coconut and the feeling of fullness seemed like a dream. Pech came down with an illness again and cried uncontrollably. Chhom assumed he was hungry for milk, and Mother had left town again.

"Chhom, what's the matter with him?" a man known as Pu Peap walked by and asked.

Pu Peap had been very close to our family. Probably Mother had been giving him food. He came to visit very often had long conversations with Mother and Tien's mom after work. He was dark and tall. He had also come very often to check on us when Mother was away. He used to be a teacher during Lon Nol's time. He told Chhom that knew of a lady who just had a baby that lived several blocks away. He told her the direction and suggested she ask her for milk.

Chhom left us all in the house and took Pech around the village seeking a nursing mother to get milk. Fortunately, despite such starving conditions, many nursing Mothers were usually not greedy when they had breast milk. Most were too malnourished to produce milk.

Chhom found the nursing lady, and Pech got fed. Chhom dropped Pech off at home after he got fed and left to seek food again. She went to search for more bats and quails but found nothing. She was heading home at nightfall empty-handed. She wanted to continue looking for food, but Mother had warned her not stay out too late after dark. She was very hungry, and she could imagine that we were as hungry as she was. She arrived home feeling very disappointed and tired. Then she saw Tien's mom and Phear's mom entering our house. It was common for people to come visit us, but not this late. From the activity of the visitors from a distance, Chhom could feel the presence of someone important coming to visit us.

When she reached the house, Tien's mom said, "Your Father is here. Go see him. He brought a lot of food for us."

When Chhom walked inside, there were more people inside our house, chatting with Mother. Some were holding a piece of meat. Some were holding a snakehead fish with two hands as if their life depended on it. They all smiled when they saw Chhom enter the house.

"Chhom is here," one of them said.

Father was lying down sleeping with one arm resting on his forehead. Chhom was glad to see Father, not only because she missed him but also because he always brought fish and other animals.

Everyone was glad to see him as well. Mother always shared the fish and animal meat with friends and neighbors.

"Your Father is here. He brought you fish. I made some soup for you and your brothers. They all have already eaten. I saved some for you in the pot," Mother said.

Chhom felt like the angels had come and rescued her. She couldn't help but smile from the overwhelming of joy. She looked at the small pot on the hearth that was waiting for her all along. Without saying a word, she walked toward the hearth. She grabbed a spoon, scooped the broth of the soup, and sipped. The soup was still warm. There were three chunks of snakehead fish and some water spinaches. Each chunk was three times the size of her wrist. She dug a spoon into the one of the pieces of fish and began eating. She shoved another chunk in her mouth before she finished chewing the other. She scooped the soup and sipped it when her mouth was already full of fish. She noticed Mother had also put some rice grains in the soup, and she could also taste the flavor of the salt.

"Eat normally! No one is going to take your food away. Your brothers and sisters are full," Tien's mom said, referring to Tien and Mao as well.

Chhom had not heard of word "full" for a long time, and the words seemed to be a myth. She'd forgotten how being full felt. Nothing could make her full.

"Be careful, or you will choke on the fish bones," Mother added.

Chhom turned around and found Mother, Tien's mom, and another lady were staring at her eating. After she felt confident that all the food belonged to her, she ate slowly.

"She just got back from searching for food for her little brothers and sister to eat. She looks very tired and hungry," Mother said.

"My niece has nothing but skin and bones. She works hard every day searching for food for her brothers and sisters and my two children," Tien's mom added. Although we were not blood related, Tien's mom referred to Chhom as her niece.

Chhom finished the soup in less than ten minutes. She ate all the fish meat and soup. She made sure there was not a single piece of fish meat left on the bones. A few of the small fish bones were stuck in her throat, but she didn't care. She dumped all the fish bones in the fire and lay next to us and dozed off. The sound of the adults' conversation didn't bother her.

"Meow! Meow!" Chhom woke up to the sound of Me-Laek. It must be close to morning by now. She had been sleeping for a long time.

When she opened her eyes, she saw Me-Laek sitting on its hind legs next to Mother as she was gutting a fish. The room was lit by a lantern that Mother placed near the cutting board. She could smell the burning of the fuel. Mother usually prepped food late at night to avoid any attention.

"Wait, I have to take the bone out for you. You might choke," Mother said to the cat and then tossed a piece of fish meat to her. The cat pinned the fish with her paws as if it was a rat and started biting from one end.

"I know you are hungry. I know how you feel, but you were luckier than I am. You could go around and find food at night. I can't. If I do that, they will kill me. Besides, you have three colors," Mother said.

Me-Laek finished the piece of fish meat, and she was pleading for more. As Mother was too busy removing the scale from the fish, she snatched the fish guts that Mother piled next to cutting board and ran to the corner of the house. After she insured that she was safe to eat, she pinned the fish guts with her paws and started biting on one end. Mother hadn't planned to throw the fish guts away. She usually cleaned them with water and cut them up into small pieces to make soup.

I woke up from light and from the sound of Mother scaling the fish. I sat up and began looking for Father. I hadn't seen him in months. I didn't think of him that much, but somehow I felt very comfortable and excited when he was around.

"Where is Father?" I asked.

"Why are you awake?" Mother asked. "Your Father is outside smoking."

I walked to the front door looking for Father. I felt a gust of cool wind brushing my face. Father was sitting on the stairway smoking. I walked down the stairs and sat right in front of him trying to get his attention. He looked at me but did not say a word and continued to puff on his hand-rolled cigar. I looked up in the sky. It was clear and beautiful and full of stars. The moon was round and bright.

Then Chhom came and sat by the doorway. "So many stars," Chhom said.

Father made a big puff and said, "Those are the Crocodile Stars."

"Where are the Crocodile Stars?" I asked.

"Over there," he pointed.

I had never seen a crocodile before and did not know what they looked like. There were too many stars in the sky, and they all looked the same except some were bigger and brighter than others. Father pointed to the other stars and told us their names. Chhom seemed to identify them quickly while I was still searching for the Crocodile Stars.

Father took the last puff of his hand-rolled cigarette and tossed the butt away. He sat silently for a few minutes and then began to make a high-pitch musical sound from his mouth.

"What is that?" I asked.

"He's whistling," Chhom answered.

"How do you do that?" I asked.

"You have to practice," Chhom answered.

Father stared at the stars and continued to whistle a beautiful tune. He changed from one tune to another. I really wanted to whistle just like him. I peeked over his face to see how he did it. Then I protruded my lip the same way he did it. Nothing but air and spit came out. I tried over and over again until I produced a faint sound.

Father stopped whistling. He appeared to be listening to me trying to whistle instead. I tried and tried until my mouth and tongue were sore. I finally stopped when I thought I wasn't making any more progress. I was happy that I was able to make some sound but would try again tomorrow.

"Go to sleep. It's very late," Father said.

Chhom and I reluctantly walked back in to sleep. Not only it was beautiful outside but we'd gotten to spend time with Father.

CHAPTER 13

Chhom woke up in the morning to the sound of Pech, Tien, and Mao playing. I was still asleep from staying up too late. She noticed the smell of the fish soup. She remembered Father had brought a lot of fish last night, and Mother probably made some more this morning. She gazed at the pot sitting on the hearth. She sat up quickly and crawled toward the pot. She opened the pot and grinned when she saw chunks of fish. Her stomach growled, begging for food. Chhom grabbed a bowl and a scooper. Her hands were trembling with anticipation to eat the soup. She noticed there were rice grains in the soup as well. Mother would normally not use too much rice, as she tried to save them for an emergency. Father must have brought the rice from Tuel Snai or traded his fish along the way home. She didn't bother checking if we'd already eaten or not. Father brought enough fish for us to last several days, and she dismissed the thought of having to feed us. She wanted to not to have to worry about us for once and feed herself, somewhere outside, alone.

When Chhom was about to walk out of the house with a bowl of soup, she saw a bottle of yellowish liquid beside and lantern. This must be the fish sauce that people talked about a lot. Mother used to talk about using fish sauce a lot to cook during Lon Nol's time. Rumor had it that fish sauce was the greatest thing to add to rice porridge or soup. Not only did it contain salt, but it was made from fish and smelled good. Chhom picked up the bottle and looked around to make sure no one was looking and then started pouring the liquid in her bowl. She'd never had fish sauce before; thus, she didn't know what the fish sauce should smell or taste like.

I woke up and focused my eyes. I saw Chhom sealing the bottle with a cork and carefully placing the bottle on the floor next to the lantern. She carried her bowl and carefully slipped out the house. The bottle caught my attention. I crawled over to the bottle. The liquid in the bottle was just about four inches from the neck. I put my nose closer to the bottle and then to the lantern. The lantern had a similar scent but mixed with a burned smell.

I wasn't interested in the liquid, so I walked outside. Father was sitting on a small hill next to our house, smoking his cigarette. He gazed far away to the horizon, beyond the rice field. The tall rice plants fluttered in the wind. Father did not realize I was here next to him. I followed his gaze, far away where the contour of mountains and tall coconut trees connected to the sky. It made me wonder how far you had to walk until the earth and the sky met. Some coconut trees stood as if they were taller than the mountains. There were more coconut trees scattering everywhere. The closer they were, the taller they appeared. The scenery took my breath away. It felt so good just to stare at the horizon. I wished I could walk there and climb those mountains.

Father took the last puff from his cigarette then tossed the butt away. I had seen him roll cigarettes before, but I didn't know what they were or why he smoked. Suddenly, he began to whistle again, but this time he made a flute-like tune. I knew the flute well. Months ago, someone played the flute just before midnight. It sounds so pleasing and sad at the same time.

"Father, how do you do that?"

"Whistle, then flick your tongue back and forth very quickly," he replied.

I practiced last night and was able to produce some sound, but nothing compared to Father's.

"Like this," Father replied and started to whistle again.

It sounded so pleasant. I wanted to learn how to whistle and do the flute-like sound. I curled my lips and pushed them out like Father did and tried. I made a faint sound for a few seconds then the sound vanished. I tried and tried, but no musical sound came out of my lips except air and saliva.

Father walked back inside the house. I had the whole hill to myself. I sat on top of the hill and continued to practice my whistle. After a while, my entire mouth was sore. I gave up trying to whistle. I was about to get off the hill and join Tien and Pech when I saw someone's head emerge from behind a tree in the distance. It looked like Chhom. I was curious and began to run closer. About halfway there, I recognized that it was really Chhom. She was vomiting and seemed to be hiding at the same time. I knew exactly how she felt. I remembered well from the experience after eating the poisonous mushroom.

When she noticed my presence, she lifted her right hand up to stop me from approaching. She could not speak. She put both hands on her stomach as she arched her back and continued to vomit. She stopped for a moment and then continued to gag and vomit again. She seemed not to want me around, so I turned around and started walking back home, afraid I would get yelled at.

"Bun, do not eat the thing inside the bottle. I think it's for the lantern. It's some type of fuel. If you eat it, you might get poisoned like you did with the mushroom," Chhom warned. "I ate some earlier. Don't tell Mother that."

I didn't reply, as I was still confused what she was trying to say or what the thing was. I simply returned home to join Pech, Tien, and Mao.

Not too far away, several of the neighboring children were talking. They were about a year or two older than I was. I ran straight toward them.

"What were you guys doing?" I asked.

"You see that man over there?" The boy pointed to the house just past the cafeteria. "He's new. He came from somewhere. He had been sharping his machetes and axes for an hour. He doesn't work, and he doesn't have any chickens. What do you think he does with his machetes and his axes?"

"To hack people," I replied.

"Yep. That's what he does with them," another boy confirmed.

"Why does he hack people?" a young girl among the group asked.

"To eat, of course," I replied with confidence. Several days ago, I heard similar conversation among another group of kids. One of them was absolutely sure the man ate human organs.

Another boy cut in, "They don't eat human meat. They eat their hearts and livers. I walked close to him yesterday. His eyes were not human. They were all red like a demon's. I heard my Mother say these demons are called the Nearadey. They are new here."

I believed every word the boy said. I saw a few of those people myself when I was eating at the dining hall. They were different and scary. Every kid about my age and older noticed the newcomers. I came back and passed the scary news to Tien and Pech. Pech didn't seem to pay attention to what I said, but Tien wanted to know more. Tien always paid attention to what I said and believed every single word.

I had been listing to Pu Peap and Mother having conversations many times. Pu Peap was a smart man. He seemed to know everything. He said he listened to this thing called "radio." One of the Mit Chah living next-door to him turned it on all the time. Pu Peap would secretly eavesdrop from his house and share what he learned with Mother and Tien's mom. It was fun to share information with other children. Surprisingly, they had learned the same thing from their parents. The rumor was the newcomers were called the Nearadey. It stood for "Southeast district of the Kampuchea." Takeo, our family hometown, was among the towns within the Nearadey part of the country. It was also the same city where K'Oeun and Ta Watt were from as well. I had not heard any rumors about K'Oeun and Ta Watt killing anyone, but something about them was not right.

More to the news, the Vietnamese were invading form the Southeast, causing the Nearadey to flee all over the country. The Nearadeys were known as a stem of the new government, and they despised the previous society more than anyone else. They arrived in large numbers fully armed. Secretly, they took over the local leaders known as Peayaup. The Peayaup had been disappearing one by one since the day the Nearadey arrived. No one had witnessed anything until a big call for a meeting at Wat Samdach a few weeks before. Only the local Mit Chahs, the Peayaup personnel, were invited. No one ever saw a single one of them return from the meeting.

Later in the evening, Chhom took us to eat supper, and then we came back to play until nightfall. She didn't spend too much time searching for food. She just picked some water spinaches and then came back because she wanted to see Father. We had more visitors asking for more fish, but Mother told them we only had a little left to feed us. Later in the night, all the guests left. It was just us.

"Puk Vea, we only have a little fish left, just enough for the next two days. I gave most of them away. What were we going to do? I feel bad for the children of those families. Every time I see the parents' faces, I can also see their dying children," Mother explained, hoping Father didn't scold her for giving the fish away.

"I don't know. I didn't tell you to give them away. You are pregnant. You will need to eat a lot," Father replied.

"Like Tien's mom, she is like our sister. Chok and Phon are your cousins. The rest of the families have dying children. If I don't give them some food, they will all die," Mother said.

"I don't know," Father replied. "Maybe have Chhom come to my place tomorrow. I will find some fish for her. But make sure she leaves early in the morning. It will take all day to get there."

"I'll go," Chhom said happily.

"By yourself?" Mother asked. "Do you know the way there?"

"I have walked that way once seeking food and almost reached his place, but I think I can find the rest of the way." Chhom said.

"All right, then. Wake up early tomorrow. I want you to get there before dark," Mother said.

Pech fell asleep. Chhom and I were lying down still listing to Father and Mother talk. Father was leaving tonight.

"Puk Vea, a lot of the new members of the government have arrived," Mother whispered. "These people are not the same as the previous government. Most of them are the elder single men and some women. They don't talk much. One of them is named Ta Kurk, and the other one is named Ta Nuy. They took over the houses owned by the previous leaders. No one knows exactly what happened to the previous leaders. Every time I look over at their houses, I saw them sharpening their machetes or their axes. That's all they do all day. And one more thing, there were two people in my group that were escorted away two days ago and never returned," Mother added.

"Maybe they took them to live in different location," Father said.

"I would hope so. And you know what else? They get along with K'Oeun well. They were from Takeo for sure. I'm glad K'Oeun seems to like me. I hope it stays that way."

"How do you know she likes you?" Father asked.

"She doesn't scold or threaten me. She's helped me get away with nearly everything."

"That is good, but you must continue to be cautious. I don't trust these people. By the way, where did you get all the rice?" Father asked.

"I stole it. I pretend to take the water I use to wash the rice to feed to the pig and hide some rice under the water. Then I chop the water spinach and other vegetables and put them right on top," Mother explained.

Mother continued to feed the pig and the chickens that she responsible for. Each day before she left work, she informed her leader that she would use the water that she used to wash the rice with some vegetable to feed the pig. When she got home, she took out the vegetables and poured the bucket in a basket to drain the water. Then she spread the rice grains around the basket. She hid the basket on the ceiling allowing the rice to dry out. She didn't cook all the rice at once. She saved it for later.

Father returned to Tuel Snai shortly after the conversation with Mother. He traveled at night to avoid being seen and questioned. He carried a pass given by his town to allow him to visit home. He had to get to Tuol Snai soon to catch fish for Chhom.

Mother woke Chhom up before the sunrise and gave her a brown bucket that she used to filter the rice water. The handle of the bucket had broken off. It was safe for children to carry a bucket around. The adults could only use them during work. Chhom began to walk along the wagon path that ran along the river. This would be a long trip. She wished she had a pair of sandals. Thorns and tree roots were everywhere. If she wasn't careful, she could step on poisonous thorns. She had tripped over roots and rocks before and nearly broke her toes. Sometimes, her toenails would rip off completely.

It was still a little dark. The adults must have been awake, but Chhom hadn't seen a single person on the road yet. Further ahead, the rice paddies sprawled on the right side of the road. Some of the rice had just begun to bloom. They were in the pregnant stage, where the stalks were still soft and the buds were bulging. When she got closer, she looked around to make sure no one was looking. She picked a handful of rice, including the stem, and shoved it in her mouth. The husks and the stalks were soft like fresh green grass. It was like eating grass except the rice buds offered her a nutty taste. If she got caught eating the rice, she would be punished, possibly executed on the spot, especially with the Nearadey regime. She chewed and walked at the same time, wishing she had the real rice grains.

A moment later she came across a fruit tree call Put Treah. It was a well-known fruit tree that grew throughout Kampuchea. The tree was short but thorny. She didn't bother searching for fruit, as the tree grew right on the roadside. Everyone that passed by would have picked the fruit. Instead, she picked the round-shaped bugs the size of her pinky. She ripped the heads off and popped them in her mouth. Every Put Treah tree had these bugs. Not everyone knew about the bugs though. They offered a delicious creamy taste. She picked and ate all she could find, but she was still hungry. Then her attention turned to the red ants crawling up and down the tree. Not all ants were edible, but the ones known as Ankrong were edible. Ankrong lived in large armies like other ants, but they made a unique large nest to store their larvae. The Khmer didn't consider Ankrong as ants. The larvae were hard to get. The Ankrong normally made their nests high up the trees, and they were very aggressive when it came to protecting their larvae. They would not abandon their nests and would fight to the death.

Bong Chhhom searched for the nest and found it on the other side of the tree. She broke off the branch that held the nest. As expected, hundreds of Ankrongs bit her hands. Some had landed on her face and neck and began biting her. This time, Chhom didn't want the Ankrong. She just wanted the larvae. She started running and shook off the Ankrong from the nest and wiped them off her body. Every bite stung.

After she got nearly all the Ankrong off the nest and her body, she began walking slowly again. She picked and ate the Ankrongs that still managed to cling to the nest. After she ate all the Ankrong, she opened the nest and saw hundreds of precious larvae. She took her time picking and eating several larvae at a time.

The sun began to rise, giving off the bright and warm light. Chhom continued to trek along the wagon road picking other edible fruits and leaves. There were the ivies known as *Slug Knung* that grew along the road. Their leaves were green and purple and tasted sour. The Khmer normally would use them to add to the soup.

As the sun inched toward its summit, the day grew hotter. Chhom became tired and thirsty. She drank water along the river when she found convenient spots. She came across other travelers along the road. None of them wanted to acknowledge her. Like Chhom, they were very skinny, dark, and their clothes were ragged. Fortunately, they were not the Mit Chah, nor the Schlope, or the militia.

She arrived in Tuel Snai a little past noon. The province was known to have many random hills and clusters of trees called Snai. She came across dozens of workers and asked for the place that produced charcoal. Fortunately, every single one of them knew about the place. Father probably had provided them the fish and meat. She followed the simple directions and arrived in an isolated house surrounded by small farms. She saw an older man cooking on the open earth a dozen feet away from the house. The man was tall and dark. He noticed Chhom's presence and asked, "Are you the daughter of Chhay? Why are you here?"

"Yes, I'm his daughter. I came to see him," Chhom replied. She was wondering how he knew her.

"He will be here shortly," the man said.

Chhom was happy to see the hearth full of fire. She began looking for a stick.

"What are you looking for?" the man asked.

"I'm looking for a stick to cook the grasshoppers," Chhom replied.

"Keep them for later. Your Father will be here shortly. I'm making a thick rice porridge and a sour fish soup," the man said.

The saliva squirted in her mouth when she heard the words "sour fish soup." She sat and waited. She looked around the area. The name of the village matched the surrounding well. There were hills everywhere she turned, and the Snai trees were scattering from the side of the house to a large hill beside the house.

Father and his crew arrived a short while later. The man had just finished cooking as well. Father scooped the rice and soup for Chhom and told her to eat as much soup as she wanted. She took advantage of the rare opportunity and ate until she could not eat another bite. Father took Chhom's bucket and filled it with fish. His friends were sitting in circle eating together with a large bowl of soup in the middle. They ate and talked loudly.

"You are done eating? Eat more so that you have energy to walk back home," one of Father's friends said.

Chhom nearly forgot that she had to return home soon. If she left late, she would be walking in the dark.

"Father, I'm leaving now," Chhom said.

"You better get going then," Father said and got up, "Where is your scarf?"

"I didn't bring a scarf," Chhom replied.

"Use mine then," Father said and took the scarf from his neck and made a coil.

Chhom walked over to check the fish in her bucket and was surprised to see how large the fish were. She had never seen fish that size up close in her life, and they were all still alive. Mother would be very happy to see these fish. She could picture Mother's reaction.

Father place the coiled scarf on Chhom's head and then lifted the bucket of fish and placed it on top of the scarf. Chhom felt a heavy pressure on her head and neck, but the thought of the precious fish gave her strength.

"Be careful when you walk. You might spill the fish," Father said.

The sun was about to set, but it was still giving off a warm and bright evening light. She wanted to reach home after nightfall so that no one would see her with a bucket of fish. At the same time, walking at night was not safe. Wolves, snakes, and tigers were known to hunt at night. Chhom shivered when she thought of it. She started walking and noticed Father appeared very concerned. He stood tall and wordless, staring at her as she left.

Chhom picked up her pace, racing against the darkness. The insects began to hum from all corners as if they were calling out for her. The mosquitoes had found her and buzzed around her ears looking for a spot to land. She brushes them off with her free hand. They went away for a few seconds and then came back. Chhom had no energy to play the chasing game. She allowed the mosquito to land on her skin, and then she smacked it and killed it.

After a while, the sun had set completely leaving faint light that was just enough for her to see a dozen feet ahead. She felt a surge of panic, but she told herself that the trip should be quick because she didn't have to search for food like she did during the daytime. Her neck and arms began to be sore. She wanted to stop and rest for just a minute, but she didn't have anybody to lift the bucket back on her head. The bucket was getting heavier and heavier. She could lift it up with a struggle, but to place it back on her head was a challenge. If she didn't do it right, she could spill all the fish.

The wolves were howling from a distant calling out for one another. If she heard it correctly, they were somewhere further ahead. Another howls came from somewhere far from the side.

The night became pitch-dark all of a sudden. She could see nothing but the thick, dark figures of trees and bushes. She could get lost easily if she wasn't not careful. Her heart was pounding. She was breathing hard and loud at the thought of getting lost. She overcame her fear slightly by ensuring herself to follow the main road all the way.

All types of night animals were taking turns pitching their strange sounds to the mix of insects and frogs. The sounds were pleasant during the daytime, but now, even the croaks of the frog sounded haunting.

Chhom continued to walk blindly in the dark. She did not know how far she had walked. It was hard to keep track of the time and the distance as her mind was occupied by fear. Suddenly, the road forked into two. One curved sharply to the left, and one slightly curved to the right. She didn't remember seeing the road split this morning and felt a sudden panic. She decided to take the left because our house was located somewhere on the left side of the road. The right may lead her further away from the house. She followed the road hoping it was the correct one. Chhom looked around for anything that might look familiar, but it was too dark. All she could see was the dark contour of the tree branches and bushes nearby.

The road became very narrow, way too small for the wagon to pass through. Some of the trees extended their branches so low and bridged over the road. She didn't remember seeing them that low when she came. She reluctantly accepted the fact that she was lost. She began to shiver uncontrollably and began to cry. Tears filled her eyes, making it more difficult to see. She needed to go back to the fork, but she was afraid she would be lost further. She continued to walk blindly. Tree branches were swiping her face from left and right. She stepped on things that weren't supposed to be there. Terrified, she nearly lost control of her arm that was holding the bucket on her head. All of a sudden, one of her feet sank into the earth as if it was swallowing her alive. She tumbles forward. The basket flew off her head. She cried frantically. She tried to lift her leg up, but something caught her ankle and she could not pull her foot free. She felt her leg and her foot was rubbing against something soft. It was too soft to be tree roots or dirt. She rotated her ankle and lifted her foot free from whatever it was. Then she used her hand to probe the ground. She probed the spot where her feet sank so she wouldn't step on the same spot. Her hands felt some sort of fabric and soft, cold flesh-like object. Her thoughts raced back to Mother's conversation with the adults, suspecting the new regime of butchering civilians and the Peayaup and burying them in one large grave. She nearly fainted from the thought of touching the corpse. But she fought to stay awake. She must bring the fish home. She needed to show Mother the fish and see her smile. She wanted to see me and Pech eat one whole fish each. Thinking of the fish, she realized she didn't even have the fish anymore. She looked around and found the dark figure of the bucket lying several feet away. She crawled and reached for the bucket and found it had flipped upside down. She flipped the bucket over and used her hands to probe for the fish. Fortunately, she found a pile of fish right underneath the bucket. She stopped crying and concentrated on gathering the fish. Some of the fish were still alive and wiggling. Chhom nearly fainted again from touching the cold, moving fish. It felt like a living human arm at first. She was determined to fight her fear and collect all the fish she could find. She even found the scarf still coiled near the bucket.

Still on her hands and knees, she dragged the bucket closer. The probed for firm ground before she decided to stand up. Once confident that she was on the firm ground, she crawled quickly away from what appeared to be some sort of grave. She noticed the bucket was a little lighter than before, but she was satisfied with the amount of fish she'd collected off the ground. She placed the coiled scarf on her head and then lifted the bucket and placed it on the coiled scarf. Her knees were wiggling from fatigue as she tried to stand up.

Just when she was ready to start searching for the path to walk, she heard the sound of a wagon and hoof steps from a distant. She wasn't sure if she was hearing a real wagon or the ghost. She'd heard stories from the adults that ghosts could make any type of sound and image to trick travelers. Ghosts liked to lure people with illusions. When the humans come close, they would use their cold hands and snap the human's neck. All the adults had told the same stories.

Uncertain whether the sound was coming from the actual ox wagon or the ghost, she determined to take the risk and follow the sound of the wagon. She didn't know where the wagon was heading, but if the wagon was real, at least it will take her to the human residents and away from the alleged grave.

She crept carefully toward the sound and came to a wagon path. She saw a faint light further ahead. The driver must have lit a lamp. It was too far to see the wagon, but she followed the light and kept her distance from the wagon. She didn't want anyone to know that she was here, especially when she had a bucket full of fish. She felt a surge of hopes. The fear of ghosts was miraculously gone.

The night became just a little cooler. She heard the wolves howling from the distance, but she was not afraid. If anything, she could call for help from the wagon driver. She followed the ox wagon for a while, easing the fear of ghosts and the dangerous animals. She didn't know exactly where she was, but she was certain that it would not lead her to another mass grave. She looked around hoping to find something familiar. Then she saw a dark figure of some sort of structural building that blended in with the trees. She squinted, trying to make sense of the shape. The closer she got, the better she could see. The figure of the building became bigger and more defined. She picked up her pace trying to figure out where she was. She was struck with joy when she learned that the figure of the building was Wat Samdach. In front of the building was the bridge. She knew exactly where she was now. Across the river was our house. As the wagon continued going straight, Chhom turned left on to the bridge. The tall tree called Ampel Tuk stood very high, greeting her by the bridge with its long and droopy branches. Chhom smiled to herself with relief. She wanted to run across the bridge and get home very quickly, but both her feet were in pain. She had just realized the sharp pain from all over of the bottoms of her feet. She must have stepped on dozens of thorns when she got lost.

Further ahead, she saw dim lights from the houses on the opposite side of the river. Most of those houses were resided by the Mit Chah. She crossed the bridge and walked up the hill. Our house was sitting on top of a small hill isolated from the rest, waiting for her. When Chhom entered the house, Mother was sitting by the door weeping. She stood up the instant she saw Chhom.

"What took you so long? And why are your clothes so muddy?" Mother asked with a croaky voice.

"I was lost for an hour," Chhom said, meaning a very long time. She wanted to tell Mother about the grave, but she was afraid Mother might not allow her to go again.

"The fish are big," Mother said happily.

"Father selected them for me."

"Wait a little. I will roast one for you and your brother. Go wash yourself."

Mother revived the fire in the hearth and began roasting one large snakehead fish that was about four times the size of her wrist. Chhom cleaned herself up using the water in the vase and changed her clothes. She couldn't remember the last time she'd changed her clothes, but this time her clothes were too muddy to sleep in. When she finished, she sat by the fire staring at the fish. It was once smooth, dark, and lively. It was now charred, crisp, and smelled heavenly. Mother didn't need to gut the fish. Most of the organs were edible.

After a moment of waiting, Mother finally said, "The fish should be done. Take half. You can have the head side. Don't eat too fast, or you will choke on the bones."

Everyone liked the head side of the fish. It was bigger and it tasted better. Most of the edible organs were located in the head side as well. Chhom retrieved the fish from the hearth and broke it in half. She took the head side of the fish like Mother said and left the other half on a plate. She began picking her favorite spot on the fish and ate. There was a lot of meat on the fish, but Chhom found the scales and skins irresistible. They were crispy and filled with flavors.

Pech and I woke up from the aroma of the roasted fish and the radiance of the fire. I normally woke up at this time to eat the food the Me-Laek brought home. Tonight, she came home sometime after nightfall without food and cuddled next to my head. I would expect a piece of dry fish. If I didn't get anything to eat, I would wail for meat until I fell back to sleep. Fortunately, Mother handed me a large chunk of fish before I begin to wail. She kept the other chunk for Pech.

CHAPTER 14

Our cat, Me-Laek, did not show up all day today. Mother was very concerned. It had been over two years since we'd discovered her. She continued to bring us food once every two to three days. She brought home mostly dried fish. Once in a while, she brought home chicken thighs or a small piece of beef. Chicken meat was rare. Although, every chicken belonged to the public, only the Mit Chah could eat them. Beef was extremely rare. Cows and oxen were used to plow only. They were butchered only when they were sick and unable to walk.

Mother had been responsible for raising four chickens for the last several months. One chicken disappeared about a month ago. She reported the missing chicken in the meeting, and she was relieved that no one was a suspect. The chickens were to roam around the neighbors' houses. Anything could happen. It was common for a chicken to disappear.

A few weeks ago, she was missing another chicken when she was trying to gather her chickens before nightfall. She could have sworn the chicken was under the house earlier that morning. As she began to trace back the last time she saw the chicken during the day time, she remembered the chicken entering Tien's house.

Mother walked to Tien's mom and asked, "Hey, Tien's mom. Have you seen my chicken?"

"No, I just got back from searching for food. I haven't seen any chickens," Tien's mom replied.

Just when she'd finished saying that, Me-Laek ran out from her house with the chicken head in her mouth.

Tien's mom looked at Mother with a guilty grin. Mother laughed uncontrollably and nearly choked from laughing too hard.

"You ate my chicken!" she continued to laugh.

"Now that you found out, are you going to take me to trial?" she asked, knowing well that Mother would never do such things.

"Are you kidding me? If you were dead, I have no one to curse at. When you are around, I get to curse any time," Mother said jokingly.

"By the way, I could hear Bun wail last night like he'd been tortured," Tien's mom said.

"He still cries every night for meat. He cries until he gets tired and falls back asleep."

Only Tien's mom knew why I cried at night. It was my habit to wake up in the middle of night eating the food that Me-Laek brought. Mother would cut the fish into small pieces and save some for the nights when Me-Laek couldn't find any food. After I ate the meat, I would go back to sleep.

During the daytime, I spent a lot of time playing with Me-Laek. Her kittens had grown big and disappeared one by one many months ago. I missed playing with her kittens, especially when they were small. None of them had three colors like Me-Laek. I remembered the day when the kittens were forced to be independent. Me-Laek normally shared her catches, mostly rats, with the kittens. One day when I was playing with the grown-up kittens, Me-Laek brought home a large rat. She normally dropped the rat in front of the kittens, and the kitten would brawl for it. This time she walked to the corner of the house away from the kittens and began eating the rat. One of the kittens approached and attempted to snatch the rat, but Me-Laek crouched and hissed defensively. I saw her behave the same way the next day. Her kittens realized she was no longer going to feed them. They would have to hunt for their own food. Unfortunately, when the kittens began to go out and hunt, they disappeared one by one and never returned. Mother believed they had all been eaten by the hungry villagers.

People would eat anything to survive. The cats were no exception, and they became very rare. Somehow Me-Laek had been very lucky to avoid all the hungry people in the village. She stayed home during the day and hunted at night.

I woke up in the middle of the night as usual, expected my midnight meat. "Mother, roast meat," I said in a toddler's tongue.

"No roast meat tonight, son," Mother replied calmly.

"Roast meat," I insisted.

"Go back to sleep, son."

"Roast meat! Roast meat!" I started to wail.

"Mother will get the roast meat for you tomorrow."

I didn't care. I continued to wail for roast meat. Mother tried to sooth me in many ways, but it didn't stop me from crying. I cried until I fell asleep.

I woke up the next morning hungrier than usual. I still remembered that I'd missed my meat last night. I remembered Mother had told me that she would get me the roast meat in the morning, but I didn't see her anywhere around.

"Mother, roast meat. Roast meat." I demanded the roast meat Mother had promised to get me this morning.

Chhom was doing her morning chores. She had gathered the wood and watered the plants. She was preparing to head out to search for food. Pech was still sleeping.

"There is no meat, and Mother is at work!" Chhom shouted.

Chhom was wearing a black sarong and long-sleeve black shirt with multiple newly sewn pockets. She was holding a dirty bucket, heading out to search for food. I was frustrated to see her leave. Mother was at work, and now Chhom was leaving. I was really hungry, and I wanted my roast meat.

"Roast meat! Roast meat!" I continued to scream, hoping Chhom would somehow give me some roast meat.

"Stop crying now! I'm not going to be here to watch Pech! When he wakes up, he's going cry until your ears fall off!" Chhom shouted angrily.

She was not afraid to spank me if she needed to. She was hungry, I was hungry, and Pech would wake up crying and hungry as well.

"Roast meat. Roast meat..." Unable help it, I continued to wail.

Chhom didn't have time to stop me from crying as she had to find food and return before noon to line up for rice porridge.

I continued crying for a while and then stopped when I got too exhausted. I looked around and saw the hearth with three crusty stones. I remembered Chhom and Mother cooked the meat, crabs, and fish there every day on that hearth. Maybe that's where they got all the meat from. I walked over and squatted next to the hearth and used my fingers to rake the ashes. My fingers brushed on something very warm. It must be the meat, I thought. I grabbed the warm object then felt an excruciation pain in my fingers. I jerked my hand out and screamed. I looked at my fingers and saw a dark spot on my thumb and my index finger. I started to cry again. Pech woke up from the sound of my screaming. He cried for a few minutes and then came and sat beside me. I grabbed a tiny stick and used it to rake the ashes for food. This time, I was cautious. After a few attempts, I found a tiny tip of a crab leg. I picked it up and popped it in my mouth. It didn't taste anything like meat, but it was crunchy and salty. The salty taste must have been from the ashes. The crab legs must have fallen off when Mother and Chhom cooked the crabs over the years. I liked the crab legs and continue to search for more. Pech found his own stick and did as I did, but he didn't seem to know what to look for. He picked up something and shoved it in his mouth, but then spit it back out instantly.

Chhom returned just before noon. She brought home a couple of small crabs and tiny frogs along with a basket of the water spinaches for us to eat. She roasted the crabs, the frogs, and the water spinaches. She brought some over to Tien and Mao. They were staying at their house today. Pech ate most of the water spinaches and demanded more food. Chhom had gotten used to seeing him cry for food. She simply said, "You can cry all you want. We don't have any more food."

After we finished eating, we played until we heard the sound of the bell. Chhom gathered us, and we begin walking to the dining hall as usual. Tien and Mao were picked up by their mom. Mother was standing beside the large pot distributing the rice porridge. After we got our share, we walked over to our normal spot and began eating. Mother came over to sit with us when she'd finished distributing the rice porridge. We hadn't seen her all morning. She had to walk far to collect vegetables. She took a small scoop from her bowl and put in Pech's bowl. The rice porridge was burning hot. Chhom was blowing Pech's bowl to cool it down. I did the same to my bowl, but it didn't seem to work. I ran out of breath very quickly and got very tired. I liked to eat my rice porridge when it was cooler.

"Eat faster before you spill it again!" Mother yelled at me. Sometimes I waited too long for the rice porridge to cool down. While waiting for the rice to cool down, I would play with a stick, swinging it around, and end up spilling all the rice porridge.

Chhom helped me cool the rice after she finished feeding Pech. She scolded me for eating too slow, but I was used to being scolded and took my time.

After a while and after much scolding, I finished my rice porridge, the same time Mother finished washing the pots. We began to walk back home. The rice porridge was good. I could eat ten more of those plates. We were about to enter our house when the distinctive voice of Phate's mom shouted with a heavy Laos accent, "You ate all the meat?" I tried not to think about her accent, afraid to get stuck again like I did once.

"Ah Khan! You ate all the meat! I'm hungry! You didn't leave any for me!" Phate's mom ran outside the house yelling at her husband.

"Who ate what meat?" Mother asked.

"Ah Khan ate all the cat meat! We caught a cat! I skinned the cat nicely! He ate it all!" she wailed.

"You killed my cat!" Mother said angrily.

"It's not your cat," she replied.

"She's the only cat around. I gave you fish and meat that I could have fed my sons. In return, you killed my cat. My cat has been with us for years, and now you killed it. More importantly, you have killed a three-colored cat. You know how much sin you have brought upon yourself?" Mother cried after she finished scolding Phate's mom.

Phate's mom didn't say a word back but continued to cry.

I woke up and wailed every midnight for roast meat. Mother was hurt when she knew that she would never able to give me roast meat at night ever again. Sometimes, she wept as she sat behind me rubbing my back to sooth me. I would cry until I fell back to sleep. I woke up each morning, squatting in front of the hearth and raking the ashes with a stick looking for crab legs. Sometimes I found several crab legs that had fallen off the crabs when Chhom roasted them the previous day. Sometimes I found nothing.

In a quiet evening, many weeks after Me-Laek had been eaten, I was squatting and raking the ashes for crab legs. "Bun, what were you doing?" a familiar, soft voice came from somewhere behind me. When I turned around, I saw Chhorn limping into the house.

"What happened to you?" Mother walked in after Chhorn and asked.

"I had a small cut about a month ago. It's spreading," Chhorn explained.

Chhorn was limping in pain. It was common for people to get a small cut and have it become infected. The infection could spread through the entire arm or legs. The Khmer had limited knowledge about infection. Some believed it was a curse.

"You have the Vietnamese infection. Sit down. I will make the medicine for you," Mother informed her.

The large infection was known as the Vietnamese infection. Mother boiled water with tamarind leaves and Sank Kae leaves. The tamarind leaves were also edible. The Khmer use the tamarind leaves to cook or add flavor to food or sauce. The Sank Kae leaves were normally used to dye our clothes black as required by the government. In her spare time, Mother collected the leaves for emergency use. She dried them on a shelf, the same place where she hid her rice.

Mother let the water boil for about thirty minutes and then she let the water to cool down.

"How did you get here?"

"I wanted to come weeks ago, but they wouldn't let me. When they saw that I couldn't do anything at all, they decided to let me come. Then I had to wait to find an ox wagon traveling this way to our house. This morning I was lucky to find an ox wagon transporting rice to somewhere around here. I begged the man for the ride."

"Come here. Let me take a look," Mother said.

Chhorn limped to Mother and lifted her right side of her trousers to show her the infection on her lower right leg. Chhorn was darker and skinnier each time she came to visit. Her legs were nothing but skin and bones. The infection was larger than the size of her palm, covering most of her ankle. The infection had destroyed her skin, exposing her yellowish flesh. She squirmed in pain when her pants touched the infected part of her ankle.

"Your foot is swollen. Try not to walk when you don't need to. Sit down," Mother said.

Chhorn sat and waited painfully. She moaned here and there. Her eyes were swollen from days of crying. When the boiled water had cooled down, Mother took a ragged cloth and dipped it in the water. She squeezed the wet cloth over her ankle, allowing the hot water to drip onto the infection. Chhorn gritted her teeth in pain as the hot water touched her foot. Tears of pain rolled down her cheeks. Mother repeated the same step over and over again until all the pot was empty. Then Mother grabbed a handful of the boiled leaves from the pot and placed them on the infection. She used the same cloth to wrap around her ankle to hold the leaves in place.

"We'll do this again before bed. Then one more time in the morning, and you will be ready to return to work the next day. Remember to continue to work hard," Mother assured. If the authority found her useless for a long period of time, she would get in trouble. Mother wished Chhorn could stay home longer so she could take care of her, but she knew well not to take the risk.

Chhorn seemed slightly relieved after Mother had finished wrapping the cloth around her ankle. She missed home. She looked very happy to be home.

"Bun looks very hungry. He's been sitting in front of the hearth raking the ashes since I got here," Chhorn said.

"Me-Laek has been killed and eaten," Mother said in disappointment.

"Who killed the cat?" Chhorn asked.

Mother explained how she found out. As the night was slowly creeping in, Chhorn walked out to the front door and sat on the stairway. She was looking for something to do to distract her pain. The adults were sitting in front of their house chatting. Pech was walking around the house with his head down as if he was having a hard time holding his head up.

"Pech!" Chhorn hollered.

Pech turned around and smiled and then continued to walk around. A surge of pain shot through her ankle when she tried to adjust her feet. Chhorn cringed and cried in pain.

"Is that you, Chhorn? What are you doing here, and what happened to you?" Tien's mom hollered.

"Yes, it me, Ming. I have the Vietnamese infection. I can't work, and they let me come home. I can't bear the pain," she replied

"Is that right? Nothing we can do but for you to bear the pain until the wound was healed," Tien's mom said and then continued to have a conversation with the neighbor.

Phate's mom was sitting on her stairway looking very depressed. Mother had not spoken to her since she killed Me-Laek.

"Is that you, Chhorn?" Phate's mom asked with her heavy Laos accent.

"Yes!"

Phate's mom began to ask Chhorn where she was staying and what she was doing. Chhorn tried to concentrate on listening and answering her normally. She wasn't mad at Phate's mom at all. She understood that most people would kill a cat when they had the opportunity. Chhorn explained what she was doing at her work and how she got the cut.

"Bear the pain. You will get well soon," Phate's mom said and walked away.

Chhorn continued to sit on the stairway and wept softly from pain. All of a sudden, a gust of wind swept over and nearly knocked Chhorn off the stairs. Chhorn heard a loud thud several yards to her right. She turned her head and saw a coconut lying right underneath a tall coconut tree. Without hesitation, Chhorn leaped from the stairs to the ground and dashed directly toward the coconut. When she was several away from the coconut, she leaped onto the coconut and landed on it with her chest. Then she grabbed the coconut with both hands and curled her entire body around it.

All the adults around the area paused and turned to where Chhorn is. Many did not know what had just happened.

"I thought your leg was hurt and you couldn't walk. You just moved like a lightning when you saw a coconut. I have been living here a long time; the coconut should be mine," Phate's mom exclaimed angrily.

A few adults had begun running toward the coconut. They stopped and looked disappointed for not getting there on time. Chhorn got up and carefully clinched the coconut tight to her chest. She carried the coconut in the house limping.

"Chhorn, what happened?" Mother asked.

"A coconut dropped to the ground, and I was the first one to claim it," Chhorn said.

Mother chuckled, "Great job, but the cloth came off your foot."

"That's all right. I got the coconut," Chhorn said and then wrenched in pain.

I was still sitting beside the hearth hoping food would appear beneath the ashes somehow. I turned around and saw Chhorn with the coconut in her hand. I leaped up with surprise.

"Coconut! Coconut! I want some coconut!" I shouted.

"Here, give this to Bun and Pech," Chhorn said and handed the coconut to Mother.

"This coconut is big and heavy," Mother said lifting the coconut up to her right ear and to shake it. "Lots of juice!" Mother said and smiled.

Mother chopped the top part of the coconut with the machete, pouring the water into a bowl. I sat next to the bowl and crouched where my face was just inches away from the bowl as Mother was pouring the coconut. When looking at the juice flowing from the coconut into the bowl, the mist of the juice brought the sweet aroma along with the dust of the husk.

"Here! Drink some but not too much. Leave some for Pech," Mother said tilting the bowl to my mouth.

I drank the sweet and delicious coconut juice. As far as I remembered, this was the second time I'd had coconut juice. I wanted to finish the whole bowl, but Mother pulled it back from my mouth.

"Here, have some." Mother handed the bowl to Chhorn.

"It's all right. Leave the rest for Pech. I'll go call him," Chhorn insisted.

"Take a sip at least. You almost broke your legs for this," Mother said. She knew Chhorn wanted some coconut juice.

"It's all right," Chhorn said as she walked out to get Pech.

When Pech found out there was coconut juice for him, he ran with his head still stooping down, nearly tripping and falling on the stairs.

Mother gave him some coconut juice and saved a little for Chhom. She split the coconut in half with the machete and used a spoon to scrape all the pulp into the bowl. There was a lot of pulp.

"Here... you have a big one." Mother handed a piece of coconut pulp to Chhorn.

Chhorn was hesitant to take the coconut pulp, but when she saw a bowl full of pulp left, she accepted the coconut pulp and munched with satisfaction. Mother gave Pech and I each a big piece. She took a small piece for herself and saved the rest for Chhom.

CHAPTER 15

I was walking along an open alley about four blocks from my house looking for something fun to do and searching for food at the same time. I tried to be cautious not to walk too far, afraid I might get lost. Chhom had taken me this way once. I had never attempted to go past where Chhom took me. There were fewer and fewer children around my house. Most were sick and had passed away. Some had disappeared with their entire families. I found a group of children who were listening to an older boy about eight years old telling a story.

"...an object that could fly in the sky. It was called "Kapal Hoh" (flying vessel [airplane]). The boy explained it, expanding his arms out and walking around in a circle and making a strange sound to demonstrate. Then he squatted down and drew a picture of the airplane on the ground with a stick. Then he drew smoke coming out the other end.

"The airplanes are made by the Americans. Normally, only gods and angels could make such talismans. The Americans must have a lot of magic to create things that can fly in the sky..." he continued.

I stopped and joined the children listening to this knowledgeable boy. It was amazing to learn that such things could exist. I believed the boy. I could almost recall seeing such an object somewhere before. The word "American" sounded very familiar to me too. Mother had spoken about the Americans every time she discussed the past stories with the neighbors.

The boy continued telling his stories. "...then I saw this thing called 'Ah Teh Plung' (Fire Wagon[train]). It's about one horizon long, and it's black. It has a big head and large teeth. It travels on the ground very fast. No oxen are used to pull. It moves by itself very fast, maybe one hundred times faster than the oxen. Not like the 'Kapal Hoh,' this thing has black smoke coming out of its head, and it makes this angry sound as it moves—a 'chook chook' and 'toot toot' sound." The boy demonstrated as he spoke.

I was amazed that such things could exist. Although, the "Ah Teh Plung" sounded familiar to me as well, but I couldn't recall where I'd seen it.

"Do you think Ah Teh Plung would eat a human?" one boy asked.

"Maybe. How else do they have strength to move? And what's the point of having big teeth?" another boy concluded.

"I hope it never comes this way. I'm scared," the other boy said.

I got goose bumps from listening to the boy, hoping the Ah Teh Plung would never come around here. The older boy jumped from one story to another, sharing everything he knew. Most of the stories were ghost stories. It was scary but irresistible. After he finished telling the story, a few other boys joined in and told more stories.

I hung out with the new children playing hide-and-go-seek to kick the can. I decided to head back home when the sun set, hoping not to bump into any of the ghosts or creatures. When I approached the house, I saw a lot of adults congregated by the doorway outside the house. Everyone was chatting happily.

"Where did you find the midwife?" one of the ladies asked the other.

"About two hours of walking from here," the other replied.

Pu Peap was among them, chatting. He was explaining something to the women. Everyone respected Pu Peap. He always knew what he was talking about. He was polite and knowledgeable. Chhom was standing holding Pech's hand and listening to Pu Peap like everyone else.

"Bun, your mom just crossed the river. Where did you come from? You are a big brother once again…" Tien's mom was the first one to talk to me. She spokes loudly and enthusiastically. I didn't understand the rest of the things she said, but she made me look so special. I didn't know what "cross the river" meant, but she was referring to something inside our house. I pictured Mother walking across the bridge to Wat Samdach. I was confused why everyone was so serious about Mother crossing the bridge. Maybe she'd found food and would share with everyone like she normally did. I liked the thought of food because I was starving. I hoped Mother had brought food home. Then I heard a cry of a baby from inside the house. I wanted to go in and see what was going on, but the adults were sitting on the stairs barricading the way in.

"Stay outside," Tien's mom said.

The night was getting darker as we stood and waited for whatever reason. We had nothing else to do. I picked up a stick and pretended it was a flying object. I held it up with one hand and raised it up above my head and moved it around. The mosquitoes were starting to swarm around my ears. I smacked the mosquitos with my free hand and continued to swirl the stick in the air to imitate the flying objects.

"You guys have a brother! Look at him. He looks like your Father. He is so white," Tien's mom said as she held something wrapped in a black cloth, crying loudly.

I walked closer to take a look, and I saw a small baby. I had never seen a human so small. Chhom seemed to understand more about the baby than me. No one had ever explained to me what babies were and what they were for.

"I gave him a name. His name is Chhook (lotus)," Pu Peap said to Chhom.

"Chhook is a nice name," Phate's mom said with her funny accent.

I covered my ears to avoid listening to Phate's mom speaking, afraid the accent might get stuck in my head again.

Everyone left soon after because they all had to wake up early in the morning to work. Chhom was holding the baby. She smiled and talked to the baby like he understood her. Miraculously, the baby stopped crying. Pech and I were very curious and could not take our eyes off him, but we were scared to touch him.

The next day, Chhom took us to line up for lunch as usual and learned that Mother was allowed to stay home for four weeks, but she was not to receive any rice at all for those weeks. Mother noticed Chhom appeared quite upset to learn such bad news. Chhom thought she would have to seek food for Mother as well. Mother noticed her concern and told Chhom, "Don't worry about the rice porridge. I have saved up a bag of rice, and your Father has buried the rice underneath the hearth, but it needs to be ground. The problem is I do not have strength to dig the hearth. You have to do it. Then I will grind the rice myself," Mother explained.

Mother explained to Chhom how she had saved the rice over the years just for an emergency. In the harvest season, she was asked to help grind and separate the rice from the husks. She collected the whole rice and hid it in her undershirt. Over two seasons, she had filled a large bag of rice. Chhom was relieved to know that.

Chhom spent her entire day unearthing the hidden rice. She had to remove the hearth and dig one meter deep to get to the rice.

"Mother, the rats found your rice. I saw one just fled the other way," Chhom said.

"Them damn rats! You Father had buried the rice so deep, and they still found their way in," Mother said.

No one was allowed to have a grinder at home; thus, it was very difficult to separate the husk from the rice kernel. Mother had collected flat rocks about twice the size of her palms. She uses the rocks to rub the rice to remove the husks. After she subbed the husks off, she needed to filter the rice from the husks. She poured the rice grains and husks in a bucket of water. The husks floated on the surface of the water, and the rice grain submerged to the bottom of the bucket. She removed all the husks from the surface of the water and drained the water, leaving just the rice kernels in the bucket.

Since the rice kernels were still wet, she needed to dry them. The rice would absorb water over time and would make it perishable very quickly. Mother cleverly spread the rice on a tray, allowing the rice to dry.

She spent most of her nighttime grinding rice. She avoided doing it during the daytime, as she's afraid she might get caught. If she got caught, it was an automatic death penalty for stealing rice from the public. Plus, she had been having a lot of visitors. Pu Peap had been coming very often to check how the baby was doing. He also came to share the news with Mother and Tien's mom.

Chhom continued to search for food and took us to the dining hall for lunch and supper. She helped Mother clean the baby when he pooped.

On the fifth day after labor, Mother was able to walk again. She got out of the house and started doing some work. She pruned the plants in the backyard that she had grown from scratch. She memorized each one by heart. Our house was sitting on a hill, making it hard to plant anything. There was already a plantain tree here when we first moved into this house. The plantain fruit never had a chance to grow. Mother normally picked the plantain's blossoms to cook. If the plantains were fully grown, people would notice and remember; thus, it would not be a good idea to steal when it was too noticeable. She knew well that when the plantains were ripe we would never get to eat them anyway. The higher officials would take the plantains for themselves.

Father came to visit about two weeks later. He brought home fish and all sorts of animals as usual. This time he brought mostly crocodile meat. Mother began to distribute them to friends and neighbors on the same night. Tien's mom and the families with the most kids got the most meat.

Father didn't like the baby's name, Chhook. "Chhook is a fancy name. If we keep that name, our entire family will be dead," he said.

"What should we name him then? I'm going to call him Poe (the youngest child) because he's our last kid," Mother said.

"Poe is still a little fancy. I will call him Poech (the last one)," Father said.

"You call him Poech, and I will call him Poe," Mother said.

Four weeks after she delivered baby Poe, Mother returned to work. She got to keep her job as the Mekong and the cook. It was a little past noon. Mother was at the water bank picking the water spinaches and lotus. She thought of the baby every single moment. She wanted to stay home and feed him, but she had to work. He was too young for Chhom to care for him. She felt helpless and in despair. As her thoughts were drifting away, she caught movements from the corner of her eye. She gazed toward the movements and saw hundreds of women and children walking among other families across the bridge. Men and women chatted as they walked. Children were trotting along. Some children were holding their smaller siblings' hands and singing. Among them, a Father was holding his small daughter on his shoulder singing "*Chab Chap* (catch the bird)", motioning his free hand to catch the imaginary birds. They must have a special meeting. Mother had noticed the new government liked to have family meetings. It must be nice to have a day off from work to attend the meeting, Mother thought and continued with her tasks.

After she finished picking the vegetables, she returned to the dining hall to cook supper for the horde. Mother brought home the water that she used to wash the rice that she'd made everyone believe was to feed the pig. After she finished cooking and distributing the rice porridge for the horde, she returned to the river to collect more vegetables to feed us.

As she began to descend to the river, Mother saw about ten men walking across the bridge toward Wat Samdach. They walked sturdily and with purpose. Some of them were carrying rifles. Some of them were carrying a metal ox wagon wheel shaft. The ox wagon wheel shafts were very common in Khmer. Some were made of rare and strong wood, and some were made from metal. Each man also had many bundles of rope hanging on his shoulders and a machete strapped around his waist.

Ah, they must be going to slaughter a cow. I'm going to ask them for the cowhide, Mother thought happily to herself. She knew for a fact that they would not give her any meat. The thought of beef reminded Mother of Me-Laek. The cat used to bring home dried beef once in a long while. She drooled from the thought of the last time she roasted the beef. She remembered taking a small bite before handing the rest of the meat to me in the middle of the night.

The cowhides were tough but edible. It would take all day to boil, but with salt and vegetables they become delicious. Cowhides could also be roasted, and they gave off a mouthwatering aroma similar to roasted meat, but they were still very chewy. The main purpose for the cowhides was to make ropes. When the cows were slaughtered, the skins were to be cut into long, thin stripes about two inches in width. The long stripes were then twisted into coils and left in the sun to dry. This was one of the accredited technologies invented by the government that led them to think they could restart the Khmer society from scratch. Other inventions included making sandals from car tires and spoons and knives from railroad tracks.

Instead of picking vegetables, Mother ran toward the bridge after the men and hollered, "Mit Bong, if you kill the cows, save me the skin. I just want the parts that you plan to discard."

The men didn't seem to hear her and disappeared to the other side of the bridge. Mother was persistent and walked briskly after them. The cowhides were worth the effort. Mother reached Wat Samdach temple and stood still, trying to figure out where the men had gone. The road split into three. One rans along the river to the left, one ran along the river to right, and one curved around the right side of the temple. Mother figured that there was nothing to the left or to the right along the river. She followed the road straight ahead. As she approached the temple, the movements through the large open window caught her attention. Mother stopped and stared through the window. One man was escorting a person with their hands tied behind their back like a prisoner. The other man stepped forward and struck the person in the head with the ox wagon wheel shaft. The person dropped to the ground. Another man dragged the lifeless body away.

Another man escorted a second bound person with a bag over their head. The man holding the ox wagon shaft bashed the bound person on the head. The bound person dropped to their knees but was still moving. Another man lashed out, lifted up the person's head, and slit their throat with a machete.

Another bound person was escorted in. This person seemed to be a woman. The executer bashed the woman in the head with the ox wagon shaft. The woman's body slumped to the ground instantly. Mother froze as she witnessed a human being butchered in front of her very own eyes. Her knees buckled and shook violently. She nearly collapsed. She wanted to walk away, but her legs didn't obey. Her guts were wrenching and twisting from confusion and terror. She stood there for a moment not believing what she saw. Then she managed to turn herself around hoping to walk away without getting caught, but a woman stood ten feet away, hands behind her back, staring at her with the piercing dark eyes like a demon that had just emerged from beneath the earth.

"Mit Yorn, what are you doing here? Did you see anything?" the woman asked.

My life is over, Mother thought.

"No, I didn't see anything. I was just looking for the Mit Bongs who came to slaughter the cow, and I wanted to ask them for the unwanted hides." Mother was surprised that she was able to speak clearly. Her entire body was still shaking violently.

Mother and the woman knew one another well. She was the new leader in Stung Chah, and Mother and all the Mekong had to follow her orders. She was known as Ta Nuy's wife. She was one of the Nearadey who'd come and taken over the village. She led all the Mit Chah in Stung Chah.

"I don't care if saw anything or not. You are not to say anything to anyone. Do you hear me? We are just cleaning up our society. Now, I want you to guard this bridge and these roads so that no one comes near this place for the rest of the night. Do you understand?"

"Yes, Mit Bong. I can do that," Mother replied.

Mother was relieved after realizing that she had just escaped death. She also realized that she had pooped her pants as well.

"I need to go home and change. I will be back to guard the bridge," Mother said with submissive tone.

"All right then, but be quick," the woman said sternly.

Mom hurried back home. Her mind was racing through her memories of the families she had seen that afternoon walking over the bridge. They didn't know that they were walking toward their death. She remembered clearly the little girl sitting on her father's shoulder singing "chap chab" and dancing. She couldn't help but picture the slaughtering process of those people. What were they going to do with the children? She wouldn't think they would do anything different to the children. They had rifles, but they chose not to use them. Instead, they used metal rods and machetes. How could anybody treat human lives like this? They must be demons. Human wouldn't do that.

Tears started to roll down her cheeks as she walked, making the road become blurry. After she reached the middle of the bridge, she cried out loud. She had to let it all out now if she wanted to make it home safely. She managed to calm herself when she reached the end of the bridge. She stopped at the river bank to wash herself up before heading home.

The sunlight was fading slowly, surrendering itself to the night. Chhom was at home just finishing feeding me and Pech. Mother stepped in the house with her clothes all soaked. Chhom noticed that something was wrong with Mother. Her eyes were watery and red.

"Mother, what's wrong? How come you are like that?"

"Chhom, I have something to do to night. Do not come to find me. I will be back in the morning."

Chhom was terrified to see Mother was so nervous and distressed.

"What about Poe?"

"I'll take him with me, but do not try to find me," Mother reassured.

Mother tied the two ends of a scarf and hung the scarf around her shoulder. She placed Poe in the scarf like a cradle. She exited the house and walks quickly toward the bridge. Chhom stepped out of the house staring at Mother walking toward the bridge.

Mother was walking across the bridge carrying Poe in the scarf. The thought of those demons in black slaughtering the victims flashed in her mind over and over again. Now she was going back to that slaughtering house. How many more people were in the temple waiting to die? She remembered seeing hundreds of men, women, and children walking to the slaughterhouse where they thought they were having a meeting.

The sky was dark. The insects were screeching, and the birds were flopping from tree to tree chirping and preparing for the night. She arrived at the temple and stood to the right side of the bridge where she could see all three roads. She didn't want to be too close to hear the sound of the slaughtering. She couldn't see the road that curved around the temple, hoping no one would come that way. It was the path she would never want to use again. The noise of the insects grew louder as if they were trying to help her fend off the sound of the horror from the inside the temple.

As her mind raced through the act of slaughtering, she looked around the road and saw a figure of a person in black on the other side of the river ascending the bridge. Her heart was pounding once again. She hadn't yet figured out what to say to the people who want to cross the bridge. She walked quickly toward the person hoping he was not one of the demons. She saw a young man in his mid-twenties, light-skinned, walking very quickly as if he was in hurry.

"Mit, I'm here to attend the meeting, but I'm late. I hope it's not over yet," the young man said.

Mother whispered, "Mit P'own [Young Comrade], you must not go in there if you want to live."

The young man paused for a few seconds and then responded, "Then...Mit Bong, thank you! Thank you!" His palms were clasped together in great appreciation, and he turned around and fled.

Mother returned to her guarding position exhausted from having to carry Poe. She was about to relax when two figures walked clumsily out of the temple toward her. One of them was holding a machete in one hand and some object in another. The other just followed. She glimpsed their faces and flinched in terror. Mother thought she had just escaped death, but her luck was about to end right here and right now with Poe.

"Mit, here! Have some livers. When you eat it, you'll become brave like us." He raised an object to Mother's face. Mother could smell the alcohol. These demons had been drinking and possibly eating human liver.

Mother squirmed and jerked her body to one side in rejection. Her whole body trembled as if she was showered with cold water. She closed her eyes, waiting to be butchered at any moment.

"Mit! Leave her alone! She's our guard. You have a lot of work to do. You need to carry all these bodies to the ditches before sunrise," Ta Nuy's wife hollered from the distant.

"I didn't do anything. I'm just offering her a fresh liver."

I'm still alive, she thought as the two men began to walk away.

For a moment, Mother forgot that Poe was with her. He was sleeping. He must have been tire from not having anything to eat this evening. She needed to sit down, as her feet were getting too tired to stand any longer. She thought she was going to die twice, but luck kept her alive. She walked closer to the temple hoping the killing was over. She sat down with her back against the concrete post of the bridge where she could easily see all three roads. She laid Poe on her lap and begin breast-feeding him.

She sat cradling Poe in the dark. Just then she realized the mosquitoes were buzzing around her biting her exposed parts of her hands and feet. They'd been sucking her blood all along, but her body was too numb from terror too feel the mosquito bites. She swatted one with her hand that was still clinging to her feet. She could feel the sticky liquid on her palm and on her foot. It had been sucking her blood for too long and became too heavy to fly. The mosquitoes were her least concern. The wolves were howling from a distance. The owls were hooting. Then a sound similar to a human laugh made by an unidentifiable creature echoed through the night. She was not afraid of the animals' attack, but the ghosts they could see. To the Khmer, the existence of ghosts was not just belief but fact. They believed the ghosts wandered around at night, sometimes even in daylight. According to Khmer, most animals could see ghosts all the time. There were ghosts known as *Bey Sach* that would guard the path they died upon. The *Bey Sach* was a female ghost that died from a brutal death and existed to seek vengeance. The humans would need to ask for her permission to pass the road. If she denied, she would float to the human, look them in the eyes, and twist their neck to death with her cold hands. Another well-known ghost was called *app* that flew around at night with guts dangling searching for the newborn babies to feast upon. The *apps* could be fended off by having pointy objects like needles, scissors, and thorny shrubs around. It's was ironic, but Mother felt a slight comfort that those men with the machetes and guns were nearby. If she saw any ghosts, she would not hesitate to scream for them to help.

Mother fought to stay awake in the long night hoping the ghosts would not come. Then she heard the faint sound of the shovels clunking against the earth from the back of the temple. Sometimes she heard a burst of laughter. Only demons laugh after murdering hundreds of people, she thought. How could less than twenty men be able to dig a grave big enough to burry hundreds of bodies? she wondered. Then she recalled that some of the women in her horde had been assigned to dig ditches somewhere across the river.

She couldn't forget Ta Nuy's wife's face when she'd confronted her earlier. Her words engraved in her mind, "cleaning up the society." They had been repeating the same phrase over and over again since they arrived here. Her feeling of terror never ceased. She was surrounded by both ghosts and demons. She jumped at every unexpected sound made by the night creatures. Every minute appeared to be an eternity. Tonight will be the longest night of my life, she thought.

It was about midnight when she was still sitting wearily with her back leaned against the bridge. She was mentally and physically exhausted. Her eyelids were getting heavier and heavier. She was too tired to worry about ghosts and demons. She just wanted a short doze and to wake up before she got caught sleeping on duty. Poe was still asleep. Maybe just one minute, she thought and began closing her eyes. Maybe just a little longer, she thought as she tried to control her short nap.

She woke up to the faint sound of a single rooster. She opened her eyes, longing for another doze, but she remembered what she had to do.

Her life depended on her staying awake. She looked around hoping it was only the early crow. She concentrated and tried to detect the sound of the shoveling, but she could hear nothing. The sound of the insects had also subsided. If anybody was doing anything behind the temple, she would hear them.

After she looked and studied her surroundings, she believed it was morning. The demons must have left. They had to walk across the bridge and see her sleeping, but they hadn't killed her. Feelings of joy surged through her. Not only she had escaped from both the ghosts and demons, but she also had a long sleep.

She returned home before sunrise and dropped Poe off with Chhom and headed to work. She was trying to figure out what she should do if she saw Ta Nuy's wife again. She could never look at her the same way again. One wrong word could get her and the family killed.

When she arrived for the morning meeting, Ta Nuy's wife didn't show up. Another woman came to replace her temporarily and held a brief meeting. No one knew why except for Mother. Mother went about her daily tasks. She thought about the horror from last night every second. She was tired but glad to be alive. She was so close to being butchered three times in just one night. The spirits of the land and the spirit of the water were definitely watching over me, she thought.

CHAPTER 16

As Chhom carried a bucket of water from the river to fill our large vase, she caught a glimpse of Pu Peap entering our house. He looked a little different. She hurriedly poured the bucket of water in the vase and then entered the house. Pu Peap was talking softly with Mother. After a moment, she noticed he'd gotten a haircut. It was rare to see anybody getting a haircut nowadays. He looked like he was up to something and looked somehow unsettled. He was supposed to be working. It was too early for him to come to visit. He'd normally come and visit us to check if things were allright in the evenings after work hour. He normally waved his hand to Chhom and acknowledged her one way or another, but this time he seemed to ignore her completely. Maybe he had learned something important from listening to the radio and would like to share his information with Mother.

"They asked me a lot of questions and then offered me a haircut. The meeting is tomorrow," Pu Peap said.

"Now you know why. It is up to you to decide what to do," Mother said.

Mother wept after her conversation with Pu Peap. Chhom didn't understand why Mother cried, but it must be serious. Pu Peap was finally aware that Chhom was standing right behind him when he walked out of the house. He gave Chhom a distressed look before he exited.

Mother when to work the next day like usual. She brought the water that she used to wash the rice home, feeling more nervous than before. She could picture what they would do to her and the family if she got caught stealing. On the other hand, if she didn't steal, we would all die of starvation and illness. She was determined to continue to steal rice but would use extra caution.

Ta Nuy's wife, the same woman who'd led the mass killing, held a meeting every day before and after work. She described her plan of cleaning up society. It was clear to everyone now that the Nearadey had seized the documents from the Pea Yaup regime and examined the documents on each family. They were looking for people who'd been in the military, people who were wealthy, people who were related to the Vietnamese, and people who were highly educated.

Since everyone knew one another well, it was obvious when someone never showed up at the meeting or to work. Normally, each worker was asked to do different tasks all the time. It was difficult to know if the workers were asked to move to other tasks or to the execution.

K'Oeun and Ta Watt seemed to get along with the Nearadey well. Mother thought it was because they came from Takeo. She was glad we were from Takeo as well.

The names of the new leaders were well known by now, even among the children. Ta Kirk was the most well-known killer. He sat in front of his house nearly every day sharpening his axes and machete. Ta Vann was living nearby, and his name sounded just as deadly. Ta Nuy was the youngest of them all, but his was as deadly as Ta Kirk. Then there was Ta Mao who was less well known than the rest, but his name made our skin prickle. Finally, Ta Watt and K'Oeun, who knew us well, now appeared as deadly as the rest. Some believed they'd submitted to the Nearadey to stay alive.

After we finished our lunch, Pech and I were walking behind Chhom who was holding Poe. As we got closer to our house, we saw adults and children crowding a house a block away. Without saying a word, Chhom marched straight toward the crowd. Pech and I followed.

When we arrived, we saw Mother was already there among the crowd. I knew the house well. It was Kru (teacher) Kuon's house. Adults and children were roaming his house. Some were standing inside his house staring up at the ceiling. Everyone was shocked and murmured softly with their friends and relatives. Chhom and I squeezed our way in the house and saw Kru Kuon's lifeless body hanging by his neck from the ceiling of his house with a scarf.

"This morning, Ta Nuy's wife requested to talk to him privately, and he was selected to go to the meeting," one of the women said.

Chhom, Pech, and I stood looking at the man hanging by his neck from the ridge of the ceiling. I had never seen a dead person before. I was trying to figure out what it was all about, but more adults flooded in and blocked my view. Some had chastised us for being there and pushed us out of the house.

When we returned home, Mother and the neighbors talked about the incident the rest of the evening, exchanging thoughts. Kru Kuon was known to be a well-educated man that worked directly with the previous regime, the Peayuap. He was responsible for writing and sending messages between our village and other villages. The messages include distributing work force, retrieving and sending rice and organize meetings base on new orders from higher officials. He was a very useful man for Peayup but the Nearadeys didn't see it that way. They wanted to get rid of him because he was educated. Kru Kuon hung himself when he learned that they want to execute him.

Early in the next morning, Mother attended the usual morning meeting before work. Ta Nuy's wife delivered a devastating message. "Today we have come up with a new plan. We are no longer providing the second meal. Each of you have experience searching for your own food after work. We give you lunch because you are busy working. The government can understand that. You no longer need the government to provide you supper. We have to be strong and live independently. Those who cannot help themselves are considered weak and lazy. Like I mentioned before, we were cleaning up our society. We want the best people in our society. We are eliminating the weak and the corrupted. They are wasting the land space. The ones that can survive are the strong, and we need every single one of them to continue to work to help our country flourish."

It was disturbing news, but Mother and everyone else pretended to agree with her. Everyone understood that disagreement would not change anything and would only put their entire family in danger. Mother could not stop thinking of Kru Kuon's death. She was hoping that the Nearadey would not have anything against our family's past. She had been living a poor life, but Puk was a truck driver. He had been driving the truck for the military, but fortunately he didn't register. Mother didn't know whether the Nearadey thought the truck drivers were part of their enemies or not. Come to think of it, most of the men living around us were truck drivers, and they had not been taken away yet for being truck drivers. She was hoping it would stay that way.

When the meeting was over, Ta Nuy's wife walked over to Mother. This was a living nightmare to Mother. She had to see her every single day. "Mit Yorn, from now on you are my messenger."

Her words were cold and evil. Mother was terrified when she was approached by the most evil woman she had ever seen in her life. She was the walking demon that had no sympathy for any human.

"I accept your offer, but I don't know anything about being a messenger. I can't read or write," Mother replied.

"Just do as I say," Ta Nuy's wife said sternly.

Mother was nervous, but she thought it might be a good thing that the demon woman trusted her.

"I have a task for you. Today I have three brave lady comrades coming to visit. They need rice. There is a transport wagon coming toward our village a little past noon. I want you to stop the wagon and request a basket of rice for our comrades." Ta Nuy's wife said firmly.

"I will do as you request," Mother replied trying not to show her content with the opportunity.

Mother worked very rapidly to cook and serve the food to the horde. After she finished distributing the rice porridge, she cleaned up the pots and then slipped away toward the river with her lunch bowl. Her hands were shaking from anticipation. She sat by the road and ate her rice porridge as she waited for the ox wagon. She was trying to determine the amount of rice she would want to keep for herself, and she had to do it in a way that was not noticeable. She needed to take some rice home since we were no longer getting supper. We were already starving. Each night without supper would be devastating. We would all die of starvation sooner or later.

Mother finished her rice porridge, but the wagon hadn't show up yet. She decided to look around the river bank and pick vegetables as she waited.

About an hour later, she heard the hoof steps and the squeaking sound of an ox wagon. She piled the vegetables on the ground and prepared herself to talk to the rice transporter. As the ox wagon was approaching, she saw a man sitting in the driver's seat holding the reins. A pair of oxen was hauling the wagon moving at a normal pace.

"Hey, Mit! Stop for a second," Mother hollered.

The man jerked the reins, and the wagon stopped. He was about an average-size man, clean shaven, with short hair. He also was obviously eating well, based on the thickness of his face. Mother could not tell if he was the Mit Chah or an ordinary laborer. Transporting rice probably was the best job to have.

"I am a messenger. I was told to get some rice for three brave lady comrades who came to visit us. They are the ones who fought in the front line," Mother said not knowing how she came up with those words.

Without saying a word, the man hopped off the ox wagon. He walked to the back of the wagon and lifted out a basket of rice.

"Here, this is for them," the man said as he placed the basket on the ground.

Mother shivered from excitement and nearly fainted. She tried to not to look directly at the man as she was having a hard time hiding her excitement.

The man hopped back onto the ox wagon and resumed his trip. Mother waited for the man to disappear. Then she looks around all the directions. When she was confident that no one was around, she pulled out a small sack. She filled the sack with rice, feeling nervous and excited at the same time. When she was satisfied, she sealed the sack with the lace and quickly tossed the sack into a bush on the side of the road.

Mother coiled the scarf and placed it on her head, and then she lifts the rice basket and rested it on the coiled scarf. She walked nervously toward Ta Nuy's wife's house and delivered her the rice.

"Good timing," Ta Nuy's wife said. "The brave ladies have just arrived. I will give them the rice. I have more tasks for you. Starting today, you will need to walk daily to the city of Swai Saw to retrieve the rice to cook for your horde. We are no longer allowed to store rice locally. Be on your way right now and get the rice for tomorrow. Just mention my husband's name and asked for five cans of rice. If you are questioned anytime during your trip, give them this note," Ta Nuy's wife said without indication of any suspicion and handed her a piece of paper.

Mother took the paper and replied, "That sounds easy. I can do that." She could not believe how lucky she was to retrieve the rice herself. She had already determined not to be too greedy—that could end her opportunity. This was a chance for the family to survive. If she couldn't control her greediness, it could mean death to the family. Mother wished she knew how to read so she could duplicate the note. She knew the Khmer alphabet, but she didn't know how to read or write. She knew exactly where Swai Saw is. She'd gone to the city to trade regularly. After Ta Nuy's wife finished giving her the instruction, she returned to the road and retrieved her hidden rice sack from the bush. She was relieved that it was still there. She concealed the rice sack in her under clothes and brought it home. She dug a small shallow ditch near the hearth and buried the rice since she didn't have time to properly hide it yet. Then she begins to walk to Swai Saw and arrived there late in the afternoon. The city was very easy to locate and very busy. People from all over the villages came to Swai Saw to retrieve the rice. Supposedly, only the authorized individuals were allowed to receive the rice. From Mother's understanding, the leaders in every village were documented and recognized in Swai Saw. Mother lined up with other men and woman to receive her rice. She spoke to a couple of women around her and found a few that could be trusted to trade with. Nearly all of them were widows and interested in cigar lighter flints, but they could only offer half a can of rice for five flints. They were all the designated cooks, and they needed flints for the cigar lighter to make fire and light their lamps. Every single one of the women came from different villages, but Mother was familiar with all the villages.

When it was Mother's turn to get her rice, the woman who was distributing the rice simply asked Mother's name and the name of the village and nothing else. The woman scooped five cans of rice and poured them in Mother's basket. Mother stood frozen as if she was being hypnotized when she saw the precious rice. She couldn't help but to smile with her eyes fixed on the rice.

"Mit! That's all you get!" the woman said.

Mother snapped back to reality and replied, "Ah, that's right,"

She began to walk back home looking for the best place to steal some more rice. She was trying picture how much awareness Ta Nuy's wife would have on the amount of rice in the basket. In any case, she was confident that there was no way Ta Nuy's wife could figure out if she just took a handful of rice.

The road was empty. A year ago, the same road was busy with many people like Mother who used the pass to travel at night and trade. Sometimes Mother would trade with them right on the road. It was a greater risk to trade on the road, as everyone was unfamiliar. They might be the Mit Chah.

Mother walked and thought over and over about her plan to steal some rice. She was also considering not stealing on her first trip. Ta Nuy's wife may have set her up to see if she was a trustful messenger, but Mother could not picture how Ta Nuy's wife could possibly do that. After a long walk and many repetitive thoughts, Mother looked around. She found herself in a familiar spot just about one kilometer from home. She walked into a small spot off the road where no one could see her from both directions. She lowered the basket of rice to the ground and quickly pulled out a small sack underneath her clothes. She stuck her head out to the road and verified that no one was approaching. Then she grabbed a handful of rice and carefully shoved it in the sack. She planned to take just one handful, but she couldn't help but to grab another and shoved the rice in the sack. She tied the sack and tossed it in the nearby bush. Then she resumed her walk toward Stung Chah feeling a little regretful for stealing more than she planned.

When she arrived in Stung Chah, she walked straight to Ta Nuy's house. She found Ta Nuy's wife was bathing outside of her house with a bucket of water.

"Here is the rice. Where do you want me to leave it?" Mother asked.

"Put it in the corner along with the other rice baskets. Tomorrow morning you can come anytime to pick it up and cook the rice."

Mother placed the basket beside another basket and returned to the spot where she'd hidden the rice sack. She felt a lot more confident now that Ta Nuy's wife would not spend her time measuring rice.

Mother used half of the rice sack to make rice porridge for us and saved the other half. As we were eating, Mother stared out through the back door looking at the pig lying on its side, breathing slowly. The pig must be hungry and tired. It was nothing but skin and bones. Mother had nothing to feed the pig for days. She felt a surge sadness and guilt. The pig was dying of starvation. It was her responsibility to feed the pig, but she never used the rice that she took from the public to feed the pig. She used that rice to feed us instead.

"I'm sorry, Mr. Pig. I hope you can forgive me. I have to feed my children. I have caused a lot of sin for starving you. I cannot do anything in this life to make it up. I will repay you in my next life," Mother said softly. She then turned to Chhom. "How was Poe? Did he cry?"

"He cried a lot. I walked around the block searching for a nursing mom, but I could not find any. So we came back home," Chhom replied.

Just when I'd almost finished my rice porridge, Ta Kloat, one of Father's close friends came holding his daughter in his arms. Ta Kloat was a tall man. He used to be chubby when we first arrived in Stung Chah, but now he was skinny like everyone else.

"Mit Yorn, my daughter is extremely sick and hungry. Please help me," Ta Kloat said.

Mother knew what he was asking for. It wasn't medicine. The little girl needed food. Mother gazed at the girl lying quietly in his arms. Her eyes were open, but she appeared very weak.

"We only have a little left, but she can have some from each of us," Mother said.

"Then I will leave her here. I will be back. I don't want to interrupt your mealtime," Ta Kloat laid his daughter on the floor and left.

Mother did not want to stop him because there was not enough food for him, and it was awkward to have him watch us eat. She grabbed an empty bowl and said, "Sons and daughter, allow Mother to split some rice for the little girl," Mother said and scooped a spoonful of rice from each of us. Pech didn't understand what Mother was saying until he saw Mother scoop the rice out of his bowl.

"My rice! Don't take my rice!" He said, kicking and swinging his hands in anger.

"The little girl needs to live. Don't you feel bad for her?" Mother said.

Pech didn't seem to pay attention to the little girl and continued to wail and wiggle his feet.

"If you kick your bowl, you will spill all your rice porridge, and you will have nothing to eat. You will starve and die," Mother said.

After Mother collected some rice porridge for each of us, she sat beside the sick girl and began feeding her. "Here, eat this. It will make you feel better."

The little girl was still lying down. She opened her mouth and sipped the rice porridge off the spoon. Mother was happy that the little girl still had the strength to eat. Mother fed her every single grain of rice in the bowl.

A short while after she ate, the little girl appeared livelier. She moved her head around looking for her father. Then she sat up after she realized she wasn't at her own house.

"Rest. This is Ming's house. Your Father or Mother will be back in a little bit," Mother assured her.

Ta Kloat's wife came just minutes after. "Mit Yorn, she's looking a lot better now. Thank you once again."

"That's all right. We have to help each other live," Mother said shortly.

"Then I will take her back home. I hope she will not get sick again," Ta Kloat's wife said.

Ta Kloat's wife appeared frail and sick. She looked like she could pass out anytime. Mother felt a surge of sympathy, but she fought against it. Everyone was dying. She could not continue to give food out. We needed food like everyone else. If she continued to give out food, we would die. As for the little girl, if she didn't do anything, she could die anytime soon—maybe within the next few days.

"Here, take this sack of rice. Don't tell anyone that I gave you rice, or you will not see me again the next time you come. And make sure your share with your husband," Mother said and handed her the sack of rice that she'd just stolen today.

It was very common for people to be unable to fight hunger and end up eating the share that belonged to their spouse and children. Mother didn't blame them. She felt like that all the time, but somehow she managed to fight the hunger and get the food to us. Mother was still very hungry. She had given all her rice porridge to the little girl. Mother looked gaunt. She was thin and frail. Now she also had to feed milk to Poe.

Pech stopped crying and finished his share. And then he cried for more, thinking that Mother had more rice porridge.

"There is no more rice, son," Mother said softly knowing that he would not listen.

Pech continued to demand more rice porridge until he got tired and stopped. Chhom and I were getting ready for bed. I didn't scavenge the hearth for crab legs that day. The rice porridge kept me occupied for the evening. We went to sleep as Mother worked on hiding rice and other useful commodities.

It was around midnight. I woke up to a soft, radiant light from the lamp. I thought Mother would wake me up to eat roast meat, but instead I heard a murmur between Mother and a man. I squinted and looked around the room searching for the person Mother was talking to. I saw a man and a woman and two boys, about a year or two older than me. They appeared ragged and scared.

"Ouen, where did you come from, and what are you doing here?" Mother asked.

"Bong Yorn, they are planning to kill us all. They were arranging for our execution. We fled this evening," the man said.

"Did anyone see you flee?" Mother asked.

"No. They thought we didn't know what they were going to do with us. We found out by accident. We fled the minute we found out," the man replied.

"What are you planning to do? If you stay here, they will find you," Mother said.

"We are not planning to stay here. We are just dropping Nup and Naem here for a while. We were going west, far away from here. We'll find a safe place to stay. When the opportunity comes, we will return the pick them up. We can't travel with our children. It's too suspicious and will get us all killed," the man explained.

"That's true. They can stay with me. They don't keep track of children. Chhom will take care of them," Mother said.

"We must get going. I know a place to hide for tonight several hours from here. We need to get there before dawn," the man said.

"Wait, Ouen. I have some rice for you," Mother said. She walked to the hearth area and came back with a small pouch of rice. "I have just dug this out and prepared to hide it deeper in the ground, but you can take it with you," Mother handed the rice pouch to the woman, who was standing with the boys on each side, holding their hands. "Do you have a pot to cook with?" Mother asked.

"Yes, I do. I must get going, Bong Yorn. Please take care of my two children. They are easy to take care of," the man said.

"All right, then go," Mother said.

"Nup. Naem. Go to sleep near your cousins. Don't be afraid. You are related. They are like your brothers and sisters."

The couple rushed out the door and left. They barely made any sound as they moved. The two boys stood still looking at me for a moment, and then they gazed at Chhom, who was still sleeping. Then they stared at Mother.

"Which one is Nup, and which one is Naem? You two look different from the last time I saw you," Mother said.

Neither of the two boys answered. They were both confused and afraid.

"Don't be scared. I'm your auntie. They are your cousins. Go lay near Bun," Mother said pointing to a spot next to me.

Neither of the boys moved. Mother walked over to the boys and grabbed their hands.

"Come." Mother led them to the spot next to me.

The boys obediently walked over and lay down beside me. I could hear them breathing very heavily.

"Who are they?" Chhom asked, still half as sleep.

"You don't remember? They are Nup and Naem. They are your cousins. They will stay here with us for a while. You are to take care of them like your brothers," Mother answered.

Mother explained to Chhom why Nup and Naem were here. She told Chhom not to say anything to anybody. Pu Ouen was Mothers' younger brother. Nup and Naem were living with us for now until Pu Ouen came back to get them. Mother told us to treat Nup and Naem like our brothers.

Nup was about my age. Naem was about a year older than I was. Both were very dark. We got along well just after we woke up. I always wanted new friends. Most kids I hung out with were too sick to play. Some had disappeared from the face of the earth.

"All of you should try to play inside the house. Avoid playing outside for too long. They might see you," Mother warned us before she went out to work.

Mother took Poe with her. She tied the scarf on both ends and hung it to one side of her shoulder and placed Poe in the scarf. We forgot

Mother's warning just minutes after she left and went outside and played anyway. It was fun to have two more people to play with. It didn't take long for Nup and Naem to be comfortable and play with us.

The two liked to wake up early in the morning and wrestle each other for fun. They reminded me of Me-Laeks' kittens. Chhom now had to take care of two more children, and she has two more mouths to feed. As usual, she left us at home and went out to search for food.

Nup and Naem could not get a share of rice because their names were not registered. Mother didn't want to register them. She feared she may attract unwanted attention.

Chhom came back home just before lunch. She caught several small frogs and snails. She cooked and shared the catch with all of us. She took me and Pech to the dining hall for lunch, leaving Nup and Naem home as Mother instructed. When we got home, Mother informed us that we had to share our rice with Nup and Naem. Chhom had to take Pech outside so he wouldn't see his share taken away. Mother used a spoon to scoop the rice from my plate to Nup's bowl. "Here, let's share our life." Then she scooped some rice from Pech and gave it to Naem. Then she took two scoops from Chhom, one to give to Nup and one to Naem.

Chhom left again right after the small meal to search for food. Mother went back to Swai Saw to get the rice regularly. She stole some each time but managed to control her greed by not taking more than three handfuls. She would come back home exhausted from having to carry Poe along with the rice. She would drop the rice off at Ta Nuy's house and returned to the road to retrieve her rice sack.

Several weeks went by, Nup and Naem were still living with us. Mother had warned us regularly to play inside the house, but we kept on forgetting and ended up playing outside with other children. So far, no one had asked us anything. No one seemed to care.

It was a warm evening. The adults were flocking from the field. I was watching Nup and Naem wrestling outside, and Mother was chopping wood. I wanted to join, but they appeared to be big and too rough for me. I decided to sit and watch instead. I had just learned why Nup and Naem woke up very early in the morning. They had this deal where the first one to wake up would fart on the face of the other. Their parents came up with this rule to make them wake up before they left for work. To avoid getting farted on the face, they both tried to wake up as early as possible. One morning, Naem, the older one, farted on Nup. Unfortunately, it wasn't just a fart that came out. Nup woke up squealing like a pig.

As I was sitting and enjoying watching Nup and Naem wrestle like the kittens in front of the house and watching Mother chopping wood, I saw Pu Kuem, a man that liked to tease Pech, holding his son in his arms approaching Mother. His son was several years older than me. His wife was trailing quickly behind him. I had never thought he had a family. More interestingly, he used to be very chubby, but he'd gotten skinny and frail like everyone else. I nearly didn't recognize him.

"Mit Yorn, my son is extremely sick. We need your help. If you don't do anything, he will not live," Pu Kuem said.

Mother dropped what she was doing and led them inside our house. I got curious and followed. Pu Kuem laid down his son on the floor. Mother walked over and knelt beside the boy. She probed his forehead with the back of her hand. Then looked at Pu Kuem and his wife's faces and knew they were not seeking medicine.

"I have nothing myself. I have two more mouths to feed. Look out there. I have two more children and this baby here," She pointed outside, and then she pointed to Poe.

"I understand, but I have no choice. My son will die if he doesn't eat," Pu Kuem pleaded.

"I will make rice porridge for him, but only him and only one meal. If you return again any sooner, my children and I will starve to death. I hope you understand," Mother explained. Mother knew there was not much they could do. It was impossible to find rice.

"I understand," they both replied at the same time. "Would you like anything from us in return? I have clothes, watches, and gold rings. I will give anything you want," Pu Kuem added.

"You know I don't take anything from anyone. Those things are meaningless to me and will only get me in trouble," Mother said as she prepared to cook rice porridge.

"The rice porridge will be done in a little bit," Mother said. "Bun, go play outside."

I went back outside. Pech was quietly playing next to the stairway by himself because he didn't feel too well. Nup and Naem took a break from wrestling and began walking around the bushes searching for something edible. Long ago, there used to be some sort of unidentified berries growing around our house. Chhom had warned us not to pick anything that was not familiar because they might be poisonous. Nowadays, there wasn't a single berry left. Someone must have taken a risk and ate them.

"I found a spider!" Naem yelled out loud holding a large spider by its back.

The spider was much larger than the size of my big toe. I had never attempted to catch a spider before because they looked scary and were fast. I had never thought spiders were edible. Naem broke a small branch off a shrub. He scraped all the leaves off and then poked the spider from its bottom to its head. He ran inside the house. I darted after him, curious to see how he was going to eat it.

Naem revived the fire in the hearth and began roasting the spider over the fire. The aroma of the roasted meat filled the air very quickly. It smelled like roast frog. My stomach growled vigorously. I really wanted to eat that spider, but I didn't think Naem would want to give it away. In just about two minutes, the spider looked well cooked. Naem blew the charred spider to cool it down and then devoured it with just one bite.

Nup and I stood watching. My saliva squirted in my mouth, as I could imagine the taste. If it smelled that good, it would taste ten times better. I didn't waste any time and dashed outside searching for spiders. I checked the same spot where Neam had found his spider. Nup was doing the same thing. We spent nearly an hour searching, but I didn't find any large spider. I found only the small ones that were barely larger than an ant. We gave up and continued to play.

It was getting dark, and there was no indication that we were going to have supper. Chhom returned home empty-handed. We were going to bed very hungry. I could not take my mind of the roasted aroma of spiders. I wanted to eat one badly. Pech was crying nonstop demanding food. He must have been as hungry as I was. Mother had gotten used to us crying for food. She was too tired to comfort Pech. She was busy sewing herself more small sacks. Pech cried until he fell as sleep.

Early in the morning, Mother was attending the meeting as usual. When everyone arrived, Ta Nuy's wife began to speak, "Mit Yorn, there have been complaints that you were taking rice from the public to feed yourself and your family, specifically, by taking the water that you wash the rice with."

Mother's heart stopped a few beats, and she nearly fainted.

"How can you accuse her? Can you see? She's skinnier than any of you," K'Ouen said defending Mother.

Mother was happy that K'Ouen was still on her side. She appeared to have as much power as Ta Nuy's wife. K'Ouen's husband, Ta Watt, seemed to have a lot of control over this village.

"How could anyone accuse me? I did everything in front all Mit Bongs. They would notice if I stole anything. I took the water I used to wash the rice to feed the pig. It's part of my job," Mother said.

"We will search your house this evening," Ta Nuy's wife said.

"You may search my house anytime. I have nothing to hide," Mother said with confidence.

Mother was glad that she had cooked the last of the rice she had to feed Pu Kim's son.

"All right then. We'll do a search this evening," Ta Nuy's wife said.

Mother continued with her daily tasks, including the walk to Swai Saw. She told Chhom to take Nup and Naem away from home to avoid suspicion. On the way back from Swai Saw, she still managed to fill a small sack with rice but she hid the sack in a different location, much further away from the previous location. When she returned to the village, she walked straight to Ta Nuys's house and dropped off the rice basket.

"How about the search? Would you like to search my house right now?" Mother said.

"I will get a few people from our group to come along so they can be witnesses."

Mother wanted to get it done so she could go back to retrieve her sack of rice. Mother told me and Pech to play outside. Chhom took Nup and Naem to search for food further down the river. Ta Nuy's wife and K'Ouen, along with people that initiated the complaints, came. They didn't specify the specific person who'd started the complaint.

Mother led them inside the house and then she stood by the wall waiting for them to examine the house. The whole house consisted of only a single room where everything thing could be seen by just standing by the door. The hearth had nothing but three stones and ashes. The floor was bare dirt. The bamboo bed raised above the ground has nothing but bare dirt floor below. There were two piles of clothes neatly folded and visible from the doorway. On top of the clothes were two rolls of yarns. The pots and a basket were hung on the wall. The rice bowls were stacked on the dirt floor beneath the pots. There was a door that led to the back yard. It was opened, exposing the backyard where the skinny pig was lying on its side with its eyes closed.

"There is nothing to search. Her house is empty," K'Ouen said dismissing the search. Everyone except K'Ouen left.

Mother was nervous about K'Ouen staying around. She wanted K'Ouen to leave so that she could go retrieve her rice sack. K'Ouen had not done any harm to anyone that she was aware of, but her husband was known as a traitor that conspired with the Nearadey to kill the Peayup.

"Say, I heard you knew about the cleanup," K'Ouen said.

"I don't know anything. I was told to guard the bridge, and I did. I don't refuse the orders from our Mit Bong," Mother said.

"Whether you know it or not, the cleanup will continue. My husband has been ordered to check the records. We still have a lot of corrupted, rotten, spoiled citizens to get rid of. Right now, he's looking into the Chuk Tang family," K'Ouen said.

Mother did not want to know who would be taken to be slaughtered. She didn't understand why K'Ouen was telling her all this. K'Ouen had so much authority and privilege, but Mother knew who Chuk Tang and his family was. They lived just a few houses a way. The name, Chuk Tang, was of Chinese descent.

"His daughter graduated from an elite school. The entire family is definitely corrupted," K'Ouen added.

Mother remembered seeing his daughter. She was about eighteen years old. She was light-skinned and beautiful. She remembered seeing other children around his house. They were possibly his children.

"Chuk Tang has done nothing wrong. He doesn't deserve to be harmed. If anything, his family should be spared," Mother said but then immediately wished she didn't. Opposing the Mit Chahs was a bad idea. "Beg Mit Bong Watt to forgive them," Mother instinctively added. She felt like she was possessed by a spirit, saying all these things she immediately regretted.

"I can't stop my husband. He's doing as he was ordered," K'Ouen said. "I must get going."

K'Ouen appeared to be losing interest in speaking with Mother and left. Mother felt dread about the news that Chuk Tang's family would be rounded up next for execution. She had no hope, and she had no way of stopping Ta Watt from taking them to execution. She had no authority or confidence. She was trying to avoid death herself, and she had been very lucky that she had gotten away with many things, including the things she had just said to K'Ouen. She didn't know how long her luck would continue to save her. She was breaking the rules every single day.

Several days later, Chuk Tang's family was taken away to Wat Samdach along with a dozen other families for execution. None of them seemed to know that they were being taken there to be slaughtered. Among them was a couple in Mother's group who had four small children between the ages of two and eight. There must have been a ploy to get the adults to go the meeting in Wat Samdach, and they were to leave the four children home. People were ordered to go places and do things all the time. No one knew if they were being summoned to their execution.

In the next morning meeting, the rumor was that Chuk Tang had escaped execution by jumping through the window. Unfortunately, his entire family had been slaughtered. Mother wanted to burst out crying. She knew too well how they had been killed. She could picture the whole slaughtering process. She tried not to show remorse in public. If she got caught feeling sympathy for a victim, she would be considered an enemy. Her mind raced toward the four children who had just become orphans living a couple houses away. The last time she saw them, they already looked gaunt. Without their parents, they would not survive long. There was no way she could help. She had four children of her own plus two nephews. Pech was sick and hungry all the time. There was no way she could help four more.

Mother held her tears throughout the day. She was walking like a zombie. Her body was doing the work, but her mind was somewhere else. The thought of knowing those four children would die slowly caused her fathomless pain. The children probably knew nothing of their parents being executed. They were probably waiting for their return to feed them.

It was past noon. Mother had finished serving the group in the dining hall. We came home and ate our rice porridge. Mother gave her share to Nup and Naem. She sat in the corner, facing away from us, and wept quietly. She had a scarf draped over her head, and she used the scarf to wipe her tears from time to time.

For the next couple of days, Mother saw the children scattered around their house. The two-year-old boy was walking and picking things off the ground to eat. The older ones were searching for food among the bushes and trees. Mother wept as she stood and watched. By far, this was the most painful thing that she'd had to bear. She could do nothing but watch them suffer.

"Angels have eyes. Please punish those demons that caused all the suffering," Mother whispered to herself.

The two-year-old boy was found dead by the side of their house several days later. One of the neighbor men picked the body up and buried it near the house.

Two days later, the oldest one was found dead by a tree. He was seen eating the leaves of a tree than produced edible potato-like roots, but the leaves were poisonous. Someone saw him eating and vomiting near the tree.

Then there was one that was a girl. She seemed to be the next oldest one. She was last seen searching for food, constantly looking down to the ground as she walked. She was found dead, facing down.

The other one was still alive walking around the house and eating whatever he found. He came to line up for rice porridge at noontime. Mother gave him a little extra rice porridge. He was nothing but skin and bones.

About two weeks later, he was found dead inside his house. His bodies lay several feet from the door. No one had any energy do anything. He probably was waiting for his mother. Like everyone else,

Mother tried to avoid looking directly at him, as it was too painful. She begged God to forgive her for not caring for the helpless children. She repeatedly asked God to send those demons to hell and let them burn for eternity. Mother knew she would remember the faces of the children the rest of her life. She would feel the guilt as long as she lived for not being able to help.

CHAPTER 17

Every morning, I woke up and squatted in front of the hearth rummaging through the ashes looking for crab legs. I hadn't found anything for a long time, but hunger made me think there might be crab legs somewhere in the ashes. The rice that was served in the dining hall was mostly water. Mother made rice at home, but the neighbors continued to bring their children to her when they were on the verge of death. We ate mostly water spinaches, but it didn't seem to help. Chhom rarely caught anything anymore. She came home empty-handed most of the time.

More families had been summoned to Wat Samdach more often for execution. It was more common than not to see orphans scattered around the village seeking food. Chhom knew most of them. Some were looking for friends just to have someone to talk to or to share food. Most wandered alone, afraid to talk to anyone.

Mother decided to stop taking the rice water for the pig. There were more complaints after the search. She didn't want to be taken away and leave us to die like other children. She made up her mind that we would die together of starvation. She wanted to be beside us if anything happened.

She had been neglecting the pig for the entire week because she couldn't find enough vegetables. She was no longer bringing home the rice water that she'd used to feed the pig. Today, she came back with a bundle of wild plants intended to feed the pig, but she found the pig unresponsive. She checked the pig and realized it was dead. She broke down crying.

"I'm sorry, Mr Pig. Because of you my sons are alive. I promise to pay you back in my next life.

Dear God, forgive me. I'm doing this for my children. If I don't do this, my children will die. Please do not give me sin," Mother whispered as she wept.

Mother reported the dead pig to Ta Nuy's wife. She and the other Mit Chahs took the pig away for themselves. The pig was nothing but skin and bones.

Several days after the pig died, Mother came up to me and Chhom as we were walking back from the river. She squatted in front of me and said, "Bun, starting tomorrow, you will be required to work. If you don't go to work, they will not give you anything to eat. You must try hard, you understand?" Mother said.

I didn't answer. I didn't quite understand what she meant.

There were a lot fewer people in the village nowadays. The labor force was getting thin, and the rice was extremely scarce. All children five years and older were required to work in order to get their share of rice.

Mother woke me up the next morning and gave me a chopping knife. I didn't recall using a knife before; maybe I never had. I had seen Mother use them to cut fish and vegetables. "Hold this tight. Do not drop it," Mother said.

I grabbed the knife by the handle. It slid and fell right to the ground.

"You have to use more strength to hold a knife, or it will drop on your feet and cut your toe," Mother explained.

I gripped the handle more tightly, and it seemed to stay in my hand. "Use this knife to cut whatever you are asked to cut, you understand?"

I didn't understand what Mother was trying to explain, but I nodded anyway.

"Follow me. From now on, you will wake up in the morning and go line up with the rest of the people. Then you do whatever your Mekong tells you to do."

I nodded without understanding a thing. I had never followed instructions in my life. I began to worry.

Mother walked me a few blocks away. I saw hundreds of children gathering in groups. I was excited to see so many children all at once. Most of the children were a few years older than me.

"This is your group. Wait here with everyone else," Mother said and left.

After a long wait, a woman came to our group and said, "Make a single line right here."

A boy about several years older than me walked over and stood facing her. Everyone rushed to stand behind the boy. I followed the flow, and the line somehow formed.

"I need all of you to tell me your name," the woman said.

The first boy was asked and responded immediately. I looked around and saw other groups were doing the same thing. Everyone seemed to know what they were doing.

"What is your name?" the woman said out loud staring at me. It appeared she had asked that question a couple times already, but I had not been paying attention.

Everyone was looking at me expecting something from me. I was scared and didn't know what to do. I looked at a girl standing close to me hoping she could help, but she gave me no hint.

The woman appeared impatient and angry. She said something else that I didn't understand. I begin to panic. No one had asked me this question before. The woman stepped past me and asked the girl who was standing right behind me. The girl said her name gracefully. Then it clicked in my mind what I needed to say. Something that everyone one called me. I stuck my head out and said, "Bun! Bun!" pointing to myself happily.

The Mekong looked at me. "Your name is Bun?"

I nodded and smile with relief. The Mekong continued getting the rest of everyone's names. She didn't seem to appreciate what I had just learned. It the first time I'd said my own name. It felt so weird.

After the Mekong finished taking our names, she walked us along the road that led to the river. Then we took the road along the river, going the same direction of the stream. Shortly after, we came to a new bridge that I had never seen before. Unlike the bridge that I normally saw, this bridge was smaller and made mostly of metal and wood. The Mekong was leading us on to the bridge.

Once in the middle of the bridge I saw a crisscross of some sort that allowed us to see the water flowing violently far below. My head spun from staring down at the flowing water. If anyone fell of the bridge, the water would sweep them away like a piece of a rag. I turned my head away and try to refrain from looking down.

"If you are scared of heights, do not look down," the Mekong said. Everyone couldn't help but to look down.

After we crossed the bridge, the Mekong led us to a small path. We arrived at a small open field covered with thick grass with spots of random brush. The Mekong stopped and looked around.

"Do what I do. Find these plans called Katreang Kaet. They look like this." She pointed to one of the bushes that she was standing by. "Cut them by the stem and make a pile…" she continued to explain.

I was not listening; my attention was elsewhere. I was confused why we needed to cut the plants, not to mention how. I waited to see how the Mekong and the other children did it. The older children seem to know exactly what they were doing. They swung the knives in a way that made the Katreang Kaet collapse to the ground. I raised the knife and swung it toward the plant. The knife struck the plant, but nothing happened.

I turned my head looking for help, but everyone was too busy. I stood around hoping someone would feel sympathy and help. I observed an older boy and learned that he was cutting much smaller plants. I searched and found smaller plants and made a second attempt. The plant collapsed to the ground, but it didn't sever. I looked closer and saw that the plants were not even cut. They were just bent. I looked around for more hints, but some children were having the same issues. I wanted to see how the Mekong did it, but she was too far away. I walked closer to the Mekong and stood by her observing.

"Why are you standing around? Get to work!" she yelled.

I jumped when she yelled at me, but I was quick enough to learn that I had been holding the knife the wrong way. I had been using the back side of the knife instead of the blade. Happy with my discovery, I found myself a small Katreang Kaet and cut it with ease.

I got bored very quickly. I wanted to talk with other children, but I didn't know any of them besides a girl name Lim who lived just few blocks from me. She was busy talking to another girl. I just stood and listened to their conversation.

"Everyone stop talking and get to work!" the Mekong yelled.

I got scared and stopped trying to talk to people and continued to cut the Katreang Kaet. I piled my cut like the others. My pile appeared to be the smallest. I got a quick surge of fear that I might get in trouble, but my attention was elsewhere shortly after.

It was noontime, and I was very thirsty. I didn't want to say anything because there was no use. I didn't see water anywhere near us. I waited. The knife was getting heavier and heavier.

A moment later, the Mekong hollered, "Gather your cuts! It's time for us to head back."

I looked at everyone for a hint of what to do. The Mekong skillfully tied her bundle using other Katreang Kaet. Her bundle was a large as her whole body. Mine and a few other kids were slightly larger than the size of our legs. Not knowing how to wrap the bundle like the Mekong, I put the knife down and awkwardly picked up the entire pile. Some of the Katreang Kaets were falling off my arms. I was hoping someone would help, but no one seemed to pay any attention to me besides the Mekong. She stood and stared at me with aggravation. She already had her bundle on her head.

I was finally able to gather the bundle and carry it on my waist with both my arms. I was the last in line, right behind Lim. We began walking back to the village the same way we came.

Once we got to the village, the Mekong led us past our houses toward the opposite side of the village. We came to an open field. Women of all ages were sitting down in line chopping the Katreang Kaets. Each one had a large pile of Katreang Kaet in front of them. I saw many columns of children emerging from other directions, possibly from many other villages, dumping their Katreang Kaet into the piles in front of each woman.

We approached the women closest to us, and I tossed my bundle in the pile.

"Wow! That's a large bundle you got there!" one of the women said and laughed.

I felt very good when the woman sounded happy. The Mekong ordered us to make a single line again. Then she led us back to the village to the dining hall.

"These are the kids that went to work," the Mekong informed the leaders.

"Well, then they can line up for rice porridge," the leader responded.

Mother was standing at the giant pot distributing the rice porridge. Unfortunately, I could no longer simply come and get my share anymore. I had to go to work to earn it. I lined up and got my share and came to see Chhom, who was walking Pech and carrying Poe in one hand and holding the rice porridge in the other.

As was our usual new routine, we walked home and gave Nup and Naem some of our share. I finished my rice porridge within a few minutes. It contained mostly water. It didn't even budge my hunger a bit. I felt like I hadn't eaten anything. Mother was sitting and watching us eat. I didn't see her eat at all. She gave all her share to Nup and Naem. Then she began to search for something, and she seemed unable to locate it.

"Bun, where is your knife?" Mother asked.

I just stood and stared at her not knowing what to say.

"You lost your knife?" Mother asked. "How are you going to work tomorrow? If you don't work, they will not give you anything to eat. You are going to starve to death," Mother said angrily. I didn't reply. I stood still feeling very guilty for losing the knife.

The next morning, Mother got me another knife about the same size and handed it to me. I gripped the knife with my hand, but my hand was sore and tired. The knife slid and dropped to the ground.

"Grip it harder," Mother said.

I tried to grip the knife harder, but the knife slid down right after. Mother paused a few seconds, and then she took off her scarf and tied the knife with one end of the scarf.

"Here, hold your scarf like this," Mother explained and showed me how to hold the scarf.

I held the scarf on one end as instructed where the opposite end was tied to the knife. Then I started walking to meet up with the group. The tip of the knife was dragging on the ground.

I arrived and lined up with my group. Everyone was tired and did not seem to care how I was holding my knife. The Mekong arrived, and she looked very tired herself. She called out everyone's name. I nearly forgot that I had to remember my own name. When the Mekong pointed to me, I paused and felt scared for a minute. Then I recalled that I had to say my own name. I said my name out loud, the way Mother called me. It was still awkward to speak out my own name, but I did it.

We walked to the same spot as yesterday and begin cutting the same plants. I felt more confident than yesterday that I knew what to do, but the long walk made me very tired. I could not focus on cutting the Katreang Kaet. Each time I lifted the knife, I felt like my whole body was going to collapse. I paused between each swing to regain my strength. I looked around for someone to talk to, hoping to distract my mind from feeling hungry. I missed staying home and wait for Chhom to bring me food. I didn't like being away from home working with the Mekong who yelled at me for everything. I got scolded several more times, but I didn't understand most of the things the Mekong said.

I learned how to use the knife a little better, but the knife was still too heavy for me to lift. It still took me three to four swings to get one Katreang Kaet down.

At noontime, the Mekong informed everyone to bundle up their cuts and get ready to march back to the village. From yesterday's experience, I was able to cut a lot more Katreang Kaet, but I was still having trouble bundling them together. When I lifted it up, most of them fell off my arm. I remembered to pick up my knife this time because it was tied to a scarf and was easy to see.

I secured the bundle on my waist with one arm and held the scarf with the other hand. I thought I was the last one in line, but I saw a girl was struggle with her bundle. I felt better that I wasn't the last person in line.

"Hurry up! Why are you so slow? You are wasting everyone's time!" the Mekong yelled at the little girl.

The little girl was probably around my age, but she was a little shorter than me and much skinnier. After she joined the line, we marched across the bridge back to the village. We arrived at the field where women were sitting down chopping the Katreang Kaet.

"Everyone, drop your bundle on the pile." the Mekong ordered. Then she had her eyes fixed on me. "Where is your bundle?" she asked, exasperated.

I looked at my bundle, and only about three small branches were left. Most of them must have fallen off along the way. I didn't pay attention because I was trying to keep up the pace. The Mekong yelled at me some more, saying things that I could not understand. Some of the elder women laughed, but some appeared sympathetic.

We took turns dumping our bundles into the piles in front of the women who chopped the Katreang Kaet to small pieces. A woman smiled lightly when I dropped my bundle into her pile; she didn't look angry.

We walked back to the dining hall in the village. I lined up to get my share of rice where Mother was serving. The Mekong was talking to Mother. Mother looks tired, but she also looked upset. She stared at me a couple of times with an angry look.

It was my turn to get my share. I noticed the new scoop that she was holding was much smaller than the normal scoop; probably half the size. Mother tried to fill it as much as possible. She was careful not tilt the scoop, which would cause the rice porridge to spill. She moved the scoop quickly to my bowl before the excess rice porridge flows off the scoop. When she pours the rice porridge, she took her time and allowed all the rice porridge to drip to my bowl.

I walked over and sat with Chhom and Pech. We waited until Mother finished distributing the rice and came over to meet us.

"Bun, I was told you didn't do your job. They told me you were not supposed to get any share, but because of Mother, they allowed you to get your share for today. From now on, you have to work hard and do as you are told. Do you understand?" Mother said.

I sat motionless. Then tears begin to roll down my cheeks. I felt hurt, confused, and guilty. I didn't know what happened. Mother sounded mad, but I knew she didn't look mad at all. Then she stared down at the scarf that I was holding.

"Where is the knife?" she asked.

I didn't response.

"Where is the knife I gave you?" she asked again.

This time I just wailed out loud.

"Let's go. Hold your bowl," Mother said and grabbed my hand.

She took Poe from Chhom and held him in her other arm.

Chhom held three bowls with the hot rice porridge. Pech was walking after her. When we got home, Mother sat right in front of me. "You didn't work hard enough, and you lost your knife. If you keep doing that, you will starve to death. You have to listen to what they tell you to do. Do you understand? If you don't, they will not give you anything thing to eat," Mother said.

Mother began to split the rice porridge with Nup and Naem. She gave nearly all her share to Nup and Naem and then scooped just the surface of our rice porridge. She lifted up her bowl and finished her rice with a single slurp.

"I'm going to get you another knife. This time, you have to be careful not to lose it," Mother said and left.

I didn't respond. I was afraid I might make her angrier. She walked outside. I began eating my rice porridge. Even after getting scolded, the rice porridge was still tasty.

The next morning, Mother brought me a new knife. She used a woven rope to tie the knife to the scarf to make it more secure. I went to work at my usual time. Things got more complicated at work. The Mekong did not like the fact that I worked too slow. She monitored me and yelled at me very often. I cried most of the time in response and did not improve much after the scolding. I was confused and scared most of the time. Mother learned that my bad performance had been reported to the higher officials. She had been asked to chastise me to help improve my performance.

"Pay attention to what you are told to do and work hard," Mother said repeatedly.

After several weeks, the Mekong was frustrated with me. Not only did I not cut enough plants, but I was always the last person in line. The girl that was normally the last person in line was no longer around. I had never thought why she never showed up again. The Mekong gave up on forcing me to work harder. Instead, she assigned me an additional task. She asked me to do whatever it took to arrive at the plant chopping site before everyone else. At least that's what I thought. When we arrived on the field where the elder women were chopping the plants, the Mekong yelled at me to run. I did as I was asked and ran toward the women. Once I got there, I got yelled at by one of the women. I think I did something wrong, but I don't know exactly what it was.

The Mekong assigned new tasks nearly every day. Sometimes she assigned me to lead the group to the working site by walking ahead of everybody. Sometimes she made me help collect other people's cuts and make a pile for them. That's what I thought. The elder children did not like my work either and yelled at me.

I worked in fear of making mistakes every day. I got more and more confused as my tasks changed all the time. To make matters worse, we were led to different locations to cut the Katreang Kaets.

This morning when I woke up, I didn't see Mother around. She must have woken up very early and traveled to another city. I realized that I'd woken up late, and I knew everyone must have left. I was scared that I would get yelled at again. Chhom was taking care of Poe and noticed I was late for work. She suggested I cut the Katreang Kaets down in the river.

I managed to find a knife and walked to the river. I hadn't been to the river for a while since after I started working. I expected the river to be full of water, but instead it was empty. Only mud and the bushes grew along the side. I descended the empty river. The Katreang Kaets were abundant. They were soft and easy to cut. I chopped down a large pile in a very short period of time. I also found some snails as I worked and collected them in my pocket.

As I continue cutting the Katreang Kaet, I noticed movements in the mud. I walked over and saw a frog wiggling. I snatched one nearby and held it by its hind feet and smashed its head against the back side of the knife. I was amazed at my own skill. I had seen Chhoeun and Chhom do it so many times. I caught another frog wiggling nearby and did the same.

I was thrilled and looked forward to getting home to cook the frog. I gathered the Katreang Kaet and rushed home. Chhom was still at home holding Poe. He was crying hard. We didn't know when Mother was coming back home. Pu Peap normally came to visit and give her some advice. We hadn't seen him for a while now.

I showed the frogs and he snails to Chhom. She was surprised. I'm sure she was very hungry herself and very happy to see two large frogs.

"When you catch frogs, watch out for snakes," Chhom said.

She revived the fire and cooked the frogs immediately. The aroma of the charred frog filled the house almost instantly. Pech, Nup, and Naem appeared from nowhere and surrounded the hearth staring at the frogs. We waited impatiently. When the frogs were cooked, Chhom picked up one of the frogs and ripped out one of the hind legs and handed it to me first because I was the one who caught the frog.

I wanted to pop the whole thing in my mouth, but I decided take my time and enjoy every bite. I picked the meat off the frog legs slowly and ate it.

Mother arrived home from her trip just before noon. Chhom explained to her why I didn't go to work and how I made up the work. It didn't surprise her that I missed work, but she was happy that I made up the work. She went and spoke with the Mekong, and they were all right with me working around home once in a while, especially when they learned that I was more productive working around home. I got my share of rice porridge.

About a week later, I woke up in the morning, and Mother was away again. I knew I was late for work. I wasn't sure if I could work at home and still get my share of rice. I begin to panic when I thought of it. A moment later, attention was on something else. I didn't feel like going to work anymore and stood idling around. Chhom was not home either. She must have left to search for food. After doing nothing for a while, it dawned on me again that I had to work or I wouldn't get anything to eat. I scrambled to get ready. I started to look for a knife, but I didn't remember carrying it back from work on the previous day. I must have dropped it somewhere. I didn't even remember where I worked yesterday. I started to panic. I had to leave soon, before Mother came back. I began walking to the river hoping to find the knife.

When I reached the river, I descended to where I thought I'd left the knife and began searching for it. After a moment, my attention was elsewhere once again, and I forgot all about my duty. I was idling in the shoreline staring at trees and plants. The knife was nowhere to be found. When I thought of my duty again, I begin to panic. Not knowing where the knife was, I begin pulling the Katreang Kaets at the root. After a few attempts, I got very tired and stopped. I gave up and stood idling around again. I saw small crabs crawling around my feet. I immediately chased after the crabs and collected them and forgot all about my responsibilities.

When the sun reached the center of the sky, I realized that I needed to deliver the Katreang Kaet to the Mekong, but I didn't have any. I panicked even more. I trekked back home not knowing what was going to happen. When I arrived home, Chhom was getting ready to get a share of rice porridge at the dining hall. I handed her several tiny crabs that I'd collected. She left the crabs near the hearth and walked us toward the dining hall.

When we arrived at the dining hall, I saw my Mekong was speaking to Mother. The Mekong was looking very angry. I was too far away to hear what they were saying, but I had a strong feeling that they were talking about me missing work.

When they finished talking, Mother walked over to me, "Why didn't you go to work?" she said very loudly.

I was too scared to answer. I didn't say anything. I wanted to explain to her that I went to work, but I didn't have a knife. But for some reason, I couldn't speak.

"You know, if you don't work you are not allowed to eat. What are you going to eat? You don't eat anything all day. If you don't eat, you will die," she said angrily and pointed her finger to my forehead. "Why didn't you go to work?" she continued.

I stood frozen. Tears started to roll down my cheeks. I sobbed softly for a little while, and then I broke out crying. Mother continued to scold, but I could not hear what she was saying.

When Mother finished scolding me, we walked back home. Nup and Naem were waiting for the rice porridge. Mother scooped some from Chhom's share and some from Pech's share, then some from her own bowl to Nup and Naem. I stood staring at the rice bowl. My mouth was watering. I know I didn't go to work and I shouldn't get anything to eat. When Mother finished splitting the rice porridge for Nup and Naem, she handed me her bowl. I looked her in the eyes just to make sure she meant to give it to me. I saw tears in her eyes. I was too hungry to figure out why she was crying, but I was glad she gave me her rice porridge. I sat down next to Pech and slurped the rice porridge slowly. Everyone was eating the rice porridge without saying a word. Mother walked out of the house and left. I thought she must be going to the dining hall to clean up.

I learned my lesson for the next several days. I understood clearly that Mother cried because of me. She spoke to herself in regret for scolding me. I didn't want to see Mother cry because of me again. I took extra caution with my knife so I wouldn't lose it again. Over time, I felt awkward without a knife in my hand. However, I still woke up late every time Mother was not home.

Several months after, the raining season began. The plants of all types flourished and became abundant. The Mekong gave up yelling at me and allowed me to work from home from now on. My new routine was to wake up and cut the Katreang Kaet down in the river by myself.

Nup and Naem were no longer with us. Their parents came back one night and took them back. I missed them. They were fun to be around. There was more rice for us to eat now. We no longer had to split our share. In addition, the rain helped the vegetation flourish. Mother had been bringing home baskets of vegetables each day. Unfortunately, the vegetables were not the same as rice. They didn't fill you up. The farm at our new house had flourished as well, but unlike our previous house, the land was smaller and crowded. Mother had secretly harvested the vegetables and skillfully covered the evidence. She learned that the lower parts of the plantain stalks were edible. At midnight she would sneak to our backyard and peel the outer layers of the stalks. She cut the lower parts of the stem into small pieces and cooked them like any other vegetables. Her yucca trees were growing very fast as well. She carefully dug up the roots at night and skillfully covered the evidence with dirt.

One morning I woke up early on my own. Mother was away. I looked around for the knife and was happy to find it by the doorway. I'd gotten better at holding the knife now. I didn't need Mother to tie it to the scarf anymore. Besides, I had lost my scarf somewhere many days ago. Chhom was up as well, holding baby Poe. He was several months old and a lot bigger now. He was too heavy for Mother to carry him around. He was the healthiest baby around. Mother fed Poe with everything we had.

"Don't forget to do your job," Chhom reminded me.

I left the house and walked toward the river, one hand holding the chopping knife. I descended the shallow river. Even after many weeks of rain, the river still remained nearly empty. The ground was damp, and the plants were a lush green. I was happy that the Katreang Kaet was abundant. I grabbed a bundle of the Katreang Kaet and chopped the lower stem. I tossed it to one side to make a pile. I stopped when I got bored. I looked around for any signs of frogs or crabs. It was harder to see frogs or crabs now as the plants grew over the once muddy river bottom. I turned my attention back to work. I stooped over and grabbed a handful of the Katreang Kaet and started cutting again. Then I noticed muddy water oozing from somewhere all around me. I stood up and looked around. The muddy water continued rising slowly submerging small plants on the riverbed. I gazed further up the river and saw an avalanche of muddy water tumbling down toward my direction. I stood frozen for a second and then realized I would be swept away if I was still standing here. I panicked then also, realizing I had just dropped my knife. I looked around and saw nothing but the muddy water rising, quickly reaching my knees. The knife has been submerged beneath the muddy water. I made my last attempt to probe for the knife in the muddy water with both of hands. I took a few steps up to avoid the current, but then I slipped on the mud and slid a few feet down. The muddy water was flowing fast. I discarded the idea of retrieving the knife and decided to get out of the river before I get swept away and drowned. I grabbed the nearby shrubs and pulled myself up. I slipped a few times along the way up, but I managed to get out of the river safely.

I was standing by the rim of the river catching my breath and looking down where I was standing earlier. The spot had been submerged by the ferocious muddy current. I would have been swept away like a piece of hay had I not climbed up in time. I was glad that I'd gotten out. After realizing that I'd nearly gotten killed, I panicked and darted home.

Chhom was roasting water spinach when I got home. "Why did you come home so early?" she asked.

"The water in the river rose," I tried to explain.

"The river is dry and empty. How can the water rise? Were you trying to skip work gain? You will not get any rice again if you skip work."

"The water really rose. If you don't believe me, come and see."

"Let's go see then," Chhom said.

I ran ahead of her, trying to prove that I hadn't lied. When we got back to the river, the water had overflowed the river; submerging the river bank and all tree trunks and bushes that grew along the bank. The logs, branches, and all sorts of lose plants were floating everywhere in the river. The water was not as muddy and wasn't flowing as violently as before, but it was deep, and the powerful force would sweep anything in its path.

Chhom gasped and turned her head to me and asked, "How did you escaped?"

"I left my knife behind and ran up as fast as I could," I explained.

She looks terrified. We stood on a slope from a distance watching the river flows with an ominous hum.

"I wonder where all the water came from," Chhom said to herself.

Chhom and I walked back home. She continuously stared at my face, as I was fortunate to make it out of the river alive. When Mother arrived from her trip moments later, Chhom explained to her my ordeal. Mother knew and explained to us where the water had come from. There was a great dam that the government forced the workers to build intended to store the water for the year-round rice irrigation. Workers from all over the country were summoned to come built the dam. Mother was among the workers building the dam. She had been selected a dozen of times within the past several months to help build the dam. Part of the project was to build the gate to control the water flow. Today, Mother was summoned to help build the gate. Luckily, she was working along the side of the river. About a hundred men and women were working on the center of the dam. The dam broke all of a sudden and swept away all the men and women as if they were small ants.

"Luckily, he's all right. My son could have been killed," Mother said to herself. She clasped her hands together pray softly, "To the Keeper of the land and the Keeper of the water, I would like to thank you for saving my son's life. Today I don't have anything to give you, but someday, when I have food, I will not forget you. I promise to provide you food along with some gifts."

I didn't get my share of rice porridge that day, but Mother gave me her share and didn't yell at me either.

CHAPTER 18

Pu Lee and his daughter were taken away yesterday for execution. Our family knew them well. He was one of Father's friends and a truck driver. He was half Chinese and half Vietnamese. Anyone with light skin was a suspect of being related to the Vietnamese, the current enemy of the Red Khmer. Being half Chinese didn't help. Chhom saw him with a haircut two days ago. By now, she knew what was going to happen to him. She remembered Pu Peap had vanished after he'd had a haircut.

I learned that nearly half the children that were working with me were orphans. They were ranging from the age of five to nine. There was a girl about four years of age. She was living with her stepmother. Rumor had it that her mother had been taking her share of rice porridge. Mother and the neighbors felt bad for her and gave her rice porridge. Over the past six months, the rice was too scarce and no one could afford to offer her rice porridge. She was so hungry and too young to look for her own food. Every day, she was found standing by the coconut tree near our house. She would hug the coconut tree and tilt her head up, staring at the coconut fruit hanging. One day she was found dead hugging the coconut tree.

Many people died during work and no one had energy to do anything. Sometimes, workers were accused of being lazy and were executed onsite. No one had the energy to deal with the dead bodies. Corpses were lying everywhere on the field.

It was late afternoon. Chhom and I had just returned from seeking food. I was walking and feeling proud of myself for working hard that day. I was able to understand most of the instructions and did what I was asked to do. When I returned home, Chhom needed my help and asked me to come along with her to seek food. When we arrived home, we saw Mother was talking to Tien's mom inside our house. They appeared serious and angry about something. Tien's mom swore more than she spoke. She sounded furious.

"My sympathy burns my heart. She was just using the fire to cook her snails, and then they shoved both her hands inside the hot water," Mother wept as she explained the incident to Tien's mom. "They took her parents away. She's living by herself. She worked hard searching for food. She just needed to use the fire to cook her snail…" Mother continued.

I stood behind Mother listening to the intense conversation, trying the figure out what Mother was talking about. After a long moment, I learned that Lim, my co-worker, had her hands burned by the Mit Chah girls. Her parents had been taken away to execution recently. She had been living by herself. She appeared more mature and more aware than I and went to work every day and got her share of rice porridge. One day, she had collected some crabs and snails as she was working. She didn't know how to make a fire. She needed a fire to cook her catches. The Mit Chah girls were aggravated that she was using their fire to cook. They scolded and warned her multiple times. Like me, the scolds had become normal for her, and we didn't pay much attention to it. As Lim was about done cooking, one of them grabbed both of her hands and shove them in the boiling water. Mother saw the whole ordeal, but there was nothing she could do about it. If she attempted to help her in any way, it would insult the Mit Chah and she would be in their hate list. Chhom didn't pay much attention to the story, as she was preparing to cook her catches. Since the pig died, we barely had rice to eat besides the rice porridge that we got from the dining hall. Mother had no more excuses to sneak some rice out. Fortunately, she was still the designated person to retrieve the rice from Swai Saw. She had been assigned to go retrieve rice once or twice a week. She continued to steal small amounts of rice using different tactics to avoid getting caught.

Lim had missed work for nearly three weeks after the incident, but I still saw her seeking food around the river and the rice field. Mother continued to talk about the incident with Tien's mom here and there.

When Chhom finished feeding us, she rested a little and began taking Pech and me to search for more food by the flooded river. She laid

Poe on the ground across the wagon road away from the flowing river. She assigned me to keep an eye on him. The water normally brought all sorts of animal from somewhere upstream. The current was too strong for Chhom to go anywhere deeper than her knees; thus, she was searching for frogs and vegetables along the river bank.

Mother was standing about twenty yards away waiting for someone. She told Chhom not to acknowledge her until she said it was all right. Mother was normally busy with sewing or pruning her plants in the backyard. Whomever she was waiting for had to be important.

I was squatting down watching Poe, who was lying quietly on the scarf. I didn't mind doing that. I was hoping Chhom wouldn't ask me to go near the river. The water current was ominous and merciless. It could overpower anybody or anything and sweep them up like a piece of a rag.

For a long moment, I heard the slow, squeaky sound of an ox wagon and the thumping of the oxen's hoofs approaching. Travelers were rare nowadays. We didn't see the ox wagon that often anymore.

"Mit! Mit! Stop!" Mother waived her hand to the ox wagon driver.

The ox wagon stopped. A man jerked the rein and stopped the wagon. "Another three brave single ladies have come to visit our village. They requested three cans of rice. Scoop me three can of rice," Mother said firmly.

"Where are they from?" the man asked.

"They didn't tell me, but I'm assuming they were the brave ones that battled the Vietnamese in the east. They looked exhausted and need rice immediately," Mother continued. Many people knew nowadays that the Vietnamese were invading the country.

The man got off and walked to the back of the wagon. He untied the woven rice bag and scooped three cans of rice and poured the rice into a sack that she'd made.

The man did not question her any further. By now, everyone should know well that stealing from the public, especially stealing rice, would get them executed.

When the ox wagon left, Mother looked around to check that no one was looking. Then she walked straight home.

Chhom stopped what she was doing and came over to pick Poe up. "Let's go," she said to me. She appeared curious to find out what Mother had done. I trotted right behind her.

When we got home, we saw Mother behaving very strangely.

"Close the door!" she said with a terrifying tone.

She didn't tell us anything, but we knew that she'd lied to the ox wagon driver for the rice. No one would take that much rice home. Even a handful of rice was impossible to find. She'd had asked for three cans.

"Don't tell anyone about this, do you understand? If anyone knew about this, we'd be dead," Mother said to Chhom.

"Yes," Chhom said shortly staring at Mother. She appeared frightened herself when she learned that Mother had taken three cans of rice from the man.

Mother spent most of the night digging the ground and rearranging the pots and pans. She hid most of the rice. She woke us up at midnight to eat rice porridge. It was delicious and special. We hadn't had this much rice porridge in one meal for a long time.

For the next couple of weeks, Mother skillfully took the hidden rice each night and left it for Chhom to make rice porridge for use to eat in the morning.

Rumor had it that the early-harvestable type of rice had just begun. This type of rice was fast to produce, but it was light and didn't taste good. Chhom had just finished feeding us the rice porridge. She was waiting for Mother to come back from her trip so that she could go out and search for food. Chhom was getting ready to collect rice grains. The children were allowed to pick the rice grains off the ground when they were dropped by the harvesters as long as they didn't pick them directly from the stalk. They still had to be careful not to collect too much.

Poe was hungry and had been crying nonstop. Chhom carried him around searching for a nursing mom. She found a lady who had just delivered a baby several blocks away from us. She begged the lady to feed Poe, but the lady did not have any milk. She was so frail and tired. Chhom returned home with Poe still crying. She waited until Mother returned home.

When Mother arrived and settled down with Poe, Chhom told Mother that she was going out to pick rice grains off the ground and hoped to return before noon.

It was still early in the morning. Chhom walked aimlessly into the alley down the corner from our house. She didn't know exactly where she could find the harvesters. Most of the houses were empty, save for the small toddlers roaming around their houses waiting for their mothers' return.

Chhom trotted along the alley and then came to a group of men and women sitting on the bench preparing to eat. It was too early for lunch and too late for breakfast. These people must have had great privilege to be eating at this time. Chhom saw a roasted chicken sitting on a plate and a bowl of soup next to the roasted chicken. A man tore off a chicken leg and took a big bite and then he talked to another man who had his head bent down slurping the soup. Another man was tearing the wing of the chicken. Each of them had a bowl of rice in front of them. Chhom stood motionless with her jaw dropped open. She had never seen so much rice in one single bowl. She had never seen a whole cooked chicken sitting on a plate with just five people eating it. She was overwhelmed with imaginations of eating the chicken. Her mouth watered.

She stood staring at the men and the women chewing their food, imagining the taste of chicken, the soup, and the steamed rice. She could almost taste the chicken from the heavenly aroma. If only she could have a bite of the chicken or maybe a spoonful of soup or maybe a scoop of steamed rice. She was only ten feet away from heavenly food but yet so far away.

She snapped out of her daydream and realized that she had been standing there for too long. These people would not hesitate to hurt her if she continued to stand there, but it was hard to turn away from the food that was just sitting there waiting to be eaten. Maybe they would throw her a piece of chicken or hand her some rice. She imagined herself chowing down on the chicken and rice and then lifting the bowl to slurp the soup. She took a deep breath to inhale the overwhelming aroma of the chicken. She could almost taste the chicken. She wanted to get a better smell of the steamed rice, so she took a few steps forward. Then the sweet and warm aroma of the rice flowed through her nostrils. It was right there. If she would just stand here a little longer, a miracle might happen.

"Get out of my face! How can I eat if you are staring at me?" the woman yelled and splashed a cup of water into Chhom's face.

Her daydream was disrupted. She snapped back to reality again and saw five angry people staring at her and wanting her to go away. Chhom flinched and reluctantly turned away. She needed to find real food that could feed herself and her hungry little brothers.

She continued to trot, still thinking about the whole chicken, the soup, and a pot of rice. How could three heavenly dishes exist side by side? She couldn't take her mind off the food. Her mouth continued to water as she walked. She thought it was a mistake to stare at the food in the first place. Now she was hungrier than ever before. She needed something in her stomach. She walked and scanned the ground hoping to find some sort of plants to chew on.

Without knowing how she got there from home or where she was now, she thought she must have passed a couple of towns and came to the interconnected rice paddies. Each of the rice paddies were crammed with tall rice stalks. The clusters of heavy rice buds made the tops of the stalks bow down. Chhom wished she could pick the rice buds. They were so green and luscious. A few stalks could offer half a can of rice grains. They were just within her reach. She would not dare to attempt to pick the rice off the stems. It had been proven that anyone who got caught picking the rice was punished, and sometimes they were executed on the spot.

Chhom randomly selected a path between the rice paddies and began to wonder, hoping to find the harvesting spot. As she walked deeper into the rice paddies, she was awed by the sight. There were millions of clusters of rice buds hanging from the stalks. She was hungry and wanted something to eat right now. These green rice buds were perfect. She could just eat them whole. Chhom looked around the area to make sure no one was around. She dove deep into the rice paddies and then crawled further away from the path. Then she laid flat on the muddy ground surrounded by the rice shrubs. She plucked a few stems from the root and chewed on the soft part of the stalk. She could taste a light flavor of sugar. If she got caught, they might not kill her since it was only the stalk. She looked around and then she plucked another stalk. This one has clusters of young rice buds. Instinctively, she shoved the whole rice clusters in her mouth. The rice grains were not meant to eat raw. The shells were still soft but they had a grass-like texture. However, the young rice buds helped make it taste more like food than the plain grass. She forced herself to chew and swallow the grass-like rice buds. After she swallowed all the rice buds, she paused and listens. When she was confident that no one was around, she leaped back up to the path. Her clothes were smeared with mud. Her arms and legs had been cut by the microscopic saw blades of the rice leaves. The cuts were painful, but she was used to it.

She continues walking with her heart pounding. She couldn't believe she had eaten the forbidden rice buds. She was still hungry, though. She was hoping to find something edible that she could eat without breaking the rules.

She got out of the maze of rice paddies and stepped into a large open plane. Just about fifty yards away, a pack of wolves were feasting on something that appeared to be a human corpse. Chhom's knees were buckling and her entire body trembling of fear. She hated wolves. Just the term alone give her a chill. If they wanted to eat her, there was no place to go or anyone to help. She felt so small and helpless. Fortunately, the wolves were busy eating the corpse. From previous encounters with dogs, Chhom learned that running was the worst thing she could do. It would attract their attention. She assumed the wolves were the same. She walked along the rim of the rice field, away from the wolves.

She trotted aimlessly away from the wolves along the rice field. Just when she was about to give up searching for the harvesters, she walked right into a group of women that were cutting and bundling the rice stems. Boys and girls as young as four were picking the rice grains off the ground. Chhom smiled and approached the crowd with joy. The women were stooping down, cutting the rice stalks with the sickle and stacking them in piles. Other women were bundling and moving the small piles to the larger piles. The rice grains were falling everywhere as the rice bundles were being moved. Chhom rushed to join the children and began picking the rice grains off the ground. Chhom has been prepared for this moment. She used a technique where she picked each grain with one hand and held them in another. When the other hand was full, she stored the rice in her pockets. The other children picked up their pace when they saw Chhom. Most of the children were much younger than

Chhom; thus, she was quicker and appeared to have better skill with picking the rice.

Each time the women moved the rice bundles from the rice paddy to the large piles, Chhom and the other children trailed after, picking the loose rice grains that fell to the ground. Chhom filled two of her shirt pockets with rice. She had a gut feeling that it was getting late and she must return home. She was very far from home and had to getting going soon before the sunset. She couldn't help but to continue collecting the rice grains. Mother would be very happy if she saw Chhom bring pockets full of rice home.

After filling all her pockets, Chhom made a pouch on the waist of her sarong by flipping the elastic band over. She collected more rice and stored them in the pouch. The mud on her clothes was now dried. She wanted to stay longer and collect more rice but she had to leave. She wasn't even sure how to get back home. She'd been daydreaming most of the time when she walked here. She decided to stop and begin walking home. She picked the dried mud chunks off her shirt as she walked.

She walked past two rice paddies, feeling relieved that the wolves were gone. Then she saw two boys walking toward her from the opposite direction. These boys were not ordinary boys. They appeared healthy and clean. They might be the Schlopes. She was trying to not to look them in the eyes. Even though she hadn't done anything wrong, these boys looked intimidating. Chhom became more and more nervous as she got closer to the boys.

When she was about a dozen feet away from the boys, she sensed that they were staring at her. Chhom noticed they each had a large stick strapped on their waist with a scarf. She began to panic. She hoped they would walk past her and leave her alone.

"Nae! What do you have there?" one of them said out loud, pointing at Chhom's bulging pocket.

"Nothing. It's the rice I collected off the ground. I swear," Chhom said.

"I don't believe you. I have to see," one of them said.

"Then take a look," Chhom said and grabbed a handful of rice from her pocket and opened her palm flat, showing it to the two Schlopes.

They both lowered their heads down examining the rice. One of them used his finger to spread the rice in her palm.

"These rice grains do not look like they were from the ground! I think you picked them off the stalks! They look so fresh!" they said out loud.

"No, I picked them off the ground, after the harvest," Chhom replied with a terrifying tone.

"You lied. You picked them off the stalks. You are a thief."

"I'll be the witness, and I say it was stolen rice," the other said.

"I didn't steal the rice," Chhom said in defiance, and she began to sob.

"You are a thief, and you must be punished," the other said and grabbed her arm.

One of the Schlopes took out his rope. The other grabbed Chhom's hand. Chhom was struggling to get free, but the boy was much stronger than she was. The two Schlopes hauled her effortlessly.

"I didn't steal the rice. I picked it off the ground," Chhom said repeatedly as she was forced to walk. She wept louder, but the Schlopes didn't seem to care.

They came to a nearby small tree and stopped. "Let's tie her here to show the passersby an example."

Chhom fought hard to escape but the two had easily overpowered her and pushed her back against the tree. Chhom felt a sharp pain on her back and head. It's not just any ordinary tree; this was Putreah tree. The Putreah tree was thorny and normally infested with red ants.

One of them grabbed her hands and twist them around the tree and tied her hands. The other Schlope used his rope and tied her body and feet to the tree. She felt more thorns piercing her arms, her legs, and her back.

"Leave her here for the ants to eat," the Schlopes said and left, leaving Chhom tied up against the thorny tree.

Chhom wailed louder when they left. This could mean the end of her life. When a person was tied up to a tree like this, it indicated that the person was a criminal of some sort. No one was allowed to help the person. To make matters worse, she was located deep in the rice paddies. The rice stalks were too tall, and the path was too narrow for anyone to see her from a distance. Someone had to come very close to be able to see her.

It didn't take long for the ants to start roaming her body and begin biting her flesh. She stretched her head forward, away from the tree. But the ants were already on her neck crawling toward her face. She shook her heat violently to get rid of the ants. Some had fallen off, but some managed to cling to her skin and continue making their way to her face. She felt a sting on her right cheek. She could smell the foul citric odor of the ants. Chhom wanted to stop crying, as it wouldn't do her any good. If she didn't get freed soon, the ants would eat her alive. She couldn't stop crying. She was terrified. More ants started to crawl and bite her head and her face. She closed her eyes to make sure they didn't crawl in her eyes.

Shaking her head and wiggling her body didn't seem to help. Chhom thought her movements probably aggravated them even more. After all, this tree was their home. She tried wiggling her hand, trying to get free, but the Schlope had tied her arm very tight.

"Help me! Please help me!" Chhom cried out. She remembered that she had walked deep into the rice paddies, far from the village. The rice around her were still young and was left to grow until they were ready to harvest. No one needed to walk this path. Thus, this path was basically abandoned until the harvest season. This was the end of her life, Chhom thought. She would be eaten alive by red ants. She kept her eyes closed and continued yelling for help. More ants were crawling on her face. Now her eyelids were being bitten. Some had already found their way between the crevices of her eyes lids.

She felt hopeless and horrified. There was no way out of this one. This was it. Then she thought of Mother's prayers. Now she knew why Mother prayed—because there was nothing else she could do. Chhom remembered Mother's prayers well. She would try, hoping it will come true.

Keeping her eyes closed, Chhom began to whisper, "To the Keeper of the land and the Keeper of the water, to spirit of all the ancestors from all cardinals, please help save me. Please save me. The Keeper and the spirit of all the ancestors, please help me..." Chhom repeated the same phrase over and over again.

After she stopped praying, she continued to wiggle her hands and feet trying to get free. Her face and her entire body were in pain from the bites. She opened her eyes slightly, but her vision was blurry from the tears. She tried to use her shoulder to wipe her tears, but every time she raised her shoulder up, she felt like the skin on her hands was tearing apart. She made a few more unsuccessful attempts. Her shoulder was too far down. The ants were relentless. They crawled under her shirts and on her legs biting her every time she moved.

She struggled until she got so tired. She had no more energy to move. Then everything went dark...

When she opened her eyes again, she was shocked to learn that it was now nightfall. Her eyes were dried. She could see a faint image of the tall rice stalks fluttering by the light wind. She noticed the light from the sky. She tilted her head up and saw the bright and round moon shining down above her head giving off a soft radiance. The brilliance of the moon was the only thing that gave her hope and strength. Somehow, it helped soothe her pain. The ants were still biting her skin, but it was not as painful as before. Maybe she was used to it, or her body was too numb to feel anything. She realized she had passed out. She didn't know how long she had been unconscious.

"The Keeper of the land and water, the spirits of the ancestors, and the angels, help me..." Chhom continued praying weakly.

Just when she finished her prayers, a figure of a person appeared just a dozen feet away. Her eyes were still blurry from the swelling and tears, but she could see the image was moving toward her.

"Who is that? You look like someone I knew," a voice of a young man said.

Chhom was still delirious and unsure if it was a dream or reality. She looked up and saw a man about five to six years older than her standing right in front of her, examining her face. The moon cast enough light for her to see his face. He has very dark-skinned and had fairly long hair for a guy. He was well-dressed and meaty. He was definitely a Schlope. Chhom didn't care if he was a Schlope or not. She was scared of being alone in the middle of nowhere. Even if he punished her some more, it would still be worth it.

"You look like Mit Chhoeun's sister. Are you Mit Chhoeun's sister?" the young man asked.

"I'm his sister. Please help me. They tied me up. I didn't do anything. They blamed me for stealing the rice," Chhom begged.

"I will help you, but you must promise me not to tell anyone that I helped you," he said. "After I untie you, you must run fast and do not look back," he added.

The young man untied her. Without a word, Chhom dashed as fast as she could like a rabbit freed from a trap. She ran and cried at the same time. She used her shirt to wipe her eyes. She was able to see well under the bright moon light. She looked back just to check that no one after her. She continues to run not knowing where she'd gotten her energy from. She ran until she was confident that no one was after her. She stopped when she reached the main road. All of the sudden, she realized that she didn't know where she is. The moonlight helped her see the surroundings but not too far. Nothing looked familiar. She didn't know if she was heading toward home or further away. She felt terrified once again and began to cry uncontrollably.

She continued to run again and cry at the same time. More tears were fillings her eyes and rolling down her cheeks. Everything had become blurry. She was afraid of getting lost and afraid of the wolves and tigers. She had seen the wolves nearly every day, but fortunately, they were feeding on the dead bodies. She had seen a tiger once on the way to get fish from Father, but the tiger was very far away. Her whole body shivered when she thought of wolves and tigers. It made her legs even weaker. She was terrified once again.

Chhom ran out of energy and stopped running. She walked at a normal pace but was still sobbing. The road branched out multiple times, but she decided to stay on the main road. The further she walked, the more frightened she was of getting lost.

Creatures of all sorts were making nightmarish sounds. The owls were among them. The wolves were howling from somewhere far away. Insects were buzzing loudly from the thick brushes and from the top of the tall trees. Small animals fled when they sensed her presence, making a nerve-racking sound.

After a long walk, she heard the flowing sound of the river from somewhere ahead. A large tree bowing down slightly to the other side looked somewhat familiar. The roads became wider. The moonlight made things look silver and different, but she could see the bridge that she used to cross very often. She looked around. Everything seemed to come together. The surroundings seemed to come alive as if the trees, the road, and the bridge were welcoming her. She felt a surge of joy and smiled. She was home.

Chhom laughed out loud. The tears continued to roll, but they were tears of joy. With a new surge of strength, she darted forward toward the intersected road in the corner, and then she ran up the slope toward the house.

When she entered the house, the room was lit up with oil lamp. She found Mother and Chhorn sitting on the high raised floor weeping.

"Where have you been?" Mother said coarsely.

"They tied me up against a tree," Chhom said and nearly broke out crying again.

"Who tied you up?" Mother asked

"The Schlopes accused me of stealing. They tied me up against a putreah tree. I was rescued by a boy that knew me."

"Mother and I were so worried. I came to visit, and then you went missing. I thought you were dead," Chhorn said.

Mother fetched the lamp and lifted it close to Chhom's face. Her whole face was swollen and nearly unrecognizable. Her clothes were muddy and ripped. Mother lowered the lamp and examined her legs.

"You have blood all over your legs. Your toe is bleeding."

Mother bent down closer looking at her feet. "One of your toenails has been ripped off," Mother said.

"I stubbed my toe on a root or rocks when I ran," Chhom said.

Chhorn was there looking at her little sister that she had not seen for a couple of months. She thought she would never see Chhom again. She was so happy to see her alive. It was past midnight. Chhom never been out that late before. She normally returned home before dark after searching for food.

"How far did you go?" Bong Chhorn asked.

"I don't know, but it's very far from here," Chhom answered.

"Go bathe and clean your clothes well. I will boil water and clean your toe before it spreads."

Chhom had been wearing the same clothes for a very long time. The weather was normally hot. She normally bathed with her clothes on and then allowed her clothes to dry as she wore them. She patched any rips or tears herself using Mother's yarns and needles. She bathed herself and laid down on the bed as Mother cleaned her toe with warm water.

CHAPTER 19

The rain was drizzling down as I stood by the door of our house watching Mother pruning her small farm. Chhom was arranging the vase and the bucket to collect the rain water. The rain would save her several days of trips carrying water. She and I were ready to catch the frogs and toads around our house. Unfortunately, it was hard to find large frogs on land nowadays. We had found a lot of toads lately. Some of them were nearly the size of bullfrog, but they were rare around our area. Mother warned us about eating toads. Some parts of their organs were known to be poisonous. Chhom made sure to discard all their organs.

After the rain subsided, the insects came to life screeching in joy. Chhom was listening to the sound of the frogs with deep croaks. They were normally big. We also learned that not all frogs were edible. We would stay away from the tiny, glossy, and colorful frogs, as most of them were poisonous. We looked for bullfrogs and also a small, tan colored frog that the Khmer called the "rice frog."

I saw my first small frog hopping from one side of the road on its way to the other side. I immediately chased after the frog trying to catch it. I leaped and pinned the frog with both of my hands and carefully secured it. I began searching for another frog. Then, out of the corner of my eye, I saw a figure of a person moving in the distance. I lifted my head up and saw a man walking and wobbling from side to side, and then he collapsed on the wet ground. I looked at Chhom who was several feet away from me. She'd seen the same thing. She dropped the bucket and yelled, "Mother, look! Who is that?"

"What is it?" Mother asked.

Chhom pointed to the man who was lying flat on the ground with his face down. Mother hesitated, but she walked slowly toward the man.

I stood still waiting for Mother's reaction. She examined the man, exchanged a few words with him, and then she yelled, "Chhom! Chhom! Come and help."

Chhom appeared confused and shocked. She dropped the bucket and ran toward Mother. I darted right after her.

"My son! My son! It's my son!" Mother yelled. "Chhom, come! Help me carry your brother!"

Mother wrapped her arms around his chest and lifted him up with great effort. Chhom was there, but she didn't seem to know how to help. She was small and very frail herself. She gripped onto his shirt and helped Mother lift him.

It must be Chhoeun. I hadn't seen him for a while. Chhoeun got up on his feet, leaning his body on Mother, and begin walking slowly. Chhom still had a grip on his shirt, helping him balance. They walked slowly and eventually made it into the house. Mother laid him down just past the doorway.

"Chhoeun, where did you come from? What happened to you?" Mother asked and wept.

"I worked near Pailin. I'm very sick," he replied weakly.

"Just rest. I will make you rice porridge to eat," Mother said.

Without waiting for Mother to ask, Chhom added wood to the hearth and revived the fire. Mother rummaged through her clothes and got a sack of rice. She dug her hand in the sack and grabbed a handful of rice and tossed it in the small pot. She added the water and place the pot right on the hearth.

I sat down and stared at Chhoeun. I had nearly forgotten the last time I saw him. He was almost a stranger to me. He was so skinny and dark. His hair was much longer than before. He lay down, trying to keep his eyes open.

"Is that rice?" he asked.

"Yes, I'm cooking rice. You are lucky. This is my last pouch. It took me weeks to save this rice," she said.

"I haven't had rice for months. I have been eating only bananas where I work. I'm hungry for rice," Chhoeun said.

"It will be done in a little bit," Mother said.

Chhoeun was so hungry for rice. He crawled closer to rice pot where his face was just a few feet away from the hearth.

I moved along and stared at the rice pot too. I felt hungry looking the rice pot, but I was also curious about Chhoeun. I want to get closer to him, but he looked too tired to acknowledge me. Mother asked him a few more questions, and he answered with great effort. Chhom and Pech went back outside looking for frogs. Pech had probably forgotten who Chhoeun was.

The water began to simmer. Chhoeun grabbed a spoon in one of the bowls nearby. He used his elbow to raise himself up and peered at the slowly simmering water.

"I'm going to take a small sample," he said, taking a scoop of rice porridge from the pot. "The rice is still raw. I'll wait a little more," he said.

He took another sample less than a minute later. He couldn't help but continue to take more samples as the water began to boil.

Mother laughed as she held Poe and watched Chhoeun eat the rice porridge as it was being cooked. He finished the entire pot before the rice had a chance to be cooked.

"They call that the 'lizard egg rice porridge,'" Mother said jokingly. "The grain is still round like the lizard egg."

Chhoeun sat up. His forehead was sweating. He appeared well and energized. He looked around, and then his eyes landed on the baby that Mother was holding.

"Whose baby is that?"

"This is your brother, Poe" Mother said.

"I have another brother," he said with a welcoming smile.

Chhoeun explained where he had been and how he'd escaped death so many times. He worked near Pailin, which was known as a cursed place. The Khmer believed that when you moved to a new place, the place had to accept you. The land would start you with an illness. If you overcame the illness, you were fine to live in the place forever. If you were overpowered by the land, the Khmer called "Chagn," and then you would have the lingering illness and eventually die if you didn't leave.

His main duty at work was to grow bananas. Rice was scarce. He had been eating bananas every day. He also made traps to catch small animals like he'd done in any other places. Nearly everyone in his horde had died from illness. Each day he spent nearly as much time burying his dead coworkers as he did the actual work. He got sick very often as well, but he was able to recover.

He requested to come home because his last illness didn't seem to go away. It was a good opportunity when the water in the river rose. It was too far to travel by land. He'd traveled by a canoe along with several other people.

A few months ago, some of his coworkers that were living near our house came to visit home. Chhoeun had sent us bananas via his coworkers. Mother had never received the bananas. Chhoeun was furious and wanted to confront his coworkers, but Mother told him not to be mad and to forget everything. Stealing from one another was very common nowadays.

Chhoeun was lying down by the hearth the rest of the day. Mother made us rice porridge mixed with vegetables and potatoes before bed. She gave most of the rice porridge to Chhoeun. He woke up the next morning like nothing had happened. He wasn't even sick. He was just starving. He was staying home with us while Mother returned to work. Chhom was taking Poe with her to search for food.

Pech and I stayed home with Chhoeun. I didn't feel like going to work today. I hoped Mother was fine with that because Chhoeun was home. I wasn't used to having any older brothers around, but I liked him a lot. Pech seemed to like him as much as I did. Pech and I were pushing and shoving for a spot to sit next to him. Chhoeun picked me up and tossed me in the air and then catches me before I landed on the ground. Then he did the same to Pech. We laughed and screamed with delight.

"Do you remember how to catch the small frogs?" he asked me.

I nodded.

"Then go catch me some small frogs, but don't kill them," he said.

I remembered faintly doing that for him some time ago. I ran outside to where I had left off yesterday with my frog catching task and returned with several small frogs and tadpoles. Chhoeun had already finished making the fishing rod. He went straight to the river and caught a pile of bullfrogs by noontime. Since the river was overflowed, the frogs were abundant and easy for him to catch.

Mother skinned and gutted the frogs and made a large pot of frog soup that night. She invited nearly everyone she knew to come and eat the soup. She invited one family at a time, trying to not to get too much attention. Chhom got to eat two whole frogs by herself. Pech and I ate one each. Mother must have added the salt to the soup; making it taste extra delicious. It has been awhile since we had this much to eat in one meal.

Four days after Chhoeun was here, we continued to eat delicious frog soup every day. Chhoeun spent all day catching frogs for us and the horde.

After lunch, Chhom, Pech, and I were standing around near the river looking for small frogs while Chhoeun was catching the bullfrogs. Mother was picking vegetables nearby. Despite the yellowish color of the water, fish were seen swimming everywhere.

"Mother, I'm going to try to catch fish the way I catch the frog. I'm going to go to the middle of the river." Chhoeun said. He untied a small canoe that he'd secured by the river bank. It was a small abandoned canoe that he'd found drifting along the side of the river yesterday.

"Be careful. When the river rises, it brings other creatures along as well," Mother warned.

"I'll be fine. I'm in a canoe. I rode the canoe from Pailin to here safely without any problem," Chhoeun assured and rowed the canoe to the middle of the river, testing his fishing tactic.

After a long wait, he hadn't had any luck. Chhoeun continued to try. Chhom and I were idling around waiting for the result.

"Chhoeun! Snake! Behind you!" Chhom screamed.

Chhoeun turned around and saw the snake about seven feet in length swimming right toward him. He stared at the snake for a few seconds and then he screamed, "Mother, help! It's a cobra!"

Chhoeun was terrified. He looked around the canoe to find a weapon to protect himself, but there was nothing in the canoe. He moved around frantically, looking for a way out. The canoe began to wobble violently. The snake was inches away when Chhoeun lost balance and fell in to the river. The canoe flipped over. Somehow it ended up on top of him and shielded him from the snake. The snake slithered over the canoe and then glided away.

Mother stood beside us, frozen from the ordeals that had happened so fast. After a moment, we saw Chhoeun emerge from the water looking around.

"Where is the snake?" Chhoeun asked.

"The snake is gone!" Mother shouted.

After he was confident that the snake was gone, he flipped the canoe back upright and climbed back in the canoe and then rowed the canoe back to shore.

"Are you all right?" Mother said.

"The snake almost killed me. Lucky the canoe flipped over and protected me. That was a cobra. I didn't know a cobra can swim," Chhoeun said breathing heavily.

"Forget about the fish. I think frogs are good enough. Snakes are everywhere after the river overflowed," Mother said.

Chhoeun docked his canoe back at the river bank and prepared himself to catch some more frogs. I hadn't gone to work since Chhoeun arrived. I didn't get any share of rice, but the rice was nothing compared to the frog soup. Chhoeun stayed home for a few more days and returned to Pailin. Mother urged him to leave, as our village was not a safe place to stay. If the higher authority knew of his presence, they would investigate and might put our entire family at risk.

"Make sure you work hard. Do whatever they ask you to do," she reminded him before he left.

A few days later, our life had returned to the way it was before. We didn't have any more frogs to eat, and I had to go back to work. It was a lot more difficult to work now since the river was flooded. I had to walk a little further to find the Katreang Kaet. I continued to miss work here and there. I got chastised by the Mekong for not following the instructions. Mainly because I either didn't understand the instructions or I forgot what the instruction was. The lack of rice and the lack of frogs made me hungry like usual. The frog soup was now just a memory.

About four weeks later, just when the memory of Chhoeun was fading, I found Chhoy and Chhorn sitting in the house chatting with Mother when I returned from work.

"Bun looks very skinny," Chhorn said when she first saw me.

"They make him work now to get his share of rice. Anyone that is five and older has to work," Mother said.

Chhoy and Chhorn felt sympathy for me, but there was nothing they could do. They had to work like oxen themselves with very little to eat. Their entire horde was forced to come home because their compound was overcrowded. More youth had been transported to their compound because the many villages had been flooded. Since it was an official move, the village leaders were aware of their presence. Chhoy and Chhorn were allowed to get a share of rice porridge.

It was lunchtime. Chhorn and Chhoy were taking us to line up to get a share of rice. It was the first time that I remembered walking with Chhoy and Chhorn to the dining hall. Chhorn was holding Pech's hand. She seemed to miss Pech a lot. Chhoy was holding Poe. Chhom was walking right behind me.

After we get our share, I noticed that Poe did not have a share. I was too excited to see my older sisters and forgot about my hunger, and for some reason I felt like I cared so much for Poe as Chhoy was holding him on her waist.

We sat in the dining hall with the other villagers. The hall was much more crowded than usual. There were many new faces. Some were familiar. Everyone was chatting and questioning one another. Everyone was eating but me. I was sitting beside Chhoy making funny faces to make Poe laugh. I wanted to give my share to Poe. Chhom and Mother often gave up their share for us. I had an urge to do the same.

"Eat your rice!" Chhom said and scowled.

I flinched and stared at her for a moment and then continued to play with Poe.

"Eat your rice!" she yelled again and smacked me right on my nose as I turned to look at her.

"I want to give my rice to Poe," I said and cried.

Then I noticed blood was oozing from my nose. Chhoy and Chhorn rushed to help me. It didn't really hurt, but when I saw the blood dripping from my nose I began to wail.

"Why did you hit him?" Chhoy scolded Chhom.

"Because he's hard-headed and slow. I have to warn him all the time," Chhom said.

"Look, you broke his nose," Chhoy yelled.

"Well, he should eat!"

"You didn't have to hit him!"

Chhoy and Chhom continued to argue. Chhorn didn't say a word, but she wiped my nose with her shirt. She did not what to be on the wrong side of Chhom. She was the youngest of the three, but she was not afraid of anyone.

Chhoy walked me back home and rinsed my nose with water. Mother was busy distributing rice porridge and wasn't aware of what was going on. When she returned home and learned that Chhom made my nose bleed, she was furious and chastised her.

Later that afternoon, Chhorn, Chhoy, and Chhom went out together to pick vegetables. They brought home a basket full of water spinach, and they had also caught a few catfish in a small puddle by the river. When the river lowered slightly, many cat fish were stranded. They carefully handled the catfish without hurting themselves. The catfish were dangerous. They had two razor-sharp fangs by their gills that were believed to have slight poison that would cause extra pain when it punctured our skin.

Chhoy and Chhom did not talk after the incident, but they didn't seem to be mad at one another. Mother made rice porridge for dinner, and she made catfish soup. She carefully dug up taro roots and a small plantain stem. We'd had plantain stem soup several times, but it was the first time for Chhorn and Chhoy. We sat in circle. It had been a long time since we'd had dinner with Chhoy and Chhorn. I sat next to Chhoy who seemed to miss me so much. Each of us had a bowl with some rice porridge. There was not much rice in our bowl, but in the center of the circle out there was a bowl of fish soup. Mother had cut the fish into six pieces so each of us could get one piece. We waited for Mother to distribute the fish meat so we didn't have to quarrel over them.

"Who wants the head?" Mother ask.

"I want the head." Chhorn said.

Everyone liked the head. It normally was the biggest piece, but it had mostly bones and gills and very little meat. The meat around the head was tastier than the rest of the fish. It was thick, fatty, and delicious.

Mother scooped the head and placed it in Chhorn's bowl. Then she scooped the tail and asked, "Who wants the tail?"

No one answered. The tail was long but thin. We all looked at each other hoping someone would take it.

"If you eat the tail, it will help you learn how to swim quickly like a fish," Chhoy said and smiled.

"Me! Me. I want the tail!" Pech and I shouted at the same time leaping from our seats. I had always wanted to learn how to swim. I saw Chhoeun swim when he came, and he was impressive. I wanted to swim just like him.

"Since both of you want the tail and there is only one tail, Bun shall get the tail because he's older," Mother explained.

"I want the tail!" Pech shouted and began crying.

"The next one was closer to the tail, so you can still learn how to swim too."

"It's a stronger part of the tail, so you might be able to learn faster than Bun," Chhoy said turning her head away to hide her smile.

"Then I want that," Pech said.

"You too can choose whichever you want," Mother said to Chhom and Chhoy.

"Leave me the smallest one," Chhoy said giving a hint to Chhom that she was offering her the option.

Without a word, Chhom scooped her piece of fish. She didn't seem to care what she got.

"Wow, the plantain stem tastes good," Chhorn said.

"Not bad for something that looks so inedible," Mother added.

As I was eating, Chhoy playfully dipped her spoon in my bowl and pretended to scoop and eat. "Oops! Wrong bowl." she said and laughed.

I was mad for a second, but I realized that she was just playing. I found that very funny, so I did the same except that I really scooped and ate some of her rice. She made a second attempt, but I pulled my bowl away from her. We continued to tease each other as we ate.

I tried the same joke with Pech, and he nearly wacked me with his spoon. He thought I really stole his rice and began crying.

"Here. Stop crying. Take mine," Chhorn said and gave a scoop of her rice porridge to Pech.

Pech stopped crying. He drew the bowl closer to himself and defensively rested one arm around the bowl as he ate.

CHAPTER 20

Chhorn had been called back to work after being home for a couple of weeks. Another compound needed more workers, and she was selected to move with the unmarried women. She was no longer considered a youth; therefore, she had to travel further from home and work on more difficult tasks. She had been selected to go to a place call Sa La Ta On (School of Ta On). There was a large river that ran across the town. The government wanted to build a controllable dam to store the water. When the dry season came, they would be able to use the water to grow rice.

Chhorn still had the infection from last year on her left foot. She woke up every morning feeling the pain of her infection. Sometimes, she woke up seeing maggots crawling out of her wound. Sometimes, she cried until she fainted. The pain was less intense during daytime.

There was no shelter for her to sleep in like when she was in the youth group. Everyone had to build their own shelter. Many people did not bother building a shelter. They simply set up their mosquito net right under a tree. Chhorn and her friends looked around for ideas, and they built a shelter that fit about five of them. They used mostly small tree branches and leaves.

On the second day, they called everyone to get together for a big meeting. The groups were already set up by the organizer. Most of Chhorn's friends were in a separate group except for Ah Nee, the Islamic girl. Each Mekong had a list of all their workers. They gathered in groups and called their names. Despite the hunger and separation from parents, the friendships between the young women were still alive and strong. Just like in school, there were popularities and cliques. Most people still used their actual name. People that had fancy names were usually from Phnom Penh.

"Prak Sori Ya (the sun)." The Mekong called out the first person's name.

Her friends cheered.

"Rak Smey (the radiant of the sun)"

Her friends cheered.

When the roll call was over, Mekong informed Ah Nee that she had been assigned to be group leader of nine women. Ah Nee's primary responsibility was to report her crew's status every day. She was required to remember everyone's name.

At bed time, Ah Nee was whispering the names of the crew to herself. "Chhorn, why do I get all the people from Phnom Penh? They have such long and complicated names, especially the sky-related ones. I can't seem to remember any of their names. Could you help me? There is one most difficult one that I can't seem to remember at all," Ah Nee said.

"Which one?" Chhorn asked.

"I don't know. The one around the sky."

"Sori Ya?"

"No. Higher."

"Bori Mey?"

"Almost there. Keep going."

"Rak Smey?"

"Ah...that's it! I can't seem to remember her name. She's way up there in the sky."

"That's right, she's the sunlight. She's very high," Chhorn said and laughed.

"I have to remember all these names, or I will be in trouble," Ah Nee said.

On the first day of work, Chhorn and her group were walking in line carrying the dirt baskets, joining thousands of other men and women. From a distance, Chhorn saw the workers carpet the large river like black ants. This was the largest number of workers she had ever seen working on the same project. To the other side, there were thousands of workers in the process of digging a nearby hill or possibly a small mountain and transporting the dirt to the river. There was a famous accomplishment in the country that one city led their group to level a small mountain in one night. The notion of this accomplishment proved that the new government believed that humans could do anything without the need of technology.

When she got closer, she heard a low, harmonic sound echoing from the workers. If she heard it correctly all the workers were singing all together. Chhorn tried to make out the words, but the song ended. Just a few minutes later, the song began again. Chhorn listened carefully.

"Yueng Kom Tup Stung, Tup Bung, Neng Tup Tonle"
We stop the lake, stop the pond, and stop the river
"Tup Oh Ho Hae, Chea Kong, Chea Kong"
Stop various brooks into many sections
"Yueng Kom Cheek Srah, On Doang Tra Paeng
We dig moats and tropic wells
"Yueng Kom Ka Sahn, Pak De Watt Tmey"
We must work hard to build the new society

"Listen to this song carefully. It represents what we are here for. All of us are required to sing this song," the Mekong who was leading the group said.

Just ahead, a large group of men were working on building a concrete dam on the ominously loud flowing river. There were three lines of men connecting from the dam to the field. They were transporting the concrete mortar from the field to the dam.

The song had subsided. Chhorn and the group walked up the hill, deep into the crowd.

"This is it. We will dig this hill and transport the dirt to the riverside," the Mekong explained simply.

This was nothing new to Chhorn and the group. They understood the job right away and began working as if they'd been here forever. This place was so crowded, and there was nothing but plain mud and dirt. It was impossible to find food here. Even if the crabs or snail lived here, they would be stomped to pieces by the hordes of workers.

Chhorn was hungry and tired. Her infection on her foot was unbearable, but there was nothing she could do. She dug and carried the dirt at a slow pace trying to preserve her energy.

Despite many thousands of workers, no one talked on the job. The sound of the loud and monotonous water falling from the dam dominated the thuds of the hoes' blades against the earth.

Just when Chhorn was thinking of lunchtime, she heard a loud crash and screams somewhere from the dam. Everyone paused and stared to the direction of the dam. It was too far for Chhorn to see what had happened, but she knew it must be very serious.

"Don't look," a lady next to her said. "The dam has broken many times, but they insist we continue. Many people, especially men, have been killed. The flood swept hundreds of them away. Right now, we are just repeating the process."

All the thudding sounds stopped. The murmuring among the workers rose.

"What were you looking at? Work!" someone yelled.

The murmuring subsided, and the thuds of the blade and dirt rose back to normal. The sound of the waterfall had vanished.

Chhorn felt sympathy for the men who had just been swept away by the river. She was glad that she was a woman and didn't have to deal with that. More men would be assigned to replace the deceased and were highly likely to face the same fate.

Lunchtime came soon after the incident. Chhorn was surprised when she got one large scoop of thick rice porridge. This was about three weeks' worth of rice porridge that she'd normally gotten from any previous youth compounds.

She returned to work with more energy than she could remember having for a long time. She wishes Chhoy was here with her enjoying the thick rice porridge. She got the same amount of thick rice porridge for dinner, except that she didn't have to go back to work. She could rest and sleep with a lot of energy.

After a few months of working here, she made many new friends like every place she'd stayed. Chhorn grew to like this place more than any other place because of the good amount of rice porridge they were given every day and the fact that the work was repetitive. If only the work was easier than digging and carrying dirt all day.

The rain was drizzling lightly while Chhorn was digging the dirt with her group. The wound on her ankle was covered with mud. She wished there was a way to make the wound go away. The wound made her job much more difficult. Just after she made the wish in her mind, a group of men wearing clean clothes walked into the area, staring at the men and women. Everyone paused and waited to see what was about to happen. Normally, that was not a good sign.

"I need five volunteers to work at the health department," a man among the group said out loud.

Chhorn raised her hand immediately. The health department normally distributed the herbal remedy known as rabbit dung to sick people. It was one of the easiest jobs around. The job would suit her well. But strangely, only about ten out a few hundred people raised their hands. Maybe they knew they had no chance of being selected.

"Mit! Come here," another man said and pointed to Chhorn. "And you, and you, and you, and you."

Chhorn was excited to be selected. She walked closer the men and stood just before them. When she turned around, she was surprised to see that the other candidates were all her new friends—Mit Pan, Mit Huey, Mit Hon, and Mit Ban. How lucky was that?

"You are coming too?" Chhorn asked her friends.

The four women had been very close to Chhorn. They slept in the same shelter and shared everything they had.

The men led Chhorn and her friends to the truck and drove. Chhorn sat in the cargo area of the truck with her friends, excited to be away from the brutal work. It has been awhile since the last time she rode a motor vehicle. She was not used to moving that fast. She soon lost her sense of direction.

After a long ride, the truck stopped at a large crowd where thousands of men and woman were being ordered to move from place to place like a large heard of oxen.

"Get off! Get off!" the men said.

"What is this place?" Mit Pan asked.

"This is town is called Veal Baek Chahn. Since no one likes to come here, we have to do it this way," one of them said.

"We have been tricked," Mit Hon said. "They made us come to work around the militants."

Veal Baek Chahn was a place known to be infested with the militants. This was where they lived. This was where they were trained to kill.

"Try to stick together. If we separate, we are in trouble," Mit Hon said.

"Come this way. That group over there could accommodate all of us," Mit Ban said and grabbed Chhorn by her arm and ran. Everyone followed, except for Mit Huey, who was hauled by a militia into another group nearby.

"You are staying here in this horde," the man said and went to the next person.

The Mekong immediately acknowledged Mit Huey as part of the horde and continued to take notes on other newcomers.

Just when the Mekong had her attention on another person, Mit Huey looked around and darted toward Chhorn and her friends.

The Mekong ran after Mit Huey and shouted, "Hey! I thought you were in my group?"

"I'm not in your group. You must be mistaking me for someone else," Mit Huey said.

"I remember exactly what you look like. You had a mole under your nose."

"Look at that person over there. She has a mole," Mit Huey said and pointed.

Everyone looked where Mit Huey was pointing and saw a woman about the same age with a mole under her nose just like Mit Huey. Chhorn and the rest of her friends couldn't help but laugh.

"What a coincidence," Chhorn said softly.

Chhorn and her friends stood in a group until everyone was settled and the chaos was over. There was no shelter available here either. They had to build their own shelter just like in Sa La Ta On. Chhorn and her friends didn't wait long and built one large shelter to fit them all. With the previous experience, they built a large shelter that could fit over six people and the roof was high enough for them to stand up. They hoisted three mosquito nets.

The work here in Veal Baek Chahn was similar to Sa La Ta On; workers were digging and carrying dirt all day. Fortunately, the thick rice porridge was provided for lunch and dinner as well. In fact, the rice porridge was even more than Sa La Ta On.

Chhorn got sick after the first week of work. For some reason, Chhorn was prone to getting sick more often than any of her friends. She could barely walk, but she had to go or else she would not get anything to eat.

Today at lunchtime, Chhorn was so sick that she couldn't even eat. Here at Veal Baek Chahn, the rice porridge was abundant enough for workers to have seconds. Chhorn wanted the seconds, but she could not eat fast enough to finish her first.

"I have an idea." Mit Pan said. "When I'm almost done with my rice porridge, I will pour the rest into your bowl so I can go up and get more."

"I will help you too," Mit Huey added.

"We all will help you," Mit Hon said.

The four girls ate as fast as possible and poured the rest of their rice porridge into Chhorn's bowl. Then they got up and walked over to get their seconds. Chhorn's bowl was full of rice. She wished she had the energy to eat faster, but her head was pounding with a migraine, and her entire body was in pain.

The four finished their seconds, and Chhorn was still working on her first. Lunchtime was almost over. The cook would begin cleaning any moment. Mit Pan came up with another idea. Each of them scooped the rest of Chhorn's rice on to their bowl. When Chhorn's plate was empty, she struggled and walked to get her seconds. When Chhorn returned, the three poured the rice back into Chhorn's bowl. Chhorn forced herself to eat even though she was weak and her mouth could not taste the flavor of the rice.

When lunchtime was almost over, a young woman wearing a clean outfit and fancy buttons came and stood in front of the large crowd in the dining hall. Two women walked behind her proudly escorting the woman. Everyone stopped talking and turned to the women.

"All Mit. You are allowed to visit your home in two days. You have worked hard and deserve a break. There is a rule. You must be able to work in order to qualify to leave. If you are sick or injured and unable to work for the next two days, you are not allowed to go. The Mekongs should know the rules." the woman said and walked away.

Everyone murmured in joy. This was a rare opportunity. All Chhorn's friends were looking at one another's faces and smiling with surprise. Chhorn heard the good news, but she was still struggling to finish her rice porridge.

"You hear that? We get to visit home?" Mit Ban said.

"I don't think I can make it to work. I don't even have the strength to eat," Chhorn groaned.

"You have to try," Mit Pan said. Mit Pan was the oldest of them all. She was probably around nineteen years old. She was taller than most women.

"We will help you. All you have to do is pretend to work. We will do the rest," Mit Huey said.

Chhorn and her friends returned to work after the lunch break was over. Chhorn was feeling miserable on top of the pain she had in her infected foot. She wobbled side to side as she walked toward the field.

As promised, all four of her friends helped her do most of her job. Chhorn pretended to dig the dirt. Her friends filled up her basket with dirt and carried it away for her. Chhorn made it through the day. She nearly gave up and asked for permission to go home a few times.

When Chhorn returned to the dining hall for dinner break, she was surprised to see that steamed rice was being served. Despite being sick and tired, she leaped to celebrate the instant she learned the good news. Not only did she get to visit home, but she got to bring steamed rice with her. When she got her share of rice, she rolled the rice with her fist into a cylinder shape and stared at the precious thing. She broke the tip of the rice and ate it and then slipped the rest of the rice into her pocket. She noticed Mit Pan and Mit Huy were doing the same thing. Chhorn thought they must have the same reason, but she didn't ask. She didn't want to let anyone know she was hiding the rice. She sat and waited for everyone in her horde to finish eating, in case there were seconds. Unfortunately, there were no seconds.

When Chhorn returned to the shelter, she picked some banana leaves and used the to wrap the steamed rice. Then she hid the steamed rice in her backpack and went to sleep, keeping the backpack very close to her.

Chhorn woke up the next day feeling slightly better. She was still unable to work, but all her friends helped her in any way they could. The thick rice porridge was served at lunch, and the steamed rice was served at dinner. She rolled the rice into another cylinder shape, ate just the tip, and then hid the rest in her pocket. She repeated the same process the next day. She had a total of three cylinders of rice hidden in her backpack.

Chhorn walked home with four of her friends the next morning when everyone was allowed to visit home. Mit Pan knew her way around very well. They left the compound very early in the morning and arrived home just before the sunset.

I'd come back from searching for food with Chhom when I got home and saw Chhorn sitting in the house chatting with Mother. She was explaining what she had been doing at Veal Baek Chahn.

"They are here just in time," Chhorn said.

"Wait to see how happy they will be when they see what you brought for them," Mother said. It was unusual to see Mother and Chhorn smiling at the same time as we entered the house.

"Do you guys want to know what I brought for you?" she said with a big grin.

Chhom was too tired to wonder. She looked at Chhorn with straight face and replied, "What did you bring us?"

Chhorn opened her backpack and took rolls of something wrapped in banana leaves. She unfolded one of the banana leaves, and it revealed something that we hadn't seen in years. It was a roll of steamed rice, slightly larger than my fist. Chhom, Pech, and I dashed toward the Chhorn staring at the roll of rice.

"That's mine! That's mine," Pech said jumping up and down.

I froze for a second in shock. I hadn't seen steamed rice for a very long time. In fact, I had forgotten the last time I saw steamed rice. I reached my arm forward hoping she would give me the rice first. Chhom was standing right behind me, speechless.

"We all have to share," Mother said. She was smiling, happy to see that we were getting to eat rice. "Let me split the rice.".

Chhorn handed the rice to Mother. She took the rice and broke the roll in half. She handed half to me and half to Pech.

I held the rice, staring at the cluster of precious oval grains in disbelieved. I was actually holding steamed rice. I felt like I was in a dream but hoped it was real. I picked a rice grain and put it deep in mouth. It was real. My hunger wanted me to devour the whole thing in one bite, but I refrained. I wanted to eat it slowly and enjoy every moment of it as long as possible. I might not be able to see this moment ever again. I looked at Pech, and he was doing exactly the same.

Mae split the other roll in half. She handed one half to Chhom and the other to Chhorn.

"I'm not eating, Mother. You can eat it," Chhorn said.

"Are you sure? You have walked a long way. You are tired and hungry," Mother said, staring at the rice as if being possessed by it.

"I'm going to take a bite and feed Poe the rest," Mae said and took a small bite.

"Then let me feed him. I want to hold him," Chhorn said.

"Say, how did you manage to get so much rice? No one gets to eat steamed rice except Mit Chah," Mae asked quietly.

"It is the harvesting season, and Veal Baek Chahn is mostly the militants. They get to eat well. Since the rice is abundant there, we get to eat thick rice porridge every day. They have given us steamed rice for dinner for the last three days. Once they told me they were allowing us to visit home, I saved the rice each day. I have been saving the rice for the past three days. When I got my share of rice, I ate just a little and saved the rest," Chhorn explained. "I let no one know that I was hiding the rice. Then during the night, I slept hugging the backpack so that no one would take it," Chhorn explained proudly.

Pech was picking and eating one rice grain at time just like me. He was singing a song that we used to hear from one the kid that disappeared months ago. This was the first time he'd actually held steamed rice.

"My rice! My rice! I dropped my rice!" Pech shouted.

"What's the matter?" Chhorn said.

"I dropped my rice! I dropped my rice! I need to get my rice!"

"Where is your rice?" Chhorn asked.

"Down there! Down there!"

"Let me get it for you. Just stay up here," Chhorn said.

"No, I want to get it myself! I want to get my rice! The chicken! Get the chicken away from my rice! Someone chase the chicken away from my rice!"

There was a new chicken underneath our house that Mother had been assigned to look after. It was lying quietly beneath the floor. Chhorn got up and walked down to the ground and pretended to chase the chicken away. We all peeked down between the crevice of the floor, and no one saw any rice on the ground.

"Here, hold my rice, but don't eat it," Pech said and handed the rice to Mother. He ran down the stairs and crawled beneath our house.

We all watched anticipating seeing how he would find the rice. Pech picked up one grain of rice and ran back up the house. We were all amazed that he was able to locate a single grain of rice among the dirt and pebbles.

"See, I told you I dropped my rice," he said and laughed, holding a grain of rice between his thumb and his index finger.

Mother and Chhorn broke out laughing.

"He found it!" Mother said.

"It was only a single grain of rice. I thought it was more than that," Chhorn said.

Pech put the retrieved rice grain in his mouth with care so that he wouldn't drop it again. Chhorn gave him his steamed rice back, and he continued eating with joy.

CHAPTER 21

Chhoy began her trip along with her group to a new location. She had been selected to work many different villages near Stung Chah and returned home when the work was completed. Today she had been selected to go to a city called Tuel Snai; the same city where Father worked. She was still with the same Mekongs, Mit Ra and Mit Rate. Most of the girls were the same girls that she had been working and staying with throughout the years. Mit Lee, Mit Vee, Mit Nee the non-Islamic, Mit Suahn, Mit Trinh Leng, and Mit Trinh Chu were all still among the group.

Chhoy was carrying the same backpack that she had two years ago with many patches over the various rips and tares. Mother neatly folded her mosquito net, which also had many patches, inside the backpack. The Mekong led the group across the bridge toward the Watt Samdach and then marched along the river toward Tuel Snai. The ground was muddy as the rain was drizzling down. No one looked happy to have to leave their family once again and head back to the brutal work. During the time of the home visit, Chhoy chatted with friends when they met. She learned nothing but bad news. Nearly half of the girls lived alone, as their Mothers and siblings had either been taken to execution or died of starvation and illness. Everyone was talking about how their family members had died. It was becoming a common conversation among friends.

Leng and Chu were walking with their heads down in sadness. They did not talk to each other or with any of their friends. They were like sisters to Chhoy. There were a few people ahead of her. She wanted to talk to them, but she didn't want to leave her friends, especially Ah Nee, who would do anything for her.

Chhoy and the group arrived in Tuel Snai in the afternoon. The rain had subsided, but the ground was still wet.

"This is our new worksite. The government has called upon us to clear this area of small trees and brush and help the local villagers with the rice plantation and harvest. We will sleep here and work here until our job is completed." the Mekong said.

"This is it? How are we going to sleep? There is no shelter. We are out in the open," Ah Nee said.

Chhoy looked around and didn't see a single shelter nearby. The place was mostly open land with random spots of trees and shrubs along with random coconut trees and palm trees. Puddles of all sizes were trapped in the bare rice paddies.

"Don't complain too loud. If someone reports you, they will take you trial," her sister Ah Vee said.

"I don't care if anyone takes me to trial. I didn't do anything wrong. Most of my family are dead anyway. Kill me or not. I don't care," Ah Nee continued.

After they arrived, the Mekongs were still trying to figure out where exactly to settle and where to get all the material to build a shelter. They left the site and returned a moment later. They found an open and flat spot up ahead. They had to march toward the new location and found boys of all ages were cutting the palm leaves and small trees to help the girls build their shelters.

Chhoy was relieved at first to have the help, but once they began building, the boys had little clue what they were doing, and the elders who were helping were too tired to do anything. Chhoy and the all the girls ended up doing most of the work.

The rain was coming down harder. The boys and men were cutting the branches while the girls were hauling the branches to build the shelter. Ah Nee was building her shelter that she was sharing with her younger sister Ah Vee. Chhoy was building a shelter with Leng and Chu where the three would share. She had not built any shelters herself before. She simply made several posts and stacked small branches and palm leaves on top of one another.

"When I'm done with mine, I will come and help you," Ah Nee said.

It was getting dark. Chhoy had just begun to stack the roof. She looked around and found some of the girls were still working on the frames. Many ended up using a tree as a shelter and set up the mosquito net below the tree.

At nightfall, Chhoy, Leng, and Chu had still not completed their shelter. They were sleeping in a mosquito net, under the rain. Only their heads were shield from the rain by the small section of the roof. Sometimes, the wind gusts blew the rain in her face. She huddled with Leng and Chu to keep warm.

Early the morning, they woke up and continued building the shelter. Somehow, they made mistakes, and the entire shelter collapsed. They had to start again from scratch. It took them three days to complete their shelter. They had been sleeping in the rain for three nights. Chhoy's shelter still had many leaks during the rain after the completion. There were holes everywhere on the roof and walls.

Leng and Chu had been working with Chhoy building the shelter, and they all slept together, but neither Leng nor Chu were talking. Chhoy thought maybe they were too busy building the shelter and didn't feel like talking. On the fourth night, just before bed, Chhoy could not help but to wonder why they were not talking. They would normally chat before they fall asleep.

"Ah Chu...Ah Leng, what's the matter with you guys?" Chhoy asked.

"Nothing," Leng replied.

"Why are you guys so quiet? You look so sad," Chhoy asked hoping for a good response.

"My Mother and Father are dead. All of my brothers and sisters are also dead," Chu said.

"What happened?" Chhoy asked.

"Starvation. All of them died of starvation," Chu said.

Chhoy felt so bad, but there was nothing she could do. It was a common story among her friends. Everyone she knew had a family member die of starvation or be taken away to execution. She wished she was wiser and had better things to say, but she couldn't think of anything.

"Really?" Chhoy said quietly and lay still, frozen by the bad news. She couldn't imagine what it would be like to lose all your family members. Leng and Chu were not the only ones who'd lost nearly all their families. The other two sisters, Peah Lee and Seung, lost their parents when the Red Khmer was taking over. They had been living with an older sister and three brothers. When they returned home, they learned that two of the brothers had been executed, and one had died of starvation.

Early in the morning, women and men were emerging from the nearby village and began to form groups in the field. Chhoy found her Mekongs, Mit Rate and Mit Ra, speaking to their superior and taking instructions. She kept herself closer to Leng and Chu trying to show that she cared a lot about them. Ah Nee and her sister Ah Vee were coming to join her. Everyone was complaining about the roof leaks and the mosquito bites that kept them up most of the night.

More youth were pouring in from all directions walking in columns. It appeared they were the newcomers looking for a place to build their shelters. Chhoy kept her eyes on them in case she spotted anyone she knew. Every single one of them appeared exhausted and miserable. Mit Rate and Mit Ra were taking attendants. By now, they knew everyone well. Everyone formed a line without being asked and followed the Mekongs to the working site.

The first assignment was to clear the shrubs off the unused land, clearing space for other groups to dig or plow the land. Chhoy and the group worked as instructed. Thin rice porridge was provided for lunch and dinner. Like all the previous compounds, Chhoy and her friends were collecting snails and crabs as they worked and spent more time searching for food after work.

Chhoy and the group finished their task about four weeks later and were assigned to help the adults dig dirt to form new rice paddies for the next season. This was one of the most grueling jobs, and it seemed there was no end to this task. Tuel Snai had a lot of land that was suitable for farming. The government wanted to use every square inch of it.

"Ah Nee, my Mother told me that my Father is working in this town. She said his house sits on a large hill. I think it's that hill over there." Chhoy said pointing to a hill about one and a half kilometers away.

"Really? You think he has rice for us to eat?" Ah Nee asked.

"Maybe. If not, I know that he has a lot of fish. My Mother told me he catches fish for his town, and he brings home fish all the time."

"You should ask the Mekong for permission to go see your Father and ask him for fish. If you share the fish with everyone, I think they will let you go," Ah Nee said.

"I'm scared they will yell at me," Chhoy said.

"Just for asking? I don't think you will get in trouble. I will ask for you."

"Are you sure?" Chhoy asked.

"Come on. Go with me," Ah Need said.

Ah Nee was the bravest girl that Chhoy had ever met. She was not afraid of anyone. She walked over to the Mekongs, and Chhoy followed.

"Mit Bong, Mit Chhoy thinks her Father lives up that hill over there. She would like permission to go see her Father and ask him for fish. He's a fisherman for this town," Ah Nee said fearlessly.

"Really? Your Father is a fisherman? As long as you share with everyone, then you can go. It is considered working because you are doing it for everyone," the Mekong said nicely.

"Can I go too?" Ah Nee asked and grinned.

"No, you can't go. There's a lot of work that needs to be done."

The two Mekongs had been very nice. They only scolded and lectured to keep everyone out of trouble. They hadn't threatened anyone like many other Mekongs would do.

Chhoy didn't waste any time and began walking toward the hill in the distance. She arrived there a little past noon. She risked losing the rice porridge for lunch and hoped to get a lot of fish in return. A tall, dark man was cooking just outside an isolated house. Chhoy approached the man nervously.

"Pu, is my Father working here?" She realized that she called him Pu (uncle) using the previous tradition of greeting.

"What is your Father's name?" the man asked, not seeming to mind being called Pu.

Chhoy paused a little. She was not used to saying Father's name. In fact, she nearly forgot his name.

"Uhhh....his name...is...Chhay. Yes, his name is Chhay," Chhoy said happily, proud of remembering Father's name.

"Was it your younger sister that came here before?" he asked.

"I have a younger sister. She might have been here before."

"He will be here shortly. He's a little late for lunch today." Just when he finished his words, a group of men emerged from a small path in the distance. Chhoy turned her head and squinted against the sunlight. She recognized Father, who was walking in the front of all the men. He was very tall and big. He was wearing a hat and black jacket with a lot of large pockets. A bundle of ropes hung from one of his shoulders. One hand was holding a large ax, and the other hand was holding some sort of dead animal. He always stood out among a group of men. Even after he'd lost a lot of weight, Father still maintained the wide frame.

Chhoy leaped up in joy and ran toward Father. He did not recognize Chhoy, even when she was about five feet away. Father squinted. He was not expecting any one.

"Father, it's me," Chhoy said.

"Chhoy. What were you doing here, and where did you come from?" he asked.

All the men stopped behind Father and stared at Chhoy. Father's and the men's clothes were still wet. Chhoy looked him in the eyes, one side was clear and other was murky, making him appear distinguished from any man in many ways. Then she turned her attention to the giant lizard that hung from Father's hand, inches away from her head. The rest of the men were holding buckets and large, wet bags that seemed to have something moving inside.

"I work right over there," Chhoy said and pointed to her new camp.

"They are not going to say anything for leaving work?" Father asked.

"I told them that you have fish. I'm coming to get fish for my group."

"Let's eat first, and then I will give you some fish."

"Is that you daughter? I have never seen her here before. I saw the little dark one often but not her," one of the men said.

"This was my daughter, Chhoy, the older of the two."

"I can tell. She looks just like you, Chhay. Even her name is similar to yours."

The men proceeded to the house. They tossed their gear aside and didn't wait long to grab their plates and head straight to the large pot sitting on the hearth. Father tossed the bundle of ropes to the side of the house and walked to the cook and tossed the giant lizard near the hearth.

"What do you think is good to make with this lizard?" Father asked.

"What else besides the sour soup? We don't have any spice to make anything else," the man said.

"It is the sour soup then. Let's keep it for dinner. Fish is enough for us for now," Father said.

After a moment, the soup was ready, and Father gave Chhoy a bowlful. Chhoy's saliva squirted all over her mouth from the aroma. She nearly choked from her own saliva when she saw several chunks of fish in a single bowl. She could smell the sour tamarind and the herbs that were floating in the soup. When she held the spoon, her hands shook from extreme hunger and long anticipation for food. She took a sip of the hot soup, and the flavor was rich with fish meat and herbs. It was the first time she had anything this good for as long as she could remember. Chhoy could also tastes the salt.

Father got a bowl of soup for himself and came and sat next to Chhoy. Father's friends had asked her some questions, but she was too busy eating the soup and simply shook her head or nodded. Father answered most of the questions for her to allow her to eat.

It took her awhile to finish the soup because it was so hot. When she was nearly finished, the dark, tall man came over with a scoop full of soup and fish chunks.

"Here, you get to finish the last ones," the man said pouring the large scoop of soup into Chhoy's bowl.

Chhoy begin eating the fish as soon as the man finished pouring the soup into her bow. She did not get a chance to acknowledge his kindness.

"She's very hungry," the man said and walked away.

Father finished his soup as Chhoy was still working on hers. He went inside the house and came back with a small woven basket.

"Ah Bao, get some fish for Chhoy. Pick the large ones for her," Father said to one of his friends as he handed him the basket.

"Yes." A young man about the age of twenty got up and walked to the bucket that they just brought back from fishing.

The young man dug his hand in the bucket and selected the fish. He filled the basket with large fish and carried it to Chhoy. He appeared to struggle carrying the basket over. It must have been heavy.

"All her fish I gave her were very big," Bao said

"Give me your scarf," Father said to Chhoy.

Chhoy had just finished her soup. She was feeling stronger than ever. It was the first time in years that she gotten to eat that much, although she could have managed another bowl if there was any left. She handed Father her scarf. He twisted the scarf until it was round like a large rope but not too tight and then he coiled the scarf into a round shape. He placed the scarf on Chhoy's head, and then he placed the basket full of fish right on the coiled scarf.

"You'd better get going before you get in trouble," Father said.

"Yes." Chhoy answered and started walking with the basket full of fish right on her head.

She had carried baskets on her head many times before, but this basket was nearly as heavy as her own weight. She had never carried than anything this heavy on her head before. It was a long trip back to the site. From the previous experience, she could not stop because she had no one to help lift the fish basket back on to her head. It was definitely too heavy to carry by hand.

After just about thirty minutes of walking with the heavy basket on her head, Chhoy was exhausted. It drained all the energy that she had gained from eating the soup. She nearly tossed some fish out to reduce the weight, but the thought of wasting the precious food changed her mind. She was determined to walk without stopping. If she stopped, she would have no choice but to toss some fish out in order to be able place the basket back on to her head.

Chhoy continued the agonizing walk and reached her camp just before dark. She hollered to anyone that she knew to come and help her unload the basket off her head. One of the girls in her group rushed to help her. With the weight off her head, Chhoy used her last bit of strength to walk over to her shelter and simply crashed to the ground to relax. Her neck was as stiff as a tree branch. Her shoulders ached. Her feet were burning.

Someone notified the Mekongs about the fish, and they came over to speak with Chhoy. Mit Rate and Mit Ra explained to her that they would cook the fish tomorrow for the group for lunch and dinner. Also, some of the fish needed to be distributed to other groups as well. They gave one whole fish for Chhoy to cook for herself tonight since she'd missed dinner.

Chhoy returned to Father's place almost every week for fish. She learned her lesson not to carry too much fish at once. She also found a couple of tree branches on along the way that stretched out slightly lower than her head and used them as a resting point. She would set the basket on the tree branch and rest without the need of another person's help. When she need to lift it back on her head, she simply lowered her head slightly and slid the basket back on to her head.

About three months had passed. Chhoy was digging the dirt when she saw more newcomers walking in line, looking for a place to settle. She had a feeling that someone she knew was coming. She observed everyone in the line looking for a familiar face, and then she couldn't believe her eyes when she saw Chhorn walking with a group of adults. Chhorn was almost unrecognizable. She had gained a lot of weight.

"Chhorn!" Chhoy hollered and waved.

Chhorn looked surprise to see Chhoy. "Chhoy! You are working here? How long have you been working here?" Chhorn asked.

"I don't know, maybe three to four months. Where are you staying?"

"I don't know yet," Chhorn answered.

"Don't talk to her. They might think you are mingling with one another and up to something," the Mekong working nearby gave a friendly warning.

Chhorn and her group continued to march further and blended with the crowd. Chhoy was relieved to have Chhorn staying nearby. Right after dinner, Chhoy begin to search for Chhorn. She began the search near the location where they'd met. Unfortunately, there were thousands of new camps, and it was dark by the time she finished eating the rice porridge, making it extremely difficult to find Chhorn. She returned to the camp after she spent about three hours of searching; it was time that she normally used to search for food after work.

Chhoy tried the second, third, and the fourth days, but she didn't have any luck. She felt like the entire ordeal of seeing Chhorn was just a dream. She had come and then vanished without a trace. If she continued to use the time that she gave up on searching for food, she would die of starvation. Chhoy decided to give up searching for Chhorn and continue her routine of searching for food. She went with Ah Nee, Ah Vee, Chu, and Leng to go catch some fish in a small pool of muddy water. Ah Nee had found this small pool hidden by trees and brush yesterday, and it appeared to be undisturbed. Chhoy and the sisters begin to drain the small pool with a bucket when she heard a voice.

"Chhoy, is that you? I have been looking for you for four days, but I couldn't find you," Chhorn said.

"I did the same thing. I have been searching everywhere for you over there," Chhoy said pointing to the direction where she been searching.

"How could you find me if I live the other way?" Chhorn said, pointing the opposite direction.

"We should come to search for food around here, so I can help you find food," Chhorn said.

There was a lot of water around here, but they didn't have anything to catch the fish with. All they could do was to find a small pool where they could drain the water to catch the fish. They spent nearly two hours draining the small pool of water and used up all their energy. They could barely walk after the water was drained. They caught several small snakehead fish and several catfish. They also caught some crabs as well. It was nearly not worth the energy they'd put in. Chhoy and her friends kept half of the catch. Chhorn and her friends kept the other half.

After several weeks, it was becoming harder and harder to find the fish nearby. All the small pools had been drained out by other people. Everyone was doing the same thing. They had to walk further and further away from the camp to seek new pools. When they get out of work, the sun had already set. By the time they found the pool and drained all the water, it would be too dark to see the fish. There were snakes and dangerous animals that came out at night. Chhoy, Chhorn, and her friends changed their routine to find crabs and vegetables instead of fish. Unfortunately, eating vegetables and crabs was not fulfilling like eating the fish.

In a late evening, the sun had sunk behind the large hills. Chhoy and Chhorn met after work to collect vegetables and crabs. Their friends decided to seek their own food, as crabs and vegetables didn't need teamwork. Today, they had no luck catching any crabs, but they had collected a basket of water spinach. As they walked picking the vegetables and searching for crabs, they came across a large pond surrounded by tall bushes and trees. They noticed there were men setting up fish nets. Some were carrying the fish trap cage looking for spots to set their traps. Chhoy and Chhorn walked closer.

"That looks like the man I met at Father's workplace," Chhoy said.

"It was him. I remember seeing him too when I visited Father," Chhorn said.

"That's Father over there in the water," Chhoy said and pointed to the pond.

"Father! Father!" They both called out to Father at the same time.

Father walked over. He was soaked from head to toe. Water was flowing down from his clothes.

"What are you doing so far from the camp?" Father asked.

"We were seeking crabs and fish," Chhorn answered.

"I don't have any fish right now, but I'm setting the net and fish trap. Meet me at the big hill over there tomorrow evening. I will be working there all day," Father said pointing to a distant, steep hill about a kilometer from where they were right now. "I will get the fish ready for you, but you must not tell anyone that you are coming to see me. Make sure not to bring anyone along," Father explained. Any fish that Father caught really belonged to the public. Any private distribution was prohibited.

Chhoy and Chhorn returned to their camp without any crab or fish for the night. It was too late to cook the vegetable the correct way. They roasted the water spinach in the fire and ate it plain.

They sneaked out right after work the next day, without telling any of their friends. They met at the pond where they saw Father yesterday. Chhorn was carrying a small knife that she normally used to cut the tough vegetables or the fangs of the cat fish. They began to walk toward the hill hoping Father would remember to meet them.

"Chhoy, wait here. I need to go pee," Chhorn said.

Chhoy waited as Chhorn walked around a small termite hill.

"Ahhhhhhh!" Chhorn screamed from the top of her lungs behind the termite hill, and then she rushed out from the hill. "A snake! Chhoy! A snake!"

Chhoy crept closer to the hill and saw a snake about the size of her wrist, stretching about four feet in length, slithering slowly near the hill.

"You know, Father used to bring snakes home for Mother. You think it's safe to catch snakes?" Chhorn asked.

"The elders said if you hold a snake by its tail it can't bite you," Chhoy said.

Chhorn dashed toward the snake and grabbed the snake by the tail. Then she swung the snake up and then slammed it back to the ground.

"What are you doing? The snake was going to bite you!" Chhoy screamed in disbelief.

"You said it was safe to catch the snakes by their tail. Now, is it dead yet?" Chhorn asked.

"No. It just lifted its head and was looking at me," Chhoy squirmed.

Chhorn slammed the snake onto the ground several more times until she was too exhausted to continue.

"How about now? Is it dead yet?" Chhorn asked again as she bent down to catch her breath.

"No. It's still alive, and it's looking at you," Chhoy said.

Chhorn swung and slammed the snake again, "Is it dead?"

"No. It's looking at me again," Chhoy said half crying.

Chhorn bent down to catch her breath. Then she hurled forward and pinned the snake by its head.

"It can't bite me if I'm on top of its head. Get me my knife over there," Chhorn said as she had both of her hands right on top of the snake and her knee on its body. The other half of the snakes was coiling around Chhorn's legs, struggling to get free.

Chhoy picked up a knife several feet away and handed it to Chhorn. Chhorn carefully freed her right hand and tilted forward to put her entire body weight on her left hand to keep the snake's head pinned to the ground. She held the knife with her right hand and pressed the blade down and then sliced its head off. Chhoy stood motionless and speechless. Her heart was still pounding.

"This will last us three days," Chhorn said as she picked up the snake and tossed it into the woven basket. "Let's go. Father is probably waiting for us."

Chhoy did not say a word. She still could not believe what had just happened. She walked but was still thinking of the whole ordeal. Chhorn could have been dead if bitten by the snake. She'd had snake meat before when she'd come to visit Mother about a year ago. Father had brought Mother snake meat along with other types of animal meat

They arrived at the large hill about an hour later. Father was fixing the ox wagon as his friends were loading the logs onto the wagon.

"Father, we were here. Do you have fish for us?" Chhorn asked.

"Come here," Father walked to the other end of the ox wagon and removed the cover from a large basket.

Chhoy and Chhorn were thrilled when they saw a basket full of fresh fish. Most of them were still alive. Chhorn lifted her basket and placed it next the fish basket.

"Chhorn, what is that?" Father asked.

"It's a snake," Chhorn answered.

"How did you get the snake?"

"I caught it on the way here," Chhorn answered.

"Who told you to catch snakes?" Father asked.

"I heard you catch snakes all the time."

"Dear God! Promise me you won't ever do that again. That's a termite hill cobra. You guys were lucky that it was very skinny and frail. Normally, they were fast and fierce. One of its bites will kill you," Father said as he lifted his hands and pressed his palms together, thanking God for sparing their lives.

Chhorn didn't say anything. She felt guilty and sad to see Father like this. She had never seen Father pray to God for anything before.

"Since it's dead and you had cut off its head, it was safe to skin it and cook it," Father said. "Here's the fish."

Father selected the fish and placed them in Chhoy's and Chhorn's baskets. "This is all I can give you without getting in trouble. These fish are for the villagers and the militants. If they found out I gave fish to anyone, I would be in big trouble. I have cooked some fish in the fire over there. It should be done shortly."

Chhoy and Chhorn walked over and sat by the fire. They stared at the fish that Father was roasting over the fire. Chhorn rotated the stick, turning the fish over and examining it.

"This side looks done. I'm going to have a taste," Chhorn said picking the fish meat that was still sizzling over the fire.

Chhoy did the same on another fish that was slightly smaller. One pick after another, they ended up eating the entire fish before it had a chance to cook thoroughly. They were too hungry to wait.

"Father, I forgot to ask if you wanted some fish," Chhorn said, with a guilty grin.

Father smiled and said, "Don't worry about me. Earlier, I had one that was twice the size of your fish. You better return to your camp soon before they start looking for you."

After eating one whole fish each, Chhorn and Chhoy had gained lot of energy. They returned to the camp quickly. It took them less than an hour to reach the camp. They shared the fish with their friends, and all was cooked and eaten in one night. Chhorn and Chhoy had one each for themselves.

CHAPTER 22

The rain had been pouring for six weeks straight, flooding most of the lower part of Tuel Snai and submerging majority of the rice paddies. The water had cut off access to the higher ground, making it impossible to work. Everyone was forced to return home. Some camps were stranded, and people had to be transported out by canoes. Chhoy and Chhorn returned home a couple days apart. They were surprised to find Father home as well. His entire cottage was flooded. He and his comrades had built a new shelter on higher ground, but the water had cut all access. There was nothing for them to do when all the roads were flooded. They were forced to come home like everyone else.

The river in front of our house continued to rise. The water ran through the channel that was routed to the rice paddies throughout the villages, overflowing a large numbers of rice paddies. Fortunately, the water brought all types of fish along.

Father and his friends took the opportunity and set fish traps along the rice paddies. He spent most of his time creating new fish traps using small bamboo trees and setting them along the rice paddies. He caught a lot fish every day and contributed more than half of the fish to the public. He secretly kept the other half for us and shared with our close friends and neighbors.

Although the fish was abundant for the families that could catch fish, the rice supply was becoming depleted. The water had submerged all the rice paddies. It was supposed to be harvesting time, but most of the rice had been destroyed. There were days when the entire town didn't get any rice porridge to eat at all. People who could not fish were starving, especially the families without a man at home and the families that did not have the tools to catch fish.

One day, Father brought home fish encased in the traps. His clothes was soaking wet. His hands and feet were muddy. I noticed a clump of some sort on his ankle.

"Father, what were those?" I asked.

He lowered his head and checked his ankle. "I didn't notice the leeches were clinching on me," he said and laughed.

He plucked the leeches out with his bare hands. The wormlike critters stretched about a foot long before they let go of Father's flesh. They were twisting and turning, hungry for more blood. He tossed each of the leeches into the fire after he plucked them from his ankle. Mother and all my sisters squirmed.

"Those were buffalo leeches," he said.

"Our family is together once again, but we are still missing Chhoeun. I'm wondering where he is right know. I'm praying that he's all right," Mother said with despair.

"I believe he is fine. That kid took care of himself since he was five," Father said.

We didn't know where Chhoeun was right now. We didn't know if he was even still alive. It was nice to be together, but Mother would not allow Father or Chhoeun to stay home long. She feared the government would ask questions and might reveal their past. Chhoeun and Father had a history of working for Lon Nol. If the new government found out, it will be the end of us.

After several weeks of fishing and distributing fish to the entire town, Father's name was becoming very popular in the Stung Chah. He didn't seem to mind, but it was Mother's worst fear. She encouraged Father to return to Tuel Snai where he could work with a group of close friends and be away from the town leaders. Father agreed to return.

"Can you take Bun with you? They make him work hard here, and he misses work most of the time. If he continues to miss work like this, they might take him to trial. I don't think they would because he's too small, but anything could happen in this town. As you can see, they've taken nearly half of the people to execution regardless of how old they are," Mother said.

"I will take him along but not today. I have to make sure we finish building the shelter first. I will come and pick him up when the shelter is ready. We don't have rice to eat either over there, but he could eat fish like me," Father said.

He informed a couple of his friends that were living nearby that he was returning to Tuel Snai. All his friends agreed to go with him. He used the canoe that he had anchored by the river and traveled to Tuel Snai. He returned a few days later with a larger canoe. Father carried and placed me in the long decorative canoe. It was about three feet wide and about forty feet long. I watched him and several more of his friends climb in the canoe. They began to row the canoe along the flowing river.

Chhoy and Chhorn were staying home. They had been assigned to work with the local men and women doing various tasks, such as draining the water from the rice paddies and clearing shrubs off the dry ground.

Within a few weeks, the rain subsided and then stopped completely. The dry season had begins. The rice that had survived the flood was ready to be harvested. Chhorn and Chhoy were selected to go back to work at Tuel Snai. They remained in separate groups. The shelters that they had built earlier had been destroyed by the flood. Since there was no more rain, there was no need to build a shelter, especially when they knew this was a temporary task. Most people would lay their mosquito net out in the open using just a bamboo tree to hold the net up. Some simply slept out in the open laying on a haystack. The job was to cut the full-grown rice using sickles and stack it up. The adults would take rice stacks and separate the rice grains from the stems using various methods. The rice grains were then gathered and taken to another location for another process to remove the hulls off the kernels.

Fortunately, the local authorities were being generous and offered enough rice to make steamed rice for everyone to eat for lunch and dinner. Chhorn and Chhoy gained so much weight after about six weeks of eating thick rice porridge and steamed rice along with the fish and crabs they caught after work. They also allowed the youth to visit home every other week. Chhorn took the opportunity to sneak the steamed rice home. They normally notified everyone about three days in advance. Once Chhorn got the notification, she began to save the steamed rice using the banana leaves.

At home, things had changed for the worse. Only one meal of rice was given at lunch each day. Mother was running out of ideas to steal the rice. The flood had caused so much damage that there were days when the entire village went without a single meal. Mother, Pech, Chhom, and Poe were starving. Mother had given up hope and accepted the fact that death was awaiting. When Bong Chhorn and Chhoy arrived with six rolls of rice every other week, she gained a little bit of hope again.

The harvest season ended quickly. A long dry season was coming. Chhoy and Chhorn returned home from Tuel Snai, waiting for further instruction. After several days, they were summoned to a city called Bung Tum. Chhoy and Chhorn were in different groups, but they were going to same location. They marched down with hundreds of other women and children and collected more people along the way. There were roughly three hundred people marching at the same time.

They arrived at the abandoned community. The houses were mostly large and tall, built to endure a flood. Most of the roofs were tiled. This community must have once belonged to the wealthy. The Mekongs got to choose a house. Chhoy's Mekong chose a decent house that sat on one side of the community. Inside, the house had two floors with nearly a dozen rooms. Chhoy really liked the house, and she was very happy that she did not have to build a shelter like she did in Tuel Snai. Unfortunately, since there were so many people, her entire group of ten was crammed in one small room. Hundreds more people poured in a few days later. All the mansions were filled quickly, forcing the newcomers to reside outside.

Most of Chhoy's friends, including Ah Vee, Ah Nee, Suan, Peak Lee, Leng, and Chu, were among the selected. Chhoy was sharing her mosquito net with Ah Vee and Ah Nee. Leng and Chu had their mosquito net just beside her.

The rice plantations were several months ahead. Normally, this was the time when the rice paddies were left untouched until it was time to plow. The plowing normally took place around the beginning of the raining season when the dirt was soft. Plowing would help loosen up the soil before spreading the rice seeds again. During the Lon Nol's time, most farmers had used oxen to haul the single blade to plow the soil. The wealthy would use a motorized plow. The current government wanted to keep everyone busy and stay ahead of schedule; they wanted to plow a month or two early. Since the oxen were rare nowadays, the majority of the work would done manually.

The brutal work began. Everyone's task was to dig the dry and hard soil. The amount of rice porridge given had been reduced each day. Just after three weeks, Chhoy and her friends could easily notice a significant amount of weight loss. Chhoy had grown a bit stronger over the years despite the lack of food. She was able to lift the hoe with less effort and learned to be efficient and not to use excessive energy. The hoes were long and heavy, designed to be used by the adults. It was very difficult for children to use the hoes.

Chhoy was digging the dirt along with her friends. "Ah Vee. Your face is becoming so black it looks like the bottom of the cooking pot," Peak Lee said.

Ah Vee replied, "*Kmao Chao Preah En, sa kdah Chen* [Dark is the descendant of the four-face angel. White is the Chinese testicle.]"

Everyone that stood nearby broke out laughing. It was one of the phrases widely used for the dark-skinned children to defend themselves from insults. It was hard work, but the girls learned that the days went by fast when they talked. The sun was beating down relentlessly. It was past noon. The lunch break seemed just seconds ago. Chhoy stood up and stretched her back when she saw two Militants come toward her. Both of them were holding rifles. Nowadays, the militants were rarely seen. The workers no longer needed to be forced the work. Everyone knew their job and understood the consequence if they were taken to trial for laziness. Chhoy stood frozen when she saw the two militants approaching.

"Trinh Leng, Trinh Chu, Peak Lee, follow us. The upper officials have a special lesson to teach you. Do not worry. They will take good care of you," one of them said politely.

Chu, Leng, and Peak Lee dropped their hoes and walked obediently with the militants. Everyone, including Chhoy, could not help but stop digging and watch.

The two sisters, Leng and Chu, were the last of their family to survive. Their entire family was all dead. Their last name, Trinh, was apparently Vietnamese. They were like sisters to Chhoy, sharing everything they had. The same with Peak Lee—she was Chhoy's close friend as well.

She had a Chinese first name, but she never mentioned her last name. Chhoy looked around and she saw hundreds of militants escorting other people around her, including the elders. A young woman about eighteen years of age who was working just ten feet from her was escorted by two militants as well. None of the militants appeared to be threatening but were calm and polite.

Mit Rate and Mit Ra appeared heedless and continued working. Chhoy noticed the two Mekongs were shivering like they were in the middle of a cold rain.

"All little sisters keep working. Do not look at their faces," Mit Ra said softly.

"Keep working hard, little sisters," Mit Rate added.

Even though Mit Rate and Mit Ra had always been nice, they never spoke with this much soothing. Everyone continued to work as usual. Chhoy had a feeling that something was wrong, but she dismissed the bad feeling and resumed digging the soil. Chhoy returned to the compound after work hoping to see Leng, Chu, and Peak Lee again, but they never showed up. She went out looking for food, hoping to see them after she returned.

At nightfall, Chhoy returned with a few catches and cooked them with Ah Nee, Ah Vee, and the new girls in the group. She still hadn't seen the three return. Chhoy was very afraid but committed to believe that they were still in training. She missed them already. She went to sleep, uncertain of the fate of her three friends.

In the morning, Chhoy woke up hoping to see the three. As the group was gathering to prepare for work, many girls and women were questioning one another about their friends and co-workers that were escorted away. No one knew where they were. Chhoy didn't bother asking any of her friends. She knew they wouldn't know the answer either. She was also afraid to learn the truth.

On the field, Chhoy was digging the soil along with her co-workers. She couldn't help but think of Leng, Chu, and Peak Lee.

"We lost Leng, Chu, and Peak Lee. I think they took them to execution," Ah Nee said.

Chhoy shivered from the statement. It was almost random that the militia just came and took them away. She could have been one of them.

"Maybe they are still in training," Chhoy said.

"There is nothing to train. I have never seen anyone being trained on anything," Ah Nee said.

Unfortunately, Ah Nee was right. Since the new government took over, there was no such thing as training. Everyone was simply forced to work and learn on their own.

"Little sisters, please continue to work hard and don't talk about what you don't know," the Mekong reassure nicely.

On the evening of the third day after many people had been escorted away, the local village leaders brought used clothes and piled them in front of each house.

"Here! Share this with anyone that needs clothes," the men who dropped the clothes off hollered.

Dozens of girls, mostly around ten years of age, happily roamed the pile and scavenged for their clothing sizes. Chhoy knew well where those clothes had come from and finally accepted the fact that her friends Leng, Chu, and Peak Lee had been executed. She felt a deep pain that she had never experienced before. She had just lost her close friends that she had spent so much time with. The images of her friends remained clear and fresh, especially the day they were escorted away. They were calm, obedient, and unaware of their fate. Every single one of their families was dead, and now they had just met the same fate.

Chhoy had been friends with them for nearly three years now. They shared everything they had, even the smallest bits of food. They slept together and shared same mosquito net and cared for one another like sisters. Chhoy wept every time she thought of them.

"You know that all the people that were taken away were all related to the Vietnamese. They were looking for anyone that has a Vietnamese last name or looks resemble to the Vietnamese," Ah Nee said as they were preparing for bedtime.

The Vietnamese normally had lighter skin than the native Khmers. Chhoy skin was lighter than most of her friends. She was scared. She was glad that her first name resembled the Chinese and her last name, Phuong, was the native Khmer. She was hoping that her first name and last name would help save her from her light skin color.

When she returned to work the next day, everyone appeared more nervous than Chhoy had ever seen. Mit Rate and Mit Ra's faces were frightened and concerned. They didn't say much except to urge the girls not talk too much about the incident.

The work became monotonous and senseless for the next few months. Everyone was digging all day every day. They were initially told to dig dirt to build the rice paddies and the water canal, but now everyone was instructed to dig without a reason. The raining season had arrived, and it was raining hard. The first wave of rain lasted several weeks, flooding the river and all the rice paddies. It was the time of the year to spread the rice seeds, but the flood made it impossible.

A few weeks later, the entire Bung Tum was flooded. All the children and the young adults were forced to go back to their home. Chhoy and Chhorn were home once again. They were working with the local hordes near the house to get a share of food until they were selected to go to another location.

Chhoy was still around fourteen years old. The age they were considered an adult was fifteen. But nowadays, age didn't matter. When they thought you were big enough to join the adults, they selected you to join the adults. Chhoy had been selected along with Chhorn to go to another location. Since most of the local towns and villages were flooded, they had no option but to travel further west, away from the flood.

On the day of the gathering, Chhoy and Chhorn saw that some of their friends had been selected as well. Ah Nee, Ah Vee, and Ah Nee the Muslim were among them. There were about forty members in the group, including the Mekong. The rest of the hordes were mostly the elder women. Mit Ra and Mit Rate were no longer with them. A new Mekong was leading them, and they knew nothing about her. Right now, she did not seem to be very friendly. In fact, she appeared to be one of the Mit Chah.

This was the rice *stoong* phase. After rice seeds had been spread and the buds had sprouted tightly, it was time to manually uproot the rice sprouts and manually plug them in other rice paddies to spread them out, giving the rice sprouts more room to grow.

It was still early morning. It had rained hard the night before. The ground was wet and muddy. It was just a drizzle now, but it was also colder than usual. After the line had been formed, the horde began to march. Since most of the members were new, no one really talked much. They walked in the rain and stopped at several places for breaks. Just before nightfall, they settled in an open rice field. The Mekong informed them that this was a city called Sra Keo. This was where they would sleep and work until the job was completed. It doesn't look anything like a city. There was not a single tree or a house. They needed to sleep, and there was nothing they could use to build a shelter. Everyone had no choice but to sleep in the rice paddies, using the rim of the rice field as their pillow.

Everyone in the horde picked their spot to sleep. They stayed close together, trying to keep warm. Chhorn had chosen a spot further away from everyone afraid others might step on her infected foot. Everyone was tired and needed to sleep. They had been walking all day without a single ounce of food. They lay down as the rain continued to drizzle. Chhorn began to feel a strong pain in her foot. The wound had no indication of going away anytime soon. She had been walking in pain all day, but when she was at rest, her mind seemed to focus on the pain and made it worse.

They fell asleep despite the rain. Chhoy and Chhorn woke up several times trying to get comfortable.

Finally, Chhorn opened her eyes like she had many times during the night, and she noticed that no one was around them. Not a single person. She began to panic.

"Chhoy! Chhoy! Wake up!" She whispered, shaking Chhoy.

Chhoy woke up and stared at Chhorn. "Why are you waking me up so early?" Chhoy asked.

"Everyone left, and I think they all left to work. We need to get there quick, but I don't know which way they went. It's too dark to see," Chhorn said and began walking.

Chhoy got up grudgingly and trudged after Chhorn. It was too dark to see. Chhorn was walking aimlessly searching for the horde. They were both scared. The Mekong was not the same as Mit Ra and Mit Rate. She was the Mit Chah, and she was talking to everyone like they were slaves.

The morning sun was still deep behind the horizon but giving off a faint radiance in the distant, enough to produce dark contrasts between objects and the empty space. Chhorn stopped and gazed around the area searching for a sign of movement. After about thirty minutes, Chhoy spotted the blurry movements about a hundred yards away.

"Are those people over there?" Chhoy pointed out.

"Where?" Chhorn asked.

Chhorn squinted and continued to walk toward the direction that Chhoy was pointing.

"Are those humans or plants moved by the wind? Let's get closer," Chhorn said and hastily strode toward the movements.

"It's them," Chhorn said happily, but she knew they were in trouble for being late. This was not the girls' group. This was the adults where everything was serious. They approached the horde expecting to be scolded by the Mekong or the group leaders. Everyone was stooping down, uprooting and wrapping the rice sprouts in small bundles. No one seemed to heed their arrival. Chhorn and Chhoy sneaked slowly and blended in with the horde. They began to work like they had been there all along.

Just when they thought they'd gotten away with it, a cold voice came from behind them. "Where have you been?"

"We had to go potty," Chhorn said. It was the only thing that she knew she could do when they were away from work. Anyone could have the excuse to go potty.

"All right then, get back to work," the Mekong said.

Ah Nee crept by slowly, pretending to work at the same time and asked, "Where were you guys? It was so dark, and I thought you were with us."

"We woke up late, and everyone had already left. It took us a while to find you guys," Chhorn said.

Stoong was one of the easiest jobs, but it required stooping down all day. Everyone worked without saying much. They took a break at noon for lunch. Somehow, the cook managed to build a fire under the light rain to cook the rice porridge. Everyone was disappointed with the amount of rice porridge they got. It was about six ounces with mostly water. They returned to work and didn't stop until dark. Normally, the Mekong would dismiss the workers after the sunset, allowing everyone to utilize the evening radiance before nightfall, but for some reason, the Mekong didn't show up until long after the sunset.

They returned to the camp area and got their share of rice porridge. After they'd finished eating, it was too dark to see anything.

"How were we going to find any food? It's so dark." Chhoy said.

"We'll have to try. The snails should be abundant because of the rain," Chhorn said.

Like everyone else in the group, they went out and searched for snails in the dark. It was too dark to pick any vegetables. They spent several hours collecting snails. They had to build a fire in the drizzle. The grasses were still green and still wet. Chhorn and Chhorn spent about an hour searching for dry twigs. They borrowed a piece of the cook's burned wood to start the fire. It took them nearly another hour to start the fire, as most of the twigs were wet.

They cooked the snails and ate them in the rain. When they finished eating, it was about midnight. They were sleeping in the rain once again. The ground was rough and uncomfortable to sleep on. They were soaking wet from head to toe. The snails did not budge their hunger, but they were too tired to think about food. It was obvious that everyone was going through the same harsh time, but no one was complaining. They don't know one another, and no one trusted anyone they didn't know.

"Wake up! Wake up! It's time to work," the voice of the Mekong called out to wake everyone up again.

Chhoy and Chhorn woke up. "I felt like I just closed my eyes, and it's time to wake up again," Chhorn said.

"I'm so sleepy," Chhoy added.

It was still pitch dark. This was way too early to wake up. The rain had subsided, but the air was very moist and cold.

"My stomach hurts," Chhoy said.

"Mine too," Chhorn said.

They went to potty while everyone was on their way to the rice paddies. Both of them had very bad diarrhea. They thought the snails they ate last night were the cause. They arrived at the site shortly and found everyone was stooping down working. Chhorn and Chhoy sneaked in slowly, blending in with the horde, hoping the Mekong would not see them. They were late yesterday and were able to pull it off. It wouldn't be that easy this time if they get caught.

Fortunately, no one seemed to care when they tiptoed in. Everyone was working, pretending they didn't see or hear them coming. They all just wanted to do their job and stay out of trouble. Chhoy and Chhorn began to work, keeping their eyes on snails and crabs, despite the common rule that no one was allowed to collect any food while working.

Several days later, the Mekong found an abandoned cottage about a kilometer away from the site. All forty people were ordered to stay in the cottage. Everyone had to squeeze in the crowded space. Some women, mostly the elders, volunteered to sleep outside. Then someone found some wood nearby and built a small additional shelter onto the cottage to fit a few more people. The cottage was a great benefit. No one had to sleep out in the rain anymore. Everyone was able to sleep much more comfortably.

About four weeks later, their task was completed. The Mekong had been instructed to move to another location about half a day of walking from there. They had begun the march right after lunch further west. Just before dark, they came to a large abandoned mansion that stood about six feet off the ground and was supported by large columns. The roof was made of tiles. The area was surrounded by banana trees and many other plants and vegetables.

"That's a mansion," someone said, afraid to add more detail.

"I have been here before. There's a prison right behind it," someone else said.

"Staying next to the prison is scary," another said softly.

The Mekong led them into the mansion. Inside, the ceiling was low, and it was obvious that there was another floor above them. Chhorn and Chhoy did not expect the house to have two floors. The second floor seemed to have its own doorway from the other side.

"We will stay here on the bottom floor. The upper floor is for our brave leaders," the Mekong said.

The night fell quickly, and the rain began to pour again. Chhoy and Chhorn were glad they were in a shelter and not outside. They had just enough room to hang their mosquito net. The room gradually became warm from the body heat of the horde. Everyone was preparing for a nice, comfortable sleep. No one spoke much except for a friendly offer to share the mosquito net.

After everyone was settled in the dark night, there was a loud murmur right above them. They must be the high officials who resided on the second floor. Chhorn was curious and tried to make out what they were saying, but the sound of the rain scrambled the words. Then she just remembered there was a prison nearby. She might not want to hear what they had to say.

The horde worked for two days in the constant pouring rain. There work wasn't productive at all. The floods in the rice paddies made it nearly impossible to uproot and plug the rice sprouts. The Mekong decided to hold off working and wait until the rain subsided.

After four days of waiting and idling, the rain didn't seem like it would ease any time soon. The entire rice fields had been flooded. The Mekong dismissed everyone to return home. She gave everyone the option to stay and wait or leave instantly. The majority decided to stay and wait until the rain subsided. Some took off the instant they got permission. Chhorn and Chhoy hesitated to leave at first, but after all her friends had left, they decided to take the risk and leave as well. The thought of staying near the prison where the Red Khmer officials were living right above them was terrifying.

Chhorn and Chhoy didn't wait for anyone to come along. They knew how to get home. The path they travelled here was mostly open land. They began walking on the flooded rice road. They reached the rice field where the rims were still visible and walked along the rims.

Along the way, they had to cross many deep parts of the flood. They held their backpacks up high and walked slowly across the flood. Some parts so were deep that they submerged their heads. They avoid swimming to save their energy and to keep their backpacks dry. Unfortunately, they came across a deep part of the flood where it took too long to walk under the water. They couldn't hold their breath that long and were forced them to swim. They were exhausted, and all the clothes and mosquito net in the backpack were soaked.

They arrived home late at night. The next morning, Chhorn and Chhoy went to check in with the local authority as required. They were told that the new law no longer allowed the young adults to stay with their parents. A new compound had been recently arranged for the young adults on the other side of the river. Chhorn and Chhoy packed and went over to the new compound as instructed. Once they arrived at the new compound, it wasn't a surprise that they met some of their friends that were in the youth group that were now considered as young adults.

Just after staying two days in the compound, Chhorn and Chhoy saw more of their friends that were living in nearby villages. The government continued to send more young women over to the compound according to the new law. The entire compound was filled from inside of building to every inch of open land. Chhorn and Chhoy had been selected to move back to Bung Tum, a town where they had been working all dry season digging soil. Bung Tum had been flooded since the beginning of the raining season. It was unknown what the government had in mind by relocating them to a flooded town.

Dozens of canoes were waiting as Chhorn and Chhoy and the selected horde were being escorted by the Mekong, the same woman who'd led them to Sra Keo. Once everyone was on the canoes, there were two men on each canoe who began to row the along the Stung Chah River. After a long ride on the wobbling and insecure canoes, they reached the town of Bung Tum. The entire town was flooded. Only the tall trees and the tall mansions were visible above the water. All the small houses and trees had been submerged. The bottom half of the mansions and tall houses were under the water.

The Mekong ordered the men to stop by the houses that were half-submerged. The wall by the ceiling had been removed to make a new entrance as all the doors were somewhere under the water. Everyone begins to hop off the canoes onto the wooden plank that sat just above the water. Chhoy and Chhorn entered the house along with Ah Nee and six other girls. The second floor has also been flooded. They were walking on the wood planks that zigzagged from the entrance to the stairs that was leading to some sort of newly built floor right on top of the main beam below the ceiling.

"This is your new place to sleep," said the Mekong, who was still sitting on the canoe.

Everyone knew well not to complain. They obediently picked a spot on the suspended floor and settled in. Chhorn and Chhoy begin to setup their mosquito net immediately. Ah Nee, the Muslim, and her new friend, Mit Nahn, were sharing a mosquito net as well. This was one of the most senseless places to stay. The houses were surrounded by water, and there was nothing for them to do here. No one spoke, as they didn't trust anyone they don't know, especially when many people had been taken to execution for any type of suspicion. The Vietnamese were closing in from the southeast. Many people had fled south to seek help from the Vietnamese. The Mekongs were ordered to monitor the girls so they could not escape. This was probably the reason why they were here, in the house surrounded by water.

Chhorn and her friends sat along the edge of the suspended floor staring at the water. The water was a little murky, but they could see fish of all types and sizes swimming beneath them. Unfortunately, they had nothing to catch the fish with. Just after one girl asked how they were going to cook, a man who rowed the canoe stopped by to distribute a scoop of rice porridge to everyone.

Before nightfall, the Mekong returned to check on the girls and left. Chhorn and Chhoy felt a little more comfortable and chatted with their friends. There was nothing else they could do but sit and watch the fish swimming right below them until the night fall. This was a big break for everyone. They didn't have to worry about digging soil for a while.

They went to sleep and woke up early in the morning because they were used to the working schedule, but they just ended up sitting around and staring at the water all day long. Chhorn made a few attempts to snatch the fish by hand while they came so close to the surface, but the fish were too quick for her.

After several weeks of staying in an enclosed spot underneath the ceiling, Chhorn came down with sudden and extreme illness. She had a high fever and vomited anything she ate. Chhorn requested to come home, knowing the chance of getting the approval was very slim. Normally, if you were not able to travel home with your own strength, you were not allowed to come home. Surprisingly, she was allowed to come home. A man came with a canoe and transported her to Stung Chah. Chhoy was separated from Chhorn once again. She's was staying with her friends and shared her mosquito net with another girl that didn't have one.

Several weeks later, Chhoy and the group were informed they were moving to another location. This time, the Mekong did not tell them the specific location. Early morning, dozens of canoes docked by the half-submerged houses and boarded everyone in the area. Ah Nee and Mit Nahn were sitting right behind her. The men rowed the canoes heading southwest along the slow-moving water, drifting Chhoy and the horde further away from home.

The canoes were floating on the water, above the fields that were once the grueling working sites that Chhoy and her friends spent time working during the dry season. This brought back Chhoy's painful memories of the day nearly half of her friends were taken away to slaughter. Chhoy was already hungry, and she knew that she would not get anything to eat at least until noontime tomorrow.

The men stopped the canoes when they reached the land just before nightfall. They came to a large hand-built dam that extended over a hundred yards. The water was overflowing the dam, causing a loud waterfall. About fifty yards away, a multilevel cottage was sitting on the pier overlooking the dam and the flooded land. The windows were visible by the faint light revealing the movements of occupants inside. Girls around Chhoy's age were roaming around the house in the gloomy evening picking vegetables.

The men anchored the canoe by the dam and helped the girls get off. Chhoy and the horde walked along the flooded dam to their new compound. Many current occupants paused and stared at the newcomers. Chhoy hadn't seen anyone older than twenty years of age yet. These were all the survivors just like her.

Chhoy remembered Father mentioned a place called Ahneam. It was the remote, hostile forest swamp, infested by dangerous animals and plants. During Lon Nol's time, Father had traveled to Ahneam and brought home all sorts of animals, including pythons, exotic monkeys, and birds. When he chatted with his friends, he would tell of his experience at Ahneam as if he had entered a demonic world and was lucky to come out alive. Father mentioned he had seen the Ahneam cobras that were twice as long as the ordinary cobra and much more aggressive. Chhoy was hoping she was nowhere near the Ahneam.

When Chhoy got closer to the compound, she saw other cottages sitting on a hill surrounded by water, scattered randomly about half-kilometers apart. The only way to get to each cottage was by canoe. The cottage that Chhoy was staying in was also isolated and surrounded by water.

When Chhoy was about to enter the housing complex, another canoe arrived. She spotted Ah Vee and Ah Nee sitting on the boat. Chhoy felt a surge of happiness after seeing them. They were like her sisters, especially Ah Nee.

Chhoy and her friends found a spot among the many rooms in the cottage and set up their mosquito nets. There were nearly two hundred girls living the same cottage. Every square inch of space were taken. As Chhoy expected, there was no indication she would get anything to eat today. She had gone the entire day without food. She had learned that this town was called Sra Keo, the same town where she had come to *stoong* with Chhorn right before the flood.

Early in the morning, Chhoy and her friends woke up waiting for the Mekong to come and assign the task for the day. As they sat and waited, they noticed many girls were still sleeping. Ah Nee asked the girl next to them, and the girl told them they hadn't had to work since they'd arrived. The girl also explained that people residing in the other cottage normally cooked and brought rice porridge for them to eat. She added that, some days, they never brought any rice porridge at all.

Similar to Bung Tum, there was nothing but water here and nothing to do. The difference was they were on the high land with a lot of space for them to walk around and find food. Chhoy and her friends didn't waste any time and began wandering around searching for food. They found the land was much bigger than they thought. It was like they had an island to themselves. Despite the large number of girls living here, there were still water spinaches available. Chhoy and her friends walked around picking the water spinaches and collecting snails. They also found small crabs along the way. They returned to the house and cooked their food that they had craved all day.

At noon, a woman rowed a boat and brought over a pot of rice porridge. Everyone get a small scoop. The amount of rice porridge given barely budged their hunger. Everyone immediately hurried out and searched for more food right after lunch.

About two weeks later, the vegetables and the snails became scarce. Everyone was focusing on catching crabs, but they were more difficult to find than snails. They lived deep in the mud or in the water. They saw fish swimming everywhere, but they have nothing to catch the fish with. Chhoy wished she had some sort of net to scoop the fish with. Sometimes, the fish came so close to the shore making it look so easy to catch them by hand. Chhoy leaped over to try to catch a fish once, but the fish swam away instantly.

It was a gloomy morning like most of the days. Chhoy and her friends walked to the water and washed their faces. It was nice to live by the water. They got to wash their faces every morning. They would bathe when they got dirty. The fish could be seen on the surface breathing the air.

"If we have a spare mosquito net, we could easily catch those fish," Ah Nee said.

"Where do we get the mosquito net? I had mine for four years. To get another mosquito net, we need about five cans of rice. We don't even have a spoon," Mit Nahn said.

"I can sacrifice mine if you let me sleep with you," Chhoy said to Mit Nahn.

"Of course you can sleep with me. We always share the mosquito net. As long as you are with me, you are guaranteed to have a mosquito net," Mit Nahn replied.

"You can sleep with me as well," Ah Nee the Muslim said.

Chhoy was confident that she would always have friends with a mosquito net. Every single person she knew since the beginning of the new government had no problem sharing anything they had. Chhoy leaped up and dashed to her sleeping spot. She untied the mosquito net and ran back down happily. She couldn't wait to catch some fish.

Ah Nee and Mit Nahn were the oldest, and they knew exactly what to do. They held each side of the net and dipped the net into the water. With one hand holding the bottom of the net and the other holding the top of the net, they walked together deeper in the river. Chhoy and the rest of her friends were flanking the fish into the net. In no time, they began to see the fish swim into the mosquito net in the murky water. Mit Nahn and Ah Nee lifted up the net and found several slick black and silver snakehead fish flipping around inside it.

"We caught some fish!" Chhoy exclaimed in joy.

"We get to eat fish again!" Ah Vee said.

Mit Nahn grabbed the fish from the mosquito net and tossed them to shore. Chhoy dashed over and picked up the fish. She held the fish with both hands and smiled. This was what she had been waiting for so many weeks. Like rice, fish always tasted good and offered so much energy. Chhoy and her friends continued to use the same technique to catch the fish. They had been doing this for so long now that it became second nature to catch the fish. Not much communication was needed. They took a break at noon and cooked the fish to eat before the rice porridge was distributed. After they ate, they continued to catch some more fish. Unfortunately, they didn't catch as many fish as they had in the morning, but they caught enough to share one fish with two people.

Chhoy and her friends woke up before sunrise the next morning and used the net the catch some more fish. They didn't have the same luck as the previous day, but they caught several smaller fish. It was much better than nothing and worth the effort and time. It didn't take long for other girls to sacrifice their mosquito nets to catch fish. Each day, more and more groups of girls appeared along the water with their mosquito nets catching the fish.

As weeks passed by, the cook came to distributed less and less frequently. It was fortunate that Chhoy and the group decided to sacrifice their mosquito nets to catch fish. Without fish, they would have starved to death by now. No one understood why they were here in the first place. No one was complaining, though, because they didn't have to work like they did before. Some believed they were here to defend the country from the Vietnamese.

A few weeks before, Chhoy had stepped on a thorn that was nearly two inches long while helping her friend flank the fish. She nearly fainted when she pulled it out. She assumed the puncture would heal quickly. She had stepped over many thorns before, and the wound had always healed.

Unfortunately, the puncture on her foot was infected and getting worse every day. This morning, she woke up weeping from the excruciating pain. She looked down at her foot and saw the puss oozing from the top of her infected foot. The infection had made a hole from the bottom of her foot all the way through to the top. She had been limping along with her friends to help them catch fish, but there was no way she could walk today.

"What's the matter?" Ah Nee asked.

"My infection is spreading. It made its way to the top of my foot," Chhoy said holding her foot with both hands. Her eyes were full of tears.

"Let's go ask the Mekong for permission to go home. They might have someone to transport you home," Mit Nee said.

"Let's try," Chhoy said.

"Can you walk? I will ask for you, but you have to be there," Ah Nee said.

"I can try," Chhoy said.

"Let's go see her then. She should be outside guarding,"

Ah Nee lifted the mosquito net and helped Chhoy stood up. Chhoy limped along the hall way with the help of Ah Nee. They came outside through the back door. The Mekong was standing looking at the yellowish water that flooded the entire town. It was not the same Mekong that had brought them here. This Mekong was quiet and different.

"Mit Bong," Ah Nee hollered.

The Mekong turned around, showing her healthy, thin, dark figure. She stood tall, towering both of them. Her long hair was tied in a bundle to the back revealing her dark and pretty face.

"Mit Bong, Mit Chhoy has a big infection on her foot. Can she go home?" Ah Nee said.

"Why do you want to go home? You have to stay here," she said, staring at Chhoy.

"I cannot walk," Chhoy said.

"There is no canoe. You have to wait until the water retreats," the Mekong said firmly. Then she turned around and continued to stare into the distance.

Chhoy was disappointed. She wanted to go home and have Mother take a look. Mother would know what to do. Chhoy and Ah Need limped slowly back to their sleeping spot. Chhoy lay down and rubbed her leg lightly to sooth the pain. Ah Nee and the girls went fishing a bit later. Chhoy had no choice but to wait until the water retreated.

CHAPTER 23

I was sitting beside Father and his friends picking at roasted fish. Father gave me a medium-size snakehead fish. There were several more fish on the fire. If I finished my fish, I would get another one. If I didn't, there would be nothing left. Father had returned to Stung Chah and picked me up with the canoes during the first flood. There was nothing for me to do during the flood. Since I was required to work to get my share of rice porridge, I had not gotten a single share of rice since the flood. We were living in an isolated cottage up on a hill. Father went to work with his friends all day and left me with an elder man that was the designated cook. He came back to the cottage just to eat lunch and then returned to work until dark. The men brought home fish every day. We ate mostly roasted fish. There was no point in making soup when there was no rice at all.

"Eat faster!" Father yelled.

For some reason, I ate very slowly. It took me hours to finish one fish. Father wanted me to eat fast so that I could get more fish. The men wouldn't mind if I got another after I finished the first, but they would not wait for me to finish. He normally reminded me to eat fast before lunch or dinner started. Father was frustrated with my slowness and scolded me nearly every day during each meal.

The elder men were eating at a normal pace. The younger men were eating as fast as they could so they would get another fish. There were two more fish left on the fire. Father knew that I would not eat fast enough to get a second fish. Normally, whoever finished their fish first got to have another one, and they often shared with someone else. Father looked over at me and saw I was just beginning to eat my fish while most men had nearly finished theirs.

"Eat faster!" he screamed and slapped me lightly on the back of my head.

Father had never yelled at me before. I looked up to him as my idol and my guardian. I felt like I had been betrayed. I begin to wail.

"You're crying because I just urged you to eat! I just touched your head a little! If you were a little bigger, I would kick you so hard!" Father said and motioned to his feet like he really wanted to kick me very hard. It hurt my feelings even more, and I wailed louder. Father got up kicked me softly from behind. I took the opportunity to make it appear like he'd really kicked me and rolled on the ground.

"Get up! Get up and eat your fish!" Father said and tapped me with his feet.

I rolled further, making it appear like he'd kicked me again. Father continued to use his feet and tell me to get up and eat. I continued to roll on the ground and wail at the same time.

"Why are you kicking your son? He is small and young. He doesn't know any better," the elder man scolded Father.

Father paused, looking guilty. "I didn't kick him. I just tapped him with my toe."

"What do mean you didn't kick him? He's tumbling everywhere on the ground."

Father stopped and stared at me with anger. "Go back and eat your fish!" he said and walked back to his seat.

I continued to cry for a few more minutes and then stopped. I walked back to my seat near Father and ate my fish. I didn't look at the men's faces, but I could sense they were all staring at me.

I was the last one to finish eating. The men ate all the fish and then built a bonfire for the water buffalos. When all the land was flooded, Father and his men brought all the water buffalo closer to the cottage. It was their responsibility to look after them. Actually, it was also my responsibility. Father had told his leaders that I was working with the group looking after the water buffalos so that I could get a share of rice. The buffalos grazed the grass around the house during daytime and slept near the haystack at night.

Many months had passed. Every night before bed, Father and the men would sit around the fire and chat. I sat and listened to their conversations. They chatted mostly about their extreme encounters during the long trip to work or their plan for the next day. A few nights before,

Father and the men killed a baby water buffalo and reported to their leaders that it had been bitten and killed by wolves. They gave most of the meat to the leaders and kept some for our group.

I must have fallen asleep during the conversation around the bonfire. I woke up the next morning and found myself in the mosquito net. Father and I were sharing the mosquito net. He normally left to work before I woke up, but for some reason he still here. I could hear him ordering his comrades to prepare the buckets and the canoes.

After a short moment, Father came over. "Bun, get up. Let's go," he said softly. If this was Mother, I would still be laying down until she called me a few more times. Since this was Father telling me to get up, I must get up. Everyone listened to him, including me. I woke up very quickly as Father ordered. I was looking forward to seeing where we were going. Normally, when I had to go along, we would travel far. I couldn't wait to see new places. I followed Father outside. All his comrades were walking ahead toward the river bank where they normally anchored their canoes.

There were three canoes, all prepared and ready to go. Father picked me up and placed me in the middle of the canoe on the right. When everyone was aboard, the men began to row and the canoes began to glide slowly. Nearly everything around was flooded. It was unfortunate for the adults that everything was flooded, but I found that fascinating. I liked to see the trees and housed half submerged under the water. Up ahead I saw fish leap in the air from the murky water.

After a long ride, the area became familiar to me, but I still couldn't figure exactly where we were. After a bridge emerged from behind the trees, I knew right away that this was Stung Chah, my hometown. The road along the river had been flooded. It was impossible to travel by the ox wagons. Father had brought me back home. I didn't know if it was just a visit or permanent. I was glad to see Mother, Chhom, Pech, and Poe again, but I didn't like the fact that I had to work and felt like I was dying of starvation every day.

Father stayed overnight and left the next morning. Now I knew that I was staying for sure. Mother did not tell me that I had to work. I didn't see how it was possible to work when everything was flooded. Other than the flood, everything else was the same. The leader of the Nearadey were still working to eliminate the unwanted. Everyone knew that the Vietnamese armies were invading. No one knew if it would lead to things being better or worse. The Khmer had a long history of conflicts with the Vietnamese before and during the time Lon Nol was in power. Father used to tell stories of how the Vietnamese soldiers killed the Khmer soldiers and took their skulls to make a hearth to cook rice. They called it *Tae Ung*. "Don't ever trust the Vietnamese," he used to tell us.

The rumor was that the Vietnamese armies had successfully taken over the southeast part of Kampuchea and driven out all the Nearadeys from their hometown, forcing them to flee all over the country, including here in Stung Chah. After the humiliating loss, the Nearadeys were seeking vengeance on anyone related to the Vietnamese. They had been walking from house to house looking for anyone of Vietnamese descent. Sometimes, they simply called a person to trial if they even looked Vietnamese. The Vietnamese normally had light skin, but the majority of the Khmer with whiter skin were Chinese descendants. Since China was a supporter of the Red Khmer, the Nearadey were loyal to the Chinese descendants. It was nearly impossible to distinguish between the Chinese and the Vietnamese.

Unfortunately, Tien's mom had extremely white skin. The native Khmer's skin, like Mother's, would turn dark after one day under the sun. The color of Tien's mom's skin wouldn't budge in the sun. Even after working under the sun for several years, her skin refused to turn dark. Several weeks ago, the militants scouted our neighbors and came across Tien's mom. They requested the local leaders take her to trial. Mother knew about the trial and nervously asked for Ta Nuy's wife and K'Oeun to be part of it. She knew that was the only way out for Tien's mom.

"Today we have brought this comrade here for trial. Our brave men have suspected her of being or having the Vietnamese blood. As you know, the Vietnamese are invading our country; thus, they are our enemies. It is our task to eliminate enemies from the inside," Ta Nuy's wife announced.

"That woman is not related to the Vietnamese. She is pure Chinese. She doesn't even have the Khmer blood in her," Mother said out loud in the meeting in front of the leaders that were ready to take her and the family for execution.

"If that is true, then this meeting was over. This comrade is free to go," Ta Nuy's wife said. The trial was dismissed seconds after Mother finished her statement. Mother nearly pissed her pants right after.

Later in the evening, Tien's mom came and thanked Mother for saving her life. "I thought I was going to die," Tien's mom said.

"Not just you. I thought that was the end of you and me. They would take me for defending you if they still thought you were Vietnamese," Mothers said. "Besides, if they killed just you, I would have no one to swear at and would die of boredom," Mother said jokingly.

"I'm glad I have a big sister I can look up to and rely on," Tien's mom said. Mother treated Tien's mom like her baby sister. She talked and swore the way only sisters would do. Tien's mom had just delivered a baby name Van Suk a few months ago. Like Father, her husband, Pu E, was away working in another town. She had no one except Chhom to take care of the newborn along with Tien and Mao.

Several days after, Phan, the Laotian woman, was summoned to trial for suspicion of being related to the Vietnamese. The Laotians normally possessed a skin tone slightly lighter than the Khmer, but Phan was lighter than the typical Laotian. The Nearadey were not familiar with her accent since Laotians were rare in Kampuchea. Laos was located north of Kampuchea, and they shared a small border.

"I have been living near this comrade for a long time. I know for sure that she is from Laos. You can tell by her broad face and her accent," Mother said, praying they would not object to her opinion. If they found Phan guilty of being related to the Vietnamese, they might find Mother guilty of defending the enemies.

Just weeks after Tien's mom initial trial, she was taken to trial again. This time she was accused of stealing the bamboo shoots that she'd found somewhere after work. No one had proof that she'd stolen the bamboo shoots. She was still taken to trial, however, and punished. She had to leave all her children home for a couple months to go to build a dam far from home. Chhom had to find food and take care of me, Pech, Poe, Tien, Mao, and Van Suk. Normally, the punishment for stealing was death. Tien's mom was lucky that she'd escaped death again. It might have had something to do with her being very close to Mother. With K'Ouen backing her up, Mother could dodge some troubles. K'Ouen had been backing up Mother in many situations, making it difficult for anyone to trial her and Tien's mom. Despite all the help, Mother still found K'Ouen fearsome. Her husband was like the grim reaper. He reviewed documents and reported anyone that he thought was corrupted. He was the only survivor of the Peayaup regime. Mother thought he'd survived by betraying his own clan. He had access to all the documents that were gathered by the Peayaup and used the documents to eliminate the unwanted. All the Peayaup in Stung Chah were wiped out in a single week, along with many workers. Ta Watt didn't stop reviewing documents even now. He was still looking for anyone that had anything to do with Lon Nol. After all the suspects had been taken to execution, he was still looking for anyone that was once wealthy or well educated.

Day by day, the names Ta Kirk, Ta Vann, Ta Mao, Ta Nuy, and his wife become well known as cold-blooded executioners. They were seen spending most of their days sharpening knives and axes.

Mother was still a personal messenger of Ta Nuy's wife, but the flood made it impossible to travel. The water continued to rise, submerging all the houses near the river. Most of the rice field had been flooded as well. No one was getting any rice to eat at all. Starvation had gone to another level. Fortunately, our house was sitting on a small hill, higher than all the houses in the village. The house that had once been inconvenient was now favorable for us. The flood brought large fish swimming visibly everywhere in the water, but it also brought many different types of snakes. Snakes of all sorts were seen cruising on the water or curling on the branches of half-submerged trees. Cobras had no problem swimming as well.

I woke up in the middle of the night from a bright light. Chhom was awake as well. I saw Mother holding an oil lamp with one hand and a machete with the other, walking out the door.

"Mother, what were you doing?" Chhom asked.

"I saw large snakehead fish swimming this evening. I'm going to sneak up on them and hack them," she said eagerly.

Chhom and I walked softly after Mother and stood in the doorway. Mother stood at the bottom of the stairs looking around. When she lowered the oil lamp, we saw dark figures of fish swimming just several feet away from the stairs. I hoped Mother knew what she was doing. I was very hungry for fish.

Mother waited for several minutes and then struck one of the fish with her machete. The water splashed and then become bubbly. We could not tell if she had hit the fish because of the bubbles. After a moment, a large fish floated to the surface of the water with its belly up.

Chhom and I smiled and looked at each other with joy. Mother grabbed the fish and walked back up the stairs and tossed the fish on the floor.

"Put it in the basket," Mother said.

Chhom hastily got a basket and tossed the fish in. Mother went back down looking for more fish. She hacked several more fish in less than an hour.

"Ey Ya...a snake! This is not good. I think I should stop for tonight," Mother said.

Mother walked swiftly through the water and up the stairs. She stopped by the doorway and lowered the lamp. I saw a large black snake about two meters long gliding slowly passed the bottom of our stairs. Chhom and I crept into the house, away from the stairs. Mother walked carefully up the stairs, closed the door, and called it a night.

She continued to catch fish every night. She shared most of the fish with the neighbors because, if she didn't, more people would starve to death. The rain continued to pour. The entire village was flooded. For most houses, the water was just inches below the bed. We were the only fortunate ones. The little hill kept us above the water.

Mother was still the designated cook. She continued to work diligently to make food for her horde. Since most parts of the land had been flooded, it was impossible for her to get around. Thus, Ta Nuy's wife provided her a palm tree canoe. Mother spent most of her day on the canoe picking vegetables. Fortunately, even during the flood, the water spinaches and several other vegetables continue to grow on the surface of the water. In fact, the water spinaches were more abundant in water than on land.

It was midnight. Mother was sitting by the oil lamp cleaning the fish. She heard a light splash of water by the doorway and then footsteps of someone walking up the stairs. Suddenly, a figure of a young woman appeared at the door. She was dressed in black, ragged clothes like an ordinary laborer. Mother knew the woman well.

"Leng! What were you doing here in the middle of the night?" Mother asked.

"Ming, don't tell anyone. They were planning to take me to execution. I'm planning an escape, but all the routes are flooded. I need to hide until the water retreats just a little. Your house is the only one that is not flooded. Please let me stay here until the opportunity comes," she begged.

"Come in. Hide behind the wall. The plants should keep you hidden. I don't have rice, but I will provide you with water spinaches. Stay as long as you need," Mother said without hesitation. Leng gave Mother more details of her situation after Mother offered to help.

Leng was the daughter of a man named Ta Lee and a mother named Chae Vooch. They were living just a few blocks away from our house. Leng was taken to trial for many different reasons and was planned for execution. For most people, there was nowhere to run, especially for those with small children. Fortunately for Leng, she was single. She would have a better chance to escape.

The next morning, Mother was rowing her boat past the meeting shack that stood just inches above water. The shack had been rebuilt and rose higher above the flood. The Nearadey leaders had been using the shack for a place to meet. The meetings were mostly about the labor plan and reviewing documents to take people to trial. Mother would normally row her boat close by the meeting shack, eavesdropping whenever she gots the opportunity so that she would know what they were up to. It was difficult to hear most of the time.

"Mit Yorn! Come here!" Ta Nuy's wife called her name.

Mother's nearly jumped out of her skin when she heard the call. Even after over one year, Mother still could not get used to working for Ta Nuy's wife, the woman behind most of the killings in Steung Chah. She hoped Ta Nuy's wife didn't know anything about her hiding Leng. If she had any slight suspicion, Mother was as good as dead. She rowed her boat closer. The boat was wobbling violently from side to side when Mother got closer to Ta Nuy's wife.

"I have an assignment for you. In a moment, I will be busy in an important meeting. I want you to spy on my husband. He has been telling me not to harm an unmarried girl named Khon, the daughter of Mit Yorn. I think he is having an affair with Mit Khon."

Mother thought this was a joke. It was the most ridiculous task she'd ever heard. However, she needed to make Ta Nuy's wife happy. Mother knew exactly who she was talking about. Khon was well known in the village as a young and beautiful girl. Her mother's name was Yorn just like hers. She had very light skin and was healthy. Mother thought her beauty kept her alive. The rumor was that Ta Nuy and few other Nearadey men had a crush on her. No one had attempted to take her trial for having light skin yet. None of the men had made any attempt to claim her as a wife yet because it was prohibited for a man to marry a single woman without official permission, including the Nearadey. It was rare nowadays for a couple to get married.

In the beginning of the Nearadey regime, there were several arranged marriages announced to the public. A few weeks after the all the couples got together, they all were taken to execution. No one knew the reason why.

"Do not use your boat. I don't want them to see you. I want you to swim. Use your boat only when you have to travel far," she added.

Ta Nuy was the youngest of all the executioners. He was about twenty-five years of age. He was handsome and tall. In Khmer, the word *Ta* means "elder" or "grandpa." It was unusual, but Nuy was called Ta because he was well known and fearsome. His wife would summon people to trial and he did the killings.

"I can swim, but I can't swim very far, especially chasing after a canoe. I need something to help me float. The best thing is sugar cane. I can use two if you have any," Mother said, not knowing where the words had come from. She couldn't believe she was asking Ta Nuy's wife for sugar cane. No one would dare ask her for anything.

Mother knew Ta Nuy's wife kept a lot of sugar cane in her house. Sugar was impossible to get, even harder to find than salt. Eating sugar cane was like eating pure sugar. It provided an instant burst of energy.

"Go to my house and get a pair of sugar canes. They're near the hearth," Ta Nuy's wife said.

Mother couldn't believe what she had just heard. She was so happy, but then she realized she was smiling involuntarily. She turned her head away trying to calm herself, "Then I must go," Mother said and started rowing the boat toward Ta Nuy's wife's house.

Her house was about a hundred yards away. Mother stopped the canoe in front of her house and secured it. She began walking up the stairs with a creepy feeling as if the house was haunted by the dead people that she and her husband had killed.

She found several dozen sugar cane stalks leaning against the wall. Mother walked up and carefully selected two larges stalks. Right before she was about to walk out, she noticed a small silver pot sitting near the hearth with a lid on. She turned her head away, fighting the temptation to open the pot. The pot was sitting on the hearth like a treasure bound by a tainted spell.

Just before she took another step to leave the house, her rational thought kicked in: "Eventually, my entire family will die anyway. I should do anything to live another day and to buy time to live a little longer."

We had not had any rice to eat for weeks. We had been eating fish that Mother caught during night time. Some nights, she saw too many snakes swimming and did not attempt to go near the water. Our lifeline was very thin, especially for Pech. He had been lying sick in bed for a few weeks now.

Mother opened the lid of the silver pot and found it nearly full of steamed rice. She noticed the scoop mark on the rice, indicating the rice had been eaten. It was safer for her to just take a little bit of rice without making it noticeable.

Mother grabbed a handful of rice and slipped it in her pocket. She had not seen steamed rice since Chhorn had brought some home last harvest season. She couldn't help herself and took another handful. Her hands and body shook violently with fear and joy.

She placed the lid back on the pot and scraped the rice off her hands and fingers with her mouth. She walked out of Ta Nuy's wife's house trying to hide her excitement and fear. Then she caught a glimpse of a canoe with several people sitting in the canoe in the distance. It was too far to see who they were. Mother was satisfied that she was able say that she saw something without having to lie. She rowed the boat straight back home.

She brought the rice home and gave us each some rice. Afterward, Mother was still in fear that Ta Nuy's wife would notice that she'd stolen her rice. Not only had she stolen rice, but she'd stolen it from the leader of the killers, a person who has the authority to take anyone for execution for any reason.

On the next day, just a little before noon, Mother came across Ta Nuy's wife again at the meeting shack. Mother explained what she saw and informed her that she didn't see any women on the boat. Ta Nuy's wife did not mention any suspicion of stolen rice. It was the moment of truth for Mother. If she got away now, her life was safe for the time being.

"I have another assignment for you. I don't feel like rowing the canoe to my house. Our comrades and I are hungry for fish. Go to my house and bring me several fish. My comrades and I will cook the fish here."

"Then I will go now," Mother said happily, hoping for more opportunities.

Mother glanced at the motion behind Ta Nuy's wife and saw K'Ouen and several other women busy chatting. They spent most of the time meeting. Mother could not think of anything else they would talk about except putting people to work and taking people to trial and execution.

Mother went to Ta Nuy's house and found a large basket full of freshly caught fish. Ta Nuy must have brought it home last night. Mother selected several fish. She wasn't sure how many fish she was supposed to get, but she made sure it exceeded the number of people in the meeting house. Then she picked one for herself. There were so many fish, and she doesn't think Ta Nuy or his wife would bother counting them. When Mother got back to her boat, she slipped one fish to the bottom of the basket full of water spinaches and delivered the rest of the fish to Ta Nuy's wife.

"Hey, Mit Yorn!" K'Oeun hollered when she saw Mother.

Mother tried to keep her distant from K'Oeun since she was one of the leaders. Because she lived so close to us, it was inevitable that Mother came face to face with her many times. At the same time, K'Oeun was the reason she had gotten away from many troubles.

Ta Nuy's wife continued to ask Mother to spy on Ta Nuy. Sometimes, Mother had to swim from one house to another, risking her life with the snakes. Sometimes, she encountered the buffalo leeches. Even though leeches were much less harmful than snakes, she feared leeches as much as the snakes. It was a phobia she wanted to get rid of but could not.

A few weeks later, the flood retreated slowly as the rainy season was coming to an end. Most of the higher ground was drying out. People were able to go back to work again. Leng had snuck out about four days after she arrived. Mother had been feeding her water spinaches while she was hiding behind the wall.

Father returned from Tuel Snai with his comrades by ox wagon and took me with him. He knew there would be nothing for me to eat here, and taking me with him would take a load off Mother's back.

Since most of the rice had been destroyed and rice planting season was over, the government had other plans for the workers. "We are behind with our tasks because of the flood. We must maximize our strength and effort to produce and make up for lost time. Since nearly all the rice was destroyed by the flood and it's too late to start all over again, we must produce other plants to sustain our country. Our village has been assigned to produce sugar cane." The phrase had been repeated over and over again every day by every leader in the village. The higher officials ordered everyone to dig ditches at least a knee deep to plant sugar cane.

Mother was no longer needed to cook since there was nothing to cook. This was one of the biggest blows to the workers. Everyone was hoping to get a small scoop of rice to survive. The lifeline for most people had been diminished. Mother has been assigned to work in the field like everyone else. Ta Nuy no longer needed her to spy on her husband or to send messages from town to town.

At first, everyone did their work and started to dig ditches as requested. The rule changed just one week after the new job had started. Everyone was required to dig thirty-five ditches a day, and each one had to be large enough to fit a person lying down. Rumor had it that the ditch was not for sugar cane but for dead bodies. Mother thought this wasn't work but rather just another way of killing people. They wanted to kill people without having to use their strength. Mother continued to gather her strength and dig thirty-five ditches a day. With no food and excessive labor, many people that she worked with simply collapsed and died in front of her. The higher Mit Chah simply stood watching like nothing had happened. Mother could not understand how she still survived. She ate once a day, mostly the plantain stalks that she still didn't believe were really considered as food. As she was digging the dirt, she tried to think of a way to get some food home for Poe, Pech, and Chhom. She was happy that I was away with Father. It was one less child to feed. Fortunately, the guards were monitoring the laborers but willing to offer palm juice to anyone that was thirsty. It was the only source of energy for Mother to continue digging ditches.

Ta Nuy's wife continued to give speeches about getting rid of the unwanted people to reduce the living space and to get rid of the lazy people. Somehow, Mother could sense that K'Ouen and Ta Nuy's wife were no longer wanted to mingle with Mother. They treated Mother like everyone else. It was the end of us if that was really the case. Mother would lose the opportunity to steal rice. She thought this was the brink of her and our family's death.

A week later, they increased the number of ditches from thirty-five to forty-five. Mother cried when she heard the news. Mother knew that they wanted to kill her along with everyone else. She fought her fear and frustration and continued looking for ways to bring food home.

"Mit Bong, I'm thirsty and I need more energy to dig more ditches. Could I have some palm juice?" Mother said to a woman who was standing and guarding the workers.

The women came over and handed her a bamboo cylinder. Mother took the bamboo cylinder and drank in front of the woman. On her last drink, she saved the palm juice in her mouth without swallowing. She continued to work with the palm juice still in her mouth. When the woman was not looking, she spit the palm juice into a small pouch that she'd made the night before and placed it in her under shirt. She had patched a small pouch using plastics and wrapped it around with a cloth. The palm juice was abundant, but no one was allowed to pick them. Only Mit Chah were allowed to climb and pick the palm juice. The palm trees were the only things that had flourished during the flood.

Palm sugars were also given during work. Mother asked for sugar to eat while working. When the Mit Chah was not looking, she slipped the sugar in a small pouch between her undershirts.

When she came home, she poured the juice and gave the juice to Chhom, Pech, and Poe. She never told Chhom or Pech how she got the palm juice, afraid they might be disgusted. She gave most of the sugar to Poe, as he was too young to eat anything else.

CHAPTER 24

I'm back in Tuel Snai with Father. I liked it much better here. I got to eat one whole fish by myself almost every meal. I didn't care if I didn't get to eat rice. The fish were delicious. I was standing by the cottage staring at the herd of the water buffalo that we were responsible to care for. Father and his friends were cutting and burning wood to make charcoal on the other side of the cottage.

I thought it was a mirage when I saw someone approaching us from a distance. Besides Father and his comrades, I hadn't seen anyone passing by this way. I squinted to see if it was one of Father's comrades, but the person had long hair and was too small to be any of the men.

After a moment, I leaped happily when I learned that it was Chhorn. I would never have imagined seeing her here. She had been away from home for many months. The last time I saw her was in the dry season when she brought us steamed rice. I remembered the incident when Pech dropped a grain of steamed rice under the house and was able to find it. I ran toward her, excited to show her where I was staying. Chhorn smiled when she saw me.

"Where is Father?" she asked.

"Over there," I said pointing to back of the cottage.

"Take me there. I need to speak to him," she said.

I skipped happily to the back of the cottage. Father and his men were busy working and unaware of my presence.

"Father, Chhorn is here," I said pointing to Chhorn.

Father turned around and frowned. "Chhorn, what are you doing here?"

"Mother told me to come and tell you to come home. We have been ordered to move soon," Chhorn said.

Father did not question her. He already knew why. The Vietnamese were approaching. Every village had been informed to move north, away from the Vietnamese. It was mandatory. Half of his men had already left to their hometowns days ago. Father had been waiting for Stung Chah to make their decision. Now it was time. Father had already prepared a small wagon and a pair of oxen. We began to ride home just minutes after Chhorn arrived.

"I'm glad I don't have to walk back home. My foot is swelling again," Chhorn said.

"What's wrong with your foot?" Father asked.

"I've had an infection almost two years now, and it doesn't go away. When I walk very long, it gets swollen," Chhorn replied.

Father didn't say anything else. He knew there was nothing he could do. He knew nothing about healing the infections.

Along the way home, we saw other men in their wagons traveling home just like us. Besides that, the road was quiet. We rode the ox wagon along the river. Chhorn was observing the path as if she was trying to remember something. We arrived home just before nightfall. Mother could not help but smile when she saw us.

"Bun got some meat back. When he was living here, he was nothing but skin and bones," Mother said.

"I just want to kick him during every meal. I had to urge him every second to eat faster. I have never seen anyone eat as slow as him," Father said staring at me.

Father parked the wagon in front of our house and tethered the oxen. He grabbed his backpack and a bucket from the wagon and entered the house.

"Many people have passed away for the past months from starvation. There is nothing to eat at all. We haven't had a single grain of rice for the last several weeks. On top of that, they made us dig ditches to death so they don't have to waste their energy on killing anyone. I'm among the few left. They told us to stop working for now and prepare to move. If I were to work a few more days, I would be dead as well. They told everyone to go to Phnom Ta Kream. They have already taken some families along. Tien's mom and her family were ready and volunteered to move first. She made the right choice. She was afraid she would get stuck here and worked to death," Mother explained. She continued to add more details about the information that she'd learned from friends and neighbors.

"Mother, I'm going back to Tuel Snai tonight. On my way there this morning, I found a hidden rice plant on a small hill surrounded by trees," Chhorn said.

"Go ahead, but be careful with snakes," Mother said.

Chhorn left for Tuel Snai to pick the rice that she'd discovered and returned sometime in the middle of the night with about half a can of rice grains. Mother grinded the rice immediately after she returned to remove all the husks. It took her nearly an hour to finish.

I woke up in the morning from the heat of the fire and the murmuring between Mother and Father. They had been having a conversation all night. Chhorn was awake as well. She was holding Poe, listening to the conversation. I saw a small pot sitting on top of the hearth. I got up and walked to the hearth and stared at the pot. I saw a handful of rice beneath the simmering water. I stooped lower with delight looking at the rice grains. I could smell the grainy aroma that I longed for every day.

"Move away from the rice pot. It might spill and burn you," Mother warned.

I took a few steps back and then sat and wait. Pech and Chhom were awake as well. Pech came and sat next to me waiting for the rice to be cooked. He heard Mother's warning and kept his distance from the hearth. As grouchy as he was, Pech always heeded Mother's warnings.

A moment later, Mother walked over and poured all the rice in a large bowl. She placed the bowl in the middle of the room and said. "Do not go near the bowl. I will let it cool down, and then we can eat together."

Pech and I leaped up and laughed with joy. We sat near the bowl waiting for it to cool down. I was so happy that we got to eat rice again.

"That's my rice," Pech said.

"No, it's mine," I said.

"It's mine," he insisted.

"No, it's mine," I argued.

"It's for all of us. We all get to eat it," Chhorn said proudly. She had walked in the night all the way back to Tuel Snai and picked the rice in the dark. All that work to feed her little brothers and sister.

I was so happy to eat rice gain. I leaped back and ran in a circle around the rice bowl. "Nah nah nah nah. I get to eat the rice. I get to eat the rice," I sang and dance.

Then, all of a sudden, I lost my balance and stomped on the bowl. The bowl flipped over, and the rice porridge splattered on my feet and on the ground. I screeched in pain from the hot rice porridge.

"Gone! The rice porridge is gone!" Chhorn screamed.

"What happened? Why is all the rice porridge spilled?" Mother asked furiously.

"Bun was dancing around the bowl, and he stepped on it. I'm going to smack you," Chhorn said to me and leaped up ready to hit me.

I ran to Mother for help. "Forget about hitting him. It will not bring back the rice porridge no matter how hard you hit him," Mother said calmly. Then she turned to me. "You deserve to eat nothing!" she scolded.

Father, Chhom, and Pech just sat and stared in disbelief. They were all looking forward to having a few slurps of rice porridge. Now it was gone right before their eyes.

"You deserve a slap in the face," Chhorn continued to scold.

I didn't cry. I stood and stared at the empty bowl feeling so guilty.

Chhom and Chhorn got up and began looking for food around the house. There were plenty of water spinaches growing by the river after the flood retreated. They didn't come across anyone all day while picking the vegetables. Most of the families had volunteered to move first.

We ate the boiled water spinach for lunch and dinner for the day. There was nothing else to eat them with. Mother snuck out at night and harvested some potatoes and plantain stalks. It was risky, but she'd taken that chance many times before. This was a good opportunity since the Nearadeys were in the middle of chaos. Mother thought they would not have the time and energy to investigate her farm. She cooked the potatoes with the plantain stalks and then she woke us up in the middle of the night to eat.

Four days later, Mother was struck by illness and barely able to walk. She struggled to go to the meeting and returned, looking very upset. "They told everyone to get ready to move the morning after tomorrow," she said out loud to Father. "What about my daughter,

Chhoy, and my son, Chhoeun? How are they going to find us? They are not allowing anyone to go anywhere without permission. They fear we might escape. I'm staying here. I'm not going anywhere without them."

"They will kill us all if we stay. I don't know about Chhoy, but Chhoeun should be able to survive on his own. Besides, we don't even know where she is, and I'm hoping she's still alive," Father said.

"You could take our other children and go first. I will stay here waiting for Chhoy. I don't care if they kill me. Chhoy is so young. She's can't be left alone," Mother said and began to weep.

"I will try to get her back." Chhorn said.

"Do you know the place?" Mother asked.

"I know the place. She's at Srah Kaev. I have been there before,"

"But everyone is prohibited from going anywhere without permission. They will kill you if you get caught. How about your infection? You can barely walk," Mother said.

"I will sneak out early in the morning. Besides, I'm young. They would not take me seriously. My infection is fine; I've gotten used to the pain," Chhorn said.

"Then go get your little sister back," Mother said with slight relief.

The next morning, Chhorn woke up and left home before sunrise. She limped with the morning pain from the infection, hoping not to bump in to anyone. She was taking extra caution by keeping herself low. She was not using the road. Instead, she decided to travel across the rice paddies. When she reached the open field, she stopped and crouched, scanning the area as far as the darkness allowed her to see. When she felt it was safe, she began walking swiftly, keeping her head low.

The morning sun was gradually rising. She crouch-walked, keeping herself low and alert. When the daylight finally swept in, the surroundings became visible and clear. Chhorn saw hordes of workers from the distance. They were probably salvaging the rice stems that had survived the flood. Normally, the workers would blanket the entire field by now. But many villages must have moved or were getting ready to move.

Chhorn trotted along the ridge of rice paddies, trying not to look suspicious but using extra caution until noon where the sun hovered high above her head, giving off steamy heat. She followed her instinct to walk normally looking like a young girl wandering around searching for food. If she was suspected of trying to flee south, her life was over.

She arrived at the canal in Srah Kaev before the sunset. Her entire body was caked with mud. The pain had spread through her entire infected foot. She limped slowly and stealthily across the dam toward the compound. When she got closer, she saw girls around her age roaming the area, picking vegetables. Some were congregating by the water using a net to catch fish. She squinted for a few seconds and caught a glimpse of Chhoy, sitting and watching her friends catching fish. Chhorn walked swiftly over, ignoring the pain.

"Chhoy!" Chhorn hollered from a distance.

"Where did you come from?" Chhoy asked.

"I come here to get you home. Our family has been asked to move to another location, but Mother isn't going anywhere until you are there," Chhorn explained.

"I can't walk. I stepped on a thorn about two months ago, and it's infected. The infection made a hole through my foot," Chhoy said showing her infected foot.

Chhorn stared at her foot and saw a lifeless, swollen foot with crusts of blood and puss mounting on top. She felt so bad for Chhoy. The pain must be much worse than hers.

All of a sudden, all her friends came and roamed around Chhorn.

"Mit Chhorn, when did you get here?" Ah Nee the Muslim asked.

"I just got here to take Chhoy back home. Everyone in the village has been told to get ready to move. That applies to all your families too," Chhorn said.

"Ah Nee asked for permission several times already, but the Mekong denied every time," Chhoy said with despair.

"I could ask again if you want," Ah Nee said.

"That's all right. I will ask myself because I'm her older sister," Chhorn said.

"All right, you ask then," Ah Nee said.

Ah Nee led Chhorn to the Mekong, where she was eating steamed rice just outside the cottage. Chhorn and Ah Nee couldn't help but stare at the rice. The Mekong had a full bowl to herself.

Chhorn walked closer to the Mekong with her eyes still on the rice bowl. "Mit Bong, I'm requesting my sister to come home."

"What's the reason?" the Mekong asked without looking at them in the face.

"Because her foot hurts."

"If her foot hurts, then she can't walk. If she can't walk, she can't go home. Then she must not go home," the Mekong said with her face still looking down at the rice bowl as if she was talking to herself.

Chhorn came back to Chhoy and gave her the bad news. "She said exactly the same thing the last time I asked her," Chhoy said.

"Then I must sneak you out," Chhorn said quietly.

"We might get in trouble if we sneak out like that," Chhoy said.

"Don't worry. Our country is in chaos right now. People were being forced to move everywhere. Nobody is keeping track of you anymore. If we can escape this place, we are free from here," Chhorn explained.

"I will help you escape," Ah Nee said.

"Me too. I will check the area to make sure it is clear. I will give you a signal," Ah Nee the Muslim said.

"I will help you as well. I will carry all your belongings. I will put all your stuff inside a basket and pretend I'm going to pick vegetables like I normally do," Ah Vee said.

"Since I cannot be seen walking with her, I will wait on the other side of the dam. I will pretend to walk back home by myself. Once you cross the dam, I can carry her home, and it would be too dark for them to find us," Chhorn explained.

Chhorn left, making it very obvious that she was leaving alone. The two Ah Nees and Ah Vee were standing by the cottage pretending to pick vegetables. They were keeping their eyes on the Mekong who was standing beside the cottage monitoring the dam. The three were waiting for the Mekong to leave.

They waited for a long time, and the woman didn't seems like she was planning to go anywhere soon. If they stood in one place for too long, they might look suspicious. Just when they were about to leave, the woman said out loud.

"I will go to potty. I will be back,"

"I'm hoping she has to go to poop and instead of pee." Ah Vee said.

Both of Ah Nees trailed slowly after the woman as she was walking down to the dry part of the canal. Then she sat down and begins her business.

"She's doing number two," they both said happily at the same time like they were special twins.

"I will go first. I will give you signal if she looking our way," Ah Vee said holding a basket full of Chhoy's belongings.

Both Ah Nees tugged under Chhoy's arms and begin walking. Chhoy could only move one foot. Her infected foot was dragging on the ground motionlessly. She hopped along with both of Ah Nees on each arm crossing the dam. They could see the Mekong squatting below the dam facing nearly parallel to the dam but slightly away to the other side. If she would shift her head slightly to the dam, she would see them. Chhoy was hopping and looking down from above praying the woman would not turn her head.

Every second seemed like forever as Chhoy continued to hop on one foot crossing the dam. She attempted to use her injured foot once in a while to help speed up, but the pain shot through her and she nearly burst out screaming. The ground was still scorching hot from the day-time heat. No one was wearing any shoes.

"Keep going. She's not looking," the Muslim Ah Nee said.

"I wish I was strong enough to just pick you up and run," the other Ah Nee said.

After a long, agonizing moment, they reached the other end of the dam. Both of Ah Nees were exhausted. They both let go of Chhoy at the same time, and Chhoy collapsed to the ground.

"My other foot is in pain. I think I have blisters on my other foot," Chhoy said.

Both Ah Nees stooped down catching their breath. They were both skinny like Chhoy. They had used up every bit of strength. Chhorn emerged from behind the bush and hollered, "You guys made it. No one saw you?"

"Mit Bong was pooping. If she saw us, she wouldn't be able to do anything anyway," Ah Nee said with a light laugh as she tried to catch her breath.

"Here is all your stuff," Ah Vee said.

"You guys should return before they find out that Mit Chhoy is missing," Chhorn said.

"True. We must go back now. I will try to sneak out probably tomorrow night," Ah Nee said and started to walk back to the cottage.

"Can you walk a little?" Chhorn asked.

"No. I cannot walk at all. Now my other foot was in pain," Chhoy said.

"Then I will carry you,"

"I don't think you can carry me. I'm too heavy for you,"

"I don't care how heavy you are; I will carry you."

Chhorn crouched down with her back turned and pulled Chhoy body against her back. She stood up and bounced a few times to adjust the position. Chhoy was surprise that Chhorn could lift her off the ground. Chhorn started walking with Chhoy on her back.

"Your foot still hurt?" Chhoy asked.

"Yeah, the wound has not healed yet. I'm hurt, but not as bad," Chhorn lied.

"I can try to walk with one foot."

"Let me carry you a little further. When I can't go any further, I will let you try to walk," Bong Chhorn said and continued to limp with Chhoy on her back.

The night had become pitch dark. Chhorn could only see several feet away. She was walking on the ridge of the rice paddies keeping her direction straight. If she changed direction, she would get lost. It was a full day of walking with just her alone to get here. With Chhoy on her back, it would take all night and possibly all morning to reach home.

After passing a dozen of rice paddies, Chhorn stopped and slid Chhoy off her back. She was breathing very hard from exhaustion.

"It's so dark. I'm scared," Chhoy said.

"There is nothing to be afraid of," Chhorn said, trying to comfort Chhoy and herself.

"Let me try to walk," Chhoy said.

"All right," Chhorn said, still breathing very hard.

"We must keep going. That woman might come after us," Chhorn said.

Chhorn lifted Chhoy's left arm and tugged her shoulder underneath her arm. Chhoy hopped with her uninjured foot and tried very hard to use her injured foot to balance. Pain shot through her body with every step she took. After about a dozen strides, Chhoy picked up a rhythm and techniques that made her walk faster and with less pain.

When Chhorn gained her strength back, she carried Chhoy on her back again and carried her until she could not take another step. Then Chhoy limped with one foot again with Chhorn assisting her on one side.

They switched back and forth. Sometimes, they came across a flooded area as deep as their neck. Chhorn carried Chhoy's backpack over her head. They both were walking slowly tilting their heads up. Chhorn didn't remember crossing this water on her way here, but she might be a little bit off her daytime route. They were glad when they reached dry land again, but the water helped cool them down a little. The coolness seemed to offer energy to Chhorn. She didn't mind being soaking wet. The water also helped clean all the mud off her clothes and body. She had Chhoy on her back again and continued to walk. The wolves were howling from somewhere in the distance. They were far, but it was uncertain how far they are. Wolves were known to have an acute sense of smell and could run very fast.

"Chhorn, I'm scared of the wolves. Are we almost home?"

"I don't know. It's too dark. I don't even know where we are," Chhorn admitted.

It was now Chhoy's turn to walk as Chhorn was too tired to carry her. They continued to walk and walk in the pitch dark until both were unable to take another step.

"Let's take a break. I can't walk anymore," Chhorn said.

Chhoy didn't reply but simply dropped to the ground. They rested for a moment. The sky seemed to get brighter from the east. They looked around as they rested. They could see a dark figure of a coconut tree standing several dozen feet away.

"It's morning. We need to get moving. It's not safe in the daytime. People might question us and cause us trouble," Chhorn said.

Without a word, Chhoy stood up painfully. Chhorn assisted her, and they continued to walk. Shortly after, they saw a group of women gathering in the field a head, preparing to work. It was risky to be seen by people, but they were lost.

"We are going to walk toward the women and as ask if they know where our town is. I don't know where we are. If we continue to walk, we might get lost further," Chhorn said.

They walked nervously toward the women.

"Um, do you know where Watt Samdach is?" Chhorn asked using the Khmer traditional title.

"Where are you from? Are you fleeing from your horde?" the woman asked.

"No. I'm visiting my Mother, and it's too dark and I'm lost," Chhorn said.

"Really? Then keep going that way. There is a wagon road along the river up north. Follow the road up that way," the woman said motioning her arm.

They followed the direction as the woman instructed and came across a wagon road about half an hour later. They walked along the open and bare wagon road. Then the thick brush and trees began to form along the side as they slowly proceeded. They knew it was a sign of the river ahead.

The morning light was shining brighter. The road was leading up north as expected. Even though they didn't know exactly where they were, they felt a little relief to have an idea where they were heading.

They limped along the road until the sun was fully rising. Moments later, the squeaking sound of a wagon and the hoof steps of the oxen were approaching. Shortly after, an ox wagon slowly emerged from behind. Chhorn turned around observing the riders, hoping to see the friendly faces.

When the wagon got closer, they saw the middle-age man and woman sitting on the driver's seat of the ox wagon. The man was holding the reigns. The woman was sitting beside him. There was no sign of children. They appeared to be normal civilians.

"Um, may I get a ride?" Chhorn asked using the previous Khmer traditional title.

The ox wagon stopped. "Come on up," the woman replied.

Chhorn didn't bother asking where they were heading. She knew that they were forced to move northwest just like us. The Vietnamese were invading from the southeast. Everyone was forced to move north.

Anyone found by the militants going in the opposite direction would be considered a fugitive and would certainly be killed.

Chhorn lifted Chhoy up onto the back of the ox wagon, and then she tugged herself up after her. There was not much behind the wagon except for a stack of hay and the cooking ware. There was no sign they had any rice with them either. Chhoy lay down, leaning her back against the side of the wagon. Chhorn sat on the back end of the ox wagon to get a better view of the road.

The ox wagon began to move. After Chhorn got settled, she looked around feeling very relieved that she didn't have to carry Chhoy. She felt a strong, throbbing pain from the infection. Her other leg was aching as well. She couldn't believe that she had walked and carried Chhoy all night with her infected foot. They both didn't get any sleep all night. She longed for sleep right now, but she was afraid she would miss the stop at home.

"Chhoy, are you sleepy? Can you stay awake? I can't keep my eyes open. Tell them when to stop," Chhorn said.

"I'm tired too, but I will try to stay awake. I can't sleep anyway. My foot is in pain."

Chhorn adjusted her position and fell asleep instantly with her back leaning against the side of the wagon. Chhoy was sitting upright, extending her legs. She looks at her injured foot and could see the puss was building up from the top of the foot. She felt a surge of relief that she didn't have to walk any further.

Her thoughts drifted back to the night before, and she was amazed by Chhorn's extraordinary willpower and determination to carry her that long way. During their life in Takeo and until Bakaeng, Chhorn was responsible for everything that Mother or Chhoeun had asked them to do. If the job didn't get done, Mother or Chhoeun would chastised Chhorn.

Chhoy was sitting, half asleep. She noticed a couple more ox wagons were catching up from behind. After a long moment, Chhoy looked around and recognized the area. It was the same road she had walk from home to Bung Tum with the hordes. She remembered the flood that submerged the entire town. The water had retreated leaving behind the damage. The tall grasses were dead. The new ones were sprouting. The tree branches were broken and twisted off the trunk. Large trees were wrapped around by other branches from other trees. Dead logs were scattered, crisscrossing one another everywhere.

Chhoy saw pots and pan lying along the road. Someone had travelled this way and decided to drop them after a long walk. Moments later, Chhoy saw a group of families traveling on foot holding pots and pan. Everyone was carrying something. They must have brought more they could handle and decided to discard some. A boy about fifteen years of age was holding a cage with a live chicken inside. He must be fortunate. The chicken was a living treasure, Chhoy thought.

The families moved to the side allowing the wagon to pass by. Some men were carrying their children on their backs. Some carried them on their shoulders. One woman had a baby curled in a scarf, hanging on one shoulder. She was also carrying a basket on her head.

The wagon drove past the families and continued to stroll along the road. Chhoy saw more families along the road. Most families were small. Many were walking nearly empty-handed.

"Chhorn! Wake up!" Chhoy said.

"Where are we?" Chhorn asked.

"We were home. See the bridge?" Chhoy said pointing to the Watt Samdach Bridge.

"Um, stop right here," Chhorn said.

The man stopped the wagon on the intersection. Chhorn hopped off the wagon and flinched from the pain on her foot. Then she assisted Chhoy who could only move one foot.

"Is your foot any better?" Chhorn asked.

"I'm feeling better, but my foot still hurts."

"Can you walk?" Chhorn asked.

"I think I can walk a little." She felt so bad for Chhorn and didn't want her to carry her anymore.

It was now midmorning. The sun was blocked by the surrounding trees. The day was beginning to get hotter. The wagon resumed its stroll while Chhorn and Chhoy stretched their arms and legs from the long ride. Chhoy looked around the area, felling very relieved to be home again. She limped toward the house wishing somehow she could shrink the distance and be in the house instantly. The pain in her foot was unbearable.

Chhoy looked up to house and noticed an ox wagon in front of our house, but there was only one ox. The neighbors were crowding in front of their house getting ready. Some of them were beginning to walk. Chhorn entered the house and crawled to an open spot and lay down. She was too tired to talk to anybody.

"Father! Chhorn is here!" Chhom shouted.

Father emerged from the back door holding a bucket full of water. "You arrived. Did you find Chhoy?"

"She's outside. She needs help walking. I can't take another step," Chhorn said.

Father walked out the door and saw Chhoy was inching forward with agony. He ran quickly toward Chhoy and picked her up.

"What happened to you?" Father asked.

"My foot hurts. It's infected," Chhoy said nearly crying.

"You came right on time. They want us to leave now, and we were getting ready. I was worried that you two were not going to make it back," Father said and carried her to the wagon.

He laid Chhoy next to Mother, Poe, and Pech. All three of them were sick. I wasn't feeling too well myself, but I was able to walk. Normally, I would be very excited to see Chhoy, but today I was too overwhelmed by the chaos. I sat in the corner of the ox wagon and stared at Chhoy who was lying down with her eyes closed. She curled her legs and holds her injured foot with her hands. I could tell she was in pain.

Father carried Chhorn over and laid her in an open spot beside me. Chhorn appeared in pain as well, but she was awake and able to move her body around. She picked up Poe who was lying by Mother, crying softly. She held Poe in her arms while Mother was lying unconscious on the wagon floor.

Father placed a bucket of water in the corner of the wagon opposite from me. It was the only open spot left. The wagon was very small. It was designed to carry no more than four people.

"Let's get moving," Father said.

Chhom came over and tossed Chhoy's backpack near the water bucket. "I'm ready," she said.

"Walk beside me," Father said and positioned himself under the hauling traces beside an ox. He tapped the ox on the shoulder, and it began to move.

Father had brought a pair of oxen from Tuel Snai, but one of them got very ill and was unable to move. He informed the Mit Chah, and they were very happy to take it away. Now he had no choice but to haul the wagon with a single ox.

CHAPTER 25

"Hurry up! Everyone is waiting!" the militant came by our house and hollered.

We were the only ones around that owned an ox wagon. All other families were walking on foot. Everyone except us was congregating by the river waiting for the line to move. Father began to haul the wagon with an ox. He was using a lot of effort to move the wagon. He slapped the ox on the ribs. "Move!"

When Chhom saw Father struggling, she walked behind the wagon and pushed it. After several paces, the wagon began to move. Once we got to the road by the river, we could see hundreds more families waiting for the line for further instruction.

"Let's begin!" A voice came from the militant group further ahead.

The line began to move slowly. Father merged in the line just in front of Phate's mom. No one was looking forward to moving. The entire village had been told that we were heading north to a place called Phnum Takream. Even thought we were leaving a place where many lives had been lost, we didn't know what the new place would be like. We would be living under the same group of killers. No one wanted to make any comments or ask any questions.

Up ahead, the militants was leading the line. Each one has a rifle strapped behind their back. Some had machetes hung loosely from their waist. The shiny white blade glistened from the reflection of the morning light.

"Remember! Anybody that resists the order is considered enemy!" a militant man walked by swiftly from behind and hollered.

He repeated the phrase over and over again until he reached another group. Chhom was walking beside the wagon. The families in front of us were moving fast. Father grunted as he applied more force to haul the wagon. Chhom immediately ran to the back of the wagon and began pushing again.

Our wagon was moving along the riverside among the crowd, taking us far away from our home. The areas were all unfamiliar to me. I had never walked this far from home before, especially in this direction. Father and the ox were tugging the wagon, struggling to keep up with the horde. I was sitting with my neck stretched over the side of the wagon.

The road suddenly merged into a broader road. We were joining another horde led by the militia just like us. There were at least two hundred people marching with us now, trailed by a group that were walking and keeping a close watch.

"Chhorn, I don't think I'm going to make it alive," Mother said softly. She had been unconscious since we left, but she seemed half awake now. He eyes were still closed. She was so skinny and frail. "Take care of your brother and sisters. You are the oldest. I don't know if Chhoeun is still alive, but now I consider you as the oldest," Mother continued.

"Yes," Chhorn said. She didn't know what to say. She was having a hard time staying awake herself. She'd nearly dropped Poe a couple times.

There was also another long line on the other side of the road. The men and women all appeared weary and scared as they observed our line. I didn't see any toddlers. All the children were around my age and older. They were walking at a fast pace keeping up with the adults. I saw many eyes staring at our wagon. I was one of the few that were riding in a wagon. There were a few more wagons ahead of us and several more behind us. Not too far behind us, I could see a man was hauling the wagon with his ox just like Father, but I couldn't see who or what was inside the wagon. Father drank water continuously as he hauled the wagon. Chhom made sure he got water right away when he requested it.

The sun slowly retreated behind the thick forest. The evening light slowly faded. The line in front of us halted, and then our wagon stopped. Father moved the wagon under a large tree.

"We are staying here for the night," Father said and began to unstrap the ox. After he finished, he filled a bowl with water and fed the ox. When the ox finished drinking the water, he tethered the ox by the tree allowing it to graze. This was our first stop since we'd left Stung Chah.

"Stay here and build a fire. I'm going to find some water," Father said to Chhom and took the bucket with him.

Chhom collected twigs and made a pile. She borrowed a piece of burned wood from the nearby adults to start the fire. The night became dark very quickly. Father emerged from the darkness with a bucket full of water and a handful of large tree branches to set up the mosquito net. It took him just minutes to erect the tree branches and setup one mosquito net on the ox wagon and one beside the wagon.

Chhom and Father were sleeping inside the mosquito net beside the wagon. The rest of us were sleeping in the wagon. The air was calm and cool. The night was quiet, save for the soft pops from the fire. The militants were a distance away from the civilians, sitting around the fire cooking their food. About half of them were women. I dozed almost immediately.

"Get up! Get up! We have to move!" someone hollered from the distance.

I opened my eyes and saw Father and Chhom were already awake and ready. The morning was bright and clear. The mosquito net had already been removed. The ox had been strapped under the hauling traces. I was very hungry as usual. We hadn't eaten since the night before we left Stung Chah.

Father began to haul the wagon with the ox. Chhom was pushing the wagon from behind. Chhorn was also awake and cradling Poe in the wagon. Pech was lying next to Mother crying softly with his eyes closed. Chhoy was curling in the corner with both of her hands cupping her infected foot. The hundreds of families were walking miserably behind us.

After a long moment, gunshots popped multiple times followed by loud screams. A wave of fear stirred the horde. Father paused for a few seconds and continued with the flow. Moments later, words rippled from somewhere up ahead. "Do not turn your face to the east. They killed four people earlier. They think we are expecting the Vietnamese to rescue us," someone said.

Father could not talk to anyone as he was hauling the wagon, but he was well aware of the situation. We were walking past mostly empty houses and farms along the road. Some residents were congregating in groups preparing to move.

The sun was rising slowly behind the forest, and then it gradually inched its way to the center of the sky, giving off the midday heat. Chhoy was moaning from the pain. Mother was deliriously speaking in her sleep. All of a sudden, we all crashed down to one side of the wagon as if the entire wagon was falling apart. We all screamed in pain and fear. Then we all realized that the front part of the wagon had collapsed. The ox was sprawled flat on the ground. Father was on his knee with the ox. He was as confused as any of us. Mother and Chhoy opened their eyes from the hard roll. Father took off the hauling trace and examined the ox. He slapped the ox on its side and shout, "Get up! Get up!"

The ox was lying still and didn't budge. Father broke a small branch nearby and tripped out all the leaves. He whipped the ox on its hind thigh multiple times, but it still would not get up. Father crouched down behind the ox and begin pushing it from behind. The ox still refused to get up. Then he walked over to front of the ox and pulled it by the rein. The ox stretched its neck but would not move to get up. No matter what Father tried, the ox was not getting up. "This ox is no longer able to walk," he said out loud.

Father unstrapped the ox form the hauling trace and set it free. Father lifted the entire hauling trace and placed it on his shoulder. He took a big huff and began to tug using all his strength. The wagon began to inch forward.

"Bun, you should get off to make the wagon lighter," Chhom said.

I jumped off the wagon immediately. We were way behind the horde. We needed to catch up, or we would be in big trouble. There was nothing on the wagon that we could toss off to make it lighter. Beside the pots and pans, the wagon was empty. Father was working very hard keep up with the horde. The afternoon sun was beating down. Father was drenched in sweats in just minutes. Up ahead, the horde had stopped for a break. It was an opportunity for Father to catch up. Unfortunately, once we reached the horde, the line began to move again. Father did not get the chance to rest.

The walk didn't really bother me. We were traveling very slowly anyway. We had caught up with families ahead of us. Several kids were walking beside their parents. Most of them were holding something because they didn't have a wagon like us. I felt a surge of excitement walking with someone my age. We didn't talk to one another but simply smiled at each other and walked side by side. Just before I realized it, over half a dozen of children were walking with me. Some of them were siblings. Suddenly, I thought of Tien and Mao. They were nowhere to be seen. In fact, I hadn't seen them for weeks. They had left Stung Chah before us.

Far away in the distance, there appeared to be some sort of sharp hill rising from underneath the earth. It rose higher and higher as we get closer. Hours later, the small hill continued to rise and became a large mountain, standing tall, stretching its tail far to one side. The front end of the mountain was a giant red cliff cleared of trees or grasses. It was shaped like some sort of ancient structure.

"That's called Phnom Som Pouv (Mountain of Ship)," Father said. He was having a conversation with the adults that were trailing behind the rest of the horde. Everyone was staring at the beautiful mountain. "The tales is that the mountain was once a ship and got stranded…" Father continued with his story.

We got closer to the mountain and trotted along the path that skirted around the outer edge. As the daylight was fading, the horde stopped in an open area with plenty of trees. Father moved the wagon by an available tree and rested. He leaned his back against the wagon and caught his breath. Chhom brought him a bowl of water. I walked over and sat next to him. My feet were burning from the heat of the earth. There were small cuts here and there on the bottoms of my feet. This was the second day without a single grain of rice in our stomachs. I was very hungry and tired from walking all day.

Without being asked, Chhom walked around began searching for twigs to build a fire. Father got up a few minutes later and began walking around searching for food and water. He returned at nightfall without any food, but he'd gotten a bucket of water. He set up the mosquito nets for us very quickly, and we spent the night on the mountain side.

We woke up early in the morning and continued our walk. Like us, most of the hordes had been walking for at least two days and two nights without food. We marched the entire morning with two short rests along the main path that swirled around the mountain. We arrived in a town known as Phnom Ta Kream in late afternoon. The local laborers were busy working in groups throughout the open field. A man wearing clean black clothes with a red and white checkered scarf caped down his neck came forward and greeted the militia. Shortly after, he came over and ordered us to settle down in a spot under several trees.

We rushed along with the horde to the area and claimed a spot. One of the trees that we were staying under was different from others. Its enormous trunk was standing firmly on a small hill. Not only was it tall and stout, but each leaf was twice the size of our heads.

"This tree is called Daum Po," Father said as he lowered the wagon and then found himself a spot by the wagon to lean on. He sat and waited for further instruction. Daum Po was a well-known tree in Khmer that was associated with mystical stories of Buddha and the other gods and goddesses. The tree was also believed to be tainted if evil spirits resided there.

The same man returned a moment later and hollered, "The thick rice porridge is ready."

"Thick rice porridge?" a woman questioned herself softly.

"They are giving us rice porridge?" Chhorn sat up looking around.

Everyone in the group stayed frozen for a short moment from the shocking news and then scrambled for their plates and bowls. Chhorn hopped off the wagon with Poe still in her arms.

"Chhom! Get all of our bowls! Chhoy! Get up! They are offering thick rice porridge!" Chhorn shouted.

Chhom rummaged around and found the rice plates for all of us. She gave two to Chhorn, one to Father, one to me, and one to Chhoy. She picked up Pech and positioned him on her waist. Chhoy managed to slide off the wagon and stood on her feet. She limped a few paces with agony but seemed determined to walk.

We begin walking behind Father toward the crowd. A line had already formed behind a large pot sitting on the hearth. The steam was swirling off the pot vigorously. Chhorn and Chhom were picking up their pace. I trotted behind them in anticipation.

"Chhoy, we will get to the line first, and I will save a spot for you," Chhorn said as Chhoy limping slowly after.

When we got to the line, there were about a dozen of people in front of us. Chhorn was in front all of us. She handed Poe to Father so that she could hold two plates. I stood right behind Father waiting for my share. Somehow, Chhoy had caught up with us and squeezed in between Chhorn and Father. I could smell the heavenly aroma of the rice. The cook was distributing the rice, and the line was inching slowly forward.

When we got closer, I saw the thick rice porridge in a large pot like we were told. My whole body shook in anticipation. Everyone behind us was pushing in to get closer to the pot. There were two more people in front of us negotiating the amount of rice for their sick relatives. Chhorn and Chhoy moved in closer to the pot. Both of them couldn't help but to stick their hands in the pot to touch the precious rice porridge. A tall, fare-skinned woman whacked Chhorn on the head with the large scoop. Chhorn shrieked and leaped back and rubbed her head in pain. The woman raised the scoop to hit Chhoy, but she leaped back very quickly. "Wait until your turn!" the woman shouted.

After the woman finished pouring the rice porridge to the people in front of us, she stared at Chhorn and Chhoy and then scooped the rice porridge for them.

"Mit, my Mother is sick. She cannot walk here. Could she get a share? I will bring it to her," Chhorn said.

"You know the rule. Sick people will not get any share," the woman said.

Chhorn didn't argue but walked over to the dining hall right behind the woman and found an open spot among the crowd. The rest of us sat next to Chhorn after we'd gotten our share. Chhorn ate a few scoops of rice porridge and then looked around. When she was sure that no one was looking, she grabbed a handful of hot rice porridge and slipped it in her pocket. She continued to put more rice porridge her pocket then snuck out the dining hall. Fortunately, the rice porridge was thick enough to handle by hand.

She came back to the wagon where Mother was still lying motionlessly. It was just her and Mother around. Everyone was still in the dining hall. She double-checked to make sure that no one was watching.

"Mother, wake up. I brought rice for you. It's the thick porridge," Chhorn whispered.

Mother spoke with her eyes still shut, "Why would you want to waste the rice on me? I'm going to die anyway."

"Just try. It's not a waste. They gave me a bowlful. I had some already," Chhorn sort of lied. She'd really only a few spoonfuls. She used her hand to scoop the rice porridge from her pocket and fed Mother with her hand. With her eyes still closed, she opened her mouth and allowed Chhorn to feed her. Chhorn made sure that Mother ate every single grain of rice.

Just when Chhorn finished feeding her with the last drop of rice porridge, Mother sat up straight and turned her head around. "I feel much better! I have my strength back!" Mother said in disbelief.

"Can you walk?" Chhorn asked.

"Let me try," Mother said. She stood up. "There was nothing wrong with me. I just needed to eat," she said and smiled in disbelief.

"It's not too late to get your share of rice porridge. I will lead you to the place," Chhorn said.

"Then take me there," Mother said.

Chhorn led Mother to line up for the rice porridge at the dining hall. Fortunately, there was still some rice porridge left. Mother explained that she was sick and unable to make it on time. The woman gave Mother her share without saying a word.

Mother was walking with her bowl of rice porridge in her hands. She nearly dropped her bowl when she came face to face with Kroo Ouwk, the man who'd taught school in Takeo. Chhoeun, Chhoy, and Chhorn had all gone to his class. He was wearing nice, clean clothes. He buttoned his shirt up to the collar with a clean red and white checkered scarf hanging loosely down from this neck. He looked healthy and well. Only the important Mit Chah would have that kind of appearance. The man seemed surprised as well when he saw Mother. He looked Mother in the eyes for a few seconds and then turned away.

Mother came to sit down next to Father who had finished his rice porridge in less than a minute. He was still very hungry from travelling three days and two nights hauling the wagons. Father was a big man and normally ate a lot. He looked around and stared at our bowls. He extended he neck as if he wanted to reach the bowl with his mouth.

"Father, you can have the rest of my rice porridge," Chhoy said and poured the rice porridge into Father's bowl.

Father sat still and stared at Chhoy's face. He blinked a few times. He must have wanted to refuse taking the food away from his daughter, but he was overwhelmed by starvation and could not resist the rice porridge. He stooped his head down and began to eat.

We returned to our wagon after we finished eating. Everyone was resting from a long walk and a generous amount of rice porridge, except for Chhorn. She'd only had about two small spoonfuls of rice porridge. She'd given all her share to Mother and was still very hungry. While all of us ate the thick rice porridge, this was Chhorn's third day without food. None of us knew that. Mother and Father were chatting with the nearby adults, including the people that we knew from Stung Chah.

A middle-age woman came by and announced. "We need few healthy and young comrades to help us grind the rice. Who wants to volunteer?"

Chhorn leaped up and darted in front of the woman. "I volunteer!" she shouted, raising both of her hands.

A few other young women came forward to volunteer. Grinding rice was hard work. The rice offered normally would not be enough to replace energy used to grind the rice. The elders did not bother with the job offer. It was better to seek frogs and snails than to grind rice for couple spoons of rice porridge.

"Mit! I pick you, you, you, and you!" The woman pointed to Chhorn and three women. A couple of younger men came to volunteer, but none were selected. Grinding rice was normally a woman's job. It required skills and patience as well as strength. The women escorted all the volunteers to a segregated warehouse to grind the rice.

With skills and the eagerness to get a meal of rice porridge, Chhorn finished her task before nightfall. She had used up her last bit of strength. This was her opportunity to eat. She was told to grab a plate in the public storage shack a few dozen yards away since our wagon was too far. Chhorn walked over the storage shack as suggested and searched for the plates.

She entered the clustered storage shack and saw mostly farming tools and haystacks. Chhorn walked slowly and searched for a plate. She was tired and needed to eat quickly. She stretched her arms to relieve her aching joints. Her right arm knocked against something hard behind the hay stacks. The object caught her attention. Chhorn turned her head and found a silver handle sticking out slightly. She reached in and grabbed the handle and discovered a heavy pot with the lid shut. She opened the lid with her other hand and found the pot half full of freshly cooked steamed rice. Chhorn's heart nearly stopped from the excitement. Without hesitation, she dug her hand in the pot and scooped as much rice as possible and shoved it in her pocket. Then she grabbed another handful and shoved it in her other pocket. She walked hastily out of the storage shack hoping no one would see her exiting the shack.

The sun had set somewhere behind the mountain giving off the dim yellowish light. Chhorn arrived at our wagon where Father and Mother were sitting on the ground surrounded by the adults under the Daum Po tree, chatting. The rest of us were sleeping with our heads resting on exposed roots of the tree. She walked slowly trying not to get any attention and then sat between Father and Mother waiting for the right time to give them the steamed rice.

"I think I smell rice. It's so close. Maybe I'm too hungry," Mother said.

"There is no rice around here, Mother," Chhorn said with a big smile. Then she stuck her hand in her pocket and came up with a handful of rice. "Here, Mother. Be careful not to let anyone see."

Father caught a glimpse of the rice. He eyes were opened wide in shock.

"Father this is yours," Chhorn said and handed him a clump of rice. Then she walked over and woke us all up. She handed each of us a handful of rice.

"Don't say anything," she whispered.

I woke up and was shocked to see a clump of rice in front of my face.

"Is this a dream?" Chhoy said softly. "Everyone is eating rice. That isn't possible."

"Chhorn, why don't you eat some?" Mother said.

"I'm fine. They will give me my share. I'm going back to get my share."

"I think I smell rice! It is so close!" an old man sitting a few yards away with his family exclaimed.

"I don't smell any rice. All I smell is someone's poop," his wife replied.

Mother and Father looked at one another and smiled. There was also a foul smell lingering in the area.

Chhorn returned to the warehouse looking forward to getting her share of rice porridge. When she arrived, everyone was finished eating and had left. She asked the cook for her share, but all the rice porridge had been distributed. Chhorn began to panic. She needed something to eat, or she will die of starvation. Then she remembered that there was about a handful of rice left in the pot that she'd found in the sack. It was risky to return to the pot. She had stolen someone's rice. But she was too hungry to care what was going to happen to her. She returned to the storage shack anyway but found the pot empty; someone had taken the rest of the rice. She returned to wagon and slept with us, hoping she wouldn't die in her sleep from starvation.

When she woke up in the morning, she felt very hungry but happy that she was still alive. She did not tell Mother or Father that she had not eaten since the morning she went to rescue Chhoy from the youth compound. Besides the couple of spoons of rice porridge she'd eaten yesterday, it had been four days and four nights now since her last meal. She lay motionless in the wagon until we were all called to eat thick rice porridge at noontime.

We stayed under the tree for several days until we were told to move near a large hill. To me, it was a mountain. It was high and steep. Many adults had climbed the hill, and they looked as small as a grasshopper from below. We were warned not to leave the area without permission. Father built a small shack beside the hill for us to stay in.

Within a few weeks, Chhorn and Chhom were assigned to harvest the rice with about thirty to forty of other workers. The rice fields were scattered all around the village. Chhoy joined them a week later when the infection on her foot had eased. Eventually, Mother had managed to persuade the local village leaders for Chhom to stay home and take care of us and still get a share of rice porridge. Backed by Ta Watt and K'Ouen, who'd come along with the other Red Khmer leaders, the local village leaders agreed. Chhom took the opportunity to seek additional food. She blended in among other children seeking fish and crabs in the rice fields, the same place where the adults were working.

Just a few days later, the sounds of artillery shelling began somewhere in the distance. Chhoy and Chhorn were working when they overheard a conversation. "Did you know the Vietnamese are approaching? My brother sneaked in from the other side and told me all about it. Whenever I'm ready, I will try to escape," one of the women working nearby said to another woman. "Or I could wait until they get here. They are almost here. Once they get here, we will be free."

"I have heard the battle from the distance for a long time, but who knows how long it will take them to get here. We will all be dead before they get here," another replied.

"We should try to run and escape," a man working nearby said.

"Yeah, we should. If we could run south or east, we would be free."

The men and women working close by continued to discuss the possibility of escaping or waiting until the Vietnamese came. Chhoy and Chhorn stayed silent as they worked. They didn't know much about the Vietnamese invasion. They were too young to know how to escape and where to run to. Besides, we had a big family. It wouldn't be easy to do such things.

They went to lunch at noon and ate their thick rice porridge and then returned to work along with the horde. They stooped down and worked among the adults cutting the rice with the sickles. All of a sudden, several militants came over and tied the hands of half a dozen of men and women working beside them. Then the militants escorted the men and women away behind the small hill in the distance. Everyone knew well not to look but to resume their work. Moments later, the sound of gunshots erupted behind the small hill and then subsided as quickly as they'd started.

Everyone was terrified and confused at first. Then they learned that the men and women were talking about the Vietnamese invasion and planning to escape. There were possibly Schlopes nearby. It must be some of the children who pretended to seek fish and crabs nearby. They must have reported all the conversations to the militants.

Mother heard the news about the execution and warned Chhorn and Chhoy not to ever talk about the Vietnamese's invasion. Besides the incident, Phnom Ta Kream was much better than Stung Chah. The rice stems were growing everywhere, including the sides of the hills and around clusters of trees. They were given two meals a day of thick rice porridge. Every single one of us had gained a lot of weight back. In fact, our entire bodies were swollen from the sudden weight gain.

Chhorn and Chhoy would not rest after work. They wandered around looking for the opportunity to steal some rice. They picked the rice here and there and slipped it in their pockets when it was dark. They brought the rice home for Mother to grind manually at nighttime.

Earlier that day, Chhorn and Chhoy found a perfect spot to pick rice at nighttime. It was hidden on the side of a mountain. Half of the rice paddy was blocked by the trees. The other side was connected an open field. Chhoy and Chhorn had been preparing all evening. Mother had sewn them large pockets on each side of their pants and shirts. They allowed the night to settle in and waited for everyone to go to sleep, and then they snuck into the hidden spot. They crawled slowly deep into the thick rice stalks looking for a comfortable place to lie down. They found a perfect spot where the rice was growing just inches off the ground. Chhorn and Chhoy lay on their backs with their ears listening to any movements.

"Stay down. I will take a peek before we start picking." Chhorn said.

Chhorn slowly stood up and tilted her face up, careful not to stick her head up too high, and then rotated her head 180 degrees to scan all the way around. Then she dipped back into the rice field. Chhoy had already started picking the rice. The rice grains had flourished well. The fruits were bundling up together tightly and thickly on the branches. It was a quiet night. There were no sounds except a light gusty wind that came and went like the waves of the ocean.

After a while, Chhorn said, "Chhoy, it's your turn to check."

Chhoy got up slowly, lifting her face up to begin scanning the area. It was important to keep her head below the surface and keep her face just above the surface to avoid being seen. When she finished checking, she crouched back down to the ground and continued picking the rice.

They both took turns checking. They had filled two of their large pockets already. Chhorn and Chhoy had their faces down as they probed for rice in the dark. Just when Chhorn was about to fill her third pocket, a voice shot out from the quiet night. "What were you guys doing? Tell us now!"

Chhorn and Chhoy turned their heads up and saw about seven people stooping over them. They couldn't see their faces well in the dark, but the silhouetted figure indicated that they were mostly young women.

"We were stealing rice, Mit Bong. Don't hurt us. It's our first time," Chhorn said in terror.

"Just kill them before we get in trouble," the other said.

"Are you the Schlope?" one of the women asked.

"No. I'm not the Schlope. I came to steal rice," Chhorn said.

"Then it is fine. We were here to steal the rice too," another woman said.

"Then we can help each other watch," Chhorn replied in relief.

Chhorn and Chhoy wasted no time and continued picking the rice. Every few minutes, one of them took turns peeking around for any comers. Chhorn laughed to herself when she saw the others were doing the same. When she rose up, she saw others crouch. When she about to crouch, she saw others rise as if they were playing a game of sitting and standing in a harmony. They returned home after all the pockets were filled.

Chhorn and Chhoy continued to pick the rice every night after work. Mother and Chhom spent most of the time at night grinding the rice to remove the husks.

A few days later, Chhoy found a small portable rice grinder when she wandered into the abandoned house, but was afraid to bring it inside our house. It was gravely forbidden to own such a thing. She told Mother about the rice grinder, and Mother warned her not bring it in the house. She did not say anything else beside that. Chhoy left the grinder on top of a nearby small hill, and she used it to grind rice at nightfall when she got the chance.

We had been eating better and better since we moved here. We had two meals a day in public and once at home before bed. Every one of us had gained thickness under our skin. Chhoy's and Chhorn's face were swollen. Pech's balloon-like belly had shrunk, but his arms and legs were thick. He was less grouchy than before and ran around like normal children. I had gained thickness under my skin as well. In fact,

I gained thickness more than anyone else in the family. I could barely see my rib lines.

I saw Mother frequently place a roll of rice the size of my thumb on a plate. She would burn a small incense stick that she'd gotten from somewhere and stood it on the rice. She placed the plate on one side of the wall and closed her eyes and started praying softly.

She normally used the same phrase, "To the spirit of the land and the spirit of the water and the spirit of all the ancestors from all generations and from all cardinals and the shining light of God, please help protect my family from sickness and from harm." She bowed three times after she finished praying.

Early in the morning, a woman came standing by the door and hollered, "Mit Yorn! There is a meeting, and you and your husband have been called."

Mother had never seen the woman before. She and Father were awake and just getting ready to start the day. Mother turned her face to Father, stunned. Chhoy and Chhorn were still asleep from exhaustion. Chhom was holding Poe as he began to cry.

Mother and Father grabbed their scarves and swung them around their necks and then followed the woman. From a distance there were about five people waiting for them. Three of them were holding rifles. One of them was a woman. There was a man without a rifle standing across from the women. Once Father saw the militants, his body began to shake violently as he walked. He was terrified. This was looking bad for both of them. Mother and Father thought this was the end of their lives.

Mother did not show her fear as she arrived and spoke clearly, "What is the reason that all Mit Bong called me here?" She looked all of them in a face and smiled. It was rare for a civilian to speak with the Mit Chah and stare directly in their eyes.

Mother looked around and was shocked to find Kroo Ouwk was among them. He looked down, avoiding eye contact when Mother glanced at his face. He was one of the leaders, but somehow Mother sensed that he was trying to hint to Mother to pretend not to recognize him.

"Sit down," a woman in the group said.

Mother and Father squatted down in front of the Mit Chah and the militants as ordered.

"We have summoned you to trial. A Schlope reported that your daughter possessed a rice grinder and left it on the hill," said the woman who seemed to be leading this meeting.

Mother looked around and tried to recall what she was talking about, and then she remembered the stone rice grinder that Chhoy had mentioned. She knew the rice grinder was a prohibited item. Anyone having such an item was considered a thief who stole rice from the public. She looked around the faces of all the individuals. If she lost this case, Mother and Father would be executed immediately.

"You know it is illegal to have a personal rice grinder," the women continued. "Only thieves would own a rice grinder."

"It's not ours. My daughter found it somewhere. I did not allow it in my house. That's why she left it on the hill," Mother explained.

"She did not discard it. She left it on the hill, intended for used. If you wanted the rice grinder that badly, you will be buried with the rice grinder on the same hill," the woman said.

Mother noticed Father was shaking violently. He knew that his life would end after this meeting. The armed militants were standing holding the rifle with both arms as if ready to shoot any time. Mother reached her hand to Father and pinched him on the side of his thigh and stared at him questioningly.

"What's wrong with him? Why is he shaking?" The other woman who escorted them asked.

"He is very sick," Mother said.

"Let's meet another day. He is sick and will not be able to think straight to answer the questions," Kroo Ouwk spoke immediately.

"Then, Mit Bong, before the next trial, could I work tonight? I would like to sprinkle the rice seeds, since that was my current task. I have nothing else to do tonight," Father managed to gain composure and spoke.

"Of course you can. A job is a job. You can add extra effort any time," Kroo Ouwk said.

Everyone left the meeting. Father and Mother were walking back home feeling so relieved that they'd walked away from the *trial* alive.

"You told them you were going to sprinkle the rice seed? Do you know this is the harvest season?" Mother said angrily.

"I don't know. I was scared to death. I just wanted to say something," Father said.

"I'm praying that they will not summon us back to the trial. I wouldn't know what to say if they do," Mother said.

The next morning, we saw several jets hovering in the distant sky firing their weapons down to the ground. The gunshots and the explosions could be heard faintly. Meanwhile, the militants came by the area with trucks and began loading the newly harvested rice onto their trucks. Mother believed they were moving. Each day after, the sound of the gun battle and artillery shelling become closer and closer. Sometimes black smoke could be seen rising in the distance.

The rumor was that the Vietnamese were closing in. Our family didn't talk much about the Vietnamese; thus, none of us knew anything about them. The local village leaders had informed everyone before work that they were banning most of the strict rules but did not mention any specific rule. The work was no longer mandatory. Everyone would get to eat two meals a day but would get an extra meal if they volunteered to work. All of us had a lot of free time to wander around, especially Chhorn. She constantly looked for ways to find food. She noticed there were lot less Mit Chah than before. The militia were nowhere to be seen. Chhorn had come across a small pond about one kilometer away from our shelter, and she saw sign of shrimp in living in the pond. She told Father about the pond when she arrived home in the evening. Father decided to sacrifice a mosquito net to use it to catch shrimps.

Father and Chhorn brought a bucket and a large basket with a mosquito net and walked into the pond. They came across a civilian carrying two buckets of water using a dong raek.

"Getting water?" the man asked.

"Yes, we are getting water," Father lied.

The man stopped and lowered the water to the ground and said, "No one was ever allowed coming to this area. This was where the militants lived, but it's all quiet now."

Chhorn and Father were relieved to hear that. Father was being cautious not to say too much besides asking for his name and where he lived. He and Chhorn continued to walk toward the pond. When they arrived, the pond was very quiet like Chhorn said. It was hidden by tall trees and shrubs. Using the same method to catch fish in the pond, Father and Chhorn caught a bucket full of shrimp in less than an hour. This was the first time in years that they'd had the opportunity to catch shrimps.

Mother arrived from work early for a lunch break because everyone had left. When she entered the house, she saw Father and Chhorn at home with a bucket and a basket full of shrimp. They were picking the weeds off the buckets and munching on the raw shrimp at the same time.

"Where did you catch the shrimps? Was it all right to catch them?" she asked.

"I don't see why not. No one was there anymore. They said the militants used to live around the pond, and now it is quiet," Father said.

"To be safe, I want to pretend that I don't know anything about the pond and ask Mit Chah if it is all right to catch the shrimp," Mother said.

Coincidently, a man who was known to be the leader of the village was walking by, scanning the area for any suspicious activities.

"Mit Bong, I have a question," Mother said with a smile. "We saw a pond somewhere over there. Is it all right to catch shrimps?" she said, waving her hand up in one direction.

The man stopped and frowned as he listened. "Anyone caught catching shrimps will be arrested and executed. Then we will dispose of the remains near the pond with several other people that have been caught catching the shrimps," the man said and left.

Mother's whole body shook from the man's comment. She turned around and looked at Chhorn and Father who were standing a few yards away. They had also heard the comments. They stood stunned side by side.

Mother walked over and said, "You were lucky that no one was there. Otherwise, you would be buried among the others."

"My daughter and I both would be dead," Father added.

After she learned that catching shrimp was prohibited, Mother hid the shrimp in one corner of the house. She took a handful of the live shrimps and munched. Then she walked over to the dining hall to get her share of rice porridge. The rest of us were already there waiting in line. She came and sat with us as usual, but she finished her rice porridge faster than normal and then decided to take off.

She was walking toward a storage shack looking for a place to rest. She'd had plenty of sleep last night, but today she still felt very tired. It was strange, but she felt more tired than usual. It was a different type of tiredness. It was a relaxing type of tired. A strong, cool breeze had swept by making her just want to stop working and take a nap. She looked around, and there was no sign of the Mit Chah around. She double-checked to make sure that no one was around, and then she walked toward the storage shack looking for a place to lie down. Work had been easy nowadays. The Mit Chah didn't seem to care too much how productive the workers were.

She entered the shack and found stacks of hay taking up most of the space with the farming tools neatly arranged in groups by the wall. The shack was nice and cool. Mother walked to the furthest corner and lay down on a haystack. She closed her eyes and dozed off almost instantly.

It was a nice, long nap until she heard a shout. "Wake up! Wake up!" an old man with a long white beard and white hair shouted. He was wearing all white. "Get your children and leave. You are free. The soldiers will come and free you."

Mother was too tired to get up. She was lying down and ignoring the old man. She just wanted to resume her nap. The old man tickled her waist and continued shouting, "Wake up! Wake up! Get your children and leave. The soldiers will come and free you."

Mother rolled her body to the side to avoid the old man, but he wouldn't stop. He repeated the same phrase over and over again and continued tickling her waist. Mother felt so ticklish and laughed. She opened her eyes and looked around for the old man, but he'd disappeared. She sat up peeking around the haystacks looking for the old man, but instead, she heard the soft murmur of several people having a secretive conversation. Mother paused and listened. She didn't want to move and make noise.

"That's all the ammunition we have. We must gather every single one of them and kill them all at once," a voice of a woman said.

"Let's start now," a man said

"Then take of this," another man said.

Mother waited for a moment and then crept over to the wall. She peeked through a hole in the wall and saw over a dozen of the militants and the Mit Chah leaving. Most of them had rifles strapped behind their backs. She waited for them to disappear and then she walked out of the shack trying to figure out what was real and what was a dream. After a long thought, everything seemed to be real, including the old man, but she couldn't figure out where old man went. She began to walk back home.

She came across Pheah's mom who had been traveling with us from Stung Chah. "Peah's mom, we should pack up our stuff. There will be soldiers coming to rescue us," Mother said in confidence.

"What are you speaking of? They will take you to execution if they hear you say that," Peah's mom said.

"I said what the old man with the white hair told me. I saw the old man with my own eyes. He tickled me until I woke up," Mother explained.

"It must be the spirit of the keeper of the land. He was trying to protect us," Pheah's mom said.

"Spirit or not, we must get ready," Mother said.

Chhorn walked over when she saw Mother. "Chhorn, pack up our belongings and get ready," Mother said.

"Ready for what?" Chhorn asked.

"Don't you know? The military force will come and rescue us. I can't explain. I need to go to potty," Mother said and walked away.

CHAPTER 26

I was playing with children around my age, trying to climb the large hill. I spent most of my time wondering around our new shelter. Just like in Stung Chah, I would never attempt to go too far from our shelter. The adults climbed the hill with ease. I made it up halfway. I turned around and looked down and nearly rolled off the hill from fear of heights. After I gained my balance, the landscape caught my eye. I looked straight ahead into the distance and noticed how beautiful the landscape was. The thick forest stretched many miles over the hills and flatland and then connected to distant mountains. Bellow, the hills were filled with men and women working together harmoniously. Elder women were stooping down, cutting rice with their sickles. The young children were roaming the area scavenging for loose rice grains. The men were loading the rice piles onto an ox wagon. The village used to be more congested with workers and the Mit Chah. There were a lot fewer people nowadays. Most of the people I saw were the same people who came with us from Stung Chah.

Father had just come back from work and was taking a break and sitting down in front of the house. The instant I saw Father, I crawled down the hill slowly and sat next to him. The sound of the artillery shells exploded somewhere in the distance. It was the closest ones we'd heard since we'd arrived. I glanced at Father's face waiting for his reaction. Father looked toward the direction of the sound and frowned.

"That is the outgoing shell, but it is so close," Father said to himself.

I didn't know much about the explosions, but it sounded very scary. After many weeks of hearing the explosions, every adult could identify if the shelling was incoming our outgoing. Everyone hoped for the outgoing.

I liked to sit with Father. Somehow, I felt safe around him. He always knew what to do when things happened. I had a toothache that had started about a week ago. It still hurt, and I didn't know what to do. One of my teeth was wiggling. I had cried a couple times that morning from the pain. I had been waiting for Father to come home.

"Father, my tooth hurts," I said.

He turned to me and said, "Open your mouth."

I opened my mouth. Father lifted up my chin with one of his hands. "Which one is causing you pain?" he asked.

I touched the wiggling teeth with my finger to show him. Then he took his finger on his right hand and wiggled my tooth gently.

"It is almost coming off. Close your eyes," he said.

I did what he said, and then I felt the unexpected force of his finger on my teeth. I felt a short, sharp pain, and then I saw blood dripping down from my mouth onto the ground.

"Here is your tooth," he said, handing me a tooth that had once been in my mouth.

Then a loud explosion went off somewhere nearby followed by the sound of gunshots. The loud explosions continued and mixed with more gunshots. The sound was getting much closer than before. It appeared there were more incoming artillery shells than the outgoing ones. Father stood up and looked around. I could see a deep concern on his face.

"The Vietnamese are invading," Father said to himself, staring intently toward the direction of the battle.

Father never discussed escaping. He was not familiar with this part of the country. More importantly, he was not quite sure whom to trust. Rumor had it that people had tried to escape toward the Vietnamese side. They were executed instantly when the Mit Chah found out their plans. From his experience, the Vietnamese had always been enemies of the Khmer. As a truck driver, he had been around almost every city in Kampuchea. He'd heard many horror stories of how the Vietnamese soldiers killed the Khmer soldiers and used their skulls to make a hearth to cook tea known as *Tae Ung*.

After a long moment, the gun battle and the explosions subsided. Everything was back to normal. Father and I continue to sit. I felt relief that the battle had subsided.

"Everybody, come to the meeting! Come to the meeting! We have a meeting over here! Everyone must come, including small children. And no talking to one another!" The militia walked around calling out to everyone.

Father got up and walked over to where we'd been instructed to go. I followed closely behind him. Every man, woman, and child around the hill were flocking toward the same direction. The adults walked and looked at one another nervously. I saw Chhom emerge from somewhere with Poe in her arms and Pech trailing after her.

All of us were walking right behind Father approaching the congregation. Chhorn and Mother were among the people sitting in the middle of a circle. About thirty to forty armed militia members were standing around the congregation. Each of them was carrying a rifle pointed at the civilians. Their grenades were wrapped around their waists along with their machetes.

Between the civilians and the militants was a large space as if it made of an invisible wall. There were small, square metal objects lying in a circle surrounding the civilians, including Mother and Chhorn. The militia members were standing away from the metal objects as if they were afraid of them and were preparing for something.

Most adults realized they were being gathered for execution. They were staring at their families' face preparing for the last moment of their lives. They knew well that crying or showing sympathy for one another was forbidden. There was nothing they could do. The children were crying in fear. The women were holding their children tightly in their arms.

Everyone was pretending they don't know what the intention of the meeting is. Some men and women asked for permission to go potty only to be monitored and escorted back to the circle. There were about four dozen civilians sitting in the middle of the circle preparing for execution. More were seen coming. There were at least a few hundred more heading to the large circle. The militia was waiting from them to come so that they could kill all of us at once.

We all walked in the circle standing beside Mother. Chhoy had just arrived as well. Mother's face had turned white. She heard about the plan just moments ago, but there was nothing she could do. This would be the end of our lives. Even with hundreds of people approaching, no one was saying anything. Everyone walked slowly and quietly to the circle.

Mother took Poe from Chhom and held him in her arms. She was sitting closely between Chhoy and Chhorn looking down nervously.

"Comrades, run!" The militants looked at one another and then started to flee. Some unstrapped their grenades and machetes and dropped their rifles and bolted away.

"Everyone, those are mines! Do not step on them!" a man yelled.

Everyone was looking at one another with cheer. The conversation erupted. Mother stared at all of our faces and couldn't help but to smile with a surge of relief. "We are safe. They all fled" Mother said.

Then everyone's eyes turned toward the rice field. Thousands of soldiers were walking in horizontal lines, cautiously holding their rifles pointing forward, sweeping the area. Each one was wearing a green and brown uniform with a round helmet of the same color pattern. Their boots were up high past their ankle. They had shiny, long blades mounted onto the tip of their rifles. Some had grenades and bullet belts strapped around their waist and shoulders. It would only take one of them to kill us all.

"Go back south," one of them said with a strange accent. "We are the Vietnamese. Go back south. Wherever you see the Vietnamese, walk to that direction," another one said in an alienlike accent.

Mother, Chhoy, and Chhorn walked out of the large circle, careful not to step on the mines. Father stood still, staring at the Vietnamese soldiers with a frightened look on his face. The people that he'd feared most in his life were here, thousands of them.

We followed the instructions and walked in line out of the circle. The adults and children alike couldn't help but to keep staring at the soldiers.

Mother walked over to Father and said softly "We are free."

"We were not free. I know the Vietnamese. They have been our enemies since before I was born. They will kill us and use our skulls to make *Tae Ung.*"

"But they just saved us," Mother said.

"They didn't come to save us. It's the war between them and the militants," Father said.

"War or not, we are still alive. Why don't you try to find our wagon and the ox that they took from us?" Mother said.

"Don't waste your energy on packing. We will die anyway, but I will get a wagon to carry my children," Father said and walked away from Mother.

Father didn't seem happy. He knew exactly where the wagon was. He'd brought a wagon from Stung Chah, but one of the village leaders threatened Father and took the wagon. He walked very quickly over to the house of the Mit Chah who'd taken his wagon.

Mother turned to Chhorn and all the families that were living beside us and asked. "Did everyone pack as I told you?"

"I packed the instant you told me, Yorn. Your dream was like the eyes of the future," a woman known as Solo's mom said. She had been living next to us for the last six months here.

"I'm done packing too, but I thought we were all going to die," Pheah's mom said.

"All of our belongings are packed, right?" Mother asked Chhorn.

Chhorn stood still. She was stunned by the whole foreseeing ordeal. "I didn't pack anything," she said.

"I worked hard making up excuses for you so that you could stay home and pack, and you didn't do anything?" Mother said furiously.

"How should I know that the soldiers would come for real?" Chhorn replied.

"Your mom has never been wrong before. Her dreams saved our lives many times before," Pheah's mom said.

We didn't have much to pack but a few pots and pans, the mosquito net, some extra clothes, and a bucket of water. Chhorn, Chhoy, and Chhom began to grab whatever we had inside our shelter and brought them outside.

Father returned empty-handed, "Someone took our wagon," he said to Mother.

"We are in trouble then. Chhorn and Chhoy still have the infection on their foot. They could walk now, but we don't know how long. Maybe you should look around. Maybe you can find another wagon," Mother said.

"There is no need to find the wagon. The Vietnamese are going to kill us all eventually," Father insisted.

Thousands more Vietnamese soldiers were pouring in. "Dee! Dee! Dee Batambang," One of them said. Nearly everyone in Khmer knew "dee" meant "go" in Vietnamese.

"Dee, your Mother! You will take my head to make *Tae Ung!* I know your plan!" Father said angrily.

"Wait for me. I will check the storage room for salt. I know where they stored the salt," Chhorn said and ran off.

She was very excited to look for things before someone else claimed them first. She went to a nearby storage shack and found a large bag of salt. She picked up the bag of salt that must have weighed more than herself and swung it on her shoulder. She took a step and then she fell flat on her back with bag landed on her chest. She got up and lifted the bag and swung it on her shoulder again and walked over to meet us.

"Everyone, help carry something," Mother said.

"Don't waste your energy. We are all going to die anyway," Father said.

Mother was holding Poe in her scarf that she'd wrapped around her shoulder. I grabbed a small pot called *Ka Mel* that was once very popular in Khmer. Every one of Lon Nol's soldiers had one. Chhorn grabbed a machete. Chhoy and Chhom were holding all the clothing and the rest of pots and pans.

As I watched my sisters gathering our belongings, it caught my attention that Mother and Father stood still staring at something. I looked around, and it seemed all the adults were looking at something. My eyes followed the crowed and saw two familiar men. One was Ta Watt, who had his hands tied to his back. Another man was walking behind him holding an axe, followed by two Vietnamese soldiers.

"That looks like Chuk Tang." Mother said. "He's the one who escaped execution. His entire family was executed."

"Ta Watt was the one who'd ordered the execution. Now, he's in Chuk Tang's hands." Pheah's mom said.

"If you do good, you will receive good. If you do bad, you will receive bad. His fate has come," a nearby elder man said.

"Yeah, he's the only one that got what he deserved. The rest of the demons had fled," a woman said angrily.

The adults continued to exchange their thoughts and knowledge. When the escort vanished behind a cluster of trees, everyone resume packing.

We started to walk along with other civilians in the crowded and long line. All of our old neighbors from Stung Chah were following Mother. It appeared they would go wherever she went. There were also new families that came and joined our group as well.

Suddenly, Pech squatted down and started to wail.

"What's the matter?" Mother asked.

"I don't want to walk," he replied and continue crying.

"Why not? You have to walk. If you don't, you going to be left here all alone," Mother said.

"I don't want to walk," he insisted.

"I'm going to smack you in the face if you don't walk!" Chhom yelled.

"Uh oh! There's a snake behind you. If you don't walk, it's going to bite you," Chhorn said.

"I'm not walking!" he shouted.

"Pech is not stupid. Pech is smart, right? He doesn't need us to tell him to walk. He is strong and outgoing. He will walk on his own. Watch..." Chhoy said, using a friendly technique.

"No, I'm not walking," he stood still facing down.

Everyone gave up trying to convince Pech to walk. The entire village had already started moving.

"Puk Vea, I think you have to carry him. He's not walking," Mother said to Father.

Father was still working on strapping his belongings, including an axe and a machete. He'd placed a dong raek on his shoulder. A basket of rice hung down from one side and a bucket of water on another side. Without a question, he lifted Pech to one side of his waist and began walking.

Just a few paces away, Chhorn noticed a tall, fair-skinned woman known as Mit Chea was walking ahead of us with an elder woman and a young woman. They were having a conversation with Mother. She was the one who'd whacked Chhorn and Chhoy on the head the first day we arrived here in Phnom Ta Kream when Chhorn instinctively stuck her hand in the rice pot. It wasn't the pain that she was angry about, but the fact that she was hit on the head with a rice scoop like an animal. Chhorn didn't like the woman at all. She would never forget what she'd done to her. She shouldn't be walking so close to our family.

"Mit Chhorn, we asked your Mother for permission to come along with you guys. I like your family. You have such a good family. I have never seen a family that is so close together," Chea said.

"Why would we want you to be around us? You hit my head with a scoop like I was a dog," Chhorn said angrily.

"I'm sorry. I don't know why I hit you. Please forgive me. We have no one to look after us. I'm living with my cousin, Huk, and her Mother. We are all girls. You have your Father," Chea added.

Chhorn did not say anything but continued to struggle walking with a heavy bag of salt on her shoulder. It was the first time she'd heard anyone say they were sorry. She must be sincere.

We marched out of the town and came to a worn path that cut through a rice field. There were dead bodies lying everywhere. The closest one was a body of a woman lying on her side in a pool of blood. A few yards away was another body of a dead woman lying on her back. A little girl about three years old was kneeling beside her crying.

More and more people were merging from all directions into the same path. The majority of the families consisted of three to four members, mostly woman and children. I noticed there were children as young as three years old without parents or sibling trying to walk along with the adults hoping they would be allowed to join. Some just stood and wept in one place not knowing what to do.

"Um, can I stay with you?" a girl about ten years old asked an elder couple who had no children walking along. There were no words of acceptance or rejection, but the girl walked along the elders anyway.

"They must have been caught in the crossfire," a man said, pointing to a dozen corpses lying just yards away off the path.

"The militants shot at everyone in sight. They knew they were losing the war. We, the civilians, were their enemies now. They tried to shoot me too, but they ran out of bullets. Otherwise, I would be one of the dead," another man said loudly, proud that he'd survived.

We continued to see dead bodies along the road. Many people believed they were killed by the Red Khmer rampage when their regime had fallen. The civilians had been looking forward to this all along.

We marched along with thousands of other people across the rice field, careful not to sway off the newly created path that could be seen zigzagging across the plane. Many men had repeatedly informed everyone that the Red Khmer had set up mines everywhere to slow down the Vietnamese. It was wise to follow the main path.

The sun was inching toward the horizon. The palm trees were standing solemnly, scattering throughout the field all the way to the contour of the distant mountains. Thick black smoke was swirling slowly up into the sky. It was too far to see what caused the smoke. The source must have been extremely large.

We came to a small village just before sunset. Most people continued walking, but Father and the elders decided to take a break. The first thing we noticed were hundreds of bags of salt laying everywhere on the side of the path.

"Had I known that the salt was abundant like this, I would have grabbed something else like rice or something. I wasted my energy carrying that stupid salt bag," Chhorn grumbled angrily and slammed the salt bag on to the ground.

Father walked around and selected an abandoned house that could accommodate our family. Father had asked Chea, Huk, and her mom to stay with us, as they were scared to stay by themselves. Everyone was still nervous about the Mit Chah. People were referring to them by their original name, the Red Khmer. No one knew for sure if they were gone forever or would come back.

We placed our belonging in the abandoned house and relaxed. I was glad that we didn't have to walk any further. I was exhausted and hungry. I sat in front of the house with Pech as Chhorn, Chhoy, and Chhom were getting ready to search for food.

Suddenly, a group of soldiers approached us. One of them was speaking Khmer and handing fliers to the passersby.

"All brothers and sisters! Read this information, and you will understand what is happening to our country," the Khmer soldier said.

"How are we going to read if none of us have stepped foot in school?" Father said sarcastically.

"I read with my forehead, not my eyes," his friend added and laughed.

"I know how to read," Huk said and took the paper from the soldiers.

Everyone looked at her in shock. In most parts of Khmer country, women weren't allowed to attend school, fearing that they might learn how to write love letters. Nonetheless, educated women were highly praised by their friends and relatives.

Huk took the paper from the soldiers and started to read. "By the name of Heng Som Rin and my allies, we were here to free all the Khmer from the grip of Pol Pot and Eang Sari. We will eliminate them forever… "

After Huk finished reading the flier, no one really knew the names of the people in the flier. No one appeared to pay much attention to the details of the information and wandered off. The sun would set in a short period of time, and they needed to get ready for the night.

"Mit Chea, where is your family?" Chhorn asked, trying to indicate she accepted her apology. She had been wanting to apologize for being mean to Chea along the way, but it was difficult. But now they were rested and she was standing beside Chea. It was a good opportunity to talk.

"All my family is dead," she said shortly.

Chhorn did not ask how. She was too tired for gruesome details. She was hungry, and she wanted to find food to eat. Chhoy and Chhom were right behind her.

"I'm going to get an ox, so I can get the meat," Chhorn said.

"Father, give me the machete. I'm going to get the oxen over there." Chhorn said pointing to a heard of oxen that were grazing freely. Since everything belonged to the public and the current regime was falling, no one was entitled to anything. Everything was free for a grab. The herds of oxen were roaming freely in the field. No one was interested in catching them.

"Forget the ox! You will attract the Vietnamese, and they will kill us for the oxen," Father scolded. "Here, take this machete, but do not try to catch the ox." Father took out the machete from a sack and handed it to Chhorn.

Chhorn did not care what Father said. She was hungry, and she wanted the oxen's meat. She walked hastily ahead of everyone toward the herd of oxen. "Everyone, help me catch the ox," Chhorn said.

"Are you crazy? What are you going to do after you catch it?" Chhoy asked.

"I don't know. I have a machete. All I'll need to do is cut it in half or something. I just need a piece of meat from the leg or at least the tail," Chhorn replied and started to run for the oxen.

"Don't do it, little sister. You are a girl, and girls don't kill oxen," Chea said.

Chhorn stopped after realizing no one was helping her. The oxen were too big, and she couldn't do it all by herself.

"If no one is going to help me catch an ox, then I'm going to find something else," Chhorn said.

She walked back to Father and handed him back the machete. "No one wanted to help me catch anything," she said to Father angrily and then walked straight into the farmhouse.

Chhom followed her in case she needed a hand. Inside the farmhouse lay pigs of all sizes. There was one that was so large it appeared unable to walk. All the pigs stared at Chhorn as she entered. Chhorn wanted to get the largest one, but she knew there was no way she could carry the pig back out. Then she eyed a smaller one that was still about three times her size just several paces away. She jumped into the barricade and hopped onto the back of the targeted pig. She used both her hands to lock the pig's front legs, and then she used her legs to lock the pig's hind legs. The pigs collapse on its stomach with Chhorn on its back. It began to squeal and struggle trying to get free. Chhorn was light and drained of energy from traveling all day. She was no match for a pig three times her size. It rolled to one side, and Chhorn fell to the ground. With determination to get the pig, her hands and legs were still locked to the pig's limbs.

Chhom was standing by the door and saw the whole ordeal. She knew Chhorn would not release the pig, and the pig was going to kill her if she didn't let go of it. "Chhorn, the Red Khmer are coming!" Chhom screamed out loud.

Chhorn dropped the pig and hopped out of the barricade. Her face and body were smeared with mud, and she smelled like pig dung. "Where are the Red Khmer?" Chhorn asked.

"I lied. I thought the pig was going to kill you. That was the only way to get you off," Chhom said, avoiding looking directly in Chhorn's eyes.

Chhorn was furious. She swore at Chhom using all sorts of words. Then she suddenly jumped across another barricade and hopped right onto another pig. This time, the pig was just slightly bigger than herself. She tugged her hands around its shoulders and its front legs and then lifted the pig off the ground. She walked out of the barricade using her leg to release the latch. The pigs' hind feet were dragging on the ground as she walked. Chhom followed her out of the farmhouse in disbelief.

Hundreds of passersby paused and stared at Chhorn, "Whose little daughter was that carrying a giant size pig?" one of them said.

"Hey, little girl. I could slaughter the pig for you if you give me half," a man on a moving wagon hollered.

"I can do this myself. Go find your own pig," Chhorn said with a grunt.

"This girl is tough," the man said and grinned.

Chhom looked around and realized that every single person had stopped and stared at Chhorn carrying a pig that was twice her size. Many ran into the farmhouse to claim other pigs.

"Father, give me the machete!" Chhorn said as she approached the house.

"What do you want the machete for?" Father asked in shock when he saw Chhorn dragging a pig.

"Just give me the machete. I need to cut the pig," she replied.

"How do know how to cut the pig?" Father asked.

"I don't know how to cut the pig, but just give me the machete. I'll just cut in in half or something."

"Don't do it. You are so little, and you are a girl." Father said.

"Just give me the machete!"

"Oh, my daughter! I don't know how to slaughter a pig, but I will do it for you since put so much effort," Father said.

Father had killed snakes, lizards, and crocodiles, but he had never killed a pig before. He took the pig from Chhorn and searched for something to tie the pig's legs. After the search, he couldn't find anything and ended up using one of the clothes. He ripped the clothes into small pieces and used it to tie its legs.

"Chhay, let me help," one of his friends said.

A couple more of his friends came over and helped.

"My daughter is a girl, but no son of anyone is better than my daughter," Father said.

"You should have seen her earlier. She wanted to kill a herd of cows," Chhoy added.

"True. And she wanted us to help her. When we refused, she got very angry," Chea said.

Father and his fellow men slaughtered the pig. None of them had any experience slaughtering a pig before. It was a slow and gruesome process. Father did the killing as the other men held the pig in place. Everyone squirmed as the machete cuts through its throat, and the pig struggled and squealed. The blood dripped into a large pot that we'd brought with us. Mother had experience cooking pig's blood before, and she knew exactly what to do with it.

"As hungry as I was, I lost my appetite. This is why I cannot be a farmer. Driving trucks is much better," Father said.

"I would never do this again. I hope it is not sinful to kill a pig," the other man said.

Mother shared the pork with the families that helped Father slaughter the pig. Mother had never killed a pig, but she knew how to cut the dead pig and separate the organs and the meat. Then she cleaned the intestines. Nothing went to waste.

"My family will get the most since this pig really belongs to my daughter," Mother said.

Each family had brought enough rice to last several days. All the rice was stolen the same way my sisters had stolen it at Phnom Ta Kream. Mother marinated the leftover pork with salt and saved it for later. She cooked all the organs that night. With plenty of salt around, Mother made real food for the first time in ages. The aroma of the boiling soup made my stomach growl and churn.

"I thought I'd lost my appetite, but the smell of the soup made me hungry," Father said and laughed.

After a long wait, the organ soup was finally ready. It was the first time I could remember that we'd gotten to eat pork. Mother had cut the intestines into smaller pieces and put them in the bowl. She gave Pech and me a bowl each.

I was hungry. I shoved one large piece into my mouth. The taste was so good that I chewed so fast and bit my tongue. I wailed in pain.

"Eat slower. No one is taking your food," Mother said. Seconds later, I could taste my own blood.

Just when the pain in my mouth had subsided, I saw Pech was choking. Mother reached into his mouth with her finger and pulled out a big chunk of pork intestine from his throat.

"Chew well before you swallow, or you will choke to death next time," Mother scolded.

All of us, including Chea, Huk, and Huk's mom, were eating happily. The flavor was rich and delicious.

"Say, Father, are you going to help me catch some oxen?" Chhorn asked as she almost finished with her bowl.

"I'm not going to catch any oxen. I no longer want to deal with rice, farming, or raising animals. I want to get back to truck driving again," Father said.

All the men that came with us were truck drivers. Like Father, none of them were interested in catching any oxen. Chhorn was frustrated trying to convince Father and everyone else to get the oxen along the way here.

After the finest dinner, Chhorn lay down in the house. Chhoy and Chea went to look for chickens. They'd seen chickens roaming around the area earlier, but no one had the energy to chase after them. The chickens were known to have bad eyesight after sunset.

CHAPTER 27

Father and Mother woke us up early the next morning. It was still very dark inside the house. The roosters crowed loudly nearby. Mother was preparing the scarf to carry Poe. She had already cleaned and packed all the pots she'd used to cook dinner. Only Pech and I were still inside the abandoned house. Everyone else was outside talking and preparing for another trip. Klo's and Peah's families were outside getting ready. I needed more sleep, but everyone seemed eager to move from this place.

Pech didn't want to get up either. Father had to lift him up and carry him outside. We started to march as soon as I stepped outside. A line of hundreds of people were already marching toward the east, where the Vietnamese soldiers had told us to go. The moon was round and bright. Although it was still nightfall, the moonlight allowed us to see a path that was built as a dam by the workers under the Red Khmer to reserve water for the rice paddies. Fireflies were flickering in the air.

"Look! The moon is following us!" Chhom said pointing to the bright, shining moon.

As I walked and stared at the moon, it seemed that Chhom was right. The moon was really following us. The moon seems to move when I moved. I took a step backward, and the moon seemed to move back a step as well.

Father was carrying Pech on one side of his waist and carrying the dong raek on his shoulder. He was the tallest man in the line. He was the only man that could carry heavy items and a child at the same time.

The sky turned brighter and brighter as we walked. Then the morning sun emerged from the horizon far ahead of us. More families emerged from the local area and joined us. The line became more crowded than earlier. Some were traveling with an ox wagon. Some were walking empty-handed. Some had makeshift cargo mounted on their backs with chickens and all their belongings inside. As the sun lit the sky, thousands of people could be seen ahead of us and behind us, all walking in one thick line.

We stopped a few times to rest along the way. Mother cooked us the chicken that Chhoy and Chea had caught last night. Chhom took the opportunity to collect more water from the local pond. Many new families that walked with us really liked our family after a long walk together and asked to go wherever we went. Some of Father's friends met their relatives along the way and decided to stay with their relatives. We just kept moving. When it got dark, we stopped under a tree to stay the night. Sometimes, we were lucky to arrive at a village at nightfall and asked for shelter for the night. Most of the residents had just claimed the house, but every single one of them kindly shared the space for the night.

Finally, we arrived in a town called Chumkah Chake (Banna Orchard). The houses were made of materials that I had never seen before. They were not made of bamboo trees and palm leaves like our houses in Stung Chah or Phnom Ta Kream. These houses stood three times taller and were shielded by some type of solid material. Even the roofs were solid. These houses seemed to be rainproof and probably would not budge against a strong wind. More interestingly, multiple houses were attached to one other like each one depended on the other. Each block had its own open door.

Father said he had been here before during Lon Nol's time. This was the housing complex used by the Lon Nol's government workers and where well-off families dwelled. Father was amazed that it was still standing up after the war and after the Red Khmer regime.

"We are going to stay here awhile since these houses are still vacant. We don't know what's ahead of us. We might not be able to find a shelter like this," Father explained to everyone.

All his friends and families, including all the new families that we'd met along the road, agreed to stay. I was glad that we'd stopped walking. I'm thirsty and tired. More interestingly, we were getting to stay in a nice place.

Father picked the first section of the house. When we walked in, the room was large and clean. It could fit us all, including Chea, Huk, and her Mother, plus more. A family known as Tuak's family was taking the one next to ours. Tuak was a boy about my age. His family had been traveling with us from Phnom Ta Kream, but I hadn't noticed his family until the last few days. I had been walking with Tuak for the last two days. Even though we didn't talk to each other, we seemed to like each other's company. Tuak had three older brothers that were around Chhorn's age. His family had a wagon, and he spent most of the time in the wagon. His Father had been killed by the Red Khmer many months ago. Along the way here, a man came up to them and threatened to take the oxen and the wagon away. He claimed that the oxen and the wagon were his. The three boys stood up and refused to give them up. After a long argument, the man gave up and left. Tuak's Mother didn't have to say a word.

Our families and friends were seeking the opportunity to harvest the rice that still had not been claimed. Chhorn, Chhoy, Chea, and Huk walked back west near Muahn Hau (Flying Chicken) village, the same path that we'd just traveled, and harvested the abandoned rice. The end of the rice harvest season was approaching. All the settlers were harvesting any rice they could find. Within weeks, thousands of men, women, and children flocked to rice fields and harvest whatever was left from the Red Khmer time. Since they don't have proper tools to harvest the rice, it took them the whole day to fill a basket with rice grains. Then they had to carry home the basket full of rice. They normally returned home after nightfall.

After the rice was brought home, we didn't have a rice grinder to grind the rice. The second popular option to remove the rice husk was to pound the rice with a round-headed piece of wood in some sort of sturdy container. Mother had wondered around the town and found piles of military helmets from Lon Nol's time. She collected several helmets and brought them home. Then she collected rocks that had rounded ends and were small enough to hold with one hand.

Mother, Huk, Chea, and all three of my sisters spent the rest of the day pounding the rice to remove the husks. After the rice was pounded, we still needed to separate he husks and the kernels. They use a large flat tray to toss the rice up in the air, allowing the air to blow the husks off the tray. It was the easiest part of the process, but it was time-consuming. This was where Mother would ask me to help.

Each day, it become more and more difficult to find rice to harvest. My sisters, Chea, and Huk had to walk further and further from home to find rice. There were times when they returned with just a few kilos of rice each. Nevertheless, it was better than nothing.

While Mother, my sisters, Chea, and Huk were looking for rice, Father went fishing with his friends in the nearby river and ponds. They also hunted for snakes and giant lizards like he'd done in Tuel Snai.

After we'd been living in the housing complex for about two months, a group of families came and claimed that the house belonged to them. They brought documents and showed them to Father. Father took a quick glance at the documents, but he had no idea what they meant since he didn't know how to read. Huk attempted to read the documents, but they were too complicated for her as well. It was nothing new that people were claiming back their properties. Unable to prove otherwise, Father and the families that came along with us gave up the house and decided to pack up.

"Let's get out of this place. We don't want to stay here and collect rice the rest of our lives anyway. If they want our house so much, let them have it, and let them live as farmers forever. I have learned the whereabouts of a few truck drivers and their families down east. There is a lot of space there. We could build shelters and live there temporarily. Then we will decide what to do next," Father said to all the families.

Everyone decided to come along. We left early in the morning the day after we were told to leave. Pech refused to walk again. Father had to carry him along with a pair of baskets using the dong raek. We walked through the town for half a day and then came to a large paved road. There were a lot less travelers nowadays, as many families had chosen their residences. Unfortunately, we continued to see dead bodies scattered along the paved road.

We arrived in a small, well-developed town in late afternoon. We cut through the alley of a neighborhood where men, women, and children of all ages were socializing in front of their houses and on a small street. We continue walking until we came to an open area where small shelters were being newly developed. Father slowly lowered Pech down and rested the baskets on the ground.

"This town is called Ma Sin Buan Bao. We will build a shelter here and live here for a while," Father said.

"Who is that? Is that Chhay?" a familiar voice suddenly hollered.

It was Pu E (Tien's father) with several of his friends. He looked like he had been here awhile. We hadn't seen Tien and Mao since we left Stung Chah.

Just as he expected, Father recognized all his old truck driver friends. Father greeted them with excitement. Mother recognized all of them. They used to come with Father to her house in Takeo.

Mother greeted them and then took us to find an open piece of land while Father was busy talking to his friends. Hundreds of families had already settled down. Some were living in the real houses made of wood. Some had just arrived and built shelters on any open land.

Mother picked an open space located just to the edge of the crowded area. There was an orange grove on one side and a small pond to the other side. She explained to Huk's mom that she wanted to be a little further away from the other houses. She was planning to purchase a cow and may plant some crops.

After a short conversation, Father, Pu E, and a few other men went to search for bamboo trees to build a house. Mother used the rice to trade for woven palm leaf planks to make the roof and walls.

The men returned shortly after with large bundles of bamboo trees. Father began building the house with a little help from Chhorn, Chhoy, Huk, and Chea. Meanwhile, Pech and I wasted no time looking for new friends. I found Tien's house up on the higher ground on the other side. He was playing with his new friends. He was surprised to see me.

Tien took me around the neighborhood. We ran most of the time. The city was larger than I thought. Some of the houses were made of solid roofs and walls similar to the apartment that we'd lived in in Cham Kah Chake. We heard loud music in the distance. We followed the music and came across an open market where mostly women were selling all sorts of food and unfamiliar materials. Nearly everyone was talking to one another at the same time. I could not understand how they even heard each other talking.

I saw a woman holding an object up high with meat on a metal tray, held together by several chains. She was sliding the metal block along the flat metal bar that somehow attached to the tray. Further in the crowd, there was a man standing by a bucket of fish negotiating with several women.

Tien took us as far as we could go, and then we returned home just before dark, right on time for supper. We slept in the open as the house was being built. It took nearly four days for our house to be completed. The house was large enough to fit all of us, including Chea, Huk, and her mother.

On the fifth day, I woke up in the morning feeling sore and tired. My head hurt like never before. I started to cough uncontrollably. I noticed Pech, Poe, and Chhom were having the same problem. I didn't feel like doing anything but lying down on the floor. We were definitely sick, but somehow Pech got sick the worst. He had been crying nonstop, complaining about his ear. Mother found out shortly that we'd all gotten the measles. Nearly every single child in the neighborhood had the measles. The four of us were lying down on the floor sleeping, not even able to get up and eat.

Measles was a well-known illness in Khmer. It was believed that people with measles needed to take a bath constantly throughout each day until it was cured. Unfortunately, the water in the small pond near our house was filthy and muddy. People pooped and peed in the water. Waste of all sorts could be seen floating in the water.

The real lake was over a kilometer away. Chhorn and Chhoy were too small to carry water from such a long distant. Chea volunteered to do the job. She had been looking for an opportunity to help the family and prove that she was not a cruel person. Unlike most women, Chea was wide and tall. In fact, she was taller than most men. She had spent all her time with Chhoy and Chhorn like sisters.

"Chhorn, I'm sorry for what I did. I love your family. I will do anything to make it up. Allow me to stay with you guys so that I can take good care of your brothers and sisters. They killed all my brothers and sisters. I survived because I gave myself to them and became one of them. The Red Khmer had drawn me in little by little," Chea pleaded.

"I don't mind you staying with us," Chhorn said. She had never experienced accepting apologies before, but she tried to show that she was fine with her around.

As we lay down feebly, Chea bathed us, fed us, and she carried buckets of water kilometers away from home. For two whole weeks, she spent most of her days carrying water from the river and bathing us.

Mother came and sat next to us and examined our progress as Chea bathed us.

"Four of my cousins' children passed away last night from measles," Mother said to Chea and wept softly. "If you can take care of them and make them well, I will do anything to pay you back."

"I don't want anything back. All I want is forgiveness from Chhorn. I don't think she forgives me yet for hitting her head with the rice scoop. I'm not the cruel person she thinks I am. Chhorn seems to be all right with me around, but I still don't see her forgiveness," Chea said.

"As her Mother, I forgive you. She's too young to know how to show you her forgiveness. If I didn't forgive you, I wouldn't let you stay with us all these days. Let's forget the past," Mother said

Chea woke up early in the morning as usual, carrying two buckets of water using the dong raek. She came back about two hours later with the buckets full of water. Without any rest, she took Poe from Mother and sat on a log. She scooped the water using the rice bowl to pour the water on his head slowly, allowing the water to run over his entire body. Since Poe was very small, she used only three bowls of water, saving the rest of water for me, Pech, and Chhom. Poe was now around one-and-a-half years old.

After she finished bathing and drying Poe, she picked Pech up, put him on her lap and bathed him. She took her time to ensure the water flowed over his entire body. After she finished with Pech, she bathed me the same way as Pech. When it was Chhom's turn, she had Chhom sit up on a small stool, and she poured water right over her head. When she finished with Chhom, Chea wasted no time and went straight back to get some more water. She stopped only to eat lunch and supper. Chea would feed each one of us first before she began eating.

Chea returned home later for dinner. Mother had saved the food in a bowl for her before we began eating.

"Ming, did all the little brothers eat yet?" she asked.

"I fed them already," Mother said.

Even after Mother had told her that we'd already eaten, Chea fed us a spoon or two of rice before she began eating.

"Chea, you have worked very hard today. If you are tired, you can rest for the day," Mother believed that without water we would die, but at the same time, Chea was way overworked. "We will find a place close to water so that we don't have carry the water that far. No one can do what you did. Not even the strongest man."

"It's all right, Ming. They are like my little brothers and sisters. I want them to get well soon," Chea replied with sincerity.

After two weeks of Chea's hard work, Chhom was able to get up and walk on her own. It took Pech and me another week to be able to walk, but I still felt so lightheaded and felt like my inner body was hollow. Pech still had a bad ear infection. We could see the white liquid clogging his ear.

We gradually got better and were able to walk, but the sickness still lingered. Pech and I could not walk far, so we hang around our house playing with whomever would come close. That fun was the only thing that made us forget about the sickness.

Weeks later, Mother was frustrated that our illness was still not going away. There were no medicines around. She was not familiar with the new land and could not find the medicine she needed. She had been searching for help from the native townsmen.

"Here, you guys go to that hill where you go poop all the time. Collect your dried poop and put it in here and bring it back to me," Mother instructed and handed me and Pech a bowl.

Pech and I were happy to do the job. We collected our dried poop from the hill and brought it back to Mother. Mother smiled and took the dried poop that we'd collected inside the house.

"Go find me some earthworms," she said.

Pech and I were not sure why she asked for earthworms, but we knew where to get them. There were plenty of them near the pond.

In just a few minutes, Pech and I came back with an earthworm each. Mother squirmed when she saw the earthworms, but she had us drop them in a coconut shell. Mother went inside the house and returned moments later.

"Go call Chhom. Tell her I have some coconut juice for her," Mother said smiling.

Pech and I didn't know why Mother was so happy, but it was fun to do what she asked. We searched the area and found Chhom talking to a group of girls around her age. It was the first time I had seen Chhom talking to anyone besides us. She always had been busy searching for food to feed us. Since Chhorn, Chhoy, Chea, and Mother had been searching for food, Chhom had a lot of free time on her hands.

We told Chhom that Mother want her home. She followed us without question. Pech and I skipped happily home. Pech had grown a lot since we'd traveled from Stung Chah. He could run as fast as me, and he was actually fun to play with.

We arrived home about thirty minutes later. Mother was working on something with our coconut shells. There was a knife and a stone grinder by the coconut shell. A woman about her age was sitting on the rug behind her talking to Chea, Chhorn, and Chhoy.

"So, these are your children too?" the lady asked Mother.

"Yes, they are my children," Mother replied.

"You are lucky that you have a lot of children left. Mine are all dead except for one," the woman said.

"Mother, what did you call me for?" Chhom asked.

"Here, drink some coconut juice," Mother said handing Chhom the coconut shell. Then she handed the other two coconut shells to me and Pech.

"All of you should drink," Mother said.

Even though the coconut trees were everywhere, the coconut juice was rare. It might be the fact that the coconut trees were too high. Only skilled people could climb them.

All three of us drank our coconut juice instantly. I realized, however, that there was an unfamiliar taste blended in with the juice.

"Why does the coconut juice taste like that?" Chhom asked.

"Don't worry about the taste. I have added medicine," Mother said smiling.

She turned her head and saw Chhorn, Chhoy, and Chea look at each other and laugh. Chhom frowned. "What did you put in there?" Chhom asked.

"Coconut juice," Mother said.

"With marijuana," Chea added.

"And with dried poop," Chhoy added and laughed.

"And with earthworms," Chhorn added.

Chhom's whole body shuddered like she had been stabbed on a chest. She held her breath trying figure out what to do. She wanted to vomit, but it was too late. Full of anger, Chhom screamed and started swearing using all the foul words she could think of.

Chea, Chhoy, and Chhorn quietly walked out of the house trying not to laugh. "Don't swear at me. I didn't do anything," Chhorn said.

"The medicine will help you get better. Four of your cousins died of illness. If I would have known you wanted to die, I wouldn't have given you the medicine," Mother said with a serious face.

Mother had a good point, but Chhom was still disgusted. She couldn't believe she'd drunk coconut juice with dried poop and earthworms. She hated and feared of any types of worms. With nothing more to do, she simply walked out of the house.

Pech and I decided to stick around inside the house. I was hoping I would get some more coconut juice; I didn't care what was in it. Neither did Pech.

"She has a bad temper," the woman said.

"The other two are fine, but this one is mean. But she is a hard worker. She's the one who took care of the little ones when I was away from home. She fed them and cleaned them during the Red Khmer time," Mother explained.

"Then her meanness is fine since she's a hard worker," the woman said. "So, these are all your children?"

"I have another one. He's the oldest one. The Red Khmer had been looking for him to kill him. I don't know where he is right now. He might not even be alive," Mother said.

"You were still luckier than me. My family is all dead. I have one son left. I used to cry every night, but my tears won't come that easily nowadays," the woman replied sadly.

Father sat nearby in one spot wordlessly. He'd laughed a little about Chhom drinking the medicine. He normally didn't talk much at home. He talked a lot when he was around other men. He had spent a lot of time chatting with his friends. He spoke mostly about his trips to far places and discussed plans to go fishing or hunting.

Since we no longer needed to bathe every minute, Chea joined Chhorn and Chhoy to search for abandoned rice and stray chickens.

Unfortunately, all the storage houses were empty. They had found nothing for the past six days. If they didn't find any rice soon, we would begin to starve again. Mother told my sisters and Chea to stop wasting time searching for abandoned storage houses and think of other ways to get food instead.

"Mother, I want to give another try to go search for more rice. Everything has been taken around here. I will walk further away from town and try to find any abandoned storage houses," Chhorn said.

"Then go. Let Chhoy and Chea start trading today. I will give them some rice, and they can use that to trade," Mother said.

Chhorn grabbed an empty basket and then walked aimlessly searching for abandoned storage houses. She walked past the open market, out of the crowded town, and followed the wagon road for a long time. Just when she was about to give up hope and return home, a large old house caught her eye. Chhorn thought the house was too large and too broken down for anyone to live there. She decided to check it out. She walked inside and was disappointed at first glance. There was nothing but piles of hay. Then a tall and light-skinned woman entered the house from another door. Chhorn hastily walked around the house searching for rice before the woman found it first.

A short moment later, a pointy object covered by hay caught her eye. She walked closer and brushed the off the hay and discovered a large bag of rice. She opened her eyes wide in excitement. She lifted the rice bag and then was shocked to find the same woman standing right behind her staring at her face.

"Mit... I mean little sister. Can I have some of the rice? I have a friend who is dying. He is very sick, and he needs something to eat," the woman begged.

"I have walked very far to find rice. I have four sick little brothers and sisters that need to eat too. I can't give it to you," Chhorn said.

"Little sister, please. My friend is dying. If he doesn't eat today, he will not live," the woman begged and began weeping.

Chhorn wasn't sure if the lady was lying or telling the truth, but she felt bad seeing an older woman cry.

"I can give you some, maybe a can or two, because you only have one sick person and I have four," Chhorn said.

"Two cans would be good. That will give him enough strength to find his own food. He helped our comrades, including myself, when we needed food. He's a very nice person," the woman said.

"Where is the person that you were helping?" Chhorn ask in suspicion. She wanted to make sure that the woman was not lying. Normally, people would help their brothers, sisters, or parents, but helping a friend was unusual.

"His name was Chhoeun. We had been living in the same compound for a year. I survived because of him. This is my opportunity to pay him back," The woman said.

Chhorn froze for a few seconds and then said, "I have a brother named Chhoeun. We haven't seen him for over a year. We thought he was dead." Chhorn was unsure if he was the same person. "What does he look like?" Chhorn asked.

"He's short and dark and has wavy hair. He said his home was located in Stung Chah," the woman said.

"That might be my brother. Take me to see him," Chhorn said quickly.

The woman appeared as shocked as Chhorn by the impossible coincidence. "Really? Then follow me," the woman said.

The woman walked Chhorn to her shelter. They exchanged a few stories along the way. Like most men and women, most of her brothers and sisters were dead. She was living with her Mother. She didn't know if her Father was dead or alive, but she was trying to find him. Chhorn was hoping the woman would have the same luck as her.

They arrived at a small hut about a kilometer away. Chhorn found Chhoeun lying unconsciously on the ground, his head resting on a small rag. He was so skinny and dark, barely unrecognizable. His distinct wavy hair and thick lip helped Chhorn confirm that it was him.

"I'm going start making thick rice porridge," the woman said and grabbed a small pot nearby.

"Bong Chhoeun," Chhorn said patting his arm slightly.

Chhoeun turned his head slightly. He opened his eyes a little and closed them back.

"Bong Chhoeun. It's me, Chhorn," Chhorn tried again.

Chhoeun opened his eyes again. "Really, is that really you?" Chhoeun asked weakly.

"We brought you rice, and we are cooking rice right now. You can continue to rest. We'll wake you up when the rice porridge was ready," Chhorn said.

Chhoeun went back to sleep. Chhorn sat beside him staring at his face. He had gotten very dark and skinny. His hair was long and messy. She was very happy to see him again. She rarely got to see him during the Red Khmer. They met at home maybe three or four times by coincidence. Her mind drifted back to Takeo and Bakaeng when they'd go fishing together. He always wanted to catch fish and sell the fish to make money to help out Mother. Since Father was always away from home, he'd had to step up and become a man before he even turned ten. He did what any adult would do to find things to sell to make money.

When the rice porridge was done, Chhorn woke him up and gave him a bowl of thick rice porridge. Chhoeun was unable to sit up straight. He turned to his side and scooped the rice porridge with a spoon and then blew on the rice porridge. He sipped the rice porridge slowly, taking his time. He didn't have to worry about grueling work after the meal anymore.

Chhorn and the woman sat beside him eating their bowls of rice porridge quietly. They were both very hungry as well.

Chhoeun seemed to be more awake after each scoop of rice porridge. After he'd eaten half of the bowl, he sat sup straight to get more comfortable. Chhorn could feel the heat from his body as he sat up. He must have a high fever. The woman gave Chhoeun another bowl after he finished the first. He finished the second bowl very quickly. Chhorn gave the woman half of the rice she'd found and then returned home with Chhoeun.

When they arrive home, Chhoeun collapsed on the ground just after he entered the door. He had used up all his energy to walk here. He was still extremely ill. Mother, Chhoy, and Chhom were shocked to see him. They swarmed around him and wept in joy and in confusion. They lifted him up and placed him on a palm leaf rug.

Mother asked if he'd had anything to eat, and Chhorn assured her that he'd eaten already. Mother didn't ask him any more questions. He appeared too weak to speak. She sat beside him probing his head, waiting for him to be conscious. Every single one of us were gathering around Chhoeun, waiting for him to wake up.

CHAPTER 28

Chhom opened her eyes in the morning hoping to see Chhoeun up and well. Unfortunately, he was still lying down unconscious. Chhoy, Chhorn, and Chea had gone out searching for food or to harvest rice.

Mother was lying down next to Chhoeun. There was a wet cloth and a bowl of hot water nearby. Mother had probably washed his face while he was sleeping. Chhom was very concerned about his condition. She didn't understand what was going on except that he was very sick. Mother had not told anyone anything about how bad his illness was. She might not even know what kind of illness he had.

She wanted to help make Chhoeun well again, but she didn't know what to do. When we were living in Stung Chah, she barely got to see him. He came home a few times and then left without a trace. He was the reason she was still alive today. His loyal friend freed her when she was tied up on the thorny tree, covered with red ants. Then he came home and caught bullfrogs for us to eat when we were on the verge of starving to death. She had not had the chance to speak with him the way normal brothers and sisters would do. He was here right now in front of her, but he lay helpless and unconscious. Chhom was frustrated and afraid that he might not make it alive. She sat up suddenly and decided to go out and look for something that might help him.

She exited the house, walking aimlessly toward the crowded area of the town. She looked around for anything that might help Chhoeun. After about an hour walking, she realized how foolish she was trying to find something that she didn't know anything about. She thought through the possibility that Chhoeun would die. She would not be able to handle that pain. She wept as she thought of bad things that might happen to Chhoeun.

She walked and wept until she came across a graveyard that was known as Mong Chen. It was one of the old Chinese graveyards that even the Red Khmer respected and left untouched. The rumor was that these graves were full of once-important Chinese people. Chhom had seen Mother pray to God and also to the spirits of the ancestors that watched over the land and water. Many times, things had happened the way Mother had prayed for.

Chhom begin walking into the graveyard with tears filling her eyes. Unfortunately, the graveyard only made her think about the possibility of Chhoeun's death. Now that she was all alone in the graveyard, she burst out crying. She stood in one place and cried for a long time. Then Chhom thought of Mother's prayers again. She wanted to pray, but she had nothing to give to the spirit. She became more and more frustrated. Then she finally decided to pray without any gifts to the spirit. She kneeled down and closed her eyes. "Dear Spirit of the Land and Spirit of the Water and all the Angels and God, please help my brother. He is very sick. If you have any medicine that could cure his illness, I beg for just one capsule. I want only one capsule. Please help me," she prayed and continued crying.

She felt like a fool when she'd finished praying. She realized it was not possible for the spirit and God just to pop out of thin air and give her the medicine she needed. Otherwise, everyone would do it. She stopped praying and cleared her eyes. She continued to walk. Just after three paces, she saw a small round object in front of her. She stooped over and picked it up and discovered a single capsule of medicine. She was so happy beyond any words. She placed the medicine in her palm and reexamined it. She had never seen medicine before, but Mother had mentioned many times that people would give her two to three cans of rice for a single capsule of the French medicines. She was very happy but still unsure if it was the medicine that could cure Chhoeun's illness. She carefully slipped the medicine in her shirt pocket ran back home as fast as she could.

She arrived home shortly and showed the medicine to Mother. Mother was stunned when she saw the medicine. She confirmed it was the French medicine that she used to take during Lon Nol's time to treat various illnesses. Chhoeun was slightly awake when Chhom arrived, but he was still lying on the ground unable to say a word. Mother gave the Medicine to Chhoeun along with the bowl of rice porridge. Chhom was staying home constantly checking Chhoeun's condition.

Later in the evening, Chhoeun ate a few more bowls of rice porridge and was able to sit up. Mother began asking him questions, and he was able to reply with a few words. Chhom was not used to talking to Chhoeun. She sat next to Mother and simply listed to the conversation. She felt so much better now that Chhoeun was getting better.

Chhoeun told Mother that he was lucky to be alive today. Most of the people he knew had either died of illness or been executed. He had been forced to move around to many different places. He explained how he was nearly taken to execution because he told them he'd joined the military. He described how they forgave him and only demoted him. He was the only one that had been forgiven. Every single one of his friends had been taken away to execution because they'd joined the military.

It took nearly two weeks for Chhoeun to recover. He was unable to do much. There were twelve of us now living together. The entire family was relying on Chhorn, Chhoy, and Chea to find food. Huk was unable to do much because of her lack of skills. They continued to look for rice, but they'd found nothing for the past several weeks. Mother was looking for the opportunity to trade, but she had nothing to start with. Both of Father's feet were swollen, probably from carrying Pech and the heavy buckets of water and rice from Chumkah Chake. He was unable to walk at all now. There were too many people for the three of them to find enough food to everyone. We no longer got to eat consistently like we had been. We would be lucky to get one meal of rice porridge a day. Everyone was hungry again just like in the Red Khmer time. We were not the only family that was facing the same problem. Many families, including Tien's family, were starving like us.

Pech, Poe, and I continued to get sick very often, and we were very hungry. Chhom wanted to help find food for us like she did in Stung Chah, but it was impossible for her to do so here. She was not familiar with the place, and most properties had been claimed, and she was feeling sick most of the time herself. She was frustrated and depressed for not being able to help the family out.

Even though she knew it was impossible to find food, Chhom continued to try anyway. She walked aimlessly down the alley, past the market, and then came to a quiet area. She looked around, but there was no sign of vegetarian. The land was too hot and too dry for the crabs and snails to live. Besides, she needed to find more than crabs and snails to feed a family of twelve. She was hungry and in despair. She knew Pech, Poe, and I, along with the rest of family, were as hungry as she was right now. Chhom had lost her hope and gave up trying to search for food. She could not think of anything else to do. She closed her eyes while she walked very slowly, and then she began to pray, "Oh, Angels and the spirit of the land and water, I'm hungry and my family is hungry. Please help me find just enough for me and my family to live. I don't want much."

Chhom was too tired to continue walking. She stopped praying and decided to sit down. The instant she opened her eyes again, she saw a small and a large sack sitting side by side near the bushes. Both of the sacks were covered with thick dust. Chhom's entire body shook from excitement. She reached her hand out and picked up the small sack. She remembered clearly praying for enough to feed the family and nothing more. She left the big sack alone. She untied the sack and found all sorts of jewelry, including gold earrings with diamonds and gold bracelets. Chhom couldn't help but laugh out loud in joy. Her prayers had come true again. She bolted back home and showed Mother the jewelry. She explained how she'd prayed and found the sack, but she didn't tell Mother that there was a bigger sack next to it. Mother confirmed they were real gold.

"Now I can trade again," Mother said and smiled.

Chhom felt so blissful to see Mother smile. She knew Mother had the skill to trade.

"Angels have eyes. The good things we have done will never be forgotten," Mother said.

Mother walked to the open market and returned with a basket full of rice. Then she began to visit people around the town looking for the opportunity to trade.

Coincidently, Chhorn, Chhoy, and Chea returned home with a basket full of rice as well. They had walked many kilometers out of town and came to a small broken-down shack that no one would have thought had anything in it. The rice was hidden underneath the haystacks. Someone must have hidden it during the Red Khmer time. After Chhom told them the news about the jewelry, the three were very happy and decided to use the rice that they'd found to trade instead. Being highly skilled in trading, Chhorn and Chhoy knew exactly what to do. They decided to use the rice to trade for fish since fish was rare around here. People were afraid to venture far to the river to catch fish because they were afraid of the Red Khmer. They carried the basket of rice to the open market and found a man standing by the ox wagon with a dozen buckets full of fish. He had just arrived from fishing. Most of the fish were still alive, flipping and flopping in the buckets. The man wanted a basket of rice for one bucket of his fish. Chhorn made a bargain and traded three buckets of fish for a basket of rice.

The three took the fish and walked around the opposite end of the market. Almost instantly, they struck a deal and traded the three buckets of fish for three baskets of rice. They returned home to keep the two baskets of rice and went back to the market to bargain with the same man. The man offered the same deal. He traded his last three buckets of fish for a basket of rice. The three took the fish and traded for another three baskets of rice. It took them longer to find the customers, but they sold all the fish well before nightfall.

Mother made steamed rice for all of us when she returned. The three were happy with the profit they'd made in one day. They could not help but to talk about their accomplishments all night. They could not wait until morning to begin trading again. They planned to stick to selling wholesale and avoid selling the fish one at a time.

They returned to the market early the next morning and began to trade gain. They didn't have the same luck as yesterday, but they were able to profit two baskets of rice before night fall. The third day was worse than the second, but they brought home a nearly basket full of rice for profit. It was still far better than searching for abandoned rice stores.

They had ups and downs thereafter. There were days where they made two baskets of rice, and there were days they made no profit at all. When they were unable to sell the fish in the market, the three carried and sold the fish door to door around to the neighbors for a very cheap price to get their investment back. Any leftover fish would be used for dinner.

We had been eating two meals a day since. In addition to eating the extra fish, Mother also cooked chicken, pork, and vegetables.

Pech and I had gotten better and had a lot of energy. We spent most of our day time playing with other children. We would come inside the house just to eat and sleep.

I was playing with a boy about my age when Mother came home with a cow. A woman and a boy were walking beside Mother. I knew the boy well. He was one of the children I played with every day. Mother tied the cow next to our house and let it graze. She informed us that she and the woman put in the money and bought the cow. They planned to let the cow eat and grow, and then they'd sell it in the near future. She also considered having the cow slaughtered and selling the meat when the time came.

As the cow was grazing peacefully behind our house, I noticed the boy was standing near the cow and would not leave it alone. I walk over and asked, "What were you doing with my cow?"

"It's my cow too. My mom said she owns half of this cow," the boy replied.

He was right. Mother said something about putting money together with another woman to buy this cow. Everyone knew that, but I don't like the fact that he was standing too close to our part of the cow. Besides, this was my house, and the cow was eating on my backyard. The boy was slightly smaller than me. I was not afraid to fight if he refused to stay away. Mother was probably the one who came up with the idea of buying the cow.

"Go away! It's my cow," I said pushing the boy aside. The boy staggered and nearly fell on his face. After he got his balance back, he walked over to front of the cow and grabbed the rein and then gave me a dirty grin. He looked at me to show me the cow belonged to him more than it belonged to me. I wanted to claim the cow, but there was nothing in the rear to hold besides the tail, and it was too high for me to reach.

"I saw the cow first, so the cow is mine," the boy said smiling even wider.

I was scared the boy would take the cow away. "It's my Mother's idea. She was the one who bought the cow, so the cow is mine," I said and then grabbed the cow on its hind leg.

"No, it's mine," the boy said and yanked the rope.

I took a step closer and stood behind one of the cow's hind legs and hugged its knee with both of my arms. "It's mine," I said. Then I tugged the cow as hard I could with both of my arms.

The cow took a step back. Its hoof stepped on my right foot and knocked me back ward. My foot was still pinned by the hoof. I shrieked in pain. I tried to push the hoof off foot but the cow's leg didn't even budge. I continue to scream in pain.

Mother burst out of the house and shouted, "What going on?" Then she realized my foot was pinned under the cow's hoof. She pushed the cow forward. The cow finally took its hoof off my foot. Mother picked me up and examined my foot. Blood begin to ooze down from the middle of my foot. I screamed so hard that I almost fainted.

"My son's foot is broken!" Mother shouted.

She took me inside the house and examined my foot further. She couldn't tell if any of the bones were broken. She began to boil water to clean my foot. She asked what I was doing near the cow, and I explained to her that the boy was trying to take the cow.

"You naïve child, the boy cannot take the cow. The cow is ours. Never go anywhere near the cow again, you hear me?" She said.

The next morning, I lay still on the floor, unable to sit up. I felt nothing but pain throughout my entire leg. I looked at my foot and saw a big piece of skin shifted to one side, leaving a small gap line above my toes. My entire foot was swollen.

Unable to get up on my feet, I lay down all day in one place. Mother woke up in the middle of the night and washed my foot with hot water. I woke up in pain each time she cleaned my foot.

CHAPTER 29

Chhoeun was staying home recovering from his illness. He had been doing much better for the past several weeks. He got up and walked around and then came back to lie down for a rest. He had gained so much weight and grown out of all his clothes. Mother had to purchase fabric to make him new clothes. His cheeks, once bony and hollow, were now thick and fluffy. He was now around eighteen years old. He was looking forward to working with Father to support the family. Father's feet were no longer swollen, and he was able to walk normally. The sufficient food had helped a lot. Chhoeun spent most of his time chatting with Father and his friends discussing their next tasks as the families were doing much better.

The men decided to make a trip to Tonle to catch fish and hunt animals along the way. Father regretted not listening to Chhorn about claiming the oxen and the wagon when they had the opportunity. Now he was relying on his friends who owned oxen and wagons. Fortunately, all of his friends were more than happy to share the wagon and split the catches. Pu Poo and Pu Kun each owned a wagon and a pair of oxen. They were eager to travel with Father and Chhoeun.

They took a trip down to Tonle Sap and returned home after two weeks. They brought home two wagons full of fish of all sorts and sizes. They also brought home snakes, lizards, and monkeys. Chhoeun had contributed more effort than the rest, as he was the youngest and most energetic. He had been waiting for this opportunity to use his skills to help the family. He'd learned so much about fishing and making traps from the past years living in the forest under the Red Khmer. In addition, Father had years of experience in fishing and hunting. With Chhoeun's and Father's skills combined, they made it simple to catch fish and wild animals. They filled the wagons with as much fish and animals as they could carry.

Father's friends praised Chhoeun highly and regularly when they spoke among the elders. Huk's mom was among the elders who were impressed with Chhoeun. She had been referred to by her first name, Yey Ngao. Huk and Yey Ngao were still living with us, but they cooked and ate separately now. Yey Ngao was pure Chinese. She had never mentioned her husband and how he had passed away. For the past several weeks, she had been making dessert for Huk to sell.

Yey Ngao had joked with Father about her interest in getting Chhoeun to marry Huk. Huk was a beautiful woman. She has light skin like Chea but has was the average height of Khmer women. She spent most of her days helping her mom bake and sell desserts. Yey Ngao was too old to do any hard work, and Huk seemed too delicate to lift anything heavy. Therefore, they could not keep up with Chhorn, Chhoy, and Chea.

Chea had overheard the jokes about Chhoeun and Huk getting married. She did not appear happy. Chhorn had been speculating about her reaction and behavior. She believed Chea had feelings for her brother.

"How come you don't speak to Bong Chhoeun," Chhorn finally asked when they were on their way to the market.

"I'm afraid Huk and her mother might think that I'm competing for Chhoeun. Plus, I'm older than Chhoeun. I am taller than any normal women, and he might not like me. I don't think I'm attractive," Chea said sadly.

"I think you are pretty. I hope they are just joking about Huk and Bong Chhoeun getting married. Maybe you can tell Father that you want to marry Bong Chhoeun," Chhorn said.

Chea couldn't help but blush. Unsuccessfully trying not to show her smile, she replied, "Are you crazy? Only parents can propose the marriage. I don't have any parents. I would be considered a whore if I were to do that myself."

"Then, if Father and Yey Ngao are serious, there was nothing we can do about it. We can't disagree with the elders," Chhorn said.

"That is true," Chea said in despair.

That was the last time they discussed Chhoeun. Chhorn felt very sympathy for Chea when she learned that she had feelings for Chhoeun.

She continued to speculate and noticed that Chea was upset that she didn't have the opportunity to talk to Chhoeun. Father and Yey Ngao continued to chat very often. Yey Ngao would throw in jokes about the marriage when the opportunity allowed.

"If he becomes my son in-law, I will let him plant all kinds of vegetables. He probably works harder than a buffalo. He's not too tall. That would make a perfect match with my daughter," she said.

Chea thought her remark directly insulted her. Chea seems to be normal with everyone else in our family. She continued to take care of Pech, Poe, and me when we were sick. She continued to put extra effort in trading and searching for rice to feed our families. She had a strong bond with Mother. Mother had been calling her by the name of Kown Chea (daughter Chea).

"You can call me Mother," Mother said a few times.

"I really want to, but I'm afraid I might insult somebody," Chea said.

Over many weeks of jokes and comments about the marriage, it turned out that Father was not really serious about engaging Huk and Chhoeun. On the other hand, Yey Ngao was very serious about trying to get the two together.

We had just finished our afternoon meal when Yey Ngao burst out of her section of the house with the terrifying face. "All of you! You must act quickly! The spirit of the land possessed me and informed me that Chhoeun and Huk must get married as soon as possible. If we don't do as the sprit has requested, something horrible will happen to everyone in this town."

"What else did the spirit say?" Mother asked. It was a common belief that the spirit could overcome a person's body and speak on its behalf. Normally, the spirit would like to pass an important message. However, it was rare that the spirit would come and possess random people. Normally, only the witchcraft person was known to call forth the spirit with lots of incense sticks, food, and gifts.

"The spirit said do whatever it takes to get them to marry. Make it simple and fast," Yey Ngao said.

Father and Mother looked at each other as they sat down resting after the meal. They believed in spirits one hundred percent. The spirits were like Mother's third eye. She had experienced it herself. Although she had never been possessed by a spirit, they had come to communicate with her through her dreams. She still remembered in incident in Phnom Ta Kream where the old man in white informed her about the incoming soldiers and woke her up from her nap. Most of her prayers and wishes had come true. Mother continued to offer the spirit food and drinks when she got the opportunity.

"Are you agreeing to offer your daughter to my son?" Mother asked.

"I must agree with the spirit, and at the same time, this is my only way to thank you for all your help to my daughter and myself. I don't know what I would do without your family. It was difficult to live without a man in the family. We had to move nearly every two months. When the country becomes stable again, I would like to have a farm where we could produce crops and raise pigs and cows. None of this is possible without a man," Yey Ngao explained. "Your son Choeun is a perfect man for my daughter. He's a hard worker," Yey Ngao added.

"Then, we must start the engagement process. We will seek a cleric and our friends and families to come to the engagement since we are the parents," Father said.

In Khmer tradition, the man's side of the family had to arrange the engagement process. A Buddha cleric was needed to witness the agreement between the man and woman to be wed. The elder friends and families would come and represent the woman to be wed or the man to be wed. The most important part of the agreement was the woman's parents' acceptance of gifts and the wedding arrangement responsibilities.

In Khmer tradition, most of the parents shared responsibility to find an unwedded man a wife. It was common that the Father or Mother would request their friends and acquaintances to marry their daughter.

While Mother, Father, and Yey Ngao were working on the engagement, Huk and Chhoeun had not spoken a word to one another. Yey Ngao seemed to have full control over Huk's decision. Mother and Father did not ask if Chhoeun wanted to marry or not. They assumed Chhoeun was interested. Chhorn didn't see any chemistry between Chhoeun and Huk at all. She was hoping to have Chea as a sister in-law instead, as they had become so close after working together to survive and to feed the family every day. Chhorn feel a great disappointment, but she was too young to say anything. Besides, she was a girl.

Early in the morning, the local cleric, along with Father's friends and the palm readers and fortunetellers, had been summoned to our house to come to the engagement. The house has been divided into two groups. One group of elders was assigned to act as the negotiators for Chhoeun, and the other group for Huk. The negotiations included the number of gifts that Mother and Father were offering now and the days before the wedding. Both Chhoeun and Huk were sitting on the opposite side of the groups.

The cleric began the meeting by chanting and summoning the spirit to come for witness. The palm readers and the fortuneteller examined Chhoeun and Huk and explained their thoughts. The elders of both sides exchanged their ideas and bargains. The term came out that Father had offered to provide food for the wedding and two baskets of rice to pay for the music band and maybe monks if they could find them.

Normally, every single one of us was supposed to sit by our parents and listen, but Chhorn, Chhoy, and Chea did not. They had left before sunrise to trade as usual. Chea was looking more depressed than ever. She had not spoken a single word all day. She had been avoiding looking at Chhorn and Chhoy in their faces. She looked like she had no life left within herself.

After the engagement, Father, Chhoeun, and the elders made another trip to the east to catch fish and hunt animals for the wedding. Pu Kun and Pu Poo volunteered to use their oxen and wagon again. They returned from the trip within six days with two wagons full of fish, along with snakes and giant lizards. The men generously took only a small share for their families and left the majority of the catches for the wedding as their gifts.

Pech, Poe, and I were sick once again. We all got a high fever and diarrhea. I was lying beside Pech and Poe on the floor, half awake. I could hear the sound of the music and the hum of the congregation somewhere not too far from our house. I knew this was the wedding Father and Mother had been talking about for many weeks. The music was different from what I'd heard in the open market. Each song was sung mostly by a woman. The tone was long and loud and consistent.

Unlike the music in the market that made me want to hop and dance, the wedding music just made me want to weep. The songs sounded like some sort of goodbye song.

I really want to get up and walk to the wedding and see all the people. There must have been hundreds of people, but I couldn't even move my legs. Chea had to lift me up to feed me rice porridge. Pech was lying on the floor breathing slowly. Chea had been holding Poe in her arms most of the time. She didn't attend the wedding. If I noticed it correctly, I saw tears in her eyes.

The wedding ended sometime in the middle of the night. The music had changed from sadness to jolting and exhilaration. There were cheers and laughter, especially toward the end of the night.

It took about six days for me to be able to get up and walk again. I felt lightheaded and weak. I was too tired to walk out of the house and play with other kids. Instead, I stood by the door with Pech looking at other children play. I noticed there were a lot less children out playing than before. My ears hurt when someone spoke too loud. I had a bad ear infection just like Pech.

Mother was chatting with the woman who'd bought the cow with her. She was speaking of the death that claimed many children's lives for the past two weeks around the town. She believed they died from the same type of illness that had made us sick. We were fortunate to be alive.

Just when they were in the middle of their conversation, a man using a loudspeaker announced, "Everyone living in this area has to move by tomorrow. The government has a special project for this place. Every single house will be torn down. If you have no place to go, you can move to a town called Kean Tmau (Rock Side) by Stung Sankae River!" The man paused for a moment and then repeated the same announcement over and over.

Mother and the woman stopped talking and looked at one another. They walked outside and found Father, Chhoeun, and all the elders speaking with one of the soldiers walking behind the announcer. Mother walked up to Father and asked. "Are they forcing us out of this place?"

"Yeah, we have to get ready today. I knew several good friends of mine that used to live in Kean Tmau. I spoke with a three-star general, and he believed most of the soldiers that survived came to claim their homes back in Kean Tmau," Father said.

Our families got ready on the same day we were notified. We woke up early the next morning and started to load our belonging onto the ox wagon. Pu Yun and Pu Kun allowed us to put anything we need in their wagons. Our families now had about six large bags of rice. We also had more pots, pans, and clothing. It was impossible to carry all those by hand or using the dong raek.

Father was carrying two baskets of clothing, hooked on to the dong raek. Chea was carrying her backpack with Pech on one side of her waist. Normally, Father would do that. Pech was still very sick, and he refused to walk.

I joined Tien and Mao, as their family was right behind us. Tien and Mao had gotten sick like Pech, Poe, and me, and they were lucky to have survived. I was very disappointed that we had to walk again. I liked this town a lot. We got to eat well and had a lot of fun.

We walked along the alley and then merged into a main wagon route and joined in with hundreds of other families that were forced to move just like us. I noticed that most families were more well off than before. Every single family had more valuable things to carry, from rice bags to blankets. Some were walking their pig on a leash like a pet. Some even had a dog, which for some reason I found very frightening. Mao had been bitten by a dog the second week we'd arrived here.

We stopped for a break around noontime to cook and eat. Then we continued to walk until we reached a paved road. The adults called it the National Road. The rain began to pour. We walked in the rain along the paved road until nightfall. We stopped and set up a spot to sleep. Father didn't have enough time to make a temporary shelter. We settled under a large tree that helped shield the rainfall. All of us circled around the trees and slept.

"The Red Khmer! The Red Khmer!" someone screamed in the middle of the night. Our family woke up, and then I saw everyone else was awake as well.

Father walked around speaking with the adults. When he returned, he informed us to get ready to move. The entire horde began to move.

No one knew exactly where we were going, but we were just moving with the flow, hoping to be far away from the Red Khmer.

We walked behind the wagon for a long time, and then the entire horde stopped. We stopped with everyone else and settled down. The rain was still drizzling. Father searched the area in the dark and found a large tree. All twelve of us lay down under the tree trying to get back to sleep partially shielded from the rain. We woke up to another scream, as confused as before. The Red Khmer had come again. None of us know where they were or where they came from. The horde began to move again, and we followed wherever they went. This time, we didn't stop. We continued walking until the surroundings become visible by the morning light. The sun was still hidden somewhere behind the mountain and trees. The horde stopped shortly before the sunrise and settled down. The rain had finally subsided. There were no trees nearby. We were all lying down to sleep in the open land.

We slept a few hours until the sun rose past the mountains and trees, making it very difficult for us to stay asleep. We got up shortly after and begin walking gain. We marched along the National Road and stopped at the destination town known as Kean Tmau. We claimed an open spot just several dozen yards from a flowing river. There were all sorts of small houses built by the river. Some had canoes anchored by a small pier. Children and adults were going about their business along the riverside. All the families that came with us claimed their spots nearby.

"Wait here. I will go find my friends that I knew from Lon Nol's time," Father said and took off.

After we settled our belongings, we walked straight to the river. I hadn't been close to the river since Stung Chah. We spent about two hours playing, dipping, and splashing in the water and then came up to shore and dried ourselves off in the afternoon sun.

Father returned with good news. He'd found several of his old friends still living in exactly the same houses as they were during Lon Nol's time. Most importantly, Pu Tuin offered Father and the families who'd come with us the materials to build a house, including metal plates for the roofs.

We slept out in the open for several nights until the house was built. Chhoeun built a separate house for his new wife, Huk, and her Mother. Chea was living with us.

Kean Tmau was as crowded as Ma Sin Buan Bao. More settlers were flooding in every day claiming any open spot, as they preferred to live by the water just like us. Within just a few weeks, the river had become polluted. Everyone was bathing, washing their clothes, and cleaning their dishes in the river. Garbage was floating on the water. It didn't bother us until we saw human feces floating nearby as we bathed along the shore.

Chhorn, Chhoy, and Chea wasted no time and started to trade. They used the same method of trading rice for fish from the wholesalers and then trade them immediately in the open market. They were lucky enough to make a little profit on their first try but stalled after the second and the third tries. Then they lost nearly a bag of rice. The harvest season had long past. The entire country was still in chaos, and no one had a chance to plant new rice yet. The existing rice was diminishing very quickly. No one was planning to trade rice for anything, especially for fish when everyone was living by the river. Most families caught their own fish.

After about four weeks of living in Kean Tmau, we'd eaten nearly half a bag of rice, and our family was unable to get any more rice at all. If we continued to live like this, our rice would be gone in a couple of months.

Chhoeun was catching fish but just enough to feed Huk and his Mother in-law. Since no one was willing to trade their rice for fish, he had no way of bringing the rice home. Besides, he had no experience in trading. Mother had been providing him and his new family with rice.

Chea had not been happy since Chhoeun got married. She had not mentioned anything to anyone, including Chhorn. She had been avoiding Chhoeun ever since. Chhorn was not the only one who knew about her feelings for Chhoeun. Mother had noticed that she was upset about Chhoeun's wedding since the engagement day. Chea was now around twenty years old. Normally, the Khmer women would have gotten married a few years ago.

Chea was feeding Poe rice porridge in a hot evening sun in front of our solid, metal roof house when Mother came over and sat down next to her.

"Chea, I have something to speak to you about. I have been thinking of you a lot. You are like my daughter. It is my responsibility to make sure you are taken care of. You are old enough to be wed. If you wait any longer, it might be difficult. It is important that you are married and have a husband to care for you. I ran into my old friend that I knew since Lon Nol named Mael. He was an important man back in Lon Nol's time. He had adopted a son who is now about your age. After I told him about you, he requested to engage you because he likes our family a lot. He will bring his son to have a formal engagement tomorrow. So be ready. If you are not satisfied with the man, you can refuse, but it is important that you are married," Mother explained thoroughly as if she had rehearsed her words.

Chea appeared shocked to hear such news. She looked at Mother, as if she was thinking of other things at the same time. She froze for a long moment after Mother finished speaking and then managed to say, "All right. I will get dressed up tomorrow."

Pu Mael and his adopted son arrived the next morning. The young man was dark and tall. Mother had summoned all the elders to prepare for the engagement. Pu Mael introduced his son to all the elders and praised him highly. He assured everyone that his son would take good care of Chea. The palm reader and the soothsayer examined the two and verified they were safe to be together.

As the elders continued chatting and planning the wedding, Mother pulled Chea aside and asked, "Are you satisfied? He isn't very attractive, but he's not ugly either. I think this is your opportunity. I have known Mael for a long time, and he was a very successful man. One day, he will regain his wealth again, and he might be able to help you in case you run into hardship in the future. They don't have much to offer now because it is a new beginning for everyone just like us." Mother paused for a moment, staring at Chea who was looking down at the ground, motionless.

"Then…are you satisfied?"

"Yes, I'm satisfied," Chea said softly.

"Then I will inform them and arrange the wedding," Mother said and returned to the elders and delivered the agreement from Chea.

Mother arranged the wedding the same week. The wedding was simple and short. The colorful garments for Chea and the groom to wear were rented for a cheap price from the local villagers. Several chickens were steamed as gifts to the spirits and the angels, along with bundles of incense sticks and candles. Chea and the groom sat before the cleric as he chanted and splashed the holy water. The wedding lasted about three hours. The normal Khmer wedding would last from morning until midnight.

Chea moved to live with her new husband right after the wedding. Chhorn and Chhoy were sad to see her leave. She had become so close to them like sisters. But Chea had never been the same after Chhoeun got married. She seemed to have been badly hurt. Chhorn was hoping that she would be happy with her husband.

Chea returned three days later with a bowl of rice porridge. She picked up Poe and placed him on her lap and then fed him the rice porridge. Pech and I sat next to her. We both missed her after not seeing her for three days. When Chea finished feeding Poe, she left without saying a word to anyone. We never saw Chea again ever since.

Chhoy and Chhorn continued to take risks and used the rice to trade for other product like fermented fish, anything that they thought that would be in the demand. They made very small to no profit. Sometimes, they lost half the rice they'd invested.

Father was very frustrated with this town. He spent most of his time fishing, but all the fish he caught were just enough to feed us. He had been speaking with his friends looking for an opportunity to drive a truck, but no such jobs existed yet. One night, the local village chief came to visit Father and his friends. The man informed everyone that this town would become even more crowded over time. He learned that there was a town call Kbal Kmouch (Skull) where most of the land was still available. The Vietnamese had just driven out all the Red Khmer. Many still feared to go claim the land. The man suggested taking a chance and going to claim the land before anyone else did. Father knew exactly where Kbal Kmouch was. He had been there several times during Lon Nol's time, transporting logs.

"Don't wait too long. Other people are probably on their way to claim the land as we speak," the man repeated.

Father talked with his friends the next day. He told them that he'd decided to take the risk. He didn't want to deal with farming, but there was nothing else to do here. We had moved around so many times. He wanted our own land where we could stay permanently. Most of his friends agreed to venture with him, including Tien's family, Pu Poo, Pu Yun, Solo's families, Um Muen, and Pu Sarin. Several other families were afraid of the Red Khmers and decided to stay.

We gathered our belongings and started to walk back to the west the next day. We used the same route that we'd taken to get here. According to the elders, Kbal Kmouch was located far to the west. There were a lot less people traveling nowadays. We were one of the few families traveling west. Most people were still heading east, toward Batam Bang. We traveled past the Ma Sin Buan Bao, Chamka Chake, and Mauan Haeu, the same path that we'd used to travel here. Since we were in no rush, we took our time traveling. The men knew exactly where they were going. We slept in places where we feel comfortable. There was no sign of the Red Khmer along the way. The rumor has it that the Red Khmer had been chased out deep into the woods.

We arrived in Kbal Kmouch on the third day. We cut through a small town and walked across a large open field and came to an abandoned warehouse sitting on the perimeter of the field. The solid building was sitting on an enormous concrete floor, stretching a few dozen yards further to the west. The wall of the building was made of hard material similar to the housing complex in Chamka Chake. The roof was made of metal plates. To the front left of the building was open grassland that stretched far into the horizon. The coconut trees were scattered everywhere. The vast and beautiful scenery took my breath away. I walked inside the building and was awed by the open space with high ceilings supported by giant columns and thick beams. The room was nice and cool by the shade. Father chose a spot by the wall. Our family placed all our belonging in the corner and begin wondering around. After all the families picked their spots, there were still more space left in the building.

Tien, Pech, Pheah, and I ran to the front of the building looking for something interesting to do. The area to the right of the building was covered with thick trees and shrubs. There was a large path that could lead to another town. About half a mile behind the building were houses scattered randomly on the field and among the trees. Some of them seemed to be abandoned. Some had cattle grazing nearby. A small figure of a man and a woman could be seen working around their house.

We walked further down and came to an open path. We saw some type of road with thick lines of metallic bar rested on the neatly arranged wood planks that ran as far we could see from one end to the other. Beneath the wood planks were millions of small rocks. I had never seen any road that looked like this before. What type of wagon would use this type of road? Maybe it was for the water buffalo wagon, I thought to myself. Then, all of the sudden, I heard a loud sound that that no human or oxen could produce. The sound got louder and louder every second. Then the sound of the whistle shot out from the same source. Tien, Pech, and Pheah looked at one another nervously. I wanted to run, but I was curious to see what was coming. I stood still, half wanting to flee but half wanting to witness what was to come. Tien, Pech, and Phear were standing right beside me. Whatever it was, I knew that it was using the strange looking metal bar as its path. Then I have just realized that we were standing too close to the path.

"Get back! You might get run over!" Pheah shouted. All of us scrambled away from the strange road. Whatever was coming, we would not want to be in its way.

As the humming sound got louder, the ground started to vibrate. The whistle blew louder and clearer. Then all four of us dropped our jaws, staring at a monster that we had talked about in Stung Chah call *Ah Teah Plung* (The Fire Wagon[train]). The head of the monster emerged from the distance. Its front teeth were as big as the nearby trees. Its head was larger than anything that I had seen in my life, except for the mountain. Black fumes thrust out from a large pipe, creating a long trail of thick, black smoke.

"The monster is coming this way!" I screamed as if this were my last day to live. Tien, Pech, Pheah, and I dashed as fast as our feet could move toward our house, hoping the adults could protect us from this monster. None of us seemed to care how the others were doing besides trying not to trip and fall.

We reached the building and found the adults were standing staring at the monster passing by. We took cover behind the adults and watched.

"That's a train," one of the adults said out loud.

"They're probably transporting logs," another one said.

Conversation among the adults erupted about this train. We learned that trains were powered by engines that could haul hundreds of attached cargo and travel across the country. It amazed me how the train could move without using a single ox.

It took a long time to see the end of the train. I wished it could go on forever. I was in awe. The thought of the engine stuck in my mind long after the train had left. I tried to imagine what could make an engine move but could not come up with anything. My friends at Stung Chah had mentioned that magic could make a lot of things move. I believed that only magic could make an engine so powerful.

We stood still hoping another train would come by, but it never did. I was now calm and relaxed. All the adults returned inside the building to set up their spots. I spent the rest of the evening observing the area with Tien, Pech, and Pheah.

CHAPTER 30

After a few days living in Kbal Kmouch, Mother and all the women trekked around the town seeking someone to speak to about claiming the available land. Unfortunately, every square inch of the land had already been taken. We were fortunate that no one wanted to claim the current warehouse that we were living in. Some said there were too many gruesome incidents in the warehouse that they wanted to forget and decided not to deal with it. That was very disappointing news. We'd travelled nearly three days just to all live under one roof. Father and the men were scrambling for ways to find food. One of the men discovered a large pond called Bung Chhook (Lotus Pond). The local residents had seen the fish in the pond, but no one had attempt to put any effort into catching the fish. Most of them were still recovering from the Red Khmer ordeal.

The next morning, nearly every single one of us flocked to the pond. Father, Chhoeun, and Pu E brought the fish nets with them. The walk to the pond was less than two hours from our building. The pond spread widely across the open field. There was a large island that stood just above the water. The other end of the pond was connected to a small stream of water flowing somewhere from the distant mountains. All sorts of plants were seen floating on the pond. The most noticeable ones were the giant green plants with leaves surrounding the flower as if someone had decorated the water.

"Those are lotus!" Chhom yelled out in excitement.

Everyone descended into the pond and started picking the lotus. Chhorn carried me down into the water. I grabbed one of the lotus plants and examined it. I had seen them before in Stung Chah, but they vanished after everyone knew that they were edible.

"Peel it like this," Chhorn said. She picked one with its flower fallen off and split the lotus in half.

Then she picked several seeds out of the lotus and ate them. I tried to do the same but was unable to get the seeds out. I gave up after the first attempt and decided to play in the water instead. I splashed the water to anyone that came nearby. The other children were doing the same.

We stayed in the pond until midafternoon. Father, Chhoeun, and Pu E somehow made their way to the small island right in the middle of the pond. They were setting up the fish net. The rest of us returned home for the day. The men returned home the next morning with three buckets of fish. Everyone was surprised to learn that that was so much fish in the pond. Father and his friends decided to take fishing more seriously. Since all the land was taken, they decided to catch the fish and trade for rice to make a living instead. Father traded a large bag of rice for a fish net. The rest of the men decided to do the same. Many families did not have as much rice as us. They used most of their rice to trade for the fish nets.

The men returned to the pond and prepared to catch fish. Chhoeun and Pu E were younger and more energetic, so they worked together draining a small pond using buckets and catching fish by hand. Father found an abandoned boat near the pond and used it to get to the small island. He began to build a small shack just above the water that could fit only one person where he could lie down and monitor the net.

The next morning, Father, Chhoeun, Pu E, and the men returned home with a dozen baskets of fish. The adults split the fish and threw away anything that was not edible. The other children and I collected the blowfish and used them to play with.

Mother roasted some of the fish for us to eat with rice. Chhorn, Chhoy, and Huk took the rest of the fish to sell in the open market. Unfortunately, they returned home without a single trade. People were not willing to give up their rice for fish. Like everywhere else, the rice was scarce. The rice planting season had already passed. No one had gotten a chance to plow and spread the rice seeds, as this part of the town was still under the control of the Red Khmer not too long ago.

Father, Chhoeun, and the men continued to catch fish. Sometimes, Father and Chhoeun brought home many different types of water-dwelling snakes along with the fish. Chhorn, Chhoy, and Huk made some more attempts to trade the fish for rice, but they had no luck. They finally gave up trading and decided to keep and eat the fish instead.

After about six weeks, the rain subsided. The fish become scarce very quickly. We had less and less fish to eat. Mother was being very cautious not to cook too much rice. If we didn't get any more rice soon, we would begin to starve again. Father and the men decided to travel and look for rice using the two wagons. They drove many kilometers searching for an abandoned storage house. They came across a small rice field located further west. It must have once belonged to the Red Khmer. It appeared unattended and abandoned. The men had simply cut the entire rice stems and brought them home because they didn't have enough time and skill like the women to separate the rice from the stems. The rice stems took most of the space on the wagon. When they got home, the women did their work to separate the rice from the stem and grind and filter the kernels from the husks. A lot of work resulted in only about two baskets of rice for the entire six families.

The men returned to look for more rice, but they had to travel twice the distance and ended up having to spend a night. Each trip took longer than the previous. Sometimes, they came home empty-handed. After returning home empty-handed twice in the row, the men sat down and discussed their next plan. One of the men suggested checking with the owner of the land to see if they could make any deal to use the land. All the lands in the area were empty and untouched. After speaking with several owners, many had offered to share the land under a simple agreement. We could use their land to grow rice. We could use their oxen and plow to plow the soil. We were also responsible to do the rest of the work. After the harvest, they would get half of the rice. Father and his friends agreed. Unfortunately, we only had the rice kernels that were for consuming. We needed the seeds for planting. Mother and the women found many villagers that were willing to trade two bags of ground rice for a bag of rice seeds for planting. Father and Mother traded two bags of kernel rice for a bag of rice seeds. That was our last two full bags of rice that we had left. Father and Mother were hoping we could find more rice in the meantime. The rest of the family contributed as much as they could to get more seeds.

Chhoeun started to plow using the oxen and the plow equipment provided by the land owner. He was more skilled with plowing than the rest of the men. He finished plowing and spreading the rice just after four days. It would take a few months before the next process of rice plantation.

In his spare time, Chhoeun went and chatted with the local villagers. He came across and spoke with the family of the village mayor, and they had offered him a job. His job was to load and transport logs to different villages. He got paid one can of rice a day, just enough to feed his wife, Huk, and his mother in-law. It was hard work for very little rice, but he had no other choice.

Mother began to panic when we started running out of rice. Father had brought home a few fish. We begin to eat just fish with a little rice porridge. I was feeling hungry almost like I was in Stung Chah again. Mother had been walking all over the village speaking with the villagers looking for any opportunity to get more rice. She'd had no luck until today. She came across a frail elder man about fifty years of age, sitting and rotating the rice grinder with a lot of effort.

Mother stopped and spoke to him. "Greetings, Pu. How come you don't let your children grind the rice for you? At your age, I would have my children do the hard work."

"All my children are dead. It's just me and my wife living here. If I don't do this, I will be dead as well," the elder man said.

"Why don't you hire a youth to do it for you? I'm sure there are plenty of them out there?" Mother asked, anticipating an opportunity.

"I know there are plenty of youth looking for work, but I cannot afford to pay them. The rice I'm harvesting is just enough for me to survive until the next harvest season. Every can of rice is important for me," the man explained.

"I have two hard-working daughters. They can work for you for free. All I request is the rice dust that you are throwing away over there," Mother said pointing to a pile of rice husk and dust.

When the rice was ground and filtered, it left behind husks and rice kernal. The rice husks were the shell of the rice, and they were not edible. However, the rice dust was made up of the loose tips of the rice that were edible but did not taste good. They tasted almost like the husk itself.

"If that is all you want, they can come and work for me. When can they start?"

"They will come today. I will head back home and tell them to come," Mother said.

"Then, let them come today," the man said.

"I'm leaving and will tell my daughters. Can I ask for your name, so my daughters can find you?"

"They called me Ta Knok," the man replied.

Mother came back home and explained to Chhorn and Chhoy about their new job. First, they got excited about having a job, but they were disappointed to learn that they would be working for free. Chhorn and Chhoy went to work that same day. The man worked beside them keeping a close eye on them to make sure they didn't steal any rice.

They stopped grinding just before sunset. Then they used the woven filtering tray to separate the husks and the rice dust. Chhorn and Chhoy spent the rest of the evening tossing and shaking the husk, filtering the rice dust. They brought home about one can of rice dust in their pocket.

Mother took the rice dust and mixed it them with water to make a dough. It was the only way to make the rice dust edible. In the Lon Nol's time, the Khmer had used the rice dust dough to feed the pigs. When we were living in Stung Chah, Mother and the villagers become very creative in making food from rice dust. Mother wrapped the dough in banana leaves and steamed it. She gave most of the dough to Chhom, Pech, Poe, me, and Tien's mom. Whatever was left was for Chhorn and Chhoy. They normally got a smaller share, as Mother believed the rest of us were more vulnerable to hunger and needed to eat more.

On the fourth morning, Chhoy and Chhorn woke up and got ready to work. On the way there, Chhoy was walking slowly behind Chhorn. Then she stopped walking when they were about halfway to work.

"Why are you standing still?" Chhorn shouted.

"I don't want to go," Chhoy said, staring down at the ground.

"You have to go. Mother told us to come. We need to get the rice dust to feed our family," Chhorn said.

"I don't care. I only get to eat a bite anyway,"

"Mother will spank you if you don't come with me. Here, hold one tray," Chhorn said handing the woven tray to Chhoy.

Chhoy thought it over and took the tray and reluctantly continued to walk after Chhorn. Her head was looking somewhere else and not on the road.

After a while of walking in silence, Chhorn turned around and looked at Chhoy, only to find her hands were empty.

"Where is the tray?" Chhorn asked.

"I don't know. I think I threw it away,"

"Where did you throw it?"

"I don't know," Chhoy said avoiding Chhorn's face.

With frustration, Chhorn returned to where they'd come from. Chhoy followed slowly behind. After nearly fifteen minutes, she found the tray lying on the road. She picked up the tray and held both of the trays.

"You lazy girl!" Chhorn shouted.

"You are the lazy one," Chhoy replied.

Chhorn continued to scold her as they walk. Chhoy responded by mocking Chhorn, but she kept her distance behind Chhorn looking down or away, avoiding any eye contact.

They arrived at Ta Knok's house later than usual. There was only one grinder. Chhorn and Chhoy would take turns grinding rice. Chhorn knew well not to ask Chhoy to start first, knowing she wouldn't do it.

"Those bags of rice over there need to be ground. You can grind as much as you want, and then the rice dust will be yours," Ta Knok reminded them, pointing to a dozen rice bags. Each bag contained about a hundred kilograms of rice, waiting to be ground.

Chhorn untied the bag and scooped the rice with a small woven basket and poured the rice in the stone grinder. She grabbed the handle of the grinder and began to rotate. The stone grinder must have weighed at least a thousand kilos. It was designed for healthy and strong adults and not frail and hungry youth. The circular motion of the grinder caused the rice to roll around, and the husks became loose and eventually separated completely from the husks.

After about an hour, Chhorn was too tired to continue so she stopped. She turned and looked at Chhoy, hoping she would understand and walk up and replace her. Instead, Chhoy squatted on the ground watching anything that captured her attention.

"Chhoy, it's your turn," Chhorn said.

"I'm not doing it," Chhoy replied.

"I'm tired, and I can't go on. I need a rest," Chhorn pleaded.

"I'm not going to work for free," Chhoy said firmly.

"We are not working for free. We get to keep the rice dust,"

"I don't get to eat it anyway,"

"But it's for our family,"

"I'm not doing it," Chhoy repeated.

"I'm going to tell Mother that you were not helping," Chhorn said trying to control her voice so Tak Knok and his wife would not hear what she said. Ta Knok and his wife were sitting a dozen yards away, tossing the ground rice in the air to separate the loose husks and dust from the rice kernels.

"Go ahead and tell,"

Chhorn gave up trying to persuade Chhoy to help and continued to grind some more rice. She rotated the grinder slower than before because she was too tired. She was angry and wanted to cry, but she was afraid she might lose this job and all of us would starve to death.

Chhorn continue to ask Chhoy to grind the rice after she finished each batch. Surprisingly, Chhoy got up and ground the rice on the last batch. As Chhoy was grinding the rice, Chhorn start to filter the rice dust from the husks as Ta Knok and his wife were filtering the rice kernels. The elder couple was doing the easiest part of job.

After Chhoy finished grinding the last batch, she came and helped filter the rice dust. She knew that the faster she worked, the sooner she got to go home. They finished filtering the rice dust shortly after midday. Chhorn transferred the rice dust from a tray to a small woven basket that she'd brought with her and returned home after.

When they arrived, Mother had cooked fish and was waiting for them to come and eat. We all sat and eat together. There were several catfish and snakehead fish on the plates. There were several pieces of the cooked rice dust dough on the other plate, but there was no rice.

"We have no more rice to eat. We have one can left that I want to save for Poe. We'll have to eat rice dust with fish from now on," Mother explained.

We all sat in circle. Mother gave Poe, Pech, Chhom, and I one piece of dough. She gave half to Chhorn and half to Chhoy.

"You are older and able to take care of yourself. You can eat more fish. Your younger ones need to eat more rice dust," Mother explained.

Chhorn and Chhoy took the dough without any sign of disappointment. Chhoy was not happy. We all looked at Father who had almost finished one whole fish all by himself. He didn't seem to care for any dough. Mother split and distributed the fish to all of us. Chhorn and Chhoy got bigger pieces, and the rest of us got the smaller pieces because we got more dough.

"I walked around the village today, and I noticed many people were butchering cows and oxen for meat. If we had any rice, I would let you trade the meat. Now we don't even have a single can of rice. If we don't get any rice soon, we will die of starvation," Mother said.

"This place is empty of everything. We drove three days just to get one squash for each family. And I would be lucky if I caught more than four fish," Father added.

I had been very hungry all day. I picked the fish meat off the bone and made sure no meat was seen anywhere on the bones. When I finished picking the meat, I sucked the bones to get any flavor of the bones. I felt like we're back in Stung Chah all over again.

"Where did you find the house that butchered the cows?" Chhorn asked.

"You can walk the same way to the market. Several houses along the way, you can see the beef hanging on the ropes everywhere," Mother explained.

While every single one of us were busy getting all the flesh of the fish bones, Chhorn got up without saying a word and walked out of the building and turned toward the market.

She arrived at the market after a long walk and began searching for the butcher's house. She walked past a dozen houses and then saw men and women working on cutting up the beef. An elder woman who seemed to be the boss of everyone was stacking a meat on a table and caught her attention.

"Ming, I would like trade rice for the meat as a wholesale. I want to take the meat and trade them in the market. How much do you want for this piece right here?" Chhorn pointed to a beef chunk about five kilograms that lay on top of the others

"That was worth two cans of rice wholesale. If I would to sell in the market, I would take about four cans...maybe more," the women said nicely.

"I beg to reduce to one and a half cans, as I'm afraid the price of the meat just went down. Everyone knows that beef are abundant nowadays."

"Then one and a half cans are fine," the women said.

The woman wrapped the beef with banana leaves and handed it to Chhorn. Chhorn couldn't help smiling as she'd already made an extra half can of rice if she could sell the meat.

"I didn't bring the rice with me, as I didn't know how much I would need to carry with me. I will give you the rice on the way back," Chhorn spoke politely with high confidence.

"That's fine," the woman said while she rushed to deal with other customers.

Chhorn was thrilled that the woman had agreed. She carried the beef and ran directly to the market hoping to sell the beef for profit. She arrived in the open market where hundreds of buyers and traders congregated. The traders were sitting on two sides. In the middle was an aisle where the buyers walked between the two rows of traders looking for products. Chhorn was planning to wholesale the beef as she had to pay the woman back on the way home. Normally, the traders would sit and wait for the customers to come to them. Chhorn needed to sell the beef quickly and did not have time to sit and wait. Instead, she walked around looking for people who were interested in buying and reselling the beef. She also pretended to ask other beef sellers for their price, so she could get a better idea of how much her beef would cost. Chhorn struck a deal with the second women she approached for three cans of rice. The market value of the beef was six cans of rice. Chhorn did not want to take a risk to seek a better deal, as Mother did not have any rice left at home. If she didn't bring home rice, we would have nothing to eat tomorrow.

Chhorn returned home after she'd paid the woman one and a half cans of rice and brought home one and a half cans of rice. She was a little disappointed for not being able to bargain for more rice, but after thinking it over, having nothing to gaining one and a half cans of rice was incredible.

Chhorn handed Mother the bulging banana leave, neatly wrapped. She looked at Mother and smiled. "You will like what's in there."

Mother opened the wrap and smile. "Where did you get this?"

"I traded beef," Chhorn said.

"With what?"

"With rice," Chhorn said.

"But you didn't have any rice."

"Your daughter has been trading since nine," Chhorn referred to herself. "I don't need the actual rice to trade," Chhorn said proudly.

"Tomorrow, your younger ones will have rice to eat, especially Poe. He gets sick very fast after eating very little rice," Mother said.

It was easy to see that Mother was extremely happy. She couldn't help but smile when she stared at the rice in the banana leaf.

As usual, Mother gave half a can of rice to Tien's family. Tien's mom had delivered a baby named Van Sok about a year ago, shortly before we were forced to move out of Stung. Van Sok was now very ill. It was unfortunate that they didn't have an older brother and sister like us. Tien's mom had been working very hard for her children's survival.

At nightfall, Mother made rice porridge using about two tablespoons for Poe. The rest of us ate fish and rice dust dough.

The next morning, Chhorn and Chhoy woke up and walked to Ta Knok's house and grinded the rice as usual. Chhorn was able convince Chhoy to help more and finish grinding the rice and filtering the rice dust. Chhoy did a little more than the previous day.

They returned home late in the afternoon but much earlier than usual. Mother made rice porridge using a quarter of a can of rice. She mixed it with the vegetable that Chhom picked from the pond. Mother saved the rice dust dough that Chhorn and Chhoy brought today for another day. She also roasted two large catfish that Father had brought home. She did not split the fish into shares, as it was too difficult.

"Leave the head part for me," Father said when Mother placed the plate on the floor.

"Whoever wants to learn how to swim, you should eat the tail. Fish use their tails to swim," Mother said, using the same trick every time we had a limited amount of fish.

"I want the tip of the tail," I said.

"No, I want the tip of the tail." Pech cried out loud.

Chhorn, Chhoy, and Chhom chuckled.

"Since Bun is older than you, he gets the tail. Since Pech is younger, he gets the upper part of the tail," Chhorn said as she broke the tail part and placed it on my plate and the upper part of the tail onto Pech's plate.

Pech and I had always wanted to know how to swim. Whenever we were brought to the pond, Chhorn or Chhoy had to carry us into the water. I could only have fun splashing the water with my hands. I would have much more fun if I knew how to swim. If I knew how, I would swim to Father in the middle of the pond and help him untangle the fish myself.

Chhorn finished her plate before everyone else. She picked up a scarf, swung in around her neck, and left.

"Where is Chhorn going?" Father asked softly.

"She's going to trade. She brought home rice last night from trading. She's going to try again without using any rice to start. She's clever," Mother said proudly.

"Very well," Father said with a big smile.

After we ate our meal, I didn't wait long and went outside immediately. It was getting dark. Tien and Phear were outside playing on the large cement floor. I noticed Chhoeun was talking to a man with a rifle in his hand. The man was several years older than him. He was known as a guard. He had spent most of his time standing on the concrete floor outside of our shelter guarding our building. I didn't quite understand who he was trying to protect us from.

I walked closer to the guard as he spoke with Chhoeun demonstrating how he would shoot. I got curious and stood between them and listened to their conversation. The two of them were exchanging stories about when they were in the military back in Lon Nol's time. They were exchanging their experience with different types of rifles.

I stood and stared at every single detail of the rifle and everything else the guard had hanging around his shoulders and waist. The guard had a belt of bullets strapped from his shoulder to his waist.

The guard noticed I was intrigued with his weapons. He stooped down and said, "Do you want to hold the rifle?"

"That's my little brother," Chhoeun said.

"Here, hold it and point it that way," the guard said and placed the rifle in my arms. The weight of the rifle yanked my entire body down. I nearly dropped the rifle. I have never thought it would be that heavy. I tightened my grip so that I wouldn't drop the rifle. I had longed to shoot a rifle since the day I saw the Vietnamese soldiers carrying them. I was excited and terrified at the same time. I was holding something that was fun but also dangerous.

"Do you want to shoot?" the guard asked.

My heart was pounding with excitement. If I said yes, I would experience shooting a rifle. I could spend the rest of my life bragging to my friends about it.

"No." For some reason, I decided to say no. I handed the rifle back to the guard feeling disappointed but glad at the same time.

"You were scared, right?" the guard asked and accepted the rifle back.

I didn't care what he thought. Instead, I left Chhoeun and the guard and walked to the area where Father was sitting in the shade speaking with Pu E. I sat next to Father hoping to hear interesting stories. He was in the middle of telling his stories about one of his trips hunting and fishing. He explained how he'd encountered large pythons and cobras in the middle of their battle. He explained how he caught them without getting bitten. Then he explained how he prepared and cooked the meat. I got hungry from listening to his story.

From the horizon, a flock of birds were flying low, just the height of the tree, with a great speed. They tweeted something that sounded like the word "Ka De Vech" very loudly. Every single one of the adults stared the birds as they approached until they flew over and past the rooftop of our building.

"We are in trouble," Father said. "The Ka De Vech have just flown over our town. There will be war coming. These birds are rare, but they bring a curse to any town they fly by," Father said in despair as if he was absolutely sure that the war was really coming again.

"True. When the war between Lon Nol and the Red Khmer started, the birds flew across our city every night. The elders knew about the curse, but I didn't believe them. Now I believe them," Pu E said.

Mother frantically emerged from inside the warehouse, holding Poe on her forearm.

"Was that the Ka De Vech? Those birds flew right across our home. These birds are extremely cursed. There will be death in the area. I have seen this happen many times before," Mother said with her face turned as white as a ghost. She went back inside the warehouse informing everyone about the birds, explaining how cursed they were.

Father and Pu E switched their stories to the time before the Red Khmer took over. Even though they had spent a lot of time driving together, there were times when they separated doing different tasks for Lon Nol. Each had had hair-raising experiences that they never got to share.

I sat on the concrete wall listening to every detail. The night breeze swept by, making me feel relaxed but also worried about the coming war that Father had mentioned. My eyelids were getting heavier and heavier. I tried to fight to stay awake and listen to Father's and Pu E's stories, but I couldn't fight the sleepiness and fell asleep.

CHAPTER 31

Chhoeun was loading the trimmed logs with his coworker onto the ox wagon under the heat of the dry season. He called his coworker by "Pu." The man stood a little taller than Chhoeun, and he didn't talk much. Many people that he'd met so far had similar characteristics. Everyone escaped the Red Khmer with the horrific memories. It wouldn't be surprising if some or all of his family was dead. Chhoeun didn't even know what his name was. It didn't matter though. His coworker was much older than him, and so he had to call him "Pu" all the time.

"This is such hard work for a can of rice," the man said.

"True. It's not even noon yet, and my gut is churning for food. I wish we could find abandoned rice storage or an abandoned farm where we could just collect food. One day of scavenging could last us up to three months," Chhoeun said.

"Since you said that, I heard a rumor from the mayor and his sons that the Vietnamese were planning to invade Prey Tum (Big Forest) in two days. That area is still infested with the Red Khmer. You will see Red Khmer flee like animals. I used to scavenge food like you. My family lived off many bags of rice until we made bad trades and lost most of our rice. We should have not gotten involved in trading. I don't know where to go look for food, and I'm scared to go far. I'm afraid the Red Khmer would kill me.

Many people will scavenge after this invasion. The raid will start at eight in the morning. The first to get there will be the lucky ones. Wait and see, the Red Khmer will flee like animals," the man said.

Chhoeun continued to exchange stories of how he used to find food to survive during the Vietnamese invasion. He tried to avoid talking about the Red Khmer regime. It was still too fresh and too painful to think about.

Chhoeun finished his work early and came home before sunset. Instead of checking in with his wife, he walked straight to Father with all his friends sitting around on a concrete floor in front of the building. The men had just returned from a trip yesterday, and they did not have any other plans yet. It was their normal routine to gather at a certain spot on the concrete floor and chat.

Chhoeun noticed that something was wrong with Father. He was sitting with his right leg extended. His lower leg appeared to be swollen. Father used his right hand to rub and squeeze his foot as he listened to his friend speak.

"Chhoeun, you came so early today," Pu Yun said.

"I have good news," Chhoeun said trying to hold his excitement. "My coworker told me there will be a raid at Prey Tum in two days. The raid will start at eight in the morning."

All the men stopped talking and paid close attention to Chhoeun. "If that's true, I know where Prey Tum is. There's a village called Pdahk, where people planted all types of vegetables. It's further that way. In Lon Nol's time, I used to drive my truck up there many times," Pu Yun said pointing somewhere to the west.

"That was the direction where all the Red Khmer had fled to. Maybe that's where they were rebuilding their forces. They can't go up further than that because that's the Thai border," Pu Poo said.

"We should stay behind the Vietnamese soldiers to be safe," Chhoeun said.

"The path that we will be traveling will be longer because it's the wagon road. There is no wagon road if we follow the Vietnamese soldiers. We will have to walk. That was not our plan. We should be the first to get there. If we are too slow, then all the food will be taken. It doesn't take long for people to pick and toss vegetables onto a wagon. There will be a lot of people ready for this opportunity. Nowadays, food is scarce," Pu Sarin said.

"As we already knew, it is impossible to find an abandoned farm or storage house nowadays. Everyone has been scavenging food just like us. I want to go too, but my foot hurts for no apparent reason," Father said.

"You can still go Bong Chhay. You don't need to move. Just sit on the wagon, and we will do everything. It's not fun without you," Pu Yun said.

"Then, I will go. I will be bored sitting at home doing nothing," Father said

"It will be great if you go. You will cook on the spot. My saliva squirts in my mouth just thinking of your cooking," Pu Sarin said.

"We should prepare our oxen and wagons and leave tomorrow before noon. If we follow the others, we won't get much. We want to be the first ones there. I know another way to get there. Instead of traveling from the south of Prey Tum, we should begin from the north. Besides, I don't know any wagon path that would lead directly from the south to Prey Tum from here. I know a place in the north where we can stay overnight. When the raid is over, we will move in before anyone else," Pu Yun explained.

Chhoeun sat down and chatted with the men until nightfall. They enjoyed the conversation, and no one was in hurry to go to bed. As night drifted further, the mosquitoes swamped the area forcing the men to leave the conversation and go to sleep.

Chhoeun and Father woke up a little after the sunrise. Chhoeun was packing pots and plates for Father and himself. Father was folding the mosquito net and coiling the cowhide ropes that he'd found from the last trip.

"Is your leg any better?" Mother asked. Mother had gotten up very early as usual.

"My leg is still in pain and swollen," Father replied.

"Then why are you going? You will not be able to walk. It might get worse. We still don't know what's wrong with your leg yet. Maybe you got punctured by some poisonous thorns," Mother spoke loudly.

"I can walk a little. I will not have to do anything. I will just sit in the wagon. Everyone else will do everything for me. Right now, we have nothing to eat. We are relying on the fish in a small lake. We are in the middle of a hot season. Soon, the lake will become dry. All of us will starve to death," Father explained.

"The Ka De Vech flew right on top of our house. Someone in this building will die, and you still want to go?" Mother scolded.

"You shouldn't say that. Our mouths are salty. Things we say might come true. Besides, I have already told them that I'm going," Father said.

"Just tell them you can't walk at all! Tell them you can't go!" Mother said even louder.

"Then I will stay home since Chhoeun is going. We'll still get a share," Father said reluctantly.

Even though Father was the tallest and biggest man in the village, Mother seemed to overpower him. Mother walked outside toward the men that were prepping for the trip. There were two wagons with a pair of oxen each. The men were tossing the tools and supplies on the wagon. Pu Poo was giving the oxen a bucket of water. Mother informed the men that Father was not going because of his injured foot. The men were disappointed to hear the bad news, but they respected Mother and did not insist.

Just when Mother was heading back inside, Tien's mom came out. "My husband cannot make it. He woke up shaking like a little baby. If you guys get anything, please share them with me," she yelled out.

"Yes, we will give you a share," one of the men replied out loud.

"Don't worry, Tien's mom. Chhoeun is going with them. I will make sure you get your share," Mother said.

Under the clear sky, the morning dew glazed over grasses and shrubs. Chhoeun and the men started their trip, moving along the wagon path that had not been used by anyone else except our families. Pu Yun decided to walk, and he was leading the way. Um Meun was driving the first wagon. Chhoeun was walking behind the first wagon. Pu Sarin was driving the second wagon. He was sitting with another man. Pu Poo was walking behind the second wagon.

Chhoeun decided to walk instead of driving the wagon. He had cut himself a fresh guiding shaft from a tree branch. He liked to hold a shaft when he walked to protect himself from snakes or to probe unknown objects.

He normally operated the ox wagon, as he was more skilled with oxen than everyone else. He had been herding oxen since he was five. Chhoeun was the youngest of all. He was still a little boy compared to the men who were all around Father's age.

The six men appeared ready and happy to start a new trip again. If Father and Pu E were here, the two would be riding together in one wagon. The men were disappointed that they were not coming. Father was not the eldest, but he normally led the group in all the trips. He normally made all the decisions and resolved any issues that they came across. Like Chhoeun, Father had grown up independent of his parents. He had been out working in the fields alone since he was very young.

Choeun has the characteristics that could almost fill the absence of Father. He was young but experienced with many aspects of traveling and survival. He didn't lead the group, but he would give good suggestions. He had escaped death many times during the Red Khmer.

It was about midafternoon. Chhoeun and the men stopped a couple of times to rest and to search for abandoned farms. They had found nothing so far. They brought two buckets of water, one bucket on each wagon. None of the men had anything to eat all morning, possibly since yesterday for most.

They were approaching a small village. The villagers were going about their business. Chhoeun noticed the villagers were still wearing all black with the red and white scarf around their waste. Some had the scarf wrapped around their head as if they were still in the Red Khmer regime. None of them appeared to take notice of Chhoeun and the men.

Pu Yun turned around and said out loud. "This place was called Padak. I have been here before. The villagers here were friendly and hard workers."

They strolled past the village moments later. The daylight became dimmer as the sun was about to set. They came across a farm full of vegetables of all sorts, including cabbage, sugar cane, corn, and squash.

Pu Yun stopped and said. "This farm might not have an owner. It's too distant from the village." Pu Yun said.

Both the wagons stopped, and all the men looked around examining the vegetables.

"These look abandoned," Um Muen said and pulled a large cabbage off the ground.

Pu Poo and Chhoeun picked a small red tomato that grew along the road and popped it in their mouths.

"This tomato is sweet. I haven't had anything to eat since last night. This is perfect," Chhoeun said and continued picking and eating the tomatoes.

Pu Yun was holding the sugar cane, peeling off the bark with his teeth. "We should sleep here tonight after we finish picking the vegetables," he said.

"I'm going to eat until my stomach is full," Um Muen said.

Chhoeun split a watermelon open with was axe and sliced one half into smaller pieces, and then he buried his face in the other half. The watermelon was fulfilling his hunger and quenching his thirst at the same time.

"Whoever wants watermelon, it's over here," he hollered.

"I'm full from the sweet potatoes. I just plucked them off the dirt like they had no roots," Pu Poo said.

Chhoeun ate until he could not take another bite. Then he started to pluck the cabbages off the ground and toss them into the wagon. The other men tethered the oxen, and they began to chop and pick other produce and toss them into the wagon. The men harvested the produce until it was too dark to see. Chhoeun set up two mosquito nets using the two wagons to sustain them. Each mosquito net could accommodate three men. The moonless night was warm but pitch black. They were too exhausted to make a fire.

"Did anyone notice there were a lot of roosters crowing earlier? They were so close to us. You think this farm belongs to someone?" Pu Sarin said.

"The roosters might have become wild without owners. The same with the hens; they must reproduce at their own will," Um Muen said.

From their exhaustion and full stomachs, no one was paying any attention to any danger. They fell asleep like they were under a spell.

Chhoeun woke up from the glare of the morning light. By now he had learned to ignore the crow of the roosters. There was no need to wake up early anymore.

"Let's get moving. We should not be late. Other people might be ahead of us," Pu Sarin said as he was eating a watermelon.

Chhoeun untied and folded the mosquito net and placed it back neatly on the wagon. He grabbed a cucumber from the wagon and ate it. Then he grabbed a sugar cane and begins peeling the leaves off. He uses his axe to slash off any rough clumps and then he used his teeth to peel the bark.

"A bowl of rice would be nice," Chhoeun said.

"When we get there, we will get a lot of rice," Um Muen said.

The men strapped the hauling traces onto the oxen and began to move. Pu Yun was leading the group on foot. Chhoeun walk about fifty yards between the first and the second wagon. Like the rest of the men, he scanned the area looking for any sign of abandoned rice. The road was straight and large enough to fit two wagons traveling opposite directions. A canopy of trees stooped over the road, giving a lot of shade.

The monkeys screeched and echoed throughout the forest. The squealing wagon and the men's footsteps caused the birds to stir and fly off. The morning became warm very quickly. In the distance, the road was gradually arcing to the left, curving its way around the sugar cane farm.

Suddenly, one of the oxen on the first wagon halted and made an eerie hiss. It jerked its head up and refused to take another step.

"What's wrong you with you? Keep moving!" Um Meun said and whipped the ox.

They followed the arc of the road to an open field with a small shack made for farmers to monitor their farms. The haystacks were lying randomly in front and around the shack. The road was slowly curving back to the right making a half circle. Chhoeun was examining the sugarcane farm as he walked. It was hard to tell if the sugar cane farm was abandoned or not, as the cane stalks didn't need much care.

All of a sudden, Chhoeun heard a loud voice coming from the first wagon, "Who is that? Are you one of us? Do you have any weapons on you?"

Chhoeun ran back to warn the men behind him, but it was too late. He saw a man with a gun pointed at Pu Sarin and the other man who sat next to him on the wagon.

"Don't be afraid. We're on the same side. How many of you are here?" the gunman asked out loud.

"There are five of us!" Pu Sarin yelled out loud.

Chhoeun understood the hint immediately. There were six people, including Chhoeun himself. Chhoeun stopped and dove into a small cluster of brush. The thorny branches whipped his face and body as he landed on the muddy ground. The cuts from the thorns began to sting immediately. Only the sticky thorn could do that. He curled his body as tight as possible. He wished he could have hidden in a better spot. The brush was out in the open surrounded by just a few Katreang Kaet shrubs. He began to pull the nearby branches to help cover his body. Then he scooped a handful of mud and began to smear it onto his hands, his feet, and his face. There was not a single tall tree to help cover him. He squeezed his body tighter, unsure if his feet were hidden or exposed. It was too late to run into the sugar cane farm. The armed men probably had begun the search right now.

He peeked between the thorny bushes and saw more armed men. They were definitely the Red Khmer. Every single one of them was wearing all black with the scarf strapped around their waist. They were questioning Pu Sarin. Chhoeun could not see the rest of the men.

"Why were you here?"

Pu Sarin was shaking violently and answered, "I'm sorry, I didn't know you were here, or else I wouldn't have come. We were just traveling looking for food."

Chhoeun begins to pray quietly, "I beg God and the spirit of the land and the spirit of the water and the spirit of all the ancestors, please do not let them see me. I'm begging you not to let them see me."

Chhoeun repeated his prayer over and over again. There was no way the small shrubs could cover him. He curled his body tighter and tighter every time he thought of being seen.

"I thought I heard a sound over there," one of them said and began to walk toward Chhoeun.

Chhoeun's heart pounded harder than ever, thinking that this man will find him.

"Please God and the spirit of the land and the spirit of the water and the spirit of all the ancestors, please do not let them see me," Chhoeun whispered his prayers.

The man stopped about three feet away from Chhoeun's face and stopped. He was wearing a pair of sandals made of tire and tire tubes. He couldn't see the man's face, but the tip of the rifle pointed right in Chhoeun's face. This was the end of his life, Chhoeun thought. He was going to be shot from the back of his head. He expected to be shot at any time now.

The armed man paused and then turned his body to the left and then to the right. Another armed man approached carrying his rifle and stood right next to the first man. The tip of the rifle was just inches away from Chhoeun's forehead. The second man was wearing the same type of sandals.

Chhoeun was thinking about getting up and surrendering. Maybe they would let him go. If he didn't get up, they would shoot him in his head. He was about to get up, but his instinct forced him to stay down.

"I was very sure that I heard a noise," one of them said.

Chhoeun realized that two men standing were not looking down at him but past him. He felt a surge of relief, and then he began to control his breathing. The men were still standing here scanning the area. Chhoeun wished they would walk away soon. Every second seemed forever now. If they decided to glance down, his life was over. Chhoeun was trying hard to calm his breathing. Every breath he took was risking being discovered.

The two men stood for another few minutes, scanning the area, and then they walked away. Chhoeun couldn't see, but he could tell that all his friends had been escorted away. About five minutes later, Chhoeun heard the gunshots *(pop-pop-pop.....)* for a good twenty seconds. His heart sank. He knew what the gunshots meant. He closed his eyes and wept softly. He was shaken by fear and sadness.

Chhoeun thought this was the opportunity to escape. He lifted his head up slightly looking left and right and was about to bolt away when the same two gunmen returned, walking right toward him again. Chhoeun dropped his face back to the muddy ground, causing him to breathe in a chunk of mud through his nose.

"These damn people have the nerve. This jungle was so far deep, and they still came," one of them said.

Chhoeun felt the mud that he breathed in sliding from his nose into his lungs, making him want to cough. He was fighting the urge. If he coughed, he would be dead. The more he breathed, the more he wanted to cough. It was only a matter of time until his lungs would force him to cough. Chhoeun decided to hold his breath completely to avoid more mud sliding down his lungs. He knew he could hold his breath for a very long time. He had done that many times when he dove under and across the river. Unfortunately, he didn't get a chance to get a deep breath like he did at the river.

He continued to hold his breath until the men walked past him. Then he managed to clear the mud from his mouth without moving his head and breathed slowly from his mouth. After holding his breath for so long, he needed to breathe very badly. He fought to calm his breathing. Then he could feel more mud sliding down from his nose to his throat. His breathing started to make a croaking sound. He tried to swallow the mud, but somehow it was stuck with his saliva onto the back of his throat.

The croaking sound become louder and louder as more mud was building up in his throat and lungs. If he continued to breathe like this, they would discover him.

Chhoeun prayed in his mind. "Dear God and the spirit of the land and the spirit of the water and the spirit of all the ancestors, please help me one more time. I need a bird of any kind to perch on the branch above my head,"

He croaked louder and louder. Then he saw a large blackbird flew out of nowhere and perched right above his head. He noticed it was the bird called *Klum* in Khmer. The bird got the name by making a croaky sound. His prayer had been answered. It was the only bird in this world that could save him. He had only one shot. He took one big cough and released the saliva and dirt out of his throat and lungs.

"What was that?" one of the gunmen said.

"It's that bird over there," the other said.

Chhoeun could not see the men, but he knew they were somewhere behind him, possibly sitting in front of the farmer's shack. He could hear them chat faintly. He continued to lie down, trying to stay calm.

The Klum flew away several minutes later. Chhoeun was concentrating on his breathing and avoiding making any movements. He couldn't see where the sun was, but the short shadow of the brush in front of him indicated it was noontime. He wished he could see exactly where the men were. He decided not to take a chance to turn his head. He continued to curl and wait. Time seemed to stand still when he really needed it to pass. When he thought of it all over again, he didn't mind the wait. He had gone through the worst part. The spirits had helped him this far, and he was not going to mess it up.

It was fortunate that the other Red Khmers did not come; only the two that nearly stepped on his head were here. The day was passing by slowly. The evening shadows of the trees were stretching and covering all the ground before him, giving him more hope. After the excruciatingly long wait, the nightfall dominated as the final savior. Chhoeun had been waiting for this moment for eternity. He felt so much safer now. He rotated his head slowly, scanning the area. He saw the shack stood empty. The two armed men must have used the small path behind the shack when they left.

Chhoeun carefully got up and crept slowly toward the road that he'd used to get here this morning. He scanned around one more time and then began to run. He ran cautiously, afraid he might run into them again. He kept his eyes and ears on high alert.

He ran for about an hour. The road split a couple of times. It was too dark to see. It was impossible to tell which roads lead him here. He simply chose from his gut feeling. He was exhausted, but he could not stop. He was still too close to the Red Khmer village. He slowed down a little but not by will. He was running as fast as his feet could move. He remembered they were walking west, and he needed to go east, back to the way home. It was pitch dark, and the jungle was too thick. He had no way of knowing which way was east and which was west. He could barely see a pace away. The fear of the Red Khmer had eased, but now he just thought of snakes and tigers. The snakes were everywhere in the jungle. The tigers were well known throughout Kampuchea. He had seen tigers before from a far distance, but he would not know what to do in a close encounter. As he thought of the tiger, he realized that he still had the small axe hanging strapped on his waist. He felt a little more secure with an axe than his bare hands.

Chhoeun could no long run. Every inch of his muscles and joints were in pain. He decided to walk and catch his breath. He wanted to cut a small tree branch to make a guiding stick, but it was too dark to see anything, and he might make too much noise. He dismissed the idea and continued to walk slowly and carefully.

He had lost track of time. He thought it should be midnight by now. He followed the wagon road, not sure if it was leading him closer to home or further away. He knew he must continue to move far away from this place.

Chhoeun walked for many hours more. He heard the faint crows of the rooster in the distance. He kept his thoughts on the distance of the rooster. Since he now knew they likely belonged to the Red Khmer, he wanted to be far away from the roosters.

As he thought of the roosters, he remembered the strange look of the villagers that he passed by earlier in the day. They all wore black with the red scarves strapped around their heads and waists. He remembered one of them stared at him strangely. Now he realized they were all Red Khmers. He and the men were walking right in to the Red Khmer's territory, more like the demons. The thought made his skin prickle.

He continued to walk, not knowing exactly where he was or where the road was taking him. It must be around five in the morning by now. Normally, the sky would give off some light, and he should be able to see the road better at this time, but the jungle was too thick. He could not see any opening to the sky. It was still pitch black.

He stopped as one of the rubbers on his slipper snapped. He took his slippers off and probed with his fingers. He noticed dozens of thorns were stuck all around his slippers. Then he probed his feet and found his feet were full of thorns. The pain was there all along, but he was too terrified of the Red Khmer to feel it. Now that the fear of the Red Khmer had eased, he could feel the pain from every puncture of the thorns. He held both of his slippers in one hand. He would fix them when he got home.

Suddenly, a loud sound of the rooster's crow ripped through the night. It was so close and so loud that it made Chhoeun jump. The Red Khmer's village must be no farther than fifty yards from where he was standing, or maybe closer. Without a second thought, he leaped of the wagon road into the bush and trees and started running again. If he stayed on the road, he might run in to the Red Khmers. He would be dead if they found him. He didn't care about the snakes or the tigers anymore. He just wanted to be far from here. He was barefoot with thorns still all over his feet. He forgot all about the pain once more.

He ran until it was bright enough to see the trees around him. Most of the trees stood over a hundred feet up, with thick leaves and large branches, leaving only a small space through the morning sky. He needed to know where the sun was rising from. There was no way to tell with this thick forest.

He began to walk after he was confident that he was further away from the village. After running all night, he felt like he could not take another step. He had not slept for one day and one night. He longed for a good sleep. He felt like his body would shut down and collapse if he didn't rest.

He looked around the area and felt confident that no one had traveled here before. It was deep in the forest and far away from the wagon road. He found a tall tree that was easy enough to climb and had two large branches side by side about forty feet above the ground. He climbed the tree and rested on the branches. He scanned the area one more time from above to make sure that no one had passed through here before. He found no sign of worn ruts nearby. He took off his long-sleeved shirt and untied the cowhide that he used to strap his axe. He used the cowhide to tie his shirt on to the tree branches to make a hammock. Then he swung an axe blade into the tree bark where the blade buried deep in the bark.

He slept with his head resting on one tree branch, his feet on the opposite branch, and his back on the shirt hammock. He felt uncomfortable with his head resting on the hard tree branch, but he was drained from running all night—a little discomfort was all right. His arms and legs were numb from fatigue and pains. He felt some of the thorns buried deep in his feet causing the most pain. His head was spinning. His eyelids were getting heavy. His mind drifted into a deep sleep that he'd been waiting for.

The sound of insects and wild animals had subsided. The only sound was the buzz in his ear from the emptiness, and then everything was a void.

"Get him! Get him!" yelled the Red Khmer.

Chhoeun tried to move, but he was stuck between the tree branches. The two men caught up with him. One of them was climbing the tree to grab him while the other one was shooting at him from below.

Chhoeun finally freed himself from the tree branches, but one of the gunmen climbed up the tree with his face stuck up to Chhoeun's face. It must be the same man that nearly discovered him yesterday.

"If you run, I will cut you to pieces," the man said.

How did he climb the tree holding the rifle and the machete? Chhoeun thought he was descending the tree. When Chhoeun got to the ground, the other man was smoking a cigarette. Why was he smoking when he was chasing him? The other man was still descending the tree.

Chhoeun found this was the good opportunity to run. He started to leap away as fast as possible, but his legs were so heavy. He couldn't move as fast as he wanted.

The man who was smoking realized Chhoeun wanted to flee. He took the rifle and aimed at Chhoeun, and then he began to shoot. Chhoeun woke up just before he got shot. His eyes were wide open trying to comprehend what had just happen. After a moment, he realized it was just a dream. He looked around, and there was not one around except the thick forest. He sighed in relief.

It was a bright day. The radiance of the sun leaked through the small opening of the canopy of the tall trees. He didn't know how long he'd slept. It seemed only about an hour or less. He was still tired and needed more sleep, but he feared being discovered. He untied his shirt from the tree branch and pulled the small axe off the tree bark and then carefully descended the tree.

He wanted to continue walking, but he did not know what direction to go. Last night, he ran without direction just to be far from the Red Khmer. Today, he wanted to start walking toward home. He need to travel east, where the sun was rising. He walked around looking for an opening to see where the sun is. He thought it was still morning. The sun should still lie to the east.

He found a tree that was tall but thin enough for him to climb. He placed his axe and slippers on the ground and began climbing the tree. About half way up the tree, he saw an opening. He couldn't see the sun directly, but the light beam indicated its position and also indicated that it was still around midmorning. He was happy that he now knew what direction to walk to. He still didn't know how far away from home he was. He worried that the time he travelled last night could have lea him further away from home.

Chhoeun descended the tree joyfully and started walking toward the sun. He was very hungry. He was no longer worried about getting captured by the Red Khmer. Now he was worried about how to get out of this thick forest. He walked at a normal pace as he scanned his eyes around for food, hoping to find fruit or lizards. He kept his attention on the sun. If it was past noon, he would need to travel the opposite direction of the sun.

He came across an area with uneven terrain that was thick with trees and brush, causing Chhoeun to lose track of the sun. He had to climb another tree over one hundred feet tall to locate the sun. The amount of effort and energy he used to climb the tree was probably more than what he'd use in a day of walk. He walked until it was too dark to see. Then he found a tree suitable to make a hammock and high enough from the wolves and set up a spot to sleep. He was hoping not to bump into tigers or bears, as they could climb the tree much better than he could.

He slept very uncomfortably at night. He woke up several times from nightmares and insect bites. He wanted to walk at night and get home faster, but he was afraid he might get lost even further.

He slept until the faint light illuminated the forest. He descended the tree and continued walking. He began to search for food. He had not found any fruit or small animals yet. The forest was a swamp with animals of all sorts, but they fled as soon as they detected his presence. Most animals were birds of all sorts living high up in the trees.

Suddenly, an open terrain spread before his eyes. Just a dozen yards away, he saw an ox wagon parked solemnly on an open field. He felt a surge of relief that he'd reached the end of the forest. On second thought, however, this might be a place where the Red Khmer lived as well. He stood in the forest and looked around the area for any sign of movements. He wanted to see what was in the wagon. There might be food. He was taking his time checking the area. If he was spotted by the Red Khmers, his life was over.

After a while, he crouched down and ran quickly toward the wagon. Then leaned his chest against the wagon and began searching. He smiled to himself when he saw several bags of some sort and two coconuts lying on top of the bags. He checked the surroundings to make sure he was still in the clear and then jumped into the wagon.

He slit the bags open and was disappointed to find that they contained nothing but salt. He was hoping to find rice. The salt was valuable, but not now. He took the coconut and carefully chopped the top part off with his axe to make a hole. He drank all the coconut juice, and then he split the coconut open and ate the pulp. The coconuts were still young. The pulp was soft and thin. He ate both coconuts almost immediately. He wished there were more coconuts. He needed more food to make it out of this place alive. There was nothing else on the wagon beside the coconuts and the bags of salt. He cut the top part of the bag open and poured out some salt. He left as much in the bag as could easily carry.

Besides the sound of birds and insects, this place seemed to be empty. He stuck his head out of the wagon and checked the area again, and then he hopped off. He crouch-walked at first and then began to run. There were no signs of anyone living around here. As much as he was happy to be out from the thick forest, he felt helpless out in the open as well. He could be easily spotted by the Red Khmers. Also, if a tiger or a pack of wolves found him, he had a little hope of escaping. There was no tree to climb or place to hide. He might be able to outrun the Red Khmer, but not the wolves or tigers.

Not knowing how he'd gotten so much energy, he continued to crouch-run in the open field with one hand holding his sandals and the other holding the bag of salt. He ran until he could no longer take another step. He stopped and lay down flat on his stomach to rest and avoid being seen at the same time.

After a short rest, Chhoeun continued to run again. He was too tired to crouch, so he ran normally. After a while, he saw the clusters of trees and two ox wagons. He stopped and carefully examined the area. He spotted a small shack and a couple of people working around the shack. Chhoeun was happy to see people, but he was not sure who they were. Then he decided to take a risk and begin to walk toward them. He studied the surroundings for hints of the Red Khmer. He was walking and keeping himself behind the clusters of trees in the distance just in case he noticed they were the Red Khmer.

As he got closer and closer, he saw several more people going about their business. The people didn't seem to take notice of his presence. Maybe they didn't see him, or maybe they saw him but didn't care. Either way, Chhoeun had to make a decision quick. He would either try to avoid them and continue walking or take a risk and ask them for directions. Even if they didn't know where Kbal Kmouch was, at least he would know what this place was. He was hungry, tired, and lost. If he continued to walk like this for another day or two, he would die from starvation or from exhaustion, or maybe be eaten by tigers or wolves. He decided to take a risk and speak to these people. He walked straight to a man standing beside the wagon rolling a long rope. The man seemed to notice Chhoeun approaching, but it did not seem to bother him.

"Pu, I'm lost. I need to get to Kbal Kmouch. Do you know where that is?" Chhoeun asked, using the traditional Khmer.

"It sounds like you are not the Red Khmer…Kbal Kmouch is that way on the other side of the mountain. Since you are traveling on foot, the best way to get there is to pass through that mountain over there," the man said pointing his hand at the distant mountain. "After you cross the mountain, you will come across a lake behind the mountain. That is part of Kbal Kmouch. I'm assuming you'll know your way once you get there," the man said.

Chhoeun was relieved that these men were not the Red Khmer.

"What happened to you, and where did you come from?" the man asked.

"I escaped Red Khmer. I was nearly captured and killed. I have been running since. I've been lost for two days and two nights now. If I don't get home soon, I will starve to death," Chhoeun answered truthfully.

The man appeared shocked and said, "Then eat some rice before you leave. We have some rice leftover from lunch. Come, follow me. Don't be afraid of us. We are oxen catchers. We catch any abandoned oxen that come our way." The man dropped his long ropes on the ground and scrambled to get rice for Chhoeun. He knew what it was like to encounter the Red Khmer.

Chhoeun followed the man to a small shack made of palm leaves. The shack was so small that it could probably fit about four people.

"Eat the rest of the rice in this pot," the man said as he opened the lid of the thick steel pot.

Chhoeun opened his eyes as wide as a chicken egg and leaped to the rice pot. His hands and body shook in anticipation. He laid down his slippers and the salt bag on one side. He grabbed a handful of steamed rice and shoved it in this mouth. Then he remembered a bag of salt in his hand. He grabbed one piece of rock salt and chewed it with rice. He nearly bit his tongue several times from chewing so fast. Then he swallowed so fast that he could feel the clump of rice forcing through his throat.

"Eat normally, so you won't choke. The water is in the bucket over there," the man said politely and stepped out the shack to speak to the other two men approaching.

"The little brother over there just escaped the Red Khmer. He's been running for two days and two nights without food. Let's leave him alone so he could eat."

"Then let the poor brother eat," the other man said, and they all went back to continue their duties.

Chhoeun tried to calm himself down from chewing and swallowing too fast. The rice and the rock salt tasted so good. Chhoeun finished about half a pot of rice in less than five minutes. He could finish five more pots, if available. He noticed he had used both hands to shove rice in this mouth. He licked every single grain of rice off his fingers. He drank the water and then walked out of the shack. He could feel the energy surging throughout his body.

"Pu, I'm leaving. I have to get home soon," Chhoeun said politely.

"All right, continue your walk," the man replied.

Chhoeun start to walk again. The day had cooled down a bit. It was only a couple more hours until sunset. Chhoeun needed to get to Kbal Kmouch before dark. He needed to find a place where he was familiar. He wouldn't feel settled until he knew exactly where he is.

He stared at the distant mountain that sprawled up and across the terrain. He was walking toward the destination knowing it was safe here; he didn't need to run anymore. He walked at a normal pace holding his slippers and bag of salt.

He reached the edge of the mountain just before dark. There were several small houses scattered throughout the area. Most were made of logs with palm leaves for the roof. He walked to the closest house and peeked through the open door. He saw an elder couple eating dinner. The couple paused and stared at Chhoeun.

"Where did you come from, Kmuey (nephew)? How come you are such as mess?" the man asked.

"I escaped the Red Khmer a couple of days and nights ago. I have to pass this mountain to get home, but it is dark and I don't know my way around this mountain. I would like to ask to sleep here for the night," Chhoeun said slowly and carefully.

"You can sleep here. Not a problem," the man said.

"You should eat before you sleep. Come, eat with us!" the woman said as she got up to get a plate.

Both the woman and the man appeared to be in their fifties. They might have been a lot younger than that. Many elders had aged faster after living through the Red Khmer. The man was thin and had lost most of his teeth. The woman looks just a little younger and cleaner. They both must have been farmers and very hard workers. Both of them were very skinny but full of energy.

The woman placed a scoop of rice on the plate and broke off a piece of fish that she was sharing with her husband. "Here, eat until you are full. I normally cook extra rice for the next morning, but you can eat the rest of the rice," the woman said.

Chhoeun took the rice plate from the woman and began to eat. The elder couple resumed their meal without asking another question. Chhoeun devoured all his rice in just a few minutes.

"I must get to sleep," Chhoeun said and moved to the nearby wall and then curled under the small window. He didn't even bother drinking any water. He felt the pains all over his feet, and taking more steps to get the water was too painful. More thorns must have made their way deeper into his feet. He closed his eyes. His mind drifted away in the cool mountain breeze, and he dozed off almost instantly.

He woke up by the crow of the rooster that must have perched right on top of the elders' roof. Then he heard the rooster flapping its wings down from the roof. He opened his eyes. The room was shining bright from the morning sun. He must have missed the early crows.

He got up and walked out the door. The woman was tossing the rice to the hen and their chicks. The hen and the chicks hurried to wherever the rice was thrown. Chhoeun looked further and saw the same man that had offered him food and place to sleep wearing a handmade hat pruning his plants as he was talking to his neighbor who was pruning his plants as well. Neither of them was acknowledging Chhoeun's present. The neighbor must have said something to him.

Suddenly, Chhoeun got a creepy feeling about this place. They might be the Red Khmer trying to blend in to avoid attacks by the Vietnamese. Even though the couple were very nice people, he knew nothing about the rest of the people. He saw more people busy working on their farm. Another man was staring at Chhoeun but did not smile in interest or greeting. He must have not trusted Chhoeun at all. This was a remote village, far from everyone else. According to his understanding of this location, it was still far down to the west where the Red Khmer were believed to have sought refuge to rebuild their force.

"Ming, Pu, I must go," Chhoeun said, feeling awkward for not knowing how to say something better.

"All right then. Get going, kmuey," the woman said nicely.

The man was too far away to hear. Chhoeun wanted to walk up to him and say goodbye, but the other man was looking suspicious and eerie. Chhoeun saw a large vase full of water nearby. He walked over and used the silver bowl floating on top of the water to scoop and drink the water, hoping the couple wouldn't mind. After he'd drunk a bowlful of water, he started to walk slowly in pain. He wished he was at a safe place right now just to sit and squeeze the thorns out of his feet. He was irritated by every single one of the thorns. He followed a small path, hoping that it will lead him to Kbal Kmouch. The forest became thicker and thicker as he ascended the slope of the mountain.

After a while, the small village disappeared from his sight. The mountain seemed to be void of humans. Walking up the mountain became harder and harder. He didn't bother holding a stick or anything to protect himself. He didn't care much about anything besides moving forward.

He continued to follow the small path that led him to a space between two peaks emerging slowly from both sides. The path started to slant downward when the sun was hovering above his head. It was noontime. About a hundred yards away, he saw a stunningly giant dam running across from one side of the mountain to the other. If his eyes told him correctly, the dam must have been thousands of feet long and thousands of feet high. The dam was reserving the water flowing from the higher part of the mountain. Chhoeun knew well the dam had been made by the hands of thousands of workers. He could imagine many lives must have been lost to build this dam. He had witnessed the loss of lives when he worked building a dam similar to this one. The dam collapsed and killed many workers. With no sympathy, the

Red Khmer forced the workers to continue building the dam until they succeeded.

The pain in his feet became worse. It was spreading higher and higher up his legs. He limped slowly across the bridge. He stopped to rest when he got too tired and continued to limp after he regained his energy. It must have taken an hour for him to cross the bridge. The path began to descend down mountain. Chhoeun's body just wanted to shut down. His arms and legs were getting heavier and heavier. He just wanted to lie down in one place and rest, but he had to continue walking.

Suddenly, he saw the villagers swarming a small river of some sort. He was too far away for anyone to notice his presence. He continued to limp slowly as his body was about to give up. He was moving half-awake and half-delirious.

It seemed like an eternity until he finally reached the flat land, closer to the villagers. His body gave up, and he collapsed onto the ground.

"That's Chhoeun over there!"

"Bong Chhoeun!" the other screamed and ran toward him.

Chhoeun squinted and focused his eyes. He noticed it one of Pu Sarin's sons.

"Have you seen all the elders? Did they come home?" Chhoeun asked knowing the answer was no, but hoping maybe the whole ordeal was just a bad dream.

"Why would you ask such a question when they all went with you?" he replied.

"Then what I heard was true. They shot all of them. They were all captured and shot," he said and then broke down weeping.

Everyone realized Chhoeun was struggling to walk and trying to stay conscious. Pu Sarin's son and another elder boy lifted Chhoeun by his arms up onto his feet.

"What happened? How did they die?" a woman asked and cried at the same time.

"We were surrounded by the Red Khmer. I was the only one that had a chance to hide. Everyone else was captured."

"Do you see them being captured?" a woman asked.

"Yes, I saw them."

"Did you see them getting shot?" she continued.

"No, they walked them away."

"How do you know they were shooting them?" another woman asked.

"I don't know, but after I heard the shots, the men came to look for me. I heard them talking, and they sounded very angry."

"Maybe they were shooting up in the air to scare you, so you could show yourself up?" a different voice asked.

"I don't know, but I don't think they were shooting up in the air. I never saw our men again. I hid until nightfall," Chhoeun explain.

The more detail Chhoeun gave, the more women and children wailed as they followed him from behind. Most of them were soaked with water.

When they reached our home, Chhoeun sat down just outside of the house in the shade. He was relieved that he no longer needed to take another step. He was surrounded by the families living in the building. They were asking more questions, hoping to hear something better. They wanted to know the possibility that their husband or father might have a chance to live.

I was playing with Pech and other children just outside the building on the concrete floor. I was terrified when I saw Chhoeun carried by two older boys, followed by all the women and children. Chhom ran inside the building calling for Father and Mother to come out and see Chhoeun. Pech and I were as curious as everyone else. We darted right into the crowd. Huk and her Mother emerged from the building in confusion.

The adults bombarded him with more questions. Many women wailed and stamped their feet in agony, demanding to have their husbands back. Chhoeun was sitting with his back leaning against the wall weeping vigorously as he explained the incident.

CHAPTER 32

It took several weeks for Chhoeun to recover from some of the cuts and bruises. The thorns that were buried deep in his feet caused infections. He had not been able to walk. He stayed home most of the time. Huk and her Mother had to go out and find food themselves. They found food just enough for the two of them. The relationship between Chhoeun and Huk was not much more than where they had started. They were living together, bound by the marriage and nothing else. Yey Ngao was not happy that Chhoeun was not supporting them. Regardless of his condition, she mocked and scolded him when opportunity allowed. Chhoeun was young and confused. He felt miserable for not being able to find food for his wife and his mother in-law like Father had promised them. He sat quietly, taking all the blame. Mother and Father were upset that Chhoeun was getting treated this way, but due to respect they ignored and pretended not to hear anything. Chhorn, on the other hand, had witnessed the mistreatment and did not hold back her anger.

"Look at him. He's as dark as a water buffalo," Yey Ngao had said.

Chhorn responded the instant Yey Ngao finished her sentence. "Yeah, there are two people that can't do anything except to rely on the water buffalo. Some people are dark as well, but they can only see others. Unfortunately, our country has no mirrors. If we had mirrors, a dark person would not call another person dark." Yey Ngao was Chinese, but her skin was very dark like the native Khmer.

It was fortunate that Chhoeun was living next us. Mother understood his situation and offered for him to come eat with us when we had food. As time went by, there were more and more conflicts between our family and Huk and her Mother. Mother was feeding him like he had no other family.

Mother, Father, Chhorn, and Chhoy were doing everything they could to bring home rice. Chhorn used all her skills, physical strength, and charisma to trade different things for rice. She continued to make people feel sympathy and build trust, and then she used the opportunity to trade without using any rice to start. Mother took some of the rice that Chhorn brought home to trade for other things like gold, which she could flip to obtain more rice.

Chhoy helped Chhorn when she could. She was still a younger sister, relying on Chhorn for everything. Her personality continued to cause conflicts with Chhorn, but at the end of each day, she contributed some time and energy to reduce the burden that Chhorn had brought upon herself.

Weeks earlier, Chhorn had brought home a can or two of rice nearly every day from trading beef. Nowadays, the beef had become rare as the cows were being slaughtered daily. Chhorn had been searching for other opportunities. She was looking for something in high demand that people would give up their rice for. She tried the Prohuk; the fermented fish nearly all the Khmer used to cook. She was able to sell some, but not as easily as beef. She was able to bring home about two cans of rice a week. There were nine of us, and Mother was still giving a share to Chhoeun. It was the same amount of rice we'd gotten when living under the Red Khmer.

Poe became sick very often from malnutrition. Mother used some rice that we had to trade for French medicine and Khmer herbs. There were days when we had nothing to eat at all. We were starving once more.

Father had lost all his friends except for Pu E. There were no more oxen or wagons he could use to go find food. He continued to catch fish in the pond, but they were getting scarce. He was lucky to catch any fish at all nowadays. He came home empty-handed most of the time.

Unlike Stung Chah, where Mother or Chhom could find vegetables along the river, there was nothing here. We ate the entire lotus and every edible plant in the pond. We had nothing to substitute for the rice. One day, we saw one of the men holding a dozen rats tied to a stick. Chhoeun quickly made traps and caught a few rats in the rice field. He learned a new trick by pouring hot water in the rats' dens to drive them out and then catch them on the surface. Nearly everyone, including the children, had learned the same trick. The rats disappeared in just a few weeks.

Nearly all the children in the building were sick. Poe had a high fever, and he had been coughing every night. Van Sok, Tien's younger brother, was very sick and had not opened his eyes for weeks. Pech had been sick off and on.

Today was hot as usual. I had been waiting for the day to cool down. It was too hot to play out on the concrete floor. I was the only one outside walking on the dirt ground. Other kids were probably too sick to come out and play or too sad because they'd lost their father. Kbal Kmouch was no longer a fun place for me. I started to dislike this place more and more. In Stung Chah, there was a river nearby where I could search for frogs, snails, or crabs. There was nothing here. The land was dry. The pond was too far for me to walk alone. Chhom had not brought anything home either. We continued to eat rice dust that Chhorn and Chhoy brought home. Mother had been gone since morning, so we didn't have anything to eat all day. I didn't expect any food until Mother called us to eat. I felt hungry every second. The only time I didn't feel hungry was when I was busy playing with other children. I was waiting for someone to come out and play jump square. In the meantime, I was drawing a new jump square. As I stooped down to draw a square in the dirt, I noticed that, for some reason, the dirt smelled so tasty. The earthy smell made me wanted to eat dirt. I had eaten dirt before in Stung Chah. It tastes satisfying at first, but then the dust becomes muddy and gross. I couldn't resist grabbing a handful of dirt and shoving it in my mouth like it was rice. I didn't chew the dirt. From previous experience, I knew it would hurt my teeth. I used my tongue to feel the taste and swallow. Then I grabbed another handful of dirt and shoved it in my mouth again.

"You're eating dirt! You are going to get yellow skin! I'm going to tell Mother to hit you!" Chhom said.

I'd heard a rumor that children who ate dirt got a disease called Yellow. Some children passed away from this disease. I was not afraid of getting spanked since I knew Mother was not home. After I'd eaten two mouthfuls of dirt, my mouth was full of mud and sand. I continue to idle around the area all by myself, searching small holes in the ground for rats. I wished I had a pot of boiling water to drive rats out of their dens. I would love to bring home a rat. They said some rats had the yellowish skin color like a pig, were nearly as big as a cat, and could possibly overpower a cat if they were to battle.

When the day became cooler, Tien, Mao, and a few other children came out and play. The guard appeared from somewhere to come and guard the building. Minutes later, Chhoeun limped down slowly to chat to the guard. I couldn't wait to listen to their conversation. I walked to the guard and Chhoeun, hoping to hear their interesting stories. I sat near the wooden stand and waited for them to tell stories.

Chhoeun started to talk about his trip to find food where all the men had gotten captured and executed. The guard was amazed as much as I was by the story.

"Well, there was a rumor that, tonight, the Red Khmer will try attack our village. I'm not sure how true it is, but we are ready for them. So, get ready," the guard said.

I was too focused on Chhoeun's story, not realizing that all the women were sitting in circle next to us discussing their own stories.

"Look at him. He is dark and strong like a water buffalo. I will take him to my hometown and make him plant ginger. He will use his strength to plow the soil. I don't need the real buffalo," Yey Ngao said to the elder women.

"I will wait for my husband to return. I believe he is still alive. I will wait forever if I have to," a woman said.

"Same as I. Chhoeun has no evidence that they were killed. They might be lost," another woman said.

Suddenly, Father and Pu E arrived from fishing. Pu E was holding a bucket and a net. Father was holding a bundle of dead snakes tied with vines. They were the only two elder men alive. The women got up to check what Father had brought.

"Take the fish and share. I will keep the snakes," Father said.

"I will distribute the fish," Pu E said and handed a fish to each of the widow women.

Mother, Chhoy, and Chhorn returned home just before dark. Mother roasted the snakes that Father brought home. He'd caught a lot of snakes today. I normally didn't pay attention to what type of snake I ate. Mother handed me and Pech one small snake each. Mine was about two feet long. I assumed it was what the adults called the frog killer snake, or possibly a water snake. They were normally small and not venomous. The snake was roasted whole. She broke off the head so we wouldn't eat their fangs by accident. I'd had snakes a couple of times before, but they were in smaller pieces. I got to eat this one whole. The charred aroma of the snake made my mouth water and my stomach churn.

"I'll take the smallest one." Chhorn said.

Like Mother, Chhorn would make sure Pech, Poe, and I got more than her.

I bit the top part and chewed. It was delicious. I ate the meat and the bones all together. By now, Pech and I were good at handling all types of bones. We instantly knew which bone was chewable. Mother never had to tell us about bones.

When I got to the midsection of the snake, I noticed this snake has a baby. I took a bite of the baby snake, and it tasted ten times better than the mother snake. It had all the taste of the mother snake plus a nutty and creamy taste that no words could describe.

"My snake has babies…My snake has the babies," I said happily.

"Let me have one," Chhom said and grabbed one baby snake from my hand.

I was going to say no, but it's too late. I continued to eat before someone else would ask me for some. Pech didn't care. He was busy eating his snake.

After I finished eating the snake, I felt a little fulfilled. I didn't ask for more. Chhorn normally would give Pech and me some of her share, but she had already picked the smallest one.

Without bothering to drink any water, I went right to sleep. The night cooled down just perfectly for bedtime. Mother and Father were still chatting. They talked in a low tone so that our neighbor would not hear the conversation. As my mind drifted away to sleep, their conversation became gibberish, and then I dozed off in the cool night.

Boooom!…Pop…pop…pop! The sound of an explosion followed by gunshots erupted in the night. I woke up frantic and confused.

Rak…rak…rak was the sound of the bullets rolling down the top of our metal roof.

I was still half-asleep, thinking it was just a dream.

"Everyone, lie down! Keep your head down!" Mother said out loud and she darted to get Poe from the scarf hammock.

Father, Mother, and Chhorn huddled around us, ensuring that we kept our heads down.

More explosions ripped through the night followed by the sound of rifles. Then I heard the clashes and clinks on the walls of the building. I knew when the enemies fired because the sound of the rifles were fainter. When the guards returned fire, they were louder.

The battle went on for about two hours before it stopped. There was no sign that any of us in the building had gotten hurt. No one said a word after the battle subsided. We weren't sure who'd won the battle. If it was the enemy, we didn't want them to know where we were.

Pech and I went back to sleep. I was too sleepy to stay awake. Mother was breastfeeding Poe to make sure he didn't cry. She spoke softly to Father so that only Father could hear her.

I woke up late in the morning and walked outside. Father and Pu E were outside exchanging ideas and thoughts about the battle last night. They were observing the bullet marks on the walls. Women and children were circling around a large crater a dozen yards away from the concrete floor, possibly a propelled grenade.

"Your prediction was right, Chhay. Ah Sat Ka Dae Vech are cursed. Six of our men died, and now we are in the middle of war," Pu E said.

"It's not over yet. A few nights ago, a few more had flown right over our house just a little past midnight. They spoke like humans, telling us their names," Father said in despair.

"What are we going to do? Have you thought of another place that we could go?" Pu E asked.

"I don't know. I thought we would have opportunity when we got here. It's turned out to be worse than where we'd started," Father said.

A few weeks later, Tien's baby brother, Van Suk, passed away from sickness. It was devastating for Tien's family and our family. Van Suk was just a few months younger than Poe. Tien's family had been eating a lot less than us. For three weeks straight, Van Suk, Tien, and Mao had been eating nothing but fish and the rice dust that Chhorn and Chhoy brought home.

Poe was as sick as Van Suk. He had been coughing and wheezing and had high fever for weeks. All of us believed that he would meet the same fate as Van Suk. Mother was scared, and she took the rice that Chhorn brought home to trade for herbs and the French medicine. Unfortunately, Poe was not getting any better, and we had no rice to eat at all.

About three weeks after Van Suk had passed away, Chhorn and Chhoy came home early in the evening without a can of rice dust, but they appeared excited about something. "Mother, we went to the new market, I saw people were wearing colored clothes and nice shoes that covered their entire feet," Chhorn said.

"They wore red, yellow, purple, and some of them even had on more than one color," Chhoy added in excitement.

"They also sold things that I have never seen in my life. They had gold necklaces, silver necklaces, and colored stoned necklaces. They were so beautiful," Chhorn added.

Chhorn and Chhoy continued to add more about they'd seen, competing to take turns talking. We had been wearing all black until now. All the new fabrics that Mother bought were all black.

After they finished, Mother said "I saw those things you were talking about too. Those things were from Thai. I have spoken to a couple of families that knew about those products."

"What is Thai?" Chhorn asked.

"Thai is a country connected to our country. You need Thai money to buy those beautiful products. Those products were brought in by the *Rut Pun* people (cross-border merchant). They sneaked into Thai and brought back those products to sell at the borders. Then border merchants sell the products to the rest of the people," Mother explained. "Remember your great uncle, Ta Hail?"

"Yes, I remember. He was living in Phnom Tom," Chhorn said.

"I remember him too. We went to visit him just before the Red Khmer took over," Chhoy said.

"Is he still alive?" Chhorn asked.

"I have sent messages through many cross-border merchants and discovered that not only is he still alive, but he is also living in the same house. He came back to claim his house right after Vietnamese invasion.

I have sent word to them to tell them where we are and described our current situation. They had urged us to go there to live with them.

Solo's mom was planning to take a trip there all by herself. I have been asked to watch her children because she trusts me. She knows I would not let her children starve. She offered me two cans of rice and promised to give me more when she comes back. People who travel there have been very successful. They got rice, gold, and wear colorful clothes," Mother explained.

Although Mother didn't know how to read or write, she was an expert at sending messages. The time she had been speaking with villagers was not just to trade but to learn about any opportunity to make a living.

The news of the products from Thai spread like wildfire. All the families in the warehouse quickly learned about the Thai products and the opportunity to make money. Some of the widows wanted to take the risk, but many still wanted to wait for their husbands to return.

Unfortunately, none of us had any oxen or wagons. From here to Phnom Tom would probably take days to walk. We didn't have any rice to eat on the way. During the first Vietnamese invasion, we were able to travel and scavenge for rice, but now everything belonged to someone. We would starve to death if we tried.

Nearly everyone was thinking about moving for one reason or another. Yey Ngao had already decided to move as well. Not only had she managed to save some rice and gold, but she had also bought a small wagon designed for a person to haul.

"We were going to Takeo in two days. Chhoeun will haul me there. It doesn't matter how long it will take. He will haul the wagon until we get there," she announced one evening.

Chhorn wept when she heard the news. As much as Chhoeun had treated her harshly when they were young, she'd always loved and respected him. He had done so much for the family. Since the age of nine, he'd brought home fish and plowed the fields to farm. He had taught her to work hard and to care for her family. She was who she was because of him. He'd taught her to do whatever it took to feed the family.

During the Red Khmer time, Chhorn never thought she would see him again. Everyone was forced to leave home, and Chhoeun had been a fugitive, and she never thought he would make it alive. Since Chhoeun had reunited with the family, she'd never had the opportunity to bond with him the way they were bonded before the Red Khmer because they had different tasks to do to support the family. Chhorn had been trading for rice, and Chhoeun was helping Father with fishing and hunting. In fact, she had not spoken to him about anything since they reunited. Now Chhoeun was leaving her again.

When Chhoy and Chhorn returned from work in the evening, they saw Chhoeun was setting the wagon and his belongings, getting ready to depart at any day.

"Chhoeun, please don't go. I will miss you," Chhorn said.

"I don't want to go, but I have to. I have a wife, and I will go wherever she goes, and she is doing whatever my mother in-law asks us to do. My wife knows I don't want to go, and she said I could return after we get there," Chhoeun explained.

"Takeo is located many horizons away. I don't believe you will ever come back again. Yey Ngao will make you stay and work for her," Chhorn said and sobbed.

Chhoeun did not reply because it was true that he would not return. In Khmer tradition, we were taught to respect the elders all the time. It was sinful to disobey them, especially a parent or parent-in-law. Huk owed her life to her mother for bringing her into this world. Since Chhoeun was her husband, the debt was now upon him.

Chhoy and Chhom wept when they spoke. Mother was very upset as well, but she felt she had no right to stop Chhoeun from going with his new family.

"You have to listen to your mother in-law. Treat her like your own mother. You go with them and take care of them like you took care of us," Mother said and wept at the same time.

Father was lying down just several paces from us resting from a day of hard work. He was expressionless. We could not tell how he felt about Chhoeun's leaving. Chhoeun and Father had been working side by side since they were reunited. Chhoeun had been a great help to Father. Not only had he offered an extra hand, but he also contributed different kinds of skills that Father didn't have.

Chhorn skipped the rice grinding job and went straight to trade. She came home early, as she was afraid she might miss the chance to say goodbye to Chhoeun. Yey Ngao would decide when to leave, and no one knew when that would be. During night, Chhorn was woken up by a slight sound, and she thought Chhoeun was leaving.

On the following night, she tried to stay awake so she would not miss saying goodbye. She waited and waited and felt asleep just after midnight. She dreamed about Chhoeun's leaving and wept in her sleep.

"Can you move faster? The sun is almost rising. We need to get moving," Yey Ngao shouted.

Chhorn woke up frantically from the clinking and clanking sound of pots and pans, not sure if she was still dreaming or not. She ran outside and saw Yey Ngao sitting on a small wagon made of two bicycle wheels with a seat slightly larger than a chair. The pots and pan were hung on the handles of the wagon and made all sorts of sounds.

"Chhoeun, don't go!" she screamed and ran to Chhoeun.

Mother ran after Chhorn. Chhoy, Chhom, Pech, and I woke up. We all ran outside. After many days of overhearing Mother and Chhorn talking, Pech and I understood that Chhoeun was leaving and would never come back.

Chhorn hugged Chhoeun and wailed, "Bong Chhoeun, please, don't go. Please, don't go..."

Chhoy went and hugged his arm. "Don't go, Chhoeun. We are going to miss you. Please stay."

Chhom hugged him and pressed her head again his waist weeping, "Bong Chhoeun, don't go."

Pech and I were weeping and hugging each of his legs. Even though we were very young and had not done much with Chhoeun, somehow, he was special to us. Having a big brother was so comforting and fun. I always wished I could grow up and chat with him the way he did with Father.

Huk was standing beside him weeping as well. She was young and obedient like Chhoeun. There was nothing she could do. Her Mother was making all the decisions. She was just following her Mother's direction like Chhoeun.

"Then, I'm not going," Chhoeun said and wept.

He released one of the handles of the wagon. Mother was standing next to him with tears rolling down her cheeks, "You must obey your mother-in-law's words. She is like your mother. It is your responsibility to take care of her," she said and grabbed his hand and placed it back on the handle. Then Chhoeun released his other hand from the other handle.

"Son, you must go. They are your family just like me and your Father. You were wed by full tradition," she said and placed his other hand onto the wagon handle.

Chhoeun released his other hand the instant Mother place one hand on the handle bar. Mother continued to reason with him and urge him to go. We continued to cry and sob around Chhoeun, hoping he would stay.

Yey Ngao was expressionless and seemed annoyed. She looked away trying to ignore the whole ordeal.

"All right, since he doesn't want to go, he can come back when we reach Phnom Penh. I used to have a lot of relatives that lived in Phnom Penh. I will look for them and ask them take me to Takeo. I need him to take me to Phnom Penh," Yey Ngao finally said.

"Then that's the deal. Son, you can come back after you have reached Phnom Penh," Mother said. Even though she urged him to go, we knew she really wanted him to stay as much as we did, but she was bound by the tradition to fulfill a parent's wishes. She sounds a little relieved that Chhoeun could come back.

Chhorn knew that Phnom Penh was half the distance to Takeo. It would take many weeks, possibly months, for Chhoeun to haul the wagon there. Besides, she didn't believe that he would return once he got there. She believed Yey Ngao would persuade him to stay. The rest of us didn't know any better and believed he would return as promised.

"Let's get going," Yey Ngao said.

All of us were still clinging to Chhoeun. "Let him go. He will be back," Mother said trying to be strong and persuasive.

All of us except for Chhorn released our grip. She continued to wail and begged for him to stay.

"I promise that I will return. No matter how long it will take," Chhoeun said.

Chhorn finally released him, but she was not planning to leave him.

"Then, I must go," Chhoeun said wiping his tears with his shoulders. He started to haul the wagon.

We all stood and wept as Chhoeun was departing. Chhorn did not give up and began walking along with Chhoeun. Chhoeun was moving slowly away from us with his new family. We all stood and cried until long after Chhoeun and his family were out of our sight.

They reached the national paved road a moment later. Many families were still traveling, seeking a place to settle. Some were fortunate enough to own a wagon. Most were traveling on foot. The small wagons similar to the one that Chhoeun was hauling were being used everywhere on the road.

Just before noon, they passed the market where Chhorn would come to trade.

"Chhorn, you should go back home. I will get hotter and too far for you to walk back," Chhoeun said.

Huk and Chhoeun did not say a single word to one another. They were nothing like husband and wife; they were like strangers to one another.

"When I get to my hometown, I will plan all types of vegetables. I'm an expert with ginger. To others, it is very difficult to plant. I have a method that no one knows about. I will make a lot of money like the rest of my Chinese relatives. I have the Chinese blood. I will succeed. I cannot believe I'm wasting my life living in poverty with these water buffalos," Yey Ngao said.

Chhorn wanted to mock her back, but she was not in the mood to argue. She wanted to spend as much time as possible with Chhoeun. This might be the last time she would ever see him again. As gullible and gentle as he was, she Yey Ngao would convince him to stay and work for her. The thought made Chhorn's chest tighten, making her want to weep again. More tears started to roll down again. She fought hard not to weep; she needed all her energy to keep up.

The road became busier with travelers and merchants later in the afternoon. Chhorn noticed every single house along the road was occupied. Women and children were hanging out in front of their houses watching the travelers while the men were busy working on the farms around their houses. Some had wagons and the oxen tethered nearby.

The surrounding activities briefly took Chhorn's attention away from Chhoeun. Yey Ngao criticized nearly everyone she laid eyes on.

"Chhorn, you should return home now. It is past noon. There is no reason you should walk with us," Huk said. She seemed like she'd wanted to say something earlier but was afraid she might hurt Chhorn's feelings. She must have never forgotten that she and her mom owed Chhorn a lot. Chhorn was the one who'd brought most of the food home since after the Vietnamese invasion. Chhorn thought Huk was right. She had no reason to walk with them. They didn't even talk to one another. She stopped for a moment, allowing Chhoeun and Huk to resume their trip. She was trying to decide whether she should continue to follow them or return home.

After a long pause, she decided to follow them. This was her last time to see Chhoeun. She was determined to spend as much time seeing him as possible. She didn't have to walk side by side with them. She could just walk behind him even if it was a distance away.

She walked and kept her distance from them until sunset. As the reflection of the evening light from the sky was getting dimmer and dimmer, it became more and more difficult for Chhorn to see Chhoeun. All of a sudden, Chhoeun and his new family blended in with the other travelers, and Chhorn could not see them again. She stopped and wept again, feeling that was the last time she would ever see him.

"All the angels and the spirit of the ancestors, please make my brother come back. Please help me bring my brother back home." She prayed out loud to ensure her prayer would be heard. "All the angels and the spirit of the ancestors, please make my brother come back," she repeated.

She had no choice now but to walk home as quickly as possible to avoid walking in the dark alone. Unfortunately, she was very far from home. She was walking on the empty road in the night alone. There was no light except from the dim lamps in the windows of the houses along the road. She arrived home just after midnight. Mother was still awake waiting for her when she arrived.

"I was scared that you were lost. Why did it take you so long to get home?" Mother asked.

"I followed them until dark," Chhorn said and lay down on the floor to sleep.

Mother lit the lamp with a lighter and placed it next to Chhorn. "Here, I saved you some fish and rice dust dough," Mother said and handed her a plate with one small snakehead fish and the steamed rice dust dough wrapped in the banana leaves. She'd had nothing to eat since morning. She'd forgotten all about her hunger, but the aroma of the roasted fish and the steamed rice dust dough made her stomach churn and made her wanted to eat again. She munched quickly and quietly in front of the lamp as Mother was lying down getting ready to sleep. She ate every piece of meat from every crevice of the fish bones. When she finished, she put the plates away and blew out the lamp light and lay down to sleep.

CHAPTER 33

I woke up midmorning from the clinking and clanking sounds of pots and pans and the squeaking of the wagon. It was like déjà vu of Chhoeun's departure.

"Damn Vietnamese! They blocked the road! Now I'm stuck in this cursed place," Yey Ngao exclaimed furiously.

I couldn't believe my eyes. Chhoeun was walking into the house carrying cooking utensils and all his clothes. All of us got up and smiled at each other. Pech and I ran to Chhoeun and hugged his legs and then jumped with joy.

"Chhoeun is back! Chhoeun is back! Chhoeun is back," Pech and I sang and danced around him.

"Why are you back?" Mother asked with a big smile.

"The Vietnamese had barred the road, not allowing anyone to leave or enter," Chhoeun explained.

"Them bastards! They blocked the road for no reason. I wasted my time and money for nothing," Yey Ngao continued to swear and complain.

Chhorn sat up, still half-asleep, but she could not stop smiling. She glanced at Yey Ngao and smiled with victory. Our day continued like nothing had happened. Chhorn and Chhoy went to work to get rice dust as usual. Mother walked over and chatted briefly with Yey Ngao and left home to continue her usual daily routine. Father did not say a word or show any kind of emotion. He grabbed his fishing net and walked out of the house toward the pond. We were very sure that he was happy that Chhoeun was back. Chhom was staying home looking after Poe. Pech and I were wondering around the building hoping to find something fun to do or anything to eat.

The rumor was that majority of the families living in the town had moved to the Thai border. Many more were getting ready to move. There was nothing but good news about the border. Many widows in our building were thinking about taking the risk and moving as well. Solo's mom had just returned from a trip to the Thai border. Mother and Chhorn had been taking turns caring for her two sons, Solo and Polok. Solo was about three years old, and Polok was about seventeen months old. She gave Mother two cans of rice as promised. She wanted to take another trip to buy products and sell them here, but she had no way to transport the products. She had no money to pay for an ox wagon, and she could not carry the products herself. She was very skinny and short. She made a bargain with Mother to have Chhoeun do the carrying, and she would pay him. She couldn't promise the exact amount because she barely had any investment to begin with. Mother explained the details to Chhoeun, and he agreed immediately. He had no other way of making a living right now except to help Father fishing. Solo's mom and Chhoeun left the next day for the Thai border and then returned a week later. Chhoeun carried all the heavy products using the dong raek with a pair of baskets. It took them over two days to walk from here to the border. It took them three days to return because Chhoeun had to carry the products. Solo's mom offered Chhoeun three cans of rice. It was very little for five days of walking, but Chhoeun did not complain. It was better than nothing. They took another trip and returned within a week. Chhoeun was offered three more cans of rice. Yey Ngao and Huk were not happy and demanded Chhoeun to ask for more. Chhoeun knew that she could not afford to pay another ounce of rice. Solo's mom had to pay Mother two cans of rice for caring for her children. Yey Ngao and Huk decided to ask Solo's mom directly. As Choeun expected, she could not afford to pay another ounce of rice. An argument erupted and got very serious. After one word led to another, Chhoeun and his wife did not speak to one another for several days.

It became impossible for Chhoeun to work with Solo's mom anymore, but he saw a lot of opportunity at the Thai border and told everyone in the building about everything he'd learned.

"Their markets are larger than here. Everyone is wearing nice clothes and shoes. They use Thai money to buy everything. You can work for other people if you don't have money to start a business. They even have their own military," Chhoeun told everyone.

Tien's mom and Pu E were aware of the opportunity, and they were thinking of taking the chance. "I want to go, but the trip will take at least a week for my family to travel. We will have nothing to eat on the way," Tien's mom said.

"If you want to go, my wife and I will go with you and help you. I have been there twice now. I might as well go with your family and give you a hand to carry stuff. If we could survive until we make it to my great uncle, Ta Hail's, house, he will provide us rice. Then we could continue on to the border. He lives right on the road that leads to the border. He loves me like his son. He will help us. That's a guarantee," Chhoeun said. "When I get there this time, I will join the *Pa Ra* and get paid right away," Chheoun said.

"What is the *Pa Ra?*" Pu E asked.

"It's the newly organized military force that was formed to defend the new camps on the Thai border. They are protecting the camps on the border from the Red Khmer and the Vietnamese. They are strong and serious. Even the Vietnamese could not break their military defense. They are the new enemy of the Vietnamese," Chhoeun said.

"Then we should take the chance, but I want to see it myself first before taking my family along," Pu E said.

Chhoeun and Pu E agreed to take the chance and traveled to the Thai border. Chhoeun brought Huk along. It was a big risk to travel empty-handed to such a far destination, but if they could make it to Ta Hail's house, they could rest and eat and resume their trip. They took a trip there, but only Pu E and Huk returned home a week later.

"Bong Chhoeun has joined the *Pa Ra,* and he cannot come home yet. He will return when he gets paid. This is how much he got when he first signed up," Huk told us and lifted up a large sack of rice wrapped in a scarf.

Pu E felt more confident now after the trip and was planning to take his family to the Thai border. Ta Hail and his wife had promised to allow his family to stay and eat at their house and then continue their trip to the border. They even gave him a sack of rice for his family to eat as they traveled.

"This is what they gave me. They are very generous. They said any friends of Bong Yorn were welcome to come and rest at their house. They will provide rice to eat as well," he said, showing a pouch of rice wrapped in a scarf. "We will use this rice for our family to travel."

Pu E and his family left the next day. The promise that Ta Hail would provide food and shelter to any friends of Mother made everyone want to go, especially Solo's mom. Unlike most of the families in the warehouse, Solo's mom had somehow managed to trade and earn some gold. She could afford to travel; however, without Chhoeun, she could not carry the heavy load of goods and walk for many days with her two toddlers. She asked Chhorn to come with her to help take care of her two sons. Chhorn agreed to come, hoping to get paid and get some rice for the family.

Chhorn and Solo's mom walked and held Solo and Polok. They switched the two from time to time. Solo was a lot heavier than Polok. They ate and slept out in the open at night and walked during the day time. After two and a half days, they arrived in the town of Phnom Tom at Ta Hail's house.

Like Father, Ta Hail was tall and big with light skin. His wife, Yey Sat, was a medium-height woman. She has light skin as well. They had not changed much since the last time Chhorn saw them before the Red Khmer. They had a daughter slightly younger than Chhorn named Nee.

"Where are your Mother and Father?" he asked

"They cannot come," Chhorn answered.

"Why wouldn't they come? There is nothing there," Yey Sat asked.

"They have nothing at all, not even a can of rice, to travel that far. It took two and a half days for us to walk. My baby brother Poe is less than two years old. He is extremely sick, and we are not sure if he is going to make it alive," Chhorn explained.

"Then I will provide them rice for the trip," Yey Sat said. "And I will make you rice to eat. Wait just a little."

Chhorn and Solo's mom chatted with Ta Hail and Yey Sat as the rice and fish were cooking. Everyone avoided talking about the horror during the Red Khmer. Instead, they talked about the times after they fled the Red Khmer.

Chhorn and Solo's mom ate rice and fish and then continued to chat until midnight. Solo's mom still wasn't sure if she was ready to take her two children to Thai border yet. She wanted to take a few more trips to make some more money. Ta Hail and Yey Sat suggested letting Solo and Polok stay with them and have Chhorn and Nee take care of them. It worked well for Solo's mom. In return, she offered to take a trip back to Kbal Kmouch to deliver rice to our family. Then she could resume her trip.

Solo mom rested for several days at Ta Hail's house then returned to Kbal Kmouch and delivered the rice to Mother as promised. Mother was now confident Ta Hail and Yey Sat would be able to provide food and shelter once we get there. Mother and Father decided to take the risk to move. If we stayed here any longer, we would all die of starvation, especially in the middle of the hot season.

Mother informed the rest of the family that we were leaving in the morning. Pu Poo's family and Pu Sarin's family were thrilled and looking forward to coming along. Um Meun's wife and Pu Yun's wife decided to stay. Um Meun's wife had discovered some relatives in another city, and they were coming to see her soon. Pu Yun's wife still believed her husband was still alive. She decided to wait. Tien's family had already left a few days ago. It was much easier for them to travel now. Tien and Mao could walk by themselves most of the time.

After Solo's mom delivered the rice to our family, she returned straight to the Thai border the next day. Yey Ngao was furious that Chhoeun had not sent her any rice. She learned that the Vietnamese would kill anyone who'd joined *Pa Ra.* Currently, Mother and Father were not seeing eye to eye with Yey Ngao. The conflicts continued to build up each day. Mother and Father were thinking of taking her and Huk along, but she was no longer able to walk far. We didn't have any wagon for her to ride. Besides, the conflicts between our family and her made it very difficult to bring her along.

It was difficult, but Mother decided to speak to Yey Ngao. "I don't know what to do. We would like to bring you and Huk along, but as you can see, we have no wagon for you to ride. The only way is for you to wait here. Chhoeun will try to earn enough rice to buy a small wagon to transport you to the Thai border."

"Tell the water buffalo not to return, or I will report him to the Vietnamese. He has not sent me any rice since he left. I do not want to go to Thai. My future is to return to my hometown and farm," Yey Ngao said furiously.

Mother knew that she was serious about not going to Thai, and maybe she was also serious about reporting Chhoeun to the Vietnamese. She seemed to despise Chhoeun more and more, especially when she was unable to return to her hometown.

We started to walk early in the morning. Surprisingly, three other families living near our building overheard our plan and decided to join us. Mother and Father didn't mind. We had travelled with many families before. Every single one of the families had nothing to carry except for the pots and pans and a few cans of rice just like us. Mother was holding Poe in a scarf. Poe had gotten a little better. He was nearly two years old now, but he was much skinnier and weighed a lot less than before. He had been eating mostly the rice dust just like us. Pech and I were walking after Chhom. Pech was about four and a half years old now. He was actually walking on his own. Father was carrying two baskets full of our belongings and a bucket of water with the dong raek. Chhom and Chhoy were carrying whatever was left.

We came to the national road after a long walk. I normally didn't see the national road unless we were traveling. The road was filled with hundreds of travelers and merchants. Most were travelling on foot. It was still common to see men hauling wagons side by side with an ox.

By noontime, every single one of us was very tired. Pech was already complaining about being too tired. He asked for someone to carry him but no one responded. Father was carrying too much already. He walked and groaned at the same time. We didn't stop to rest, as Mother feared we would take too long to reach Phnom Tom. If we stopped, it would delay the time to get to Phnom Tom where Ta Hail and his wife would cook rice for us when we got there. Right now, we had no rice with us at all. Mother shared some of the rice that Solo's mom delivered with another family, and we ate the rest.

By evening, the day had become slightly cooler. The road became more crowded. We trekked on the hard paved road. My feet became heavy and heavier. We were walking at a much slower pace. The sun would set soon.

"We've almost reached Tmah Koal. If we get to Tma Koal, we'll be halfway to Phnom Tom. We will need to find a place to sleep. We have a long way to go," Father said.

We arrive in Tmah Kaol just before nightfall. We stopped near a small house sitting just off the road among other houses. "I will ask for a place to sleep," Father said and walked toward one of the houses.

A woman slightly younger than Mother stood by the door smiling.

"What were you looking for?" she asked.

"We are traveling to Phnom Tom. We need a place to sleep. Could you let us stay for the night?" Father asked.

"You can stay, but my house is small. If you don't mind squeezing in with my children, you are welcome to stay," the woman replied with a smile.

"We don't mind the small space. We just want to be inside," Mother said happily.

"Then come in," the woman said.

We walked into the house as Pu Poo's family, Pu Sarin's family, and the others were asking other families nearby to stay for the night.

Inside, two beds built from bamboo trees stood about four feet off the ground. Three boys and one girl ranging from four to twelve were on the bed prepared to sleep. They were all skinny and dark just like us.

Pech, Chhom, and I hopped on the bed with relief. We had been waiting for a long rest. Chhoy, Mother, and Father sat on the floor against the wall. Mother was cradling Poe on her lap and breastfeeding him.

"Where is your husband?" Mother asked.

"My husband has departed this world. It's just me and my four children living here," the woman replied.

"That is very sad. I won't ask you more about your husband. I'm afraid it might bring back bad memories," Mother said.

Mother and Father chatted with the woman some more trying to avoid talking about the painful past. Pech, Chhom, and I dozed off very quickly in spite of the crowded bed. We slept through the night without waking up once. We didn't even hear the crow of the rooster. Father and Mother had to shake us to wake us up in the morning.

On the way out of the house, Mother and Father thanked the woman for letting us sleep in her house. Other families that were traveling with us were already ready, waiting for us to resume the trip. We congregated by the road to ensure everyone was ready, and then we began walking. Just a few yards away, we saw other travelers were sleeping along the street on their wagon or under the tree with a mosquito net. Many other travelers had already begun walking in the dark.

The road became more and more crowded as the morning passed. The mountain was rising slowly in the distance, stretching across the land like a giant sleeping alligator. The merchants were standing in a small shack selling food. The customers purchased what they wanted and then rested around the shack to eat. Then all of us turned our attention to a young man standing a few yards away eating some sort of dessert. Every single one of us stared hungrily as he was biting the round and yellow dessert.

"That's *Num Kroach,*" Chhoy said.

"How do you know?" Chhom asked.

"I had that before in Phnom Phen in Lon Nol's time. I think you had some too," Chhoy said.

"I don't remember. What does it taste like?"

"It's very delicious. It's soft, sweet, and creamy."

Pech and I could not help but fix our eyes on the people munching on their dessert around the merchants. We walked slowly, not paying any attention to where we were walking. We all wanted to stop and stare at the people eating.

"Don't look at them. It will make you hungrier," Mother said.

I turn away from them as Mother suggested. The man was so lucky to eat such things. I turned my attention to the landscape of the country. Men and women worked on their farms along the road. Some of them were using the water buffalo to plow their land. Some were digging the soil beside their houses using hoes. The people were now living without fear. They were on their own going about their normal life.

We saw houses of all shapes and sizes. Most were very small and would fit only about four people. It probably took the people one day to build them. Some were made of mostly straw. Some were made of palm leaves. Once in a while, we saw a huge house built with a large wood frame and a roof made of metal plates.

"I can't walk anymore. My feet hurt," Pech suddenly complained.

Pech had been very good so far. It was surprising that he even walked. Maybe he saw other children walking and saw Father was carrying a heavy load. He knew Chhom was no longer able to carry him. Pech had grown a lot since we'd left Phnom Ta Kream. He was a lot taller but still skinny.

"Let's all take a rest. We have been walking nonstop. Our children need to take a break. This is a good place to rest. There are a lot of trees here," Mother said.

"Then we should rest. My feet hurt," one of the women said.

I was happy that we got to stop. The sun made the ground very hot, and it was burning my feet.

"I will go ask people for more water. We're almost out of water," Father said carrying a bucket.

Mother led us to a large tree with branches spreading wide all around. We all sat down around the tree, exhausted. Each family found their own tree to rest under. No one said a word. Everyone was too tired and hungry to talk. We sat and watched other travelers passing by. Some of them stopped and rested beside us.

A short while later, a woman screamed, "My son! My son! My son is not moving."

The men and women surrounded a boy name Tuen, one of Pu Sarin's sons. I had seen Tuen very often but never gotten to speak to him. One adult confirmed that he was dead. He was just sitting by the tree resting and then passed away. He was ill when we began the trip, but he had no choice but to come along. In addition, we'd had nothing to eat since the night before, possibly longer for some families. Starvation might have been a factor in his death. It was devastating for the family. Pu Sarin had been captured and executed not long ago, and now Tuen was dead as well.

His brothers, sister, and Mother wept uncontrollably. The adults borrowed tools from the local villagers and dug a shallow grave just off the road. They buried him and then said brief prayers.

"We must keep walking soon. If we stay here any longer, we will die as well. We need to get to Phnom Tom and get something to eat," one of the adults said.

Everyone was relying on Ta Hail and Yey Sat to give them rice to eat when we get there.

"I have strong faith in my great aunt and my great uncle. They will feed us when we get there," Mother said.

We resumed walking right after. Pu Sarin's family was walking and weeping along the way. The mountain was getting closer and closer. The path stretched slowly toward the mountain. The hill slowly began to elevate, making it difficult to walk. Some of the families that had tagged along with us on the way met their relatives along the road and decided to leave us and follow their relatives.

We reached the mountainside in late afternoon and followed the road along the waist of the mountain. Merchants were sitting along the road behind their product stations. Most of the products were strange to me. Nothing but food would catch my attention. Houses of all sorts and sizes were stacked beside one another to one side of the mountain. Most of the houses were built from solid wood.

"We are in Phnom Tom. From here on, the road will become steeper and steeper, but we are very close. I don't remember exactly where Yey Sat lives, but in this city, everyone knew one another," Mother said. "That was during Lon Nol's time. I hope it's still the same. You can ask about any family, and they will tell you exactly where they live," Mother added.

We ascended the elevated road for an hour but didn't see the house that she was looking for yet. "Stop here. I will go ask them where the house is," Mother said as she walked toward a large wooden-frame house.

Everyone stopped and waited, hoping to get the good news. She returned just a short moment later with a big smile. "We are almost there. Their house is easy to find. It's right on the main road travelers use to walk to the Thai border. We need to continue straight on this road. Then there is a big road that leads to the Thai border. It's the first house on the right off that road. The house is surrounded by coconut trees and palm trees. We can't miss it," Mother said happily.

"Let's continue," Father said and positioned the dong raek on his shoulder.

We resumed our walk and reached the house sitting on the corner of the intersection a little after nightfall. Ta Hail was outside watering his farm. "Is that Chhay and Yorn?" he asked.

"Yes, it is me, Chhay," Father replied.

All the adults approached Ta Hail happily. "Greetings!" everyone said.

"Greetings to everyone," he replied. "I thought you guys would never come. I have been waiting for you to come. This road here leads to the Thai border. It's a long walk from here, but many who left don't want to return. They must like it over there. If I were young like you guys, I would take the chance. But I'm too old to walk that far. Come inside and rest. I will ask your aunt to make some rice to eat."

"And these are all your friends?" Ta Hail asked and looked around. There were almost thirty of us.

"Yes, most of them were our friends since Lon Nol's time. The husbands passed away recently. They heard about your generosity and would like to take the risk and come. We'll discuss some more once we are settled down," Mother explained.

Ta Hail led us into the large house. Yey Sat began to cook rice. Chhorn sat inside the house cradling Polok to sleep.

"I thought I would never see you and the family again. I thought you would never survive the Red Khmer. Since I found out that you were alive, I have been waiting to see you. Your uncle and I are too old to travel, but I would like to help you with anything you need. You are among the few of our families that I knew that survived. I have not heard anything about the rest of our families," Yey Sat said.

Mother explained our hardship living in Kbal Kmouch and how Chhoeun escaped the Red Khmer a few months ago. Yey sat and instructed Chhorn to cook more to feed all of us.

"We all came empty-handed. We don't have a single grain of rice. All the women here are widows. All the children here are without a Father. They were looking for opportunities to make a living where they would be able to bring food home," Mother explained.

"Your uncle and I don't have much ourselves. As you can see, we are too old to do anything. We pay people to plant and harvest rice and plants. We lease our land. We'll get some share at the harvest season. But we will do anything to help get you get started," Yey Sat said.

While Mother and Yey Sat were chatting, the rest of us picked a spot to sleep. It was a big house but not for thirty people. We took every square inch of space in the house. My entire legs were in pain. I just wanted to go to sleep, but the thought of having the steamed rice before bed made me stay awake.

The rice was done in less than an hour. Everyone was literally starving and could not wait to eat. This was the second day without food for us. Chhorn distributed the rice to all of us, and we began to eat like hungry wolves. We didn't bother using a spoon and devoured our share within a few minutes with our hands.

After we finished our rice, most of us found a spot to rest and dozed off almost instantly from exhaustion.

CHAPTER 34

After three days living in Ta Hail's house, everyone understood that they could not stay here long. The house was too crowded, and Ta Hail would not be able to continue to feed nearly thirty of us. Each day we reduced one month's worth of rice for his family. Every family quickly began to search for places to live nearby, and they knew they had to make a decision quickly. Yey Lap, Yey Rom, and Pu Sarin's family were among the other families that came along with our families. Fortunately, they had discovered friends and relatives living nearby. They were able to borrow money and rice from their friends and relatives to continue their trip to the Thai border. Pu Poo's family found an abandoned house in the town and decided to move into the house until they could find enough rice to resume their trip.

It was then just our family and Solo and Polok now living in Ta Hail's house. He and Yey Sat did not put any pressure on Mother or Father to move. In fact, they had encouraged them to stay until we could save enough rice to make the trip. We were using one section of the house just for our family. Mother collected several stones to make a hearth. We use our own pots and pans to make food. Chhorn was living in a lower part of the house that was much smaller. Solo's mom had made a deal to give Ta Hail some rice when she returned for the room that Chhorn and her two children were living in.

Ta Hail had over three dozen palm trees on his land. He said Mother and Father could harvest the palm juice to trade. Unfortunately, the palm trees were very high, and Father did not know how to climb them or harvest the palm juice.

"It's been over ten years since the last time I climbed the palm trees. I'm too old for that, but I will try to climb and harvest the palm juice for you guys," Ta Hail said.

Ta Hail gathered all his gear, mostly bamboo cylinders, that he had stored away a decade ago, somehow undisturbed by the Red Khmer. Then he started to climb the palm trees and set up the bamboo cylinders to collect the palm juice.

The next morning, he climbed the palm trees and retrieved the bamboo cylinders and gave the cylinders full of palm juice to Mother to sell.

We woke up a little after sunrise from the noise of the travelers. Moments later, Mother came in with several of the bamboo cylinders in each hand. "Here, all of you help me carry these. I will go and sell them. If we don't sell the palm juice, your little brothers will have nothing to eat for today. Ta Hail no longer can afford to provide us rice. We've eaten nearly all the rice that he'd reserved for the rest of the year," Mother explained. She handed Chhom, Chhoy, and me a bamboo cylinder each.

Mother led us on the main road to the open market. We found a spot and sat down on one side of the road waiting for the thirsty travelers. There were several other women selling palm juice just a few yards away. Our product was obvious. We didn't have to say out loud what we were selling. Everyone knew we were selling palm juice.

We sat for an hour. The customers came and bought dessert, fish, and chicken just beside us. Some were walking, and some were riding their bicycles passing by. Not a single person was interested in purchasing the palm juice.

Chhom and I became bored very quickly having to sit that long time. Chhoy was used to selling products, so she was used to sitting and waiting. She looked very patient. I got up and walked around the area looking for something interesting to do and hoping we could go home soon.

I turned around and saw Mother smiling and holding the bamboo cylinder asking the customers, "Would you like to buy some palm juice?"

"No, I don't need any palm juice," the customer replied.

Mother went to the next customer and then the next and asked the same question over and over again. Some customers did not even reply. It was humiliating to walk around the market and ask customers to buy your product. Normally, the customer knew what you were selling and would come to you if they were interested.

It was long past afternoon, and not a single person showed any interest in buying the palm juice. No customers meant no rice for us to eat that night.

Mother gave up on the customers who were walking on foot. She walked to the middle of the road targeting people on their bicycles instead.

"Would you like to buy some palm juice?" Mother said to nearest man on a bicycle as she lifted up the bamboo cylinder. The man simply swerved around Mother and gave her an angry look. Mother ignored the man and continued on the next person. Mother attempted to approach other bicyclists, but they swerved around her left and right. "Why are you standing in the middle of the road?" one of them yelled after nearly crashing into her.

It was evening. Mother was growing more desperate to sell some palm juice to get some rice to feed us. There was a man on a bicycle with a basket on a rack behind him. Mother fixed her eyes on the man. He was riding more slowly than everyone, as his bike was heavy with a basket of rice.

"Hey brother, could you offer me some rice for my children? Take some palm juice to drink," Mother begged and gripped the man's arm with her hand. The man nearly lost his balance.

"Why did you do that?" the man asked angrily.

"Give me some rice for my children, and you can have some palm juice," Mother pleaded with a can in her hand. She had given up selling and begun begging instead.

The man got off his bike and dug his hand into the tightly secured basket on the rack on his bike and grabbed a fistful of rice and put it into Mother's can.

"Here. This is not my rice; this is all I can give you," he said.

"Here, have some palm juice," Mother said, handing the bamboo cylinder to the man.

"No, I don't want any palm juice. I have to get going," he said as he hopped on his bike and peddled away slowly.

Mother made a few more attempts to get bicyclists to buy palm juice, but she had no luck. She returned to her spot and stood still. She kept a straight face, not showing her frustration and despair, but we knew.

"Let's go home. I got some rice for your little brothers to eat. We will try again tomorrow," Mother said.

We followed Mother home, looking forward to eating some rice. I was very hungry as usual. Mother made rice porridge with the rice she'd gotten. It was not enough to make steamed rice.

When the rice was cooked, Mother scooped out the rice for Pech, Poe, and me. However, there wasn't enough rice for everyone, so Father, Mother, Chhom, and Chhoy just sat and watched us eat.

"That's all we have. The rest of us will have nothing for today. We have to try harder tomorrow," Mother said

We still had a lot of palm juice left. Mother woke up early the next morning and walked up to the intersection of the street to sell the palm juice. She did not bother walking to the market.

"Is anyone interested in palm juice?" she said to the passersby.

No one paid any attention to her. Mother continued to repeat her words patiently to everyone that passed by. She kept an eye out for any bicyclists who might have rice on their bicycle. When she saw one, she would run up to them and asked them to buy the palm juice.

Just before noon, Mother saw a man with a large basket on his bicycle. Mother ran to the middle of the road and stopped in front of him, forcing him to stop. "Help me. Buy some palm juice. I need rice for my children," she begged.

"I don't need the palm juice, but I will give you one can of rice," the man said.

He got off his bike and scooped out a can of rice and handed it to Mother. Mother smiled with joy.

"Thank you. You should drink some palm juice to give you strength," Mother suggested.

"That's all right. I'm in hurry," the man replied.

"Then good luck," Mother said.

Mother returned home immediately after she'd gotten a can of rice. When she entered the house, she saw Chhom sitting and crying softly, holding her feet. There was blood all over her hands and on her foot.

"What's the matter with you? Why are you bleeding?" Mother asked.

"I was looking for vegetables, and I stepped on a vase shard," she said sobbing.

"You need to wash it with hot water before an infection spreads," Mother said. "I will make rice porridge first. Your brothers are hungry. I will boil water to wash your feet after that," Mother said.

Chhom did not complain. As much pain she was in, her hunger was even greater. The thought of rice porridge made her stop crying.

Mother made rice porridge using only half a can of rice. She saved the other half just in case she was unable to get more rice tomorrow. All of us got to eat rice porridge in the afternoon. We did not have any vegetables to eat, as there were no rivers or abandoned land here to search for food.

By now, Mother knew for sure that no one wanted to buy palm juice. She would have better luck begging for rice. She continued to beg the passersby for rice. There were beggars everywhere on the road, but the only difference between her and the beggars was that she has palm juice to offer. She didn't ask much from the passersby. She just asked for a fistful of rice to feed the children. Luckily, she got some rice every day. Sometimes, she got two to three cans of rice.

Father had been staying home with nothing to do. There was no lake nearby where he could go and catch fish. He didn't have a wagon to travel far. He was becoming very frustrated not being able to find food.

"Mae Vea, we cannot live like this. We need to take a risk and move to Thai. Look at Solo's mom. She went to Thai and was able to earn enough money to come back and take her children with her. And she's a widow. If she can do that, we can too," he said to Mother during mealtime.

"How were we going to move if we have nothing to eat on the way? We came here from Kbal Kmouch with no food, but we knew we would get something to eat when we got here. We have no one in Thai who could give us rice to eat. We will die of starvation if we try," Mother said.

"Then what are we going to do? You can't beg for food forever. There is nothing for me to do here," Father said.

"As you know, Ta Hail has found many more of his children living in this city. I was thinking we should ask him to borrow some Thai money from them. I'm sure some of his children are well off by now. I noticed everyone is using Thai money in this city," Mother said.

"We should try. I really want to take the risk and go to the Thai border. I have heard everyone is doing well there. If things go well, we should be able to pay them back soon," Father said.

Mother and Father agreed and talked with Ta Hail about their plan, including borrowing money from his children. Ta Hail agreed. He saw us struggle, and there was nothing he could do to help. He went to every one of his children the next day and explained our situation.

Ta Hail came back in the same evening with the good news. "I talked with my children about your plan. They were willing to offer some money. The total is seven hundred baht. You could make the trip easily. I will miss you again when you leave. I will miss all my grandchildren too. If you could let me keep one of your children, I would do anything to get you the money. Plus, you have so many children, and I love them all. You know I'm capable of caring for them. Since Chhom is injured and unable to walk, she could stay here and live with us," Ta Hail said. "My children are like your brothers and sisters. Each of them would give me some money. They don't expect anything back, but if you were able to pay them back, you could just give the money to me and I would pay them back myself. You don't need to look for them to return the money," Ta Hail said.

Mother and Father looked at each other in disbelief. Seven hundred baht was a lot. Not only would it provide us food to travel, but we'd also be able to survive for six months. They agreed to have Chhom live here with them and take the money to travel. Ta Hail returned to his children the next day and came up with seven hundred baht as promised.

"We should have done this long ago. I didn't know Ta Hail could come up with seven hundred baht. I could buy things and trade with this much money," Mother said

"We should head for Thai soon before the Vietnamese block the road," Father said.

After Mother and Father made the decision to walk to Thai, Mother told all the families that came from Kbal Kmouch that we were going to the Thai border. She told them that we had some money, and she would buy rice for everyone to eat when we got there.

Early in the morning, we gathered in front of Ta Hail's house getting ready to make another trip. Pu Poo's family had been waiting for the opportunity all along. His son, Pat, and his daughter, Peah, were standing beside us with their mother. It was sad that their father, Pu Poo, had passed away on the trip to search for food with Chhoeun. He could have made their lives much better right now.

Several families that were living near Ta Hail's house overheard Mother and Father's plan and decided to come as well. Yey Sat was crying nonstop when she saw us preparing to leave. "You're all leaving me again. I have been waiting for you for so long. It is unfortunate that I am unable to support you. I will take good care of Chhom. I promise."

Mother was in tears as well. Besides us, Yey Sat was her next closest relative alive that she knew of. She had very little doubt that her brothers and sisters would have survived the Red Khmer. "If fates allow, we will meet again," Mother said.

Chhom was sitting in front of the door weeping. She was being left behind to live with a great aunt and uncle she had just gotten to know. She really wanted to come, but she couldn't walk. She understood that our family could not stay. We would starve to death if we did.

Father carried all the belongings using the dong raek. Pech and I were carrying one pot each. Chhoy and Chhorn were carrying the rest of our belongings that Father couldn't fit in the bucket. Mother was carrying Poe, wrapped in a scarf.

I didn't like the idea of walking again after we'd walked two days not too long ago. I still had small cuts from walking from Kbal Kmouch. Some of the cuts had been infected, and the infection was spreading. There was always some sort of infection on my feet, but most of them were no bigger than my thumb.

Just as we began walking, I saw at least a dozen more families getting ready to walk right behind us. Everyone was afraid to travel alone. Once they heard someone was going, they rushed to join. It was a last-minute decision for most families.

Today was a warm and cloudy. We began to march on the wide and clear road that was large enough to fit two ox wagons traveling in opposite directions. The vegetables and sugar cane were growing along both sides of the road. I felt like it was the Vietnamese invasion all over again. Pat, Pech, Peah, and I were walking together trying to make the best of this miserable walk. Pat had become our good friend since living in Kbal

Kmouch. He was the only boy around our age nearby here. We enjoyed any type of company to keep us from feeling hungry or tired. Pat kept looking at Father. Everyone knew he missed his own father. Peah, Pat's older sister, was about Chhom's age. She normally walked closely with Chhom on every trip. They normally didn't talk much, but they seemed to enjoy each other's company on the trip from Kbal Kmouch. Since Chhom was not here, she was walking with us.

After walking for a while, I turned my head around and saw that Ta Hail's house had gotten much smaller. Everything else around his house appeared small as well. The figures of the travelers around his house were ant-size from this distance.

The road gradually curved left, and then it curved right. Then all the trees and plants blocked all the houses from view.

"My legs hurt. I cannot walk anymore," Pech said as he stopped walking.

"You have to keep walking. No one is going to carry you," Mother said.

"I'm not walking," Pech said.

"There is a giant right behind you. It will eat you if you don't walk," Chhorn said.

"I'm not walking," Pech said.

"Puk Vea, carry him. He hasn't felt well for the last few days. He just walked two days straight recently. It's not a good idea to let him walk that far again," Mother said.

Without a word, Father stopped. He stooped down and lifted Pech up and placed him on his chest. Pech wrapped his feet around Father's body and then wrapped his hands around Father's neck. Father adjusted his dong raek and used one of his hands to support Pech from the bottom and continued walking. We stopped just a moment waiting for Father and then continued to walk. Pat was staring at Pech and Father, probably wishing someone could carry him too.

The sky became mostly clear. The afternoon sun was hovering above our heads, giving off its mighty heat. The trees were too far away to cast any shade. The plants along the road were too short. My feet were burning. I could feel every pain from the small cuts on my feet. This was a lot worse than the trip from Kbal Kmouch.

"Mother, I can't walk anymore. My feet hurt," I said.

I had never complained about walking before. I'd walked from Stung Chah to Ta Kream and from Ta Kream to many other towns that took us many days. This was my first time. I was hungry, exhausted, and my feet were in pain from the small infections.

"Chhorn, you should carry the dong raek and have you Father carry Bun on his back," Mother said.

"What's the matter with your feet?" Chhorn said angrily.

"My feet hurt," I replied.

"You should walk. Don't let Father carry you," Chhorn said.

I started to cry and said, "I can't walk."

"Here, carry this," Father squatted down and removed the dong raek from his shoulder.

"Climb on my back," Father said to me.

I smiled and climbed onto Father's back. I wrapped my legs around Father's waist just below Pech's legs and clung to Father's shoulders with my hands.

Father continued to walk with Pech in front and me in the back. I noticed everyone stopped and looked at us. Father was big and tall. He walked like it was nothing.

"Pech and Bun are lucky. They have a dad. If my dad was here, he would do the same. Right, Mom?" Pat said as he stared at us.

"Yes, he would do the same," Pat's mom said and started weeping.

We stopped to rest about three hours later. Father squatted down to allow me to get off his back.

"All right, you should walk again," Father said.

After spending three hours sitting on Father's back, my legs had become numb and unresponsive. I feel a light tingling through my legs, but I couldn't move them at all. I sat on the ground the same way I sat on Father's back. I tried to stand up, but my legs did not respond.

"I can't move my legs," I said and started to cry.

"I don't think he can walk. Carry him," Mother said.

After a short rest, Father picked Pech and me up and continued walking again. Pech and I clung to Father as he walked. Chhorn was angry that she had to carry all the things that Father had been carrying. It was way too heavy for her.

After about two hours later, Father got very tired and he stopped again.

"Chhorn, help me carry Pech. I will carry the dong raek and Bun," Father said.

"That's fine," Chhorn said.

Father positioned me on his chest and squatted down to secure the dong raek on his shoulder. Chhorn placed Pech on her back where he could use his feet to secure himself.

A while later, dark clouds began forming in the sky. Thunder rumbled from above. Lighting flashed in the distance.

"It's going to rain. There is no shelter around. We'll have to walk in the rain. We should not stop in the open field like this. It's too dangerous," Mother said.

The dark cloud continued to build up and inched closer and closer. The rain began to drizzle. The wind gust picked up its speed, blowing anything within its path. The day became dark like night in just a few minutes. The thunders cracked through the air like a demon ripping the sky apart. Then a loud explosion burst somewhere in the sky, louder than the artillery shelling. I was terrified. I would normally run inside the house for cover when I heard loud thunder. The rain began to pour very hard. There was no sign of anyone stopping. We were walking against the force of the wind and the heavy rain.

About two hours later, the heavy rain and the strong winds subsided. It was now just sprinkles with light wind. The skies were partially clear. Our clothes were soaking wet, but I didn't mind. It was nice and cool. The path become much narrower than before, and the road elevated drastically as if we were climbing a hill. Gradually, the sun dipped behind the distant trees and mountain. The calm and cool night took over. We were now walking in the dark. There was no sign that the adults would stop and rest.

Pop! Pop! Pop! The sound of gunshots erupted in the night.

"Get down!" Mother screamed.

Father crouched down suddenly with both of his arms securing the buckets to avoid spilling them. Then he used one hand to scoop me off his back.

"Get to the rice field. Stick together," Mother said.

Father lifted the dong raek up with his shoulder and carried me with one arm. Chhorn had Pech on her back running after Mother with Chhoy trailing behind. Poe was crying from the sound of the gunshots and from the sudden jerk.

Pop! Pop! Pop! More gunshots erupted.

Everyone dove for cover beside the ridge of the rice paddies. Mother rocked Poe and tapped him with her hand gently to stop him from crying. Father laid me beside his shoulder. The rice paddy was flooded from the rain. Our entire bodies were submerged in the water. We rested our heads on the rim of the rice paddy to keep our faces up.

"Maybe the Vietnamese and the Red Khmer are fighting," Mother whispered.

"Maybe that's true," Father replied.

"We should sleep here tonight. If we walk, we might get caught in the crossfire," Mother said.

"It's better if we sleep here just leaving our heads up like this. It's too dark to see where we are going," Peah's mom added.

Lightning flashed somewhere in the distance, revealing hundreds of travelers hiding in the rice paddies just like us. Peah's family was lying right next to us. Another baby somewhere nearby cried. I cringed and hoped the gunmen would not hear the sound of the crying baby.

After a while, the gun battle subsided. The night became completely silent.

"Let sleep here tonight. I don't think we should try to get up," Mother said.

"We all should sleep now," Father said. Then he turned over and picked Pech up from Chhorn and laid his head on his arm. Then he laid my head on his other arm. When he was satisfied with our position, he rested his head on the rim of the rice paddy. It was very uncomfortable sleeping with the rest of our bodies under the water, but I felt safe. Chhorn and Chhoy were lying between us and Mother.

I closed my eyes and dozed off. I woke up when Pech or Father moved, but I went back to sleep almost immediately. Chhorn and Chhoy were awake most of the time. They turned side to side trying to get comfortable.

The sound of loud, mushy footstep woke me up.

"What happen up there?" a man asked.

"There was a robbery back there. The robbers had guns and robbed the travelers. The Pa Ra surrounded the robbers and killed them all," another man said.

I didn't know anything about robbers, but they sounded dreadful. They sounded nearly as bad as the Red Khmers. I wondered what the robbers would look like. I could only imagine a bunch of skinny men in black carrying rifles. Maybe that's who they were.

Just when I was about to fall back asleep, the sound of thunder rumbled in the sky and lightning flashed everywhere. I opened my eyes, and then another flash of lightning lit up the sky. I closed my eyes and tried to get some more sleep. Then I dozed off despite the drizzling rain on my face.

"Get up! Get up!" Father shook me and Pech.

I opened my eyes. The rain had ceased. It was morning, but it was still dark. Our families normally started to walk before the sunrise just to get a head start. I could move my legs a little now, but I wasn't going to let anyone know. I didn't want to walk. I might not get a chance be on Father's back again.

Pech and I got up and crawled out of the water. Father squatted down and picked me up off the ground and positioned me on his back. Then he picked up Pech and positioned him in front.

Chhorn gathered the pots and pan that had fallen off the bucket and hooked the handle of the bucket onto the dong raek and placed it on her shoulder. Father waited until Chhorn was ready, and then he began to walk. Chhoy picked up the utensils that she had been carrying and walked right behind Chhorn. Mother was trailing after us with Poe snuggled down in the scarf on her shoulder. Pat was staring at me and Pech, longing for someone to carry him.

The sun was rising slowly. The brilliant light radiated from the eastern sky. We could see everything around us. Every single one of us were soaked and smeared with mud. Some people still had rice stalks stuck to their clothes and hair.

About two hours later, we came to a steep incline. The hill was blocking everything ahead. Father was walking slowly up the hill. He stopped when we reached the top of the hill and lowered Pech and I down. For some reason, my legs were numb again. I couldn't even get up to extend my leg to stretch. Every time I tried, I felt intense pain and soreness. I struggled on the ground, trying to extend my legs, but they would not respond.

The landscape caught my attention. I looked around and saw thick forest. There was not a single farm in the area. I felt like we'd arrived in another world.

"Let's rest. I'm very tired," Father said.

"Father, these things are heavy. Can I toss a few things away that we don't need? Maybe some plates? We have so many plates," Chhorn asked.

"Throw some away," Father replied as he was trying to catch his breath.

Chhorn grabbed a few plates and tossed them aside.

After a short rest, Father picked up Pech and me and placed us on his back and chest again and then continued walking. The hill began to decline very slowly. I could see hundreds of travelers from both directions of the road since we were on the hill. Most of these people weren't here yesterday. Somehow, they had caught up with us.

About an hour later Chhorn asked, "Father, can I throw a few more things away?"

"Go head. Make sure you don't throw away our pots. They are very important to us," Father said.

Chhorn was struggling with the dong raek. The load was meant for Father to carry. He was the biggest and strongest man around. It was not for a young and frail girl like Chhorn.

Nearly an hour later, Chhorn asked again, "Father, can I toss the machete and the axe out? They were heavy."

"You can toss out one, but keep the other. It doesn't matter which one," Father said.

Chhorn stopped and lowered the dong raek. She grabbed the axe and tossed it onto the side of the road. Then she placed the dong raek back on her shoulders. It doesn't appear to be any better for her after she'd tossed the axe away.

Moments later, Chhorn asked again, "Father, my shoulder hurts. Could you carry the dong raek now, and I will carry Bun?"

"All right, we'll trade," Father said.

Father lowered me down on the ground. My legs were curling lifelessly as I was being transferred. Chhorn picked me up and placed me on her back.

Father was now carrying the dong raek on his shoulders and Pech on his chest.

At first, I was comfortable because Chhorn had a smaller body to wrap my feet around, but unlike Father, she didn't use her hand to support me. My legs slid down as she walked.

"Move up!" she said.

I moved up a little but then slid back down.

"Move up!" she repeated.

I moved up again but then slid down almost immediately. Then I felt an excruciating pain from a pinch on my lap.

"Ow!" I screamed.

"I *said* move up!"

I leaped up and tried to stay up on her back, hanging onto her shoulders as best I could. Then, after a few moments, my legs started to slide down again. I felt another pinch on my thigh, and then I leaped up again. Chhorn stopped telling me to get up. Instead, she pinched me every time my legs slid down. I did what I could to keep my legs up.

"This is the fourth Vietnamese *ksae tream* (preparation line). We passed the first and second yesterday. We are still in the battle zone," Mother said.

Somehow, Mother was able to recognize the line where the Vietnamese set up. I looked around, but I didn't see any type of lines. The adults seemed to understand and knew what Mother was talking about.

"We must walk in a single line to be safe from mines," Father said.

Just when Father finished telling everyone, another traveler yelled out, "There was one over there. That's from the work of the Red Khmer. The Vietnamese would not plant mines."

I looked at where the man pointed, but I could not see any mines except for a small pile of dirt like a child had been playing with it.

When we walked further away from the mines, Chhorn asked Father to switch me for Pech. I was getting too heavy for her. I was glad Father was carrying me again.

After a long walk, the sun was ready to set. We came to a crowded area where hundreds of travelers were resting and chatting with other travelers. Some people made a camp to sleep and eat. Some were cooking rice and roasting fish.

"We passed all the *ksae tream.* I think this was the Pa Ra territory," Mother said.

"I think we are here," Chhorn said happily.

There were merchants walking in groups carrying heavy loads of baskets on a dong raek heading back to Phnom Tom. This was like a preparation spot for merchants and travelers. Some even had nice bicycles. Everyone was wearing colorful clothes. Our clothes were still black, ripped, and dirty.

There was a man pouring a pot of steamed rice onto a large plate on an abandoned hearth. There was no one around to eat the rice. It seemed he was giving the rice away.

"Chhorn, look at the rice over there! See?" Pech said and pointed.

Chhorn knew the man was giving the rice away, but for some reason she was embarrassed to fetch the rice. She had risked her life stealing rice many times during Red Khmer but never had to take the rice from someone who left it out in the open like that.

"Be quiet!" Chhorn said and pinched Pech on his legs. "We have our own rice. We will cook our own rice to eat," Chhorn said.

"I want that rice. I'm hungry," Pech continue.

The strange feeling made Chhorn hesitate to get the free rice, but she was very hungry. It was the second straight day of walk without eating. She squatted down and lowered Pech to the ground. Then she began walking toward the plate full of rice. Then a woman and two children came and picked up the rice and left. Chhorn gritted her teeth with anger and disappointment. She came back and picked Pech up and then continued walking.

"Chhorn, talk louder so maybe Chhoeun or Tien's mom could hear us," Peah's mom said as they tried to squeeze through the crowd.

"We don't even know if they are here. It doesn't matter how loud we speak, they will not hear us," Chhorn replied.

"Who is that? It sounds like Chhorn," said a woman's voice from somewhere in the crowd.

"Ming! It is me, Chhorn!" Chhorn screamed in surprise.

Tien's mom emerged from the crowd like a phantom. Chhoeun was walking right behind her carrying two heavy baskets with a dong raek. Father, Mother, Chhoeun, and everyone laughed in disbelief that they'd found each other in such a crowded place and in a perfect time.

"Chhoeun and I were about to head back to Phnom Tom to give you some rice and to go see my daughter, Mao. Since you all are here, we don't have to go. It will save me a lot of energy," Tien's mom said.

"Where is Mao? I thought you all came together," Mother asked.

"I had to give her up to a wealthy man. She was very sick and hungry. I thought she was going to die like Van Suk. The man gave me some rice in return so that I could continue to travel. Without the rice, all of us would have died on the way here," Tien's mom explained.

"You are a lunatic. I don't who care who you gave Mao to, I want her back. She's like my daughter. We raised her together since the beginning of the Red Khmer. We will not give her up," Mother scolded.

"After your family is settled down, we can talk about it. By the way, where is Chhom?" Tien's mom asked.

"I gave her to my uncle, but I had a good reason. He gave me seven hundred baht, and Chhom was injured. She would not have been able to walk anyway," Mother said.

"Why would you give my niece away? Mao is small, but Chhom is a full-grown girl. She worked hard to raise her little brothers and my children. I would do anything to get her back. I will get her back myself then."

"We can talk later when my family gets settled down," Mother replied.

"Speaking of rice, we are hungry. We haven't eaten for two days. Let's cook the rice and eat." Peah's mom said.

The plan was to get here and buy some rice to cook. We had a little rice but not enough to feed everybody. Since Chhoeun had a lot of rice, we did not have to buy any.

"Here! I brought cooked rice with us intended to surprise you when we got there. Since you are here, we can eat right now. Chhoeun has a pot, and I have a pot."

"Let's eat. I'm so hungry that my stomach is churning," Peah's mom said.

Everyone walked in and squatted down around the two pots. Chhoeun was the only one that didn't want to eat. He'd probably eaten already. He just stood and watched us eat.

As we were digging our hands into the pots, competing for rice like wolves, a young man a little older than Chhoeun was standing and holding a small knife just a few feet from us. He was watching us eat, and he looked very hungry. His eyes were fixed on the rice pots.

Mother noticed the young man and asked, "Are you hungry, *Kmuy*?"

"Yes," the young man said and swallowed his saliva.

"Then come and eat," Mother said.

The young man did not hesitate but came and knelt down in the circle and dug his hand into the pot like he was one of us. He shoved one handful of rice into his mouth while using the other hand to grab some more rice in the pot.

"Pat, eat faster. This guy here eats very fast. He's going to eat all the rice. If he continues to eat that fast, there will be no more rice for us," Peah's mom said.

"*Kmuy*, eat a little slower, all right?" Mother said gently.

"Yes," the young man replied politely.

We ate until there wasn't a single grain of rice in the pot, and then we sat still in the same spot and relaxed. I wish there was more rice. I was still very hungry.

"Is there any water?" Mother asked.

"Water is scarce around here. It is as valuable as rice. You need to trade rice for water, not like back where we live where water is abundant. Over here, we have to dig a well. People are making a living from selling water," Tien's mom explained.

"If I knew the water was scarce like that, I would have collected more during the storm. Then I could have traded it for rice," Mother said.

"Now I know why the man was standing there with a bucket of water in front of him," Chhorn said. "I can't wait to get there to sell some water."

Chhoeun scooped a can of rice and went to trade for water with the man standing with a bucket full of water.

"This was all I get for a can of rice," Chhoeun said, handing Mother a coconut bowl of water.

"My God! That's two meals of rice for our family," Mother exclaimed. "Then carefully share the water. Make sure everyone get some. Include the young man here,"

"What? We just fed him rice, and now we're giving him water too?" Peah's mom exclaimed.

"Who would eat and not drink water? If he doesn't drink water, he will die from thirst," Mother said.

After we drank the water, the adults sat on the ground and chatted.

"Chhoeun, your mother in-law is very angry at you for not bringing any rice for her. She said if she sees you, she will report you to the Vietnamese. She will tell them that you joined Pa Ra, and she really meant it. It's up to you if you want to go back or not," Mother said briefly.

"I'm not going back. I could never make her happy. She insulted me every minute. This was a perfect time for me to depart from her," Chhoeun said.

Everyone knew that was true, but Chhoeun didn't look happy after saying that. It was hard to tell how he felt about not returning to Huk and her Mother. He rarely spoke of them, but he had been working hard to support them like Father had promised them.

After a short rest, we followed Tien's mom to her new shelter. Pu E came shortly after and informed us that he'd found a vacant shelter not too far from here. We followed him to the new shelter made of bamboo and hay. Father laid me down on the floor. My legs were in pain, and I begin to sob. Pech was having the same problem. He was crying as well.

Mother was staring at us with curiosity. We had walked two days from Kbal Kmouch to Phnom Tom, and we were fine. This time, we didn't have to walk that much. We'd spent most of the time on Father's and Chhorn's backs.

"Let me take your pants off and see what was wrong with your legs," Mother said and pulled my ragged pants off.

Mother wailed when she saw my legs. I looked down and saw dozens of bruises on each of my legs. She cried and walked over to Pech and took off his pants. She saw bruises everywhere on his legs as well.

"What did you do to them?" Mother shouted.

"I was tired of trying to hold them up on my back. Their legs kept on sliding down making it very hard for me to walk. When I pinched them, they moved their legs up for a while. When their legs slid down again, I pinched them some more. I was very tired. I can't even walk straight myself. Having them on my back made it even harder," Chhorn explained, nearly in tears herself.

Mother continued to scold Chhorn for pinching us. Meanwhile, Father was lying on the ground motionless. He'd been carrying us and the dong raek for two days straight.

Moments later, Tien's mom came and gave us fish and steamed rice. She told us that every family got a share of salty fish, known as *pla thu,* once a week. Sometimes, they gave out rice. We ate the rice that Tien's mom brought with the fish. The fish were strange looking and salty, but they were good.

This was the first time in a long time that we'd gotten to eat streamed rice twice in the same day. I ate until I could no long take another bite. It was the first time as far as I could remember that I could eat until I was full. Tien't mom was still chatting with Mother.

The next day, Pech and I didn't wait long to venture out in the new place. Our legs were still sore from the pinches, but I could walk and run without a problem. This town captured my attention. Unlike any other place we'd lived in, this place was well-organized and crowded. The trees grew everywhere. The entire town was covered by the canopies of the trees. According to Tien's mom, this place was called Jum Rum Tmey (New Camp). This was a hidden city in the jungle. Children of all ages were running wild, having so much fun. They appeared to have a lot of energy.

We walked slowly further into a spacious area. Hundreds of adults and children were walking and chatting at a normal pace. It was amazing just to see what the people were wearing. Everyone here, especially the grownups, was wearing colorful clothes. Many men and woman wore colorful rubber sandals and shoes that covered most of their feet. A dozen yards away, several men were walking together wearing black shoes that covered their feet. Women wore ornaments on their necks, in their hair, and on their wrists.

Clothing was not the only thing that was abundant; the food was too. People were eating everywhere I turned. They walked and ate food on a stick or sometimes in some type of package.

Then a boy about our age, well dressed, walked past us while eating some type of dry food with one hand and holding a yellowish package in the other. The smell of the food was so good and exotic that it was indescribable.

"I wonder what he was eating," I said to Pech.

"It smells good. I want some," he said.

The boy immediately noticed that we were new to this place and stopped. "This was called *mee*. It's noodles, but it comes in a package. You're supposed to cook it before you eat it, but it tastes good raw too," he said.

"Can we have some?" I asked.

The boy paused for a long moment. He looked at Pech who could not take his eyes off the noodles. "You can have a bite, but I bought this with my money," the boy said and broke of a small piece of noodle and handed to me. Then he broke off another small piece of noodle and handed it to Pech.

I didn't know what he meant by money, but it sounded important. I popped the piece of noodle in my mouth, and the taste was delicious. Rice tasted good, but *mee* was like rice times ten. I really wanted some more, a lot more. I could eat it all day if it was available.

"Can I have a little more?" I asked. I had never had to ask another person for food before because I knew no one would give up their food, but this boy seemed to have a lot in his hand.

"If you want more, you have to buy it yourself," the boy said and walked away.

I was disappointed and felt a little ashamed for asking, but I saw something had fallen out of the package that he was holding.

"Look what he dropped!" Pech picked up two small packages. One was clear with blue stripes, and one was silver with decorative figures on it.

Pech gave me the clear package, and he kept the silver one for himself. I ripped the package open, and some sort of liquid was oozing out. Then I was overwhelmed by the indescribable, heavenly aroma. Instinctively, I sipped the liquid. It tasted like oil but was rich in flavor. I had tasted plain oil before, and it was delicious, but this liquid offered the hidden creamy and satisfying taste with some sort of garlic or roasted herb. In fact, it tasted so much better than the noodle itself.

"I'm going to tell Mother you ate something bad," Pech said and ran toward the house.

The last time he told Mother when I ate the poison mushroom, she whipped me so hard that red marks appeared instantly all over my skin. I learned my lesson and would not go near Mother when Pech told on me. Instead, I sucked on the oily package until nothing was left. I continue to wander around the area looking for someone to play with or some more things to eat.

Unlike me, Pech would never eat something without knowing what it was. He wouldn't hesitate to tell Mother if I'd eat anything we didn't know about. He returned to the open area to play later that day. There was no indication that Mother was looking to whip me. He seemed normal and acted like nothing had happened.

CHAPTER 35

I continued to like Jum Rum Tmey more and more. We had been eating well. I was having a lot of fun, and more importantly, I felt safe here. We were living in a congregated place hidden in the forest, protected by the Pa Ra, the newly formed military system probably funded by the Thai. Their main purpose was to keep the Vietnamese away from the Thai border since the Thai and the Vietnamese had been enemies since the beginning of time. The Pa Ra also kept the Red Khmer away, making Jum Rum Tmey free of the Vietnamese and the Red Khmer.

Everyone was doing well here. It was only our fourth day here, but I got to eat pla thu fish twice a day. I never got tired of the fish. It came in many different types and sizes. The largest fish I had seen Mother cook was the size of an adult's hand. I couldn't eat the entire fish by myself because it was too salty, and I had to eat it with rice.

We got most of the rice from a man known as Pu Young, who had been living in Stung Chah with us all along. He had everyone fooled into thinking he was mentally disabled. Pu E notified Pu Young the second day we arrived. He was escorted by several heavily armed Pa Ras when he came to greet us. All the Pa Ra called him by the title Loak (sir).

"I thought you had mental problems?" Father asked.

"If I didn't act like I had mental problems, I would have been taken to execution long ago," Pu Young replied. "I inadvertently spilled my military background to them when they first started asking questions. When I discovered they were killing the Lon Nol's soldiers, I pretended I had a mental illness and didn't know anything. If not for that, I would not be living today."

"I could give you a basket of rice every week for free, but that would be too obvious. I'm not allowed to give away rice, but if you work for me, I could give you rice," Pu Young said.

"What do you want me to do?" Father asked.

"All you need to do is carry water from the well to the military base. You are the strongest man around. The job will fit you."

"A basket of rice per week is a lot. I can carry water all day," Father said.

"Then you should start soon. But tonight, you should drink with me. I have ordered all-you-can-eat blood clams. Come to my house, and we will eat and drink," Pu Young said.

Father went with Pu Young that evening. He returned home after midnight drunk and sick. He vomited before entering the house. Then he continued to vomit and had diarrhea all night until morning. He was so weak that he could not even stand up.

"I think I was poisoned by the blood clams. I don't think I'm going to make it alive," he said.

"You shouldn't have gone drinking last night. You just walked carrying two children for two days. Your body is still recovering from the hard work," Mother scolded.

"I thought it was all right. I've had blood clams before. I've never had this problem. I think I might die today," Father said in agony.

"Don't say that. Just lie down and rest," Mother said. Mother began to weep. Father had never been this sick before. He was vomiting and having diarrhea all night. He could barely move now.

Chhorn and Chhoy were crying and messaging his arms and legs. They were praying nonstop. "Father, don't leave us. We need you. Please get better. Please God, help Father," Chhorn said.

Father was lying down on the floor almost motionless. Mother continuously checked on him to make sure he was still breathing. He woke up several hours later feeling well again, "I thought I was going to die. I have never been that sick in my whole life. Now I feel normal gain. Maybe I can even work. A basket of rice is a lot," Father said.

We were happy that Father was up and well again. He went to work later on that day. It was an opportunity he didn't want to miss. He came back home at night explaining how his job went. "It's hard work. I had to carry two buckets of water from a well to the military base for the Pa Ra to cook and drink. The distance from the well to the military base is about two kilometers. I have to make four trips a day, but it's well worth it."

Pu Young came to visit our house regularly. He was impressed by Father's work. He offered the job to Chhorn and Chhoy as well if they wanted to work. Chhorn and Chhoy accepted the job and began working the next day. Carrying two buckets of water for two kilometers was easy for Father, but not for Chhorn and Chhoy. Pu Young noticed they were struggling to make just one trip on their first day. He offered them another option.

"Why don't you register for the military like your brother did? You would get more rice," he said to Chhorn.

"I don't know how to carry a rifle, and I don't want to shoot anyone," Chhorn replied.

"You don't have to carry a rifle or shoot. You just need to be there and work in the kitchen," he said.

Father told Chhoy to stop working. She was too small and too frail for the job. Chhorn registered with the military as Pu Young suggested. She worked in the kitchen with the chef collecting firewood, cutting vegetables, carrying light water for short distances, and serving food to the Pa Ra military. She got paid a basket of rice per week as well. However, she was terrified of the Pa Ra. One day, one of the member of the Pa Ra requested a glass of water while they were training. Chhorn was nervous and spilled the water. The Pa Ra member was upset and grabbed a rifle and fired a few shots up the air to tease her. Chhorn pissed her pants and wailed.

With a lot of incoming rice, Mother cooked two meals a day every day with a side dish, such as stir-fried meat and vegetables. Mother sold some rice for Thai money. Then she used the money to purchase meat, vegetables, salt, sugar, MSG, garlic, and other spices to cook with.

After the second week, Mother was planning to get Chhom and Mao back. She cried every time she thought of them. She talked with Solo's mom and offered to pay her to get Chhom back. Solo's mom was still exporting products from here to Phnom Tum. Her children were still living with Ta Hail. His daughter Nee was taking care of them.

"Tell my uncle that I miss my daughter every day. Tell him I am extremely sick from thinking of her. If I don't see her, I will die of sickness," Mother said to Solo's mom.

Solo's mom accepted the task and kindly refused to accept any payment. She returned from Phnom Tum a week later with Chhom. Her injury was not completely healed, but she was able to walk and made it here with us. After Solo's mom brought Chhom home, she told Mother that this was her last time in Jum Rum Tmey. She had made enough money to buy land and open a business at Kbal Kmouch. She had saved enough rice to last a year, and she had saved enough money to buy Thai products and sell them in Kbal Kmouch. She still had faith that her husband was alive, and she would continue to wait for him.

A few days after Chhom arrived, Mother urged Tien's mom to get Mao back. Mao's case was more complicated because Tien's mom had given her up to a stranger for the price of rice. She had no right to get her back. Like Mother, Tien's mom cried every time she thought of Mao. She missed her a lot.

"I don't care how you get her back, but you must get her back," Mother urged Tien's mom every time.

Mother had asked Chhoeun to sneak out from the Pa Ra camp and help get Mao. Chhoeun agreed and led Tien's mom to a city call Sisophon, where Mao was.

They returned six days later with Mao on Chhoeun's back. Every single one of us was extremely happy to see her back, especially Chhom. She had been taking care of her like her own sister for many years.

"I pretended to go visit just by myself. Chhoueun was hiding in a bush nearby. Then I convinced the husband that I would take Mao to the potty. I placed her on my back and started running toward Chhoeun. When I reached Chhoeun, he put her on his back and ran. We ran until we were out of breath and almost died of exhaustion," Tien's mom explained and laughed.

Tien's mom was very excited and relieved that Mao was back. She thanked Mother for encouraging her to get Mao back and thanked Chhoeun every time she talked about Mao's rescue story.

Pech and I began to hang out with Tien and Mao again. Tien was very hyper and outgoing. He was the opposite of me. We liked to play together, but we argued a lot and even had fistfights sometimes. Then we'd get a long the next day like nothing had happened.

Every day was a fun day for us. The moment we got out of bed, we immediately met up in the open field where the Pa Ra soldiers trained. We also made new friends with other children about the same age. Most of them had been here much longer than us. They had seen more things, and they loved to share their stories.

"Yesterday, I saw three French people," a boy said.

"What is French?" I asked. Pech and Tien were behind me waiting for answers.

"The French have white skin and white hair, and they are big like the giants," the boy said, stretching his arms up high and lifting his heel up to make himself look taller.

"Do they eat human like the giants?" I asked.

"Maybe the French eat humans. Their stomachs are always bulged out, and they always carry large backpacks," the boy said.

I was so anxious to see the French and hoped they didn't eat humans. I couldn't wait to tell my other friends about the French.

Just when the boy finished telling the story, the sound of thousands of footsteps came down like a heavy rain. Thousands of Pa Ra soldiers were walking in perfectly aligned columns marching down from somewhere. Every single one of the soldiers was wearing a camouflage uniform and holding a rifle. They were singing some sort of song that I could not decipher. However, I was mesmerized by the harmonious movements and the tune of the song.

After the training was over, Tien found other children to play with and left. Pech and I continued to play in the open field. Today must have been the pla thu fish distribution day. We saw that large trucks had just unloaded piles of pla thu fish. Each pile must have been three times my height. I grinned in delight when I saw the fish.

"I'm going to steal some fish," I said to Pech.

"How? They going to arrest you," Pech said.

"Don't worry. Just pretend we're playing around the fish. I will look around. When no one is looking, I will grab some fish and run," I explained.

Pech did not say anything. He knew what I was going to do was wrong. He normally didn't do anything wrong. I picked up a stick about three feet long. I held the stick and pretended to play with it as we walked toward a pile of fish. Pech was walking behind me looking very nervous. When I got closer to the fish, I looked around for any adults nearby. A couple of adults were busy making another pile of fish from the truck and didn't seem to pay any attention. I dropped the stick and grabbed as much fish as I could with my two hands and ran as fast as I could toward our house. I didn't pay attention to what Pech was doing.

I didn't stop until I reached the front door of our house. Chhom was at home preparing something for Mother to cook. She was not paying any attention to us.

"I got fish! I got fish!" I said happily showing Chhom several pla thu fish.

Pech was right behind me, laughing in excitement. "I got some fish too!" He was holding one fish on each hand.

"You stole the fish?" Chhom said and smiled. I knew Chhom wouldn't get mad at me. She stole rice to feed us all the time in Stung Chah.

It was fun to steal something that could feed our family. I had always wanted to help feed the family like Chhom, Chhorn, and Chhoy. Pech and I went back and stole some more fish until one of the adults took notice.

"Nae! Stop taking the fish. It's for sharing," the man said from a distance motioning his hand angrily.

Pech and I tossed the fish back onto the pile and ran home. We were scared to death. We rested at home for a while, hoping no one was after us. We went back later in the evening. I was sure the man who'd seen us steal the fish would not remember us. There were way too many kids around.

Pech and I spent most of our days hanging out in the same open field. Chhom would come and call us for lunch and dinner. The Pa Ra soldiers held their training here every three to four days. Sometime people gathered in the middle of the field for meetings where one person would speak and the rest would sit and listen.

As Pech and I trotted home from a long fun of day, we saw a group of children standing and listening to a boy about three years older than me. "Last night, the play was about the giant putting a spell on the princess. Then the prince broke the giant's spell with his own magic and shot the giant with his magic arrow," the boy described. "The prince sang, and he danced like this." He started to dance with a stick in his hand as his imaginary bow and arrow.

This was not the first time someone mentioned the play. There were activities going on at the other side of the camp that I don't know about. Whatever it was, it sounded interesting. The boy continued to tell us other parts of the play. He moved and danced as he told the story. It was about giants, wizards, the prince, and the princes. Pech was standing next to me paying very close attention to the story.

As the boy was telling the story, I noticed a group of men were cutting a tree about two dozen feet away. They had been doing this since we came to listen to the story, but I didn't really pay attention to what they were doing. Just when I was about to turn my attention to the men, the tree gave out a loud crack sound. Then I saw the top of the tree slowly moving toward us.

"Get out of there!" a man yelled.

It was too late. The entire tree crashed to the ground so fast, I didn't get a chance to warn Pech, who was standing closer to the tree than I was. One of the branches caught Pech on the side of his head and knocked him on to the ground.

Pech was lying motionless on the ground. I didn't know what to do. I walked over to Pech, hoping he was all right.

"Are you guys all right?" a familiar voice said. "F***! It's Pech!"

It was Chhoeun who was cutting the tree with the other men. He picked Pech up. Then Pech opened his eyes and started to wail. Chhoeun checked all over his head and found no blood. "Go home and see Mother," Chhoeun said and left.

I walked Pech home for a moment, and then he stopped and stood in one place, both of his hands cupping his jaw. He cried with his jaw fixed open as if it was too painful to close it. I had never felt so bad for Pech in my whole life. Since we'd grown up together, we were always competing for food and telling Mother on each other. Today I realized I was his older brother, and for some reason, I felt like this incident was my fault.

I knew if the tree that size had fallen on him, it must have broken his bones somewhere. It must be his jaw. He seemed to have trouble closing his jaw. I panicked. I didn't know what to do. I grabbed Pech's hand and tried to make him walk home, but he pulled his hands away and used it to cup his jaw again.

I decided to run home. I found Chhom lying inside the house, resting after some hard work. She couldn't resist taking the job of carrying and selling water.

"Chhom, Pech got hit by a tree!" I said frantically.

"Where?" she asked.

"This way."

I ran and led her to Pech, who was still crying and cupping his jaw with both hands.

"What's the matter?" she asked Pech.

Pech didn't answer but continued to cry. She peeled his hand off his face and examined him. There were bruises on his left jaw, but she doesn't know what else to check.

"I don't know if his jaw is broken, but we can find out. I'm going buy him a pack of mee. If he can eat, then he might be all right," she said.

Chhom left for the nearby merchant and returned less than ten minutes later with a pack of mee. She ripped the package open and broke the mee in half. She gave him half and gave me the other half.

"I don't want it. Give it all to Pech," I said, hoping Pech was all right.

Pech stopped crying and took a bite of the mee. He cringed in pain when he chewed, but he continued to eat it any way.

"Let's go home," Chhom said.

Pech walked and ate at the same time. I followed him and scrutinized him, hoping he was all right. I got hungry as I watched him eat. I really wanted some mee too, but today I wanted to be his real big brother and fought my hunger and allowed him to eat the rest of the mee.

When we got home, Pech sat down and finished the entire package.

"Are you going to eat the oil?" I asked. Every package came with the delicious flavored oil.

"No," he replied.

"Can I have it?" I asked.

"Yeah," he said and handed me the tiny package of flavored oil.

I ripped the oil package open and sucked on it until nothing was left. Chhom told Mother about the incident. Mother was very upset and nearly spanked us for not taking care of Pech. Chhom and I ran outside when she grabbed a small stick.

Pech woke up the next day crying and cupping his jaw with his hands. Chhom bought him another pack of mee to try to make him stop crying. Pech took a bite and threw it away. It was too painful for him to chew. There was nothing she could do to help. She left to go to work that morning, leaving just me and Pech at home.

Staying home didn't help Pech either. I thought maybe if we went out to play, Pech might forget his pain. I walked him back to the field to play and hoped to ease the pain.

"Burglar! Burglar!" someone screamed.

Pop! Pop! Pop! The gunshots erupted and then subsided very quickly.

Normally, I would dive to the ground and lie flat on my stomach, but it happened so fast that I didn't have a chance to react. Strangely, everyone was flocking toward the incident instead of running away. Pech and I looked at each other, curious what was going on. Then we followed the crowd.

"They caught a burglar!" a boy yelled out from a distance, looking proud to have witnessed the incident.

"Have you seen a burglar before?" asked a well-dressed boy about my height who walked beside us.

"No. What do they look like?" I asked.

"I don't know, but I heard from other people that they can run very fast. Their toes have thin skins between them like duck feet. That's how they run so fast. They also carry rifles," he explained with a serious face.

I had seen ducks before in Stung Chah. They did have the thin skins between their feet, and they did run very fast. I believed the boy and continued to follow the others toward the burglar. The crowd seemed to move toward the military base.

A moment later, we arrived at the military base. There was a thick circle of people surrounding the suspect. Pech and I could not pass through the circle, but we waited patiently.

"He's a burglar and part of the Red Khmer. He must be lost and hungry. He came to rob for food," one of the adults said.

It didn't take long for people to lose interest and return to their normal life. There were still a dozen of men and women standing around discussing the incident. It was an opportunity for us to get closer to the suspected burglar. In the center was a thin man wearing black. His hands were bound together behind his back, and he was squatting down. He didn't look afraid as I thought he would. In fact, he looked very angry.

The Pa Ra left his rifle leaning against his face with the barrel pointing upward. They were confident he couldn't do anything, and it helped prove who he was. This was my first time looking at a burglar. Now I knew what a burglar looked like. They were skinny. They wore black clothes. They had a rifle, and they looked very angry.

I was afraid of the burglars, but at the same time, I was excited to see one. I had an urge to do something crazy, something Pech would go tell Mother about right away. I looked around the area and found a pointy blue pen cover just a few yards away from the burglar. I had seen the blue pen covers everywhere lately. The adults used the pens to write, and sometimes they dropped the cover.

I walked over and picked up the pen cover and leaped over to the burglar and shoved the pen cover into the barrel of his rifle. Then I immediately dashed away as fast as I could. I looked back and saw Pech running right behind me. I expected someone to yell or throw something at me. Instead, I heard a loud laughter from all the adults. I was scared, but it was a thrill. This was, by far, the most exciting day of my life. I'd insulted the Red Khmer, whom I had been living in fear of for so long. He was also a burglar, whom everyone feared of as well. I had never done something so wrong and felt so good.

We ran until we got home. Pech and I were exhausted. Normally, Pech would have told Mother on me already, but this time he didn't. Maybe his jaw still hurting and he couldn't talk, or maybe he liked what I did. He stooped down laughing and trying to catch his breath at the same time.

It took two weeks for Pech's jaw to heal. He was now able to eat steamed rice and salty fish. He could also eat hard food like beef or pork. After his face stopped swelling, there was a big mark underneath his facial skin that indicated either a broken bone or dislocated jaw. There were also two dimple-like marks on both sides of his jaw as well. The left dimple was larger than the right.

After several weeks or maybe months had passed by, Pech and I ventured further and further away from home, wandering around this amazing place. We saw more new settlers building new houses around the area. The camp became more and more crowded.

In midafternoon, Pech and I had just finished eating lunch. Mother had just given us two Thai coins before she left the house. I knew what to do with the money, but I had never actually done it. Then we came across the thing that the other children were talking about. "That's the male French," I told Pech.

"Wow! It looks like a human. It is so tall and big like the giants," Pech said.

We followed the French as he was walking with a couple of men that stood just below its shoulders. The French was holding a rectangular white package with a large red cross sign. We examined the French from a distance, and now I believed everything the boy had said. We ran and got closer, trying to get a better look. The French realized it had been followed and turned around and looked at us straight in the eyes and smiled. My heart stopped a few beats from the stare. The French had a sharp, pointy nose and bizarre-colored eyes. His face was as pale as his arms with lots of hair.

"Bonjour!" the French said.

"Run!" I screamed. Pech and I leaped like we had been chased by tigers and fled. No one was paying attention to the French, but we didn't care. We didn't want to take any chances. We wanted to get as far away as possible. We ran as fast has our feet could move.

We slowed down after a while and then looked back. When we saw that no one was following us, we stopped.

"That was close!" I said.

"The French nearly got me," Pech said.

We came to an area that we had never been to before. It was very crowded like an open market. We saw a man standing by a bicycle with a large box in the back. Children were buying something from the man. It was some sort of dessert on a stick.

"We have money. Let's go buy some," I said to Pech.

We waited in line to buy some. By the look of the boys and girls and the man exchanging the dessert for money, we learned that the man was selling popsicles. When it was our turn, the man wanted just one of my coins and gave us two popsicles. I took a bite of the popsicle. It tasted so good and so cold. I thought the mee oil was delicious, but the popsicle was ten times better. It was creamy and sweet. There were also some beans in the middle that made it even more delicious. The chill from the popsicle ran through my lips and teeth. Maybe that's why it was so good. This was the coldest object that I had ever touched. It amazed me how the merchant made the popsicles so cold on such a hot day.

I enjoyed nearly everything about Jum Rum Tmey except for the time I needed to go to the bathroom. I used to have my private spot to do my business, but someone discovered my spot and did their business there as well. And there were a lot of them. I got disgusted every time I had to go, especially on rainy days. Sometimes, I lost my appetite thinking about it. I had never lost my appetite before. I was always hungry. It was something new.

My thought of this place as a sanctuary ended when I heard the gun battle and explosions erupt. The rumor was the Vietnamese were forming a force and attacking this place. It was just a matter of time before they would break the barrier. Then there were also rumors of a suicide and murders near our house. Jum Rum Tmey was not as safe as I'd thought.

Father continued to spend time eating and drinking with Pu Young, who knew more about this camp than anyone else. He told Father that there were trucks transporting anyone who wanted to go live in a new camp on Thai soil. All we needed to do was to register. Father discussed with Mother and agreed to take the risk to live on Thai soil. He went and registered our names as instructed.

A few days later, Chhom told me a date that we would depart to Thai and told me not to go out of the house on that day. I wasn't sure what she was talking about, but it sounded serious.

Several days later, I was playing hide and seek with Tien and Mao around their house when Chhom furiously marched toward me and Pech.

"I thought I told you not to go anywhere today! The truck is waiting for us. If we don't get there on time, our family will leave without us! Now, let's go!" she yelled and nearly slapped me. It was fortunate that she came right on time. It was my turn to hide in the game of hide-and-go-seek. Pech was hiding behind the closest tree and noticed how much Chhom wanted us to follow her.

Pech and I were running after Chhom. Not too far away, I saw several trucks full of men, women, and children parked in front of the camp gate. Some people were standing along the side of the truck, and some were sitting in the center. Mother, Father, Chhoy, and Chhorn were already on the truck. The truck engine had just started and moved forward a little.

Families were still climbing onto the trucks. Some people were weeping as they said goodbye to their friends and families. Most people were scared. This was almost like the beginning of Red Khmer all over again. People we were being transported to an unknown destination. Some were smiling for having a chance to be on the truck.

"Run faster! The truck will move any time now!" Chhoy yelled.

Chhom, Pech, and I ran as fast as we could, hoping the truck would not move. We hopped into the truck with the help of Chhoy and Father.

"Chhoeun, it's time to get on now," Mother said.

I hadn't seen Chhoeun earlier, but he stood hidden behind several people that were saying farewell to their families. Chhoen looked around and leaped onto the truck. He was wearing his civilian clothes today.

"Go…go...go!" Chhorn urged the truck to move.

Soon enough, the gate magically rose up, and the truck began to move. The sudden jerk nearly knocked me and Pech off our feet. Now I understood why some people were sitting down instead of standing up. Pech and I laughed from the new experience. When the truck picked up speed, I felt like someone was playing with my guts. I felt scared and excited at the same time. I'd had this feeling before, but I could not recall when. Even sitting in the ox wagon was not like this.

I got used to the motion of the truck and turned my attention to the scenery. Every single one of adults were sitting down on the floorboards of the truck, giving Pech and I the chance to see the scenery as the truck was moving. This was another sort of excitement. Looking out to the side of the truck, I could see trees, shrubs, and grasses were moving. The closer they were to the truck, the faster they moved. The distant objects, such as palm trees, were rotating around the closer object. In fact, the entire earth was moving. The only things that seem to be standing still were the trucks behind us.

"Pech look! Everything is moving fast!"

"Yeah...yeah...everything is moving!" Pech replied happily in agreement.

"Everything is not moving! We are moving, idiots!" said Chhom, annoyed by our naïve conversation.

We stopped talking and continued to enjoy our view. I wished we could sit here forever. It was a good feeling to travel a great distance at great speed without having to take a single step. We could even eat while we were moving if we had any food.

The truck went over a bump and tossed us slightly up in the air. "Ya!" Pech screamed in excitement.

The adult didn't seem to care, but Pech and I loved it. The landscape changed from thick trees to grassland and to hills. Small houses sat on the plain isolated from others. Cows were grazing on the grasses peacefully. The farmers were wearing umbrella-like hats and pruning or picking vegetables.

A while later, the truck slowed down and made a right turn onto a narrow road. It continued to move at a slower speed. I got very disappointed, as my thrill had reduced to almost nothing. I hoped the slowdown was only temporary, and we would pick up speed again. The ride was so addictive and fun.

Unfortunately, the truck never picked up its speed again. It moved at a constant slow speed. The other trucks were just a dozen yards behind us. I was curious why the truck slowed down, so I stuck my head out. I saw two soldiers wearing camouflage uniforms, each holding a rifle. One motioning his hand across his throat as if he was going slit our throats.

Then the truck stopped completely.

"Mother, why did he move his hand across his throat like that?" Chhorn asked in fear. "Maybe they are going to slit our throats like the Red Khmer."

"Don't say that. They might get angry and shoot us for real." Mother replied. She sounded unsure herself.

"See the building over there with the red plus sign? That's call the Red Cross," Father said. "Red Cross helps save anyone in need. They are like the angels. We are safe now."

The gate magically rose up. The truck started to move again. I was happy the ride was not over yet. Maybe the stop was just temporary. The truck was moving toward the large building with the humongous red cross sign on it. It stopped at the open paved space. The other trucks stopped close by.

The soldiers came to our truck and opened the back of the truck. "Get down! Get down!" one said with a strange accent.

After we got off the truck, there were several French standing on both sides of the door of the building. All of them were wearing light-colored uniforms with the red plus sign on their shoulders. Two of them were women. I had seen male French before with Pech, but I would have never thought that females existed. They looked similar to the male French but without the hair on their faces. They were standing tall with different hair colors, smiling. Maybe they were the angels that the adults prayed to all the time. I was scared at first, but since Father was here, he would never let them hurt me. I hoped Father was right about the Red Cross people, or else we were walking into the French trap.

We followed the soldiers' lead into the building. All the French smiled and said "Bonjour!" One of the French women took the lead, saying something that started and ended with hissing sounds, and motioned her hand for us to follow. I thought the Vietnamese soldiers sounded strange, but the French sounded even stranger. I didn't know how they could communicate when they spoke with such fast and hissing sounds. Maybe they had special hearing power. That's right. Of course they had special powers—just like the giants in the Khmer story.

Inside the building was a wide-open space with tables and several blocks of enclosed small rooms. On the tables were neatly organized cases with Red Cross signs. There were several Khmer women who seemed to expect us to be here, each standing beside a table across from the French.

"Hello, brothers and sisters. Welcome to Jum Rum Kao E Dang," one woman said with a friendly tone of voice. "Before you are sent to live here, the Red Cross will get your name, take your physical exam, take your blood, and they will also give you preventive shots."

Chhoeun and Father seemed to understand what they needed, and they spoke with the woman. The woman scribbled our information on pieces of paper. It took over an hour for Chhoeun to answer all her questions.

After the papers were completed, we were told to stand in a line with other people that had come on the trucks. Each of us took turns entering the enclosed room.

I entered the room when it was my turn. Before I realized what was happening, the French woman poked me with sharp needles on both sides of my shoulders and then smiled. I screamed after I realized what the French woman had done. The pain was not too bad, but the thought of the needle penetrating deep in my shoulder gave me a chill. I thought they were angels. What angels poke two needles on my shoulders and smile?

After I had just recovered from my pain, the French woman pulled my pants down and checked my area where I never thought another person would ever see. This was one of the most humiliating things that I had encountered in my life. I didn't think I would ever forget this moment. That explained why every adult came out of the room smiling with embarrassment.

"I lived in my Kampuchea all my life. No one dared touch my privates. I came here less than two hours, and they flicked it like some type of game," one of the men said trying to hold his laugh.

After the children found out about the shots, some wailed when they stepped inside the room. When we were finished with the Red Cross, we hopped back onto the same truck that transported us here. The truck moved slowly along a gravel road. There were more buildings behind the first building surrounded by tall trees. The truck moved past the building compound and came to an open land. Small palm leaf houses were built neatly in rows and columns. Civilians like us were living here and going about their daily lives like they had been here forever. Children were waving their hands to greet us. Some were running after us.

Along the edge of the road stood an extremely high tower made from cement. Multiple black cables linked between the towers. There were coils on each end of the cables. At the top of each tower, and arm holding some type of lamp stretched out.

Further up the road, the mountain with thick forest stood firmly, stretching across the horizon. The road slightly elevated as we approached the mountain. The slope didn't seem to slow the truck down. We continued to move forward, closer and closer to the mountain. The closer we got, the bigger the mountain grew and the further it stretched to both sides and didn't seem to end.

Minutes later, we reached the side skirt of the mountain. The truck took a left turn and continued to move along the edge of the mountain. Thick trees and shrubs drooped over from both sides of the road. Some trees were freshly cut to clear the road.

The truck stopped shortly after we reached an intersection of another road. We hopped off the truck and waited for further instruction. A woman that we saw in the Red Cross building explained something to Father and Chhoeun and pointed her fingers to the first row of houses to the right. Father and Chhoeun walked toward the house as instructed. We all followed them to a house made of palm leaves that stood between other houses.

Inside the house, there was one main open space for cooking and guests and one large room on each side. Each room had a bamboo board floor suspended about three feet off the ground.

I noticed there were windows in each room. The children and adults who were currently residing in the area were peeking from their windows looking at us. Pech and I couldn't help but to smile. We were looking forward to making friends and playing with the children.

After I saw the inside of the house, my attention was now back to the mountain that stood just a short walk away. Thick forest blanketed the entire mountain, except for a large boulder that was five times the size of our house, which protruded out from the surrounding trees.

Pech and I walked across the road and ascended the edge of the mountain, exploring the nearby area. We stopped once when got up high enough, and I looked straight down, I saw hundreds of rows of houses divided by the inner walkways into blocks. The tall cement towers connected by the cables stood along the main road from the edge of the mountain to other side of the Jum Rum as if it was eternal. I couldn't wait to find out how far the main road extended.

When Pech and I returned home from the mountainside, the rice was already cooked. Besides the aroma of the steamed rice, I could smell a stir-fry of some sort. We had not had anything to eat since we left Jum Rum Tmey. My stomach was rumbling in anticipation of food, especially the stir-fry.

Mother made stir-fried chicken with some sort of cabbage. I didn't remember Mother bringing any chicken or cabbage. This new place must have provided them to us. All of us were sitting in circle in the middle of the main room and eating. Mother was holding Poe on her lap and feeding him rice and the stir-fry. Poe was around two years old now. He had gained a lot of weight from living Jum Rum Tmey.

Chhorn was sitting right next to Pech, constantly helping Pech moving the rice off the rim of the plate back to the middle to prevent the rice from falling off.

Chhoy sat next to me. Once in a while, she teased me by scooping rice off my bowl and said, "Oops! Wrong bowl!" I knew it was a joke, and I did it back to her and laughed.

Chhom was sitting between Chhoeun and Father, constantly asking if they wanted more rice. Father and Chhoeun had finished their third plates as I was still working on my first. Then Father took a break from eating and leaned back, resting his hands on the ground. Mother and Father looked at each one of us as we ate and smiled.

"From today on, we know we will live," Mother said.

"From today on, we don't have to run anymore," Father added.

CPSIA information can be obtained
at www.ICGtesting.com
Printed in the USA
FFOW03n1408151017
41104FF